# IOWA'S ARCHAEOLOGICAL PAST

D1244856

**A Bur Oak
Book**

# IOWA'S ARCHAEOLOGICAL PAST

By Lynn M. Alex

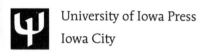

University of Iowa Press
Iowa City

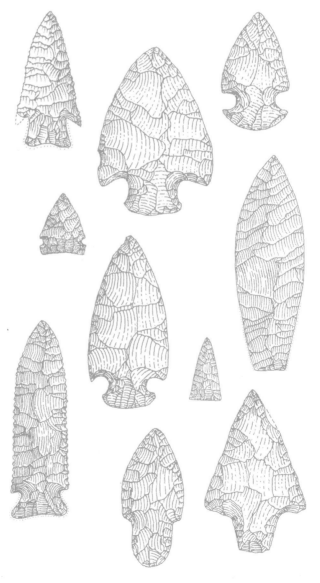

University of Iowa Press, Iowa City 52242
Copyright © 2000 by the University of Iowa Press
All rights reserved
Printed in the United States of America

Design by Omega Clay

www.uiowapress.org

Printed on acid-free paper

Library of Congress Cataloging-in-Publication Data
Alex, Lynn Marie
    Iowa's archaeological past / by Lynn M. Alex.
        p.   cm. — (A Bur oak book)
    Includes bibliographical references (p.   ) and index.
    ISBN 978-0-87745-680-3, ISBN 0-87745-680-1(cloth)
    ISBN 978-0-87745-681-0, ISBN 0-87745-681-X (pbk.)
        1. Iowa—Antiquities. 2. Excavations (Archaeology)—
    Iowa. 3. Archaeology—Iowa. 4. Indians of North
    America—Iowa—Antiquities. 5. Historic sites—Iowa.
    I. Title. II. Series.
    F623.A54   2000
    977.7'01—dc21         99-33566

Among the Mandan, it was believed that children choose the mother they want. —Alfred W. Bowers

To Mary M., my choice

# Contents

# Preface

Archaeology is fascinating to people when it is communicated to them in plain language.
—Marquardt 1996:2

**IN 1980** the University of Iowa Press published *Exploring Iowa's Past: A Guide to Prehistoric Archaeology*. Favorably received throughout Iowa and the Midwest, the book has since become a standard source in public libraries and schools statewide as well as a guide for cultural resources planners.

In the period since the publication of *Exploring Iowa's Past*, an enormous amount of archaeological work has been conducted in Iowa and throughout the Midwest, much of it generated by Cultural Resource Management (CRM) studies and compliance with state and federal legislation that had only just taken effect in the 1970s. This research has transformed our knowledge of Iowa's human past, and yet much of what we have learned remains buried in the "gray literature" of technical reports and conference papers.

The current volume offers a comprehensive summary of Iowa's archaeological heritage that should have particular relevance for educators, cultural resources planners, and professional and avocational archaeologists alike. It synthesizes the research of the past two decades and presents the culture history of Iowa within a

framework familiar to readers of the earlier publication. New topics of discussion include environmental change and its challenge to early human inhabitants, geological events and their influence on ancient landscapes and site preservation, historic Native American peoples and the impact of Euroamerican immigrants, and recent legislation and its effect on archaeological research.

For anyone who considers archaeology a static field because its subject matter is the past, the current volume is intended to show otherwise. Archaeology is a dynamic science, and new interpretations result as much from the way we approach and question the past as from innovative research methods and techniques. Both our questions and our methods are affected by developments in other disciplines and by changing historical perspectives.

The face of Iowa archaeology at the start of the new millennium is different than it was just a few decades ago, and there is no reason to doubt that in another twenty years a new face will have emerged. While for some, space travel may promise the trip of a lifetime, for others a trip back in time still delivers a pretty good ride.

# Acknowledgments

THIS BOOK is largely a synthesis and as such draws on the discoveries of the many avocational and professional scientists who have worked and continue to work to elucidate Iowa's archaeological past. While many of these individuals might have written this book, thanks to William Green, Iowa's State Archaeologist; Holly Carver, director of the University of Iowa Press; and the Iowa Department of Transportation (DOT), I was fortunate enough to be given the opportunity.

I would like to thank the Iowa DOT for its financial support of this project through an Intermodal Surface Transportation Efficiency Act (ISTEA) grant and the University of Iowa Press which for a number of years has encouraged production and offered support for a revised volume on Iowa archaeology.

I am especially grateful to the following individuals who read versions of the manuscript or parts thereof and offered constructive criticism and helpful suggestions: Mark Anderson, Joe Artz, William Billeck, Rich Fishel, Lance Foster, William Green, John Hedden, Julianne Hoyer, Marlin Ingalls, Stephen Lensink, Carl Merry, Julie Morrow, Toby Morrow, Blane Nansel, Mike Perry, Cindy Peterson, Jean Prior, Don Raker, Shirley Schermer, Susan Snow, Joseph Tiffany, and Larry Zimmerman. Linea Sundstrom, Joseph Tiffany, Jim Collins, John Doershuk, Kris Hirst, George Horton, and Marshall McKusick were helpful with sources. John Cordell, Linda Forman, Julianne Hoyer, Robin Lillie, and Tim Weitzel assisted with site records, archival materials, photographs, and artifacts curated at the Office of the State Archaeologist. Allison Alex double-checked site records. Jeff Carr and Jason Titcomb researched photographs at the Iowa State University Archaeological Laboratory. Mary Bennett of the State Historical Society of Iowa in Iowa City was particularly helpful with archival materials in the Keyes Collection. Linda Langenberg and Patti Streicher of the Office of the State Archaeologist helped me navigate through a series of unavoidable bureaucratic and computer jams.

The works of several very fine artists illustrate this volume. They include David Crawford, Lance Foster, Julie Morrow, Toby Morrow, and Mary Slattery. I am especially grateful to Julie and Toby Morrow, who permitted unrestricted access to many of their excellent artifact illustrations. Lance Foster's cover painting captured my attention the first time I saw it, and I was delighted to be given permission to use it. Permission to use additional photographs, drawings, and items for illustration was provided by the Anthropological Archives of the Smithsonian Institution, David Benn, E. Arthur Bettis, Steven De Vore, William Edwards, Brian Glenister, Julia Golden, the Goodhue County Historical Society of Minnesota, David Gradwohl, Mary Helgevold, R. Eric Hollinger, the Iowa Department of Natural Resources, Iowa State University Archaeological Laboratory, Stephen Lensink, Louis Berger and Associates, Nancy Osborn, Maria Pearson (Running Moccasins), Jean Prior, the Putnam Museum of History and Natural Science, Robert L. Rankin, the Sanford Museum and Planetarium, the State Historical Society of Iowa, the State Historical Society of Nebraska, and Joseph Tiffany.

Permission to reproduce previously published images came from these individuals and institutions as well as from the *Journal of the Iowa Archeological Society,* the Office of the State Archaeologist, and the *Plains Anthropologist.* Diana Brayton, graphic specialist at the University of Iowa, prepared maps showing sites discussed in the text.

Holly Carver, my editor at the University of Iowa Press, remained enthusiastic, patient, and constantly supportive. Robert Burchfield served the manuscript, and thus the author, through his consummate skills as copyeditor. Two anonymous colleagues carefully read and critiqued the text at an early stage, and the final product is better by far as a result of their suggestions. The index was prepared by Barbara E. Cohen.

I would also like to express my appreciation to the many readers of the earlier *Exploring Iowa's Past* volume, most of whom remain kindred spirits in the Iowa Archeological Society. Over the years they have offered personal support and the kind of generous praise that encouraged me to try again.

This book could not have been completed without the monumental assistance and encouragement given me by Stephen Lensink and Joseph Tiffany. Steve provided all of the calibrations and discussion of radiocarbon dates. Joe's tremendous personal knowledge of midwestern archaeology and willingness to share it proved a constant resource.

Finally, thanks for the patience and forthright suggestions of Allison, Brendan, Stacey, and Kim Alex, who are growing up around and in spite of me.

# Introduction

None of the dead can rise up and answer our questions. But from all they have left behind, their imperishable or slowly dissolving gear, we may perhaps hear voices, which only now are able to whisper, when everything else has become silent. —Björn Kurtén

ARCHAEOLOGY interests almost everyone. The spirit of adventure and discovery that entices many mingles with a fascination for the past, the appeal of the exotic, and the excitement of an imagined treasure hunt or detective's case. Even those who come to understand that hard uncomfortable work, attention to detail, and tedious study of seemingly mundane discoveries lie at the core of archaeology rarely lose their enthusiasm or attraction for this field. While most of us have long since abandoned our image of Indiana Jones or an absentminded professor as the prototypical archaeologist, we are still drawn to the past and the lure of its discovery that such characters evoke.

This book tells the story of Iowa's human past as revealed by more than a century of archaeology conducted here and elsewhere throughout the Midwest. The story begins 13,000 years ago with the arrival of the first immigrants trickling across the continent in small groups, presumably unaware that they were populating a vast new land. It closes almost within living memory as new settlers, this time from a different shore and with a conscious deliberation, asserted their authority over a territory they knew to be bountiful and within a few generations claimed it as their own.

The challenge, as well as much of the appeal, for modern archaeologists is trying to understand and perhaps explain events such as these

without the benefit of living informants, with much of the evidence missing, and perched as they are at the beginning of the twenty-first century. Chapter 1 describes how this challenge is being met by today's researchers, who are armed with innovative new techniques for the discovery and recovery of archaeological remains and increasingly refined temporal and interpretive frameworks.

More than 18,000 archaeological sites have been recorded in Iowa, the product of thousands of discoveries and the research of many individuals. To understand how we have come this far and perhaps where we are going, Chapter 2 looks at the history of archaeology in Iowa, noting events and people who have been important and recent legislation that promises to influence the discipline well into the future.

The human experience in Iowa has been in part a series of adaptations to a variety of distinctive geographical regions that over time underwent significant changes in landform and vegetation and were affected by continental-wide climatic shifts. The preservation of archaeological sites is itself related to their position on the land. Chapter 3 summarizes Iowa's natural setting as first depicted by Euroamericans at the time of historic contact. This setting contrasts, at times sharply, with the landscapes encountered by earlier Iowans, which are described in succeeding chapters.

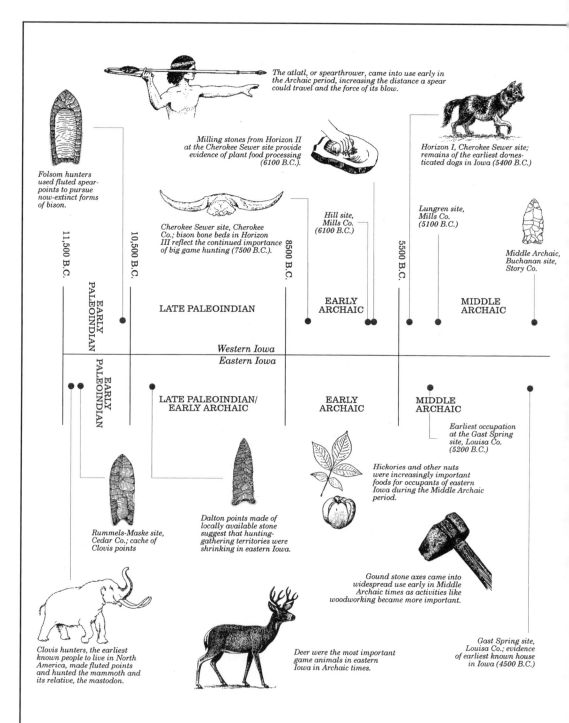

The atlatl, or spearthrower, came into use early in the Archaic period, increasing the distance a spear could travel and the force of its blow.

Milling stones from Horizon II at the Cherokee Sewer site provide evidence of plant food processing (6100 B.C.).

Horizon I, Cherokee Sewer site; remains of the earliest domesticated dogs in Iowa (5400 B.C.)

Folsom hunters used fluted spearpoints to pursue now-extinct forms of bison.

Cherokee Sewer site, Cherokee Co.; bison bone beds in Horizon III reflect the continued importance of big game hunting (7500 B.C.).

Hill site, Mills Co. (6100 B.C.)

Lungren site, Mills Co. (5100 B.C.)

Middle Archaic, Buchanan site, Story Co.

11,500 B.C.

10,500 B.C.

8500 B.C.

5500 B.C.

EARLY PALEOINDIAN

LATE PALEOINDIAN

EARLY ARCHAIC

MIDDLE ARCHAIC

Western Iowa
Eastern Iowa

EARLY PALEOINDIAN

LATE PALEOINDIAN/ EARLY ARCHAIC

EARLY ARCHAIC

MIDDLE ARCHAIC

Earliest occupation at the Gast Spring site, Louisa Co. (5200 B.C.)

Hickories and other nuts were increasingly important foods for occupants of eastern Iowa during the Middle Archaic period.

Dalton points made of locally available stone suggest that hunting-gathering territories were shrinking in eastern Iowa.

Rummels-Maske site, Cedar Co.; cache of Clovis points

Gound stone axes came into widespread use early in Middle Archaic times as activities like woodworking became more important.

Clovis hunters, the earliest known people to live in North America, made fluted points and hunted the mammoth and its relative, the mastodon.

Deer were the most important game animals in eastern Iowa in Archaic times.

Gast Spring site, Louisa Co.; evidence of earliest known house in Iowa (4500 B.C.)

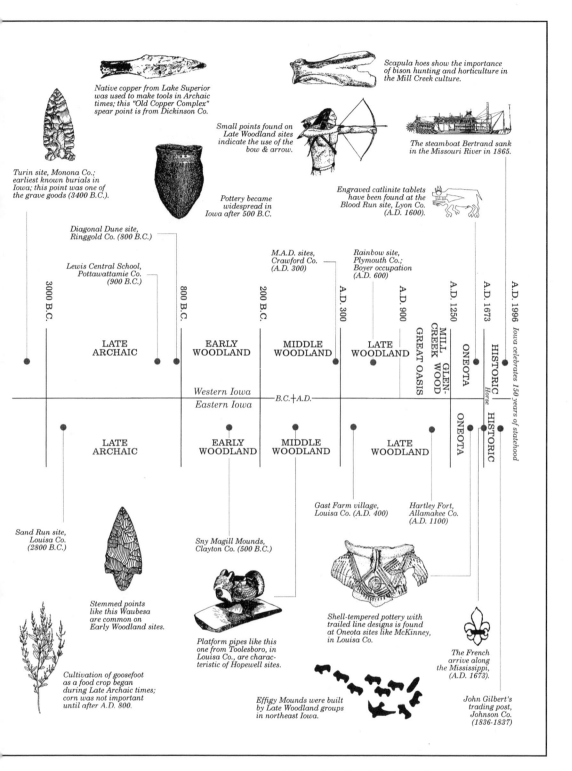

Native copper from Lake Superior was used to make tools in Archaic times; this "Old Copper Complex" spear point is from Dickinson Co.

Scapula hoes show the importance of bison hunting and horticulture in the Mill Creek culture.

Small points found on Late Woodland sites indicate the use of the bow & arrow.

The steamboat Bertrand sank in the Missouri River in 1865.

Turin site, Monona Co.; earliest known burials in Iowa; this point was one of the grave goods (3400 B.C.).

Pottery became widespread in Iowa after 500 B.C.

Engraved catlinite tablets have been found at the Blood Run site, Lyon Co. (A.D. 1600).

Diagonal Dune site, Ringgold Co. (800 B.C.)

Lewis Central School, Pottawattamie Co. (900 B.C.)

M.A.D. sites, Crawford Co. (A.D. 300)

Rainbow site, Plymouth Co.; Boyer occupation (A.D. 600)

3000 B.C.

800 B.C.

200 B.C.

A.D. 300

A.D. 900

A.D. 1250

A.D. 1673

A.D. 1996 *Iowa celebrates 150 years of statehood*

LATE ARCHAIC

EARLY WOODLAND

MIDDLE WOODLAND

LATE WOODLAND

GREAT OASIS

MILL CREEK

GLEN-WOOD

ONEOTA

HISTORIC

Horse

*Western Iowa*
—B.C.—A.D.—
*Eastern Iowa*

LATE ARCHAIC

EARLY WOODLAND

MIDDLE WOODLAND

LATE WOODLAND

ONEOTA

HISTORIC

Gast Farm village, Louisa Co. (A.D. 400)

Hartley Fort, Allamakee Co. (A.D. 1100)

Sand Run site, Louisa Co. (2800 B.C.)

Sny Magill Mounds, Clayton Co. (500 B.C.)

Stemmed points like this Waubesa are common on Early Woodland sites.

Shell-tempered pottery with trailed line designs is found at Oneota sites like McKinney, in Louisa Co.

Platform pipes like this one from Toolesboro, in Louisa Co., are characteristic of Hopewell sites.

The French arrive along the Mississippi, (A.D. 1673).

Cultivation of goosefoot as a food crop began during Late Archaic times; corn was not important until after A.D. 800.

Effigy Mounds were built by Late Woodland groups in northeast Iowa.

John Gilbert's trading post, Johnson Co. (1836-1837)

**I.1.** Iowa's archaeological time line. From an original prepared by Linda Forman, Timothy S. Weitzel, and Lynn M. Alex.

Although Iowa hardly seems an exotic setting, to many its archaeological past is as fascinating as that found anywhere. The remainder of the book explores in some detail what archaeologists have learned about this past from the study of material remains and their contexts. (fig. I.1) Chapters 4 through 11 are organized chronologically. Within this framework, more specific topics are addressed. These include the nature of the earliest settlement of Iowa, the development of farming cultures, interaction among native societies, tribal affiliation of early historic groups, and the arrival and impact of Euroamericans. While the intent is to outline these events as we interpret them in Iowa, they have meaning only when explained within a larger midwestern and, at times, North American context. Modern political boundaries are an artificial construct, the product of recent history. Native peoples had their own sense of place, and their activities and interactions ranged well beyond the piece of land we call Iowa.

The final chapter of this book examines the question of stewardship. Although state and federal legislation affords some protection for archaeological resources, there are many ways individuals can insure the survival of finds and sites.

To help breathe some life into the projectile points, potsherds, and patterns that make up the archaeological record, the text is sprinkled with examples of customs and beliefs recorded among more recent native peoples. This kind of ethnographic analogy has long been used in archaeology but is always strongest when some kind of link between prehistoric remains and known societies can be made. Therefore, the ethnographic examples presented here come from societies believed to be similar to the archaeological cultures described or possibly descended from them. Additional information on topics introduced throughout the book are briefly explored in appendixes at the end of chapters. A glossary and an extensive bibliography close the volume.

*Iowa's Archaeological Past* is intended for anyone interested in the archaeology of the state, and many people are. The public's fascination with archaeology is growing, and Iowa has an admirable history of avocational interest and involvement. This volume hopes to foster that interest and involvement by synthesizing what we know about the past from Iowa's archaeological resources and by encouraging everyone to play a part in their discovery, preservation, and protection.

# IOWA'S ARCHAEOLOGICAL PAST

# 1 The Science of Archaeology

For now we see through a glass, darkly.
                    —I Corinthians 13:12

**ARCHAEOLOGISTS** are not dinosaur hunters. The last of the huge dinosaurs were long gone and their remains well fossilized before the first humans came on the scene. The dinosaur detectives of books and films such as *Jurassic Park* are paleontologists, geologists who specialize in the study of ancient, generally nonhuman life and the natural world in which it developed. Paleontological remains are by and large fossil evidence of plants and animals. Because these ancient remains are buried, sometimes at great depths, paleontologists use techniques similar to those of archaeologists to recover this data. Devonian Fossil Gorge, the 375-million-year-old fossil bed in Johnson County exposed by flooding at Coralville Lake Reservoir in 1993, is a good example of a paleontological site (fig. 1.1).

The domain of archaeology is the human past and the cultural world in which it unfolded. Since much of the human past transpired before the advent of written records, that is during prehistoric times, archaeologists recover the byproducts of human behavior in an attempt to reconstruct these remote periods. People who lived during the historic era, for which there is written documentation, also left physical evidence of their behavior. Archaeological investigation of historic sites can extend or sometimes even challenge the conclusions drawn from written sources alone.

Archaeological remains include the portable artifacts people made and used; nonportable features such as burials, trash pits, and fireplaces;

and floral (plant) and faunal (animal) evidence —sometimes referred to as ecofacts. Artifacts, features, and ecofacts are found at archaeological sites. A site is any location where there is evidence of past human activity. It could be as small as the find spot of a single artifact or as large as an entire city. In Iowa, common types of sites include lithic scatters, open camps, work stations, villages, cemeteries, rockshelters, quarries, fish traps, rock art, and standing structures (Appendix 1.1).

Archaeologists find sites and recover the material remains of the past and their contexts using a whole set of careful and specialized techniques, including archaeological survey, excavation, and analysis. To make interpretations about past human behavior, however, the archaeologist must wear the broader hat of the anthropologist.

## Archaeology, Anthropology, and Science

Archaeologists are anthropologists who specialize in the culture of past societies. Anthropologists believe that the key to understanding human behavior is in understanding the development of culture and how it has allowed humans to cope with their world in increasingly complex ways. Unlike most cultural anthropologists, such as the late Margaret Mead, who may live within a particular society and observe its culture firsthand, archaeologists must find and recover the material remains left by former societies. From these "things" they hope to reconstruct both the material and nonmaterial aspects

**1.1.** Devonian Fossil Gorge in Johnson County is a good example of a paleontological site. Courtesy of Brian Glenister. From *Iowa Geology* 1994.

of earlier societies. Archaeologists cannot "dig up" a prehistoric society's language, religion, or social organization. Yet they hope that the patterns observed in the material remains and their contexts, when combined with the insights anthropologists have contributed from their studies of living peoples, will help them make inferences about all aspects of past cultures.

People are sometimes frustrated with the explanations about the past that archaeologists provide. Often the explanations seem uncertain or ambiguous and are liberally peppered with qualifiers such as "probably," "perhaps," or "possibly." This is because archaeology, like most sciences, rarely can provide absolute answers. The scientific method requires that hypotheses, which are really explanations about the nature of things, be validated or confirmed by testing either through repeated experimentation or as the result of the repeatability of discoveries. Because historical sciences such as archaeology, paleontology, and even astronomy deal with events that happened in the past, their hypotheses are not subject to experimentation. Therefore, an ar-

chaeological hypothesis can be strengthened or confirmed only by the repeated discovery and careful observation, recording, and interpretation of similar evidence. The hypothesis that stone spear points were used by ancient Ice Age hunters, for instance, as first proposed on the basis of points found in association with extinct animal remains, was only "confirmed" after the repeated discovery of similar remains in similar contexts at other sites and was eventually verified by radiocarbon dating.

Historical sciences must also contend with an often incomplete and imperfect record. What we know about the past depends upon meager evidence when only certain kinds of data have survived, and incompletely so at that. Thus coming to firm conclusions about the archaeological past is doubly difficult because many of the pieces of the puzzle are missing.

Finally, the archaeological record is an incomplete chronicle of human behavior. Cultural anthropologists have demonstrated that, while there are patterns to human culture and certain universal needs that all human societies must meet, formulating absolute laws about human behavior is difficult if not impossible. Therefore, more than most scientists, archaeologists must recognize that the material evidence they recover may stem from a myriad of past situations that cannot always be elucidated. And, given our twenty-first-century perspective, with its own cultural biases, we may not always be clever enough to devise explanations.

## Fieldwork

### Finding Sites

While accident has frequently played a part in the discovery of ancient remains, archaeologists also make deliberate, systematic searches for prehistoric and historic sites. This is called archaeological reconnaissance or survey. Almost all survey ultimately involves the inspection of a region on foot for signs of artifacts or surface features that might disclose the presence of sites. However, sites cannot always be detected from surface evidence alone.

In the past, deeply buried sites, especially on certain Iowa landforms, were frequently overlooked unless they happened to be eroding along streams or were exposed during the course of large construction projects (fig. 1.2). Today surveyors use a variety of techniques, from mechanical augers and coring devices to more high-tech remote-sensing methods such as proton magnetometry, to help them detect subsurface archaeological remains (fig. 1.3). They also employ geomorphologists who can identify the landforms and soils present in a region that might have potential for buried sites (fig. 1.4). In addition, low-altitude aerial photographs and high-altitude infrared photographs sometimes reveal unusual features of the ground surface and distinctive vegetation patterns that could indicate the presence of sites (see plates 1 and 2; fig. 1.5).

Computer technology now permits Iowa archaeologists to develop maps that combine various types of information useful when planning research. Geographic Information Systems (GIS) technology overlays information from various spatial databases to produce customized maps that can be quickly updated as new information becomes available (Ludvigson et al. 1994:23).

Space-age technology has also provided a new tool to record the position of sites on the landscape more accurately. The Global Positioning System (GPS) is a relatively inexpensive technology consisting of a handheld or tripod-mounted unit capable of receiving satellite signals. The unit processes signals received from multiple satellites to ascertain latitude and longitude. With the appropriate signals and data processing, the archaeologist's position can be located to a meter or less on the earth's surface. The Midwest Archaeological Center in Lincoln, Nebraska, used digitized maps from the late nineteenth and early twentieth centuries, GPS, and GIS in an attempt to relocate and map many of the features known to have existed at the Oneota Blood Run/Rock Island site, a National Historic Landmark in northwestern Iowa and southeastern South Dakota (Vawser and Hampton 1997).

### Excavation

When people think of archaeology, they probably imagine a checkerboard landscape of excavation pits—mounds of dirt piled high to one side—occupied by dusty khaki- and denim-clad excavators armed with shovels, buckets, and trowels. This is not an unrealistic scene (see plate 3). The primary technique for recovering information about human prehistory is excavation.

All excavation is designed to recover data and their context, which will help answer specific questions about the past. While North American archaeologists ultimately hope to extend our knowledge of culture history and culture processes into the past and to elucidate past lifeways, each project has more specific objectives. The nature of the site, the goals of the research, and the level of funding influence the specific recovery techniques used—from dental picks and hand trowels to total station transits, from tripod-mounted sifting screens to water flotation, and

**1.2.** The multicomponent Cherokee Sewer site in Cherokee County was discovered when construction for a new town sewage treatment plant began. Photo by Richard G. Slattery. Photo archives, Office of the State Archaeologist, University of Iowa.

**1.3.** A geologist using the Giddings rig, a subsurface coring device, to detect buried cultural deposits. Courtesy of E. Arthur Bettis III.

**1.4.** Remote sensing at the Oneota McKinney site in Louisa County tests for the presence of subsurface storage pits and possible burials. Photo by the author.

**1.5.** USDA aerial photographs scanned and manipulated for information on the Turkey River Mound Group in Clayton County reveal features unrecorded in conventional surveys. Photo scanned and manipulated by Mark L. Anderson. Photo archives, Office of the State Archaeologist, University of Iowa.

from the use of a makeshift photo tower to the employment of professional geomorphologists (see plate 4; figs. 1.6–1.8). Even weather conditions must be considered in project planning and execution.

Throughout each excavation the archaeologist pays particular attention to provenience—the context and relationship of remains. Recovering and recording archaeological remains in situ, that is, in place, permits inferences about their function and observations about their relation-

ship in space and time. Archaeologists follow the law of association, which suggests that items found together in the same level are contemporary with one another.

By mapping the location of all materials at a site both horizontally and vertically, the archaeologist can recognize potentially significant patterns (fig. 1.9). Clusters of artifacts and features, for instance, might indicate the presence of specific activity areas and could reflect patterns of prehistoric social organization. Historic accounts

**1.6.** Careful troweling lies at the heart of archaeological excavation. The Marshalltown Trowel Company of Marshalltown, Iowa, manufactures most of the trowels used by North American archaeologists. Photo archives, Office of the State Archaeologist, University of Iowa.

**1.7.** Makeshift photo tower in use at the Mill Creek Lange site, O'Brien County. Photo archives, Office of the State Archaeologist, University of Iowa.

of native Plains women, for example, suggest that they were usually the hide dressers and seamstresses in their communities. The presence of artifacts believed to represent hide-dressing kits—scrapers, fleshers, awls, and needles—accompanying female burials indicates that women in prehistoric Plains societies performed similar tasks.

Stratification, or the vertical layering of natural and cultural deposits at a site, provides important information about the association of materials relative to one another in time. Unless

**1.8.** A geomorphologist examines DeForest Formation deposits in Jones County. Photo archives, Office of the State Archaeologist, University of Iowa.

**1.9.** Careful mapping and record keeping are as important to archaeological interpretation as excavation. Photo archives, Office of the State Archaeologist, University of Iowa.

something has happened to disturb the order of deposition, archaeologists expect that the youngest remains will be those first encountered as the site is excavated. This is the law of superposition and is a basic premise upon which archaeological dating relies.

## Archaeological Dating

Archaeologists depend on a host of both "relative" and "absolute" techniques to determine the age of archaeological remains. Stratigraphic dating, applying the principle of superposition, is probably the most widely used method for placing cultural events in a sequence from older to younger. Stratified sites are particularly valuable in demonstrating the relative order of occupations. Where there are clear breaks between layers and relatively undisturbed deposits, it may be possible to establish a cultural sequence that can serve as a model for an entire region. In some cases overlapping sequences at a number of stratified sites can be linked to produce a regional guide to the culture history of an area.

### Radiometric Dating

Radiocarbon dating, also called $^{14}C$ dating, is the most important "absolute" or chronometric technique for determining the actual age of organic materials less than about 50,000 years old. Only organic remains or items in direct association with them can be used to date cultural events by this method. Thus a ceramic vessel cannot be dated directly by $^{14}C$, but the charred food residue found inside could be.

The radiocarbon method measures the amount of a radioactive isotope of carbon, carbon 14 ($^{14}C$), found in organic remains. Organic materials in an archaeological context usually survive in the form of charred wood and seeds, antlers, bones, and shells. A live organism regularly takes in $^{14}C$ as the result of the carbon dioxide interchange (in plants through photosynthesis, in animals by eating plants). As long as the organism is alive, $^{14}C$ is continuously replenished. However, when the organism dies, no new

$^{14}C$ is taken in, and the amount of $^{14}C$ begins to decline through radioactive disintegration. Scientists have been able to measure the disintegration rate of $^{14}C$, and they know that after 5,730 years half of the $^{14}C$ present in an organism at the time of death will be gone. This is the half-life of $^{14}C$. By measuring the average emission rate of the $^{14}C$ remaining in an archaeological sample, scientists can tell how much is left and thus calculate the length of time that has elapsed since the organism died.

A $^{14}C$ date is expressed in years before present (B.P.), with "present" conventionally set at A.D. 1950. A statistical error is also included in a $^{14}C$ date. A sample of charred seeds radiocarbon dated at 2550 ± 80 B.P., for instance, means that there is better than a 67 percent chance that the seeds were deposited at the site from a plant that died between 2,470 and 2,630 years B.P. (i.e., 80 years before or after 2550 B.P.).

Traditionally, the methodology used in determining a radiocarbon date involved counting the actual disintegration of radioactive atoms from the sample over an extended period using a Geiger counter or liquid scintillation counter. The larger the sample size or the longer the counting time, the more reliable the date. Recently, however, physicists have devised a new way of ascertaining a date by directly measuring the amount of radioactive carbon present in a sample relative to the quantity of the stable form of carbon, $^{12}C$. This technique, called Accelerator Mass Spectroscopy (AMS), uses a tandem accelerator and requires a much smaller sample of datable material. AMS dating, while costly, has opened up the possibility of dating sites where very minor amounts of organic material are preserved. The conventional method of $^{14}C$ dating required about a handful-sized sample; now only a few milligrams are needed. Priceless antiquities like rare cave paintings or the Shroud of Turin might have gone undated were it not for the AMS technique.

After the $^{14}C$ method was developed, scientists discovered that the amount of radioactive carbon produced in the upper atmosphere has not always remained constant. At times there has been more, at times less. As a result, the radiocarbon clock at times has run faster and at times slower. This means that the actual length of time that has passed since an organism died as suggested by a radiocarbon date might not reflect its true calendar age. By dating wood from long-lived trees, such as the Bristlecone pine which can survive for thousands of years and whose exact age can be determined by counting annual growth rings, it is possible to see how far off radiocarbon ages are from true calendar dates. This has allowed scientists to produce a calibration curve to help bring radiocarbon dates more in line with true calendar dates.

Today, most radiocarbon dates are run through a computer program to determine their calibrated date, which is expressed in calendar years B.C. or A.D. While most radiocarbon determinations from archaeological sites in Iowa previously have been published as uncalibrated dates, throughout this book $^{14}C$ dates have been calibrated to calendric dates (Appendix 1.2). As a result, the dates that appear here may vary considerably from uncalibrated dates presented in other publications. This is especially true for the oldest sites in Iowa.

Thermoluminescence dating (TL) of fire-cracked rock or other lithics also has been used at a few sites in Iowa. TL measures the amount of energy trapped within the crystal lattice of the material, such as pottery or fire-cracked rock, since the time the material was last exposed to high temperatures. The amount of energy trapped is proportional to the dose of radiation absorbed by the material from the surrounding soil or from inherent radiation in certain minerals found in the material itself. When the specimen is reheated in the laboratory, this energy is released as light. The older the artifact, the greater the amount of light released.

### Cross-Dating and Seriation

Once archaeological remains have been placed in a relative sequence or have been dated in absolute years, they can serve as a kind of reference point or chronological marker for dating similar finds and similar sites elsewhere. This is the process of cross-dating, and it has been a standard practice in archaeology for more than a century.

In certain instances, artifact types also can be ordered by seriation. Like most aspects of technology, artifacts changed over time. If, for instance, you collected models of cookstoves used in the United States since the 1800s, you would probably be able to arrange them in a sequence from the simplest wood stoves to the latest microwaves. Should someone donate another model to your collection, say the first gas burner, you would probably be able to place it accurately in the sequence by comparing it to the models that immediately preceded and followed. Artifact types can sometimes be ordered in a similar manner. In many cases, this is from the simple to the more complex, but not always. The resurgence in the popularity of woodburning stoves today might confuse your sequence in the case of the cookstove example. However, if the developmental sequence of artifact types can be confirmed through the discovery of their actual stratigraphic context at a site or by absolute dating, then such types become useful in cross-dating.

## Analysis, Classification, and Interpretation

Excavation, while perhaps the most celebrated part of archaeological research, is just one step in the process intended to produce insights into past human behavior. Once fieldwork has ended and the site backfilled, the job of analyzing the site begins. For every day spent in excavating, two to five days may be needed in the lab sorting, cleaning, quantifying, identifying, and describing the remains; classifying and comparing artifacts and features; and evaluating field notes and maps. The archaeologist must be able to reconstruct a site and describe its contents in a report that will stand as the only documentation of something that is now gone.

Broken artifacts including stone tools and pottery can often be refitted if most of the pieces are found. Refitting a stone artifact from a mass of debitage may indicate the sequence of steps used by the ancient flintknapper in producing a tool (fig. 1.10). Refitting vessels from potsherds scattered across a site may help to determine the population size of the community and the relationship of households. If the archaeologist is able to refit a large number of artifacts from a site, it may suggest whether the site was significantly altered through various transformational processes following its abandonment and whether these have affected the preservation of material remains.

The detailed examination, description, and classification of artifacts according to their indi-

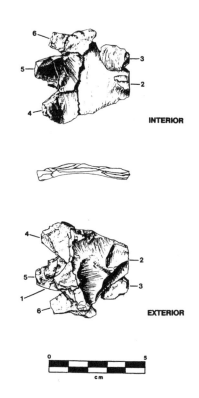

**1.10.** Refitted flakes from the Ed's Meadow site in Des Moines County provide clues to the sequence of flake removal. Illustration by Toby Morrow. From Morrow 1996c.

vidual characteristics or attributes allows the archaeologist to define specific types. A *type* represents a class of artifacts that share similar attributes. The presence of similar types at sites in a region may be a clue that the sites are the same age or were related in some way.

The careful examination of artifacts also provides clues as to how they were made and used. Signs of use-wear in the form of striations, chipping, and abrasion often can be detected microscopically on lithic artifacts. Techniques such as X-ray fluorescence have made it possible to identify the specific sources of various raw materials. Clay, stone, and metal artifacts typically possess a distinctive geochemical signature. If the archaeologist, with the help of specialists, can identify these geochemical "fingerprints," the source of the material can often be determined. Pipestone, also termed flint clay, for instance, has a unique mineral fingerprint depending on its source. The red catlinite from quarries in southwestern Minnesota consists of the minerals pyrophyllite, muscovite, and diaspore. Purplish pipestone from the Baraboo Hills in eastern Wisconsin contains muscovite, pyrophyllite, and kaolinite (Boszhardt 1997a).

By knowing the source of particular raw materials used in the past, archaeologists have a better understanding of the efforts ancient peoples expended to acquire favored raw materials and the direction of trade and travel. Copper, obsidian, and certain pipestone artifacts found in Iowa are now known to have originated hundreds of kilometers from their find spots. The Elkhorn Creek pipestone used to make Middle Woodland pipes and once thought to have been acquired in Ohio has now been sourced to the Sterling–Rock Falls area of northern Illinois (Alex and Green 1995; Berres et al. 1993; Gray 1995) (see plate 5).

Although the detailed analysis of artifacts lies at the heart of archaeological interpretation, the reconstruction of ancient environments and diet relies upon the recovery and identification of faunal and floral remains, sometimes micro-

scopic in size. Typically these materials are collected from water flotation (fig. 1.11) of soil samples and are analyzed by specialists in paleobotany, palynology, malacology, and chemistry. Biochemical analyses of blood residues detected on some stone artifacts, for example, can pinpoint the animal species killed or butchered (Loy 1983). Carbon encrustations on potsherds may contain plant phytoliths that identify the plants cooked by prehistoric peoples. Bones, shells, carbonized plant remains, fish scales, and other ecofacts recovered from a site may also provide clues as to the season of site occupation.

Reconstructing the culture history of any area begins with the careful evaluation of individual sites. Detailed analysis and classification of artifacts, features, and ecofacts found from each site allows the archaeologist to formulate an impression of the lifeway of the people who lived there. As the material remains from different sites are dated and compared, it may be possible to suggest the relationship between sites and to construct local sequences. Information on site features, site size, and the kind and distribution of

**1.11.** Dauseman Flote-Tech machine in use at the Wever Terrace project in Lee County allows recovery of microscopic artifacts and ecofacts. Photo by Jeffrey K. Yelton. Courtesy of R. Eric Hollinger and Louis Berger and Associates.

sites on the landscape provides an understanding of the settlement pattern and social systems of local societies. As sites in ever widening circles of space and time become better known, archaeologists may begin to interpret the observed relationships and account for the suspected changes that occurred using concepts and theories from anthropology.

In the end, the goal is not merely to document how individual societies coped with environmental change, or what plants native gardeners first grew in a region, or when people first populated an area, or where the oldest sites are, but why these events occurred in human societies worldwide and why they took on the particular form they did in Iowa, in North America, or anywhere for that matter.

## Taxonomy

The prehistory of Iowa is the story of the succession and interrelationships of once-dynamic cultures, the remnants of which are known only from unevenly preserved material remains and some oral traditions. The archaeologist recovers the "things" of these cultures and then tries to reconstruct flesh and bone and narrative. Today, some would say that "construct" might be a more apt description of this process, hampered as we are by an incomplete record and by our own cultural biases.

In the following chapters, the culture history of Iowa as archaeologists now understand it is presented. Each chapter represents a slice of time, a period that undoubtedly was populated by a multitude of individual societies, each of which shared a common identity and culture. The archaeologist attempts to define these individual cultures through patterning in the archaeological record. The defining characteristics of individual societies and cultures in the remote past are blurred, and their material remains seem similar over broad areas of space and time. Thus, in describing Paleoindian and Archaic remains in Iowa, archaeologists paint with a fairly wide brush. In contrast, discussions of later discoveries from Woodland and late prehistoric sites are both more complete and more specific.

Those unfamiliar with the professional jargon of archaeology are frequently confused by the vocabulary used to organize materials. Paleoindian might modify such terms as period, tradition, stage, or even culture. The same is true with the terms Archaic, Woodland, and Mississippian. Mill Creek, Great Oasis, Nebraska, and Oneota might refer to a people, a culture, a focus, or an aspect. Words such as period, aspect, focus, phase, culture, stage, and tradition are really organizing terms intended to group archaeological remains in ways that might reflect similarities in their form or content, spatial distribution, and age. In order to understand these distinctions, it is necessary to know a little something about taxonomy, the system archaeologists use to order or classify data.

In the past, two taxonomic systems were used to organize archaeological data from Iowa—the Midwest Taxonomic System (MTS) developed by William C. McKern (1939), curator of anthropology at the Milwaukee Public Museum, and the Willey and Phillips system (W&P) proposed by two Harvard archaeologists, Gordon Willey and Philip Phillips (Willey and Phillips 1958). Until the 1960s the McKern system, which organized data by form, was the predominant one used throughout the Midwest. This scheme consisted of five major divisions—focus, aspect, phase, pattern, and base—proceeding from lower order, more specialized classes to larger, more generalized ones (McKern 1939:307).

The W&P system proposed a three-dimensional system of taxonomic units that ranged from fairly exclusive to more and more inclusive. Its advantage over the MTS was that it could incorporate all three variables of content, space, and time. Lower order terms such as component and phase were used to relate local sites and their contents. Higher order terms such as culture, stage, and tradition were proposed to integrate data into broader relationships and connections, sometimes over fairly wide areas.

According to the W&P system, individual sites, or a level within a site, characterized by similar types of artifacts and features would define the component. One would expect similar components to occur within a fairly circumscribed geographical area called the locality. Contemporary components within a locality with a demonstrated similarity of content are assumed to be related in some way and are said to belong to a particular phase. A site could be characterized by a single component or contain multiple components. The chronological succession of components or phases within a locality makes up the local sequence.

If the archaeologist can assume that taxonomic units have any social reality, then the equivalent of the component would be the community and the equivalent of the phase would be the society or the tribe. Related phases could represent a particular ethnic group that shared a common culture. Of this we can never be sure. At best taxonomy is a tool to bring order to archaeological data.

Archaeological remains in a region can show formal similarities to those over a broader area. This could indicate actual contact or movement between people in various regions, or it might suggest the success of particular aspects of culture content. Widely distributed styles in culture content are the basis for the definition of the horizon. Sites in a region can also show similarity in form to one another over long periods of time. This might reflect an actual antecedent-descendant relationship or the persistence of a particularly successful way of life and technology. The longer-term trajectories of similar culture content are usually referred to as traditions. Traditions can sometimes be subdivided into sequential variants.

At the broadest level of archaeological synthesis for New World prehistory are cultural stages: Lithic, Archaic, Formative, Classic, and Postclassic. Each emphasizes a dominant economic pattern and associated technologies. Stages are somewhat equivalent to the more familiar Old World sequence of ages: Paleolithic, Mesolithic, Neolithic, Bronze, and Iron. The stage is considered to be a segment of a historical sequence in a given area defined by content alone, devoid of time. In contrast, the definition of a period depends on the recognition of both content and especially of time (Krieger in Willey and Phillips 1958:247). As an area becomes better known and dated, it is possible to define a sequence of periods.

Since the introduction of the W&P system, prehistorians throughout the Midwest have generally been abandoning the MTS. Difficulties have arisen in applying either system to the local data. Some archaeologists continue to mix the two systems or simply to replace terminology from the MTS with that from W&P. The MTS term "focus," for instance, is often replaced by the "phase" of the W&P system when the temporal dimension can be added.

In this book, an attempt has been made to follow the W&P taxonomy and to order Iowa's archaeological past chronologically. The reader should be aware, however, that cultural traditions crosscut both temporal and spatial boundaries. Woodland developments did not mean the end of Archaic lifeways, and people in western Iowa continued to follow the traditions of their Paleoindian ancestors as their neighbors adopted the customs of Archaic societies elsewhere.

Classification systems are artificial frameworks intended to serve as tools to organize and compare material remains in order to learn something about the people who left them. It is often easy to forget that the ultimate goal is to try to understand the culture of the people behind the projectile points, potsherds, and post molds. We can hope that our classifications have some meaning in reality, but of this we can never be sure. As might be expected, the past was probably a lot "messier" than our taxonomies indicate.

## APPENDIX 1.1.

### Site Nomenclature

Each recorded site in Iowa is assigned a three-part notation according to a standardized system developed by the Smithsonian Institution and used throughout the U.S. (Frankforter 1953). The Helen Smith site, for example, is 13LA71. The number 13 represents Iowa, which is thirteenth when the contiguous states are alphabetized; the letters LA, the abbreviation for Louisa County, where the site is located; and 71, the number assigned to this particular site to distinguish it from all others previously recorded in that county.

## APPENDIX 1.2.

### Radiocarbon Calibration

The chronology presented in this text is based on the Gregorian calendar with dates expressed in B.C. and A.D. Because dates obtained from the radiocarbon dating method do not correspond to dates in true calendar years, the radiocarbon age determination and the general chronologies derived from such "raw" [14]C results have been calibrated to Gregorian calendar dates. All calibrations were done with the Radiocarbon Calibration Program 1993, Revision 3.0.3 (CALIB 3.0.3), Quaternary Isotope Lab, University of Washington (Stuiver and Reimer 1993). For [14]C dates between 6000 and 20,000 B.C. calibrated (ca. 10,000–20,000 radiocarbon years before present [RCYBP]), a combined dataset based on bidecadal tree-ring and coral data was used. For dates younger than 6000 B.C. calibrated, the decadal tree-ring dataset was used. For all radiocarbon dates, the respective calibration curves were smoothed using a five-point moving average. For dates older than 6000 B.C., this is equivalent to a 100-year moving average; for dates later than 6000 B.C., it is equivalent to a 50-year moving average. The moving averages were used because most radiocarbon dates are based on carbon produced over a period of time. For example, a single piece of wood charcoal may be easily comprised

of 5–50 annual tree rings, and many [14]C dates are obtained from multiple pieces of carbonized material spanning several years. When multiple [14]C dates are available from a single component at a site, a weighted mean of the dates was calculated prior to calibration.

Because the radiocarbon dating method is based on the random decay of a radioactive isotope, there is an associated counting error reported by the laboratory. In addition to this statistical error, there are systematic errors from other sources, such as sample contamination and counting equipment instabilities. The size and nature of these latter errors are almost never reported by [14]C laboratories but are generally assumed to be as much as one or two times as large as the counting error itself. To allow the dates in this text to reflect the various sources of error associated with radiocarbon dating, the one-sigma ranges provided by the CALIB calibration program were utilized to represent the associated counting error. Then the oldest end point of each range was rounded to the next older 100-year value if a B.C. date and to the next older 50-year value if an A.D. date. The youngest end point of the range was rounded to the next younger 100-year value if a B.C. date and to the next younger 50-year value if an A.D. date. As an example of this rounding procedure, a radiocarbon age of 1350 ± 70 RCYBP produces a calibrated date of A.D. 670 with a one-sigma range of A.D. 646–757. This rounded range will be A.D. 600–800. Thus, if a site yields a radiocarbon result of 1350 ± 70 RCYBP, we can be reasonably confident that it was inhabited sometime between A.D. 600 and 800 in actual calendar years.

The rounding of the one-sigma errors accomplishes two goals. First, it increases the range somewhat so that the actual activities of interest are more likely to have occurred within the range than if just the one-sigma results of the calibration program were reported unaltered. Second, and more important, it helps prevent the reader from attributing more precision to a date than is warranted when both sources of error are considered. The larger rounding factor is used for B.C. dates because, compared to younger dates, older dates generally have larger counting errors and can have larger systematic error resulting from sample contamination.

Overall, the preceding procedures were adhered to when reporting dates in the text. There are a few exceptions. First, if an author had already provided a calibrated chronology and adhered to a rounding scheme similar to that outlined above, the date was used as published. Second, in some cases authors provided approximate dates for events in radiocarbon years before present based on a general assessment of the radiocarbon chronology. These dates were then calibrated and a calendar date reported after rounding the intercept provided by the CALIB program. Generally, original dates reported in a radiocarbon time frame were rounded to the same number of significant digits after calibrating. If an author, for example, had reported an event such as the end of the Wisconsin glacial maximum as occurring at approximately 14,000 RCYBP (i.e., to the nearest 1000 years or two significant digits), the same event would be dated to approximately 15,000 B.C. in this text.

# 2   History of Iowa Archaeology

We believe strongly, and a great many people in Indian country believe strongly, that no human remains or grave goods should be excavated, housed, and/or subjected to studies in museums and other academic institutions without tribal consent.
>                —National Indian Education Association,
>          February 22, 1990, *SAA Bulletin* 11(3):9

A CENTURY AGO there were people who dug into archaeological sites, particularly burial mounds, to acquire the unusual artifacts within and to obtain evidence to support theories concerning mysterious "moundbuilders" (fig. 2.1). The more enlightened of these individuals were aware of the necessity of careful excavation, had a rudimentary understanding of the importance of context and stratigraphy, and published the results of their fieldwork. Their insights were limited, however, because important premises upon which the modern discipline of archaeology is based were not yet widely recognized and because these investigators primarily sought "objects," not information. They also lacked certain essential tools that would allow them to date finds accurately and relate them to others.

## The Moundbuilders

As Euroamericans advanced across North America throughout the nineteenth century, they encountered large earthen enclosures and huge mounds that became the object of fanciful speculation. Although a few individuals—including Thomas Jefferson, who excavated mounds on his own property—suggested that these were the works of prehistoric American Indians, most were unwilling to credit these people with such monumental achievements. To account for the earthworks, the "moundbuilder theory" came

into vogue. Central to this theory was a belief in the existence of an earlier race of people derived from one of the more "advanced" Old World civilizations. This race was thought to have built the mounds and then to have been exterminated or amalgamated by arriving American Indian peoples. Demonstrating the existence and identity of the moundbuilders became a primary motive behind the archaeological explorations of most nineteenth-century North American antiquarians (Silverberg 1968).

### The Davenport Conspiracy

In Iowa as elsewhere, the moundbuilder controversy inspired the earliest excavation, and burial mounds were the focus. These projects only rarely resulted in useful details of mound structure and content. Instead, the initial period in Iowa is characterized by the destructive looting of mounds to gain the exotic "treasures" they were thought to contain.

Private scientific academies such as the Iowa Academy of Science, the Muscatine Academy of Science, and the Davenport Academy of Natural Sciences sponsored many excavations in the period between 1870 and the 1890s (fig 2.2). Beginning in 1874, the Reverend Jacob Gass reported discoveries from the Cook Farm Mounds (13ST82) in Davenport and from two other locations in Louisa County. In addition to artifacts

**2.1.** Dismantling of the Middle Woodland Boone Mound, Boone County, in 1908. Courtesy of the State Historical Society of Iowa, Des Moines.

that later would be placed within the Middle Woodland Havana-Hopewell complex, Reverend Gass presented some rather amazing finds, including slate tablets inscribed with a zodiac and various Near Eastern signs and symbols. If accepted as credible, these items reinforced the postulated link between the moundbuilders and Old World civilizations. Stone pipes carved in the shape of elephants, included in Gass's discoveries, also seemed to demonstrate the contemporaneity of the moundbuilders with ancient mastodons—another archaeological conundrum of the day (McKusick 1970, 1991).

Many in the Davenport Academy supported Gass and his discoveries. Others, however, did not. By the 1880s opposition to the moundbuilder theory was gaining strength. Careful surveys and excavations in the eastern United States, particularly those of Cyrus Thomas and the Division of Mound Exploration under the Smithsonian's Bureau of Ethnology, were dem-

**2.2.** William H. Pratt, charter member and first salaried president of the Davenport Academy of Natural Sciences and one of the excavators of the Toolesboro Mounds. Courtesy of the Putnam Museum of History and Natural Science, Davenport, Iowa.

onstrating that the mounds and their contents represented the accomplishments of earlier American Indian peoples, not a mysterious moundbuilding race. On viewing the Davenport finds, the Bureau charged that the tablets and pipes were fraudulent and questioned not only the authenticity of the artifacts themselves but the circumstances surrounding their discovery.

The debate that followed this incident and the dispute it created shattered the Davenport Academy. Secret testimony disclosed that the entire event was the result of a series of hoaxes and subsequent efforts to conceal them. The artifacts had been manufactured and planted primarily to deceive Reverend Gass. Unfortunately, this evidence was largely suppressed, and almost a century would pass before the full nature of the fraud was publicly disclosed (McKusick 1970, 1991).

### The Development of the Discipline in Iowa

The speculative nature of archaeology that characterized the earliest investigations in Iowa gradually gave way to fieldwork and publications of a higher quality. While mounds continued to be the focus of investigation into the twentieth century, greater attention was paid to excavation, site survey, and mapping and to the description and classification of artifacts. This more rigorous approach helped to refute the moundbuilder theory and to gain recognition and acceptance of American Indian peoples as the true moundbuilders. This recognition in turn affected the nature of fieldwork and the development of archaeology as an established discipline. Archaeologists now considered a wider variety of sites worthy of study since, as Charles R. Keyes was later to observe, "if the American Indians built the mounds, and if it is his past that we are studying, then not the mounds only become, but everything that this past produces becomes, the object of our quest" (Keyes 1920:361). Consequently, because American archaeology was recognized as an extension of American Indian studies, it became an integral part of the developing field of anthropology.

Iowa shared in the more exacting quality of archaeological fieldwork that typified the late nineteenth century and contributed individuals who advanced the cause of the discipline itself. The efforts of Colonel P. W. Norris on behalf of

Cyrus Thomas's mound survey of eastern North America in the early 1880s, Theodore Lewis for the Northwestern Archaeological Survey between 1883 and 1898 (Haury 1993; Keyes 1928a, 1930), and Duren Ward during the first decade of the twentieth century reflect a more systematic approach to fieldwork than that found among many of their contemporaries.

In 1882 Norris prepared the first map of sites on the Hartley Terrace in Allamakee County and test excavated mounds there (McKusick 1973; Thomas 1887b, 1894). Lewis recorded a wide variety of sites, surveying not only a large number of mounds but numerous earthwork enclosures and rock art (fig. 2.3). Ward, a Universalist minister from Iowa City, displayed an awareness and attention to detail remarkable for his day. He described a mound excavated at Lake Okoboji in Dickinson County and provided a discussion of the finds and a site plan and profile (Ward 1905a). Ward photographed "important" objects in situ and bagged each object, noting its provenience (fig. 2.4). His recognition of stratigraphy and intrusive features is a particularly significant achievement since throughout most of North America stratigraphic work was neglected until after World War I (fig. 2.5). In addition, Ward was one of the first to call for an interdisciplinary approach to archaeology, suggesting the need to employ specialists from other sciences in order to fully interpret archaeological sites and their environmental context. He also stressed the importance of soil analysis and lithic sourcing (McKusick 1975a:37).

One of the most important contributions during this period was an annotated bibliography and summary of Iowa antiquities published by Frederick Starr in 1897, which described the fieldwork and archaeological discoveries in Iowa to that date. While Starr's publication clearly illustrates the emphasis on mound exploration characteristic of the time—of the 244 papers listed in the bibliography, 197 describe mound sites—it also shows that other information was being recovered. This data would form the basis

**2.3.** Theodore Hayes Lewis conducted surveys and mapping in Iowa for the Northwestern Archaeological Survey during the 1880s and 1890s. Courtesy of the Goodhue County Historical Society, Red Wing, Minnesota. From Haury 1993.

and the Iowa General Assembly expanded the functions of the State Historical Society to include anthropological survey. Despite these achievements, none of the state's institutions of higher learning established an anthropology program for several decades, and the Iowa Anthropological Association itself collapsed when Ward left Iowa in 1907.

Other individuals and private institutions continued explorations throughout this period. In 1910 members of the Sioux City Academy of Science and Letters excavated sites in Plymouth County, including the Mill Creek Broken Kettle site (13PM1) (Banks and Lilly 1968; Powers 1910) (fig. 2.6). The State Historical Museum in Des Moines sponsored excavations at the Middle Woodland Boone Mound (13BN29) on the Des Moines River under the direction of Thompson Van Hyning (Van Hyning 1910a, 1910b) (fig. 2.7). The Davenport Museum, reorganized from the shattered Davenport Academy, redeemed its reputation by enlisting the professional services of William B. Nickerson at the Albany Mounds'

for defining the major prehistoric cultures in the state.

Starr also outlined a more systematic approach to research and advanced the cause of anthropology as an academic discipline by teaching its first course in Iowa at Coe College in 1887. Ward likewise urged the establishment of anthropology as an academic pursuit and supported the development of institutions that would improve its status (Ward 1903b). Through his efforts, the Iowa Anthropological Association was organized in 1903,

**2.4.** Duren Ward. The excavations of Duren Ward in the early twentieth century exemplify an attention to detail missing in the work of most of his contemporaries. Courtesy of the State Historical Society of Iowa, Iowa City.

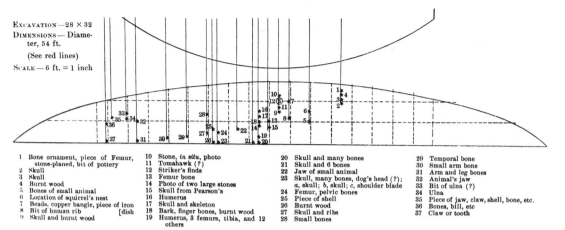

EXCAVATION—28 × 32
DIMENSIONS — Diame-
ter, 54 ft.
(See red lines)
SCALE — 6 ft. = 1 inch

1   Bone ornament, piece of Femur, stone-planed, bit of pottery
2   Skull
3   Skull
4   Burnt wood
5   Bones of small animal
6   Location of squirrel's nest
7   Beads, copper bangle, piece of iron [dish
8   Bit of human rib
9   Skull and burnt wood
10   Stone, *in situ*, photo
11   Tomahawk (?)
12   Striker's finds
13   Femur bone
14   Photo of two large stones
15   Skull from Pearson's
16   Humerus
17   Skull and skeleton
18   Bark, finger bones, burnt wood
19   Humerus, 3 femurs, tibia, and 12 others
20   Skull and many bones
21   Skull and 6 bones
22   Jaw of small animal
23   Skull, many bones, dog's head (?); *a*, skull; *b*, skull; *c*, shoulder blade
24   Femur, pelvic bones
25   Piece of shell
26   Burnt wood
27   Skull and ribs
28   Small bones
29   Temporal bone
30   Small arm bone
31   Arm and leg bones
32   Animal's jaw
33   Bit of ulna (?)
34   Ulna
35   Piece of jaw, claw, shell, bone, etc.
36   Bones, bill, etc
37   Claw or tooth

**2.5.** Profile of a mound excavated by Duren Ward at Lake Okoboji. Courtesy of the State Historical Society of Iowa, Iowa City.

**2.6.** Early excavation of a Mill Creek midden at the Broken Kettle site, Plymouth County. Courtesy of the State Historical Society of Iowa, Iowa City.

site in Illinois in 1908 and Truman Michelson from the Smithsonian at the Pine Creek Mounds (13MC44) in Iowa in 1914. At both sites mounds were professionally surveyed and topographic maps prepared (DeWys-Van Hecke 1990; Herold 1971; Hodges 1989).

**2.7.** Thompson Van Hyning (lower right) and assistants, excavators of the Boone Mound, Boone County.
Courtesy of the State Historical Society of Iowa, Des Moines.

## Culture History: The Contributions of Keyes and Orr

The increasing number of excavations across the country during the early twentieth century created large collections of archaeological materials. Between World War I and World War II archaeologists classified and compared artifacts from these collections in order to establish regional chronologies that served as the basis for outlining the culture history of North America as a whole. These goals were facilitated by the growing attention given to stratigraphic excavation and to artifact seriation.

Although a number of Iowa researchers shared in these pursuits between 1920 and 1950, the ef-

forts of two individuals, Charles R. Keyes and his assistant, Ellison Orr, dominated Iowa archaeology throughout this period. Their field investigations and publications established the prehistoric outline of the state, and as a result of their efforts, the public recognized and accepted archaeology as a respected endeavor (Green 1992).

Keyes, a professor of German language and literature at Cornell College in Mt. Vernon, Iowa, had an active interest in archaeology (fig. 2.8). This curiosity led him to examine artifact collections and sites and to record his observations carefully. In 1920 he presented a paper, "Some Materials for the Study of Iowa Archaeology," at the Iowa Academy of Science meeting. This paper summarized and evaluated the archaeological accomplishments in the state and emphasized the potential of Iowa antiquities. The presentation came to the attention of Benjamin F. Shambaugh, superintendent of the State Historical Society of Iowa, who in 1921 arranged for Keyes's appointment as research associate under the auspices of the Society and the University of Iowa. Keyes came to assume the title of Director of the State Archaeological Survey, a position he retained until his death 30 years later (Keyes 1929).

Early in his career with the Survey, Keyes prepared a bibliography and summary of available sources dealing with Iowa archaeology. In researching this publication Keyes collected all available literature on the subject, visited libraries and institutions in Iowa and surrounding states, and consulted individual collectors and examined collections and sites in every Iowa county. As a result, Keyes published his first outline of Iowa prehistory in 1927. In this scheme, he named four prehistoric cultures: Oneota, Mill Creek, Effigy Mound, and Glenwood (Keyes 1927b). During these years he also engaged in extensive research that attempted to dem-

onstrate that certain early historic archaeological sites were the product of known American Indian tribes.

Until 1934 Keyes conducted only minimal field investigations. In that year he directed the first of several field projects for the Survey, utilizing crews provided by federal programs such as the Federal Emergency Relief Administration and the Work Projects Administration. His field assistant until 1939 was Ellison Orr. Orr, a civil engineer, had a lifetime interest in archaeology and was a competent surveyor and field technician, having spent the better part of his 77 years locating and recording sites near his home in northeastern Iowa (fig. 2.9). In his position with the Survey, Orr conducted surveys and excavations, sometimes devoting as much as six to eight months in the field. Orr's detailed maps, photographs, and descriptive reports provide a substantial contribution to the database on Iowa prehistory (Orr 1963).

Keyes consciously fostered public awareness of archaeology. He presented lectures and published popular articles such as those that appeared in the *Palimpsest,* the State Historical Society's magazine of popular history. He described the types of sites that might be expected in Iowa and continued to discourage the tenacious moundbuilder myth. This involvement with the public paved the way for the establishment of a state archaeological society and the eventual acquisition of public funds.

By the early 1940s Keyes again proposed an outline of five archaeological manifestations present in Iowa: Woodland, Hopewell, Oneota, Glenwood, and Mill Creek (Keyes 1941b). While much of his synthesis was based on the results of the Survey, he and Orr benefited from their contacts with contemporaries working in the state. Prominent among these were A. A. Christensen, Frank Ellis, Henry Field, MacKinley Kantor, Mildred Mott, Paul Rowe, Paul Sagers (fig. 2.10), Nestor Stiles, and Frank Van Voorhis (Billeck and Rowe 1992; Cordell et al. 1991; Green et al. 1992).

**2.8.** Charles R. Keyes is often credited as the "Father of Iowa Archaeology." Courtesy of the State Historical Society of Iowa, Iowa City.

**2.9.** Pioneer archaeologist Ellison Orr excavating a burial in Allamakee County. Courtesy of the State Historical Society of Iowa, Iowa City.

**2.10.** Paul Sagers in front of the Levsen Rockshelter, Jackson County, in 1933. Photo by Charles R. Keyes. Courtesy of the State Historical Society of Iowa, Iowa City. From Cordell et al. 1991.

Keyes and Orr employed the techniques and methodology current to the discipline at the time and networked with archaeologists elsewhere. The organization of the State Archaeological Survey itself was patterned after that established by Clark Wissler and the National Research Council, which funded a committee on state archaeological surveys. Keyes utilized the Direct Historical Approach (Strong 1935; see chapter 12) and the Midwestern Taxonomic System (MTS) (McKern 1939; see chapter 1). He attended regional and national conferences and presented papers on Iowa archaeology. Keyes organized the third Plains Conference for archaeology, held in 1936 at Mt. Vernon, Iowa, where archaeologists were invited to discuss the newly developed MTS (Green 1992:81).

By the time Keyes and Orr died in 1951, their efforts to popularize and promote archaeology were bearing fruit. The Iowa Archeological Society (IAS) was a reality, Effigy Mounds was designated a National Monument, and archaeologists were on staff there and at the Sanford Museum in Cherokee (Green 1992:83). Shortly thereafter, an archaeology program was established at the University of Iowa. The Keyes Collection, now at the Office of the State Archaeologist (OSA) in Iowa City, today contains over 108,000 artifacts and supporting documentation systematically gathered from surface survey, donations, and Work Projects Administration-sponsored research (Alex et al. 1998). The accomplishments of these two men justify their recognition as leaders in Iowa archaeology (Anderson 1975a; Green 1992; McKusick 1975a, 1979; Petersen 1951).

## Past Lifeways and Culture Process: 1950s–1970s

Although Iowans contributed little to the development of professional methodology in the decade following the deaths of Keyes and Orr (Anderson 1975a:79), the prehistoric framework elucidated by them was expanded and clarified. Responsibility for this can be attributed to the

IAS and its local chapters, to the archaeology program established at the University of Iowa in 1952, and to the surveys and excavations in the Effigy Mounds region initiated by the National Park Service and conducted by Paul Beaubien and Wilfred Logan. Members of the Northeast Chapter of the IAS participated in the National Park Service projects and undertook individual research. The Central Chapter of the IAS, founded by R. W. Breckenridge and G. S. Guynnes, supported the work of individuals such as Paul Rowe and Donald Davis in the southwestern part of the state. The Northwest Chapter, centered around Cherokee, was particularly active during the 1950s and 1960s. Guided by the Sanford Museum and its director, W. D. Frankforter and later Duane Anderson, members such as A. C. Thompson, Clinton Lawver, Chuck Smith, Shirley Smith, Nestor Stiles, Joe Beals, Roger Banks, Ruth Thornton, and David Lilly conducted fieldwork at a number of important northwestern Iowa sites.

At the same time, Reynold Ruppé, appointed to the University of Iowa's Department of Sociology and Anthropology in 1952, together with David Stout organized the archaeological program at the University of Iowa. Ruppé directed numerous field projects over the next few years, and many of his students, including Adrian Anderson, Dale Henning, John Ives, Eugene Fugle, and George Cowgill, subsequently became prominent archaeologists.

Prior to 1960 there was limited public funding for fieldwork in Iowa. Keyes's appointment had been state supported through a joint sponsorship by the State Historical Society and the University of Iowa. Ruppé had minimal support from the University of Iowa. He also received funds from the American Philosophical Foundation and the Old Gold Foundation. After its formation, the IAS was an ardent supporter of many field projects. Reports of finds and excavations were published in the *Journal of the Iowa Archeological Society* (*JIAS*) and in the newsletters of the Society and its Northwest Chapter.

As the rate of site destruction increased through the years, the State Historical Society and the University of Iowa were unable to provide sufficient support for salvage excavations. Nor was there any concerted preservation plan to protect remaining antiquities. As a result, Ruppé urged the legislature to consider the establishment of a state office that might coordinate archaeological research. In 1959 the OSA was established, with Ruppé at its head. It was not until he had resigned this position and left the state, however, that the new State Archaeologist, Marshall McKusick, began to receive the support necessary to establish an effective archaeological program.

Throughout this period archaeologists continued to clarify the prehistoric outline of North America. Extensive, federally sponsored programs such as the massive public works projects of the 1930s and the reservoir salvage programs of the 1940s through the 1960s produced a wealth of new information and reflected public attention to archaeology. In the process of inventorying and salvaging information from sites slated for inundation by massive dam construction, small armies of young archaeologists cut their eyeteeth on sites within the Missouri and Mississippi river basins as part of the Smithsonian Institution's River Basin Surveys. In Iowa important new sites were recorded and excavated in the Saylorville, Red Rock, and Coralville reservoirs (fig. 2.11).

The discovery of the radiocarbon dating technique in 1949, a by-product of the Manhattan Project, greatly facilitated the archaeologist's ability to order prehistoric events in time. Although establishing secure chronologies was essential, the goals for many archaeologists began

**2.11.** Iowa State University excavations at the Saylorville Reservoir. Photo archives, Iowa State University Archaeological Laboratory, Ames.

to shift from the construction of culture history to an attempt to understand past lifeways within a broader social and environmental context and to explain culture process within a wider cultural evolutionary framework.

To some extent, Iowa shared in these loftier pursuits, as reflected in many of the reports and papers that appeared in the *JIAS* and the publication series of the OSA, which began in 1970. During this time archaeology was strongly affected by scientific developments and by a confidence in the methodology and philosophy of science in general. Archaeologists were admonished to make their research rigorous and "explicit" and to integrate scientific methodology with archaeological inquiry.

As the discipline of archaeology became more standardized with a rigorous methodology and theoretical base, the gap between professional and avocational archaeologists seemed to widen. In Iowa the *JIAS* became increasingly technical, with fewer contributions by nonprofessionals, and fewer field projects encouraged the public's participation. Although Marshall McKusick produced a film series on Iowa archaeology as well as a popular text, it was during Duane Anderson's tenure as State Archaeologist (1975–1986) that a conscientious effort was made to encourage avocational interests and to develop a program in public education (fig. 2.12). The results included a certification program, field schools, teacher workshops, filmstrips and films, publications, and correspondence courses. Archaeology Week, officially sanctioned by a governor's proclamation in 1993, and a World Wide Web home page on Iowa archaeology are recent additions to these endeavors (Alex et al. 1998).

## Archaeology and the Law

Beginning in the 1960s, federal and state legislatures have enacted laws that have had a tremendous impact on the protection of prehistoric and historic sites and on the practice of archaeology in Iowa and throughout North America. While the earliest laws were designed to protect

**2.12.** Duane Anderson, Iowa's State Archaeologist 1975–1986, excavating at the Lewis Central School site, Pottawattamie County. Photo archives, Office of the State Archaeologist, University of Iowa.

archaeological remains from destruction, the most recent legislation seems intended to protect some of these same remains from the archaeologist.

Federal laws to protect archaeological resources in North America are not new. The Federal Antiquities Act of 1906 made federal officials responsible for protecting archaeological sites as public resources and for combating looting and vandalism (Stuart and McManamon 1996:31). In the 1960s and 1970s additional legislation greatly altered the practice of archaeology in the United States and as a result expanded the job market for archaeologists. The National Historic Preservation Act of 1966, with its Sections 106 and 110, required federal agencies and those receiving federal funds or permits to assess the effect of their "undertakings" on archaeological resources. The Archaeological Resources Protection Act of 1979 established major criminal and civil penalties for violators of the Federal Antiquities Act. In 1988 the law was amended to simplify prosecutions and to make the intent to loot a felony. Amendments also required federal agencies to undertake surveys of archaeological resources and to expand public education programs (Stuart and McManamon 1996:32).

As a result of these laws, there has been a tremendous increase in the number of archaeological surveys and excavations supported by federal agencies or by private companies. This has meant that many new sites have been discovered and others preserved. Some sites have been nominated to the National Register of Historic Places, and others have been incorporated into national and state parks, such as the Iowa State Preserves system. In those instances where sites have not been saved, important information has been acquired as a result of phased testing and excavation. Such research has promoted an increased public awareness of the nation's antiquities and the role archaeology plays in their preservation.

Iowa has been exemplary in its efforts to preserve and protect prehistoric and historic antiquities. Attempts to salvage archaeological sites were well under way in Iowa before the national legislation of the 1960s and 1970s. The strong public interest in the state's cultural resources was a major factor in drawing official attention to historically important sites and obtaining their National Register status. The Division of Historic Preservation, now the Community Programs Bureau of the State Historical Society of Iowa, has been a national leader in the nomination of sites to the National Register of Historic Places and has arranged for many ongoing cultural resources studies. The Bureau keeps an archive of reports on archaeological and historic architectural surveys conducted in Iowa and maintains a database on historic structures.

Because of their familiarity with local areas, avocational archaeologists are valuable assets in recognizing and preserving archaeological sites in the state. Since its establishment almost fifty years ago, the IAS and its six regional chapters have located, helped investigate, and preserved many sites throughout Iowa.

### Cultural Resource Management

With the greater demand for archaeological surveys and excavations required by federal legislation, employment possibilities for archaeologists expanded, and a new subdiscipline, Cultural Resource Management (CRM), evolved. Today more than two-thirds of all archaeologists in the United States are employed in CRM archaeology (Green and Doershuk 1998:3). While CRM programs are often part of public institutions and offices, numerous programs also exist within private firms. The primary state agency with a major CRM program in Iowa is the OSA. The OSA is charged with compiling, disseminating, and preserving information on Iowa's prehistoric and historic past and maintains a database on over 18,000 archaeological sites. More than two-thirds of the OSA staff are employed in two CRM divisions, the Highway Archaeology Program and the General Contracts Program. Iowa State University also has an active CRM program. In addition, several private firms conduct CRM archaeology in the state (Green and Doershuk 1998).

### Protection of Human Remains and Sacred Sites

The treatment of ancient human remains is currently one of the most important issues affecting North American archaeology. The last few decades have seen heated encounters between members of the archaeological community and native peoples regarding the issue of native burials and ceremonial sites, including their disturbance, handling, and interpretation by non-natives and the disposition of the remains (Green and Doershuk 1998). During this period, a number of incidents in Iowa and elsewhere demonstrated the differential treatment extended to historic Euroamerican sites as opposed to their prehistoric native counterparts (Appendix 2.1). Although it was unlawful to disturb or vandalize historic cemeteries, prehistoric burial grounds were not afforded equal protection.

The recognition that the excavation of native burial sites might constitute a form of desecration was expressed early on in Iowa but was largely disregarded (Toole 1868:53). In 1976 a state burial law was enacted, the first of its kind in the country. This legislation was designed to prohibit unauthorized excavation of ancient human remains, that is, human remains older than 150 years, on all lands in Iowa. To do so is considered an act of criminal mischief in the third degree. The law also outlined a procedure for the investigation and reinterment of those burials unavoidably disturbed. As specified in the Iowa Code, the OSA is responsible for the protection of and reburial of ancient human remains. An Indian Advisory Committee, made up of Native Americans in Iowa, works closely with the OSA to implement the law and to insure compliance with new federal legislation (fig. 2.13).

**2.13.** Maria Pearson (Running Moccasins) and grandson Nick Jensen. Pearson, a Yankton Sioux, has been a key figure in shaping Iowa's legal position with regard to the protection of ancient burial sites and the reburial of human remains. Courtesy of the State Historical Society of Iowa, Iowa City. Original in possession of Maria Pearson.

In 1990 the Native American Graves Protection and Repatriation Act (NAGPRA) was enacted by Congress and signed into law. It requires federal agencies and most museums in the United States to inventory Native American human remains, burial artifacts, sacred objects, and objects formerly owned communally by tribes and to offer to return them to the tribes clearly affiliated with them (Stuart and McManamon 1996:32).

NAGPRA legislation represents the beginning of a new era for North American archaeology. The debate surrounding the law and its application has already necessitated a greater level of dialogue and cooperation between archaeologists and the Native American community and more thoughtful concern on the part of the profession regarding the disposition of ancient remains. While the law does not resolve many important issues and is viewed by some native peoples as yet another tactic to delay the return of what is considered rightfully theirs, it has already changed the face of the profession and is likely to continue to do so well into the future.

## Recent Developments

The reconstruction of culture history and the protection and preservation of diminishing cultural resources remain fundamental goals for North American and Iowa archaeologists. New methods and techniques, many an outgrowth of advances in computer technology, have been added to older procedures. As the number of professional archaeologists in the state has grown—membership in the Association of Iowa Archaeologists, the state professional organization, totaled over 60 in 1998—research continues to mirror the objectives and theoretical perspectives of the discipline in general. One of the most enduring of these perspectives has been the ecosystem model, which views human culture as a dynamic entity linked to a much larger environmental and social system. In practice this encourages the archaeologist to gather detailed information about the interrelationship between past culture, landscape, and environment. Such an approach has inspired improved data-recovery methods, particularly those related to the retrieval of environmental and geomorphologic information. Because no individual archaeologist can be a master of many disciplines, it has also promoted an interdisciplinary effort that brings together specialists from many sciences working toward common goals. The large multidisciplinary projects at the Cherokee Sewer (13CK405) and Gast Farm (13LA12) sites are good examples.

While archaeological research throughout North America continues to emphasize the importance of rigorous testing and analysis, some archaeologists have lost confidence in the ability of science to provide explanations for the cultural behaviors of the past. Many believe that our own cultural biases and twenty-first-century "boundedness" restrict our ability to understand the prehistory and history of others. Some have suggested that there are multiple interpretations of the past and that archaeologists no longer have exclusive rights to formulate these (Miller 1998).

These concerns, coupled with a renewed awareness of the social and ethical responsibilities to sites, to Native Americans, and to other minorities, are inspiring new directions in the discipline. Archaeologists are more frequently relying on native oral tradition in the analysis and interpretation of some prehistoric remains. Native Iowa peoples, including the Meskwaki and the Ioway, have their own stories to tell, and modern archaeologists seem more willing to listen. Gender issues are now a part of the discipline, and archaeologists are devising ways both to recognize gender in the archaeological record and, more important, to counter gender bias in archaeological interpretation. These and other issues are not unique to archaeology but mirror concerns in other academic disciplines and in society at large. They are likely to guide the direction of archaeology for some time to come.

## APPENDIX 2.1.
### Maria Pearson (Running Moccasins)

Maria Pearson (Running Moccasins), a member of the Yankton Sioux tribe who has lived in Iowa for 40 years, was a key figure in convincing Iowa's legislators to pass a law protecting ancient Indian burial sites. Born in Springfield, South Dakota, she was living in a small Iowa town in 1969 when her husband, John, an engineer for the Iowa Department of Transportation, informed her of the disturbance of a pioneer cemetery and the subsequent reburial of all but one of its 27 occupants. The one unburied individual was identified as an American Indian woman and was removed to the University of Iowa for further study. Angered at the differential treatment afforded this individual, Pearson demanded a hearing with the governor. The incident, the media attention, and the public support it drew weighed on state legislators, who in 1976 passed a law protecting ancient burial sites, the first of its kind enacted in the United States. Today, Pearson remains an activist for American Indian rights, serving on the Indian Advisory Council of the Office of the State Archaeologist and the State Historical Society of Iowa and as the Governor's Liaison for Indian Affairs (from Frese 1993 and Ruth 1993).

# 3  Iowa Landscapes

Loose,
the windblown silt
of glacial melt,
and loose these hills,
as if they might wander
over the broken prairie.
—From "Wind-borne,"
   by Neal Bowers (Mutel
   and Swander 1994)

IOWA LIES at the intersection of the Eastern Woodlands and the Western Prairie-Plains. For this reason the history of its native peoples reflects adaptations to a diversity of landscapes as well as lifeways shared with societies in more woodland settings to the east and in grasslands to the west. At the time of historic Euroamerican contact, Iowa was described as a sea of tall-grass prairie with ribbons of deciduous woodland along the river valleys and slopes and in fire-protected gullies and hollows elsewhere (fig. 3.1). The late-seventeenth-century journal entries of explorers, traders, missionaries, military men, and settlers provide the first written impressions of the Iowa landscape at the time of contact. While accounts such as those of Marquette and Joliet in 1673 or Lewis and Clark in 1804 and 1806 often reflect little more than fleeting comments as these early travelers canoed down the Mississippi or keeled up the Missouri, later descriptions are more detailed.

The Government Land Office (GLO) surveyors who mapped the new Iowa Territory for settlement beginning in 1832 recorded the distinctive combinations of relief, drainage, prairie, and woodlands, as well as the resource potential for human settlement, in each of the areas in which they worked. According to their surveys, grass-land covered about 85 percent of the state (Bowles 1975:19). Their maps and notes, in combination with modern soils maps, have become valuable resources for archaeologists attempting to reconstruct the immediate precontact landscape of Iowa (fig. 3.2).

For the prehistoric period there are no such accounts. Archaeologists rely on geologists, geomorphologists, and paleoecologists to help them interpret earlier landscape events and their effect on the archaeological record. Knowledge of such events makes it possible to reconstruct ancient environments, to predict where sites might be located, and to select methods that will make it easier to find them. In later chapters these topics will be revisited, and Iowa's prehistoric environments will be described in some detail.

Geologist Jean C. Prior (1991) has divided the state into a series of seven natural regions, distinct in both topography and vegetation. Each of these regions represents an intricate combination of geology, climate, vegetation, and animal life subsequently modified by people. Her descriptions, already classic and beautifully composed, serve as a convenient backdrop against which to begin a study of Iowa's archaeological past. They are paraphrased in the discussion that follows (fig. 3.3).

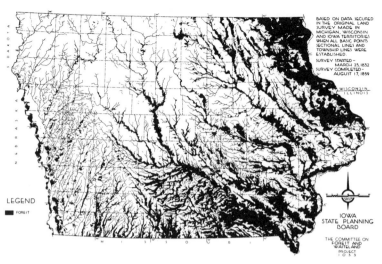

BASED ON DATA SECURED
IN THE ORIGINAL LAND
SURVEY MADE IN
MICHIGAN, WISCONSIN
AND IOWA TERRITORIES
WHEN ALL BASIC POINTS
SECTIONAL LINES AND
TOWNSHIP LINES WERE
ESTABLISHED.
SURVEY STARTED—
MARCH 25, 1832
SURVEY COMPLETED—
AUGUST 17, 1859

LEGEND
■ FOREST

IOWA
STATE PLANNING
BOARD

THE COMMITTEE ON
FOREST AND
WASTELAND
PROJECT
1033

**3.1.** Original forest cover in Iowa. Prepared by Iowa State Planning Board Project 1033 from data secured in the original land surveys, 1832–1859. From Oschwald et al. 1965.

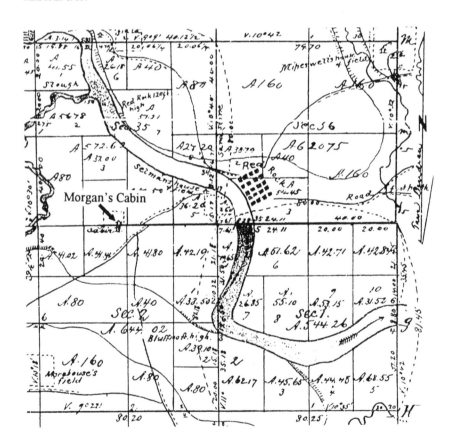

Morgan's Cabin

**3.2.** Original Government Land Office land survey plat of the Red Rock area, 1846–1848, with more recently identified Morgan's Cabin site superimposed. From Rogers 1993.

Framing the state of Iowa on its eastern and western borders, like uneven parenthetical brackets, are segments of two of the continent's mighty river valleys—the Mississippi and Missouri. These broad lowlands were literally being transformed into their modern configurations by massive glacial meltwater and sediment as the very first Iowans watched. Later they became major arteries for trade and exploration by prehistoric and early historic wayfarers. Throughout its recent history the Mississippi River alluvial plain has a broad, biotically rich wooded floodplain rimmed by high bluffs and upland prairie beyond. As the channel downcut through older deposits, a series of alluvial terraces and benches were left standing like progressively younger steps through time. High and dry from subsequent flooding, such locations attracted settlement by the earliest Iowans, while backwater sloughs and oxbow lakes supported rich habitats

for a myriad of plant and animal species and served as important stopovers for hundreds of migratory waterfowl. Here prehistoric people established campsites on sand bars and ridges and later cultivated rich, tillable soils.

Marquette and Joliet began the checklist of resources for this area, noting the presence of bison and deer along the Mississippi River near McGregor in 1673. Marsh and stream-bank communities of canary-reed grass, cattail, bulrush, amaranth, goosefoot, willow, yellow lotus, duck potato, and marshelder shared habitats with turtles, lizards, frogs, snakes, river otters, muskrats, beavers, mink, and migratory waterfowl (Benn 1987:10; Guldner 1960). Dozens of species of fish and various "fat" mussels drew the attention of early explorers. The woodlands on floodplains and slopes were home to species like turkey, opossum, porcupine, raccoon, squirrel, and skunk. Above the bluffs the mid- to tall-

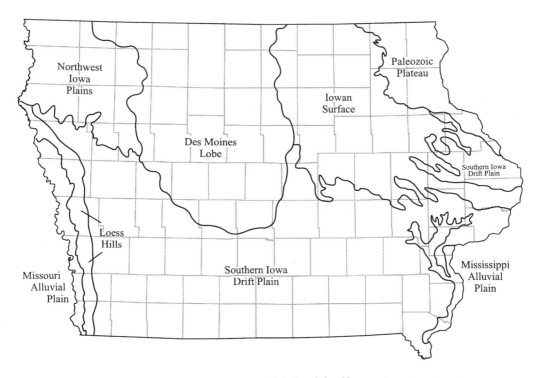

**3.3.** Iowa's landform regions. From Prior 1991.

grass prairie supported a variety of mammals, including rabbit, deer, coyote, elk, and bison. The intersection of prairie and woodlands provided a habitat for numerous songbirds as well as species sought after for food such as prairie chicken, quail, and passenger pigeon. In the more than 150 years that have passed since Iowa became a territory, 17 species of nesting birds have disappeared and 39 species of mammals are gone or are on the decline (Collins 1991:23).

Although its geological history is less well known, the Missouri River alluvial plain presents a more open setting with a wide, pancake-flat valley created by tremendous meltwater floods during the late Pleistocene and a lively, winding river. Throughout its recent history, the river has been known for its massive, disastrous floods and ever-shifting course. The installation of a series of dams by the Army Corps of Engineers has ameliorated the effects of such events but also vastly altered the traditional personality of the river.

A third of Iowa's rivers—including the Big Sioux, Rock, Floyd, Little Sioux, Maple, Soldier, Boyer, Nishnabotna, Nodaway, Platte, Thompson, and Chariton—drain south or southwestward into the Missouri (fig. 3.4). Alluvial fans spread outward from small tributary streams, creating the potential for deeply buried archaeological sites. Historically, woodlands were found in the valleys and fingering up the tributaries, with prairie dominant elsewhere. Sloughgrass predominated in the bottoms, existing as pure stands or accompanying cattail in the swamps (Bowles 1975:20; Weaver and Fitzpatrick 1934:146). Cottonwood was ubiquitous on the floodplain, and Lewis and Clark reported groves of timber with willow, cotton, mulberry, elm, sycamore, linden, hickory, walnut, oak, and coffee tree near their camp at Council Bluffs, where the Missouri meandered "the open and butifull Plains" (Thwaites 1969:1:95). They also noted the presence of hazelnut, plum, currants, raspberries, grapes, and a unique kind of honeysuckle in the same vicinity.

Bison, elk, and deer attracted human settlers to the Missouri River valley throughout prehistory, although smaller species such as ground squirrel, sharp-tailed grouse, prairie chicken, turtle, frog, and fish were also utilized. Like the Mississippi, the Missouri River is an important flyway for migrating raptors and waterfowl, particularly geese.

Steeply perched like gigantic snowdrifts along the Missouri River valley to the east is the picturesque, prairie-covered Loess Hills region (fig. 3.5). Created by the deposition of massive amounts of fine, wind-borne silt produced by the grinding of sediments beneath the weight of Pleistocene ice, the Loess Hills have become one of the state's unique and most fragile environments. The topographic relief of the Loess Hills presents a dramatic contrast to most of the Iowa landscape (Bowles 1975:15). Steeply dissected, their narrow gullies provided shelter, protection from fire, and special habitats for unique plant and animal communities. Throughout prehistory the Loess Hills were touched by influences and incursions of people from the central and eastern Plains. They were also one of the first Iowa landscapes seen and noted by Euroamerican travelers following the Missouri River into the country's interior. Finding traces of early Iowans here presents the challenge of locating sites in deeply buried contexts.

Pre-Illinoian ice sheets dated to more than 500,000 years old carried massive amounts of glacial drift that over time was reshaped by erosion and weathering, periodically downcutting to form the Southern Iowa Drift Plain, the largest landform region in the state. Stretching eastward from beneath the Loess Hills to the Mississippi River and immortalized in the landscape paintings of Grant Wood, the region today is stereotypic Iowa, with gently undulating cornfields and scenic valleys. West of the state drainage divide, the Little Sioux, Maple, and Boyer rivers flow through a portion of the region to the west, supporting gallery forests in a vast expanse of prairie. Major tributaries like the Maquoketa,

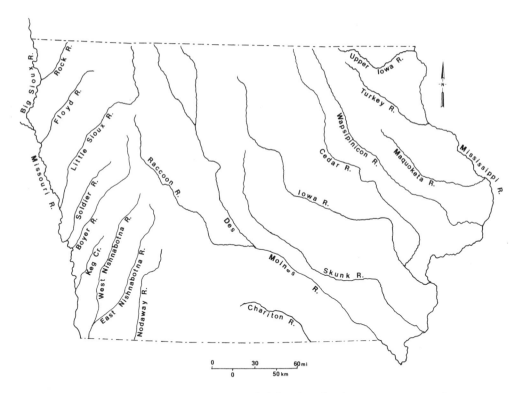

**3.4.** Iowa's major rivers. Photo archives, Office of the State Archaeologist, University of Iowa.

**3.5.** The Loess Hills, a unique western Iowa landform. Photo by Gary Hightshoe. From Prior 1991.

Cedar, Iowa, English, Skunk and Des Moines create a diversity of landscapes as they traverse the region in a southeasterly direction to join the Mississippi. Many of these streams have wide, steep valleys that support dense stands of hardwood forests. Where they cut through flat, tabular uplands in the southeastern portion of the region, they expose chert deposits embedded in Mississippian-age strata. Varieties such as Burlington, Keokuk, Maynes Creek, and Croton tabular were widely sought and exchanged by prehistoric peoples (fig. 3.6).

Throughout its history, Northeast Iowa's scenic Paleozoic Plateau, a rugged, heavily dissected region formerly referred to as the "Driftless Region" because of its lack of glacial deposits, has

shared with adjacent parts of Wisconsin, Minnesota, and Illinois a common geology, distinctive microenvironments, prehistoric cultures, and historic influences. Swift-flowing streams and rivers such as the Upper Iowa, Turkey, and Yellow cut deeply through the bedrock-dominated terrain, producing steep-sided, timber-covered valleys and towering bluffs. Extensive stands of sugar maple and basswood developed on the cool, moist lower slopes, while boreal species included white pine and white birch.

Limestones and dolomites underlay this landscape, creating a karst topography riddled with sinkholes, springs, and caves. Rockshelters were a common habitation for prehistoric peoples (fig. 3.7). The numerous exposed bedrock faces served as a canvas for prehistoric rock art—engravings and paintings—most of it still undated. Lead ore, or galena, occurs in veins along crevices in the Ordovician dolomites. An important resource for thousands of years, it was traded by American Indian people throughout the eastern United States. Euroamericans were quick to learn of its abundance in the Upper Mississippi Valley through brokers such as the Ioway and Meskwaki and soon established lucrative mining enterprises, such as Julien Dubuque's in the late eighteenth century.

To the west of the ancient rocks of the Paleozoic Plateau is the pre-Illinoian, drift-dominated Iowan Surface region. This landscape of gentle relief—with its long slopes and broad, shallow valleys of the Cedar, Shell Rock, and Wapsipinicon rivers—extends southeastward to the Mississippi. Once resembling the Southern Iowa Drift Plain, its proximity to Wisconsinan glacial advances created extremes of weathering and erosion that overwhelmed earlier landscape contours. Fieldstones, known as glacial erratics, dot its surface. Along the larger stream valleys in the southern part of the region, elongated, loess-capped ridges, called pahas, exist. Their alignment parallel to the river valleys suggests an origin combining erosional remnants of glacial drift mantled with dunes that accumulated as

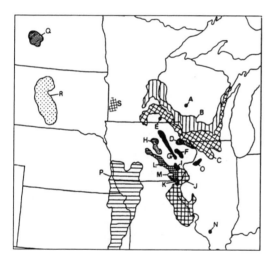

**3.6.** Outcrop locations of lithic materials commonly found in Iowa sites. (A) Hixton silicified sandstone; (B) Prairie du Chien cherts; (C) Galena/Platteville chert; (D) various Silurian cherts; (E) Grand Meadow chert; (F) Wapsipinicon chert; (G) Rapid chert; (H) Maynes Creek cherts; (I) Wassonville chert; (J) Burlington cherts; (K) Keokuk chert; (L) Croton cherts; (M) Spergen chert; (N) Cobden chert; (O) Moline chert; (P) Missourian and Virgilian series cherts; (Q) Knife River flint; (R) Bijou Hills silicified sediment; (S) Minnesota catlinite, or pipestone. After Morrow 1994.

**3.7.** Horsethief Cave, Johnson County. The caves and rock overhangs in the Paleozoic Plateau provided shelter for Iowa's residents throughout prehistory. Photo archives, Office of the State Archaeologist, University of Iowa.

strong northwesterly winds scoured the Iowan Surface during glacial times. The northern part of the region contains a botanically varied landscape, from tall-grass prairie to ancient aspen bogs and oak-savanna. Hardwood forests line the river valleys and may once have capped the larger pahas.

The Des Moines Lobe region in north-central Iowa, the thumbprint of the final Wisconsinan glacial advance, is the only region in Iowa that still displays landscape features directly created by glacial action. A series of concentric ridges, called terminal moraines, outline the position of successive glacial advances throughout the region. The Bemis moraine at Des Moines marks the southernmost extent of the ice. As the ice retreated it left kettleholes, prairie potholes, lakes, and other visible features on the landscape. The Iowa Great Lakes—Spirit Lake, Clear Lake, Storm Lake, and Lake Okoboji—as well as a variety of ponds, sloughs, marshes, and bogs make up the northern portion. Before most of these wetlands were tiled and drained, they provided a habitat for large flocks of nesting and migrating waterfowl, including Canada geese, Sandhill cranes, Trumpeter swans, ducks, and coots. Aquatic plants such as cattail, arrowhead, bulrush, water lily, and yellow lotus, traditionally important to native peoples, were also present. Euroamericans reported wild rice after 1820, although it is not known whether it was utilized in the area prehistorically. Oak-hickory groves grew on glacial moraines between the wetlands and sloughs.

Deeply entrenched in its valley along the axis of the Lobe is the Des Moines River. Its thick outwash deposits were downcut into a series of postglacial terraces. Recent studies from central Iowa demonstrate that these terraces contain deeply buried archaeological sites in good geological context (Bettis and Hoyer 1986).

To the west, the gently rolling Northwest Iowa Plains served throughout prehistory as a kind of topographic and cultural gateway to the High Plains, reflecting developments common to both the Coteau des Prairies of southwestern Minnesota and eastern South Dakota and the Missouri River valley. The uplands in the western part of this region are underlain by pre-Illinoian tills, but in the east younger Wisconsinan-age drift represents an extension of glacial events documented on the Des Moines Lobe. Windblown loess covers most of the area but is thicker in the west, closer to its source in the Big Sioux and Missouri River valleys. Before modern settlement, tall-grass prairie blanketed the region, with gallery forests along the Big Sioux, Rock, Floyd, and Little Sioux rivers and their tributaries.

As a means of transportation and a source of food, the western rivers proved of crucial importance to native peoples. Here, too, the state's youngest rocks—Cretaceous-age sandstone, chalk, limestone, and shale—rest directly on the state's oldest Pre-Cambrian rocks. Reddish Pre-Cambrian Sioux quartzite outcrops in the extreme northwest corner of the region. Where it extends north into southern Minnesota it contains a layer of red mudstone, also called catlinite, a material utilized by native peoples in late prehistoric and historic times as an important source for pipes and carvings (fig. 3.8).

There is more than a touch of irony in the fact that archaeologists rely upon descriptions of the Iowa landscapes and the lifeways of Iowa's native peoples made by Euroamericans, whose arrival would drastically alter both. The explorers, traders, and settlers who provided these first accounts set in motion changes to the land unequaled in rate and magnitude since the melting of the Ice Age glaciers (Baker, Schwert, Bettis, and Chumbley 1993:314). They also set in motion unprecedented changes for the native inhabitants.

**3.8.** The catlinite quarries of western Minnesota were a coveted source of pipestone beginning in late prehistoric times. Photo by Samuel Calvin taken in the 1890s. Photo archives, Office of the State Archaeologist, University of Iowa.

# 4 Paleoindian Discoveries

In the beginning, Mao (The Earthmaker) made the earth and all the universe. Then there was a man who fasted under an elm tree. His face was blackened with charcoal and he strove to gain a vision. While he was there four bears came out from under the ground. They were the four who became the ancestors of the Bear gens, and whose names are borne by the sub-gentes of that division. He told the faster that they would give him power and that they would become people. At the time that he saw them they had the appearance of bears, but acted like human beings.

—Account of Chief David Tohee, Ioway, obtained in 1914 (Skinner 1926:218)

---

**ARCHAEOLOGISTS BELIEVE** that people have lived in Iowa for at least 13,000 years. The world and the lifeways of the first inhabitants were different from those of any people living today or any within modern memory. The first Iowans encountered some landscapes recently delivered from the grips of the Ice Age that would be unrecognizable to us now. They were migratory hunters, but they pursued animals that no living hunter has ever seen and in an abundance that is rivaled only in areas of Africa today. Their societies were tiny and scattered over enormous distances. They did not struggle to survive on the margins of more populated communities but held dominion over vast and bountiful lands. Anthropologists can provide few clues from the study of modern peoples to help in the interpretation of these early societies. They were the first and only people to see, hear, smell, taste, and try to comprehend a world that is now gone.

The earliest archaeological sites in Iowa are called Paleoindian. The term was first used by the doyen of eastern United States prehistory, James B. Griffin (Griffin 1946), to denote a period when early Americans hunted Ice Age fauna. The earliest Paleoindian artifacts throughout North America consist of stone weapons, specifically a series of lanceolate (leaf-shaped) projectile points, used as spears or darts to hunt large Pleistocene game (fig. 4.1). Almost all of the Iowa ex-amples were discovered as surface finds. We do not know what animals early Paleoindian people in Iowa hunted or even the exact age of the earliest sites. Contemporary paleontological and geological sites provide some clues, as do archaeological finds from other states.

Traditionally, archaeologists have used projectile point types as a kind of index fossil or chronological marker of specific time periods and cultural complexes. Lanceolate, fluted forms such as Clovis and Folsom represent early Paleoindian types. Lanceolate, generally unfluted points like Agate Basin and Dalton and the first stemmed types come later. It should always be remembered, however, that the appearance, contemporaneity, and disappearance of particular point styles across the Midwest varied, and the situation in Iowa, if ever fully known, may not exactly mirror that found elsewhere.

Paleoindian finds in Iowa are poorly known. Currently, only one early Paleoindian site in the state has been excavated, although significant sites have been investigated in nearby states. One of the oldest, best-preserved, and most complete human burials, for example, was found more than half a century ago in western Minnesota (Wormington 1957). This find, termed the Browns Valley skeleton, has been dated to about 10,000 years ago by the AMS technique (Shane 1991). More recently, the excavation of sites such as Kimmswick just south of St. Louis (Graham et al. 1981) and Lange-Ferguson in the South Dakota Badlands (Hannus 1990) has resulted in a broader understanding of early Paleoindian economies.

The scarcity of Paleoindian sites in Iowa is the result of many factors (fig. 4.2). Sites of such a great age are not usually well preserved, and some may be deeply buried by deposits in the uplands or under thick alluvial sediments beneath fans and on the valley floor. The small size of the Paleoindian population, its mobility, and the perishable nature of most of its material culture mean little has been left for archaeologists to discover. Many researchers are attracted to more visible sites of later periods, which promise more abundant remains. CRM investigations, with their budgetary and temporal restraints, often disregard the potential importance of certain kinds of sites, such as lithic scatters, or fail to test deep enough for buried deposits that might contain ancient remains. Many Paleoindian discoveries have been made by avocational archaeologists who have the time and persistence to get to know a local area and who recognize potentially early finds.

Paleoindian materials date to the end of the Pleistocene (the most recent of the "Ice Ages") and the beginning of the Holocene (Recent)

**4.1.** Hafted Clovis point. Illustration by Mary M. Slattery. From L. Alex 1980.

epochs, times of dramatic change in the climate and landscape of North America. After the last episode of extreme cold had ended around 15,000 B.C. (Hoffecker et al. 1993:47), global warming resulted in glacial melt and retreat and rising sea levels. Coastlines and land bridges were submerged, new land surfaces and drainage systems were created, and older ones were buried under glacial drift or rearranged into new configurations. Rainfall patterns changed, and seasonal differences in temperatures increased. Entire plant and animal communities, depressed southward during times of cold, gradually shifted their ranges northward, while mass extinctions of large and small mammal species occurred.

For centuries following their arrival in North America, generations of Paleoindian people coped with these environmental changes. Trying to tell their story—finding and dating sites and interpreting the human behavior they reflect in light of what is known about the environmental setting—takes the combined effort of archaeologists, geologists, soil scientists, and paleontologists. The prehistory of this early period is as much natural history as it is anything.

**The First Americans**

Archaeologists believe that early immigrants entered the New World from northeastern Asia, possibly on numerous occasions during the past 20,000 years. The first migrations probably occurred at times when vast ice sheets covered parts of the Northern Hemisphere. These glaciers locked up thousands of cubic meters of water, thereby lowering sea levels on a worldwide scale and exposing many areas of land. One of these was a vast region that included the Bering Strait, the ocean passageway that currently separates northeastern Siberia and western Alaska. At times during the late Pleistocene, with sea levels lowered as much as 120 m, the two continents were joined by a 3,000 km wide land bridge called Beringia, a subcontinent in itself. Across this open plain both plant and animal

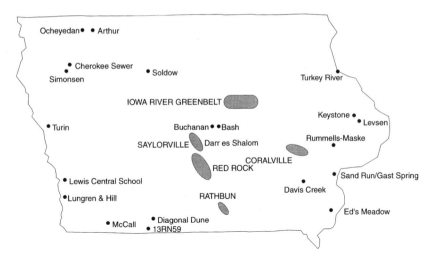

**4.2.** Paleoindian and Archaic sites mentioned in the text. Map by Diana Brayton.

species gradually migrated, including the first humans. No undisputed evidence has yet been found to establish that earlier immigrants occupied North America south of the ice sheets (Taylor et al. 1996; see Dillehay 1997 and Meltzer 1997 for recent information on the early occupation in South America). Even at times when sea levels rose and flooded the land connection, and certainly after the Bering Strait was permanently established, perhaps as late as 11,000–9000 B.C. (Hoeffecker et al. 1993:46), new arrivals could have journeyed across this same region by boat.

During periods of glacial retreat, the continent's two great ice masses, the Cordilleran to the west and the Laurentide to the east, melted apart from one another, creating an open corridor along the east slope of the Rockies into interior North America (Reeves 1973a). This corridor may have been ice-free even during most of the last glacial maximum (Hoeffecker et al. 1993:47), allowing generation after generation of early Americans to make their way southward. Although at times the route was probably inhospitable and difficult, numerous early Paleoindian sites occur at its southern end in Wyoming and Colorado, and some Paleoindian finds have been made in the vicinity of the corridor itself. It is

also possible that early immigrants followed a course along the southern margin of Beringia, around the present Aleutian chain, and down the west coast of Canada and the United States. If so, that route is now under water, drowned by the rising post-Pleistocene seas.

Descendants of these very earliest Americans reached Iowa as the last ice sheets of the Wisconsin stage had begun their retreat from the mid-continent. Perhaps these people followed major east-west drainages like the Missouri, Platte, and Arkansas across the Plains into the Midwest (Anderson 1990). At its maximum around 14,800–14,400 B.C., the lower margin of the Wisconsin ice sagged as far south as the city of Des Moines in a U-shaped configuration known as the Des Moines Lobe (Baker et al. 1986; Bettis et al. 1996; Kemmis 1991; Prior 1991). Evidence suggests that this ice was withdrawing from Iowa a thousand years later and before humans arrived. Although no early Paleoindian sites in Iowa have been dated, other early sites in North America suggest a range in age from 11,100 to 10,750 B.C. (Taylor et al. 1996).

As the ice advanced and then melted and receded, it redesigned the north-central part of the state as well as many river valleys. Irregular drift and meltwater deposits formed along the ice margins, producing rounded hills and poorly drained depressions and potholes, characteristic features of the Des Moines Lobe landform region (Anderson 1983:226; Prior 1991). Enormous amounts of glacial meltwater periodically gushed out from the ice and from glacial lakes, flooding river valleys and carrying massive amounts of sand and gravel to be deposited downstream. The force of the water carved broad and deep trenches and cut steplike benches into the valley sides (Baker, Bettis, and Horton 1993; Bettis et al. 1992). In general the higher terraces are older, and the lower terraces date to progressively younger periods of flooding (Rogers and Green 1995:7).

Both the Mississippi and Missouri rivers deepened and partially filled their valleys with alluvium during episodes of meltwater flooding. The Mississippi valley south of the Quad Cities was diverted westward to its present course by earlier outwash flows from advancing Wisconsin glaciers in Illinois about 23,000 B.C. Two of the last episodes of massive late Wisconsinan flooding produced the thick sand-and-gravel deposits that form the Savannah and the lower Kingston terraces along the Mississippi valley (Hajic 1989). The deposits that form the High Terrace in the Des Moines River valley began to collect after 11,000 B.C. Subsequent episodes of downcutting and stream channel meandering left these deposits as sandy terrace remnants, which attracted settlement by people seeking access to rich wetlands and safe locations away from the more unstable floodplain (Benn 1992:66; Bettis and Hoyer 1986; Bettis and Benn 1984; Bettis et al. 1992).

The fine silt produced by the grinding of sediments beneath the weight of the ice and released in meltwater was picked up during droughty episodes throughout the Pleistocene and carried by strong winds to be deposited over broad areas as blankets of loess. In regions closer to the source of this fine "rock dust," such as the broad Missouri River valley in western Iowa,

conditions were ripe for a thick mantle of Wisconsinan-age loess to collect across the landscape, producing one of the state's most distinctive topographic regions, the Loess Hills (Prior 1991:48). Elsewhere across Iowa such eolian, or windblown, silt deposits are thinner and have less of an impact on the appearance of the terrain. While geologic evidence suggests that major episodes of loess formation occurred late in the Wisconsin, occasional and localized loess deposits may have accumulated early in the Holocene. Although not all geologists agree that these early Holocene materials meet the definition of loess, such deposits do create the potential for buried sites in upland settings (Abbott 1980; Abbott and Tiffany 1986; Artz 1993a, 1993b; Collins 1991; Tiffany et al. 1977). Eolian sand originating in nearby stream valleys was also carried and deposited as dunes and ridges. Subsequent reworking of all Quaternary deposits by wind, erosion, and slumping has created the upland topography familiar in Iowa today.

## Iowa's Paleoenvironments

During the late Pleistocene, with ice still present as far south as Des Moines, the average air temperature in Iowa was probably around 0°C compared with an average today of approximately 8°C (Anderson 1983:226). Paleoclimatic evidence, particularly that inferred from pollen and plant macrofossils and mammalian fossil sites, suggests that a mosaic environment of boreal hardwoods and coniferous trees distributed in an open, meadowlike grassland covered much of the state. As the ice retreated and the climate became warmer, forests of spruce and larch moved in to be replaced later by fir and a succession of deciduous trees (Anderson 1983:226; Baker et al. 1980; Baker et al. 1990; Baker, Bettis, and Horton 1993; Rhodes and Semken 1986). With the increasing influence of warmer and drier Pacific air masses, prairie vegetation—grasses, sagebrush, ragweed, chenopods, and composite plants—extended eastward, to northwest Iowa by about 8100 B.C. (Baker et al. 1992;

Van Zant 1979), to central Iowa by around 7400 B.C. (Baker et al. 1990), and finally around 4400 B.C. to the northeastern part of the state (Baker et al. 1990; Baker et al. 1992; Chumbley et al. 1990; Dorale et al. 1992).

At the height of the Atlantic, or Hypsithermal, of the mid-Holocene, a period marked by average temperatures that were warmer than current temperatures, prairie dominated most of the state. The maximum period of dryness in central and western Iowa began around 5500–5200 B.C. and lasted around 1,300 years. In eastern Iowa dry conditions prevailed between 4400 B.C. and about 1700–1200 B.C. After this time deciduous forest returned to eastern Iowa, marking a more humid trend. In the west, however, prairie vegetation remained in place, with oak returning in isolated stands (Baker et al. 1990; 1992). By 1200 B.C. the climate and vegetation throughout the state were similar to that reported by Euroamerican settlers—a sea of tall-grass prairie with ribbons of timbered stream valleys, slopes, and uplands.

Except perhaps for lingering pockets on the Des Moines Lobe, the ice was probably gone when Paleoindian populations arrived. They encountered a climate that was still relatively cold and moist. Warmer conditions brought the northward shift of entire plant communities and climatic zones and a diverse mosaic of flora and fauna that occupied ecological niches unlike any in the state today (Prior 1991:28). Late Pleistocene mammals inhabiting Iowa presumably would have been a major attraction for hunting societies whose own ancestors were probably drawn to North America in pursuit of the large herds of caribou, musk ox, and mammoth that occupied Beringia. Pleistocene fossil evidence in Iowa documents the presence of mammoth, mastodon, ground sloth, horse, peccary, camel, deer, elk, moose, musk ox, bison, giant beaver, and bear (Anderson 1983; Prior 1991) (fig. 4.3). Bones and teeth of the mammoth, a grazer, and the woodland-browsing mastodon have been documented in all ninety-nine Iowa counties

(Anderson and Williams 1974; Prior 1991:27) (fig. 4.4). Remains of both the Woolly mammoth (*Mammuthus primigenius*) and Jefferson's mammoth (*Mammuthus jeffersonii*) occur. So far, no early Paleoindian artifacts have been found in context with these animals in Iowa. Such discoveries, however, have been made in other states.

The diversity of animal species present was greater than that available to later Iowans, and Paleoindian peoples must have been familiar with the habits of animals no hunter after them ever saw. Archaeologists can make inferences as to how some of these animals might have been stalked and killed by observing living animals, such as elephants, whose behavior may be a clue to that of their ancient relatives, such as the mammoth. For other animals it is more of a guess. In general, large game appear to have been dispersed across the landscape, perhaps ranging widely in their annual movements. The human population apparently followed suit, with small bands of hunters and their families utilizing territories of perhaps several thousand square kilometers. With the end of the Pleistocene 10,000 years ago, many animals became extinct, including over 30 genera of mammals. While major extinctions occurred at this time on other continents, none were as severe as those in North America. Environmental change, disease, or predation by hunters leading to overkill—or a combination of all three—have been suggested as possible causes (Martin 1973; Martin and Klein 1984; Meltzer and Mead 1984).

## Discovering Early Sites

The often dramatic natural setting of the late Pleistocene must be considered when archaeologists attempt to discover early sites and to interpret early human adaptation. It is important to remember that not all areas of the state would necessarily have attracted occupation or have been equally hospitable. Large river valleys, for instance, which possibly drew early humans and the animals they sought, would also have been dangerous for permanent settlement due to the

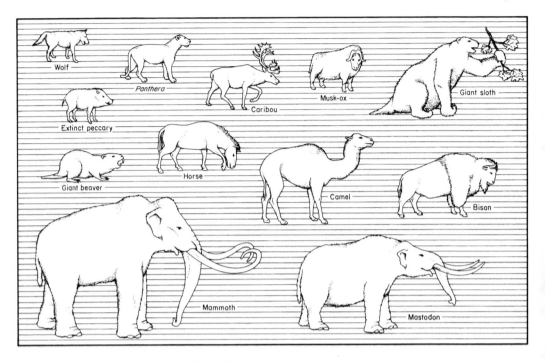

**4.3.** Mammals known to have occupied Iowa during the Pleistocene. Illustration by Patricia J. Lohmann. From Prior 1991.

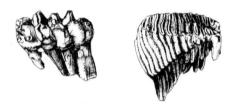

**4.4.** The cusp pattern on the teeth of Ice Age fauna demonstrates dietary preferences and helps paleontologists make identifications. The tooth of the young mastodon (left) is that of a browser, while the mammoth tooth (right) is that of a grazer. Illustration by David A. Crawford.

threat of massive flooding from late glacial outwash and early postglacial downcutting (Benn and Rogers 1985:27).

Paleoindian peoples likely camped in areas that offered suitable conditions for shelter and abundant resources, especially game, water, wood, and lithic raw material. Drainages or tributary streams, springs with salt licks, outcrops of high-quality stone or secondary lithic sources such as tills and outwash deposits represent settings where ancient sites might occur. Prominent features of the landscape could have served as beacons for social gatherings or marked the location of sacred spots.

Unfortunately, the dynamic nature of the late Pleistocene and early Holocene environment was not often conducive to the preservation of ancient sites. Sites left on high benches, terraces, or upland landscapes were often eroded if not fortuitously protected by later deposits. Flooding, downcutting, and erosion frequently destroyed floodplain and lower terrace locations not protected by alluvial fans or colluvial slopewash.

The geologic context of these early sites can sometimes be a clue to their location and to their extreme age. Study and dating of valley terraces and alluvial fans provide information about the potential for buried sites and other resources that might have attracted early humans (Prior 1991:107). The discovery of sites in or under sediments of known late Pleistocene or early Holocene age can verify their antiquity, as can the association of artifacts with extinct fauna. The discovery of stone spear points with the bones of extinct bison at sites on the southern Plains in the 1920s originally convinced scientists of the contemporaneity of human populations with Ice Age fauna and led to the definition of the Paleoindian period itself (Wormington 1957).

## Late Pleistocene Hunters (11,000–10,500 B.C.)

The oldest human occupation of Iowa is documented by hundreds of lanceolate projectile points collected from throughout the state (J. Morrow 1994; Morrow and Morrow 1994, 1996; Morrow 1996b). More than 250 are fluted forms belonging to the Clovis, Gainey, and Folsom types (Morrow 1984, 1996a). Since these artifacts have not been found in datable contexts in Iowa, their exact age is unknown. At sites elsewhere, stratigraphic evidence, the association of similar points with extinct Pleistocene fauna, and radiocarbon dates indicate their great antiquity. While some researchers propose that the use of Clovis and Folsom types actually may have overlapped in time, recent radiocarbon evidence suggests that the latest Clovis components predate the earliest Folsom components by as much as 100 years (Taylor et al. 1996). Clovis materials have also been found underlying Folsom remains on the High Plains. In addition, the lack of mammoth remains at Folsom sites could indicate that Folsom occupations postdate those of Clovis. The current time range suggested for Clovis is from approximately 11,100 to 10,750 B.C.

and for Folsom from 10,750 to 10,450 B.C. (Taylor et al. 1996), but the chronological issue is far from settled. The temporal position and nature of Gainey are as yet unresolved.

Projectile points constitute almost all we know of the earliest occupation of Iowa. While points would seem to provide limited information about the lifeways of Paleoindian people, study of how the points were made, from what raw materials, and where they occur allows archaeologists to make inferences about the organization of early human technology, resource use, and settlement.

The relative scarcity but wide distribution of early Paleoindian remains across North America indicates that early population levels were low but that Paleoindian peoples were considerably mobile. Perhaps 1,000 to 2,000 people occupied Iowa at the time of first settlement, calculating on the basis of one person for every 75–100 km$^2$ of the state's 145,000 km$^2$—an estimate that parallels that for nomadic Subarctic hunting bands of more recent times.

Band-level societies such as these generally consist of upward of 25 to 30 people who typically reside and travel together throughout the year. On occasion and at particular seasons, larger groups may gather to undertake cooperative hunts, meet prospective marriage partners, trade raw materials, conduct various ceremonies, and bury their dead. Paleoindian societies, like many small-scale societies of the recent past, were probably egalitarian in nature—with age and gender the primary criteria for differences in roles and duties among members. However, in order to track and hunt large game animals some level of cooperation and social control must have been maintained.

The oldest Paleoindian remains in Iowa rarely occur except as single finds, suggesting that settlement was short-term and did not result in the substantial accumulation of materials. This observation must be tempered with the reminder that no intact early Paleoindian living site has yet been excavated in the state. Points in private collections usually represent surface finds collected from upland settings or high terraces, locations where in situ sites are unlikely to be preserved unless fortuitously buried (Benn and Bowers 1994; Henning 1990; Stevens 1980). Paleoindian sites containing large numbers of artifacts probably represent locations reoccupied over long periods of time. The occurrence of nonlocal lithics at Iowa sites supports the likelihood of a highly mobile population that may have traversed broad distances to acquire desirable raw material from specific quarries (Morrow 1996:1).

## Making a Living

Across North America, both kill and camp sites indicate that Paleoindian peoples hunted large animals. The original discoveries of Clovis and Folsom projectile points at western kill sites in direct association with now-extinct animals such as mammoth, camelids, and early forms of horse and bison led archaeologists to refer to this era of North American prehistory as a "big-game hunting stage." Subsequent finds have reinforced this association. Close to Iowa, fluted points were discovered with the remains of mammoth at the Lange-Ferguson site in western South Dakota (Hannus 1990) and with mastodon (*Mammut americanum*) at the Kimmswick site in eastern Missouri (Graham et al. 1981; Graham and Kay 1988; Morrow 1996:112; Morrow 1996c:8). A possible mastodon-human association was documented in southwestern Wisconsin almost a hundred years ago when four boys digging in a swollen creek bed found the skeleton of a mastodon in the same deposits as a fluted projectile point (Palmer and Stoltman 1976).

Hunting behavior for such megafauna probably involved a number of strategies, some deliberate and planned, others fortuitous and opportunistic. These strategies may have included wounding and following game until they became too weak to escape, entrapping large animals in timber corrals or surrounds, driving small herds off precipices, and scavenging wounded or juvenile individuals or those that had become

trapped in bogs or marshes (Frison 1989; Morrow 1996:30–31) (fig. 4.5). Experiments using Paleoindian weaponry to hunt African elephants demonstrate that the hunter must get close enough to thrust or throw a weapon at a spot most likely to penetrate the hide and reach a vital organ. The elephant's poor eyesight but well-developed sense of smell leads modern African hunters to carry small bags of fine dust to continuously check the direction of the wind so as to maintain a position on the leeward side of the animal (Frison 1991:146–147).

Archaeologists realize that Paleoindian peoples ate more than just big game. Regional differences in subsistence practices existed, and smaller animals as well as some plants were utilized (Meltzer and Smith 1986). At the Kimmswick site, in addition to mastodon, white-tailed deer, hare, turtle, and possibly ground sloth made their way to the table. At Lange-Ferguson, early South Dakotans also utilized deer and rabbit (Hannus 1990). Paleobotanical remains, while less commonly reported, occasionally come to light when archaeologists use recovery techniques such as water flotation and fine screening. At the Shawnee-Minisink site in Pennsylvania, hawthorn seeds were found associated with Clovis artifacts (McNett 1985).

The subsistence economy of early Paleoindian peoples thus appears to have been somewhat more diverse, at least for some groups, than previously thought and certainly included plants and small as well as large animals. Mosaic landscapes of the late Pleistocene and early Holocene likely fostered adaptations to a variety of settings. The apparent emphasis on megafauna seen at many early sites could also result from factors such as differential preservation or site function (Morrow 1996:32). Large, massive bone and ivory elements may stand a better chance of preservation if quickly buried and then covered for tens of millennia than do the bones of smaller species. Residential sites, though rarely excavated, could contain evidence of other types of animals and plants used by Paleoindian peoples.

**4.5.** Stalking and killing large Pleistocene megafauna required hunters to get close to the animal and to aim their spears at a vulnerable spot, such as the lungs or heart. Illustration by David A. Crawford.

If big-game hunts were favored, perhaps it was because these were the most economical way of procuring a prehistoric supermarket of supplies—meat, fat, hide, sinew, bone, and ivory—in a single, though presumably risky, venture (Morrow 1996:32). Then again, since Paleoindian hunters were a relatively new element on the North American scene, perhaps the large, gregarious species they sought had no natural fear of the two-legged predator and were less dangerous to stalk and kill than we might imagine. In the end, the occasional mammoth killed and butchered by Clovis hunters may have been the equivalent of a truly "big fish" story—an event bragged about for years afterward but seldom repeated. At present we know little about these aspects of human behavior directly from the archaeological record in Iowa.

### Fluting: North America's First Invention?

Whatever their target, fluted projectile points like Clovis and Folsom represent impressive hunting devices, probably manufactured as part of a composite weapon, typically a thrusting spear, a dart (smaller spear), or an atlatl (spear-thrower). While the technology that Paleoindian peoples used in producing bifacial points harkens back to their Old World roots, fluting seems to be one of the first native North American inventions, despite recent claims to the contrary (King and Slobodin 1996).

Fluting was a technique used to thin and taper the basal portion of the projectile point in order to create a smooth juncture for its insertion or attachment to a bone, ivory, or wooden foreshaft (Morrow and Morrow 1996:11). When hafted to the foreshaft with sinew binding and an adhesive such as pitch or resin, the foreshaft was inserted into a wooden mainshaft to create a very effective weapon. Once an animal had been killed, the point and foreshaft having penetrated a vulnerable spot, the hunter would have a means of retracting the mainshaft for reuse. While most Paleoindian hunters probably packed a supply of point preforms and some finished points, replacing a mainshaft represented a more time-consuming effort, and one that a hunter likely avoided if possible.

### Clovis: Iowa's Mammoth Hunters?

Clovis is currently the oldest well-documented archaeological complex in North America. Best known from a series of kill and processing sites in the western United States dated between 11,100 and 10,750 B.C. (Taylor et al. 1996), the characteristic Clovis point is typically associated with the remains of mammoth and now-extinct forms of bison, *Bison bison occidentalis* and *Bison bison antiquus*. Other lesser known site types include habitations, quarries, meat caches, and burials. In addition to a distinctive chipped stone technology used in the production of bifacial artifacts, Clovis assemblages include formal flake tools such as side and end scrapers, gravers, and small wedge-shaped flakes sometimes referred to as *pieces d'esquile*. Unretouched utilized flakes and retouched blades and flakes, as well as a number of bone or ivory pieces including foreshafts, have also been found at Clovis sites.

Most Clovis artifacts probably relate to the hunting and processing of animals, the preparation of hides, and bone cutting and engraving. A small Clovis blade found in Lee County (Morrow 1996) (fig. 4.6) probably functioned to cut and groove long slivers of bone or ivory for use as needles and awls. A preference for high-quality lithic raw material, the use of red ocher (in very rare instances associated with burials), and a tendency to place points or preforms in caches either for storage or as part of burials characterize Clovis assemblages (Frison 1989).

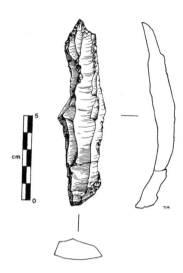

**4.6.** Clovis blade tool from Lee County. Illustration by Toby Morrow. From Morrow 1996a.

Avocational archaeologists have found Clovis points in the form of both preforms and finished projectiles throughout Iowa. For example, five points were recovered as surface finds from one site in Hardin County (Collins 1990, 1991). The known distribution of points suggests a concentration in the southeastern corner of the state in Des Moines, Henry, Lee, Louisa, and Van Buren counties, where ample supplies of Burlington chert exist. Other features attractive for human settlement in this area may have included streams, springs and sinkholes, upland game overlooks and depressions, and a variety of plants (Morrow and Morrow 1994; Morrow 1996:54).

Clovis points have not been found with mammoth remains at any site in Iowa. Mammoth remains have been dated in Iowa as late as 12,600 B.C., almost contemporary with the recession of Pleistocene ice (Rhodes and Semken 1986). Paleoenvironmental studies suggest that about the time that early Paleoindian peoples arrived, the rich boreal grasslands that supported megafauna such as mammoth were being replaced by forests. By around 9000 B.C., Pleistocene megafauna were gone (Rhodes and Semken 1986: 108–109). Whether early hunters in Iowa had a hand in their extinction is unknown.

While the majority of Clovis points were manufactured from Burlington chert, stone acquired from outside the state was also utilized, including Moline chert from western Illinois, Hixton silicified sandstone from Wisconsin, and Knife River flint from North Dakota. Knife River flint is a distinctive root-beer-colored stone that comes from Dunn and Mercer counties in west-central North Dakota, where at least 29 native quarries have been located (Clayton et al. 1970). These "exotic" materials indicate that Paleoindian peoples had wide-ranging contacts and roamed over broad territories. The average distance between finished Clovis points in Iowa and the source of their raw material was over 100 km, with a maximum distance of nearly 1,000 km (J. Morrow 1994), which suggests that Clovis artisans preferred good-quality lithic material and went to considerable lengths to travel or trade over long distances to obtain it. The presence of unfinished preforms of imported stone demonstrates that weapons were often transported home in an incomplete state. Clovis people likely roughed out transportable preforms and flake blanks at quarry locations to carry with them to replace exhausted and lost tools.

### Gainey—A New Paleopoint for Iowa?

Certain Clovis points, including examples from Iowa, seem to grade into another fluted form called Gainey, named for the type site in Michigan (Deller and Ellis 1988; Morrow and Morrow 1996:6; Roosa 1965:96; Simons et al. 1984). Gainey is part of a complex, sometimes called Bull Brook–Gainey or Bull Brook–Gainey–Clovis, that followed or slightly overlapped Clovis. The Gainey point is similar to Clovis points in overall appearance, size, and proportions but is typically thinner between the flutes and has a deeper concave base and a more pronounced flute (Morrow 1996c:8). At Rummells-Maske (13CD15) (fig. 4.7), an upland site on a trib-

utary of the Cedar River in east-central Iowa, archaeologists excavated a cache of 20 finished fluted points and point fragments from the plow zone. This represents the only instance of an Early Paleoindian site excavation in Iowa (Anderson and Tiffany 1972). The points from Rummells-Maske include some that resemble Clovis, others typical of Gainey, and some that may be intermediate between the two (Morrow 1996c:8).

Clovis and Gainey points, although similar in appearance, differ in the way they were made (fig. 4.8). In this respect, the Gainey point seems to share a greater affinity with the Folsom type. Archaeologists can surmise how points were made by examining the flake scar pattern visible on stone points and point preforms discarded or cached at various stages of manufacture. Some archaeologists have become adept as flint-knappers themselves and, through experimentation, have gained a better understanding of how early peoples produced stone tools. By knowing what kind of techniques result in the flake scars

4.7. Excavation at the Paleoindian Rummells-Maske site, Cedar County. Photo archives, Office of the State Archaeologist, University of Iowa.

seen on ancient stone artifacts, inferences can be made about how such tools were produced. The discovery of the by-products of stone tool manufacture, particularly the original cores, flakes, preforms, and debitage that exist at sites where Paleoindian flintknappers worked, can strengthen and perhaps confirm these inferences.

These lines of evidence indicate that Paleoindian groups had preferred ways to produce stone points. Such differences may reflect cultural or regional preferences or changes over time. The superb artisanship evident in points from some caches found in western North America may imply the existence of highly skilled knappers who were sought after to produce points. This level of individual specialization is not typical of most band-level societies, and some archaeologists argue that Paleoindian flintworking, however well executed, was within the grasp of any competent flintknapper who had knowledge of the preferred ways to create a point.

Clovis people had a true blade technology missing from both Gainey and later Folsom assemblages. Long, thin, relatively heavy flakes called blades were struck from both ends of prepared conical cores (fig. 4.9). Evidence for this is retained on the blades in the form of a portion of the prepared platform and long, parallel flake scars, which mark the removal of previous flakes. From such blades, distinctive bifaces were produced—bifaces that could be made into more formal tools such as knives and projectile points or could serve as sources for additional flake blanks.

Clovis points were thinned and fluted by careful and well-controlled soft hammer percussion, while Gainey points may have been fluted by indirect percussion. The position of the striking platforms and the direction of the flake scars produced in thinning the points also differ. The flute was removed from the Clovis type at a stage when the point preform was still relatively thick. Fluting sometimes consisted of the removal of more than one fluting flake, resulting in overlapping flake scars (Morrow 1996:213–214). Fol-

**4.8.** Early Paleoindian projectile points from the Rummells-Maske site, Cedar County. Photo archives, Office of the State Archaeologist, University of Iowa.

**4.9.** Paleoindian blade core from a Missouri site. Illustration by Toby Morrow and Julie Morrow. Courtesy of Toby Morrow and Julie Morrow.

lowing the removal of the flute, the point was additionally thinned by soft hammer percussion, and the basal and lower lateral edges were ground to prevent cutting through the hafting material. The Gainey point was fluted at a stage when the preform already had been thinned closer to its finished form. The final flaking appears to have been completed by pressure flaking. Both of these techniques characterize Folsom technology (Morrow and Morrow 1996:12–14).

### Folsom: The Fluting Tradition Continues but the Mammoths Are Gone

Folsom points occur most frequently at Great Plains sites ranging in age from 10,750 to 10,450 B.C. (Taylor et al. 1996). Folsom points, like Clovis points, are found only as surface discoveries in Iowa, most from the southwestern corner of the state, particularly Mills County (Morrow 1996b; Morrow and Morrow 1994). The Folsom point is usually smaller than the Clovis or Gainey point, with bifacial fluting produced by the removal of a single channel flake over most or all of both surfaces (Wormington 1957). This created a relatively thin artifact (Morrow 1996c:9). The flute was probably removed by indirect percussion or pressure in a manner similar to that for Gainey. Following fluting the knapper trimmed and shaped the point by pressure flaking (Morrow and Morrow 1996:14–16) (fig. 4.10).

Though likely a hafting device, Folsom fluting may also have served another function, perhaps with ceremonial significance. By successfully fluting a point, the hunter may have been attempting to insure the outcome of a more important event to follow, such as a successful hunt (Bradley 1993:255). Anthropologists usually refer to this kind of practice as a form of sympathetic magic. Whether or not fluting served such a purpose for Folsom hunters, there is no question that many of their stone and bone tools were among some of the finest made in ancient North America. Although as yet unknown in Iowa, the thin, delicate eyed-bone needles,

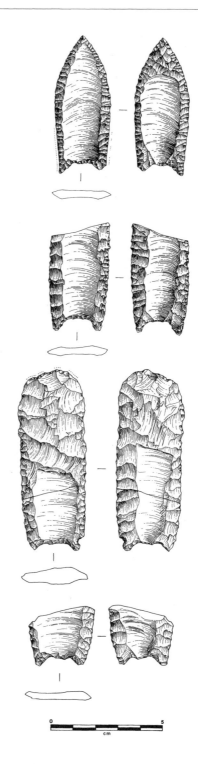

**4.10.** Folsom points and preforms from Mills County. Illustration by Toby Morrow. From Morrow 1996b.

tiny bone beads, and other finely incised bone pieces found at Folsom sites on the western Plains reflect a very high standard of artisanship (Frison 1991:51).

### Clovis-Gainey-Folsom?

The relationship among the three early Paleoindian point types in Iowa is as yet unclear, especially without dated sites. Gainey points appear to be intermediate in form between Clovis points found at western sites and those from eastern North America. Gainey and Folsom were made in similar ways. Gainey occurs over much of the eastern and the midwestern United States but has not been reported in the West. Folsom, however, is by and large a western type. At sites across the High Plains, Folsom points are frequently encountered in the context of large kill sites in association with extinct forms of bison. Little is known about the subsistence of Gainey hunters.

Perhaps Gainey represents an intermediate or transitional type that links Clovis and Folsom in some areas. On the other hand, its technological affinity to Folsom but more easterly distribution could mean that Gainey is contemporaneous with Folsom but is a geographically distinct type. This might suggest that some early Paleoindian point complexes represent separate but coexisting peoples who exploited different resources (Morrow 1996c). If so, this would appear to be a trend that continues in Iowa in the early Holocene. Until archaeologists discover, excavate, and date in situ Paleoindian sites in Iowa, we can say little about the lifeways of people who made Clovis, Gainey, and Folsom points.

### Early Holocene Hunters and Foragers (10,500–8500 B.C.)

The people who follow the Folsom hunters in Iowa were adapting to a climate and landscape that would be more familiar to us today. In western Iowa, as the climate became warmer and drier, the prairie gradually replaced the deciduous forest that had expanded across the Midwest (Baker et al. 1990; Baker and Van Zant 1980:

126). East of the Des Moines valley, woodlands remained the dominant vegetation for some time. The more varied nature of local environments was accompanied by greater diversity in human adaptation as well. Regional traditions in subsistence patterns, projectile point styles, and tool assemblages began to emerge. A number of new technological innovations appeared, including the use of heat treating to improve the workability of stone and the first chipped stone adzes, indicating that woodworking was becoming important.

In the eastern United States about 10,500 B.C., the lanceolate Dalton point type and a similar Iowa form called Fayette appear to continue the lanceolate point-making tradition of earlier Paleoindian people (fig. 4.11). Sites where these points occur, however, show the use of a wide range of fauna including deer, small mammals, waterfowl, and fish, as well as fruits and nuts, suggesting a more generalized subsistence pattern that would continue over the next 10,000 years—the broad foraging model, a hallmark of the Archaic tradition (Morrow 1996c:11) (table 1).

In the western United States, a variety of unfluted lanceolate projectile points predominate, and the earliest stemmed types appear (Morrow

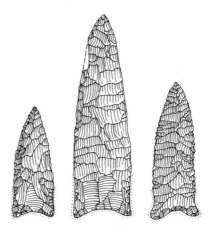

**4.11.** Dalton points from (left to right) Iowa, Van Buren, and Muscatine counties. Illustration by Toby Morrow. From Morrow 1984.

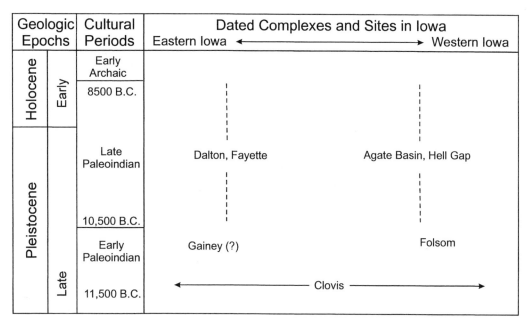

| Geologic Epochs | | Cultural Periods | Dated Complexes and Sites in Iowa |
|---|---|---|---|
| | | | Eastern Iowa ← → Western Iowa |
| Holocene | Early | Early Archaic | |
| | | 8500 B.C. | |
| Pleistocene | | Late Paleoindian | Dalton, Fayette          Agate Basin, Hell Gap |
| | | 10,500 B.C. | |
| | Late | Early Paleoindian | Gainey (?)          Folsom |
| | | 11,500 B.C. | ← Clovis → |

Table 1

1984). Originally discovered at sites on the High Plains, many of these points were associated with early Holocene-age kill sites and campsites containing fauna such as bison and antelope. The Agate Basin point has been dated at 10,500 B.C. in Wyoming. The contracting-stemmed Hell Gap type may be contemporary but appears to have outlasted Agate Basin perhaps for centuries (Frison 1991; O'Brien and Wood 1998:115) (fig. 4.12).

Iowa is geographically positioned between the Great Plains and the Eastern Woodlands, and Early Holocene artifacts found here reflect the traditions of both areas. Finds in western Iowa seem to imply a greater affinity in technology and perhaps subsistence with Paleoindian sites on the High Plains. Finds in eastern Iowa compare more favorably with those of the Early Archaic tradition in the eastern United States. However, both diagnostic eastern and western point forms are recovered throughout the state (Morrow 1997a).

Although little is known about other aspects of prehistoric life during this period, it is as-

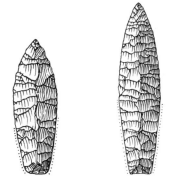

**4.12.** Agate Basin points from Iowa County. Illustration by Toby Morrow. From Morrow 1984.

sumed that people in western Iowa, like those on the Plains, continued a more specialized big-game hunting way of life in an increasingly prairie-type setting. Their contemporaries along the Mississippi River and its tributaries may have begun to concentrate on a range of plant and smaller animal species, essentially becoming efficient hunters and foragers. Finds from central Iowa likewise suggest eastern associations (Benn and Rogers 1985:30; Collins 1991). At the same time, the occurrence of varied point styles throughout the state indicates the possibility that contemporaneous societies with perhaps different lifeways coexisted for a time during the Early Holocene (Morrow 1996c:10).

In eastern Iowa, Dalton and Agate Basin points may have been in use by 10,500 B.C. Each form exhibits a distinct pattern of raw material use and distribution, which suggests manufacture by separate groups of people. The Dalton point is a lanceolate form with basal thinning and occasionally exhibits fluting reminiscent of earlier lanceolate styles (Morrow 1996c:10). It is the descendant of the fluted point tradition in the southeastern United States and is similar to the contemporaneous Meserve point known largely from Great Plains sites. However, blade edge serration and alternate beveling as a re-sharpening technique first appear on Dalton points, indicating use of these artifacts as cutting and sawing implements in addition to projectile tips. Dalton flintknappers used locally derived low-grade cherts and applied heat treating to improve the rock's flaking qualities. In Iowa, the distribution of Dalton points is generally close to these chert sources, suggesting that Dalton groups occupied restricted territories and were perhaps less mobile than contemporaneous Agate Basin groups (Morrow 1996c:10).

The more broadly based foraging pattern characteristic of Dalton people in the eastern United States was probably characteristic in eastern Iowa as well, where a wide diversity of plant and animal species was available. Within the Mississippi valley, the majority of known finds occur on sand ridges adjacent to environmentally rich backwater sloughs and lakes, a pattern that continued well into Woodland times (Benn 1992:68). Chipped stone adzes also make their appearance during this time (Morse and Goodyear 1973). No pure Dalton component in a clearly dated stratigraphic context has been excavated in Iowa, although the points have been reported at both open sites and rockshelters such

as Keystone (13JK23) in Jackson County (Anderson 1987a).

In contrast, Agate Basin points from western Great Plains contexts typically occur at sites where large game, particularly bison, were hunted. The Agate Basin point is long and narrow with almost straight blade edges produced by delicate final retouch. The corners of the base are rounded and achieved by an ever-increasing inward taper, which usually begins about one-third the distance from the base to tip (Frison 1978:159). In Iowa, Agate Basin points were made of high-quality lithic material, particularly Burlington chert and Hixton silicified sandstone, which was not heat treated. The broad distribution of these points far from the source of raw materials suggests that Agate Basin people ranged over wider territories than contemporaneous Dalton groups (Morrow 1996c:11). Although projectile points from the lowest levels at the Cherokee Sewer site in northwestern Iowa were originally classified as Agate Basin, the late date of this component and comparison of these points to Agate Basin points found elsewhere makes the classification of these finds more problematic (see chapter 5).

Hell Gap points represent one of the earliest contracting-stemmed types and are best known from Great Plains sites (fig. 4.13). Common in Iowa, they are typically made of local cherts that

**4.13.** Hell Gap points from Johnson (left) and Linn (right) counties. Illustrations by Toby Morrow. From Morrow 1984.

were frequently heat treated, a pattern similar to that of Dalton (Morrow 1996c).

Although virtually nothing else is known about Early Holocene subsistence or site types in Iowa, the position of known sites on the landscape provides clues. Sites situated in sheltered areas close to springs or perennial creeks may represent base camps from which people ventured out for various tasks, such as hunting, gathering, and the acquisition of resources on a seasonal basis. In most river valleys, sites are probably buried by later Holocene alluvial fans or colluvial deposits.

The arrival in Iowa of stemmed and notched varieties of projectile points that elsewhere date after 8500 B.C. marks the end of the Paleoindian tradition in many parts of the state. Although projectile point styles for some time would continue to include types shared with Plains bison hunters to the west and woodland hunters and foragers to the east, these artifacts are found at sites that reflect the increasingly varied nature of Iowa's Holocene landscape and the diversity of subsistence and settlement patterns that developed after this time.

# 5 Archaic Developments

Nowadays, the first questions we ask about a region's prehistory are: where in the landscape are sites most likely to be located, and what conditions of preservation can be anticipated? —Benn 1987:231

OUR UNDERSTANDING of the lifeways of ancient Iowans 10,000 years ago is remarkably poor. We know that they made new types of spear points and dart points of a variety of shapes and sizes and other stone tools with which they hunted and butchered modern species of animals. Evidence is found in sparse amounts and widely scattered across a variety of landscapes, usually at small campsites. We assume that their societies were small and migratory and that much of their food supply and material culture was perishable.

Thousands of years later, as the final millennium B.C. began its countdown, entire chapters had been added to this story. By then the population in Iowa probably had more than doubled, and people in some areas were beginning to settle down in familiar territories marked by communal cemeteries. By this time, almost all of the tools and techniques ever used by aboriginal hunters and gatherers had been invented, including metalworking and ceramics. At sites that were occupied for long periods, thick garbage heaps, called middens, gradually accumulated. Their contents demonstrate that hunting and gathering remained important but that wild plants were being supplemented with a few cultivated ones. People also made more frequent connections with one another over long distances, and the first hints of social inequality appear.

This longest period of Iowa prehistory is characterized by sites of the Archaic tradition. Ar-chaeologists generally group Archaic sites into three periods, Early (8500–5500 B.C.), Middle (5500–3000 B.C.), and Late (3000–800 B.C.). Currently, more than 600 Archaic sites have been documented in Iowa, a minimum number since many more await discovery and recording (fig. 5.1). Still, Archaic remains are more numerous than Paleoindian finds, and more sites have been investigated. This relates to the preservation of sites, the level of archaeological recording, and ultimately to the lifeways of Archaic peoples themselves.

## People and Climate: The Prairie Peninsula

Archaic people lived during times of major climatic and vegetational change throughout the Midwest. Archaeologists have been especially interested in the effect of climatic change on Archaic societies during the Hypsithermal, a time when warm and dry conditions encouraged the eastward spread of tall grasslands across the Midwest, creating the Prairie Peninsula (Transeau 1935). The emergence of the Prairie Peninsula is documented in regional pollen diagrams, which show a rise in pollen from forbs and grasses and a drop in tree pollen, as continental-wide climatic change affected local vegetation.

Pollen cores from several locations across Iowa indicate that post-Pleistocene forests dominated by oak and elm were replaced by prairie grasslands in a time-transgressive manner

(Baker et al. 1980; Baker et al. 1990; Chumbley et al. 1990). The prairie had expanded into western Iowa by 8100 B.C. (Baker et al. 1992) but did not reach parts of eastern Iowa for more than another 3,500 years (Baker et al. 1990; Baker et al. 1992; Baker et al. 1996; Bettis et al. 1992; Chumbley et al. 1990; Winkler et al. 1986). Climatologists believe that during the Hypsithermal the climate throughout the Midwest was warmer and drier than at any time during the Holocene (Bettis et al. 1992:3). Understanding Holocene paleoclimatic change is crucial to understanding Archaic patterns of human adaptation. It is also important because the preservation of Archaic sites is related to their position on the landscape, something that ultimately was affected by climate.

## Geomorphology and Archaeology

Geomorphology, or the study of landforms, has significantly enhanced our knowledge of the Holocene in Iowa. Until archaeologists recognized that many Archaic sites were deeply buried in alluvial settings and that particular geologic contexts had archaeological potential, they were missing half the pieces to the Archaic puzzle.

The beginning of the Holocene marked the end of significant accumulations of wind-transported sediments, chiefly loess, in the uplands. As deposition halted, erosion, weathering, and soil formation became the dominant geological processes in these areas (Prior 1991; Rhodes and Semken 1986:109; Ruhe 1969). Many Holocene-age sites in upland locations are not deeply buried and have been significantly altered or even destroyed by erosion and weathering. In particular, bone artifacts and faunal remains are less likely to be preserved in such contexts. Other upland sites lie beneath deposits up to a meter in depth. These sites have the potential to provide important archaeological information and cannot be overlooked on the basis of meager surface discoveries (Benn 1997; Hirst 1997:2–3).

While upland deposition virtually ceased during the Holocene, sediments from these locations were being eroded and then redeposited on

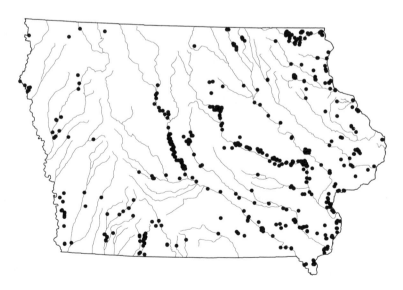

**5.1.** Recorded Archaic sites in Iowa. Data compiled from site records. Office of the State Archaeologist, University of Iowa. Courtesy of Timothy S. Weitzel and Stephen C. Lensink.

a massive scale in river valleys across Iowa. Alluvial fans and thick deposits dumped by rivers across valley floors grew to depths of many meters in some spots. The deposits composing the High Terrace of the Des Moines River, for instance, accumulated to a thickness of 8 m (Benn and Rogers 1985:31). Archaic sites in valley settings are buried in these "sediment packages," often at great depths, and are frequently very well preserved (fig. 5.2). Subsequent downcutting, however, sometimes has resulted in the loss of sites such deposits contain.

Archaeologists must understand and be able to identify geologic contexts. The presence and relative ages of some sites can be predicted from their stratigraphic position (Appendix 5.1). The absence of an expected deposit could mean that the archaeological record from a particular time period is missing. In western Iowa, for example, many Early and Middle Archaic sites have been almost completely eroded from small valleys (Bettis 1981:IIA–120). The absence of sites sometimes has led to the false conclusion that a region was depopulated or abandoned (Bettis and Hajic 1995:101–102). Archaeologists now realize that there may be a geologic explanation. Landform study in the Saylorville Reservoir in central Iowa, for instance, has recorded the presence of numerous Middle Archaic sites on Holocene river terraces where earlier research had concluded that no sites existed (Benn and Rogers 1985; Bettis and Hoyer 1986). Researchers are now advised to prepare a field strategy that employs deep testing and evaluation by geomorphologists in those areas where buried sites might be anticipated (Association of Iowa Archaeologists 1993:1–19; Zimmerman et al. 1994:1–2).

## Making a Living

Archaic societies adapted to continental-wide environmental change and to a myriad of local settings. People utilized a broad range of food resources, including large and small mammals, waterfowl, fish, shellfish, and wild plants. For the first time they began cultivating plants. In order to take advantage of this diversity, Archaic people developed an increasingly varied technology.

In Iowa the most diagnostic artifacts of the Archaic are projectile points. Archaic hunters manufactured a greater variety of point types than their Paleoindian ancestors. Most points were probably used on darts or spears and propelled with the atlatl (fig. 5.3). Old World hunters had invented this device by the end of the Ice Age, and some Paleoindian hunters may have used it as well. The atlatl was a composite weapon consisting of a wooden shaft fitted with a hook of wood or antler on one end and a handle at the other. Perforated shell or stone weights sometimes were fitted onto the shaft. Certain ground and pol-

**5.2.** Cultural deposits in Gunder Member alluvium eroding 6 m below the surface at 13PM105 in Plymouth County. The individual is pointing out eroding artifacts and faunal remains. Photo archives, Office of the State Archaeologist, University of Iowa.

**5.3.** The atlatl, or spearthrower. Illustration by Toby Morrow. From Morrow 1984.

**5.4.** Items such as these ground and polished gorgets from Iowa (top) and Johnson (bottom) counties may have served as spearthrower weights. On display, Iowa Hall, University of Iowa. Photo archives, Office of the State Archaeologist, University of Iowa.

ished stone artifacts, called bannerstones, boatstones, and gorgets, probably served as atlatl weights and handles (fig. 5.4). By using the atlatl, hunters could throw their weapons greater distances and with greater force.

Archaic points in Iowa appear to be less well made than Paleoindian types (fig. 5.5). There was an emphasis on the use of local cherts and an increase in the frequency of heat treating when poorer quality stone was used. Some styles apparently remained popular for long periods, and people in different areas favored particular types. Use-wear analysis has shown that certain types, such as the broad, thick Thebes point, also functioned as knives. Thus it is not always clear

whether different styles of points represent temporal, spatial, or functional types.

Ground and polished stone artifacts occur in profusion at Archaic sites. The pecking and grinding processes involved in their production allowed for the use of harder, less easily worked igneous and metamorphic rock such as granite and quartzite. Ground stone adzes, axes, grinding stones, and grinding slabs reflect the greater need for woodworking or plant-processing tools at a time when such resources were readily available (fig. 5.6). Bone artifacts such as awls, probably used in sewing and basket-making, and bone scrapers commonly occur by this time. More unusual are items like the bone flute found at the Cherokee Sewer site (fig. 5.7).

Archaic sites also provide the first evidence for the beginning of metalworking. Raw copper acquired from deposits in the Great Lakes region was cold hammered into a variety of artifacts that found their way throughout eastern North America. Iowa examples are rare and generally come from poorly documented contexts but suggest an affinity with the Old Copper complex of Wisconsin.

While not all technological innovations are directly evidenced in the archaeological record, we can infer the presence of others from the kinds of animal and plant remains left at Archaic sites. Butchered bison bone implies the practice of communal hunts that involved driving portions of herds over jumps or trapping them in dead-end gullies, corrals, or surrounds. A wide variety of fish species suggests the existence of nets, traps, or other devices that left no discernible trace. Waterfowl and small fur-bearing animals, whose butchered bones appear in archaeological contexts, were probably caught with small traps, nets, or snares. Freshwater mollusks, whose shells comprise many Archaic middens, may have been collected in woven baskets, in bags, or in bark or wooden containers.

The domestic dog, found for the first time in Iowa at Archaic sites, represents the earliest instance of an animal kept for a nondietary pur-

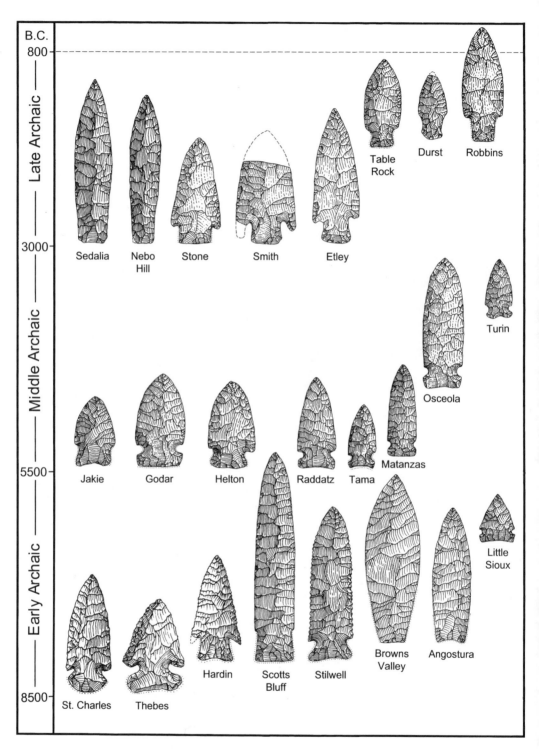

**5.5.** Archaic projectile point types found at Iowa sites.

Illustrations by Toby Morrow. From Morrow 1984.

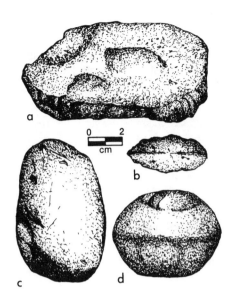

**5.6.** Ground stone artifacts like these from the multi-component Keystone site in Jackson County appear in profusion during Archaic times: (a) anvil stone; (b) axe or celt blade fragment, probably a Woodland period item; (c) utilized cobble; (d) shaped hammer-stone. From Anderson 1987a.

pose, perhaps for use in hunting, as a pack animal, or as a pet. The family Canidae includes wolves, coyotes, foxes, and domestic dogs. Bones of these animals found in archaeological sites can be distinguished from one another but often only with difficulty. There is also the problem of dogs crossing with both wolves and coyotes, creating the possibility of some interesting osteological mixes. Criteria used to distinguish these animals largely center on quantitative and qualitative differences in the skull, teeth, and long bones (Howard 1949; Krantz 1959; Olsen 1980; Schwartz 1997; Walker and Frison 1982).

Cultural changes during the Archaic were time-transgressive, as sites in eastern Iowa seem to display new forms of technology and subsistence adaptations earlier than sites in the west. This probably relates to a greater continuity in the subsistence economy of western Iowa, where bison hunting continued the big game–hunting pattern characteristic of earlier times. To the east, a broader-based hunting and foraging pattern with emphasis on deer, elk, smaller animals, birds, fish, shellfish, and plants was established

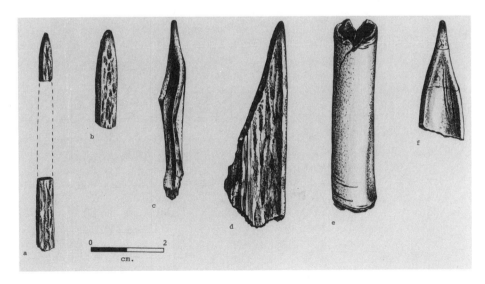

**5.7.** Bone artifacts from Horizon I at the Cherokee Sewer site, Cherokee County: (a–d, f) awls; (e) bird bone flute. From Shutler 1974.

early. It is not clear whether this adaptation was due to the more varied environments in eastern Iowa or to the cultural preferences of eastern Archaic people; probably it was both.

That plants—nuts, fruits, and tubers in particular—became important in some areas is evident both in the floral remains from archaeological contexts and in the presence of plant-processing tools such as grinding stones, or manos, and grinding slabs, or metates. Certain features also appear for the first time. Pits for roasting and boiling occur at many Iowa sites, some still containing signs of the materials that were cooked. Numerous ethnographic and historic accounts attest to the variety of customs among Native Americans that might account for such pits archaeologically (Alex 1996; Wandsnider 1997). The Lewis and Clark party, for instance, suffered exceedingly from gorging themselves on camas roots cooked in earth ovens by the Nez Percé. Fire-cracked rock, the by-product of cooking activities involving stone boiling or pit roasting, be-

gins to appear in profusion at many Archaic sites (fig. 5.8). Other pits represent storage facilities characteristic of more permanent habitations.

By the time people occupied the latest Archaic sites in Iowa, native varieties of plants of the so-called Eastern Agricultural Complex were being cultivated. Charred seeds of little barley (*Hordeum pusillum*) and goosefoot (*Chenopodium berlandieri*), often considered weeds today, occur alongside charred squash seeds and rind at a few sites in the southeastern part of the state. Cultivation represents one of the most important developments in the prehistory of America, a development that ultimately revolutionized the economy and lifeways of many native groups (Appendix 5.2).

## A Sense of Place

Throughout the Holocene, the growing number and variety of sites imply increasing populations. In certain regions societies began to occupy smaller territories and gradually became less mo-

**5.8.** Fire-cracked rock, the by-product of cooking activities such as stone boiling and pit roasting, appears in huge quantities beginning in Archaic times. From Roper 1994.

bile. As people adapted to local areas, they responded with hunting, fishing, and gathering
strategies, new food preparation methods, and
technologies that allowed them to utilize nearby
resources more efficiently. As a result, in some
areas settlement patterns began to change.

A highly mobile way of life marked by frequent
moves and resettlement on the part of small
family bands characterized Paleoindian society.
Throughout the Holocene, such a pattern was replaced in some areas by a more settled lifeway.
People began occupying larger, semipermanent,
seasonal base camps where several families remained for longer periods of time carrying out a
range of everyday tasks. On occasion, men and
women ventured out on periodic forays to collect
food and other resources. Archaeologists sometimes describe this change as a shift from a "for-
ager" to a "collector" strategy (Binford 1980).
Through the intensive utilization of especially
abundant and predictable resources, Archaic
people eventually occupied some sites year-round
and established the first small villages.

The occupation of smaller territories and increasing sedentism are important trends of the
Archaic. Such trends may explain a conspicuous
custom that first makes its appearance in Iowa
by the end of the period—communal burial. Anthropologists have documented that many societies throughout the world ritually mark the territories they occupy by establishing communal
cemeteries. By burying their dead at particular
locations, communities make a strong symbolic
statement regarding their connection to the land
(Charles and Buikstra 1983). Communal ossuaries and the first earthen burial mounds occur
in Iowa as testimony to the greater territorialism
felt by late Archaic communities. Some of the artifacts found accompanying the burials include
items made of shell, copper, and imported lithics
brought from distant sources. Their presence
implies the beginning of a wider sphere of trade
and contact among midwestern societies that is
a harbinger of broader interaction networks to
come.

## Women and Children in Archaic Society

Archaeologists assume that Archaic societies
were basically egalitarian and that most adults
would have participated in food gathering and
preparation, toolmaking, house construction,
and other everyday tasks. Any differences in roles
probably related to age and gender. Thus children
would not have been expected to perform all the
tasks of adults, and the responsibilities of men
and women probably varied. Although individuals might have been recognized and admired for
their special skills as hunters, basketmakers, or
storytellers, it is unlikely that anyone was born
with special status.

Paleoindian remains, mainly weapons found
at kill and processing sites, are believed by most
archaeologists to reflect the activities of male
hunters. While women and children were obviously part of Paleoindian society, there is little
concrete evidence for their existence. From Archaic times on, however, the archaeological record more accurately reflects the makeup of ancient society, and definitive evidence for both
women and children appears at Iowa sites. Burials of women and children, like those uncovered
at the Turin site (13MN2) and finds such as deciduous (baby) teeth at the Cherokee Sewer site
confirm the presence of entire families. In addition, artifacts such as bone awls and needles, and
stone scrapers, essential parts of prehistoric sewing and hideworking kits, become more common. Most archaeologists believe that as in later
times, these items were made and used largely by
women, although such gender interpretations
have not gone unchallenged (see Balme and Beck
1994; Gero and Conkey 1991).

## Early Archaic Discoveries
## (8500–5500 B.C.)

Early Archaic discoveries in Iowa consist of a variety of stemmed and notched projectile points,
most found at surface sites. The first stone tool
complex to succeed Dalton in eastern Iowa is
known as the Thebes Cluster and is comprised of

corner-notched St. Charles points and corner-notched Thebes knives. Although the age, contemporaneity, and duration of Early Archaic stone tool complexes is not well established, sites in west-central Illinois and elsewhere suggest that the Thebes Cluster may have begun as early as 8500–8100 B.C. (Morrow 1996e; O'Brien and Wood 1998). Stemmed Hardin points and corner-notched points of the Kirk Cluster follow around 8100–7500 B.C. (Morrow 1996c:11). Bifurcate base types such as St. Albans and LeCroy are found in contexts dating as early as 8000–7400 B.C. (Broyles 1971; Morrow 1996c, 1997a). Chipped stone adzes like those found with Dalton points accompany these complexes (Morrow 1997a:8). Early Archaic sites coincide with the Early and early Middle Holocene (table 2).

### Eastern and Central Iowa

Early Archaic point styles are widely distributed in parts of southeastern Iowa and the Mississippi valley. Although little else is known about the lifeways of people who made these weapons, their settlement pattern is assumed to have been seasonally mobile with subsistence based on hunting and foraging. Sites in the Iowa River Greenbelt in Hardin County yielded points of these types that provide clues to Early Archaic settlement (Collins 1990, 1991:29). Site types apparently were positioned to take advantage of a variety of resources. Residential camps may have been situated along the base and crest of the Iowa River bluff line, with seasonal camps and specialized activity sites outside the valley (Collins 1990, 1991:30). The Soldow site (13HB1) on the Des Moines River in Humboldt County produced a series of Hardin Barbed points (Flanders 1977; Benn and Rogers 1985:30), and the Kirk Corner Notched point type has been found south of there in the Saylorville–Red Rock area (Benn and Rogers 1985).

Contemporary stemmed and lanceolate projectile point styles are also found over much of Iowa. These include the contracting stemmed Alberta type, which is partially contemporaneous with the Thebes Cluster dating to 8200–6300 B.C. on the Great Plains (Frison 1991), and parallel-sided and stemmed Scottsbluff and Eden points contemporaneous with Hardin points. A series of parallel-oblique flaked to randomly flaked lanceolate types, such as Allen, Angostura, Browns Valley, Frederick, and Lusk, roughly contemporary with the bifurcate base series, follow between 7500 and 6300 B.C. (see fig. 5.5). Distinctions in the way these points were made, preferences for exotic or local lithics, and the differential use of heat treating suggest that these tools were used by contemporaneous groups of people who were exploiting slightly different ecological niches across the state (Morrow 1996c:10).

### The Cherokee Sewer Site and Early Archaic Hunters in Western Iowa

The Cherokee Sewer site south of the town of Cherokee in northwestern Iowa is the oldest extensively investigated site in the state. In the early 1970s construction of a sewage treatment plant revealed the remains of stratified components buried within an alluvial fan developed on the floodplain just west of the Little Sioux River (Hoyer 1980; Shutler et al. 1980:2) (see fig. 1.2). Archaeological investigations followed in 1973 and 1976, with the goal of determining the effect of climate and environment on human adaptation during the Middle Holocene (Shutler et al. 1980:2). To that end an interdisciplinary team of archaeologists, geologists, and paleontologists was assembled. Together they uncovered and interpreted four major, superimposed cultural zones or horizons at the site: Horizons I, II, IIIa, and IIIb, each associated with buried soils. Sediment cores taken from four other alluvial fans in the Little Sioux valley indicate the presence of contemporaneous, superimposed paleosols that could contain similar cultural materials (Hoyer 1980:61).

Analysis of lithic and bone tool assemblages, features, and faunal and floral remains suggests that groups of hunters ambushed and killed bison near the Cherokee Sewer site throughout its his-

| Geologic Epochs | Cultural Periods | Dated Complexes and Sites in Iowa |
|---|---|---|
| | | Eastern Iowa ←——————————→ Western Iowa |

| Geologic Epochs | | Cultural Periods | Dated Complexes and Sites in Iowa (Eastern Iowa ← → Western Iowa) |
|---|---|---|---|
| Holocene | Late | 800 B.C. | Red Ocher    Stemmed point complexes (Dryoff, Springley, Mo-Pac)    Diagonal Dune    Lewis Central School |
| | | | Darr es Shalom |
| | | | Davis Creek    Stemmed and notched point complexes (Table Rock, Durst, Ft. Dodge) |
| | | Late Archaic | O l d |
| | Middle | | C o p Sand Run p e r    T-S-N-like complexes (Wadlow, Karnak, Sedalia, Nebo Hill, Etley) |
| | | 3000 B.C. | Hemphill-like complexes (Godar, Matanzas, Osceola, Raddatz, Helton)    Turin |
| | | | Helton-like complexes (Godar, Matanzas, Helton, Karnak) |
| | | Middle Archaic | Gast Springs house    Stemmed and notched point complexes (Jakie, Brannan, Matanzas, Raddatz, Godar)    Cherokee Sewer Horizon I |
| | | 5500 B.C. | Cherokee Sewer Horizon II |
| | | | Prairie expansion across Iowa |
| | | Early Archaic | Parallel oblique, randomly flaked lanceolate point complexes (Allen, Angostura, Browns Valley)    Cherokee Sewer Horizon III |
| | Early | 8500 B.C. | Stemmed, notched, bifurcate-based point complexes (Thebes, Kirk, Hardin, St. Albans, LeCroy)    Unfluted lanceolate and stemmed point complexes (Alberta, Scottsbluff, Eden) |
| Pleistocene | Late | Late Paleo-indian | Dalton, Fayette    Agate Basin, Hell Gap |

Table 2

tory. A small tributary valley descending onto the floodplain of the Little Sioux River probably served as a game trail (Tatum and Shutler 1980: 252). Camps and processing areas occupied by small family bands were located on the nearby alluvial fan and adjacent floodplain (fig. 5.9).

*Horizon III*  Cultural material in Horizon IIIa, the oldest of the three main occupations, was dated to 7600–7200 B.C. Pollen studies from nearby Lake Okoboji revealed that the uplands surrounding the site at that time were covered with prairie, while in the valley lowland gallery forest prevailed (Baker and Van Zant 1980). The artifact assemblages from Horizon III consisted of lanceolate and stemmed projectile points found with the bones of *Bison bison*, possibly one of the now-extinct forms that was larger than modern buffalo (Pyle 1980:181). The lanceolate specimens, originally identified as the Agate Basin type, may be more similar to parallel-oblique and randomly flaked lanceolates found at con-

temporary sites throughout the Midwest (Anderson 1980; Anderson et al. 1980:262; Morrow 1984:32, 1997a:9) (fig. 5.10).

Other stone tools from Horizon III included bifaces, end scrapers, utilized and retouched flakes, a chopper, and a utilized cobble. Throughout the site's history, the inhabitants used Tongue River silicified sediment found in gravel deposits in northwest Iowa (Anderson 1980). This is a poor-quality material for knapping, so the Cherokee toolmakers used heat treating to improve its workability. Other stone tools were also made of locally available raw materials derived primarily from glacial outwash deposits in the region. Bone artifacts from Horizon III included chopping tools made of lower limb elements, a deer antler tine, and a worked beaver incisor (Tatum and Shutler 1980).

Horizon III contained the site's first hearths and a possible boiling pit, features characteristic of all horizons at the site. In later times, Native

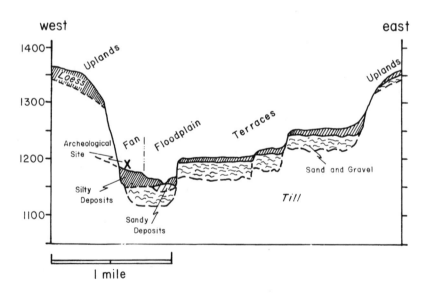

**5.9.** Schematic cross section of the Little Sioux valley with the position of the Cherokee Sewer site, Cherokee County, indicated. Photo archives, Office of the State Archaeologist, University of Iowa. From Hallberg et al. 1974.

Americans used boiling pits to render the fat and marrow from smashed and broken bone. Archaeologists surmise that the activities of the Horizon III occupants centered around the butchering and processing of bison, bone grease and marrow extraction, hide working, and stone and bone tool manufacturing and maintenance (Anderson et al. 1980:266). Women probably worked and sewed skins to make clothing, containers, and shelter.

Fifty percent of the Horizon III bison were calves and juvenile animals, and females dominated the assemblage (Anderson and Shutler 1978:136–137; Pyle 1980) (fig. 5.11). Reanalysis of the bison bone suggests that the earliest kills at the site probably took place during the early winter and that hunters deliberately selected calves and young bison (Whittaker 1998).

The nearby Simonsen site (13CK61) on the Little Sioux River 16 km south of Cherokee produced a component contemporary with Horizon

III (Agogino and Frankforter 1960; Frankforter 1959a; Frankforter and Agogino 1959a, 1960). Zone 7, buried 5 m below the surface, contained the remains of the extinct *Bison bison occidentalis*, identified from one skull only, side-notched

**5.10.** Lanceolate projectile point from Horizon III at the Cherokee Sewer site, Cherokee County. Illustration by Mary M. Slattery. From L. Alex 1980.

**5.11.** Articulated bison bone elements from Horizon III at the Cherokee Sewer site, Cherokee County. Photo archives, Office of the State Archaeologist, University of Iowa.

projectile points, other chipped stone artifacts, and a ground stone ax (Beals 1965a:3–5). Although 25 individual bison were originally reported, this figure could not be confirmed by subsequent study (Pyle 1980).

While the one radiocarbon date from Simonsen would seem to make the component in Zone 7 contemporary with Horizon III, the side-notched points are more similar to the projectile points from Horizon II dated almost a millennium later (Anderson et al. 1980:262) and to those from similarly dated sites in the region, including Hill (13ML62) (Frankforter and Agogino 1959a), Logan Creek (25BT3) (Kivett 1962), Turin (Fisher et al. 1985), and Pisgah (13HR2) (Frankforter 1961). The large standard deviation of 500 years on the date from Simonsen may suggest that the actual age of the site is closer to the later components just cited. The points and the date on the early occupation at Simonsen imply that *Bison bison occidentalis* survived for some time into the Holocene on the eastern Plains. Points from Simonsen have sometimes been referred to as the Simonsen type (Benn and Rogers 1985:30). Other archaeologists include them with the side-notched forms from Horizon II in a Little Sioux type (Morrow 1984) (see fig. 5.5).

At the Arthur site (13DK27) on the Des Moines Lobe at East Lake Okoboji, archaeologists recovered a lanceolate projectile point and lanceolate point fragments, all with ground bases, in mixed and undated contexts (Anderson and Spriestersbach 1982:113, 116; Tiffany ed. 1982). Lanceolate and stemmed points similar to those from Horizon III also occur in surface collections from western Iowa (Anderson and Shutler 1974:167).

*Horizon II*  By the time Horizon II at the Cherokee Sewer site was occupied, ca. 6200–5900 B.C., the uplands surrounding the Archaic camp were covered by prairie brought on by an increasingly warmer and drier climate (Shutler et al. 1980:12). Such an environment supported important game, particularly elk and bison, and

cooperative hunting continued as a key element of the economy.

As in earlier times, the site functioned as a kill and processing camp where at least 15 bison were butchered and dressed, possibly the by-products of multiple hunts (Whittaker 1997). The faunal remains, including the bones of very young animals, suggest occupation during the late fall and early winter (Whittaker 1998). Judging by the number of hearths associated with this component, 30 to 60 people may have lived there during Horizon II times.

Although initial analyses concluded that all horizons at the Cherokee Sewer site reflected a similar pattern in settlement and subsistence, this conclusion has since been disputed (Ahler 1995; Whittaker 1997, 1998). Reanalysis of the age classes of bison remains, for instance, indicates that Horizon II hunters may have been less selective in the animals they took, conducting numerous kills over a relatively short period of time (Whittaker 1997:26–31).

A side-notched projectile point, classified as the Little Sioux type (Morrow 1984:61), had come into use by Horizon II times, perhaps reflecting a more efficient hafting design (Musil 1988:382). The points exhibit basal grinding, and most were made of locally available Tongue River silicified sediment. A variety of chipped and ground stone tools rounded out the stone tool inventory. Scrapers, bison limb bone choppers, and splinter awls from Horizon II underscore the continued importance of hideworking to the Archaic inhabitants. A cut bone fragment with worn edges and a smooth surface may have functioned as a pendant.

Points similar to those from Horizon II occur elsewhere in western Iowa—at the Hill site on Pony Creek north of Glenwood, at Pisgah (13HR2) in Harrison County, and, as mentioned, at Simonsen (Agogino and Frankforter 1960; Anderson et al. 1980:264; Beals 1965a; Frankforter 1959a, 1961). Hill and Simonsen are deeply buried in Corrington Member alluvial fans and Gunder Member terraces, and the date from Hill is close to that from Horizon II (Benn 1990:76). The artifacts and features found at these locations identify them as base camps occupied for several weeks or even months at a time. Other sites known from upland and high terrace locations and identified from lithic scatters are probably the remains of shorter-term camps and resource procurement spots.

Previous researchers grouped many of these sites into a complex called Logan Creek after the Logan Creek site in Burt County, Nebraska, just across the Iowa border (McKusick 1964b). Radiocarbon dates indicate that the inhabitants of Logan Creek, Hill, and Horizon II at the Cherokee Sewer site were utilizing the eastern Plains and western prairie in similar ways (Kivett 1962; McKusick 1964b). Hypsithermal drought apparently had little effect on the economy, and bison hunting continued. Assuming that western Iowa may actually have received more rainfall than locations to the west, perhaps both herds and hunters were attracted there during dry episodes (Benn 1990:77). Elk, deer, and smaller mammals, as well as birds, turtle, fish, and mussels, rounded out the diet of these early western Archaic people.

## Middle Archaic Discoveries (5500–3000 B.C.)

The occupation of Middle Archaic sites in Iowa coincided with the most arid part of the Holocene. Archaic peoples responded to the extreme conditions of the Hypsithermal by moving to a number of so-called refuges—stream valleys, lakesides, marshlands—where more reliable sources of water, surviving stands of timber, and more diverse resources could be found. Middle Archaic base camps as well as shorter-term camps and workshops often exist deeply buried in most river valleys. Surveys of the Des Moines Lobe have demonstrated the existence of numerous briefly occupied encampments or procurement sites, as well as larger base camps, around the margins of prairie lakes, marshes, and sloughs (Lensink 1984; Mallam and Bettis

1980). During extremely dry episodes, groundwater levels dropped, and some of the shallower Iowa Great Lakes, such as East Okoboji, nearly dried up, becoming marshes (Abbott 1982a:9; Baker and Van Zant 1980). Droughty episodes appear to have enhanced wetland resources in the prairie lakes region, and occupation appears to have increased during the Middle Holocene (Lensink 1984).

Northeastern Iowa remained free from prairie for several millennia longer than other areas of the state and may itself have become a refuge for Middle Archaic groups, although sites from this time period are not well known. Pollen studies from southeast Iowa are more ambiguous as to the time of prairie encroachment and its effect on human settlement (Baker et al. 1992; Baker et al. 1996; Baker and Whelan 1992; Nations et al. 1989).

Traditionally, uplands were viewed by archaeologists as less desirable locations for permanent habitation during the Middle Holocene. Recent studies, however, show that sites do occur in the uplands and demonstrate their continued use despite drier conditions and prairie cover (Benn and Bowers 1994; Green and Rogers 1995:9; Hirst 1997). By the Late Archaic, the number of upland sites began to increase, as people rapidly spilled over into new territories and intensified their subsistence strategies in response to the milder environmental conditions at the close of the Hypsithermal (Benn and Bowers 1994:I–91).

### Site Types

In many parts of the Midwest, small bands of Middle Archaic people moved throughout the year in order to harvest important plant and animal species (Brown and Vierra 1983). In other areas where favored resources were abundant and available for lengthy periods, some societies started to concentrate on particular species, and a trend toward longer settlement at large base camps began. These differences in subsistence and settlement resulted in a greater variety of living sites found in the Midwest at this time.

At present, so little is known about the Middle Archaic in Iowa that it is difficult to evaluate whether the trends noted elsewhere in the Midwest were under way. The increasing numbers of sites and greater variety of site types—for example, base camps, short-term camps, and special purpose sites such as quarries (Anderson and Semken 1980; Collins 1995; Collins et al. 1991; Fisher et al. 1985; Green and Rogers 1995; Lensink ed. 1986)—indicate that the population was growing.

Sites in eastern Iowa show that Middle Archaic subsistence was dependent on the hunting and gathering of a wide range of resources. The presence of both upland and lowland sites with varying functions implies that people were moving between resources, most likely on a seasonal basis. Middle Archaic hunting and foraging groups in the Prairie Lakes area in the northern portion of the Des Moines Lobe also inhabited a variety of site types following the establishment of tall-grass prairie. Substantial lithic scatters consisting of debitage and finished artifacts characterize base camps where people "tooled up" for periodic forays to avail themselves of lake and marshland resources. Diagnostic points found in the uplands surrounding the prairie lakes also suggest the seasonal exploitation of bison herds during Middle Archaic times (Lensink 1984). Discoveries in the South Skunk River valley near Ames in central Iowa indicate a preference for narrower, steep-sided valleys rather than the broader valleys favored during Early Archaic times and considerable differences in land and resource use even over short distances (Bower and Bettis 1991). In western Iowa, bison hunting remained important.

Mortuary sites also occur for the first time in Iowa during the Middle Archaic. Most notable are the multiple pit burials at Turin in northwestern Iowa. Impressive collections of Middle Archaic points and polished and ground stone tools found together at blufftop and other upland locations elsewhere may also represent former burial sites whose context has been destroyed by plowing (Benn and Bowers 1994: I–89).

### Stone Tools

Once again, projectile point types, especially a wide range of medium-sized stemmed and notched forms, are the diagnostic indicators of Middle Archaic components (see fig. 5.5). Stemmed types include Stanley, White Springs, and Jakie, as well as unnamed corner-notched styles similar to those from the early Middle Archaic levels of the Koster site in the lower Illinois River valley and from the upper horizon of the Campbell Hollow site, also in Illinois (Brown and Vierra 1983; Justice 1987; Stafford ed. 1985). Jakie stemmed points have been tentatively dated at 5800–4800 B.C. (O'Brien and Wood 1998:132).

After 5500 B.C. side-notched forms known by a variety of names—including Brannan, Matanzas, Godar, Osceola, Raddatz, Robinson, and Tama—predominate and carry over into Late Archaic components (Morrow 1996c:12, 1997a: 10). A late Middle Archaic complex at the Koster site, known as the Helton phase and dating to 4400–3700 B.C. (Brown and Vierra 1983), is characterized by Godar, Matanzas, Helton, and Karnak points. Sites similar to the Helton phase are found in eastern Iowa (Morrow 1996c). Osceola points are both widespread and common throughout the Upper Mississippi basin, while Matanzas and Godar points appear less numerous in the Mississippi valley north of Clinton (Benn et al. 1994:61). Osceola points were associated with deposits radiocarbon dated to 4500–4300 B.C. at the multicomponent Buchanan site (13SR153) near Ames. Here Archaic to Woodland cultural remains were distributed throughout the alluvial deposits of a small sidewall valley of the South Skunk River (Bower and Bettis 1991; Hainlin 1992; Van Nest 1987). Tama points at Buchanan were dated at 4100–3900 B.C. and Raddatz points from the same site at 2900–2700 B.C.

Middle Archaic flake tools are smaller, less formally patterned, and less well made than earlier Archaic types. In addition to projectile points, chipped stone artifacts include winged T-shaped drills, bifaces, and large unifacial scrapers. Fire-cracked rock and quantities of debitage are common at some sites. Many flake tools were manufactured from local cherts that were frequently heat treated. Such changes could relate to the smaller territories and decreased mobility of Middle Archaic people, making it more difficult to acquire choice lithic raw material (Morrow 1996c:12).

At the multicomponent Bash site (13MR228) in Marshall County, excavations uncovered a late Early Archaic or early Middle Archaic chert quarry and lithic workshop buried in a Corrington Member fan. Throughout its occupation, the site served as a processing location for Maynes Creek and Warsaw Formation cherts. Archaeologists uncovered heat-treatment facilities and pit features, the latter containing large pitted anvil stones used in bipolar core reduction, chert raw material, and cores. The site's residents may have cached these materials for later use (Collins 1995; Collins et al. 1991).

In contrast to the decline in size and quality of chipped stone items, ground stone artifacts proliferate during the Middle Archaic. Fully grooved axes appear early, followed by rounded-polled three-quarter grooved axes (fig. 5.12). Flat-polled three-quarter grooved axes were being made by the end of the Middle Archaic (Morrow 1996c:12). Skillfully made ground and polished bannerstones are common throughout the Middle Archaic, most probably functioning as atlatl weights (Benn 1992:68). The function of objects referred to as plummets as well as small ground and polished pieces of hematite still remains a mystery.

### A Middle Archaic House in the Mississippi River Alluvial Plain

Work along the Mississippi River has shown the presence of sites in well-drained settings along backwater lakes and sloughs (Benn 1992:68). Coring, deep trenching, and subsequent excavation at 10 alluvial fans lining the bluff base in

**5.12.** Three-quarter grooved ax from Allamakee County. On display, Iowa Hall, University of Iowa. Photo archives, Office of the State Archaeologist, University of Iowa.

the Muscatine Island–Lake Odessa locality revealed similar developmental sequences of Corrington Member fan deposits overlain by paleosols in their upper regions. Geomorphologists have demonstrated similar cycles of fan deposition and soil formation throughout much of the Midwest during the Early to Middle Holocene, which are possibly linked to climatic factors (Benn et al. 1988; Bettis and Hoyer 1986; Bettis and Hajic 1995; Hajic 1990). Additional work may help in dating the arrival of Middle Holocene prairie in this part of the state and determining its effect on local adaptation by Middle Archaic people (Artz 1995).

Interdisciplinary study at the Gast Spring site (13LA152) situated on a small fan adjacent to Muscatine Slough revealed a substantial Middle Archaic midden. Associated with the midden was a basin-shaped feature buried 4.5 to 5 m below the surface. The feature appears to be the floor of a structure into which the inhabitants had excavated a shallow oval pit. Midden deposits filled the pit and covered the floor of the feature, yielding the remains of fish, turtle, bird, mammals, seeds, and gastropods; abundant charcoal; fire-cracked rock; flake tools; a biface; and a micro-

blade core (Baker and Whelan 1992). Charcoal
from the subfloor pit and midden dated to
5200–4500 B.C. If this is indeed a house, it
would be the oldest one known in Iowa (Bettis et
al. 1992:39; Goldman-Finn et al. 1991; Green et
al. 1994).

### Middle Archaic Hunters on the Southern Iowa Drift Plain

The Ed's Meadow site (13DM712) on a narrow
ridge spur above Flint Creek in Des Moines
County exemplifies use of an upland setting by
Middle Archaic people (Morrow 1996c). While
surface collections at the site were sparse, subsequent excavation revealed the presence of significant prehistoric deposits (Morrow 1996c:
49). One area at the site represents a single occupation dating to the early Middle Archaic.

A Jakie point and a type similar to corner-
notched forms from western Illinois were found
near a dense concentration of debitage believed
to represent a feature where the site's occupants
prepared bifaces (Morrow 1996c:49) (fig. 5.13).
The feature was apparently part of a broader habitation area utilized as a hunting camp. Use-wear
study of the flake tools from the living area at
Ed's Meadow indicates activities related to the
cutting of soft or medium-hard materials, scraping or planing of medium-hard to hard substances, and the splitting of wood or antler
(Morrow 1996c). Most of the chipped stone
materials found across the site were made of locally obtainable cherts, particularly Burlington
and Keokuk types. The presence of abraded hematite fragments and an igneous rock fragment
covered with red hematite suggests the processing of ocher for use as a pigment or as a hide pre-
servative. Hematite, a form of iron oxide, was
used throughout the prehistoric world. Ground
to form a powder called ocher, it was sometimes
mixed with an emollient such as animal fat to
produce a paint. Ocher was commonly placed
over burials.

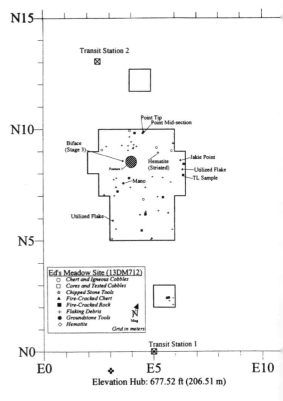

**5.13.** Middle Archaic feature at the Ed's Meadow site, Des Moines County. From Morrow 1996c.

### Middle Archaic Hunters in Western Iowa

Later components in western Iowa, such as Horizon I at the Cherokee Sewer site, Lungren
(13ML224) on Pony Creek north of Glenwood
(Reeves 1973b), and Ocheyedan (13OA401)
west of the Iowa Great Lakes (Anderson ed.
1973), offer a glimpse into the life of western
Iowa bison hunters during the very height of the
Hypsithermal. There is little evidence to suggest
that drought greatly affected the lifeways of Middle Archaic societies here.

At the Cherokee Sewer site, hunting bands
established a final encampment around 5500–
5200 B.C. The climate during this period would
have been up to 2°C warmer than present, with
precipitation reduced by about 10 percent

(Wendland 1980). Prairies covered the uplands, while the floodplain supported an impoverished gallery forest consisting largely of willows and hackberries (Shutler et al. 1980:12). Despite the occupation of the site during times of drought, human activities showed little discernible differences from the two earlier periods of occupation. The Middle Archaic residents killed and butchered at least nine bison and processed their meat and hides. Disarticulated canid bones indicate that dog had been added to the diet (Pyle 1980).

The lithic tool kit of the last residents at Cherokee included medium-sized side-notched projectile points with slightly concave to straight bases (fig. 5.14). An elk antler knapper, a bone tube, and what has been interpreted as a flute fashioned from the limb bone of a turkey-sized bird composed the bone tool inventory (see fig. 5.7). The flute is the earliest instance of a musical instrument in the Midwest and one of the oldest in North America (Tatum and Shutler 1980:240).

Three hearth areas uncovered on Horizon I imply the presence of a small hunting band of perhaps 15 to 30 people (Tatum and Shutler 1980:242). While it has always been assumed that groups of families camped at the Cherokee Sewer site throughout its history, the discovery of three deciduous human baby teeth confirmed the presence of children during Middle Archaic times.

Evidence for a contemporary hunting camp was found at the Lungren site in Mills County, where at the base of a stratified deposit a side-notched projectile point similar to that from Horizon I occurred in a context with a roasting or boiling pit and a varied stone tool assemblage dated at 5200–5000 B.C. (Brown 1967a; Reeves 1973b). A surface collection at the Ocheyedan site in Osceola County produced similar points and bison remains (Anderson ed. 1973).

*Turin*

The Turin site in Monona County provides the first evidence for deliberate human burial in western Iowa during Middle Holocene times. In 1955 gravel pit operators accidentally uncovered four separate burials (Fisher et al. 1985; Ives 1955a). Because the burials were observed in loess, archaeologists assumed they dated to the Late Pleistocene, and the site received national notoriety (*Life* 1955) (fig. 5.15). Since then, better understanding of western Iowa geomorphology and a radiocarbon date has established a Middle Holocene age for the component. The burials are now known to have occupied a Gunder Member fill in a gully cut into Wisconsinan-age loess and dated at 3800–3000 B.C. (fig. 5.16).

Although the gravel pit workers disturbed the first burial at Turin, that of a young adult male, archaeologists carefully excavated the remaining three, identifying an infant and two children, one possibly female. All were found in a flexed position. One of the children, estimated at about 10 years of age, was placed in a shallow pit, and red ocher was sprinkled over the body. Beads of *Anculosa* shell were associated with this burial, and a side-notched projectile point lay in the region of the pelvis. *Anculosa* is a freshwater mollusk that originates in streams east of the Mississippi River. The projectile point was made of Knife River flint and resembled types from Cherokee, Lungren, and the Late Archaic Lewis Central School site (13PW5).

**5.14.** Side-notched points from Horizon I at the Cherokee Sewer site, Cherokee County. Illustration by Mary M. Slattery. From L. Alex 1980.

*Anculosa* shell and Knife River flint represent materials widely exchanged throughout the prehistoric world. The use of red ocher and other aspects of the Turin site duplicate known Middle Archaic burial customs found elsewhere. The flexed position of the individually buried skeletons, with at least one placed in a shallow pit, and the occurrence of *Anculosa* shell, perhaps used as a necklace or sewn to clothing, are common finds at other burial sites of this period in the eastern United States. Neither the burial mode nor the finds themselves imply that the people buried at Turin had special status within the society, although the *Anculosa* shell was probably considered a valued possession.

**5.15.** The excavations at the Turin site in Monona County created local as well as national interest. Photo archives, Sanford Museum and Planetarium, Cherokee, Iowa. From Fisher et al. 1985.

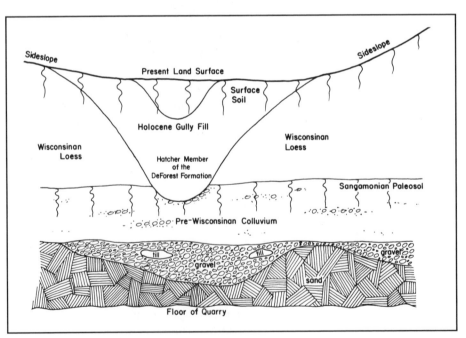

**5.16.** Turin site location in DeForest Formation deposits, east-west cross section. Photo archives, Office of the State Archaeologist, University of Iowa. From Fisher et al. 1985.

## Late Archaic Discoveries: Winds of Change (3000–800 B.C.)

The Late Archaic coincides with the Late Holocene, a time of cooler temperatures and increased moisture throughout the Midwest that continues to the present. Most areas of Iowa probably appeared much as they did at historic contact. A milder climate may have encouraged the reoccupation of areas vacated during the Hypsithermal, although use of prairie wetlands on the Des Moines Lobe apparently decreased (Lensink 1984). Late Archaic sites in Iowa, identified on the basis of diagnostic artifacts, radiocarbon dates, and geomorphologic contexts, are more numerous and are somewhat better known than earlier Archaic sites as a result of the excavation of deeply buried contexts. The increase in sites and finds and the greater variety of projectile point types suggest that the population was increasing (Morrow 1995a).

By the end of the Late Archaic, people were making greater use of the uplands both for temporary and more permanent habitation. In eastern Iowa, the presence of reliable and abundant resources apparently encouraged the year-round occupation of large base camps in the Mississippi valley as well as temporary camps or procurement sites (Benn 1987, 1992). At some of these locations, native species of plants were first cultivated, marking the earliest evidence for gardening in Iowa. A similar pattern is found at Terminal Archaic sites along the Mississippi and Illinois rivers in Illinois (Emerson and McElrath 1983). In contrast, research in central and western Iowa suggests that a more mobile, seasonal pattern of site occupation prevailed.

### Complexes and Phases

Archaeologists recognize four Late Archaic artifact complexes in Iowa that are similar to four phases or complexes identified in nearby states. The earliest complex compares to the Hemphill phase of west-central Illinois, a transitional Middle to Late Archaic phase that succeeds the Helton phase and dates to 3800–2800 B.C. (Benn et al. 1994:66; Conrad 1981:43; Cook 1976; Stoltman 1980:139). The Hemphill phase is characterized by small to medium-sized side-notched points, like Matanzas and Godar types, with many more of the larger side-notched Osceola points. Expanding stemmed Helton-like points, winged T-drills, and rectangular three-quarter grooved axes also occur (Benn 1987; Benn and Bowers 1994; Morrow 1996c:13). This complex was present in the lowest levels at the Sand Run Slough West site (13LA38) in Louisa County, where it dates to 2900–2600 B.C. (Benn 1987).

Artifacts characteristic of a second complex, sometimes referred to as the Titterington–Sedalia–Nebo Hill (TSN) culture (McElrath et al. 1993:150), are found at sites across southern Iowa (Benn et al. 1988; Benn and Bowers 1994: I-92; Collins 1990:379; Henning 1990: G-2). In west-central Illinois, the Titterington phase dates between 2900 and 1700 B.C. (Cook 1976) and is in part contemporary with the Sedalia complex of northeastern Missouri (Chapman 1975) and the Nebo Hill phase of central and northwestern Missouri and northeastern Kansas. Nebo Hill sites have been dated to 2900–700 B.C. (O'Brien and Wood 1998: 122). Diagnostic points or bifaces in this complex include the lanceolate-shaped Wadlow, Karnak, Sedalia, and Nebo Hill types; the large, stemmed Etley type; and, less commonly, Stone Squared Stemmed and Smith Basal Notched points (Benn et al. 1994:66). Chipped stone gouges and polished Sedalia diggers functioned as digging and chopping tools. Thick bifaces, drills, heavy scrapers, axes, and grinding equipment—especially flat or trough-bottomed three-quarter grooved axes—are also typical (Benn 1992:70; Benn and Bowers 1994:I-91; Morrow 1996c:13). Fiber-tempered pottery occurs at some Nebo Hill phase sites in northwestern Missouri.

Although chipped stone gouges and diggers are rare in Iowa, other artifacts of this complex are found in the upper Mississippi valley near Muscatine, in the lower Skunk valley and the lower central Des Moines valley above Des Moines at Saylorville Lake, and as far north as the Iowa valley in central Iowa (Artz 1995; Benn et al. 1988; Benn and Rogers 1985; Benn and Bowers 1994: I-92; Collins 1990:379; Henning 1990:G-2). Other sites occur in southwestern Iowa in Page and Ringgold counties. Points identified as the Sedalia type found at the Buchanan site were associated with a date of 1500–1000 B.C. (Hainlin 1992; Van Nest 1987).

A third complex is identified by smaller stemmed point types including Table Rock, Springly, Durst, Robbins, and Merom; by broad side-notched types such as Fort Dodge and Conrad; and by small corner-notched Vosberg points (Benn 1992; Benn et al. 1994; Morrow 1996c) (see fig. 5.5). Thermoluminescence dating on burned rock associated with Table Rock points from the Davis Creek site (13WS122) in Washington County suggests an age between 1600 and 1000 B.C. (Lensink ed. 1986:198). A Table Rock point was found above, and possibly contemporary with, a Terminal Archaic feature dated to 900–800 B.C. at the Diagonal Dune site (13RN54) in Ringgold County (Hirst and Artz 1993). Durst or Table Rock points were identified at the Darr-es-Shalom site (13PK149) in the central Des Moines valley in association with a date of 1100–800 B.C. (Osborn and Gradwohl 1981:131, 154; Timberlake 1981). Durst points are the diagnostic type for the Durst phase of Wisconsin, dated to 900–700 B.C. (Stoltman 1986a:227). Durst points, a common type in eastern Iowa, occurred in the Keystone rockshelter (Anderson 1987a:2) and in the Henry Schnoor shelter (13JK20) in Jackson County (Jaehnig 1975:139; Marcucci et al. 1993:28). A Durst point from 13CT228, an occupation along the Turkey River in Clayton County, was associated with a radiocarbon date contemporary with the Durst phase of Wisconsin (Green 1990). A point identified as a Fort Dodge type from the Buchanan site was associated with deposits dated to 1400–1200 B.C. (Bower and Bettis 1991; Van Nest 1987).

The presence of a fourth complex characterized by Terminal Late Archaic points matching types in the Mississippi and Illinois valleys is known from surface discoveries in southeast Iowa. Points include the Dryoff and Springly types, medium-sized stemmed points with barbed shoulders, and expanding-stemmed Mo-Pac points. Scrapers, drills, gravers, celts, grinding stones, pipes, plummets, galena, and worked hematite represent other elements of this complex (Benn et al. 1994:67–68). In the American Bottom region of west-central Illinois, these materials comprise the Prairie Lakes phase, believed to range between 1100 and 700 B.C. (McElrath et al. 1984:49–58; Morrow 1996c:14).

The similarity of Iowa materials to these four varied complexes suggests that Late Archaic communities here interacted with others over a broad area of the Midwest, sharing styles of points and other artifacts. Iowa on occasion may have been included within the territorial range of some outside groups. There is evidence that by Late Archaic times people in the Midwest began to establish local territorial allegiances at the same time they were trading and interacting with groups over wide areas.

### The Old Copper Complex and Early Metallurgy

Numerous finds from eastern Iowa illustrate that the region was within the sphere of the Old Copper complex, best known from Middle and Late Archaic sites in Wisconsin, the majority dating to 3800–1100 B.C. (Gibbon 1998). Old Copper sites represent the earliest evidence for metalworking in North America. Archaic people made distinctive copper artifacts from deposits surrounding Lake Superior. The crystalline rock matrix in which the rock occurred was first heated and then doused with cold water, causing it to crack. The copper was then extracted with stone hammers and cold hammered into a wide variety of utilitarian and ornamental artifacts (Stoltman 1986a:220). At some point, native metalworkers discovered that by heating and then cooling the copper they could counteract its

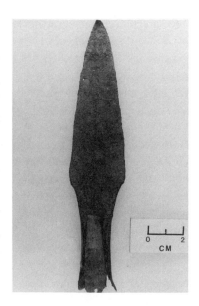

**5.17.** A socketed copper point from Dickinson County. Photo archives, Office of the State Archaeologist, University of Iowa. From Green 1990b.

tendency to become brittle and crack, thereby increasing its workability. This process, known as annealing, allowed for the production of very thin objects.

Copper items found in Old Copper burial sites in Wisconsin include utilitarian artifacts such as socketed spear points, harpoons, hooks, gorges, spuds, celts, axes, adzes, chisels, gouges, wedges, awls, punches, drills, spatulas, and distinctive single-edged semilunar knives similar to the Eskimo ulu. Archaic woodworkers may have used the copper axes and chisels to make dugout canoes. Other burial items, including tabular and spherical beads, C-shaped bracelets, pendants, and a headdress adorned with sheet copper strips, perhaps served ornamental functions (Stoltman 1986a:217). Sites also yield distinctive large side-notched Osceola points and smaller side-notched Raddatz forms. Sites in east-central Minnesota are associated with assemblages containing both Raddatz and Durst points (Gibbon 1998:45).

Archaeologists have not yet identified the camps and living sites of Old Copper people in Wisconsin. In the southwestern part of the state, however, there are a number of rockshelters where Raddatz points and a variety of utilitarian artifacts occur. Study of the faunal remains from these sites suggests that they represent short-term winter hunting camps where residents sought deer and smaller game. Although copper items are missing from these sites, the presence of artifacts, particularly projectile points, diagnostic of the Old Copper complex may identify the sites as the temporary hunting encampments of Old Copper people (Wittry 1959a, 1959b).

Artifacts that may be associated with the Old Copper complex appear in Iowa as far west as Dickinson County (Green ed. 1990b) (fig. 5.17). Most, however, have been found in the eastern part of the state, particularly in Allamakee, Winneshiek, and Clayton counties (Logan 1976; Mallam 1978). One of the more distinctive is the long rattail spearpoint (see plate 6). Like the copper pin and the Osceola point dredged from a depth of more than 10 m below the surface of the Wapsipinicon River in Jones County, none of these items have been excavated in situ (Ruppé 1954). They likely represent trade items acquired from Old Copper people to the north.

Other Iowa sites, such as the Levsen Rockshelter (13JK4) near Maquoketa, have yielded Raddatz and Osceola points without copper items. Osceola points occur in the earliest occupations at Sand Run Slough West. They are considered contemporary with other midwestern Osceola finds and with sites of the early Late Archaic Hemphill phase. Hemphill phase sites, in turn, have produced copper artifacts and other items similar to those of Wisconsin's Old Copper and related complexes (Stoltman 1980). The presence of Osceola and Raddatz points at Iowa sites suggests the potential of these sites to provide further details about the lifeways of people who began to participate in a wider interaction network throughout the Midwest.

## Settling Down in the Mississippi River Alluvial Plain?

By the Late Archaic, the settlement pattern along the Mississippi River in southeastern Iowa apparently included some intensively occupied base camps situated on well-drained landforms. As might be expected, these sites contain thick midden deposits with large quantities of artifacts and features perhaps reflecting year-round occupation (Artz 1995; Benn 1992, 1987). At floodplain locations more ephemeral sites occur, marked by thin scatters of fire-cracked rock and low frequencies of artifacts (Benn 1992:92). Paleobotanical remains indicate that the cultivation of plants was part of the subsistence strategy for some Late Archaic people in this area. A similar subsistence-settlement pattern is duplicated at contemporary sites in large river valleys throughout the eastern United States (Emerson and McElrath 1983).

The Sand Run Slough West site covers two small alluvial fans and a Mississippi River terrace beneath the bluff south of Lake Odessa in Louisa County. Excavations in 1986 revealed several discrete occupations within a narrow band of cultural deposits eroding along the west bank of Sand Run Slough. Stratum III, the earliest component, contained Late Archaic artifacts found within a dense midden, midden-filled pits, and roasting pits. One pit appeared to contain the remains of a deliberately buried dog. This occupation is believed to represent a base camp, possibly occupied year-round (Benn 1987).

Excavations at Sand Run Slough West uncovered large and small projectile point types together throughout the midden. Heavy side-notched Osceola points dominated the assemblage, occurring alongside Godar, Raddatz, and smaller Matanzas points. This diverse point complex is typical of the early Late Archaic Hemphill phase (Conrad 1981). Many of the "points" at Sand Run Slough West served multiple functions, including use as knives.

The faunal and floral remains from the site reflect the kind of abundant and locally reliable resources that could support a permanently occupied base camp on a backwater channel of the Mississippi River. Although acidic soils resulted in relatively poor faunal preservation, archaeologists identified the remains of deer, small mammals, turkey, duck, turtle, catfish, and freshwater drum in the Late Archaic levels. Seasonal growth rings on fish bone suggest year-round catches. Floral remains show an emphasis on nuts, seeds, and possibly tubers. Plant foods include hickory nuts, walnuts, acorns, wild rice, and the seeds of ragweed, sunflower, goosefoot, and marshelder (Lopinot 1987). The presence of goosefoot, marshelder, and sunflower, all known to have been under cultivation elsewhere in the Midwest by this time, suggests that the Sand Run Slough West inhabitants were experimenting with gardening.

Some items found in Late Archaic sites indicate increasing social complexity. At Sand Run Slough West, items such as bannerstones, celts, hematite and limonite pebbles, and galena may have functioned as items of social exchange and certainly imply interregional contact and trade. Galena, a natural form of lead sulfide found in the Paleozoic Plateau region, occurs in the shape of small cubes. Archaic people traded galena widely throughout the eastern United States (Walthall 1981). Its presence at Sand Run Slough West demonstrates the interregional connections southeast Iowa populations had developed by this time.

Communal burial sites are a conspicuous custom of the Late Archaic throughout the eastern United States. People used Sand Run Slough West itself as a cemetery soon after its abandonment as a habitation site. Archaeologists encountered a basin-shaped pit, 70 by 70 cm, containing individual flexed and bundle burials (Benn et al. 1992). Features like this may be present at contemporary settlements but, if so, lie deeply buried and undetected (Benn and Bowers 1994:1–89).

The Gast Spring site, not far from Sand Run Slough West, provides evidence for Late Archaic plant cultivation. Here, archaeologists encountered a small basin-shaped feature lying at the base of the oldest of four paleosols. The feature was densely packed with charcoal, burned tufa, fire-cracked rock, and important paleobotanical information. Remains of little barley, goosefoot, and squash rind, all believed to have been under cultivation, were dated to 1000–800 B.C. (Dunne 1997). This represents the oldest known occurrence of cultivated little barley in the Midwest.

### Hunting and Toolmaking on the Southern Iowa Drift Plain

Late Archaic settlements on the Southern Iowa Drift Plain apparently were not occupied year-round. Excavations at the multicomponent Davis Creek site, situated on a stream bench above Davis Creek in Washington County, revealed a Late Archaic component containing 22 Table Rock projectile points. This point type, first found in mixed context at the Rice Rock shelter in Missouri, is estimated to date between about 2500 and 1100 B.C. (O'Brien and Wood 1998:132). Thermoluminescence dates from a heat-treated chert flake and a piece of fire-cracked granite at Davis Creek suggest an occupation falling between 1600 and 1000 B.C. Seventy-three percent of the Table Rock points at Davis Creek were made of Maynes Creek chert, a type from east-central Iowa whose nearest source is 150 km from the site. The majority represent the fractured bases of dart points probably discarded during rehafting, and all but one were heat-treated (Billeck 1986a).

Many of the features found at the Davis Creek site contained large quantities of stone tool debris along with some domestic refuse. A shallow pit filled with fire-cracked rock was probably

**5.18.** Fire pit or hearth at the Davis Creek site, Washington County, a characteristic feature of Archaic sites. Photo archives, Office of the State Archaeologist, University of Iowa.

used for roasting or stone boiling (fig. 5.18). In one part of the site, a cluster of materials enclosed a relatively cleared area, possibly indicative of material discarded around the perimeter of a shelter. The features, artifacts, and floral remains found at the site imply that the inhabitants engaged in hunting, collecting of hickory nuts and hawthorn fruits, and possibly hide processing or other scraping activities. The quantities of chipped stone debris, especially locally available Wassonville chert, identified the site as an important knapping station for toolmaking and the repair or replacement of artifacts broken during hunting.

Late Archaic sites on the central Des Moines River below Des Moines are comparatively rare, as are sites of the Archaic in general (Benn and Rogers 1985; Moffat et al. 1990; Rogers and Koldehoff 1987; Roper 1986). Archaeologists do not know if this is the result of survey bias, the deep burial of sites in alluvial settings, or environmental or cultural factors. Recorded sites apparently represent small habitations or short-term extractive camps (Roper 1986).

### Late Archaic Hunters and Foragers on the Des Moines Lobe

Evidence for Late Archaic occupation along the central Des Moines River at the southern end of the Des Moines Lobe is abundant. Sites here are three times as numerous as those of the Middle Archaic (Benn and Rogers 1985:36). Excavations at the multicomponent Darr-es-Shalom site, situated on a terrace of the Des Moines River, provided additional information about Iowa's Table Rock inhabitants. A buried occupation radiocarbon dated between 1300 and 1100 B.C. (Osborn and Gradwohl 1981; Timberlake 1981) revealed the diagnostic point type in association with a possible structure defined by a dark oval stain and a concentration of cultural remains. The structure, apparently made of willow saplings and possibly covered with thatch or mats, surrounded several features, including hearths and storage pits. A single post mold occurred at its

center (Timberlake 1981:268). The site yielded a broad range of fauna, such as deer, turtle, beaver, bird, and mollusks, suggesting an extended residency from summer throughout the winter (Timberlake 1981).

Archaeological survey and study of private artifact collections demonstrate that, while population levels in the Prairie Lakes region in the northern portion of the Des Moines Lobe rose continuously throughout the Archaic, the cooler and wetter conditions of the Late Archaic apparently discouraged utilization (Lensink 1984). Rejuvenation of prairie marshes depends upon their periodic desiccation and subsequent reflooding. While the degree of reliance on these habitats by hunting and gathering groups remained remarkably stable throughout the Holocene, subsistence resources saw maximum exploitation following droughts, when the wetland habitat recycled to a more productive state (Lensink 1984:168–169). Evidently, fewer droughts and the longer recovery time required for the recycling of marsh resources diminished Late Archaic utilization (Lensink 1984).

### Western Iowa: Where Are the Bison Hunters?

Excavated materials from Late Archaic components in western Iowa reflect the use of local and varied resources at camps or procurement sites occupied for brief periods (Hedden 1996). Neither sedentary base camps nor sites containing large quantities of bison bone are recorded. The low frequency of bison bone at prehistoric sites in the Loess Hills region marks a trend that continues into the late prehistoric. Overall, the settlement pattern apparently remained fairly mobile. Two Late Archaic components found deeply buried in Roberts Creek Member deposits suggest short-term, seasonal encampments. Sites are situated near the confluence of major waterways and close to habitats with varied floral and faunal resources and locally available lithic raw materials (Hedden 1996).

Excavation at the McCall site (13PA38), buried 2 m below Roberts Creek Member deposits on the floodplain of the West Nodaway River in Page County, revealed a Late Archaic occupation with associated point types resembling the Matanzas type (Mehrer 1989). Two small, well-defined activity areas, identified by discrete concentrations of occupational debris, were interpreted as short-term outdoor work areas utilized on a seasonal basis. Both contained hearth features associated with a limited set of activities. A slab of scratched and battered catlinite may have been used as a cutting board and as a source of red pigment. Archaeologists recovered faunal remains of amphibians and reptiles, as well as seeds of a moist, low-lying sedge not incompatible with the inferred site setting on the margin of an abandoned river channel.

A Late Archaic campsite in Ringgold County appears to be a variation on this same theme. The multicomponent Diagonal Dune site, situated on a narrow sand ridge above the Grand River, contained a substantial fire pit believed to represent a Terminal Archaic occupation dating between 900 and 800 B.C. Although diagnostics were not associated with the hearth, a Table Rock point found nearby may provide a cultural affiliation for the occupation. The excavators propose that the site was used during a brief stopover by hunters (Hirst and Artz 1993:89).

### Central Plains Connections in Southwestern Iowa?

Research in southwestern Iowa indicates that throughout prehistory it was part of the territorial round of Central Plains groups (Artz 1993c; Reid 1980, 1983). Thirty Etley stemmed points made of Burlington chert cached on a ridge top overlooking the West Nodaway River in Page County suggest the presence of Nebo Hill phase people (Reid 1980, 1983). Another potentially significant site is 13RN59 in Ringgold County, where archaeologists uncovered evidence for a Late Archaic campsite with distinct activity areas buried 40–60 cm beneath a historic farmstead (Artz 1993c). Test excavations yielded a medium-sized corner-notched point comparable to those from Nebo Hill phase sites and to others from Walnut Hill phase sites in northeastern Kansas and northwestern Missouri. The base of an expanding-stemmed dart point appears similar to the Late Archaic Stone Square Stemmed point of Missouri, a type that commonly occurs at Late Archaic Sedalia and Titterington phase sites and is found in small percentages at Nebo Hill phase sites (Artz 1993c:33; Chapman 1975). Bifaces of Knife River flint and other chipped and ground stone items completed the stone tool inventory.

The core areas for Nebo Hill and Sedalia phase peoples include the lower reaches of the Platte and Grand river basins, whose headwaters originate in southwestern Iowa (Artz 1993c). The variety of point styles documented in this part of the state may indicate that the area served as a hinterlands region by such outside groups (Artz 1993c). Fiber-tempered ceramics are a defining characteristic of some Nebo Hill sites. The earliest ceramics in western Iowa were probably introduced to Woodland communities who may already have been familiar with ceramic-making from their contacts with Late Archaic Nebo Hill phase people (Benn 1990:129–130).

### Sacred Places: Red Ocher Mounds and Late Archaic Ossuaries

Communal burial sites are a defining feature of the Terminal Archaic throughout the Midwest. In Iowa, communal burial sites occur in both the extreme eastern and western portions of the state. Sites in eastern Iowa fall within the sphere of the Red Ocher complex, which extends throughout the upper Mississippi valley region of Iowa, Wisconsin, and northern Illinois and as far east as Michigan and Ohio. Red Ocher sites represent the earliest evidence in the Midwest for communal burial in earthen mounds. Artifacts found in Red Ocher burials or caches often include items fashioned from exotic raw materials such as copper beads, celts, and awls; nonlocal lithics; galena cubes; slate and other polished stone gorgets; large Turkey Tail bifaces of blue-gray hornstone; and bar-style and boatstone at-latl weights. A hallmark of Red Ocher is the coating of these artifacts and associated burials with red pigment (Overstreet et al. 1996:36).

Many Red Ocher Mounds in Iowa, northern Illinois, and southwestern Wisconsin contain Marion Thick ceramics and, as such, are defined as Early Woodland sites (Esarey 1986a). The only radiocarbon dates from Red Ocher Mounds in Iowa indicate their use sometime within the first half of the first millennium B.C. Thus they could be affiliated with either Terminal Archaic or Early Woodland peoples. A number of these mounds lack pottery, suggesting that Terminal Archaic groups initiated the practice of earthen mound burial (Green and Schermer 1988). Most archaeologists now believe that Red Ocher represents a complex that spans the Terminal Archaic to Early Woodland transition (Overstreet et al. 1996:36; Ritzenthaler and Quimby 1962; Stoltman 1986a).

The best-known Red Ocher site in Iowa, the Turkey River Mound Group (13CT1) in Clayton County, occupies a ridge 60 m above the Turkey River at its confluence with the Mississippi (Green and Schermer 1988; McKusick 1964a). Mounds here were the scene of two important archaeological surveys, first by Theodore Lewis in 1885 and again by Ellison Orr in 1932. Mounds within the group were excavated in 1964 (McKusick 1964a). One of the mounds in the Turkey River Mound Group, Mound 38, and another mound in the Sny-Magill Mound Group (13CT18) in Clayton County, Mound 43, contained no pottery. They did contain red-ocher-covered burials, ellipsoid bifaces, straight-stemmed Adena-like projectile points, a bar amulet, cylindrical copper beads, and a copper awl (fig. 5.19). These are classic Red Ocher features. Although another mound in the Turkey River Mound Group, Mound 37, produced tiny, sandy-tempered sherds that were first thought to have an Early Woodland Prairie phase affiliation (Green and Schermer 1988; see chapter 6), a radiocarbon date indicates the mound was con-structed sometime between 800 and 500 B.C., probably too early for Prairie phase people.

The presence of communal cemeteries like the Red Ocher Mounds implies that Terminal Archaic groups had settled more permanently in local territories and perhaps had begun to claim both the territory and its resources for their own. The unusual artifacts that appear in the mounds may signal the presence of higher-status individuals within the community. Such people had access to rare materials acquired from distant sources. The ellipsoid biface from Mound 38 is the only known example made from Knife River flint. The bar amulet was beautifully worked from a piece of banded slate that originated in Ohio. Both types of artifacts rarely occur west of the Mississippi River. Archaeologists discovered a large number of marine shell beads in the mouth of one of the 11 individuals in Mound 38. The prominent positions of the Turkey River and other Red Ocher mounds in northeastern Iowa suggest strategic locations, perhaps way stations along important trade routes through the upper Mississippi valley.

The construction of a new elementary school in Pottawattamie County in western Iowa brought to light a communal burial site of a different nature. Skeletal remains uncovered at the Lewis Central School site provided evidence for a Terminal Archaic ossuary dated to 1100–800 B.C. (fig. 5.20). Working under hasty and constrained conditions, excavators identified the remains of at least six children and 19 adults, including nine males and two females. All of the associated chipped stone artifacts appeared to be utilitarian in nature and were made of local Nehawka chert and Tongue River silicified sediment. Bone awls of both mammal and bird, deer antler artifacts, and worked shell are evidence of diet as well as the bone technology present. The highly worn teeth on almost all the burials reflect a relatively gritty diet. The more complete and articulated nature of some of these individuals suggest their burial occurred immediately following their death. Others, however, probably

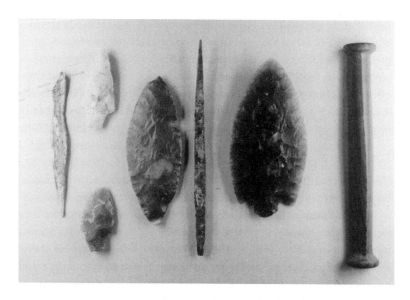

**5.19.** Bone awl, stemmed points, ellipsoid bifaces, copper awl, and bar amulet from Turkey River Mound 38, Clayton County. Photo by Robert A. Alex.

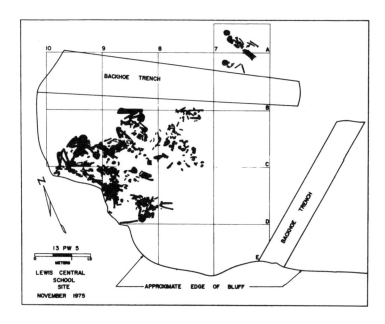

**5.20.** Plan view of Lewis Central School ossuary, Pottawattamie County. Photo archives, Office of the State Archaeologist, University of Iowa. From Anderson et al. 1978.

lay elsewhere for a period of time before being bundled up and added to the ossuary. This implies that the site functioned as a communal cemetery over some length of time and may indicate the beginning of territorialism among Late Archaic hunting and gathering bands in western Iowa.

## Conclusion

Communal cemeteries and other kinds of developments make the lifeways and customs of Archaic people seem more familiar to us. The baby teeth and bone flute from the Cherokee Sewer site, the dog buried at Sand Run Slough West, and the shell jewelry kept perhaps as a valued possession and interred with the young people at Turin reflect events and customs that are poignantly human. We can more closely identify with Archaic societies because they inhabited a state that looked much as it does today and hunted, collected, and utilized familiar types of animals and plants in ways that were still used until recent times. We have evidence that they mourned their dead, cared for their children, and had a sense of place. Our window into their world is wider than it is for their Paleoindian ancestors, and as a result we have a view that, while not exactly a reflection, is certainly not foreign. By the end of the period there are hints that some communities had begun to develop a system where social inequality was recognized and where access to exotic material possessions may have been a sign of status. From our twenty-first-century perspective, customs such as these may seem more than a little familiar.

## APPENDIX 5.1.
## The DeForest Formation

Geologists have determined that in small and medium-sized valleys across Iowa episodes of deposition and subsequent downcutting were occurring at approximately similar intervals throughout the Holocene, ultimately in response to climatic events (Bettis and Hoyer 1986; Bettis

and Littke 1987:45). This has resulted in a stratigraphic sequence of alluvial fill deposits that can be identified, mapped, and correlated from stream valley to stream valley across the state (Bettis 1990). These alluvial deposits are referred to collectively as the DeForest Formation (Daniels and Jordan 1966) and include the Gunder, Corrington, Roberts Creek, and Camp Creek members (fig. 5.21). Each member is separated by either erosional surfaces called disconformities or soils called paleosols. The latter formed during periods when the land surface was stable (Bettis 1990). Similar alluvial sequences have been identified elsewhere in the Midwest and throughout the eastern Plains (Artz 1996:3).

The Corrington and Gunder members of the Early and Middle Holocene are dated between ca. 8000 and 800 B.C. During this climatic episode water tables were lowered and flood frequency was reduced, although high-magnitude flooding became more prevalent (Bettis and Littke 1987: 45; Collins 1991:18). Corrington Member deposits make up alluvial fans created by periodic erosion of small and moderate-sized valley sediments into larger valleys (Artz 1996:10; Bettis 1990:8). Within such fans are stratified paleosols representing long periods of stability when soils formed. Alluvial fans at the foot of bluffs offered early peoples well-drained locations for campsites and access up small side valleys to upland prairie resources (Artz 1996:10).

Corrington Member deposits interfinger with Gunder Member alluvial terraces, which accumulated as the result of overbank flooding and hillside erosion called colluvial slopewash (Bettis and Littke 1987). Late Paleoindian through Woodland sites are buried within the Corrington and Gunder members. Good examples of sites found within Corrington alluvial fans are the upper two horizons of the Cherokee Sewer site and the Archaic components at the Gast Spring site. The Turin site burials, once thought to date to the Late Pleistocene because of the loessic deposits in which the site is buried, are now known to have occupied a position in Gunder Member

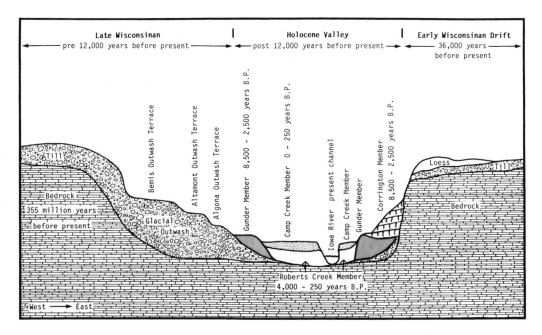

**5.21.** Schematic cross section of the Iowa River valley in Hardin County indicates position and age of DeForest Formation alluvial deposits. From Collins 1991.

alluvial fill consisting of loess redeposited in a gully setting (Fisher et al. 1985). The Des Moines High Terrace is a Gunder Member terrace and contains numerous Early and Middle Archaic sites (Benn 1985; Bettis and Hoyer 1986).

The Roberts Creek Member represents floodplain deposits that began to accumulate about 4,000 years ago as a result of a new episode of downcutting and stream channel meandering seen throughout the Midwest during the Late Holocene. During this time cooler and wetter conditions prevailed across the state, increasing the frequency of low-magnitude floods and higher water tables, which resulted in the expansion of deciduous forests (Bettis and Littke 1987:46; Collins 1991:18). The Roberts Creek Member contains Late Archaic through early historic cultural components (Anderson 1995:12). Late Archaic components may be preserved at great depths in floodplain locations under Roberts Creek Member deposits (Hedden 1996:143).

Overlying these earlier sediments of the De-

Forest Formation is the Camp Creek Member, sometimes referred to as postsettlement alluvium, which is very late prehistoric to historic in age and represents the active floodplain of streams in Iowa over the past 400 years (Bettis 1990; Bettis et al. 1992:3; Collins 1991:18). The Camp Creek Member contains buried and unburied historic components. In certain locations, Camp Creek Member deposits may be more than 5 m in thickness. Finding early sites buried beneath recent deposits of such great depth requires deep testing, usually by auguring or drilling (Artz 1996:3).

## APPENDIX 5.2.

### Plant Cultivation and Domestication

Paleobotanists generally agree that the prehistoric inhabitants of eastern North America cultivated at least eight indigenous plant species between Late Archaic and protohistoric times; of these eight, five are widely recognized to have been domesticated (Asch and Asch 1985; Asch and Green 1992; Fritz 1990; Watson 1989, 1991; Yarnell 1989, 1993). The five indigenous domesticates are *Cucurbita pepo* (ornamental gourds and summer and winter squash), *Lagenaria siceraria* (bottle gourd), *Iva annua* var. *macrocarpa* (sumpweed, marshelder), *Helianthus annuus* var. *macrocarpus* (common sunflower), and *Chenopodium berlandieri* ssp. *jonesianum* (goosefoot, chenopod). In addition to these domesticates, other species accepted as cultigens include *Phalaris caroliniana* (maygrass), *Polygonum erectum* (knotweed), and *Hordeum pusillum* (little barley). Of these eight, seven have been found in prehistoric contexts in Iowa (Asch and Green 1992). The only exception is bottle gourd, which does occur in prehistoric sites near Iowa and likely was one of the cultigens grown by early residents here (Asch and Green 1992; Dunne 1997).

Archaeologists generally use the term "cultivation" to refer to the process whereby humans deliberately encouraged the reproduction of certain plant species by various means such as watering, weeding, or sheltering (Asch 1992:9–10; Asch and Asch 1985). Annuals like oily-seeded sunflower and marshelder, and starchy-seeded goosefoot become very prolific in soils disturbed by human activity (Ford 1977: 174–176). By Late Archaic times humans had recognized this, and native North American plants were deliberately tended to use as a food source. Archaeologically, the occurrence of abundant amounts of seeds from plants known to occur beyond their natural range is one clue that cultivation was under way. The discovery of the seeds of starchy-seeded plants including maygrass, knotweed, and little barley at sites known to be beyond the natural distribution of these species suggests that these plants were being cultivated.

Plant domestication is assumed to have occurred when actual genetic changes resulting from human selection, either deliberate or otherwise, are detectable (Asch and Asch 1985; Asch 1992:10–11). In the case of plants such as squashes and gourds, genetic changes associated with domestication include larger seeds and a thicker rind. Domesticated sunflower and marshelder also show an increase in seed size. On the other hand, domesticated goosefoot maintains a small seed similar to wild varieties but exhibits a thinner seed coat and other detectable morphological changes (Asch and Sidell 1992).

*Cucurbita pepo* probably represent the first plants cultivated in the Midwest (Asch and Green 1992:11). Small carbonized rind fragments of *Cucurbita pepo* have been found at the Koster and Napoleon Hollow sites in west-central Illinois (Asch and Asch 1985; Conard et al. 1984) and at the Anderson site in Tennessee dating 6000 to 5700 B.C. (Crites 1991). While early forms of this plant were domesticated in Mexico, paleoethnobotanists believe that people in the eastern United States independently produced a domesticated variety (Cowan 1997). Bottle gourd has been dated as early as *Cucurbita pepo* at several sites in Florida and Missouri (Asch 1992:18). It may have reached North American shores from South America or via a transatlantic float trip from Africa (Fritz 1990). Evidence for the domestication of marshelder, a native North American plant, comes from a 2700–2300 B.C. context at Napoleon Hollow.

At Late Archaic sites in west-central Illinois, significant increases in the quantity of goosefoot around the same time probably signal early cultivation (Asch and Asch 1985). The first clearly domesticated goosefoot seeds have been directly dated by the AMS technique to 1700 B.C. at sites in Kentucky. Little barley and goosefoot found in the same feature with squash rind at Gast Spring are believed to have been cultivated and are almost as old (Dunne 1997).

# 6   Woodland Innovations

It must be remembered, too, that food-production
does not all at once supersede food gathering.
—Childe 1951:70

**TODAY WE** think of Iowa as an agricultural
state, a patchwork of corn and soybean fields,
cattle yards, and hog lots. Soybeans, cattle, and
pigs were originally domesticated in Europe and
Asia and only introduced quite recently to North
America. Corn, or maize, however, is a Native
American plant first brought under cultivation
in central America by native people. Woodland
societies started growing corn in Iowa after varieties were developed that could withstand the
shorter growing season of northern climates
(Green ed. 1994). By A.D. 1000 corn had become
a staple crop for many people and was fostering
new types of settlements and lifeways.

Traditionally, the presence of three cultural
hallmarks—mound burial, pottery, and plant
cultivation—have defined the Woodland in Iowa
and much of the Midwest (fig. 6.1). While each
of these customs originated within Archaic
society (Phillips and Brown 1983), their broad
occurrence and elaboration mark the Woodland
as a time of major technological, economic, and
social change. Yet not all people adopted these
practices nor did so at the same time. Many
societies continued the successful lifeways they
had established earlier.

Hundreds of Woodland habitation sites have
been recorded and investigated in Iowa over the
past three decades, yet many others probably remain undiscovered, buried under alluvium in
Iowa's river valleys (fig. 6.2). Woodland sites occupy diverse settings, including upland, lowland-
riverine, and lakeside locations (Tiffany 1986a:

167). Prehistoric people utilized rockshelters as
well as open sites repeatedly throughout the period. Population size increased. Because of the
widespread custom of earthen mound burial,
mound groups are a prominent type of site. Conical-shaped mounds were constructed by Early
Woodland people and remained popular for
more than 1,000 years. The famous effigy forms
were a Late Woodland custom. Pottery was used
throughout the state, and new styles of projectile
points were introduced. Cultivated plants became increasingly important.

In Iowa, archaeologists generally subdivide
this period into Early (800–200 B.C.), Middle
(200 B.C.–A.D. 400), early Late (A.D. 400–650),
and late Late (A.D. 650–1200). Each interval is
defined through distinctive styles of pottery and
projectile points and by associated radiocarbon
dates. Ceramics, the distinguishing characteristic of the Woodland, provide a useful tool to relate sites to one another and to subdivide prehistoric time. Ceramics dominate any discussion of
the Woodland and often seem to have taken on a
life of their own. The ceramic chronology used in
Iowa, especially in the eastern part of the state,
has been strongly influenced by that developed
in adjacent states, particularly Illinois, where the
Woodland cultural sequence was first established. Thus many of the ceramic types named
here are the same as those used in areas to the
east, and their age and time span often are assumed to be the same as well. In western Iowa,
there are stronger ties to the eastern and central

**6.1.** Woodland pottery. Photo by Charles R. Keyes.
Courtesy of the State Historical Society of Iowa, Iowa City.

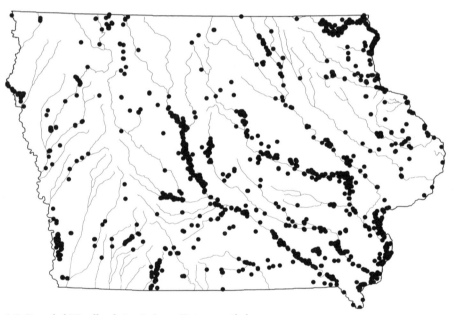

**6.2.** Recorded Woodland sites in Iowa. Data compiled
from site records, Office of the State Archaeologist,
University of Iowa. Courtesy of Timothy S. Weitzel and
Stephen C. Lensink.

Plains and in the northern part of the state to
Minnesota and Wisconsin.

Pottery evidently was not a native Iowa inven-
tion but entered the state early in the first millennium b.c. Changes in ceramics took place in-
crementally throughout the next 2,000 years,
not unlike improvements seen over the past three
decades in computer technology. The big, boxy
IBM 360, which in the 1960s occupied a room to

itself and had a megabyte of memory, has been streamlined and upgraded to the sleek notebook equipped with 32 megabytes and available in designer colors. In a similar manner, the first thick, chunky Woodland pots gradually gave way to thinner-walled, more heat-resistant and efficient vessels, and decoration became more of a consideration.

Despite the addition of ceramics, the lifeways of Early Woodland peoples in Iowa appear to have changed little from that of their Late Archaic predecessors. A migratory seasonal residence pattern probably prevailed. Small base camps, some occupied year-round, existed in both upland and lowland settings. Cultivated plants, including gourd or squash, sunflower, goosefoot, and marshelder, were raised by some Early Woodland peoples, although cultivated plants seem to have affected the overall economy very little. Hunting and gathering continued to dominate subsistence activities. Mound burial was practiced especially in the east, and some exotic grave offerings indicate interaction and trade with societies far from Iowa.

By Middle Woodland times, there are measurable changes in the fabric of social and ceremonial life in some areas. These developments reached a threshold around the first century B.C., when societies throughout the Midwest began participating in what archaeologists call the Hopewellian Interaction Sphere (HIS), constructing impressive earthworks and large earthen burial mounds, trading in beautifully crafted items and raw materials from distant areas, and sharing widespread patterns of ritual and ideology (Green 1986). A series of remarkable sites along the Mississippi River attests to the full participation by some Iowa societies in this intriguing phenomenon.

By the end of the Woodland almost a millennium ago, native Iowans had developed the full range of cultural achievements handed down to their historic descendants and were living in prairie-forest settings like those described by the first Euroamerican settlers. Economies depen-

dent on corn, reliance on the bow and arrow, substantial wattle and daub houses, intricate technologies including weaving and fine pottery-making, artistic symbols that reflect rich mythological traditions, settled village life, and tribal-level society had all come about.

By this time, less desirable aspects of life can also be documented. Nutritional and dental deficiencies increased as corn, a food high in carbohydrates, became a staple (Buikstra 1979). More compact settlements, growing populations, and more intensive farming practices in some places altered local landscapes. Storable garden produce and desirable trade items cached in large, semi-permanent villages, coupled with growing populations and the desire for new territory, ultimately fostered the need for defense, and the incidence of intervillage violence and ultimately warfare increased. These phenomena are not peculiar to Iowa, to the Midwest, or even to the rest of North America but seem to go hand in hand with growing populations and the development of village farming life.

## Early Woodland Discoveries (800–200 B.C.)

Two ceramic-making complexes called Marion and Black Sand signal the beginning of the Early Woodland in Iowa. Most archaeologists believe that these complexes represent the influx of new ideas and technologies, if not actual people, into Iowa from farther east. Marion Thick pottery, according to some, marks the beginning of a long ceramic tradition that ultimately became the Middle Woodland Havana-Hopewell (Munson 1982, 1986a). Black Sand may represent a slightly later, separate, but partially coeval tradition. In Iowa, Marion sites and later Middle Woodland Havana sites are confined largely to the Mississippi River and the lower reaches of its tributaries, although Havana influences were felt elsewhere. Black Sand and possibly its later ceramic "descendants" occur throughout the state. Where the distribution of these traditions overlaps, archaeologists must determine what kind of interaction, if any, took place between the peoples who left these ceramics (fig. 6.3; table 3).

### The Marion Ceramic Tradition

The oldest pottery in Iowa and in many areas of the Midwest is called Marion Thick. People were making Marion Thick pottery perhaps as early as the ninth century B.C. Radiocarbon dates from early ceramic sites in Iowa overlap with others considered Terminal Archaic. The distribution of Marion Thick pottery spans the Midwest from the eastern part of Iowa to central Indiana and southern Michigan and from St. Louis north to southeastern Minnesota. In southern Minnesota, a similar pottery type called LaMoille Thick occurs (Anfinson ed. 1979:117; Anfinson 1997). Other thick-bodied ceramics are found throughout eastern North America, serving as a kind of horizon marker for the Early Woodland.

The shape and style of Marion Thick pots and the occurrence of textured impressions on their interior surface suggest that the potter formed the clay around a basketry, leather, or wooden container (fig. 6.4). Vessels resemble clay flowerpots with thick walls (1–2 cm), straight sides, and a flat bottom. Typically pots contain grit temper made from chunks of crushed igneous rock larger than .5 cm. In the central Illinois valley, Marion Thick ceramics and straight-stemmed Kramer projectile points are the defining artifact types of the Marion phase, dated to about 800–400 B.C. (Munson 1982). Comparable phases include Schultz in southern Michigan, Seehorn in west-central Illinois, and Carr Creek in the American Bottom, the rich floodplain region below the confluence of the Missouri and Mississippi rivers.

The thick walls and flat bases of Marion pots are believed to have enhanced their use as cooking vessels. Encrusted, charred organic material on Marion Thick sherds from the Ambrose Flick site in the Sny Bottom of west-central Illinois suggests direct boiling of food over hearths (Stafford 1992b), although others propose that stone boiling was the cooking method used (Goldman-Finn et al. 1991; Reid 1990). Perhaps the tough seeds of some early cultivated plants could only be processed by sustained simmering in pottery vessels (Benn 1990:128–129). Cultivated plants associated with Marion culture sites include squash, goosefoot, little barley, and possibly maygrass (Asch and Sidell 1992). In Iowa,

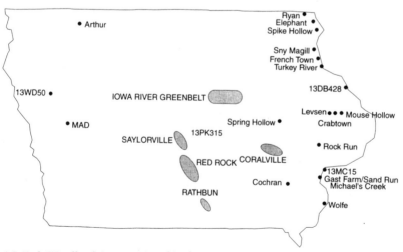

**6.3.** Early Woodland sites mentioned in the text. Map by Diana Brayton.

## Suggested Woodland Phases and Ceramic Complexes

Eastern Iowa ⟵⟶ Western Iowa

| Time | Eastern Iowa ←→ Western Iowa |
|------|------------------------------|
| **1200 A.D.** | Hartley (Hartley Ware) |
| | Lake Benton (Lake Benton Ware) |
| | (Maples Mills)  (Minott's Ware)  Saylor (Saylor Ware)  Loseke (Loseke Ware) |
| | Louisa  Keyes (Madison Ware) |
| | Late Fox Lake |
| **A.D. 650** | Lane Farm (Lane Farm Cord Impressed) |
| | Sterns Creek (Sterns Creek Ware) |
| | Henry  Randolph  Floyd |
| | Gast  (Henry Ware) (unnamed)  Riverbend  (Held Creek Ware) |
| **A.D. 400** | (Weaver Ware)  (Madrid Ware) |
| | Allamakee (Linn Ware)  H |
| | a |
| **A.D. 200** | v  Middle Fox Lake  Valley (Valley Ware) |
| | McGregor (Havana pottery)  a  Van Hyning (High Bridge)  (Rowe Ware) ? |
| | n |
| | a  Early Fox Lake |
| **200 B.C.** | Prairie Phase (Prairie Incised) |
| | (Glenwood Trailed) |
| | Polk City (McBride Trailed)  Crawford (Crawford Ware) |
| | Black Sand Complexes (Black Sand Incised/Liverpool Ware) |
| **500 B.C.** | R e d |
| | O  Marion Complexes/Ryan Phase (Marion Thick) |
| | c h e |
| **800 B.C.** | r |

Table 3

sumpweed appears to have been under cultivation by people using Durst points and living at 13CT228 in the Turkey River valley around 900–700 B.C. (Green ed. 1988). Little barley, squash, and goosefoot apparently were grown by the Terminal Archaic residents at Gast Spring even before this time and by later Early Woodland occupants of the site who were using Marion Thick pottery (Dunne 1997).

Marion Thick pottery occurs in Iowa at sites along or very close to the Mississippi River (Benn 1987:67) (fig. 6.5). The pottery has not been confirmed in interior Iowa. Sites containing Marion Thick pottery cluster along the shoreline of Lake Odessa and Muscatine Slough in the southeast (Benn et al. 1994). Calibrated radiocarbon dates from Mound 43 of the Sny-Magill Group, Mound 37 of the Turkey River Group (Green and Schermer 1988; Steventon and

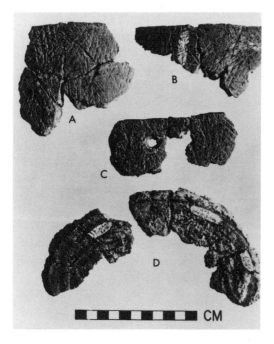

**6.4.** Rim sherds (a–c) and base (d) from a Marion Thick vessel found at the Smith site, Louisa County. Basketry or woven impressions are clearly visible on the interior of the base. From Anderson 1971a.

Kutzbach 1990:209–210), and Early Woodland features at the Gast Spring site (Dunne 1997; Goldman-Finn et al. 1991) suggest a beginning date for Early Woodland finds in Iowa sometime during the 800–400 B.C. time period (Appendix 6.1).

Archaeologists know little about the relationship between Early Woodland people and their Late Archaic predecessors in Iowa. Certainly ceramic-making and perhaps new styles of projectile points were introduced from outside the state at this time, although older point styles continued in use. At Gast Spring, Early Woodland Marion occupations appear to follow immediately those of the Late Archaic, indicating rapid succession or transformation. The people who made Marion Thick pottery may have constructed many of the Red Ocher burial mounds, thus suggesting a link with Late Archaic people in northeast Iowa (Boszhardt et al. 1986; Esarey 1986a; Stoltman 1986b). In addition, the Early Woodland subsistence-settlement pattern in Iowa does not seem to show appreciable change from the Late Archaic, again suggesting continuity. Whether new populations brought the points and ceramics that mark the Early Woodland or whether these artifacts resulted from new ideas that spread throughout midwestern populations is not known; probably it was both.

In eastern Iowa, some Red Ocher mound sites, particularly Mounds 38 and 39 of the Turkey River Group, and habitation sites containing Marion Thick pottery, such as the Elephant Terrace site (13AM59), were first grouped into the Ryan focus (Logan 1976) and more recently have been reclassified as part of the Ryan phase (Stoltman 1986b). Although neither Mound 38 nor 39 contained pottery, the presence of Early Woodland Adena-like and Kramer-like points suggests a Ryan phase affiliation (Green ed. 1988). Other Ryan phase Red Ocher Mounds include Mound 10 of the French Town Group (13CT166), Mound 2 of the Ryan Mound Group (13AM17), and the Houlihan Mound (13AM117) (Tiffany 1986a:160). The Smith site (13LA2), a blufftop

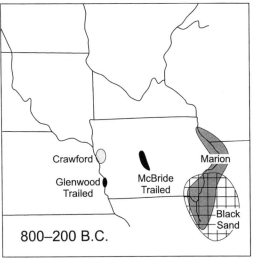

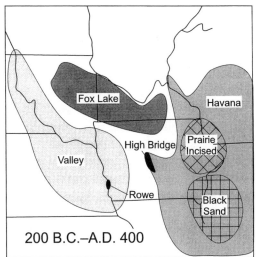

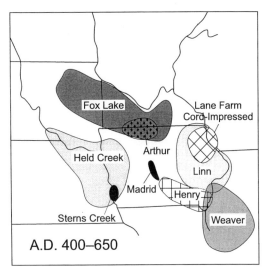

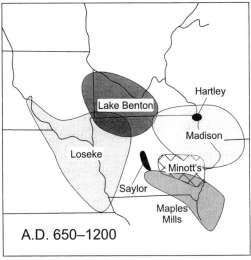

**6.5.** Distribution of major Woodland ceramic complexes in Iowa. From Perry 1996.

habitation in Louisa County that contains the largest known Iowa sample of Marion Thick pottery, would seem to be a related southeast Iowa counterpart (Tiffany 1986a:165).

The Ryan phase apparently parallels the Marion phase of the central Illinois valley and the slightly later Indian Isle phase in the Prairie du Chien region of Wisconsin (Green and Schermer 1988; Logan 1976; Stoltman 1986b, 1990; Tiffany 1986a). The ceramic type from the

Indian Isle phase, Indian Isle Punched, is similar to Marion Thick pottery but lacks interior cord-marking (Stoltman 1990).

In addition to the Elephant and Smith sites, Marion Thick pottery has been found in mixed deposits at Sand Run Slough West, at 13LA3 near Sand Run (Anderson 1971a:3; Billeck 1985, 1986c), at three sites on Lake Odessa north of Sand Run Slough (Benn 1987:67; Benn et al. 1988), at Gast Farm (Green and Wallace 1991), at the Wolfe site (13DM1) (Straffin 1971a; Titus et al. 1991), at 13LA56 (Perry 1982), and at Helen Smith (13LA71) (L. Alex 1976; Billeck 1995). An ephemeral Marion component may also exist at 13MC15 on Muscatine Island (Artz 1995). Marion Thick pottery occurred in a feature dated to 800–500 B.C. that was associated with the uppermost paleosol and overlying deposits at the Gast Spring site (Dunne 1997; Goldman-Finn et al. 1991). A single sherd has been reported from mixed deposits at the Dolomite Ridge site (13DB428) near Dubuque (Collins 1996a). The Cochran site (13WS7) in Washington County also has produced Marion Thick ceramics (Tiffany 1986a).

The base of a Marion Thick vessel and a nearly complete Kramer point were found at 13CT254 on a blufftop in Clayton County when a windstorm toppled a large basswood tree, revealing a pocket of artifacts exposed in the underlying crater. Although pottery of the Late Woodland Keyes phase also occurred, the Marion Thick vessel and Kramer point indicate the presence of a Ryan phase component (Collins and Green 1988:119–120). Kramer-type points and Marion Thick pottery were also reported from the multicomponent Aulwes site (13CT47) in the same county (Collins and Forman 1995:19; Roggman 1974, 1990). Kramer projectile points or related points are found with Marion Thick pottery at a number of sites, and collectors commonly find the points on surveys in eastern Iowa (fig. 6.6). In Iowa, the distribution of the point type appears both wider and extends later in time than Marion Thick ceramics.

The Red Ocher Mounds of the Ryan phase possibly extend burial customs begun during Terminal Archaic times into the Early Woodland. These are conical earthen mounds built over the ground surface after the topsoil was removed. People interred their dead in subfloor pits or within the mound fill itself, most commonly as bundle burials but also as semiflexed and extended inhumations. Red ocher was applied over and surrounding the remains. Grave goods include leaf-shaped blades, straight-stemmed points, and cylindrical copper beads (Green and Schermer 1988; Logan 1976). Although Red Ocher Mounds have not been identified elsewhere in Iowa, artifact caches of possible Red Ocher affiliation occur at some locations. A collection of bipointed bifaces of exotic blue-gray chert found above the Skunk River in Henry County represents one example (Morrow 1996c:14; Thomas 1992).

Although archaeologists know little about the subsistence-settlement pattern of people who made Marion Thick pottery in Iowa, the presence of diagnostic artifacts in a variety of landscape settings indicates successful exploitation of several major biotic communities, including prairies, forests, marshlands, and lakes, probably as part of a seasonal round (Tiffany 1986a:167). Such a pattern is supported by faunal and floral evidence from excavated contexts, which reflects the use of aquatic and terrestrial plants and animals and a few cultigens. Marion sites in Illinois also show a marked increase in the use of tubers (Asch and Sidell 1992).

For the most part, habitation sites containing Marion ceramics in the Midwest are believed to represent widely dispersed, short-term residences and special purpose camps left by small groups who were highly mobile. The Elephant Terrace site may be one such example. Marion Thick ceramics at Sand Run Slough West, a possible lowland base camp, and the Smith site, a habitation on the blufftop above the Iowa River in Louisa County, suggest that this pottery occurs in other settlement types as well.

### The Black Sand Ceramic Tradition

After some Early Woodland people in Iowa began making Marion Thick pottery, another ceramic tradition appeared over a broad area of the Prairie Peninsula. In Illinois and eastern Iowa, this pottery is referred to as Liverpool ware and includes types such as Black Sand Incised and Liverpool Cordmarked (Griffin 1952b). Black Sand and Liverpool vessels are thinner than

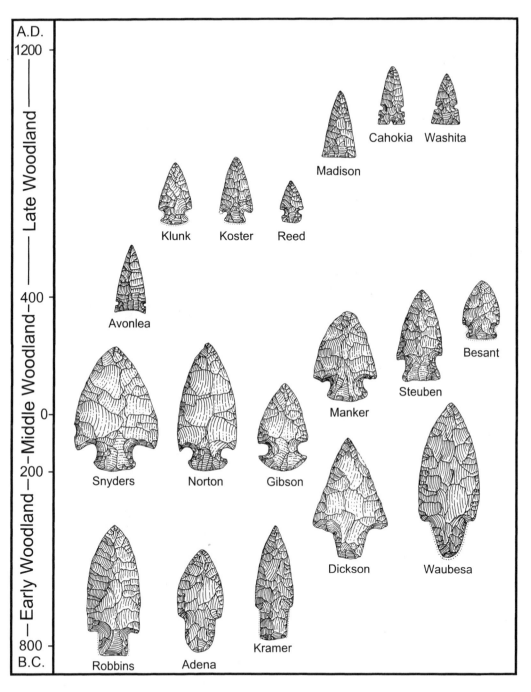

**6.6.** Woodland point sequence from Iowa. Illustrations by Toby Morrow. From Morrow 1984.

Marion Thick, are conoidal or baglike in shape, and have a sandy paste. Rims generally are straight. Decoration consists of carefully incised rectilinear designs over exterior cordmarking and, occasionally, of exterior nodes, or bosses, set close to the lip (fig. 6.7). Contracting-stemmed projectile points, particularly the Waubesa and Dickson types, or Dickson cluster, are also typical (Justice 1987; Montet-White 1968) (see fig. 6.6). Sites where these ceramics and point types are found together have been classified as part of the Black Sand culture. However, the broad distribution of Black Sand sites over the Prairie Peninsula makes it unlikely that these sites actually represent a single culture. While some early Black Sand sites in Iowa might represent immigrant groups, later sites could reflect their descendants or local people who copied the pottery.

Pottery types in Iowa classified as regional versions of Black Sand Incised include McBride Trailed from the central Des Moines valley (Benn and Rogers 1985), Fox Lake Trailed from the Prairie Lakes area of southern Minnesota and Iowa (Benn 1982a; Hudak 1976), Crawford Trailed found at sites in extreme western Iowa (Benn 1983a), and Glenwood Trailed (including Pony Creek Punctate and Keg Creek Twisted Cord) in the southwestern corner of the state (Tiffany 1977). Some archaeologists classify similar pottery in southwestern Wisconsin and northeastern Iowa as Prairie Incised (Stoltman 1986b), including the Iowa type formerly called Spring Hollow Incised (Logan 1976). Not all archaeologists, however, agree with this classification (Benn 1987).

Phases of the Black Sand tradition defined largely on the basis of the ceramics include the Prairie phase of southwestern Wisconsin and northeastern and north-central Iowa (Collins 1990:383; Stoltman 1986b; Theler 1983), the Fox Lake phase of southwestern Minnesota and

**6.7.** Early Woodland Black Sand pottery from Iowa sites. Left to right: dentate stamped sherd from the Benson site, Woodbury County; stamped sherd from Muscatine County; embossed, cordmarked rim sherd from Harvey's Island Mound Group, Clayton County. On display, Iowa Hall, University of Iowa. Photo archives, Office of the State Archaeologist, University of Iowa.

northwestern Iowa (Anfinson 1982, 1997; Benn 1982a, 1982b), and the Polk City phase in the central Des Moines valley (Benn and Rogers 1985). It is important to keep in mind that these regional phases are not all contemporary but appear in a time-transgressive manner across the state (see fig. 6.5). In the south and east, sites containing Black Sand ceramics fall within the time span of those with Marion Thick pottery, and at some locations both ceramics are found. Of 16 Early Woodland sites along a 25 km stretch near Sand Run Slough, most contain mixed components, and almost all, including those with Marion Thick pottery, contain Liverpool ware as well (Benn 1987:237).

Radiocarbon dates in the latter half of the first millennium B.C. have been reported from sites containing McBride Trailed pottery in the central Des Moines valley (Benn and Rogers 1985; Emerson and Finney 1984) and Crawford ware in western Iowa (Benn 1981, 1990; Benn et al. 1994:71). Elsewhere, pottery types possibly derived from Black Sand, such as Prairie Incised and Fox Lake Incised, have been dated centuries later and occur with Middle Woodland Havana assemblages. Prairie phase sites in southwestern Wisconsin generally date to the first century A.D., but a few sites in northeastern Iowa suggest somewhat older dates (Collins 1996a, 1996b; Collins and Forman 1995; Stoltman 1986b, 1990). The Fox Lake ceramic series exhibits a particular conservatism. Initial dates suggest that Fox Lake components began in the first or second century A.D., while later components fall within the final centuries of the millennium (Anfinson 1997). The relationship between Marion and Black Sand, and ultimately their relationship to traditions such as the Middle Woodland Havana, probably varied throughout the Midwest (Farnsworth 1986:638).

Black Sand ceramics typically occur at sites on low, sandy locations along rivers or lakes. Sites in the Coralville Reservoir are found on sandy knolls and judging from private collections, probably once existed on natural levees along the

Iowa River (Anderson 1971a:3; Tiffany 1986a: 160; Zalesky 1977). Black Sand pottery is also reported from rockshelters such as Levsen, Mouse Hollow (13JK59), Crabtown (13JK62), Spike Hollow (13AM47), and Rock Run (13CD10) (Alex 1970; Logan 1976). Archaeologists propose that subsistence and settlement centered on floodplain lakes, sloughs, and swamps and were maintained by small, loosely organized groups that moved frequently (Asch et al. 1979; Farnsworth 1986). Black Sand sites, in contrast to those containing Marion Thick pottery, produce little evidence for cultivation and few signs of mortuary ritual, social stratification, or long-distance trade.

Prairie phase sites near Guttenberg, Iowa, and Prairie du Chien, Wisconsin, occur on the Mississippi floodplain and on the high terraces of large tributaries. These sites show clear evidence for intensive utilization of floodplain resources and in Wisconsin represent the earliest known shell middens on the islands and Mississippi floodplain (Stoltman 1986b, 1990:255; Theler 1983, 1987).

Prairie phase mortuary sites have not been identified in Wisconsin. The discovery of two sherds of sandy-tempered pottery in Turkey River Mound 37 in Iowa suggested use of the mound by Prairie phase people (Schermer and Green 1988:133), although this is now considered unlikely (Collins and Forman 1995). More definitive evidence of Prairie phase burial practices comes from Buck Creek Mound (13CT34) in Clayton County north of Guttenberg. Excavations of a circular mound disclosed a burial capped with limestone slabs and associated Prairie phase ceramics. The mound dated between A.D. 0 and 350 (Collins and Forman 1995:127).

In the central Des Moines valley, Polk City phase sites are recorded on fans, benches, and uplands but are generally absent from river terraces and side valleys. This pattern contrasts with Black Sand locations to the east. Polk City phase sites appear as seasonal base camps whose distribution and, by inference, subsistence parallel that of local Late Archaic sites (Benn and Rogers 1985). At least 33 sites have been recorded in the Saylorville Reservoir area based on discoveries of McBride Ware and stemmed points, particularly the Kramer and Poag types (Benn and Rogers 1985:37). At 13PK315, McBride Trailed pottery occurred in association with charcoal dated to between 400 B.C. and A.D. 0 (Emerson and Finney 1984).

### Early Woodland on the Western Prairie Peninsula

Little is known about the earliest Woodland occupation of the western Iowa prairies. Subsistence probably was broadly based, and resources from prairie, lacustrine, riverine, and timbered environments remained important, a pattern not unlike that of the Late Archaic. To this was added new projectile point forms and ceramics.

Two adjacent multicomponent sites, 13CF101 and 13CF102, occupy Holocene floodplain and alluvial fan deposits along the west bank of the Boyer River in Crawford County in western Iowa. These sites were named the M.A.D. sites after the landowners, Mahaphy, Akers, and Denison. Throughout the Woodland, small family bands apparently occupied the M.A.D. sites on a seasonal basis, carrying out everyday tasks associated with hunting, stone tool manufacture, hide working, cooking, and heating (Anderson et al. 1981:Table 28; Benn 1981, 1990).

At 13CF101 incised-over-cordmarked Crawford ware (fig. 6.8) occurred in the lowest midden deposits (Benn 1981, 1990; Benn ed. 1990). A radiocarbon date suggests occupation by Early Woodland residents sometime between 750 and 150 B.C. (Benn 1981). Sherds from two small Crawford ware vessels and other occupational debris were scattered in a 5 m area surrounding a hearth, and a post mold occurred at the center of the scatter. An ovate side-notched projectile point similar to those from Early Woodland components at Mouse Hollow and Levsen rockshelters in Jackson County and the Spring Hollow 2 shelter (13LN212) in Linn County

(Anderson et al. 1981:V–51) occurred in the vicinity. Faunal remains of deer, a single bison, and a number of smaller mammals documented subsistence resources. A narrow range of plants including walnuts, acorns, squash or gourd, sunflowers, grasses, and goosefoot were identified from flotation samples. None were reported as domesticated.

Crawford ware also has been found at 13WD50 in Woodbury County (Thompson and Benn 1983), and similar pottery occurs at sites in North Dakota with suggested ages in the sixth and fifth century B.C. (Swenson 1987). The

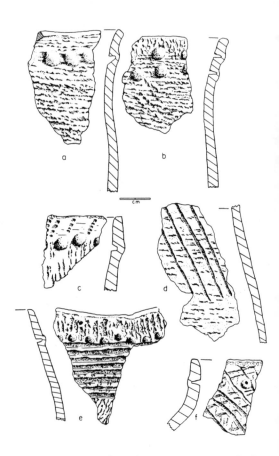

**6.8.** Crawford ware from the M.A.D. sites, Crawford County: (a–c) Crawford Cord Roughened; (d–f) Crawford Trailed. From Benn ed. 1990.

Crawford phase has been proposed as an early member of the Valley variant on the western Prairies. It appears to represent the adoption of a complete ceramic technology by people who were already familiar with the molding and firing of clays, as demonstrated at Late Archaic Nebo Hill phase sites (Benn ed. 1990:129–130).

## Prairie Lakes Potters

In the Prairie Lakes region, systematic survey and examination of private collections have documented the full range of Early Woodland projectile point types found elsewhere in the upper Midwest, suggesting that lacustrine resources were frequently utilized at this time (Lensink 1984; Tiffany 1986a). Intensive use of the Prairie Lakes region possibly resulted from population increase, greater sophistication in resource exploitation, or seasonal occupation by hunting and gathering groups from other areas, such as the Iowa River valley where similar point type distributions occur (Tiffany 1986a:167).

Ceramic-bearing sites of the Fox Lake phase are distributed from southwest and south-central Minnesota into north-central Iowa and eastern South Dakota (Anfinson 1997). Early Fox Lake Trailed ceramics occur in the earliest Woodland component at the Arthur site on the east side of East Lake Okoboji in Dickinson County (Tiffany ed. 1982). Aceramic, including Paleoindian and Archaic materials, through late prehistoric Oneota remains document intermittent use of this location throughout most of prehistory. Stratification over much of the site was complex and mixed, and it is virtually impossible to separate individual components. Features, particularly trash-filled pits, intrude into earlier occupations. No structures were identified, and no radiocarbon dates exist. The vertical distribution of pottery was used as a means to infer the sequence of cultural occupations (Benn 1982a). The horizontal distribution of both ceramics and lithics helped in identifying significant episodes of occupation (Anderson and Spriestersbach 1982:86–118; Benn 1982a). Several triangular

side-notched and stemmed dart point types, including one resembling the Fox Lake Stemmed type, were apparently used over long periods of time, beginning in the Late Archaic.

Early ceramics at Arthur included sherds decorated with rows of slashes over cordmarking, a type possibly reminiscent of LaMoille Thick, which has not been found in Iowa. Eleven vessels of early Fox Lake ware more similar to Black Sand Incised were also present. Early Fox Lake vessels are squat and conoidal in shape with irregularly formed walls, thinner at the lip and rim, and thicker in the body. Patchy, vertically oriented cordmarking is characteristic. Decoration consists of fine notches on the lip and a row of bosses on the upper rim. Rim and body decoration consists of rows of slashes and/or closely spaced, parallel trailed lines oriented horizontally or obliquely (fig. 6.9). Other Iowa sites with Fox Lake ceramics are known from collections made around Lake Okoboji and in Winnebago and Hancock counties to the east (Benn 1982b:164–168).

In the Prairie Lakes region of Minnesota, the few dated early Fox Lake components are late and indicate contemporaneity with Middle and early Late Woodland complexes (Gibbon 1986:89). Early Fox Lake ceramics followed the LaMoille Thick type around 200 B.C. and apparently continued in use until the seventh century A.D. (Anfinson 1997). Although vessels became thinner through time and frequently display a smoothed exterior surface, the pottery remained relatively thick, and bold exterior cordmarking was popular throughout. Simple, wide-trailed line decoration gradually gave way to more complex designs of narrow trailing (Anfinson 1997:62–65).

Sites occur on islands or peninsulas in the Prairie Lakes region and on terraces of the Minnesota River. Site locations usually feature water on at least two sides, and it is likely that protection from prairie fires influenced the choice of site setting (Anfinson 1997:71). This settlement pattern persisted into the late prehistoric. Overall, Fox Lake represents the late arrival of pottery

**6.9.** Fox Lake ceramics from the Arthur site, Dickinson County: (a–c) Early Fox Lake Trailed; (d–f, h) Middle Fox Lake Trailed; (g, j) Late Fox Lake Trailed; (I) Fox Lake Cord-Wrapped Stick Stamped. Benn ed. 1990.

making in the Prairie Lakes area and a conservatism in lifeways that persisted for a long time.

## Middle Woodland Discoveries (200 B.C.–A.D. 400)

Many people are familiar with features and artifacts archaeologists call Middle Woodland. Two thousand years ago American Indian peoples in eastern North America were premier moundbuilders. Thousands of mounds once existed in Iowa alone, many constructed by Middle Woodland communities. Sites such as Toolesboro Mounds (13LA29) above the Iowa River in

Louisa County, Cook Farm Mounds in Davenport, Weed Park Mounds (13MC43) and Pine Creek Mounds in Muscatine County (fig. 6.10), and Boone Mound on the central Des Moines River were impressive monuments that inspired the earliest archaeological exploration in the state. In addition, many of the artifacts interred with the dead at these sites exemplify the artistic skills of prehistoric Native American peoples.

Middle Woodland mounds were conical features made by piling up earth, one basketload at a time (fig. 6.11). Such "loading" has been documented in Iowa at both the Buck Creek Mounds and the Keller Mounds (Benn et al. 1978; Collins and Forman 1995). Study of mound profiles shows that special soils, frequently selected from off-site locations, were brought to the burial site and incorporated in the mound fill (Van Nest and Vogel 1999). Sometimes mounds covered central log crypts, roofed with timbers or slabs of limestone. Inside this tomb the dead were laid out in extended fashion, often on top of a prepared floor coated with a special clay or sand or covered with imported soils of different colors. Ritual fires and perhaps the ceremonial "killing" of pottery by deliberate breakage seem to have been part of the burial ritual at some sites (Anderson 1958). The Boone Mound in the central Des Moines valley may contain the remains of a charnel house, a special structure where the deceased were laid out for a period of time prior to interment.

### The Earthdiver and Middle Woodland Burial Ritual

Where archaeologists are able to record the finer details of Middle Woodland mortuary customs, it is possible to speculate about the nature of funerary rituals. Mounds at Toolesboro, for instance, contained small, narrow copper pins surrounding the burials and set vertically in the tomb's clay subfloor pit (Alex and Green 1995:68) (fig. 6.12). Similarly, in Mound 3 at Pine Creek, excavated by the Davenport Academy in 1914 with assistance from the Smithsonian Institution, eight bone awls believed to be the tibiae of large birds, pos-

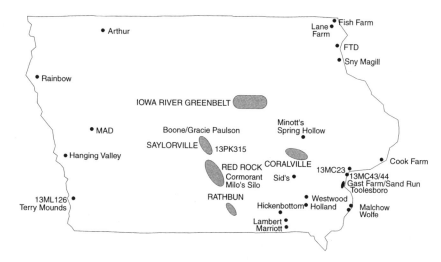

**6.10.** Middle Woodland sites mentioned in the text.
Map by Diana Brayton.

**6.11.** Profile of the Boone Mound, Boone County, during Van Hyning's excavation in 1908. Courtesy of the State Historical Society of Iowa, Des Moines.

sibly crane, were found surrounding the burials. The excavators found remnants of matting still attached to the bone (Paarmann 1914). In Mound 23 at the Albany Mounds site in Illinois, bone pins made from the radius of the trumpeter swan were set in a similar configuration around the burial pit (Herold ed. 1971:39–40). Archaeologists believe that such pins secured some sort of burial shroud, cloth, or skin over the dead.

It is possible that the entire burial arrangement within the mounds—the preparation of the clay floor, the positioning of the bodies, the placement of the pins, and the use of bird bones—was a dramatization of an important origin story in the religion of Middle Woodland people. For many Algonkian and Siouan groups, the creation of the earth began with the Earthdiver's quest to bring up primordial muck or mud from the depths of the ocean and to secure it between sea and sky with anchors or weights, which among some people represented water spirits (Hall 1979:260). The Earthdiver was frequently said to be a bird or a water creature such as an otter or muskrat. In addition to the swan bone pins at Albany, a muskrat skeleton and skull accompanied the burials. Many of the exquisite effigy pipes found in Middle Woodland mounds are carved in the likeness of birds, such as ducks, or other aquatic animals like otters, beavers, turtles, and frogs. One of the pipe bowls from Toolesboro is shaped like a wildcat (fig. 6.13). Since one of the chief water spirits among groups in the upper Mississippi valley and Great Lakes region was the Water Panther, that may be the image depicted. Perhaps all of these figures and the burial ritual of which they were a part represent a reenactment of the widespread Earthdiver myth and as such served as an act of renewal for Middle Woodland people (Hall 1979:261).

### Hopewellian Interaction Sphere

Although distinct local traditions of pottery making and flintknapping continued during the Middle Woodland, many of the funerary artifacts from Middle Woodland mounds are similar throughout the eastern United States. These include fine, thin, highly decorated pottery; beautifully carved stone and ceramic platform pipes; human and animal figurines; copper axes; copper-covered panpipes, breastplates, and earspools; carved sheets of mica; galena cubes; marine shell containers; and quartz, pipestone, and finely chipped obsidian, chalcedony, and chert projectile points (Seeman 1979:410). Mounds and village sites in the Mississippi valley reflect the use of nonlocal materials that originated from the Atlantic Coast to the Rocky Mountains and from the Great Lakes to the Gulf of Mexico. These include obsidian, mica, pipestone, bear canines, meteoric iron, galena, gypsum, steatite, copper, hematite, freshwater pearls, marine shell, Wyandotte chert, Flint Ridge flint, Knife River flint, and a variety of other chert types (Alex and Green 1995:2–3). Although rarely reported as a mound inclusion, silver, in the form of a "hemisphere," was found at the Cook Farm Mounds in Davenport (Herold 1970:527). Copper artifacts in some instances exhibit the residue of woven fabric bags or wrappings preserved by the copper salts (see plate 7). Fabric pieces removed from the surface of a copper breastplate found in Mound 57, a Middle Woodland feature at Effigy Mounds Monument, contained woven fibers from the basswood tree (*Tilia americana*). On the undersurface of the artifact was a substance believed to be buckskin (Beaubien 1953:134–135).

Moundbuilding is a widespread trait of the Middle Woodland. Among some societies it signaled their participation in what has been termed the Hopewell Interaction Sphere (HIS). The HIS represents a broad exchange network that existed throughout eastern North America and extended west onto the Plains. Participants traded the exotic materials and artifacts found in the mounds and participated in shared practices of moundbuilding and funerary ritual. Many archaeologists believe that these customs reflect new forms of authority in some Middle Wood-

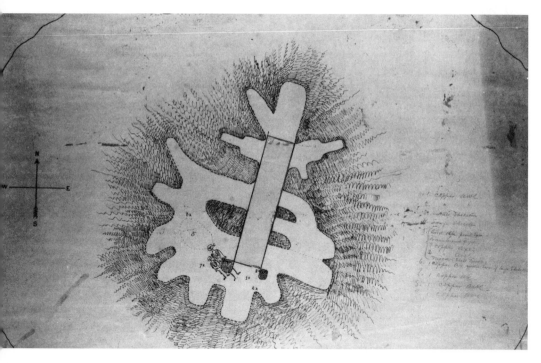

**6.12.** Interior of Mound 7 at Toolesboro Mounds, Louisa County, excavated in 1886 by the Davenport Academy of Natural Sciences. Numbers denote the position of artifacts, including six copper pins located at points 1–2, 5, 8–9. Courtesy of the Putnam Museum of History and Natural Science, Davenport, Iowa. From Alex and Green 1995.

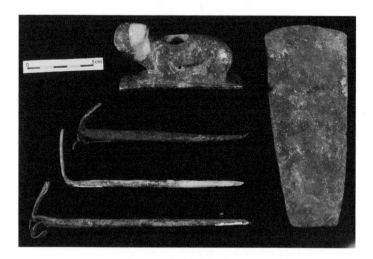

**6.13.** Animal effigy pipe, copper pins or awls, and copper celt from a Middle Woodland mound on the Parsons farm at Toolesboro, Louisa County, excavated by local residents in 1875. Courtesy of the Putnam Museum of History and Natural Science, Davenport, Iowa.

land societies, perhaps the power and prestige of corporate families or clans, guided by important leaders. Although most Woodland societies probably had important elders and clan heads, the mounded tombs and their elaborate contents likely reflect and symbolize the solidarity and influence of the clan itself. It seems probable that by Middle Woodland times tribal society had emerged among some native groups.

### Havana Tradition

The Havana tradition, whose heartland was the central and lower Illinois valley and adjacent parts of the Mississippi valley, is one of a number of regional Middle Woodland traditions whose local societies were united by their participation in the HIS. Two others are the Crab Orchard tradition in southern Illinois and the Scioto tradition in Ohio. Scioto probably arose in some way from the Early Woodland Adena culture, which was contemporary with Red Ocher in Iowa and in which similar elements of mound burial and mortuary ritual occur. Hopewell was first recognized and defined at a series of spectacular Scioto tradition mound sites and earthworks in central Ohio. Although archaeologists do not completely understand the relationship between the various Middle Woodland traditions, they generally believe that many elements of Hopewell originated in the central Illinois valley and radiated outward to surrounding regions (Salzer 1986:263).

The Havana tradition appeared during the final centuries of the first millennium B.C. and continued in Illinois until about A.D. 400. It is divided into a sequence of phases called Morton/Caldwell, Fulton, Ogden, and Steuben or Frazier. The Ogden phase represents the classic Hopewell phase of the Havana tradition and is marked by the first appearance of fine Hopewell burial pottery. Diagnostic of Havana are a series of well-known ceramic types collectively called Havana ware (Griffin 1952b). Morton/Caldwell and Fulton, pre-Hopewell phases, contain Havana pottery types such as Sister Creeks Punc-

tate, Morton Incised and Fettie Incised, which may owe some inspiration to influence from Black Sand (Munson 1986a). Later phases, including Ogden and Frazier, are frequently referred to as Havana-Hopewell proper and represent the peak and close of the HIS. Hopewell, Havana Zoned, Hummel, Naples, and Baehr are some of the ceramic types of the later phases.

Variation in the style of Havana and Hopewell ceramics from region to region may indicate that local people adopted certain design elements of Illinois pottery and reworked them into their own styles, just as they also selectively adopted other aspects of Hopewell ideology, ceremony, and belief (Logan 1976:177; Nansel 1996:6; Perry 1991a:115). This regionalization of Havana is evident in Iowa, where a more limited range of Havana pottery types occurs and where certain decorative elements appear on locally made vessels. People in areas at a greater distance from the Havana heartland apparently received even fewer artifacts and influences from groups to the east and very little in the way of Hopewell ideology or ritual. This seems especially true in western and north-central Iowa.

In general, Havana pottery is thick, with coarse rock or grit temper. The typical vessel is a large, elongated jar with a subconoidal base and poorly demarcated shoulder. The rim is usually straight and almost vertical, and the lip is often beveled. Decoration includes lip notching, short vertical or oblique impressions on the outer rim edge produced by a cord-wrapped stick or dentate stamp, and bosses evenly spaced around the vessel below the rim. In contrast, Hopewell pottery is fine pasted, thin walled, and often limestone tempered. It has a channeled or at times slightly S-shaped rim and exterior zones of decoration. The stylized talon of the hawk or falcon or other bird motifs envelopes the body of many Hopewell vessels (see plate 8).

Although contracting-stemmed projectile points carried over from the Early Woodland, points with corner notching and broad, flat flaking are key traits of the Middle Woodland period.

Another is the extensive use of exotic cherts and heat treating (Benn 1987:239; Morrow 1996c: 15). Typical chipped stone artifacts include corner-notched and side-notched points of the Snyders Cluster (Justice 1987:204), such as the broad, ovate Snyders and Gibson types and the smaller Manker and narrower Norton forms (see fig. 6.6). Long, thin, parallel-sided (lamellar) blades averaging between 50 and 75 mm in length and smaller bladelets about 30 mm in length, made from prepared prismatic cores, characterize many Middle Woodland lithic assemblages. Rectangular chipped stone "hoes," elongated end scrapers with rounded working ends, and steeply retouched unifacial flake tools represent other stone artifacts typical of the period in the Upper Midwest (Morrow 1996c:15).

In addition to the use of exotic lithic materials such as Knife River flint imported from North Dakota, Rocky Mountain obsidian, and Cobden/Dongola chert from southern Illinois, groups in eastern Iowa had a strong preference for Burlington and Croton tabular cherts. Croton tabular chert was formerly attributed to the Warsaw Formation in southeastern Iowa, but geological work has shown that this distinctive tabular chert occurs in the Croton Member of the St. Louis Formation (Witzke et al. 1990:26). Thus Croton tabular chert is now the proper name for materials previously called Warsaw tabular and Warsaw banded chert in southeastern Iowa (Morrow 1996c:38). Southeast Iowa is a major source of these materials, although some pieces may have been imported from Missouri or west-central Illinois. The Havana residents at the Gast Farm site apparently processed Croton tabular and Croton banded cherts, possibly for export (Hare 1992). Finished artifacts manufactured from these cherts may represent one of Iowa's contributions to the HIS.

*The Spread of Havana into Iowa*  The Mississippi River and its tributaries in western Illinois were major arteries for the spread of Havana to the west, and the strongest and most direct Havana presence in Iowa is along the Mississippi and up its major tributary streams to the eastern interior. Major mound groups and villages occur on both sides of the river from Clinton south, and from these locations Havana probably spread north and west, eventually replacing, interacting with, or assimilating some Black Sand and related complexes in Iowa, Minnesota, and Wisconsin (Farnsworth 1986). Whether this process involved an actual migration of people or strong Havana influences on local populations is not known; most likely it was both.

Black Sand pottery has been noted as a minor type in most Havana habitation sites in eastern Iowa, and many Mississippi valley sites contain both Black Sand and early Havana ceramics (Alex 1970; Perry 1991a; Tiffany 1986a). At Gast Farm, the distribution of surface artifacts suggests that Black Sand and Havana components may be separate entities, although some early Havana pottery exhibits characteristics of both (Nansel 1996). At Sand Run Slough West, the stratigraphy indicates that a Black Sand component(s) was contemporary with the early Havana components (Morton/Caldwell and Fulton phases). Other Iowa sites with Black Sand and early Havana Morton-like ceramics include the Levsen and Crabtown rockshelters and the Rogers site (13CD20) (Anderson 1971a; Logan 1976; Tiffany 1986a:160). The Wolfe site, Boone Mound, and Milo's Silo (13MA41) have produced Black Sand Incised pottery in association with Havana or Havana-like material (Gradwohl 1974; Straffin 1971a). Havana assemblages with Morton-like decoration and characteristic lithics, including Snyders points and lamellar blades, also occur at large bottomland sites downstream from Lake Red Rock in the Eddyville locality (Henning 1990 cited in Benn and Green 1997).

Artifact styles of the latter half of the Havana tradition, including Hopewellian items, are found throughout eastern Iowa. In addition to the well-known villages and mound groups along the Mississippi, interior eastern Iowa sites include the Holland site (13JF303) on the Skunk

River (Till and Nansel 1981a) and mounds in the vicinity of the Westwood site (13HN4) near Mt. Pleasant (Collins 1997:9–10; Ruppé 1960). Other interior Iowa societies related to Havana extend as far as the central Des Moines River basin. The best-known of these interior sites are rockshelters along the Maquoketa River in Jackson and Jones counties (Logan 1976:92–93, 105–107; Perry 1991a:109, 115), central Des Moines valley sites of the Van Hyning phase in the Saylorville Reservoir area (Benn and Rogers 1985), others to the south at Lake Red Rock (Moffat et al. 1988; Roper 1984, 1986), field camps and residential bases in the Cedar River valley (Perry 1985, 1991a), and a number of mound and habitation sites in the Rathbun Reservoir (Brown 1967b; Perry 1991a:109).

While sporadic finds of early Havana ceramics appear in northeastern Iowa, Havana probably arrived here fairly late, with Hopewell. Havana in northeastern Iowa is termed the McGregor phase (Benn 1978, 1979). A similar, related phase in Wisconsin is the Trempealeau phase (Stoltman 1979). Typical Hopewellian items have been found at Sny-Magill and in many burial mounds within Effigy Mounds National Monument, such as Mounds 55 and 57 situated on a terrace of the Mississippi River. Archaeologists discovered partially cremated bundle burials at the center of Mound 55 in association with a drilled bear canine and a Snyders projectile point. Nearby Mound 57 contained a subfloor rectilinear burial pit with a prepared floor and at least 12 bundle burials, one wearing a copper breastplate (Beaubien 1953).

Although the lifeway of McGregor phase people in northeastern Iowa is not well known, sites such as FTD (13AM210) in Allamakee County are typical of the landscape setting preferred by Havana-related groups in this area. FTD is a multicomponent Woodland site situated on a low terrace above the Mississippi River (Benn 1978). Such locations would have provided elevated settings protected from most floods, high bluff backdrops, and access to major transportation routes and rich floodplain resources (Benn 1978:231).

Contemporary ethnic groups like the Prairie phase people represented at local sites such as Buck Creek Mound 1 may have been in close contact with McGregor phase people, acting as trading partners but declining to or prevented from participating in the outward trappings of Hopewell status, ritual, and exchange. Groups like these may eventually have intermingled (Collins 1996a:127–129; Collins and Forman 1995:139).

It has not been established whether Black Sand descendants in other areas lived alongside Havana communities. Chronologically later, incised-over-cordmarked ceramics may be the product of Black Sand descendants who were displaced by Havana people or the work of local populations who lived in areas where the Havana tradition made little headway (Alex 1970).

*Havana-Hopewell Settlements and Cemeteries along the Mississippi Alluvial Plain*  Sites along the Mississippi River south of Clinton and up the lower reaches of the major tributaries exhibit the strongest expression of the Havana tradition. Large bluff-base villages such as Gast Farm and Wolfe were probably occupied throughout most of the Middle Woodland, and mound groups such as Cook Farm, Pine Creek, Toolesboro, and Malchow (13DM4) suggest that people on the west side of the Mississippi valley were full participants in the HIS. The Van Hyning phase of the central Des Moines valley, defined on the basis of exotic materials and imported Hopewell ware from the Boone Mound, the adjacent Gracie Paulson Village (13BN30), and nearby sites (Benn and Bowers 1994; Benn and Rogers 1985), represents clear but attenuated Havana influence in central Iowa.

Starting with the Albany, Illinois, site across from Clinton, Iowa (Benchley et al. 1977; Herold ed. 1971), major mound groups once existed on both sides of the Mississippi River as far south as Burlington. In Iowa, these include the Cook Farm Mounds in Davenport, Pine Creek and other mounds in and around Muscatine, mounds and earthworks near Toolesboro, Malchow and Poisel (13DM226) mound groups near Kingston, and another complex near Burlington. Numerous Middle Woodland mounds like the Fish Farm Group (13AM100) occur along the Mississippi River north of Davenport but are generally less well known (Marcucci 1997, 1998) (see plate 9; fig. 6.14).

In 1879 a Muscatine antiquarian reported that in a 30 km stretch along the Mississippi River beginning a short distance east of Muscatine to a point near Toolesboro, groups of from 2 to 100 or more mounds occurred on all the higher points. He noted the presence of 50 mounds and long earthworks near Muscatine, and he estimated that 2,500 existed throughout

the entire stretch, including both the Iowa and Illinois sides (Stevenson 1879). If the latter figure is close to accurate, and if half of these were constructed during even 400 years of Middle Woodland occupation, then some 6,250 to 12,500 people may have been buried in these sepulchers, assuming an average of 5 to 10 individuals per mound.

The mound sites of eastern Iowa were the object of the first archaeological explorations in the state, and their structure and contents have been studied for more than 100 years. Unfortunately, few of these sites were subjected to modern standards of excavation and recording, and hundreds are now gone—looted, plowed away, or destroyed by urban and rural development. A few descriptions, maps, and letters pertaining to

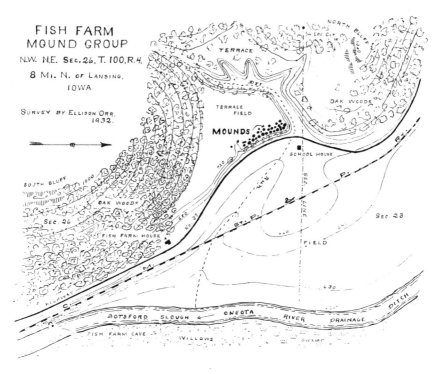

**6.14.** Fish Farm Mound Group near Lansing, Allamakee County, as mapped by Ellison Orr. Courtesy of the State Historical Society of Iowa, Iowa City.

some of the original excavations still exist, and a handful of the extant artifacts are curated at the Putnam Museum of History and Natural Science in Davenport and at a few other institutions (fig. 6.15). However, critical details about the mounds and their contents have been lost. Recent burial legislation and the respect now afforded mounds as cemeteries prohibit additional disturbance for scientific purposes or otherwise.

Fortunately, a number of the larger Middle Woodland village sites are still intact. The Wolfe site has been test excavated (Straffin 1971a), and both Gast Farm and Sand Run Slough West have been the scene of more extensive research (Benn 1987; Benn et al. 1988; Green and Wallace 1991; Hare 1992; Nansel 1996). In addition, related information comes from adjacent western Illinois villages such as Albany and Putney Landing (Benchley et al. 1977, 1979; Gregg 1974; Markman ed. 1988). These studies indicate that these large riverine settlements were probably occupied year-round. Gast Farm and Sand Run Slough West are situated on alluvial fans adjacent to backwater channels at the base of the bluffs, and the Wolfe site also occupies a fan at the edge of the floodplain. Such locations provided shelter, proximity to the river, and ready access to both forest and aquatic resources.

Subsistence at a site like Wolfe or Gast Farm revolved around hunting, fishing, gathering of wild plants, and gardening. Small plots of squash, knotweed, goosefoot, and sumpweed were maintained. Tobacco occurs as early as A.D. 150–300 at Middle Woodland sites in Illinois and was probably cultivated in Iowa by this time as well. Although American Indian peoples smoked other plants, including sumac, dogwood, and bearberry, the beautiful platform pipes characteristic of Hopewell probably held tobacco (see plate 5). The use of flotation and fine-screen recovery techniques likely will confirm the presence of tobacco at Middle Woodland sites in Iowa (Asch and Green 1992).

Each of the known Havana villages in southeastern Iowa is associated with a nearby mound or mound group. The Malchow and Poisel mounds are situated on bluffs just above the Wolfe village. Consisting of more than 60 mostly conical mounds that remain largely unexcavated, these are perhaps the best preserved of all the Iowa examples. At Gast Farm, a large mound once existed within the village area, and earthen enclosures were recorded nearby and on the bluff above (Benn 1987; Till 1977). Although destroyed more than three decades ago, the Gast Farm Mound produced a large collection of HIS items, including copper axes, sheet mica, and platform pipes (Nansel 1996). While not excavated, the Airline Railroad Village (13LA104), located on a large alluvial fan north of Toolesboro, also appears to contain a mound with an associated mound group on the bluff above (Benn 1987:245).

The large mounds in the vicinity of Toolesboro, which probably numbered close to 20 when first recorded in the mid-nineteenth century, were rich in evidence for mortuary ceremony and exotic artifacts (Alex and Green 1995). An adjacent earthwork, first described as octagonal in shape and more than a meter in height (fig. 6.16), may have been constructed by local Middle Woodland populations. Large geometric earthworks, some with possible astronomical significance, are characteristic of Ohio Hopewell (Lepper 1996; Pacheco 1996). When excavated in the 1870s and 1880s, the mounds at Toolesboro were reported to be free of habitation debris, which suggests that an adjacent village area was not the source for the mound fill (Alex and Green 1995). However, if such a site were located at the base of the bluff on the terrace below the mounds, the shifting channel of the Iowa River may well have destroyed any archaeological evidence (Benn et al. 1988:133).

The distribution of the major Mississippi valley mound groups and associated villages at 10 to 15 km intervals between Muscatine and Burlington indicates a settlement pattern similar to that noted for Havana-Hopewell communities in the central Illinois River valley (Benn 1987; Gregg

**6.15.** Topographic map of the Pine Creek Mounds, Muscatine County. Courtesy of the Putnam Museum of History and Natural Science, Davenport, Iowa.

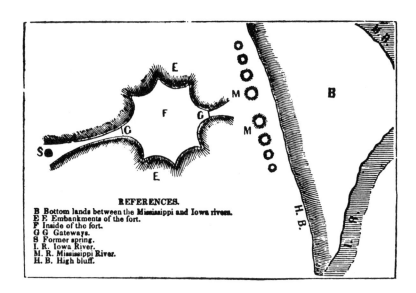

REFERENCES.

B Bottom lands between the Mississippi and Iowa rivers.
E E Embankments of the fort.
F Inside of the fort.
G G Gateways.
S Former spring.
I. R. Iowa River.
M. R. Mississippi River.
H. B. High bluff.

**6.16.** First known sketch of the earthwork and mounds at Toolesboro, Louisa County. From Newhall 1841.

1974). Archaeologists believe that these mound-village clusters marked the individual territories controlled by important Middle Woodland lineages or clans. If so, then the mounds themselves were probably the cemeteries of these important families and were highly visible symbols reminding everyone of the clans' authority.

The presence of considerable quantities of HIS artifacts within the village sites suggests that these communities served as important centers for ritual, trade, and the manufacture of valued craft items. Artisans at Gast Farm, for instance, may have produced and exported Croton tabular chert bifaces and blades (Hare 1992; Nansel 1992, 1996). The sheer quantity of Hopewellian items found at Toolesboro and Albany mark both as major regional centers. The strategic position of these sites along major waterways that likely served as routes of trade and communication must have promoted such activities. Overland routes were possibly used as well (Bailey 1977; Braun et al. 1982; Cantwell 1987; Clark 1984; Farnsworth and Koski 1985). The Holland site on the Skunk River in Jefferson County, near the source area for Croton tabular chert, may represent an acquisition point for lithic material traded overland to sites such as Gast Farm (Nansel 1992, 1996; Till and Nansel 1981a).

While the large mound groups and nearby villages are perhaps the most well known of the Havana culture sites in eastern Iowa, many smaller occupations with similar but less prolific artifact inventories and little to no HIS items also exist between the major clusters. Such an occupation is the Sid's site (13KK16) (see plate 3), a small campsite on a low terrace of the North Skunk River near Sigourney in Keokuk County, which was apparently reoccupied seasonally from Early to Late Woodland times. Lithic material used by the site's inhabitants included Croton tabular chert brought upriver to the site from its outcrop about 32 km downstream and Keokuk chert imported from Van Buren and Lee counties 64 to 80 km away. A thermoluminescence date of 200 B.C. to A.D. 300

was obtained from one of the Middle Woodland sherds (Benn 1984a).

Throughout interior eastern Iowa, field camps on high terraces adjacent to small tributaries and residential bases in upland settings overlooking major river valleys distinguish the Havana settlement pattern from that along the Mississippi River valley. Numerous rockshelters have also yielded high quantities of Havana ware, suggesting their intermittent use. These locations imply that Havana people in the eastern interior of Iowa may have focused on a more narrow range of habitats than the residents of the better known villages along the Mississippi (Perry 1991a:115).

*The Boone Mound and Hopewell in the Central Des Moines River Valley*  The Des Moines River surely served as the route by which Havana-Hopewell influences reached areas of central Iowa. Dramatic and direct evidence occurs in the Van Hyning phase sites north of Des Moines (Benn and Bowers 1994; Benn and Rogers 1985:40–46; Gradwohl 1974, 1975; Lensink 1968; Osborn and Gradwohl 1982). Two sites south of Boone, the huge Boone Mound and the adjacent Gracie Paulson village, compose part of a local cluster of at least 12 habitation sites that contained significant amounts of High Bridge ware, a local Middle Woodland pottery. Madrid ware, a later pottery that developed out of High Bridge, was probably used after the final construction of the Boone Mound since it was not a major component in the mound fill (Benn and Rogers 1985:46).

The Boone Mound and the Gracie Paulson site may have been outposts for Havana-Hopewell immigrants and centers where local people gathered to trade and carry on ritual activities (Gradwohl 1974; Osborn and Gradwohl 1982). It is also possible that they represent local populations who emulated the customs and styles of Havana people farther east (Benn and Rogers 1985; Gradwohl 1974, 1975).

Located on the high terrace of the Des Moines River, the Boone Mound measured 4.7 m in height and 39.5 by 48.8 m when excavated in 1908 by Thompson Van Hyning of the State Historical Department (Van Hyning 1910a: 157) (fig. 6.17). Despite the spectacular structural contents within the mound, no detailed report was ever prepared, and Van Hyning's own records were destroyed in a hurricane after he moved to Florida (Lensink 1968: 1).

The Boone Mound apparently was composed of layers of village midden probably scooped up from the adjacent Gracie Paulson site. Material within the fill included stone implements, large amounts of High Bridge ware, and some Hopewell ceramics (Benn and Rogers 1985; Harlan 1908; Lensink 1968). Van Hyning also discovered several thousand shells of freshwater mussels (Unionidae) deposited in layers and pockets within the mound fill.

The mound floor consisted of closely spaced limestone paving measuring 8 by 5.5 m and raised above the terrace surface. A rectangular log structure about 3 by 4 m was erected above the floor. Upright limestone slabs were set against the outside to form an enclosure. Smaller enclosures, which Van Hyning thought were individual stone crypts, occurred at the four corners of the larger structure (fig. 6.18). Van Hyning said that the larger structure had a roof of wooden timbers and a covering of poles and brush with small glacial boulders placed on top. Later examination of the human remains recovered by Van Hyning suggests that skulls from the mound showed signs of the kind of shaping that typically results from cradle board flattening or habitually transporting heavy loads on the back using a strap or trump-line around the head (Fisher 1986; Holland 1983).

The structure uncovered at the Boone Mound may have served as a crypt or charnel house not unlike similar features at Hopewell sites in Ohio (Benn and Rogers 1985:43). Ash heaps and human remains scattered across the stone pavement could reflect mortuary rituals involving cremation and the display of the deceased prior to burial. Van Hyning reported that the human bone was heavily gnawed, as if it had been exposed and subject to rodent chewing for a period of time. However, such marks can also result from small burrowing rodents gnawing dry bone buried within the mound (Benn and Rogers 1985:43; Fisher 1986; Van Hyning 1910a:162). If the stone feature did function as a charnel house, it may have provided a focus for public mourning by Middle Woodland populations living in nearby settlements.

Although the Boone Mound contained few HIS items, Hopewell ceramics and some exotics, including obsidian, occurred in the mound, at the adjacent Gracie Paulson village, and in other Van Hyning phase sites (Benn and Rogers 1985; Lensink 1968; Osborn and Gradwohl 1982). Since Gracie Paulson was investigated many years after the demolition of the mound, it is possible that some of the mound artifacts found in the village represent spoilage from the destruction of the mound. Dickson and Manker points of Knife River flint were recovered from three other Van Hyning phase sites, and at 13BN262 a rim of what was probably an imported Hopewell Zoned vessel occurred (Benn and Rogers 1985).

In addition to the large Boone Mound, 17 known or reported mounds or mound groups once existed in the Saylorville area. Fifteen of these occur in Boone County within a linear distance of 8 to 11 km above and below the Boone Mound (Ashworth and McKusick 1964; Benn and Rogers 1985:41; Gradwohl 1974). Since these groups include both linear and low conicals, they may date to either the Middle or Late Woodland periods. A sample of wood charcoal from the Middle Woodland cultural zone at Gracie Paulson produced a date of 400 B.C.–200 A.D., while the Middle Woodland Sparks site (13BN121) just 3.2 km south produced dates of A.D. 400–500 (Gradwohl 1975:100–121). The date at Gracie Paulson could indicate a fairly early Middle Woodland presence in the central Des Moines valley, while Sparks seems unusually late.

Larger Van Hyning phase habitation sites may

**6.17.** The Boone Mound, Boone County, with the
Boone High Bridge in the background. Courtesy of the
State Historical Society of Iowa, Des Moines.

**6.18.** Limestone flooring and possible crypts in the
interior of the Boone Mound, Boone County. Courtesy
of the State Historical Society of Iowa, Des Moines.

represent sizable base camps situated on the river terraces. Smaller sites have been recorded in the uplands. The broad range of faunal remains recovered from these sites suggests that Middle Woodland populations utilized deer, birds, turtles, fish, and shellfish. Features include trash and roasting pits containing considerable amounts of fire-cracked rock, lithics, and ceramics. In addition to High Bridge ceramics, diagnostic dart points include the Dickson type, which carries over from the Early Woodland, and more typical Middle Woodland Snyders and Manker styles. Other large, ovate-bladed styles, such as Gibson, and triangular Creston and Pelican Lake types are also reported. Sandstone abraders, drills, hematite celts, bifaces, and end scrapers round out the lithic inventory (Osborn and Gradwohl 1981:637).

The nature of Havana settlement downriver from the Van Hyning phase sites is poorly known. Archaeologists have recorded smaller habitations that could represent seasonal locations of people from the larger villages upstream or a more dispersed population on the periphery of influence from the Van Hyning phase people (Benn and Rogers 1985:44).

Havana-like ceramics have been found at sites in the Lake Red Rock area, such as Cormorant (13MA387) (Moffat et al. 1988:75). At least 30 mounds have been recorded in the area, and excavation indicates that some are Middle Woodland (Gradwohl 1965, 1973, 1974; Roper 1986:366). The Milo's Silo site produced Havana-like and Black Sand–like materials associated with roasting pits and a varied chipped stone tool inventory (Gradwohl 1974; Roper 1986:365).

Some large Havana-related sites including mounds occur along the South River in Warren County, in the Eddyville area, and possibly on other Des Moines River tributaries. The existence of these and many other sites of varied function demonstrates that the mound/village complex is only one aspect of the Havana settlement system

in the eastern half of Iowa, a system that is still imperfectly known.

## Conservative Communities in the Prairie Lakes Region

To the north and west of the Havana heartland, local cultures exhibit only fleeting indications of Havana-Hopewell influences. Fox Lake phase communities in the Prairie Lakes region continued a regional conservatism that lasted for centuries. Mounds are rare, and the earliest postdate A.D. 800 (Anfinson 1997:71). The impression archaeologists obtain from sites such as Arthur and those in southern Minnesota is of general continuity in subsistence, settlement, and technology throughout the Woodland, possibly fostered by the environment itself. The region offered a variety of mammalian, aquatic, and plant resources available only during certain seasons. Coupled with long, harsh winters and wet springs, which turned the prairie into a marsh, the seasonal resources acted as constraining factors on the choices of resident hunters and gatherers (Benn ed. 1990:133).

Faunal material from the Arthur site and from numerous sites in southern Minnesota and eastern South Dakota indicate that Middle Woodland people utilized a diversity of mammals, especially bison and muskrat, and a wide variety of fish. Plant use is largely unknown due to poor conditions for preservation and spotty archaeological recovery, but varieties important to later peoples, such as arrowhead tubers and wild rice, may have been harvested. The occurrence of some ground stone artifacts, including manos and metates, a celt, and a nutting stone at Arthur, possibly indicate plant processing. Chipped stone tools also reflect hunting and hide working.

Prairie Lakes people were probably aware of certain Middle Woodland trends emanating from Havana and possibly from Laurel societies to the north, although such influence remained limited (Anfinson 1997:58). Ceramics show the use of dentate and cord-wrapped stick stamping, and a few sites have produced small amounts of exotic lithic materials. An obsidian flake was found at Arthur, and some of the cherts, including fusilinid and Maynes Creek types, derive from southwestern and central Iowa (Anderson and Spriestersbach 1982:116). In general, however, local raw materials predominate. Projectile point styles associated with Fox Lake ceramics at Arthur include styles similar to St. Croix Corner-Notched, Steuben Stemmed, and Monona Stemmed. More diagnostic Middle Woodland point types are rare, and in general there is a greater affinity with Plains types over time (Anfinson 1997:68).

### Hard Times Out West?

Although Havana people appear to have extended as far west as the Kansas City area (Johnson 1976, 1979, 1981; Wedel 1938a), Hopewell items north of the Missouri and Kansas borders on the eastern Plains are rare. There are only a few indications that new forms of burial ritual and long-distance trade influenced the everyday life of eastern Plains peoples (Neuman 1975; Snortland 1994). Even then such influences appear to have been rather modest.

A few mounds, such as the Terry Mound Group (13ML49), are recorded in the Loess Hills in southwest Iowa (Billeck 1993). A Middle Woodland mound may have existed on the site of a later Glenwood earthlodge at 13ML126, where a Hopewell-type rim and chipped stone tools were reported (Billeck 1993:74). Hopewell-like pottery, Knife River flint corner-notched points and blades, and Dongola chert artifacts also occur in private collections from Mills and Fremont counties (Billeck 1993:77). These may relate to the development termed "Kansas City Hopewell," a complex in northwestern Missouri and northeastern Kansas that reflects the western extension of the HIS (Johnson 1979; O'Brien 1971; Shippee 1967; Wedel 1943, 1961).

Middle Woodland sites in western Iowa are not well known, largely because remains are deeply buried in alluvial settings. Private collec-

tions and early work by Keyes and Orr in the Loess Hills suggested a Middle Woodland presence whose details remain largely unexplored. More recent work has been conducted at several key sites, including the M.A.D. sites (Benn 1981), Rainbow (13PM91) north of Sioux City in Plymouth County (Benn ed. 1981a, 1990), and Hanging Valley (13HR28) in Harrison County (Tiffany et al. 1988). These sites have been grouped into a Valley variant or phase of a larger Mid-American Woodland tradition (Benn ed. 1990; Haas 1983). Suggested dates for the Middle Woodland here range from 50 B.C. to as late as A.D. 650 for sites in the eastern Dakotas (Benn ed. 1990:223). Radiocarbon dates from the Middle Woodland Valley phase at Rainbow indicate an occupation somewhere between A.D. 200 and 450 (Benn ed. 1990).

Overall, Valley ware, which follows the earlier Crawford ware at the M.A.D. sites and occurs in the earliest component at Rainbow, the contemporary Rowe ware of the Glenwood area (fig. 6.19), and Sonota pottery from the Middle Missouri in the Dakotas all show traits such as embossing, punctating, stamping, and zoning that were probably inspired by Havana. At the same time, these decorative treatments were applied to pots with narrow trailing and with exterior cord-marking swirled diagonally rather than longitudinally around the exterior surface (fig. 6.20), characteristics preferred by other Plains potters (Benn ed. 1990; Tiffany 1978a). Thus western prairie and eastern Plains cultures exhibit a mix of both borrowed and locally derived ceramic characteristics.

At the Rainbow site, dark humic cultural deposits alternated with lighter layers of Roberts Creek Member alluvium that accumulated in an ancient gully of Held Creek just north of its confluence with the Floyd River. This produced a "frozen" record of prehistoric life spanning the Middle to Late Woodland period (Benn ed. 1990:53). Lithics from the relatively ephemeral Valley phase occupation show an increase in the use of imported cherts, a trend of the Middle

**6.19.** Middle Woodland Rowe ware rim sherds from southwest Iowa. From Tiffany 1978a.

Woodland, although the typical broad-bladed corner-notched projectile point styles like Snyders and Norton are absent from Rainbow and most of western Iowa.

At 13CF101, the Middle Woodland residents may have erected a circular structure marked by dense scatters of Valley ware pottery, lithic debris, and bone fragments surrounding a hearth (Benn ed. 1990:130). Such scatters of encircling detritus typically represent the "drop and toss zones" (Binford 1978) that often accumulate within a habitation area as the occupants discard by-products of household activities (Benn ed. 1990:57) (fig. 6.21).

Floral and faunal materials from Rainbow and M.A.D. indicate a seasonal cycle of hunting and gathering supplemented with some cultivation of plants such as squash, chenopodium, and sunflower. A single kernel of corn was assigned to the Valley component at Rainbow (Benn ed. 1981b, 1981c). If substantiated, this find would be as old as the earliest corn dated at sites in Tennessee and Ohio (Asch 1992:93).

**6.20.** Valley ware vessel fragment from 13WD50. Photo archives, Office of the State Archaeologist, University of Iowa.

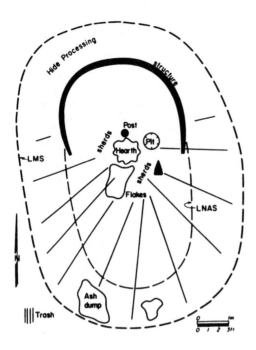

**6.21.** Disposal pattern of artifacts and debris surrounding features at the M.A.D. sites in Crawford County forms an inner ring, the Limit of Nuclear Area Scatter (LNAS), that marks the primary area of activities and trash discard, or "drop zone," while a wide outer ring, the Limit of Most Scatter (LMS), consisting of a secondary area of trash disposal forms the "toss zone." From Benn ed. 1990.

Small triangular and subtriangular points interpreted as arrowheads were found at Rainbow and M.A.D. and were associated with both the Valley (A.D. 200–450) and subsequent early Boyer components (A.D. 400–650) (Benn ed. 1990:85). While Old World hunters had been using the bow and arrow since the end of the Ice Age, its first occurrence on the North American Plains is not confirmed in most locations until after ca. A.D. 450 (Frison 1991:29–36).

The Woodland components at Rainbow and M.A.D. suggest a pattern of shifting residence and the reoccupation of small communities by family-sized bands of upward of perhaps 15 people. Other sites near M.A.D. interpreted as game-watching, hunting, and animal-processing stations may reflect other kinds of habitations and features created by local Middle Woodland residents (Benn ed. 1990:66).

Evidence from the Hanging Valley site, a reported Middle Woodland cemetery in Harrison County, demonstrates that not everyone during this time period was buried with the kind of elaborate ritual or offerings that accompanied the death of some Havana-Hopewell people. At Hanging Valley, the skeletal remains of seven individuals were found eroding from a gully wall in Gunder Member deposits northeast of the juncture of the Little Sioux River with the Missouri (Tiffany et al. 1988). The depositional context of the site was similar to that of the Late Archaic Turin burials. Dated wood charcoal associated with cultural deposits suggests use of the site sometime between A.D. 450 and 600 (Tiffany et al. 1988:224–225).

Two of the buried individuals from Hanging Valley were adult females, while the remainder were juveniles and an infant. Four individuals had been laid out in a flexed position, two in a shallow, basin-shaped pit. The bones of one of the young adults apparently were placed within one of seven Middle Woodland vessels. In addition to the pottery, a small sample of artifacts was found, including an antelope cranium coated with red pigment. This was the first verified example of antelope found at an archaeological site in Iowa. Other faunal remains included bison, deer, pocket gopher, squirrel, rabbit, fish, turtle, amphibian, and mollusks. Seeds of domestic sunflower, black walnut, black cherry, and wild rose were also recovered. All of these are known to have had medicinal or food value to native peoples.

The condition of the human remains from Hanging Valley indicates that the population was under considerable dietary and social stress. The teeth exhibited the kind of defects that typically result from periods of starvation, malnutrition, disease, and traumatic injury. X-rays of the long bones brought to light transverse lines that often mark episodes of arrested growth following malnutrition or disease. Small pits or lesions in the skulls and at the back of the eye sockets, typical of iron deficiency anemia, probably reflected iron-poor diets, poor iron absorption, or weaning with iron-poor supplemental foods. When paleoanthropologists measured the lengths of the juvenile long bones and compared them to the growth curves of similar-aged American Indian children, they concluded that the young people buried at Hanging Valley had been subjected to metabolic stress throughout most of their short lives (Benn 1989a; Tiffany et al. 1988:239–250, 1989).

Although the teeth of the Hanging Valley burials displayed the kind of chipping and extreme wear characteristic of an abrasive diet, they did not show signs of dental caries (cavities). Physical anthropologists have documented a decline in the oral health of populations when they switch from a hunting and gathering diet to one that contains well-processed garden plants such as corn (Tiffany et al. 1988:242).

One of the adult burials from Hanging Valley exhibited the kind of cut marks seen on the skulls of scalping victims. If this was the fate of this individual, it would represent one of the oldest examples in North America of a worldwide practice commonly associated with warfare.

### Trade Routes across Iowa?

Since some of the exotic materials found at Havana-Hopewell sites, such as obsidian and Knife River flint, came from sources in the western United States, they may well have passed through Iowa on their way to destinations along the Mississippi River and farther east (Anderson et al. 1986; Boszhardt 1995). Archaeologists know little about the mechanisms of this trade or the role that Iowa communities played. Were these items passed from settlement to settlement in a down-the-line fashion? Did people in the Rocky Mountains or those living near the Knife River flint quarries in North Dakota acquire these materials themselves and transport them

eastward? Or were they sought by ambitious traders from Havana communities who ventured west? Perhaps Havana-inspired techniques in ceramic decoration seen in Middle Woodland sites in western and north-central Iowa, and the mounds and Hopewell-like items present in the Loess Hills were the result of early Iowans acting as brokers in the exchange of items to Havana-Hopewell people or represent actual way stations for traders heading across the Midwest.

While archaeologists often assume that major rivers represent the highways of prehistoric exchange and communication, overland routes also must be considered (Braun et al. 1982; Cantwell 1987; Clark 1984; Farnsworth and Koski 1985). This makes the discovery of a cache of five ovate bifaces of Knife River flint in a plowed field near the Winnebago River in Hancock County in north-central Iowa particularly tantalizing. The cache occurred near an Adena-Dickson–like point and a drilled bear canine, and Middle Woodland pottery was found nearby (Braun et al. 1982:67). Perhaps this was the hoard of an overland trader traveling to the Havana-Hopewell centers along the Mississippi.

### Late Woodland Discoveries (A.D. 400–1200)

By the fifth century A.D. the long-distance exchange in exotic artifacts, the construction of large earthworks, and evidence for broadly shared ritual and belief that marked Hopewell ended throughout the Midwest. People in Iowa continued to build mounds, but the mounds were smaller and lacked exotic trade items. This was a time when populations seemed to disconnect from one another (Tainter 1983), when large communities dispersed, and when hinterlands were reoccupied (Green 1987). After the apparent drama of Havana-Hopewell, Late Woodland sites in the Upper Midwest seem to "pale" in comparison. The term "Good Grey Cultures," adopted by one archaeologist, portrays this sense of blandness (Williams cited in Fowler 1973:51).

What brought about the decline and eventual disappearance of the HIS is unknown. Although various causes have been proposed, including the effect of climatic or economic changes, breakdown of trade alliances, or defiance of authority (Green 1993a, 1995d), none have satisfactorily answered this question. Nevertheless, as one archaeologist maintains, the idea of some sort of cultural decline following Hopewell probably has little relevance in Iowa since only certain areas of the state would have been directly affected (Benn 1980:199). For most people life probably went along very much as it had before.

The Late Woodland in Iowa is represented by more sites than any earlier period (fig. 6.22). Populations were larger and in some areas more nucleated, so archaeological materials are more numerous. Sites generally exist closer to the surface and are thus more easily located, and testing has been able to uncover the remains of shallowly buried components (Perry 1987). Archaeologists now realize that this was a rather dynamic period in midwestern prehistory, a time when societies increased in size, settlements expanded into the uplands and small secondary valleys, and horticulture became a mainstay rather than a supplement to the economy. People maintained contact with one another as evidenced by the rapid spread of new ideas in pottery-making, weaponry, and horticulture. Communities may have been locally based, but they were not isolated. By the time the latest Woodland sites were occupied, a series of distinctive late prehistoric cultures had emerged in parts of northwestern and central Iowa.

### Late Woodland Subsistence and Settlement

Although settlement patterns varied regionally throughout the Late Woodland, dozens of small villages or hamlets of one or only a few seasonally inhabited structures are known from open sites scattered across the state. These include Sand Run Slough West, Helen Smith (L. Alex 1976; Billeck 1995), the Smith site (Anderson 1958; Iowa Archeological Society *Newsletter*

1958), Walters (13JH42) (Anderson 1971b), Darr-es-Shalom (Osborn and Gradwohl 1981; Timberlake 1981), 13LC17 (Roper 1992), Saylorvillage (13PK165) (Osborn et al. 1978, 1989), Cormorant (Moffat et al. 1988; Rogers and Koldehoff 1987), Arthur (Tiffany ed. 1982), M.A.D. (Benn 1981), Rainbow (Benn ed. 1981a, 1990), Sharps (13ML142) (Tiffany 1977), and Thomas (13ML204) (Brown 1967a).

Late Woodland people also occupied numerous rockshelters throughout eastern Iowa, many investigated by Charles R. Keyes and Ellison Orr as part of the State Archaeological Survey and later by Wilfred Logan (Benn and Marcucci 1981; Cordell et al. 1991; Finney and Logan 1993; Marcucci et al. 1994; Roetzel et al. 1980; Schermer 1996). Well known are Woodpecker Cave (13JH202) (Caldwell 1961; Emerson et al. 1984; Overstreet 1985; Wheeler 1949); Rock Run (Alex 1968); Minott's shelter (13LN210) (Keyes 1943; Logan 1976), Spring Hollow shelters 1–3 (13LN211–213) and Gingerstairs 1 and 2 (13LN215 and 13LN220) in Palisades-Kepler State Park and Palisades-Dow State Preserve; Mouse Hollow (Logan 1976); Horsethief Cave (13JN8) (Morrow 1997b); the Highway Thirteen shelter (13CT231) (Logan 1976); Spike Hollow (Logan 1959, 1976); and Henry Schnoor (Jaehnig 1975). Since the time of Keyes and Orr, excavations have been conducted at Keystone (Anderson 1987a), Hadfields Cave (13JN3) (Benn 1976, 1980), and Carroll (13DB486) (Collins 1996b; Collins et al. 1997).

Late Woodland communities maintained traditional subsistence patterns, with the mainstays of hunting, fishing, and gathering increasingly supplemented by cultivated plants. This is evident from the remains of a variety of domesticated plants and by the presence of numerous subsurface storage and processing facilities. Goosefoot, little barley, maygrass, sunflower, marshelder, and knotweed were cultivated in the east, while western Iowa people tended squash or pumpkin, sunflower, gourd, goosefoot, and marsh elder. Tobacco occurs at the Gast Farm

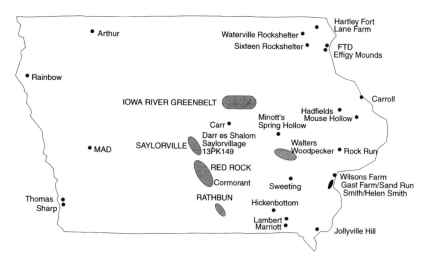

**6.22.** Late Woodland sites mentioned in the text. Map by Diana Brayton.

site in Louisa County by the fifth century A.D. and in early Late Woodland components dated after about A.D. 400 at the Rainbow and M.A.D. sites in the west (Benn ed. 1990).

### Burial Customs

In northeastern Iowa, people continued to build conical-shaped burial mounds and to erect new linear forms. Archaeologists find evidence of prepared rock "altars," burial pits, rock-lined cysts, and cremations inside and beneath these mounds (Beaubien 1953; Benn et al. 1978; Benn et al. 1993; Logan 1959; Orr 1963).

Along the Skunk, Des Moines, Iowa, and Chariton rivers and their tributaries, people built low circular, oval, and linear mounds at ridge-top settings. Excavations at the Marriott (13VB455), Lambert (13VB82), and Hickenbottom (13JF52) sites, all in southeastern Iowa, have produced evidence of bundle burials covered with limestone slabs or enclosed in limestone cysts (Benn and Green 1997; Caldwell 1961; Collins 1997; Fulmer et al. 1977; Thomas 1887b; Thompson and Fisher 1977; Ward 1904).

### Technological Leaps

During the Late Woodlands, improvements were made in both weaponry and cooking vessels. In some regions, dart points were used for a while, with later Middle Woodland expanding-stemmed Steuben and Ansell types continuing (see fig. 6.6). In the west, early Late Woodland dart points resemble the Besant style of the Plains. Heat treating of lithics was commonly practiced, but the use of exotic raw cherts and the blade technology typical of the Middle Woodland largely disappeared (Morrow 1996c:17). The increased use of local cherts may suggest that some groups controlled access to specific quarries (Collins 1991:40, 1997).

The presence of small triangular projectile points, perhaps as early as A.D. 500, documents the adoption of the bow and arrow from west to east across the state. In the west, points similar to the Avonlea style occur. Elsewhere, small types include notched Klunk, Koster, and Scallorn and the unnotched triangular Madison type. The side-notched Klunk point has been identified as the earliest dated arrow point in Illinois and northeastern Missouri (Perino 1971:100). Distinctly triangular side-notched Reed and Washita types and tri-notched Cahokia-like points are characteristic as early as A.D. 800 (Morrow 1996c:18). Late Woodland projectiles are small, thin, and light and were often made by retouching the margins of thin flakes.

Although derived from Middle Woodland wares such as Havana and Valley, most early Late Woodland ceramics show important stylistic and technological changes. Pottery decoration in most areas was less abundant and less ornate. This is particularly true of Weaver and Henry wares in southeast Iowa (Perry 1987; Weitzel and Green 1994) and Held Creek ware in the west (Benn ed. 1990). Decoration typically involved the application of simple notching of the lip/rim margin made with a straight-edged tool, cord-wrapped stick, or fingernail (Stoltman 1990: 247). In northeast and north-central Iowa, there is a greater stylistic continuation of Middle Woodland, with dentate stamping predominating on the more highly decorated Linn ware.

Compared to Middle Woodland ceramics, Late Woodland vessels are more globular in shape, as the widening of the shoulders produced a more rounded body and pronounced shoulders. Late Woodland potters reduced the thickness of their vessel walls by about 30 percent (Benn 1996:6–7). Vessel wall thinning also may have been accompanied by an increased selection of certain tempering materials—finer grit, sand, and, late in the period, shell—that made pots more heat resistant (Braun 1983). Potters produced a cord-marked or smoothed-over-cord-marked surface by thinning the vessel walls with a cord-wrapped paddle and sealed the surface by smoothing (Benn 1996:8).

The thinner-walled pottery and finer pastes of Late Woodland vessels possibly derived from the technology used to produce Middle Woodland Hopewell ceramics. These improvements may be related to the adoption of new cooking methods and the increased use of boiling as a means to process native cultigens, especially starchy plants

(Braun 1983). The increased efficiency in pottery is believed to have promoted population growth, as more thermally efficient pottery allowed women for the first time to prepare soft, highly palatable weaning food from boiled starchy seeds. As a result, children could be weaned at a younger age, perhaps increasing the chances that birth spacing became shorter (Buikstra et al. 1987; Cook and Buikstra 1979).

### Early Late Woodland Ceramics and Regional Phases

Early Late Woodland sites in Iowa have been organized into a series of local phases characterized by diagnostic pottery types. In parts of eastern Iowa, early Late Woodland ceramics are called Weaver. Weaver pottery first occurs in the latest phases of the Havana sequence as a utilitarian type alongside Baehr ware. Sites in the central Illinois valley containing Weaver pottery form the basis for a Weaver phase (Griffin 1952b; McGregor 1947, 1952; Wray and MacNeish 1961). Weaver ceramics tend to be plain surfaced, with decorations limited to lip margins. Decoration usually consists of a row of bosses below the rim or a series of tool impressions or cord-wrapped stick impressions near the lip (Benn 1987) (fig. 6.23). Sites with Weaver pottery in Iowa generally occur in the Mississippi alluvial plain and adjacent areas of the interior south of Clinton. A Weaver variant has been defined for these sites, with the Gast phase a charter member. Gast phase sites occur in an area from Muscatine south to Kingston (Benn and Green 1997).

Other possible initial Late Woodland phases in Iowa are associated with related or contemporary ceramics. These include the Henry phase of the lower Des Moines, Skunk, and Cedar rivers in interior southeastern Iowa characterized by Henry ware (Benn and Green 1997; Perry 1987); the Randolph phase extending from Lake Red Rock south to the Chariton River basin of northern Missouri (Chapman 1980; Roper 1992, 1994); and the Riverbend phase in the Saylorville Lake area and the central Des Moines Lobe with

**6.23.** Plain tool-notched Weaver rims from the Gast Farm site, Louisa County. From Weitzel and Green 1994.

associated Madrid ware (Benn and Rogers 1985; Osborn and Gradwohl 1981).

In northeast and north-central Iowa, the Allamakee phase with its defining pottery, Linn ware, spans the Middle to Late Woodland transition (Benn et al. 1993; Logan 1976). Radiocarbon dates from Allamakee phase Buck Creek (13CT36) Mound 2 produced dates averaging A.D. 300–450. The Millville phase represents a closely related phase in southwestern Wisconsin, with radiocarbon dates falling within the period of A.D. 300 to 700 (Arzigian 1987; Stoltman 1990). Linn ware is more highly decorated than Weaver and usually displays zones of dentate-stamped or cord-wrapped stick decoration (fig. 6.24).

All of these Iowa phases have been placed within the Weaver variant (Benn and Green 1997). Steuben and Ansell projectile points, flake tools, and small cores carry over Middle Woodland traits into some Weaver variant assemblages, and some communities continued to use small amounts of copper, galena, and imported cherts (Benn 1978:232, 1992:73).

**6.24.** Levsen stamped vessel, a type of Linn ware, from Harvey's Island Mound Group, Clayton County. On display, Iowa Hall, University of Iowa. Photo archives, Office of the State Archaeologist, University of Iowa.

In the Prairie Lakes region, the early Late Woodland is represented by late Fox Lake pottery and by contemporary Arthur Cordroughened ceramics at the Arthur site on East Lake Okoboji and in collections from nearby sites in Iowa. Similar pottery occurs at the Pederson site in southwest Minnesota (Anfinson 1997; Benn ed. 1990; Tiffany ed. 1982).

The initial Late Woodland of western Iowa is defined by Floyd phase components at the Rainbow and M.A.D. sites. Vessels with a subconoidal form classified as Held Creek ware occur. Scalp ware is a contemporary ceramic on the eastern Plains (Hurt 1952). The Floyd phase sites are considered part of the Boyer variant of the Mid-American Woodland tradition (Benn ed. 1990; Benn and Green 1997). Radiocarbon dates on initial Boyer occupations at Rainbow were A.D. 400–650; later Boyer dated A.D. 600–700 (Benn ed. 1990). Just as the Weaver potteries in eastern Iowa appear to have developed from Middle Woodland Havana forms, so pottery such as Held Creek ware appears as a thinner, more efficient, and minimally decorated pottery derived from earlier Valley ware (fig. 6.25). These changes seem to represent widespread ceramic trends across the Midwest at the beginning of the Late Woodland (Benn ed. 1990:138).

In Mills County, sites such as Thomas and Sharps belong to the Sterns Creek phase, characteristic of the Missouri River valley in southwest Iowa and eastern Nebraska (Brown 1967a; Haas 1983; Orr 1963; Strong 1935; Tiffany 1977). Charles R. Keyes found Sterns Creek ware, a subconoidal cordmarked pottery with simple lip notching, underlying later Missouri Bluffs ware, suggesting an early Late Woodland affiliation (Billeck 1992a cited in Butler and Hoffman 1992; Keyes 1949; Strong 1935; Tiffany 1977; Tiffany ed. 1982) (fig. 6.26). Some later investigations also indicate an early Late Woodland position for Sterns Creek (Hirst and Artz 1993; Tiffany 1977; Tiffany ed. 1982). However, other archaeologists argue that late radiocarbon dates from Walker-Gilmore, the type site for Sterns

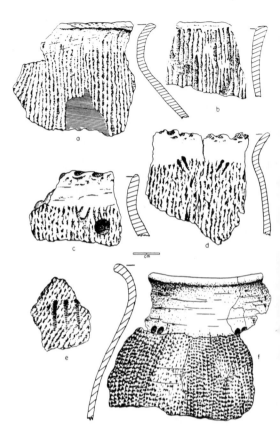

**6.25.** Held Creek ware from the Rainbow site, Plymouth County: (a–b) Held Cord Roughened; (c–f) Held Tool Impressed. From Benn ed. 1990.

Creek in Nebraska, and certain ceramic characteristics point to a late Late Woodland affiliation for this same phase (Benn ed. 1990; Benn and Green 1997; Haas 1983).

*The Mississippi Alluvial Plain: The Gast Farm Site*  The Gast Farm site on an alluvial fan at the edge of the Mississippi valley is the type site for the Gast phase of the Weaver variant (Benn and Green 1997). Calibrated radiocarbon dates indicate that early Late Woodland people occupied Gast Farm as early as A.D. 400–450 (Weitzel and Green 1994) and were living at other regional sites such as Helen Smith perhaps as late as A.D. 600–700 (Billeck 1995). Other Gast phase settlements on large tributaries like the Iowa River or on smaller secondary streams several kilometers inland were smaller and were probably seasonally occupied. In addition to Helen Smith, Gast phase components exist at Sand Run Slough West, Wolfe, Wilson Farm (13LA56) (Fokken and Finn 1984), and 13MC23 (Perry 1984). The discovery of Late Woodland Steuben points in the uplands to the west of these sites may reflect Gast phase people on hunting forays. Many of the low conical mounds that once existed throughout eastern Iowa are believed to represent the burial sites of these early Late Woodland people, although few have been excavated (Benn and Green 1997).

Gast Farm appears to be a ring midden settlement, defined archaeologically by a circular concentration of midden and features surrounding a relatively clear area. This distinctive type of community, home to 100 or more residents, occurred throughout a broad area of the Midwest ranging from southern Wisconsin and eastern Iowa to Kentucky and Tennessee.

**6.26.** Sterns Creek vessel found northwest of Glenwood, Mills County, and restored by Paul Rowe. Courtesy of the State Historical Society of Iowa, Iowa City.

The diameter of the ring midden at Gast Farm is 100 m, and the entire settlement occupied an area of about 1 ha. The central zone contained numerous hearths and animal bones, suggesting that it might have served as an open plaza for communal feasting. The surrounding midden, .5 m thick in some places, is presumed to represent the former location of houses, undetected at Gast Farm but described from sites in Illinois as small, oval, or rectangular post structures covered with wattle and daub (Jackson and McConaughy 1983; Whelan and Green 1991; Wray and MacNeish 1961). Pieces of daub were discovered at Gast Farm, indicating that houses such as these possibly once existed (Whelan et al. 1992).

Numerous pit features and hearths of several types were exposed in the Weaver component at Gast Farm during four seasons of excavations. Archaeologists uncovered pits that may have held large jars and some that were probably big storage chambers. Others may have functioned as earth ovens or roasting pits. One such feature contained thousands of charred acorns, possibly the result of a fire that went out of control while the nuts were being roasted (Hodgson 1992) (fig. 6.27). Acorns were an important staple for many native groups as early as Archaic times and required considerable processing to remove the tannic acid they contain. Native peoples devised numerous techniques for this purpose. Acorns were parched and roasted, buried, mixed with iron-bearing earth, and soaked and boiled in freshwater or in ash-treated water. Kernels were often then dried or roasted before storing (Hodgson 1992:36). Other plants utilized by the Gast Farm site occupants include a variety of nuts and fruits and cultigens such as goosefoot, little barley, maygrass, and sunflower (Hodgson 1992).

The Gast Farm site location, which offered access to floodplain marshes, upland prairie and forests, and forested waterways, provided a wide variety of fish, aquatic and terrestrial birds, mammals, and reptiles. Over 9,000 animal bones found during the excavations reflect the

**6.27.** Roasting pit filled with burned acorns at the Gast Farm site, Louisa County. Photo archives, Office of the State Archaeologist, University of Iowa.

significance of local environments as sources for key elements in the diet of Gast phase people. Deer, muskrat, fish, and turtle predominate. Nearby Muscatine Slough was a convenient route to and from the main channel of the Mississippi for people and for spawning fish (Neverett 1996). The importance of fish is well established at Gast Farm, where 48 varieties have been identified. Fifteen different kinds occurred in a single coprolite sample, probably from a dog. One feature found close to the acorn-filled pit was full of fish bone. As a major flyway, the Mississippi River would have provided an abundance of migratory birds, particularly during spring and fall. Thus archaeologists were surprised to discover so few bird bones among the faunal remains.

Gast Farm flintknappers favored local lithics, particularly Burlington chert. Steuben points and retouched flakes dominate the assemblage.

Quickly made, disposable or "expedient" flake tools are typical of early Late Woodland assemblages. A small amount of galena, mica, and green-gray pipestone also occurred. While Gast phase people may still have been importing these materials, it seems more likely that they occasionally picked up such items from the vicinity of the older nearby Havana settlement and mound.

By the end of the Gast phase, sites such as Gast Farm and Helen Smith, situated on an alluvial fan of the Iowa River a short distance south (L. Alex 1976; Billeck 1995; Van Nest 1995), were apparently abandoned in favor of single households or small settlements of a few structures scattered in the uplands (Green 1993a). The shift to a more dispersed settlement pattern may have been related to growing populations, intensified cultivation, local game depletion, or greater territoriality (Markman ed. 1988:352–535). In addition, a wetter climate may have encouraged settlement in the uplands (Green 1987).

*The Western Iowa Prairies: The Rainbow and M.A.D. Sites* Work at the Rainbow and M.A.D. sites forms the basis for much of what is known about early Late Woodland remains on the western Iowa prairies. Excavations in the Floyd phase component at Rainbow revealed a narrow, cigar-shaped house constructed over a shallow basin (Benn ed. 1990). Post molds spaced at 1 m intervals marked the position of the side walls. The doorways opened from both the north and south ends. No evidence of daub was found, and it is likely that the wooden wall posts and beams supported an arched roof and walls covered with a woven framework of wands and poles. The exterior surface of the structure probably consisted of bark slabs, reed mats, or skins.

Small interior posts may have supported wind deflectors or other hearth furniture. A line of interior trash pits and post molds divided the house into two halves. Fourteen vessels discarded evenly in each half suggest the living quarters of two separate groups. Midden areas outside the house with similar pottery indicate the residents also maintained distinct spots for trash disposal.

Most likely the two groups living in this Floyd phase structure were related families (fig. 6.28).

Unlined basin-shaped hearths positioned in front of the doorways and pits, some super-imposed, show that the house was reoccupied on at least two occasions. Some of the larger features may have been built for food or raw material storage, while smaller basins could have supported conoidal Held Creek vessels or served as containers themselves. A smaller round structure with an internal hearth and trash pit stood adjacent to the northwest end of the Rainbow house (Benn ed. 1990).

Small triangular and subtriangular points interpreted as arrowheads were associated with the Floyd phase components at the Rainbow and M.A.D. sites. Lithic assemblages reflect the use of quartzite and other local materials, with little im-ported chert. Mussel shell obtained from nearby creeks was commonly made into scrapers. Artifacts and debris within the structure at Rainbow imply the existence of activities such as raw material processing, food production, tool manufacture, and hideworking. Archaeologists think that empty spots adjacent to the hearths and along the walls might represent former sitting and sleeping areas kept clean of artifacts and trash.

The settlement system displayed in the Floyd phase components at the Rainbow and M.A.D. sites shows few differences from the earlier Middle Woodland Valley occupation of western Iowa. The M.A.D. sites may have accommodated a few nuclear families or small extended families who occupied temporary lean-tos set up in protected areas. At Rainbow, longer-term camps in more permanent structures were probably occu-

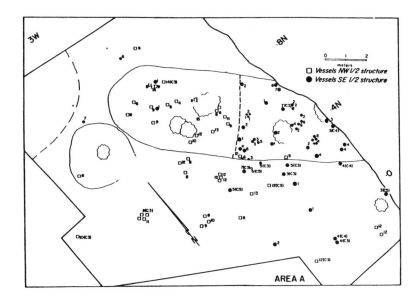

**6.28.** Late Woodland Boyer structures at the Rainbow site, Plymouth County. This view indicates the position of reconstructed and numbered vessels in and around the larger cigar-shaped house and the smaller round structure at its northwest end. The evenly spaced distribution of 14 vessels between the two halves of the larger structure suggests the presence of two groups of inhabitants. From Benn ed. 1990.

pied by similar-sized family groups or by slightly larger family bands. Both sites would have been revisited and reoccupied over the course of several seasons or years by hunting and gathering peoples familiar with the resources of the area. Cached food and other raw material such as stone and house-building supplies awaited the occupants' return. Historic peoples such as the Ioway and Winnebago (Ho-Chunk) prepared bark slabs two years before they needed them to build their oval, bark-covered lodges (Plank 1908; Radin 1923; Skinner 1926; all cited in Benn ed. 1990:69–70).

Settlements elsewhere across many areas of the Midwest and eastern Plains during the early Late Woodland reflect a similar pattern of small, seasonal occupations not unlike their Middle Woodland predecessors. Structures of poles probably covered with bark, mat, or hides or wattle and daub walls were common. At 13PK149, a multicomponent site on the Des Moines Lobe in the Saylorville Lake area, two long oval pit clusters about 10 m apart were associated with the early Late Woodland Riverbend phase dated to around A.D. 400–550 (Osborn and Gradwohl 1981; Timberlake 1981). At the Thomas site in Mills County, a large, irregular basin-shaped pit was reportedly associated with a Sterns Creek component (Brown 1967a:54–56, 61–64). Evidence of pole dwellings covered with wattle and daub or bark walls and a thatched roof of reeds or grass was also found at Walker-Gilmore in Nebraska (Strong 1935; Tiffany 1977:86–87).

### Late Late Woodland: Corded Ceramics, Effigy Mounds, and Rockshelters

The ceramics that follow Weaver, Linn ware, and other initial Late Woodland pottery are characterized by the use of complex, twisted cord impressions and lavish fabric decoration, customs that swept across the Prairie Peninsula among widely scattered communities. The intricate patterns indelibly impressed on the exterior surface of these vessels reveal the ingenuity and artistry of prehistoric weavers and potters, probably women.

The initial inspiration for the Late Woodland corded ceramics was likely the Lane Farm Cord Impressed type (see plate 10), which probably derives from Linn ware ceramics and is the hallmark of the Mill phase of southwestern Wisconsin and a newly proposed Lane Farm phase of northeastern Iowa (Stoltman 1990; Stoltman and Christiansen 1997). Lane Farm Cord Impressed pottery combines some Middle Woodland decorative attributes, particularly rocker stamping, with Late Woodland cord-impressed rim designs applied to Late Woodland vessel forms. Lane Farm Cord Impressed ceramics in Wisconsin are stratigraphically and chronologically sandwiched between Allamakee/Millville phase components and components associated with the later Effigy Mounds (Stoltman 1990). At the FTD site in Iowa, Lane Farm Cord Impressed pottery occurs below late Late Woodland Keyes phase levels and above those containing Middle Woodland McGregor phase materials (Benn 1978:250). Two Wisconsin radiocarbon dates suggest that Mill–Lane Farm phase components fall within the period A.D. 750–1000. Sites show a continuation of local resource exploitation similar to that seen at earlier Millville phase sites (Stoltman 1990).

Cord-decorated ceramics find their full expression in Madison ware, the *pièce de résistance* of Keyes phase people, most likely the architects of northeast Iowa's effigy mounds (fig. 6.29). Keyes phase occupations occur at open sites and in rockshelters. Radiocarbon dates associated with domestic and mound sites fall within  the seventh to the twelfth centuries A.D. (Collins 1996b; Collins et al. 1997; Stoltman and Christiansen 1997). The heartland of the Effigy Mound tradition was southern Wisconsin, where most sites are placed in an Eastman phase (Stoltman 1990).

In Iowa, effigy mounds and associated conical, linear, and compound mounds are concentrated along the upper Mississippi River north of Dubuque and along the lower reaches of the Turkey, Yellow, and Upper Iowa rivers (Benn and Green 1997). Contemporary linear mounds occur throughout east-central Iowa along the middle

**6.29.** Bird-shaped effigy mounds, Allamakee County, outlined in lime. Photographed by R. Clark Mallam. Courtesy of Lori A. Stanley, Luther College.

reaches of the Iowa, Cedar, and Wapsipinicon rivers. These mounds and nearby habitation sites also contain Madison ware; however, the possible affiliation of these sites with the people who built the effigy mounds has not been established (Benn and Green 1997; Collins 1990; Perry 1993).

In the Mississippi valley south of Clinton, numerous mounds may have been the cemeteries for people who occupied small campsites where cord-impressed pottery and Madison projectile points were used. Many of these sites, including a late occupation at Sand Run Slough West, commonly occur on natural levees in the bottomlands. These sites have been grouped into a proposed Louisa phase (Benn 1987; Benn and Green 1997).

Like earlier conical mounds, effigy mounds were the focus of archaeological interest as early as the mid-nineteenth century, and many were mapped, classified, and opened before that century ended. While opinions vary, it is now thought that the mounds depict animal shapes—panthers, bears, birds, turtles, humans, and possibly bison and wildcats (Mallam 1976b). However, some mounds were built in stages, and their shapes may have shifted in the process (Hurley 1986:195).

Building an effigy mound generally involved the removal of the surface soil and the excavation of an outline shape, or intaglio. The mound form typically followed this same shape. Single or multiple burials occasionally were placed in a primary pit dug in the intaglio, were included within the mound itself as cremations, or were added later as secondary bundles. The mound interior sometimes had a hearth or rock feature, occasionally referred to as an altar (Hurley

1986:295). Artifacts occur in the mound but frequently represent unintentional inclusions scooped up as fill with the dirt from nearby habitation areas. Gone are the exotic grave goods typical of Hopewell. And, unlike earlier Middle Woodland mounds, which sometimes reached heights of several meters, effigy mounds are typically less than a meter high.

While few people actually occupied the dark, inner recesses of caves, numerous rocky overhangs along cliff faces and other rock exposures were sought for habitation (Benn and Marcucci 1981; Schermer 1996). The protection provided by such shelters was apparent to native Iowans throughout prehistory, so most rockshelters contain numerous components stratified one above the other. Unfortunately, because soil accumulates slowly in such contexts and because prehistoric peoples dug pits into their living floors, rockshelter deposits are often disturbed, and the remains of different occupations are usually mixed and difficult to interpret.

*Hadfields Cave*  At least two Late Woodland components were identified in excavations conducted at Hadfields Cave along the North Fork of the Maquoketa River on the western edge of Iowa's Paleozoic Plateau. Woodland peoples utilized the front and largest of three contiguous rooms, an area about 30 by 12 m, where they had access to sunlight at the entrance and enjoyed a constant temperature of about 10°C (Benn 1976, 1980:31). While many caves and rockshelters were chosen for their warm, south-facing openings, Hadfields and the Carroll Rockshelter, another Keyes phase shelter excavated south of Dubuque (Collins 1996b; Collins et al. 1997), face eastward. The entrance to Hadfields was perched at the summit of a talus slope 15 m below the top of the cliff face (Benn 1980:12). This position would have provided morning sunlight and protection from northwesterly winds.

Hadfields exhibited extensive mixing of cultural deposits due to the reuse of the living area over numerous seasons and the earthmoving activities of the prehistoric residents (Benn 1980:

19). Small, shallow pits and surface hearths were dug into earlier deposits, and older materials were displaced upward (fig. 6.30). This created a palimpsest of debris and makes interpretations about the relationship of the prehistoric materials difficult.

The presence of Linn ware in the lower of two major strata of midden deposits defined an early Late Woodland occupation dating ca. A.D. 400–550. The upper stratum contained both Linn ware and Madison ware. Two dates averaging A.D. 650–700 came from this layer, although neither was associated directly with the ceramics. The apparent overlap in time and similar stratigraphic position of both types of ceramics in the lower portion of the upper strata suggest separate use of the rockshelter for a brief period by two separate groups or else their rapid succession (Benn 1980:31–36). Eventually the Keyes phase occupants prevailed.

The wide variety of artifacts, floral materials, and faunal remains at Hadfields reflect repeated visits to the shelter by small family bands or hunting parties. White-tailed deer, the animal most frequently associated with Keyes phase sites, elk, raccoon, and beaver contributed over 80 percent of the diet, with turkey, passenger pigeon, prairie chicken, fish, turtles, and freshwater mussels serving as supplementary meat sources. Hickory nuts, black walnuts, and butternuts were important wild plant foods. In addition, domesticated sunflower, corn, and goosefoot occurred in the flotation samples. Corn is rare in archaeological sites at this time, and its precise age at Hadfields has not been established (Asch 1992:94).

Archaeologists also found evidence that Hadfields' residents used plants for other purposes. Dogbane or Indian hemp may represent the raw material used as cordage and the source of the intricate woven collars that characterize Madison ware pottery (Benn 1980:149) (fig. 6.31). Twenty-four vessels from the site were decorated with fabric impressions created when a woven sheet was applied as a collar before the vessel was

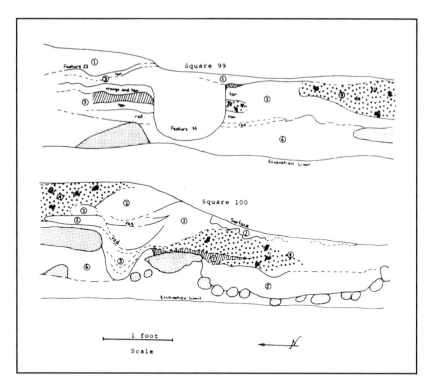

**6.30.** East wall profile at the Hadfields Cave site in Jones County illustrates the difficulty archaeologists encounter when interpreting a site with complex stratification where younger features intrude into and disturb older deposits. From Benn 1980.

fired. Archaeologists believe this collar was an integral part of the manufacturing process, intended to help shape and give structure to the pot before it was fired. Since such fabrics were quite rigid and could not be pulled off once the vessel was dry, they probably remained on the pot during firing. The intricate woven motifs recorded on hundreds of Late Woodland vessels appear to be as different as snowflakes. Once a woven collar was applied to a pot, the artisan apparently never used it or the same design again (Benn 1980).

The floral and faunal evidence from Hadfields indicates residency at the site was one part of an annual subsistence and settlement cycle for Keyes phase people. Small family bands probably moved upstream from larger river valleys into the wooded interior where they occupied rock-shelters and similarly protected sites in the early fall. Here they remained throughout the winter, subsisting on a variety of mammals, particularly white-tailed deer, and on stores of nuts and aquatic tubers such as arrowhead (*Sagittaria latifolia*) and yellow lotus (*Nelumbo lutea*), so important to Sauk and Meskwaki people in historic times (Smith 1933:105 cited in Benn 1980:185).

Toward the end of winter and early in the spring the sap from various trees begins to flow, and from it Late Woodland people may have produced quantities of syrup and sugar. Descriptions of maple sugaring by the Potawatomie, Winnebago, Sauk, and Meskwaki exist in county histories (Ahern 1938; Hartman 1915:1:105; Hirst 1993; Hoffman 1965), and archaeologists

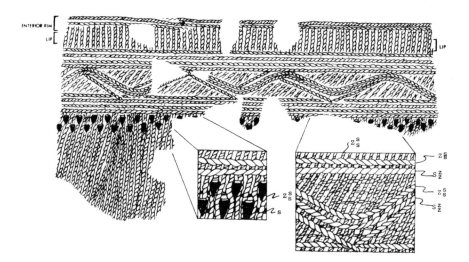

**6.31.** Elaborate woven collars or fabric sheets were used to create Madison ware pottery. Impressions like this one taken from a vessel at the Hadfields Cave site in Jones County allow archaeologists to determine the actual form and structure of the twined fabrics. From Benn 1980.

have proposed that several prehistoric sites in eastern Iowa may have been sugar camps (Billeck 1987; Hirst 1993:69). Other researchers, however, have concluded that maple sugaring was fostered by Euroamerican influence and may not have been practiced prehistorically (see Holman 1984, 1986; Holman and Egan 1985; Mason 1987, 1990).

In the summer Hadfields Cave apparently was abandoned. During this season Keyes phase people probably returned to the larger Mississippi, Iowa, Cedar, and Des Moines river valleys, as well as to smaller rivers with broad floodplains. Here families may have congregated into larger lineage bands at big summer villages where wild resources could be collectively exploited and cultigens raised in mudflat gardens. During these social gatherings, it seems likely that acquaintances were renewed, marriage partners selected, and lineage identity reaffirmed. If theories concerning the function and meaning of the effigy mounds and their animal shapes are correct,

then families also congregated to bury their dead and construct or add to the effigy mounds, which represented important territorial markers for the assembled lineages (Benn 1980; Mallam 1976b).

*Conservative Communities in the Prairie Lakes Region and Western Prairies*  In the Prairie Lakes region of southern Minnesota and north-central Iowa, Lake Benton phase people lived at small lakeside habitations such as the Arthur site on East Lake Okoboji about the same time as the Keyes phase occupation of Hadfields Cave (Benn 1982b; Tiffany ed. 1982). Lake Benton pottery, which probably developed out of Fox Lake ceramics and is found as far south as Des Moines, is predominantly decorated with cord-wrapped-stick stamping (Anfinson 1997; Benn 1982a, 1982b) (fig. 6.32). Neither twisted-cord nor fabric-decorated ceramics are common in the Prairie Lakes region (Anfinson 1997:87–88). By A.D. 700 the bow and arrow had probably been in use for a couple centuries, and the construction of burial mounds was widespread (Anfinson 1997:75). Beyond these trends, populations in the region seem to have ignored other Late Woodland innovations and continued earlier Fox Lake patterns, occupying the same locations and undertaking similar subsistence pursuits. While the arrival or emergence of Great Oasis people introduced new pottery styles to these resident hunters and gatherers, there are indications that the Lake Benton phase continued well into the Late Prehistoric (Anfinson 1997; Benn and Green 1997).

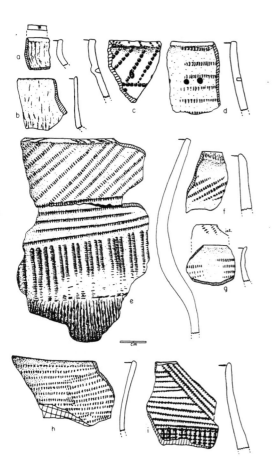

**6.32.** Lake Benton ware from the Arthur site, Dickinson County: (a) Late Benton Cordmarked; (b) Lake Benton Plain; (c–d) Lake Benton Stamped; (e–i) Lake Benton Cord-Wrapped Stick. From Benn ed. 1990.

Late Woodland moundbuilding evidently was not widely practiced on the western Prairie Peninsula in Iowa. Low conical mounds are documented in northeastern Nebraska and at sites along the Missouri, James, and Big Sioux rivers in South Dakota (Hurt 1952; Kant 1979; Myer 1922; Neuman 1960), but some of these are known to belong to the Middle Missouri tradition (see chapter 8). Small Late Woodland habitation sites occur in western Iowa on river and stream terraces and along the shores of the northwest Iowa lakes, indicating an orientation toward floodplain and lacustrine resources.

These habitation sites produce a globular-shaped, vertically cordmarked and cord-decorated pottery classified as Loseke ware (Benn ed. 1990:114; Kivett 1952). Similar pottery is common at sites along the Missouri River drainage in southeastern South Dakota, such as Scalp Creek, and in eastern Nebraska, including the Loseke Creek type site. Several eastern Plains pottery types—for example, Missouri Bluffs Cord Impressed, Feye Cord Impressed, Feye Cord Roughened, and Ellis and Scalp Cord Impressed (Hurt 1952; Keyes 1949; Kivett 1952)—have been grouped within the Loseke ware category (Benn 1982a, 1982b; Benn ed. 1990) (fig. 6.33). It is doubtful, however, that all of these distinctive high- and low-rim, subglobular- and globular-shaped types should be considered part of a single ceramic ware, particularly since their relative contemporaneity has not been well established.

At 13CF102, a Loseke occupation dates between A.D. 750 and 900. Sites such as Arthur on the Prairie Lakes also contain cord-impressed pottery originally classified as Missouri Bluffs Cord Impressed and considered part of Loseke ware (Benn 1982a, 1982b; Benn ed. 1990:140). Both the classification and age of this pottery at Arthur have been challenged, however (Tiffany ed. 1982). The presence of sites containing Loseke ware in both the western prairies and the Prairie Lakes region is paralleled soon afterward in the distribution of Great Oasis sites (Benn ed. 1990:143).

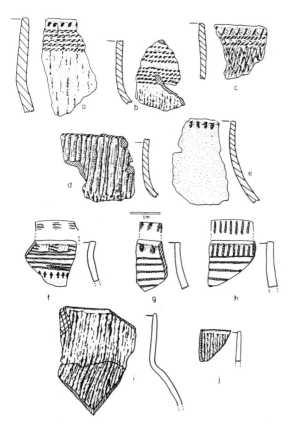

**6.33.** Loseke ware from the M.A.D. (Plymouth County) and Arthur (Dickinson County) sites: (a–d) Loseke Plain from the M.A.D. sites; (f–h) Loseke Cord Impressed from Arthur; (i–j) Loseke Cord Roughened from Arthur. From Benn ed. 1990.

### Corn Farmers and Cahokia: The End of the Woodland in Iowa

Two events originating outside the state greatly affected the lifeways of Iowa's inhabitants after A.D. 900: the arrival of corn and interaction with Middle Mississippian societies (Appendix 6.2). Analysis of paleobotanical remains and carbon isotope studies of human bone demonstrate that after a long period of only minor use, corn became an important part of the human diet over a broad area of the Midwest (Asch 1992:86). The bones of people who eat corn have a higher ratio of $^{13}C$ to $^{12}C$ than do the bones of those who do

not because $^{13}C$ is more common in plants such as corn. Study of the isotopic carbon ratio of prehistoric skeletal remains gives paleoanthropologists clues as to when corn became an important component in the diet (Buikstra et al. 1989; Price and Feinman 1993:182–183).

In Iowa, small amounts of corn have been reported from pre-A.D. 900 components at Hadfields Cave, Rainbow, and the Cormorant site in Marion County. However, the earliest conclusive dates on assemblages with large amounts of corn in Iowa are after ca. A.D. 1000 (Asch 1992:95, 1996; Green 1995a, 1995b). By that time maize had become suited for more northerly climates, allowing Iowa farmers to produce a reliable, storable food that ultimately permitted a more sedentary lifeway. Corn became an established part of subsistence, and other changes in technology, settlement, and perhaps even ideology may be related to the importance that this plant attained. Combined with bison hunting, now facilitated by the use of the bow and arrow, the presence of corn helped to foster new types of compatible semisedentary hunting-horticultural economies that characterize Late Prehistoric cultures.

As Iowa cultures were changing around A.D. 900, even greater changes were occurring not far to the south. Between A.D. 800 and 1000 in the American Bottom, local Late Woodland cultures were being transformed into more complex Middle Mississippian communities (Appendix 6.2), culminating at the site of Cahokia, the largest site in prehistoric America north of Mexico. Surrounded by a network of smaller farmsteads and hamlets that thrived on the intensive harvesting of natural floodplain resources and the cultivation of maize, by A.D. 1050–1100 the site had developed into a regional center whose population may have reached a maximum of 10,000 to 15,000, a size slightly larger than estimates for first-century A.D. Pompeii (Pauketat and Lopinot 1997:115; Storey 1997). Surrounding Cahokia—including the area that today is East St. Louis, Illinois, and St. Louis, Missouri—were other major towns and mound-residence clusters (Pauketat and Lopinot 1997:117). Public and private buildings, flat-topped mounds that served as the base for both political and religious structures and the homes of the elite, and large, rounded, earthen burial mounds created a community unique in pre-Columbian North America (Fowler 1989; Pauketat and Emerson eds. 1997; Stoltman 1986c). Completing the picture were craft workshops, a huge open plaza, a series of "woodhenges" for solstice watching, and a surrounding stockade of wooden wall posts set in trenches (see plate 11).

Cahokia represents the first instance in North America of community planning and organization that probably required a political system directed by a complex chiefdom. Iowa would not see a similar-sized town until Dubuque and Davenport reached population figures over 10,000 in the mid-1800s (Doudy and Burke 1995). However, people here and throughout the upper Mississippi valley were drawn into the orbit of events at Cahokia. As a result, far from being isolated, communities were frequently in contact and in conflict with one another.

A few sites in the upper Mississippi valley, such as Trempealeau in western Wisconsin, show early Mississippian features in the form of platform mounds and Cahokia ceramics (red-filmed seed jars and Fine Grog ware), suggesting an actual movement by a few people from the American Bottom (Green and Rodell 1994). Although there are no Middle Mississippian sites in Iowa, Mississippian-like materials, especially ceramics, are found here. The presence of traded goods, local copies, and stylistic influences demonstrate that by A.D. 1050 people in parts of Iowa, Minnesota, and Wisconsin interacted directly or indirectly with Cahokia's residents.

Cahokia-like ceramics typical of ca. A.D. 1100–1200 occur at a number of Iowa locations, including Gast Farm, Mouse Hollow rockshelter (Logan 1976), Horsethief Cave (Morrow 1997b), and Hartley Fort (13AM103) (Benn 1992; Finney 1992a; Finney and Stoltman 1991; McKusick 1965, 1973; Stoltman 1986c). A hooded water bottle (fig. 6.34), another Mississippian vessel type, was reportedly found in the Aicher Mound group (13JH1) just north of Iowa City (*History of Johnson County Iowa* 1883; Howe 1882; Starr 1897c; Webster 1889). In addition, the peaked, or castellated, and square-cornered rims of late Late Woodland wares such as Minott's (Logan 1976), Saylor (Osborn et al. 1978), and Maples Mills (Cole and Deuel 1937) (fig. 6.35) have been interpreted as Mississippian inspired (Tiffany 1986c:37). A Mississippian-style design appears on a shell gorget discovered more than 50 years ago on the floor of Hadfields Cave (Tiffany 1986:37) (see plate 12). Late Prehistoric Mill Creek sites in northwest Iowa show abundant evidence of Mississippian contact (see chapter 8) (Hall 1967; Harn 1991; D. Henning 1967, 1991).

Most late Late Woodland sites in Iowa are small and dispersed across the uplands and small interior valleys. River-valley communities such as Gast Farm or Sand Run Slough West apparently were abandoned or occupied by only small groups at this time. Habitation sites display middens, storage pits, hearths, earth ovens, one or a few houses, and a diverse array of artifact types. Occupations, although repeated, appear to have been temporary, and small camps, work stations, and other kinds of sites were also maintained. Most of these dispersed communities appear to have been largely autonomous but maintained contact with related groups across the region.

Sites such as Cormorant (Moffat et al. 1988) and Saylorvillage, both in the central Des Moines River valley (Osborn et al. 1978, 1989), Walters in the Iowa River valley (Anderson 1971b), Marriott in the lower Des Moines River valley (Collins 1985), Wilson Farm on a Mississippi River valley alluvial fan south of Muscatine (Fokken and Finn 1984), and Sweeting (13WS61) on a small tributary of the Iowa River in east-central Iowa (Lensink ed. 1986) typify the small hamlets and base camps of late Late Woodland people in Iowa. By this time communities had adopted both corn farming and bow and arrow hunting as significant aspects of their lifeways.

**6.34.** Hooded water bottle. Photo archives, Office of the State Archaeologist, University of Iowa.

Late Late Woodland ceramics in Iowa generally display single cord impressions, often applied as geometric designs on the high rims of globular-shaped jars. Rims were frequently castellated or thickened to produce a collar. This broad surface area provided the potter with a wide "canvas" upon which to display a variety of pan-midwestern motifs, many probably inspired by events to the south. Elaborate chevron designs executed in cord impressions may have been stylized renditions of the wings of the falcon or thunderbird, important symbols of the warrior and warfare in midwestern iconography (see chapter 10) (Benn 1989b, 1995; Hall 1983; Lothson 1976).

Regional late Late Woodland ceramics in Iowa include Minott's ware found along the Mississippi valley and west to the central Des Moines valley (Benn 1987; Logan 1976); Maples Mills, part of Canton ware, an Illinois pottery that appears commonly in southeastern Iowa (Fowler

**6.35.** Reconstructed Late Woodland Maples Mills type vessel from the Sand Run Slough West site, Louisa County. Photo archives, Office of the State Archaeologist, University of Iowa.

1955; Riggle 1981); Saylor ware, characteristic of the central Des Moines valley (fig. 6.36); and late Loseke and Great Oasis pottery on the western prairies and in the Prairie Lakes area. Hartley ware is found at sites along the Upper Iowa in the northeast (Tiffany 1982a). Accompanying these ceramics are small, triangular, notched and unnotched arrowpoints.

Effigy mound building apparently had ceased in northeastern Iowa by the time the latest Woodland sites were occupied. In southeastern Iowa, low conical mounds placed in defined cemetery areas, such as the Jollyville Hill site (13LE12) in Lee County, were erected by people who made ceramics similar to Minott's and Maples Mills Cord Impressed (McKusick and Anderson 1966; Tiffany 1986b:244).

*Homesteads on the Southern Iowa Drift Plain*
The Cormorant site on an upland ridge spur at Lake Red Rock in the central Des Moines valley contains a late Late Woodland component that

appears related to sites found to the north at Saylorville Lake. Pottery is characterized by castellated, cord-impressed rims similar to Minott's ware (Benn and Green 1997; Benn and Rogers 1985; Moffat et al. 1988:200). Radiocarbon dates suggest an occupation falling within the tenth to eleventh centuries A.D. Excavations at Cormorant uncovered typical Late Woodland features such as earth ovens, fire pits, and storage pits. Fragments of daub with impressions of wattle and pole thatching indicate the presence of structures.

Unfortunately, the faunal remains from Cormorant were poorly preserved, and the floral sample was also small. Edible wild plants including hickory, butternut or walnut, hazelnut, wild plum, and ground nut reflect use of both bottomland and upland resources near the site. Corn was present, but it is not known whether it was grown near the site or was transported from elsewhere. Many of the chipped stone artifacts

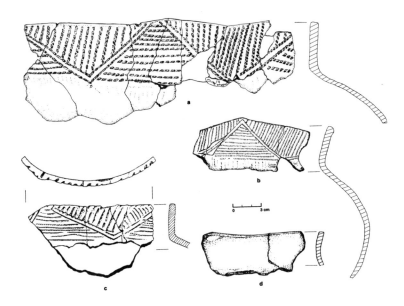

**6.36.** Saylor ware from the Late Woodland Saylorville site in Polk County illustrates early cord-impressed triangular designs: (a–c) Saylor Cord Impressed; (d) Saylor Plain. From Osborn et al. 1989.

were made of chert obtained from nearby glacial tills.

The Sweeting site is situated on a loess-mantled, upland ridge spur in Washington County. It may have been occupied for one or more brief periods between A.D. 1000 and 1200. When discovered and test-excavated in the early 1980s, a midden and 15 features were uncovered. Ceramics related to Minott's Cord Impressed and 94 small triangular Cahokia-type side-notched and unnotched Madison projectile points were found (Billeck 1991; Lensink ed. 1986) (see fig. 6.6).

Features at Sweeting included shallow, basin-shaped pits as well as post molds, artifact concentrations, and rock clusters. The association of 10 post molds with pit features and several vessels suggest the location of a structure possibly resembling a historic wickiup (Hill and Lensink 1986:73). Twenty to 50 pottery vessels had been discarded at the site, along with a broad array of ground and chipped stone artifacts, including hundreds of expedient flake tools and stone tools under production. Almost all the stone tools were made of local raw materials. Utilizing ceramic figures, archaeologists estimate that the site might have been occupied by one household for 5 to 12 months or by two households for 2.5 to 6 months if each household broke pottery at a rate of 50 percent per year (Anderson 1985b; Lensink ed. 1986:113).

The Late Woodland ceramics from Sweeting are similar to several late Late Woodland ceramic types in eastern Iowa, such as Hartley Tool Impressed (Tiffany 1982a:140–141), Minott's Plain, Minott's Cord Impressed, and Maples Mills. One rim appears to be a copy of a Powell Plain or Ramey Incised vessel, both Middle Mississippian types (Fowler and Hall 1975; Hall 1991; Tiffany 1986b). Regional sites with similar ceramics include Minott's Rockshelter in Linn County; Walters in the Coralville Reservoir in Johnson County, in addition to other sites in the Iowa valley; the Carr site (13MR31) in Marshall County (Griffin 1948); and sites in the central Des Moines valley at Saylorville (Tiffany 1986b). The diverse ceramic assemblages found at sites like Sweeting may reflect the interaction and intermarriage between Late Woodland bands, where new brides brought to their husbands' community the ceramic-making customs learned in their own households (Tiffany 1986b:243–245).

Faunal remains were not well preserved at Sweeting, although the presence of numerous arrowpoints suggests that hunting was important. Carbonized corn kernels, cobs, and stalk fragments imply that gardens existed nearby, possibly in the small valley south of the site. Fire-cracked rock clusters probably represent food preparation by stone boiling and pit roasting. Evidence suggests the site was inhabited year-round.

Sweeting, Cormorant, Saylorvillage, and other sites represent only a few of the many small communities in Iowa that were adopting the technologies and new subsistence practices that swept across the Midwest during the late Late Woodland. While groups at these sites maintained autonomy, interacting with one another, others took on a more direct role in the events of the outside world.

*Hartley Fort: Traders or Intruders?* The presence of fortifications and evidence of trade with outside communities make Hartley Fort on the Iowa River a unique site in northeastern Iowa (Finney 1992a, 1994; Finney et al. 1993; Finney and Hollinger 1994; McKusick 1965, 1973; Tiffany 1982a). It is one of a complex of Woodland and Oneota components on the Hartley Terrace first investigated in the 1880s by Colonel P. W. Norris as part of Cyrus Thomas's and the Smithsonian Institution's study of archaeological sites in eastern North America (Thomas 1887b, 1894). Later, Ellison Orr conducted extensive studies here (Orr 1963).

The residents of Hartley Fort interacted directly with late prehistoric Mill Creek people (see chapter 8) and with the world beyond Iowa, perhaps actually hosting outside visitors. This openness may have placed them in a precarious position, especially if they possessed surplus commodities and desirable trade items. As a result, Hartley Fort inhabitants, like those at many of the Mill Creek communities in northwest Iowa, maintained a defensive posture, constructing some of the earliest fortifications in the state.

The Late Woodland fortification at Hartley includes an earthen embankment forming a square enclosure about 60 m across. The embankment today is less than 1 m high and about 5 m wide, half its reported size in 1882 (Finney and Hollinger 1994) (fig. 6.37). Excavations at the site were conducted by the University of Iowa in 1964. Additional excavations undertaken in 1993 and 1994 revealed the presence of a basin-shaped structure with a double row of posts around the perimeter. Excavation also confirmed the existence of two 3 m wide ditches on both the interior and exterior sides of the palisade line. Hartley Fort is believed to date between A.D. 1100 and 1200 based on radiocarbon dates and ceramic cross-dating.

Ceramics from the early excavation at Hartley Fort formed the basis for the definition of the Hartley phase (Tiffany 1980, 1982a). Archaeologists believe that the Hartley phase reflects interaction between local Late Woodland communities and Mill Creek communities in northwest Iowa. There is also good evidence for contact with terminal Late Woodland people in southern Wisconsin and with Middle Mississippian groups.

The ceramics from Hartley include samples of local Late Woodland types (Hartley Plain and French Creek Cord Impressed), pottery that resembles Mill Creek ceramics (Hartley Cross Hatched and Hartley Tool Impressed) (fig. 6.38), and actual Mill Creek vessels that may have been produced by Mill Creek women living at the site (Benn 1995; Tiffany 1982a). Mill Creek ceramics have been found in at least three other sites in Allamakee County (Lensink and Finney 1994; Tiffany 1991a). Thin-section analysis has confirmed that Ramey Incised (see chapter 8) and Powell Plain type vessels at Hartley originated in the American Bottom, possibly at Cahokia itself (Stoltman 1991). In addition, Hartley Fort potters were copying the Ramey vessel style in a

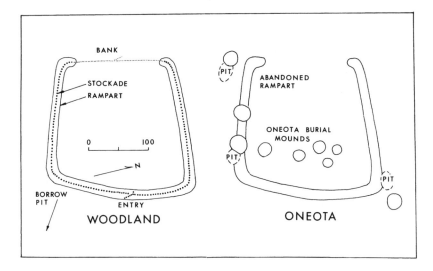

**6.37.** Hartley Fort, Allamakee County, Late Woodland stockade and rampart (left) and Oneota occupation (right), as delineated by McKusick. From Tiffany 1982a.

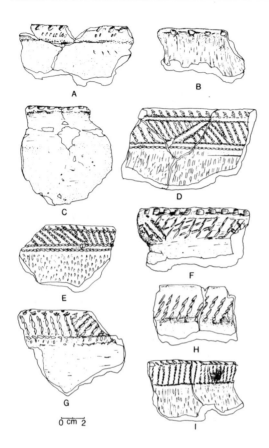

**6.38.** Hartley Fort pottery: (A–C) Hartley Tool Impressed; (D–I) French Creek Tool Impressed. From Tiffany 1982a.

local, grit-tempered form. Thin-section analysis has also revealed that pottery made at Hartley was traded to the Fred Edwards site in southwestern Wisconsin, to at least six other eastern Iowa sites, and to the Chan-ya-ta site (13BV1), a Mill Creek village in northwest Iowa (Finney 1992a; Stoltman and Finney 1991; Stoltman 1991, 1993; Tiffany 1978c).

Hematite, found in abundance at Hartley Fort, may have served as a trade item among Hartley phase people and others in the region (Finney and Hollinger 1994). Hartley Fort's involvement in trade was enhanced by its position at the east end of a transportation route connecting the upper Mississippi River and the Missouri River (Tiffany 1991a). This route likely pro-

vided a pathway for trade to the eastern Plains. Materials exchanged along this route included prestige items of marine shell, copper, pipestone, nonlocal lithics, and finished artifacts, as well as information, evidently an important commodity to Middle Mississippian chiefs (Brown et al. 1990; Green and Rodell 1994; Moore 1983).

The mechanisms of this exchange in Iowa are uncertain. There seems to have been no centralized political entity directing the acquisition and movement of goods between regions. In addition, there are no clear indications of Middle Mississippian enclaves in the state similar to those proposed for some sites in Wisconsin and Minnesota (Gibbon 1991; Rodell 1991, 1997). Only the Mill Creek communities and Hartley Fort seem to have participated in direct, two-way, and perhaps somewhat extended Middle Mississippian exchange. Elsewhere, it appears that people had only intermittent contact with groups outside Iowa. Artifacts such as the engraved shell gorget from Hadfields Cave could illustrate isolated instances of gift-giving between trading partners or emblems of prestige worn by local peoples to show off Mississippian connections. Then again, perhaps the gorget represents the actual calling card of a Mississippian trader.

### Conclusion

Corn agriculture and contact with Mississippian cultures helped to transform Late Woodland economies and lifeways. Between A.D. 950 and 1200 several distinct cultures emerged in western and central Iowa—Great Oasis, Mill Creek, and Glenwood. They were partially contemporary, and they interacted with late Late Woodland communities in eastern Iowa and Mississippian societies outside the state. During the thirteenth century, however, Iowa became the "heart" of the Oneota world, and Woodland communities disappeared. The fate of Woodland peoples in eastern Iowa is still unclear. Most likely they "became" Oneota, although probably not the earliest. While Oneota people are likely descended from earlier Late Woodland groups under strong influence from Middle Mississippians (Rodell 1997; Stoltman 1986c), this transformation has not been confirmed as yet in Iowa. Perhaps this kind of change occurred so quickly that it is difficult for archaeologists to detect, an instance of what paleontologists call "punctuated equilibrium." Then again, perhaps the latest Woodland people abandoned eastern Iowa to move to a number of Mississippian centers. Only after the florescence of sites such as Cahokia did their descendants return, then wearing Oneota symbols and making Oneota pots.

## APPENDIX 6.1.
### Problems with the Radiocarbon Calendar

Radiocarbon dates provide little helpful information about the true ages of sites from the first millennium B.C. because of erratic production of atmospheric $^{14}C$ during this time interval. Calibration curves suggest that samples with true ages of 400–750 B.C. will be collapsed into a short period of radiocarbon time—450–550 B.C. (Goldman-Finn et al. 1991). This indicates that the true age of Early Woodland sites cannot be addressed through radiocarbon dating. A similar situation exists for Late Woodland and Late Prehistoric dates between A.D. 1000 and 1150.

## APPENDIX 6.2.
### Woodland and Mississippian Traditions

Long-term cultural continuities are referred to by North American archaeologists as "tradi-tions." The Woodland and Mississippian represent two of these traditions in eastern North America. Although both persisted until European contact, in regions such as the upper and central Mississippi valley the Mississippian tradition supplanted the earlier Woodland tradition after A.D. 1000. Prehistorians divide the Mississippian tradition into two stages: Middle Mississippi and Upper Mississippi, each of which is subdivided into temporal and regional variants or cultures that are divisible into phases. One of the regional variants of the Middle Mississippi stage is the American Bottom culture associated with the rise and florescence of Cahokia. The Upper Mississippi stage is considered an offshoot of the Middle Mississippi stage and has two major regional variants, Oneota and Fort Ancient. No phases of the Middle Mississippi stage occur in Iowa, although Late Prehistoric peoples here were influenced by Middle Mississippi developments (Stoltman 1986c:2–3).

Phases used at Cahokia:
   Lohmann (A.D. 1050–1100)
   Stirling (A.D. 1100–1200), formerly
     called Old Village Cahokia
   Moorehead (A.D. 1200–1275)
   Sand Prairie (A.D. 1275–1350)
   Vulcan (Oneota) (post 1350)(Hall 1991:10)

Payment for training was so highly developed in Mandan society that a young woman assisting her mother in the making of clay pots would prepare a simple feast to which the females of the household were invited in order to receive the right to assist in the making of pots and to make vessels of her own after her mother had died. Within the family group the payments were usually insignificant so far as the value of the goods was concerned. It was felt that the small payment in goods expressed the young woman's respect for her mother. The Mandan also believed that payments expressed societal values. The mother would explain each step in pottery-making, the selection of the clay and grit, the molding of the mass, the introduction of decorations, and the drying and baking of the vessels. Mandan vessels had a variety of decorations and the persons buying the right to make pottery acquired only the right to employ such decorations as the mother had a right to use. If she wished to utilize other decorations, she was obliged to seek another woman entitled to make the particular decoration and buy the right of her.

—Bowers 1950:92

---

**ARCHAEOLOGISTS** have identified four distinct late prehistoric cultures in Iowa: Great Oasis, Mill Creek, Glenwood, and Oneota (fig. 7.1 and fig. 10.2). Their appearance marks an important development in the prehistory of the Midwest—the widespread establishment of semi-permanent villages dependent on corn farming. Although Woodland societies initiated this pattern by cultivating gardens of native squash and small seed crops of the Eastern Agricultural Complex, the addition of maize and later beans both encouraged and required new patterns of residence and scheduling of economic activities among native societies. The outcome is evident in the late prehistoric cultures of Iowa.

Our ability to distinguish these cultures relies upon the distinctive "signatures" each produced in the nature of their distribution, subsistence economy, settlement pattern, and artifacts. There is also good evidence that the earliest of these late prehistoric societies interacted with the latest Woodland communities in eastern Iowa. Sites such as Hartley Fort, in fact, may have functioned as points of liaison between western Iowa peoples and Middle Mississippian groups (Tiffany 1983). In addition, Mill Creek and Glenwood are believed to have interacted with one another, and early Oneota people in western Iowa may have affected both.

In the past, archaeologists believed that the appearance of farming societies such as Great Oasis and Mill Creek was fostered by the onset of climatic conditions favorable to corn growing. The Neo-Atlantic climatic episode, radiocarbon dated between A.D. 800 and 1250, seemed to signal the arrival of a warmer, moist climate over the Prairie Peninsula, one that promoted semi-permanent settlements increasingly dependent upon corn (Baerreis and Bryson 1965; Bryson et al. 1970; Bryson and Wendland 1967). Further analysis of some of the original climatic data, as well as new research, has called into question the validity of the climatic model as it was originally proposed and in turn its implications for prehistoric occupation of the Prairie Peninsula (Clark 1990; Laird, Fritz, Maasch, and Cumming 1996; Laird, Fritz, Grimm, and Mueller 1996; Lensink 1993a, 1997, 1998b; Zalucha 1982). Current hypotheses look toward cultural factors, particularly those related to resource depletion, and socio-political events, which may also have encouraged the first horticultural villages in western Iowa and affected their history.

Great Oasis culture was first named and

investigated in southwestern Minnesota, where sites were situated in protected or oasislike settings adjacent to woodlands and lakes that provided a buffer against prairie fires (Wilford 1945). Although the culture was first recognized in Minnesota, archaeologists have recorded more than 100 Great Oasis sites in Iowa, extending from the central and upper Des Moines valley to the Missouri River (Anderson 1971a; Anderson 1995; Banks 1965; Broihahn 1997; Flanders and Hansman 1961; Gradwohl 1974; A. Henning 1966; Henning 1969a, 1970a, 1971a, 1996a, 1996b; Henning comp. 1980, 1982; Henning 1981; Henning and Henning 1978; McAllister 1972; Peterson 1967a; Williams 1975). Sites also occur in southeastern South Dakota and stretch along the Missouri River as far north as the big bend below Pierre (Beissel et al. 1984; Buechler 1982; Cooper 1949; Gillen 1993; Haberman 1993a, 1993b; Hall 1961; Johnston 1967; Neuman 1964). Additional Great Oasis materials are reported in northeastern Nebraska (Anderson 1995:62; Frantz 1958a, 1958b; Ludwickson et al. 1981), southeastern North Dakota, and southern Manitoba (Anfinson 1979, 1997; Nicholson

1989; Wilford 1945, 1955, 1960). Great Oasis pottery found in late Late Woodland components such as Woodpecker Cave in Johnson County, Iowa (Caldwell 1961), probably represent trade items.

## Settlement Pattern

Great Oasis sites are found in two different environmental settings that possibly fostered different lifeways for their inhabitants. Lakeside communities such as those on the Prairie Coteau of eastern South Dakota and southwestern Minnesota may have remained more conservative, with a diverse hunting and gathering economy similar to that of their Woodland ancestors. Great Oasis people who settled along the Missouri River and tributary streams in Iowa, South Dakota, and Nebraska appear to have adopted both corn growing and bison hunting and in some areas established small, semisedentary villages. Access to river routes likely encouraged trade and interaction regionally and over longer distances. The same groups of Great Oasis people may also have occupied both types of settings, migrating seasonally between the two (Anfinson 1997:195).

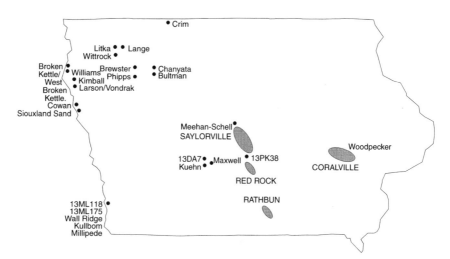

7.1. Great Oasis, Mill Creek, and Glenwood sites mentioned in the text. Map by Diana Brayton.

In Iowa, two distinct clusters of Great Oasis sites occur, one in the extreme northwest along the lower terraces of the Little and Big Sioux drainages and the Floyd River, and a second in central Iowa along the Des Moines, Raccoon, and South Raccoon rivers (Broihahn 1997; Gradwohl 1974) (fig. 7.2). Sites in the central Des Moines drainage are grouped into the Maxwell phase (Green and Doershuk 1996:38). Maxwell phase sites include habitation sites such as Maxwell (13DA264) (Doershuk and Finney 1996), Kuehn (13DA110) (Lensink and Finney 1995), Meehan-Schell (13BN110) (Gradwohl 1974, 1975; Mead 1981), and 13DA12, as well as cemeteries like the West Des Moines Burial site (13PK38), the De Camp site (13DA64), and the Paardekooper site (13DA11) (Hotopp et al. 1979; Knauth 1963; Tiffany and Alex 1999; Till et al. 1979). The Larson site (13PM61) and nearby

13PM60 in the Perry Creek drainage north of Sioux City have been placed in a proposed Perry Creek phase believed to represent a dual occupation by contemporaneous Great Oasis and Mill Creek peoples (Henning comp. 1982; Henning 1996a, 1998). Great Oasis sites near Fort Dodge (Flanders and Hansman 1961) and others in northwest Iowa, including West Broken Kettle (13PM25) and Cowan (13WD88), have not yet been assigned to a phase. Although little known at this time, additional Great Oasis remains are reported in the Prairie Lakes region of north-central Iowa, a setting similar to that in southwestern Minnesota.

Sites in Iowa include what appear to be semi-permanent winter villages such as West Broken Kettle and smaller, more dispersed homesteads or campsites such as Williams (13PM50), Cowan, and Kuehn, which could represent

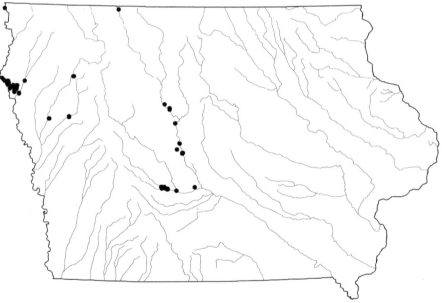

7.2. Recorded Great Oasis sites in Iowa. Data compiled from site records, Office of the State Archaeologist, University of Iowa. Courtesy of Timothy S. Weitzel and Stephen C. Lensink.

summer locations where activities centered around gardening or hunting. This pattern, originally proposed for Iowa by Williams (1975) and elaborated upon by Anderson (1995), has generally been confirmed by recent excavation, although few additional large primary villages or hunting camps have come to light. The house depressions typical of villages such as West Broken Kettle may be obscured at other sites by overburden (Johnson 1974:7). Recent archaeological research at Great Oasis sites has been of a salvage nature designed to retrieve information from sites damaged by flooding or threatened by construction. Knowledge of site types may be less than representative. These studies demonstrate that some sites may be deeply buried beneath Camp Creek Member and Roberts Creek Member deposits (Anderson 1995; Doershuk and Finney 1996).

Only two sites in Iowa have disclosed good evidence for houses. At West Broken Kettle in Plymouth County, the remains of four semisubterranean rectangular lodges 6 to 12 m long were found and excavated along the terrace overlooking Broken Kettle Creek. Each structure faced south-southeast and was built within a semisubterranean basin (Johnson 1974; Henning 1969a; Peterson 1967a) (fig. 7.3). Inside, a central fire pit and numerous cache pits reaching depths of 1 m dotted the floor area. Single or double rows of posts outlined the exterior walls. House 1 exhibited a double row of posts along the side walls and a single row at the front and rear walls. House 4 had a double row of posts along all four walls. The fire pits in House 1 and House 4 were surrounded by a set of large posts, possibly the support for stringers that extended to the side walls to form the roof (fig. 7.4). Animal remains found in the storage pits suggest the site was occupied throughout the fall, winter, and spring (Baerreis et al. 1970). Evidence for a house similar to those at West Broken Kettle comes from the Heath site in Lincoln County, South Dakota, where one end of a rectangular "earthlodge" was reported (Hannus 1974; Hannus et al. 1986).

At the Maxwell site on the floodplain of the South Raccoon River in Dallas County, one or possibly two house basins were identified (Doershuk and Finney 1996). These structures were truncated by the river and only partially preserved. Excavation indicated a rectangular configuration with an extended entryway facing west, a single line of side wall posts, possible central support posts, and numerous interior cache pits.

Better known in Iowa are the remains of smaller horticultural settlements such as Williams, Cowan, and Kuehn. While daub and isolated post molds occurred at these sites, evidence for more substantive structures was missing. Artifact density was low, but the wide range of artifact types, activity areas, and pits filled with horticultural remains indicate these were small farming communities occupied seasonally. A similar situation may exist at the Bonander site in southeastern South Dakota (Haberman 1993b).

Daub occurs at a number of Great Oasis sites in Iowa, although wattle has rarely been reported. The frequency of daub suggests the possibility that wattle and daub houses were being built by Great Oasis people (fig. 7.5). There is no evidence that the exterior of these structures was banked with soil or covered with sod, as was the case with some later Plains village houses (see plate 13).

The Vondrak site (13PM62) in the Perry Creek drainage is the only Great Oasis site that has produced evidence of a possible fortification (Henning comp. 1982; Henning 1996a). A row of 24 post molds forming a straight line oriented northwest to southeast and roughly paralleling the terrace edge was uncovered in excavation. The diameter of the post molds (20–25 cm), their depth (almost 1 m), and their distance from one another (25–35 cm) suggest a fairly substantial construction. However, the position of this alignment near the base of a hillslope would have provided little protection from unwanted visitors who might easily have seen over the top and into the encampment (Henning 1996a).

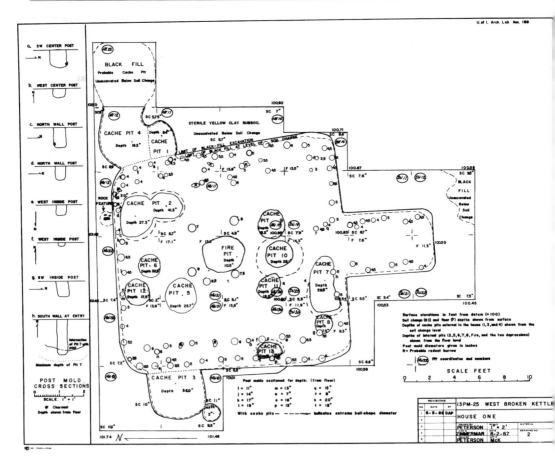

**7.3.** Floor plan of a Great Oasis house at the West Broken Kettle site, Plymouth County. Drawing by Drexel A. Peterson. Archives, Office of the State Archaeologist, University of Iowa.

### Early Corn Farmers in Iowa

There was once some question as to whether Great Oasis farmers grew corn. There is now no doubt that corn was important. Whenever fine-screen recovery and adequate paleobotanical analyses are conducted, the importance of corn farming has been demonstrated. Although corn is the most common cultigen recovered, a domesticated variety of goosefoot also appears to have been prevalent (Green 1995a:38). In addition, remains of domestic sunflower, gourd, squash, little barley, and reed canary grass or maygrass are found.

Charred plant remains are generally recovered from the contents of the numerous cache pits that dot the living area of Great Oasis sites. We know from historic accounts of the Mandan and Hidatsa that cache pits were designed to store food and other items (fig. 7.6; see Appendix 7.1). Once the contents of these pits had spoiled or were disturbed by rodents, they would be removed. Since it was dangerous to have a large, open hole on the house floor, the residents quickly swept rubbish into the empty pits. A Pawnee account tells of a woman who fell into an open pit before it had been filled (Weltfish 1965). When archaeologists excavate these pits,

**7.4.** Excavation of a Great Oasis house at the West Broken Kettle site, Plymouth County. Photo archives, Office of the State Archaeologist, University of Iowa.

**7.5.** Wattle impressions mark the surface of these pieces of clay daub. Photo archives, Office of the State Archaeologist, University of Iowa.

they often find an abundance of broken pottery, discarded stone and bone tools, chipped stone flakes, and animal and plant remains. The analysis of these materials provides information about the diet of Great Oasis people and helps to determine the season of year the house was occupied.

Although hoes made from bison scapulae are present at Great Oasis sites, they are a minor element in most assemblages. This may only imply that other sorts of horticultural implements, such as wooden digging sticks, were used or that early farmers used a type of broadcast sowing. It may also indicate that Great Oasis people were not hunting bison in large numbers. Great Oasis sites on the eastern Plains, such as Heath, contain larger amounts of bison remains than those farther east. Other bone tools include awls, needles, spatulas, bracelets or bow guards, shaft wrenches, serrated fleshers, antler flakers, deer jaw sickles, and spatula knives.

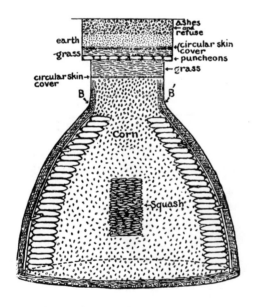

7.6. Cache pits like this Hidatsa one served as winter root cellars for storing corn, beans, sunflower seeds, and dried squash or large packages of dried meat and bladders full of bone grease. From Wilson 1977.

Great Oasis people utilized a wide diversity of wild plants and animals. At sites where faunal remains are well preserved, evidence exists for hunting and trapping of numerous mammal species including deer, elk, bison, gopher, ground squirrel, coyote, wolf, beaver, and rabbit. Birds, especially waterfowl, and fish, particularly catfish and bullheads, were also favored. Raptors such as falcons, hawks, and eagles, so important to Mill Creek people, were absent from the West Broken Kettle site, although a breast plate made from golden eagle bones accompanied the De Camp site burials. As with the majority of Native American groups, dog was the only domesticated animal kept by Great Oasis people. Plants like hackberry, hazelnut, black walnut, grape, wild plum, bush clover, nightshade, smartweed, ground cherry, sumac, elderberry, and several pond weeds were being harvested (Asch 1992, 1996; Asch and Green 1992; Green 1995a, 1995b; Mead 1981; Treat et al. 1970).

Stone artifacts associated with hunting include small triangular and corner-notched projectile points often unifacially worked and not always particularly well made. A side-notched projectile point similar to the Reed point has been identified as a typical Great Oasis point (Anderson 1995:58) (see fig. 6.6). Stemmed and corner-notched points found at some sites are similar to Woodland types. Other chipped stone tools are scrapers, bifaces, gravers, and a variety of worked and utilized flakes. A bipolar technology may characterize Great Oasis flake tool production. Bipolar technologies are believed to relate to stone tool industries that utilized relatively poor quality materials. This technique would have allowed the knapper to get the most out of the raw material available (Anderson 1995:55).

A variety of ground stone items are characteristic of Great Oasis sites. These include paired shaft abraders, manos, metates, celts, and thin sandstone palettes (fig. 7.7). Grooved mauls, common to Mill Creek sites, are rare. Assuming these were used to crack and smash large bones

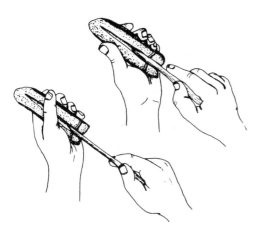

**7.7.** Shaft abraders. Illustration by Mary M. Slattery. From L. Alex 1980.

in the production of grease and marrow, their infrequency again may reflect the small amounts of bison at Iowa locations. Minerals such as limonite and hematite, the raw materials for paint and pigment, are commonly reported from Great Oasis sites. Abraders of pumice or clinker seem to have been preferred as well.

## Connections

Much of the chert and quartzite used by Great Oasis people was obtained locally. However, communities in both northwest and central Iowa seem to have been exchanging these materials between their respective regions, and they were also tapping distant quarries to the west. Chadron and Republican jasper and Nehawka chert from Nebraska, Knife River flint from west-central North Dakota, and Bijou Hills silicified sediment from central South Dakota occur at Iowa sites and reflect a strong western network of communication and contact. In addition, ceramics characteristic of Initial Middle Missouri tradition sites to the west have been reported in the central Des Moines valley, possibly associated with the Great Oasis occupation there (Broihahn 1997; Broihahn and Gradwohl 1997).

The large pieces of Burlington chert in the Dallas County sites and examples from the

Cowan site in Woodbury County show that lithic materials were also derived from the southeast. This is just one indication of a more extensive eastern exchange network that stretched beyond the Mississippi River. *Anculosa* shell collected from the Ohio and Alabama river systems and perhaps a small amount of marine shell made their way across the Midwest to sites like Williams, West Broken Kettle, and Larson. These shells may reflect the emerging interaction between Iowa communities and the Mississippian world (Henning 1991).

## Running Deer and Turkey Tracks

Ceramics have been the distinguishing characteristic of Great Oasis sites. The typical vessel is a globular-shaped pot with a rounded shoulder and bottom, constricted neck, outflaring rim, flat lip, thin walls, and fine grit or grog temper (Zimmerman 1985:79–80). Pots were made by paddle and anvil modeling, as evidenced in their smooth or smoothed-over-cordmarked surface. Buffing and polishing of the upper rim and interior lip surface are also characteristic.

A variety of decorative elements were precisely executed on the exterior of the rim and flattened lip of most vessels. Upper rim decoration consists of fine trailed (incised) horizontal or oblique lines, elongated punctate impressions, tool impressions, and cross-hatching. Additional designs were placed within a plain or horizontally trailed lower rim zone and consist of triangles, diamonds, pendant triangles, trapezoids, pendant chevrons, upright or inverted turkey tracks, and stylized maize, tree, and running deer (flag and dot) motifs (Anderson 1995:19; Johnson 1969; Henning and Henning 1978; Ludwickson et al. 1981:138) (fig. 7.8). The precision or "neatness" in the execution of Great Oasis ceramic decoration is a hallmark trait (Henning 1996a). One study has demonstrated that much of the fine, evenly spaced horizontal trailing was executed a line at a time and generally in a left-to-right direction (Edwards 1993). In addition to pottery vessels, untempered ceramic beads have

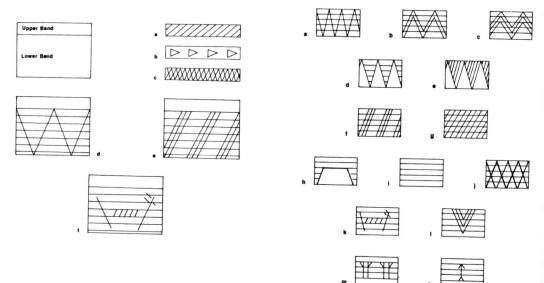

**7.8.** Great Oasis High Rim design element subdivisions. Left: (a–c) upper band motifs; (d–f) lower band motifs. Right (lower band motifs): (a–c) zigzag; (d–e) pendant triangle; (f) spaced oblique; (g) continuous oblique; (h) trapezoid; (I) horizontal line; (j) diamond; (k) running deer; (l) pendant chevron; (m) conventional maize; (n) arrow. From Edwards 1993.

been found at Williams and West Broken Kettle in Iowa and at the Great Oasis Village in Minnesota.

Great Oasis ceramics from Iowa sites are generally classified according to a hierarchical scheme used elsewhere on the Plains based on wares and types (Lehmer 1954:42). The more inclusive "ware" contains a group of "types" that share a majority of basic characteristics: fabric (paste, temper, firing, hardness, color, method of manufacture), general vessel form, surface finish, and basic rim form. Types are defined on the basis of decorative elements. Three "ware groupings" have been proposed: High Rim, Wedge Lip, and S-shaped rim. Each of these consists of two or more named "wares" commonly found at Great Oasis and Mill Creek contexts (fig. 7.9). These ware groupings imply a close, ancestral-descendant relationship between Great Oasis

and Mill Creek, particularly in the lower Big Sioux region (Henning 1996a:3).

There are no defined types in any of the three named Great Oasis wares, although the presence/absence of decorative elements would seem to provide the basis for such definition (Anfinson 1979; Doershuk and Finney 1996:28; Henning and Henning 1978; Wilford 1945, 1955). Great Oasis High Rim is common to all identified Great Oasis sites. Great Oasis Wedge Lip seems rare in southern Minnesota; south of South Sioux City, Nebraska; and the Des Moines valley. It constitutes over 50 percent of the ceramics at some northwest Iowa sites (Henning 1991:1) and is consistently found in southeast South Dakota. Great Oasis S-shaped is present but rare at both the northwest and central Iowa sites, having been previously classified as an aberrant rim form in most reports. Its occur-

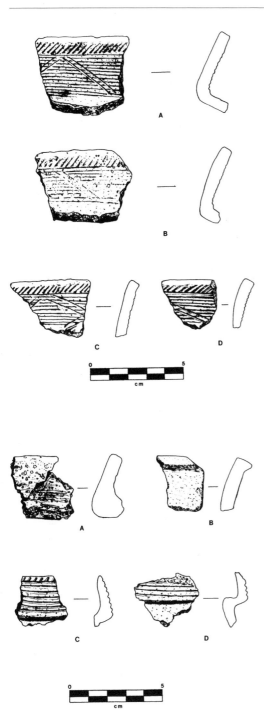

**7.9.** Great Oasis rim sherds from the Maxwell site, Dallas County. Upper: (A–D) Great Oasis High Rim. Lower: (A) uncertain; (B) Great Oasis Wedge Lip; (C–D) Great Oasis S-Shaped Rim. From Doershuk and Finney 1996.

rence elsewhere has not been tabulated. At sites such as West Broken Kettle and Ferber in Nebraska, S-shaped rims are identified as Mill Creek Foreman ware (Edwards 1993). These examples deserve reexamination in light of the S-shaped ware category now recognized at other Great Oasis sites. The regional variation in percentages of Great Oasis wares may represent temporal, geographical, functional, or social factors (Henning and Henning 1978).

Although archaeologists know quite a bit about where and how Great Oasis people lived, they know little about their social structure or their religious beliefs. Archaeologists generally believe that regional and local differences in pottery may be a reflection of the prehistoric social system, particularly that part of it related to marriage and residence patterns (Deetz 1965). The regional and local patterning displayed by Great Oasis pottery could be interpreted as a reflection of matrilocal residence (Henning 1996a:90). In such a situation a newly married couple lives with the wife's family after marriage. The crafts produced by women, such as pottery, are similar from generation to generation because daughters continue to live with and be influenced by their female relatives. Among some historic Plains village people—for example, the Mandan—communities were composed of several clans of related matrilineages who were affiliated by a common ancestry through the female line. Matrilocal residence was also the rule among the Mandan.

Isolated human skeletal elements are scattered throughout Great Oasis sites and may reflect customs such as scaffold burial. The Mandan, and in later years the Hidatsa, typically collected the bones of their relatives from around the scaffolds after these structures had rotted and fallen to the ground. Most bones were gathered and wrapped in hides before being buried in the village refuse or along river or creek banks (Bowers 1950:101). Known burial locations associated with Great Oasis sites occur primarily as hilltop cemeteries of single or multiple interments (ossuaries), or as secondary burials in older Woodland mounds, or in mixed contexts.

The West Des Moines Burial site is one of the better known Great Oasis cemeteries. Here dozens of burials were uncovered, many found in a flexed position. Grave goods included whole pots, dozens of *Anculosa* shell beads, local freshwater artifacts, and two dozen pieces of freshwater clamshell cut in a cross shape (fig. 7.10). At the De Camp site near Redfield, a larger cemetery with similar remains occurred. Some of the De Camp burials were covered with large stone slabs (Tiffany and Alex 1999). Numerous other burial sites have been documented in the vicinity of Great Oasis sites. Some, such as the Siouxland Sand and Gravel site (13WD402), contain additional examples of nonlocal exotics, particularly marine shell. However, the context of the exotic shell is not well documented, and since only Mill Creek pottery occurs at the site, the Great Oasis affiliation of these materials is unlikely (Anderson et al. 1979).

### From Where? To Where?

Woodland pottery is found at many Great Oasis sites. Most of the Great Oasis components recorded between the Gavins Point and the Big Bend dams in South Dakota contain Woodland ceramics (Johnston 1967:70). At approximately a third of the Great Oasis sites in Iowa, Woodland

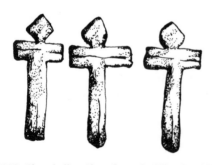

**7.10.** Clamshell artifacts from the West Des Moines Burial Site, Polk County. Illustration by Mary M. Slattery. From L. Alex 1980.

materials are also reported. Since it has not been determined if these contexts represent mixed or multiple components, most researchers conclude that such associations could be the result of one or all of three possible situations: the disturbance of earlier Woodland components by later Great Oasis people occupying the same site, incidences of actual Woodland–Great Oasis contact, or sites transitional between the two.

It is virtually certain that Great Oasis had its origin in regional Late Woodland cultures. The single cord-impressed decoration typical of Late Woodland pottery seems to have been translated into the fine, trailed decoration characteristic of Great Oasis. The broad-based subsistence, nonnucleated settlements, and evidence of wattle and daub houses typical of many Great Oasis sites are viewed as essentially a continuation of a Woodland pattern. To this was added the growing importance of corn farming, which may have encouraged more permanent settlement by some groups. Radiocarbon dates indicate that Great Oasis was under way by A.D. 950 (Lensink 1996), contemporary with late Late Woodland sites elsewhere in Iowa. Some archaeologists, in fact, would identify Great Oasis as a Late Woodland culture (Benn and Rogers 1985; Tiffany 1983).

Other archaeologists view the corn farming, bison hunting, and more nucleated settlement seen at some Great Oasis sites as signaling the emergence of a new Plains Village pattern, an adaptation to the tall-grass prairie/short-grass Plains ecotone and best exemplified at later Mill Creek and Nebraska phase sites. Supporters of this view argue that Great Oasis displays most of the features characteristic of the earliest Plains villagers, whose cultures are assigned to the Middle Missouri tradition (Lehmer 1954). According to these archaeologists, Great Oasis is no longer a member of the Woodland tradition but instead is a charter member in the emerging Middle Missouri tradition (Johnson 1974, 1996; Johnston 1967; Henning and Henning 1978).

A more persistent problem in Great Oasis research concerns the historical relationship between Great Oasis and Mill Creek. Archaeologists for decades have pointed out the close spatial association between Great Oasis and Mill Creek sites (Henning 1981:35), their overlapping chronology, and similarities in settlement and material culture. Ceramics such as Great Oasis High Rim are viewed as directly antecedent to Mill Creek Chamberlain ware and Great Oasis Wedge Lip to Sanford ware (Henning and Henning 1978). It is also possible that the S-shaped Great Oasis pottery inspired the Mill Creek Foreman types.

Significant differences between the two cultures, however, have also been noted. Located in riverine, terrace, and lakeside settings, Great Oasis sites are found over a much broader area than Mill Creek sites. With the exception of the West Broken Kettle and perhaps Maxwell sites, Great Oasis sites have a less nucleated settlement pattern. Iowa sites show little evidence of intensive bison utilization and have fewer numbers of bone tools, particularly bison scapula hoes suggestive of horticulture. In the past, the importance of corn was questioned. Mill Creek sites also demonstrate a high incidence of Mississippian trade materials, especially pottery, while at Great Oasis sites such contacts are suggested only by the presence of *Anculosa* shell and possibly small amounts of marine shell and by early types of Mississippian pottery (Henning 1991).

These different perspectives have resulted in a number of hypotheses concerning the relationship between Great Oasis and Mill Creek and underscore the difficulty archaeologists have in figuring out links between prehistoric cultures. Some archaeologists suggest that in Iowa, at least, Great Oasis was both ancestral to and contemporaneous with Mill Creek (Henning and Henning 1978) and that a symbiotic relationship existed between the two, with Great Oasis hunter-gatherers perhaps trading for the corn harvest of Mill Creek farmers (Henning 1981). A modern analogy might be the nineteenth century–like lifestyle of the Amish persisting alongside that of their twentieth-century neighbors. Proponents of this view suggest that while Great Oasis may have begun the trade with emerging Mississippian societies, Mill Creek eventually usurped and expanded upon it.

More recently, it has been proposed that Great Oasis and Mill Creek peoples not only lived near one another, as suggested by the West Broken Kettle site which sits across the creek from the Mill Creek Broken Kettle village, but in the case of Larson and 13PM60 in Plymouth County actually shared the same village (Henning 1996a). According to this view, Great Oasis persisted alongside Mill Creek for some 300 years (Henning 1998; Johnson 1996:197–199).

Proponents of the "Great Oasis and Mill Creek as neighbors" view have relied on what appear to be overlapping sets of radiocarbon dates and evidence from a very small number of sites, such as Larson, where ceramics from both cultures seem to occur together. In the past, the apparent scarcity of corn and bison scapula hoes implied that Great Oasis people rarely farmed, thus reinforcing the possibility of economic dependence on Mill Creek and a reason for periodic interaction between the two groups.

Other archaeologists propose that Mill Creek developed out of Great Oasis in Iowa and that the two were not contemporaneous (Peterson 1967b). The greater interaction with the Mississippian world exemplified at Mill Creek sites is seen as an intensification of an earlier pattern initiated by Great Oasis. According to this scheme, the development of Mill Creek from Great Oasis is attributed to more direct contact and trade with Mississippian societies to the east and Plains settlements to the west, to an intensification of both corn farming and bison hunting, and to increased nucleation of settlement and changes in socio-political organization (Lensink 1998b). Archaeologists who favor this view see Mill Creek society shaped by its position as the power broker in the trade between the eastern Plains and Middle Mississippian communities.

Proponents of the "Great Oasis becoming Mill Creek" hypothesis point out that radiocarbon dates cannot be used to settle this argument. The radiocarbon clock is not that fine-tuned, and there are problems with the dates from this part of the late prehistoric period due to fluctuating levels of atmospheric radiocarbon. They also point out that the few sites that contain both Mill Creek and Great Oasis materials are essentially Mill Creek components with smaller amounts of Great Oasis, not the reverse. Even the Larson site, which has been placed in a "fused" Great Oasis–Mill Creek phase called Perry Creek, is described as "principally" reflecting the Mill Creek tradition and "minimally" Great Oasis (Henning 1996a:15). If the two cultures were contemporaneous, archaeologists might also expect to find Great Oasis sites with Mill Creek materials on them. Sites such as Larson could reflect sequential components or a transitional situation (Tiffany et al. 1998).

In addition, the items of presumed Mississippian trade found on Great Oasis sites do not include the Ramey ceramic type, which generally coincides with the Stirling phase at Cahokia dated between A.D. 1100 and 1200 and which does occur at Mill Creek sites. The absence of material like this on Great Oasis sites supports the argument that Great Oasis in northwest Iowa had ended or become Mill Creek by A.D. 1100.

There is at this time no definitive evidence that settles the question of the relationship between Great Oasis and Mill Creek. That corn farming was an important element in the subsistence of Great Oasis is now well established. The discovery of abundant remains of corn kernels as well as cob fragments at the Cowan, Kuehn, Maxwell, Meehan-Schell, and Larson sites suggests that Great Oasis may be worthy of distinction as having the first real corn-producing economy in Iowa. Thus, if Great Oasis and Mill Creek shared some sort of symbiotic relationship, trade in corn was unlikely to have been a principal item of exchange. If the Great Oasis materials found at the Larson site are indeed in reliable archaeological context, and this is not

without question (Tiffany et al. 1998), then the fact remains that once again Larson appears to represent a Mill Creek site with a Great Oasis presence, not the reverse. Although the radiocarbon dates from the site imply a thirteenth-century occupation, the Mississippian trade pottery that occurs is at least a century older. While these vessels could represent heirloom pieces kept as valuables by Mill Creek people (Henning 1996a, 1998), the simplest explanation might be that the component or components at the Larson site are actually older than the dates suggest (Tiffany et al. 1998).

## APPENDIX 7.1.
### Preparation of a Cache Pit

The Hidatsa cache pit as described by Buffalo Bird Woman, who was born around 1839, began with the excavation of a "jug-shaped" pit, less than 1 m wide at the mouth dug to a depth sometimes requiring the use of a ladder in descending. Women were responsible for its preparation and filling. Prehistorically, the hole was probably dug with a bone hoe, scooping the dirt into a bowl that was handed to a helper who emptied it. The excavation took more than two days. Once dug, the base of the pit was lined with dead and dried willow sticks and long, dried grass. The same grass was kept in place by vertical willow sticks nailed in place with willow pins lining the interior walls. Over top of the flooring was a large skin, sometimes the cover from a bullboat with its willow frame removed. Inside strings of braided corn of 54 or 55 ears, folded over once, were laid snugly against the sides of the pit with the tips of the ears pointed inward. Two layers of braided strings, creating a tier 4 ears deep, completed the first phase of the cache. Following this, loose, shelled corn kernels were poured into the pit to the level of the top of the four tiers of braided corn strings. A string of dried squash was coiled onto and piled up in the center of the loose corn. Strings of braided corn were added around the wall of the pit to the top of the squash heap coil in the center. Afterward, loose corn was once again poured into the pit until the squash pile was covered and the topmost row of braided ears was reached. The process was repeated until the pit was almost full. A circular piece of thick, bull buffalo hide was snugly fitted over all, and a puncheon cover made from small split logs was placed over the first skin. A layer of grass was trampled down hard over the mouth of the pit and covered with a second cut buffalo hide. Final layers of dirt, ashes, and refuse were then added.

Approximately 30 or more strings of braided corn lined the walls of an average-sized pit. Four seven-fathom strings of dried squash were usually coiled and stored in the center. A fathom was described as the distance between the tips of the fingers of one hand to the tips of the other with both hands outstretched at either side. The dried squash was placed in the center of the shelled corn to protect it from dampness (Wilson 1977:87–97).

# 8  Late Prehistoric Mill Creek

A long time ago the Missouri River flowed into the Mississippi River and thence into the ocean. On the right bank there was a high point on the ocean shore that the Mandan came from. They were said to have come from under the ground at that place and brought corn up. Their chief was named Good Furred Robe. He had one brother named Cornhusk Earrings and another younger brother called No Hair on Him or Head for Rattle after the gourds. They had a sister named Corn Stalk.

When they came out of the ground, there were many people but they had no clothing on. They said, "We have found Ma'tahara." "ha" was what they called the river as it was like a stranger. It is also the word for "stranger." They went a short distance and planted corn, even though they were naked. They were located there for a few years, and all that time they planted corn. Then they moved north, and no one knows the number of years they stopped at different places. At last they came to the place where the river flowed into the ocean. When they came to the mouth of this river, they saw people on the other side who could understand their language and they thought they were Mandan too. The village on the other side had a chief whose name was Maninga. It was a very large village.

While they were stopping there, they found that the people on the other side owned bowls made of shells. At Good Furred Robe's village they would kill the rabbits for the hides. They also killed the meadowlarks for the yellow crescents. They took them to the people of the other village to trade for shell bowls. They would also take the rabbit hides painted red and trade for the shells.
—Mandan origin myth related
by Wolf Chief in Bowers 1950:156

---

**THE LATE** prehistoric Mill Creek culture of northwest Iowa, defined and named by Charles R. Keyes after a tributary of the Little Sioux River (Keyes 1927b, 1951; Vis and Henning 1969:254), is perhaps the best studied of Iowa's prehistoric cultures (fig. 8.1). The characteristically large rich midden mounds have attracted the attention of collectors and archaeologists throughout the twentieth century. In many ways Mill Creek sites are like mini "tells," mounds of village debris and mud-walled houses whose disintegration provided the base upon which subsequent structures were built. In time, an entire village area could be elevated 2–3 m above the original ground surface. At some sites there is evidence that Mill Creek people deliberately raised the village surface with the addition of soil brought in from outside the site (Fishel 1995a, 1996; Van Nest 1995).

While the rich content of the highly visible Mill Creek sites drew early interest, it was climate change and its role in the settlement and eventual abandonment of Iowa by Mill Creek people that became the focus of later investigations (Henning ed. 1968). More recently, the direction of research has shifted again, as archaeologists attempt to understand what impact Mill Creek people may have had on their local environment and whether their interactions with other peoples ultimately prompted their exodus from northwest Iowa (Lensink 1993a; Lensink et al. 1995).

### Big and Little Sioux Localities

Thirty-five Mill Creek sites are recorded in two localities in northwestern Iowa. Seven settlements or burial sites occur in the Big Sioux locality in Plymouth County along the Big Sioux River and its tributaries such as Broken Kettle Creek (fig. 8.2; see also fig. 7.1). They appear in pairs, each member of which is separated by a distance of 2–2.5 km. One isolated site, 13PM7, exists 6

**8.1.** Mill Creek pottery. Photo by Charles R. Keyes. Courtesy of the State Historical Society of Iowa, Iowa City.

km beyond its nearest Mill Creek neighbor to the northwest (Fishel 1995a:69). Two of the Big Sioux locality sites, Broken Kettle and Kimball (13PM4), have been excavated. All are assigned to the Big Sioux phase.

Twenty-eight sites are found in the Little Sioux locality along the Little Sioux River and three tributaries: Mill Creek, Brooke Creek, and Waterman Creek in Cherokee, Buena Vista, and O'Brien counties. Six of these Little Sioux phase villages—Brewster (13CK15), Chan-ya-ta, Phipps (13CK21), Lange (13OB7), Double Ditch (13OB8), and Wittrock (13OB4)—have been excavated. Most of the Little Sioux phase sites occur in clusters of two to eight, with each site situated within 6 km of the other. Three of the five clusters contain at least one site that was fortified (Fishel 1995a:69). The Crim site (13ET403) in Emmet County was test excavated, but its identity as a Mill Creek settlement remains questionable (Anderson 1977).

The Big and Little Sioux phases belong to the Initial variant (formerly horizon) of the Middle Missouri tradition of the Plains Village pattern (Appendix 8.1). Mill Creek sites are linked to other members of the Initial variant by a constel-

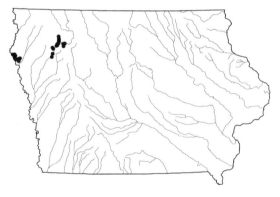

**8.2.** Recorded Mill Creek sites in Iowa. Data compiled from site records. Office of the State Archaeologist, University of Iowa. Courtesy of Timothy S. Weitzel and Stephen C. Lensink.

lation of traits relating to settlement, economy, and technology. Closely allied sites are those of the Lower James phase in southeastern South Dakota (Alex 1981a). The Lower James phase sites most likely represent contemporary settlements of related populations, although it is possible that some may be descendant communities of Mill Creek people who moved west and north.

Many researchers believe that Initial Middle Missouri sites are the ancestral communities of Mandan and some Hidatsa peoples. Physical anthropological study of a small number of human remains from the Broken Kettle site shows a possible affiliation with ancestral Arikara people (Owsley et al. 1981). However, these remains could represent trophy skulls, possibly of Central Plains origin, that were brought back to Mill Creek settlements following incidences of warfare (Bozell and Ludwickson 1994:147–148).

Calibrated radiocarbon dates and ceramic cross-dating suggest an A.D. 1100–1250 time span for the entire Mill Creek occupation of the Big and Little Sioux localities (Lensink 1992, 1997, 1998a). The earlier sites show strong Middle Mississippian influences in the way of ceramics, trade items, and high incidences of tri-notched projectile points (Billeck 1993:199–200). Interaction between Mill Creek and Nebraska phase people in the Glenwood area, while apparently infrequent, also appears to have been early (Billeck 1993:124, 270–277). A proposed division of the Little Sioux phase into early and late subphases has not been supported by recent research.

## Settlement Pattern

Mill Creek people situated all but one of their villages on river or creek terraces, although they avoided broad, flat, treeless valleys, such as the Floyd. No sites are recorded in the upper portion of the Little Sioux in the Iowa Great Lakes region or south of Correctionville in the Little Sioux valley (Tiffany 1982b:11–12). The most important factors affecting the location of Mill Creek sites appear to have been the availability of water, tillable soil, large game, and timber (Tiffany 1982b:11). Western Iowa was covered by tallgrass prairie, with timber growth largely confined to stream valleys. Mill Creek villages contained substantial timber houses that frequently needed repair or rebuilding, requiring abundant supplies of wood. In addition, the presence of wooden palisades, drying racks, and outbuildings and the use of timber for fuel would have placed a premium

on locations with plentiful tree growth. Nineteenth-century GLO surveys reveal a correlation between the distribution of many former Mill Creek villages and areas that were once timbered (Bryson and Baerreis 1968:17).

### Houses

Mill Creek sites are typically compact, nucleated villages that cover less than .4 ha (about an acre) (Fishel 1995a). Apparently these were year-round settlements composed of substantial semisubterranean wattle and daub houses with timber superstructures and extended entryways. Investigations at Chan-ya-ta in Buena Vista County (Tiffany 1975), the scene of the first Iowa Archeological Society field school (Anderson 1974), produced evidence of house walls of thatching tied over a wattle frame daubed with mud. Thatch also appears to have been used to cover the roof timbers (Tiffany 1982b). While a rectangular house pattern typifies most sites, square or even diamond-shaped houses were uncovered at Chan-ya-ta and Wittrock. The post mold pattern of Mill Creek structures suggests houses were fairly large and composed of walls held up by vertical timber posts set in individual post holes. The Kimball site produced house dimensions of 6 by 9 m or more. Smaller houses at some sites may indicate shorter periods of occupation or residence by nuclear rather than extended families.

At some settlements, including Chan-ya-ta, Kimball, Wittrock, and Double Ditch, evidence of considerable community planning exists (fig. 8.3). Houses may have been situated in rows, possibly arranged in streetlike fashion (Orr 1963). At the Double Ditch site, the northernmost recorded village, the double parallel fortification ditches surrounding the site and the houses themselves were apparently planned and constructed prior to the time people moved into the village. Among matrilineal Mandan people, the household was held together by related females, and the lodge belonged to their clan (see Appendix 8.2). When a village was first built,

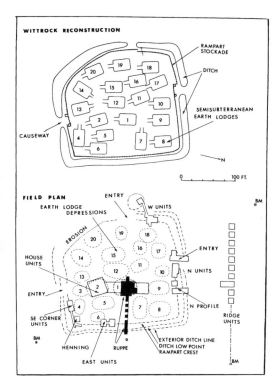

**8.3.** Suggested village layout at the Wittrock site, O'Brien County. Prepared by Marshall McKusick. Map archives, Office of the State Archaeologist, University of Iowa.

each household selected a site for its lodge, corn scaffolds, and caches. These lodge sites were held permanently within the female line. If villages were abandoned for extended periods and then reoccupied, the female descendants of the original builders were entitled to their former lodge sites (Bowers 1950:26).

### Defense

Fortifications that include single or double rows of ditches surrounding all or a portion of the village and an interior palisade occur at some Mill Creek sites (fig. 8.4). Fortification ditches have been recorded at Wittrock, Bultman (13BV2), Double Ditch, Chan-ya-ta, Lange, and possibly Phipps (see plate 1). Plowing and other kinds of disturbance over the past century probably obliterated evidence of fortifications at some sites.

Ditches may have functioned like dry moats, the depth and width of the ditch deterring unwanted intruders. The palisade at the Wittrock site on Waterman Creek consisted of a wooden wall of posts set in individual holes. Erecting the palisade just behind the ditch effectively increased the height of the protecting wall as much as a meter or more. The post molds in the south wall at Wittrock averaged 33 cm in diameter and were spaced 65–80 cm apart. This wide distance between individual post molds suggests that some kind of walling, perhaps intertwined branches or hides, filled the space between the posts.

The defensive features at Double Ditch include two 4 m wide parallel ditches. The site is set back several meters from the terrace edge to the west, a position requiring potential attackers to scale the terrace prior to launching an assault (fig. 8.5). However, rising above the site in the opposite direction is a higher terrace that must have provided a clear view over the top of the palisade and into the village for any hostile party approaching from the east. Perhaps this defensive weakness was quickly realized, as the paucity of archaeological remains at Double Ditch suggests a very brief occupation.

Presumably the defensive system at Mill Creek sites was designed to protect the village and its nearby gardens from attack, although direct evidence of violent encounters is almost nonexistent. Four skulls from the Broken Kettle village suggest the possibility of trophy head-taking. One of the skulls had two holes drilled in the frontal area, possibly for suspension (Bozell and Ludwickson 1994; Owsley et al. 1981).

The reasons for Mill Creek fortifications are unknown. The Missouri River seems to have marked a territorial boundary between Mill Creek and Central Plains tradition peoples. Contemporary Nebraska phase sites occur just south of the Big and Little Sioux locations, while those of the St. Helena phase exist to the west across the Missouri River in Nebraska. Mill Creek sites are not recorded on the Nebraska side, although items of Mill Creek origin or copies of Mill Creek

**8.4.** A double set of fortification ditches and interior
house depressions are visible in this aerial photo of
the Mill Creek Double Ditch site in O'Brien County.
Photo by Mary Helgevold. Photo archives, Office of the State
Archaeologist, University of Iowa.

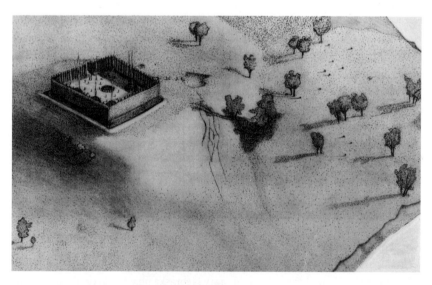

**8.5.** Artist's rendition of the Double Ditch site,
O'Brien County. Illustration by David M. Crawford.

ceramics occur in St. Helena sites (Blakeslee 1988:6). One idea, as yet untested, is that Nebraska phase people threatened to disrupt the waning trade between Mill Creek and Mississippian communities (Bozell and Ludwickson 1994).

Oneota succeeds the Mill Creek occupation in northwest Iowa. None of the late Nebraska phase sites in Iowa, nor the Oneota components, contain evidence of "friendly" interaction with Mill Creek in the form of trade pottery or other items of exchange. Such contact apparently did occur between late Nebraska phase people and Oneota groups. Mill Creek communities could have been fortified against Central Plains tradition people, against Oneota groups who were beginning to encroach into Mill Creek territory, or even against one another. Perhaps hostilities occurred between the Little and Big Sioux phase villages themselves. There is also the possibility that more nomadic groups, perhaps from southwestern Minnesota or the eastern Dakotas, raided the Mill Creek area.

Excavation of large Mill Creek midden mounds demonstrates the superposition of house floors, one atop the other. This evidence and radiocarbon data led earlier archaeologists to hypothesize that Mill Creek sites were occupied over very long periods of time, 500 years or more. Careful analysis of the radiocarbon dates has shortened the chronology, making it improbable that villages lasted for hundreds of years (Lensink 1997, 1998a). Hidatsa and Omaha peoples maintained similar houses for 10 to 20 years before they were abandoned. If villages had been rebuilt at the same location over extended periods, a community likely would have overtaxed local resources, particularly timber and game and perhaps arable soil as well. Sedentary tribes such as the Mandan and Arikara describe the abandonment of Missouri River villages once local resources, especially timber, became depleted. Pierre Antoine Tabeau wrote in the early nineteenth century that the Arikara "cultivate only new lands being forced to change their habitation

often for want of wood which they exhaust in five or six years" (Abel 1939:69). The changing course of the river also could destroy or cut off floodplain gardens. To avoid walking great distances to new gardens, the Mandan would relocate the village itself (Bowers 1950).

## Mill Creek "Tells"

How might the deep midden mounds at sites such as Brewster, Phipps, and Broken Kettle be explained if not by the gradual accumulation of village debris over long periods of occupation? The presence of introduced fill at sites such as Phipps, as a means to deliberately raise the level of the village, has already been mentioned. It is also possible that some sites were abandoned and then reoccupied, giving local resources time to rebound. At Phipps, stratigraphic evidence and ceramic seriation suggest two separate periods of occupation. In addition, the nature of house construction possibly contributed to the depth of the midden deposits. Banking or berming of exterior house walls with earth as a structural support may have produced substantial deposition (R. Alex 1973; Baerreis and Alex 1974). Digging of pits, rebuilding of houses, and shifting midden areas also may have added to the deposits; if so, two or three short occupations at a site could account for the production of thick midden mounds. Probably a combination of these factors explains the accumulated deposits at some Mill Creek sites (Anderson 1985b, 1986; Fishel 1996).

In addition to permanent villages, Mill Creek sites include cemeteries, gardens, and possibly fish traps or weirs. The burial practices of Mill Creek people, like those of Great Oasis, probably involved a number of customs, such as blufftop ossuaries, mounds, and primary interments within villages. The discovery of isolated skeletal remains in village middens and cache pits also suggests the dismantling and relocation of bodies from scaffolds (Banks and Lilly 1965; Tiffany 1991a:319).

At the Siouxland Sand and Gravel site on a loess bluff overlooking the Big Sioux River, more than 100 limestone slab–covered extended burials were uncovered in one portion of the cemetery (Lillie and Schermer 1990). Marine shell recovered with the burials included a portion of a Long-nosed god mask made of whelk (*Busycon* sp.) (fig. 8.6), dozens of disc and barrel beads of the same material, 45 *Conus* sp. shells, and 36 freshwater *Anculosa* sp. shell beads. Mill Creek pottery and other items, including the shell mask, a portion of an imported engraved vessel similar to a pottery type from the Caddoan area of Texas called Holly Fine Engraved (Anderson and Tiffany 1987; Ekland-Olson 1981; Newell and Krieger 1949) (fig. 8.7), and a local copy of the Mississippian Ramey Incised pottery indicate a Mill Creek affiliation (Anderson 1975c; Anderson et al. 1979). The engraved vessel has very thin walls and very fine temper, probably of powdered shell. This suggests its origin was actually the Cahokia area, where similar pottery referred to as Fine-Line Incised is associated with the Lohmann phase (Holley 1989). The similarity between the Fine-Line Incised pottery and the Holly Fine Engraved type reflects contact between the Mississippian and Caddoan worlds and the sharing of ceramic styles.

### Ridged Field Farming

Mill Creek people were highly successful farmers whose economy relied upon intensive maize horticulture. Large cache pits, the root cellars of prehistoric times, dot the living surface of Mill Creek villages, both on the interior and exterior of lodges. These straight-sided, basin-shaped, and bell-shaped features, sometimes as much as 1–2 m deep, were designed to store food surplus, both plants and meat, dried after harvesting (see fig. 7.6). Analysis of cache pit contents has identified a variety of domesticated plants, including maize and common beans (Wegner 1979), as well as sunflower, gourd/squash, goosefoot, little barley, knotweed, maygrass, and sumpweed or marshelder (Jones 1993). Corn, in the form of both kernels and cob fragments (cupules), and goosefoot dominate the crop assem

blage at sites where paleobotanical analysis has been undertaken. Goosefoot, harvested in the fall, was valued for its starchy seeds, although today it is collected primarily as a green (Asch 1992:47). In contrast, sumpweed produces oily seeds which in some archaeological contexts are found together with other plants like squash and sunflower, suggesting that some sort of prehistoric succotash may have been concocted (Asch 1992). Beans, probably a late arrival in North America, first occur in Iowa at Mill Creek and Glenwood sites.

Some Mill Creek gardens probably were situated in fields along creeks and rivers where the soil could be easily worked with hand tools and was replenished periodically by flooding. Prior to European settlement, Native American horticulturists farmed the loose, rich bottomland using wooden digging sticks, bone hoes made from the scapula or skull of bison (fig. 8.8), scapula and deer mandible sickles, and antler rakes. In addition to floodplain gardening, Mill Creek farmers possibly established gardens on other landforms and enhanced crop productivity with a number of specialized agricultural techniques. At the Litka site (13OB31) in O'Brien County, a small field (ca. 1 ha) of east-west trending earthen ridges spaced 1.5 to 2.0 m apart occupies an upland bench above Waterman Creek and is directly north of the Lange village site (see plate 2). These features were part of a ridged field or raised bed system, probably associated with the Mill Creek occupation nearby. Ridged fields also may exist on a terrace near the Wittrock site farther downstream (Lensink 1992; Lensink and Gartner 1994) and are known from at least two other locations in eastern Iowa (Billeck 1986d, 1987; Keyes 1927a, 1927b, 1941a, 1951) (fig. 8.9). Although destroyed by modern plowing, ridged fields may once have been a regular part of Mill Creek agriculture.

Ridges within a raised-bed field may have formed the supportive base for plants, particularly corn. In addition to providing a mounded base for the stalks, the ridges may have enhanced

**8.6.** Long-nosed god mask made from marine whelk shell: (A) front view; (B) side view. From Anderson 1975b.

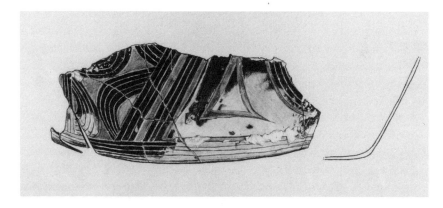

**8.7.** Thin, engraved vessel from the Siouxland Sand and Gravel site, Woodbury County, appears to be an import with ties to both the Mississippian and Caddoan areas. Illustration by David M. Crawford. From Anderson and Tiffany 1987.

drainage or offered frost protection. The shallow ditches between the ridges may have helped to retain moisture and/or sheltered beds of squash and pumpkins shaded by the corn stalks planted in the adjacent ridges. Ridged field sites are common in Wisconsin and Michigan, where several have been associated with Late Woodland or Oneota sites (Gallagher et al. 1985; Riley et al. 1981).

A high phosphate content in the soil at the Litka ridged field suggests the addition of ash, perhaps to increase soil fertility. On the floodplain just below the Double Ditch site and immediately to the northeast of Litka across Waterman Creek, two large fields of small, enigmatic

earthen mounds occur. These mounds, each no wider than .5–1 m and about .25 m high, may represent the former corn hills of Double Ditch farmers (see fig. 8.4). Such hills served as supports for clusters of corn plants, though not within a raised-bed system.

Mill Creek people utilized a variety of wild plants, including bulrush, plum, sumac, ground cherries, various berries, bearberry, and nuts such as black walnut and hazelnut (Wegner 1979). The fruits, flowers, leaves, vines, roots, bark, stems, pods, seeds, bulbs, and shoots of both domesticated and wild plants had dietary, medicinal, and ceremonial value to native peoples when ingested, applied as poultices or

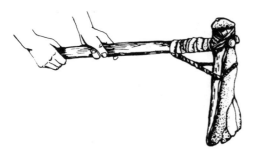

**8.8.** The type of scapula hoe used by Mill Creek peoples. Illustration by Mary M. Slattery. From L. Alex 1980.

**8.9.** A ridged field or raised garden beds at 13BH1 in Black Hawk County. Original photo by Karl Von Lackum, 1927, retouched to emphasize the garden beds. Photo archives, Office of the State Archaeologist, University of Iowa. From Billeck 1986d.

powders, and smoked. Many of these plants provided raw materials for containers, basketry, matting, pit lining, brushes, brooms, dyes, and paints. Plants also may have functioned in ways otherwise invisible to the eye of the archaeologist. Goldenrod, for example, was part of the floral calendar for the Omaha. Its bloom reminded far-ranging bison hunters to return to the village for the corn harvest (Gilmore 1977). Seeds of goldenrod are one of many wildflower types that occur in the botanical assemblages at Mill Creek sites.

### Bison Hunters

Although horticulture probably provided the mainstay of the Mill Creek diet, the Plains village economy relied heavily on hunting. While the maintenance of gardens required fairly permanent residence in the village, the communal nature of bison hunting likely prompted villagers to leave their settlements on occasion. Archaeologists have never identified a Mill Creek kill site, but the nature of the butchered bone found in some villages suggests that occasionally hunts took place at distant locations. Many big game hunters utilized certain parts of the animal right away or left them at the kill site because they were less desirable or more difficult to transport home. The pelvis and skull, for instance, are commonly absent or rare at village sites, suggesting that some hunts were conducted far from the village (Jans-Langel and Fishel 1995).

Bison, deer, and elk were the most important large game hunted by Mill Creek people in terms of usable amounts of meat, although the primacy of either deer or bison varies from site to site and within sites over time (Dallman 1983; Lensink 1993a). In general there appears to be an increase in bison utilization up to A.D. 1200 (Lensink 1993a, 1998b). These patterns, once thought to reflect climate change, may be related to the external contacts of Mill Creek people and to the role that bison products played in the trade with Mississippian societies to the east (Lensink and Finney 1994; Tiffany 1987, 1991a).

While large ungulates dominate the faunal record, smaller mammals including the plains pocket gopher, beaver, dog, and various rodents were probably regular supplements to the Mill Creek diet. The large number of gopher bones at sites such as Brewster and the cut marks detected on the bones suggest that these small animals were butchered and cooked, possibly like later Hidatsa people did by roasting them whole over spits (R. Alex cited in Dallman 1983; Wilson 1978b). Gophers can be serious pests in gardens and may have been harvested in an attempt to reduce their impact on crops as well as to supplement the diet (Rhodes and Semken 1986:116–117). Fish, turtle, and birds provided additional food resources (Jans-Langel and Fishel 1995).

Mill Creek people also utilized the now-extinct passenger pigeon and the redhorse sucker, no longer native to northwestern Iowa. Two possible fish weirs, or traps, are recorded on Waterman Creek, one near the Wittrock village and the other just below the Lange site. Another on Mill Creek near the Brewster site was documented years ago by Ellison Orr. Historically, such traps consisted of large stone boulders aligned across the creek in a U- or V-shaped formation pointing downstream (see plate 14). The rocks served as the base for a brush and pole trap used to capture species such as catfish. Although the age of the Waterman and Mill creek alignments is unknown, their proximity to Mill Creek villages and the occurrence of numerous catfish bones in nearby sites suggest a possible affiliation.

In addition to food, by-products of hunting included a wide variety of bone tools (fig. 8.10). Fleshers, hide grainers, shaft straighteners, hoes, knives, sickles, flaking tools, awls, beamers, fishhooks, and quill flatteners were manufactured from the bone of bison, elk, and deer. Fine bone needles and pointed awls of bison or bird bone or the dorsal spine of the drum fish allowed Mill Creek people to sew hides and work basket fibers. *Anculosa* and marine conch shell beads and pendants, carved bone pins and beads, and a variety of teeth including those of bear, dog, and beaver likely adorned the clothing, covers, and containers fashioned by Mill Creek women (see plate 15). Although no direct evidence exists, porcupine quillwork possibly began as an art form during Mill Creek times.

### A Rich Material Culture

Many archaeologists believe that the bone, hides, skins, and feathers procured by Mill Creek hunters were incorporated into ceremonial clothing, headdresses, containers and other items important in trade. The case of birds is particularly interesting. We know from ethnographic accounts of historic Plains groups, such as the Osage, Omaha, and Arikara, that the skins of birds filled with sacred objects were part of ceremonial bundles or medicine bags. Stuffed bird skins served as personal fetishes believed to bring good luck to their owners and became part of larger group ceremonies to cure the sick or bring success to hunting or war ventures. In order to give some form to the bundle, the skull and bones of the wing and feet would be left attached to the skin. Although the use of such bird bundles in prehistoric times is unknown, the occurrence of large numbers of bird bones from the feet, wings, and skull at Mill Creek sites strongly suggests their existence.

At both the Phipps and Brewster sites the wings and legs of raptorial birds are particularly abundant (Fishel 1997; Jans-Langel and Fishel

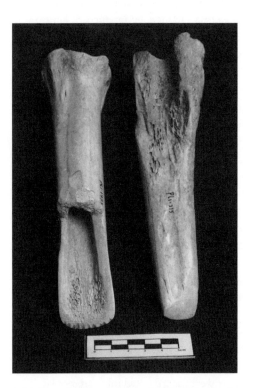

**8.10.** Bone flesher, probably a hide-working tool, from a Mill Creek site in Plymouth County. Mill Creek peoples were bone toolmakers par excellence. On display, Iowa Hall, University of Iowa. Photo archives, Office of the State Archaeologist, University of Iowa.

1995:38–39). Hawks, falcons, and eagles were important to the ceremonial and symbolic systems of midwestern societies aboriginally, and their feathers and other body parts were used as bags, fans, and headdresses and for decoration. Hunters went to great and sometimes precarious lengths to capture and kill these raptors. The Hidatsa, for instance, excavated eagle trapping–pits in which they concealed themselves, luring unsuspecting animals with bits of meat. Once the bird had landed, the hunter reached up through the brush covering the trap and grabbed its legs, wrestling it into the pit where it was captured. The frequent occurrence of raptor bones at sites such as Brewster and Phipps may relate to similar customs and possibly to trade in feathers or bird-skin bags (Fishel 1997).

Mill Creek potters manufactured a wide variety of characteristic grit-tempered vessels, including wide-mouthed subglobular jars (ollas), bowls, "seed jars," hooded water bottles, and miniatures (Ives 1962). These ceramics have been classified into four major wares: Sanford (low rim), Chamberlain (high rim), Foreman (S-shaped rim), and Mill Creek (fig. 8.11). Except for Mill Creek ware, each ware is distinguished primarily on the basis of a flaring or S-shaped rim form, with specific types defined largely by exterior lip and rim decoration. Mill Creek ware consists of four distinct vessel types believed to have been inspired by Middle Mississippian forms. Sanford, Chamberlain, and possibly Foreman ware types have antecedents in earlier Great Oasis types.

Mill Creek ceramic decoration typically includes incised geometric patterns such as triangles, rectangles, and diamonds or horizontal bands of trailing applied to the shoulders. Other motifs include the running deer (flag and dot), turkey track, and weeping eye. Cross-hatching, tool impressions, and trailing also occur on the rims of some types (fig. 8.12). Carinated shoulders characteristic of some vessels, as well as curvilinear designs, are probably Mississippian imitations. Some of the pots have loop handles

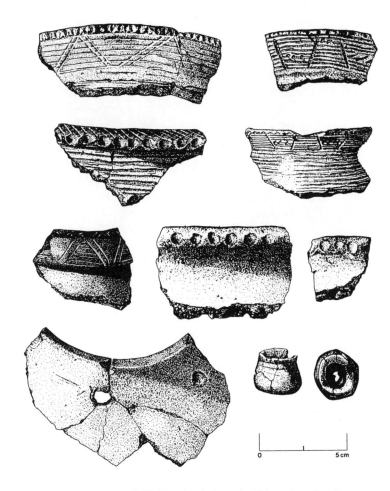

**8.11.** Rim sherds from the Phipps site, Cherokee County. From top row to bottom row: Chamberlain Incised; Mitchell Modified Lip and Chamberlain Incised; Foreman Incised Triangle and Kimball Modified Lip; Mill Creek seed jar and miniature. From Fishel 1995a; Tiffany and Adams 1998.

or effigy handles representing small mammals and birds (see plate 16).

Higher percentages of certain pottery styles at particular villages may indicate a matrilocal residence pattern. The effigy handles on some Mill Creek vessels could symbolize the totem animal of the potter's lineage or clan. Within the Sanford ware category, the larger Kimball type vessels may represent the Revere ware and Tupperware of Mill Creek society designed for cooking

and storage, while the more highly decorated and smaller Mitchell-type pots might have been reserved for serving (Anderson 1981a; Tiffany 1982b).

## Northwest Iowa: Gateway to the Plains?

Many artifacts found at Mill Creek sites reflect the wide-ranging contacts these northwest Iowa communities had with other peoples. Contact undoubtedly occurred with other Initial variant

**8.12.** Rim sherds from sites in Plymouth County illustrate the diversity of rim form and decoration found in Mill Creek ceramics. Upper row, center: running deer; middle row, center: weeping eye; lower left corner: diamond. Photo by Charles R. Keyes. Courtesy of the State Historical Society of Iowa, Iowa City.

members to the west and north, late Late Woodland societies to the east, and Middle Mississippian communities to the east and south. Much of this interaction undoubtedly transpired in the context of trade. The similarities between Mill Creek and Lower James phase sites in southeastern South Dakota suggest that these communities were closely related and frequently in contact. Resources from the Plains, including bison and certain lithics, are common at Mill Creek sites. There is no local bedrock source for the stone tools made by Mill Creek people. Many tools were fashioned from materials extracted from local glacial till or stream and river gravels. However, the presence of large pieces of Knife River flint and Bijou Hills silicified sediment point to trade or to direct procurement from locations in North and South Dakota.

Certain raw materials and specific artifact types also suggest a strong eastern exchange network. Burlington and other cherts and chalcedonies derive from sources in central and southeastern Iowa. Mill Creek chert from southern Illinois, which circulated within the Mississippian world most commonly in the form of finished hoes, has been identified at the Phipps site (Finney 1995:60). Tri-notched projectile points similar to Cahokia points (see fig. 6.6) occur alongside the more typical Plains side-notched forms. Artifacts such as earspools (pulley-shaped stone or bone earrings), chunkey stones (fig. 8.13), elbow-shaped pipes, shell pendants, scalloped-edge shell gorgets, carved bone pins, shell-tempered ceramics, *Anculosa* shell beads, and Gulf or Atlantic Coast marine shell are common at Mill Creek sites and at Middle Mississippian sites, including the metropolis of Cahokia itself. Iconography displayed in the Long-nosed god masks, now known from two Mill Creek contexts (Anderson 1975b, 1975c), and design motifs such as the scroll or the weeping eye imply a shared ideology with Mississippian societies.

Ceramics offer the most convincing evidence in favor of interaction. Mill Creek pottery or local imitations occur in early Nebraska phase sites in the Glenwood locality in southwest Iowa (Billeck 1993:124–125; Green ed. 1992; Ives 1955b) and in sites of the Itskari and St. Helena phases of northern Nebraska (Blakeslee 1988:6). Late Late Woodland sites in Allamakee County, including Hartley Fort, Waterville Rockshelter (13AM124), and Sixteen Rockshelter (13AM122) (Logan 1976; Orr 1963; Tiffany 1983, 1991a); sites of the Eveland phase of the Spoon River culture in the central Illinois River valley (Conrad 1991; Harn 1991; Tiffany 1991a); and the Diamond Bluff site in western Wisconsin contain Mill Creek ceramic imports. Hartley Fort pottery also occurs at Chan-ya-ta and at the Fred Edwards site in Wisconsin (Finney and Stoltman 1991:243; Stoltman 1991; Tiffany 1991a:320). The local Hartley Fort ware itself shows such strong influence from Mill Creek rim forms that Mill Creek women may actually have lived at this northeast Iowa location (Benn 1995:115). Imported Mississippian Powell Plain and Ramey Incised vessels (fig. 8.14), red-slipped seed jars, and polished bowls with finely ground shell temper occur at Mill Creek sites and suggest direct interaction with the American Bottom. Locally made copies of these Middle Mississippian pottery types constitute up to 20 percent of some Mill Creek ceramic assemblages. Thin-section analysis of the paste and temper of Mill Creek sherds helps to distinguish between imported vessels and locally made copies (Stoltman 1989).

## Postcards from the Edge?

At one time researchers proposed that Mill Creek communities represented the migration of Middle Mississippian people to northwest Iowa from the Mississippi valley through sites such as Aztalan in Wisconsin and Cambria in Minnesota. Archaeologically, this is referred to as site unit intrusion and is believed to reflect the actual movement of an outside group into a new area.

**8.13.** Stone discoidals sometimes called chunkey stones may have been used in a game by Mill Creek and other Late Prehistoric peoples. Photo archives, Office of the State Archaeologist, University of Iowa.

**8.14.** Ramey Incised Vessel, a Mississippian type, from the Mill Creek Chan-ya-ta site, Buena Vista County. Photo archives, Office of the State Archaeologist, University of Iowa. From Tiffany 1982b.

However, radiocarbon and ceramic cross-dating now demonstrate that some Mill Creek sites are as early as their supposed prototypes in the Mississippi valley and probably developed from local cultures like Great Oasis. Therefore, the Mississippian items found in Mill Creek sites likely resulted from direct contact and trade, a situation referred to as trait unit intrusion. Long-distance travel or down-the-line exchange along major rivers such as the Missouri, Mississippi, and the Des Moines or via overland trade routes across northern Iowa or southern Minnesota may explain the introduction of foreign ideas or items to the Mill Creek area.

While some archaeologists believe that actual Mississippian traders roamed throughout the upper Midwest, this remains an unconfirmed hypothesis (Porter 1969). It is also unlikely that Mill Creek people had the specialized traders or artisans characteristic of more centralized societies. Thus the nature of Mill Creek–Mississippian interaction remains an intriguing though largely unresolved issue. Some Mill Creek people, possibly important men and their relatives, may

have traveled to communities like Cahokia, where they participated in a form of ritual exchange designed to establish friendly relations and an atmosphere of mutual trust with their Mississippian hosts prior to more substantive trade (Tiffany 1991a). This might have included a kind of ceremonial adoption designed to create a fictive kinship between trading partners who otherwise were unrelated. Fictive kinship, a worldwide custom, serves as a way for people from different societies to develop alliance networks. On the North American Plains and in the Midwest historically, ceremonial adoption was associated with the well-known calumet, or "peace pipe," ceremony (Blakeslee 1975; Hall 1983).

The initial exchange may have involved the transfer of prestigious gifts to the elite at Cahokia, for example, bird-wing fans, hawk- and eagle-skin medicine bags, feathered capes and headdresses, quilled and beaded bison robes, and pottery or other containers filled with desirable plants, perhaps sage or sweet grass. In exchange, Mississippian peoples might have offered their

Mill Creek trading partners the rights to perform certain rituals, songs, and dances as well as ceremonial paraphernalia, iconography, and special artifacts (Tiffany 1991a:328). Tangible evidence of these items from Mill Creek sites include earspools, marine shell, and chunkey stones or door-knob discoidals (Baerreis 1968:187; Orr 1963) possibly used in a game similar to chunkey, or "chungke," recorded historically among southeastern peoples such as the Natchez and Choctaw (Tabeau 1775; Fugle 1962:6; Tiffany 1978b) (see Appendix 8.3). Sacred water or substances having hallucinogenic, medicinal, or emetic properties or even corn or tobacco may also have been transported in certain highly polished and decorated Mississippian ceramic vessels. Long-nosed god and short-nosed god maskettes manufactured from marine whelk shell or in some instances from copper are found in Mississippian and contemporary sites, including Mill Creek (Anderson 1975b, 1975c; Anderson et al. 1979). Their discovery alongside human burials and their depiction on artifacts and in pictographs suggest that they were worn as ear ornaments. The Pinochio-like figure may represent a character in an ancient Siouan myth involving a hero known as Red Horn or He-Who-Wears-Human-Heads-As-Earrings (Salzer 1990).

Accompanying the feasting and gift exchange, more practical items such as bison scapula hoes, bone bracelets, dressed bison robes, bird feathers, and jerked meat might have been offered by Mill Creek traders for shell-tempered ceramics, marine shell beads, and possibly small amounts of copper. Salt may also have been a commodity exchanged by Mississippian peoples. It is estimated that during the Stirling phase, 1,500 Mississippian vessels and 50,000 marine shell items moved northwestward into Mill Creek sites (Tiffany 1991a:334–336).

Calculations based on the quantity of bison bone found at Mill Creek and other Initial variant sites indicate that at times these communities were producing surpluses in meat and hides (Tiffany 1991a). In addition, the large number of

meat-processing and hide-dressing tools—knives, scrapers, bone fleshers, awls, and quill flatteners—strongly implies the preparation of jerked meat and dressed hides at Initial variant sites. In contrast, the number of projectile points and scrapers found at Stirling phase Mississippian sites in the American Bottom is quite low. It may be that Cahokia residents desired imported meat and hides. In addition, evidence for the importance of hawks and eagles at sites such as Phipps and Brewster and, inferentially, their by-products in the way of feathers, skins, fans, and headdresses makes a strong case for the kind of commodities Initial variant communities were offering in trade (Alex 1971; Alex 1993; Fishel 1997; Tiffany 1991a).

How items were transferred over distances of 800 km is suggested by ethnographic analogy. While pack dogs could have carried loads overland, river travel using canoes or large hide-covered frame boats similar to the bullboats of the Mandan and Hidatsa might represent another means of transporting heavy loads of jerked meat (fig. 8.15), hides, and finished artifacts between northwest Iowa and the Mississippi valley. Mill Creek traders could have completed a round-trip journey by canoe to Cahokia in 30 days (Little 1987). The hide boat, though more difficult to navigate, could be built quickly and transported overland, and it could carry large loads. Historically, flotillas of bullboats lashed one to the other carried bundles of hides and dried meat weighing 200–900 kg. The weight of the load actually increased the stability of the boat (Tiffany 1991a:340).

Items from Cahokia and other Mississippian communities likely endowed their Mill Creek owners with considerable honor and prestige and by association raised the status of certain lineages. Mill Creek society was likely both matrilineal and matrilocal. Since many of the postulated items of exchange, such as quilled hides, feathered items, and bone tools, were probably produced by women, the prestige afforded the northwest Iowa communities by their distant

**8.15.** George Catlin's lithograph of the bullboats being used by the Mandan below their village on the Missouri River bluffs. Courtesy of the Putnam Museum of History and Natural Science, Davenport, Iowa.

trading ventures was largely made possible and perhaps to an extent fostered by Mill Creek women. It is possible that on occasion Mississippian peoples returned to northwest Iowa with their Mill Creek visitors or that Mill Creek women stayed in the Mississippi valley. Among some societies, women and children were exchanged as a commodity within the alliance network. Perhaps the ceramic evidence actually reflects the exchange of women or intermarriage between the two societies (Tiffany 1991a).

### Exodus from Iowa

Although Mill Creek people apparently traded peacefully with late Late Woodland and Mississippian societies, their abandonment of northwest Iowa was under way by A.D. 1250. Hostile groups, perhaps Oneota, may have fostered this exodus. The earliest Oneota sites in northwest Iowa are in the Dixon-Correctionville area about 40 km downstream from the Mill Creek villages. These sites appear to postdate Mill Creek, but perhaps they represent the eventual occupation of Oneota people following an extended period of hunting and raiding into Mill Creek territory (Lensink 1992:194). Another intriguing though unsubstantiated proposal is that some Mill Creek and other Initial Middle Missouri people were absorbed into the rapidly expanding Oneota world (Gibbon 1995:191).

Past interpretations about the existence and disappearance of Mill Creek society emphasized the role of climate (Bryson and Baerreis 1968; Dallman 1983; Henning ed. 1968, 1969). The climatic model was based on a multidisciplinary study of data such as pollen, soils, gastropods, fauna, and flora, and it was outstanding for its time. Reexamination of some of the earlier data and new studies have questioned the validity of the model and challenged the conclusions of the original research (Clark 1990; Laird, Fritz, Maasch, and Cumming 1996; Laird, Fritz, Grimm, and Mueller 1996; Lensink 1997; Zalucha 1982). The pattern of declining deer and increasing bison at some sites, for instance, once thought to reflect an increase in grasslands and the effect of drought on the Mill Creek exodus, could actually relate to certain cultural practices, particularly trade in bison products. A diminution in woodlands over time may suggest the exhaustion of timber resources as trees were cut down and utilized in village construction. This in turn may have reduced the deer habitat and led to their decline (Lensink 1993a). Thus depletion of local resources, coupled with increasing threats from outside groups, may have had more to do with the Mill Creek abandonment of northwest Iowa than did climatic change.

Later sites of the Middle Missouri tradition in South Dakota may best answer the question, Where did the Mill Creek people go? Sites along the Missouri River belonging to the Extended variant seem to display many of the characteristics found in Mill Creek sites. In addition, lesser known communities in the prairie lakes region of eastern South Dakota (Alex 1981b) and southwestern Minnesota, such as those of the Big Stone phase (Anfinson 1997; Haug 1981a, 1981b), may somehow be related. From such traditions, Siouan-speaking groups such as the Mandan and some of the Hidatsa peoples may have developed. They were living a lifeway not unlike that of earlier Mill Creek people when first contacted by eighteenth-century French explorers and traders at their compact earthlodge villages on the Missouri River. Their long experience with the interband trade system placed them in a particularly favorable position to serve as brokers between increasing numbers of Euroamericans and more nomadic groups on the Plains.

## APPENDIX 8.1.
### Middle Missouri Tradition

In northwest Iowa and along the Missouri River and its tributaries in South and North Dakota, a series of archaeological cultures occur that represent the remains of compact/nucleated villages of sedentary horticulturists and intense bison hunters. Archaeologists have grouped these cultures into the Middle Missouri tradition. This tradition is further subdivided into sequential variants (formerly called horizons) from early to late: Initial, Extended, and Terminal. One member of the Initial variant of the Middle Missouri tradition is the Mill Creek culture of northwest Iowa. Whether Great Oasis also belongs to this tradition is still debated (Johnson 1996; Tiffany 1983, 1991b). Members of the Middle Missouri tradition share a number of cultural features. As originally defined by Donald J. Lehmer (1954), these include subsistence based about equally on hunting and agriculture; semipermanent villages of rectangular structures usually twice as long as wide, with entrances at one end; villages with houses arranged in rows; occasional fortification ditches; cache pits in and between houses; grit-tempered, paddle-marked pottery with flared or S-shaped rims (cordmarking on vessel bodies predominate in the Initial variant); small, light, multiple-notched projectile points; plate chalcedony knives; small, evenly flaked end scrapers; polished celts; grooved mauls; broad, splinter-type awls; quill flatteners; split metapodial fleshers; and scapula knives. Contemporary cultures in Nebraska, Kansas, Missouri, and southwest Iowa belong to the Central Plains tradition. Most archaeologists believe that the people who left the sites of the Middle Missouri tradition were gradually forced up the Missouri River by later Central Plains emigrants. Eventually the two traditions appear to have merged to form the Coalescent tradition. By historic times, participants in the Coalescent tradition on the Northern Plains can be identified as the Mandan, Hidatsa, and Arikara.

## APPENDIX 8.2.
### The Mandan Earthlodge

The Mandan household was the smallest economic unit and was composed of one or more biological families related through the females. There was a tendency for related families to select adjacent quarters, while those intimately connected with the Okipa ceremony selected lodge sites adjacent to the open circle. Among the Mandan, the household was held together by females so long as their lineage was unbroken, and the lodge belonged to the clan of which the females were members. When a village was first built on a new site, each household selected a site for its lodge, corn scaffolds, and caches. These lodge sites within the village were held permanently within the female line, and when returning to rebuild after a temporary abandonment of the village, female descendants of the original builders were entitled to their former sites. When a family died out, the lodge belonged to the clan of the females and could be occupied by another group of the same clan or could be sold to females of a different clan (Bowers 1950:26).

## APPENDIX 8.3.
### Discoidals and the Game of Chunkey

Disc-shaped ground stone artifacts have been interpreted as gaming pieces possibly used in the manner of the chunkey, or "chungke," game of historic southeastern Indians like the Natchez and Choctaw (Tabeau 1775; Fugle 1962:6; Tiffany 1978b). Mill Creek examples have a thin, narrow edge and biconvex face in contrast to Middle Mississippian examples, which have a flat, broad edge and concave face. They are usually termed door-knob discoidals (Baerreis 1968:187; Orr 1963). Oneota discoidals also exist (Harvey 1971). Whether these items were used in a game similar to chunkey is conjectural. If they were, that game may have gone something like this:

> The warriors have another favorite game called chungke, which, with propriety of language, may be called "running hard labor." They have near their state-house a square piece of ground, well cleaned, and fine sand is carefully strewn over it, when requisite, to promote a swifter motion to what they throw along the surface.
>
> Only one or two on a side play at this ancient game. They have a stone about two fingers broad at the edge, and two spans round; each party has a pole of about eight feet long, smooth and tapering at each end, the point flat. They set off abreast one of each other at six yards from the end of the playground; then one of them hurls the stone on its edge, in as direct a line as he can, a considerable distance toward the middle of the other end of the square; when they have run a few yards, each darts his pole anointed with bear's oil, with a proper force, as near as he can guess in proportion to the motion of the stone, that the end may lie close to the stone; when this is the case, the person counts two of the game, and, in proportion to the nearness of the poles to the mark, one is counted, unless by measuring both are found to be at an equal distance from the stone. In this manner, the players will keep running most part of the day, at half speed, under the violent heat of the sun, staking their silver ornaments, their nose, finger, and ear rings; their breast, arm and wrist plates; and even all their wearing apparel, except that which barely covers their middle. (Tabeau 1775:401)

# 9 Late Prehistoric Glenwood

Viewed archeologically, settlement patterns are, like any prehistoric residue, the incomplete and fragmentary oddments of something that was once vital and whole. Nevertheless, settlements are a more direct reflection of social and economic activities than are most other aspects of material culture available to the archeologist. —Willey 1956:1

AT THE TIME that northwestern Iowa was dotted with compact Mill Creek villages, to the south along the dramatic loess bluffs paralleling the Missouri River and opposite the mouth of the Platte the settlements of the Glenwood culture were established (fig. 9.1). Glenwood sites have been classified within the Nebraska phase, one of several phases belonging to the Central Plains Tradition (fig. 9.2; Appendix 9.1).

Nebraska phase sites straddle the Missouri River for approximately 120 km from northeastern Kansas and northwestern Missouri through eastern Nebraska and extreme western Iowa (fig. 9.3). The Glenwood locality in Iowa is one of nine localities occupied by Nebraska phase people and is the only one east of the Missouri River. The first excavations of sites assigned to the Nebraska phase were conducted in Iowa during the late nineteenth century (Blakeslee and Caldwell 1979:4; Dean 1881; Proudfit 1881). Since that time, numerous Glenwood house sites have been excavated by avocational and professional archaeologists, making them some of the most intensively investigated structures in Iowa (see plate 17). In Mills County, avocational archaeologist Paul Rowe (Appendix 9.2) and his colleagues documented dozens of Glenwood sites through surface collecting and occasional excavation. His work revealed the close relationship between sites of the Glenwood Culture and other Nebraska phase sites of the Central Plains tradition (Green et al. 1992:1–4).

Years of research and the high visibility of Nebraska phase settlements have allowed archaeologists to conduct detailed studies of settlement pattern and its relationship to the landscape (Anderson and Zimmerman 1976; Tiffany and Abbott 1982). The history of Glenwood archaeology in fact has largely been about the nature of settlement pattern (Perry 1998:1). This work has posed the question: Do sites of Nebraska phase people in Iowa represent individual homesteads spread along the bluffs like beads on a string or small villages clustered like knots on a net at the mouths of important drainages? Both interpretations have had their supporters.

Because many sites do consist of isolated structures representing single occupations, it has also been possible to model individual site histories and suggest the size and composition of the households that occupied them. Analysis of data related to house construction and study of the distribution of artifacts and interior features give archaeologists clues as to the way a house was constructed and used and indicate why it was ultimately abandoned.

## Settlement Pattern

Approximately 240 Nebraska phase lodges or probable lodges have been recorded within the

**9.1.** Nebraska phase pottery from Mills County, Iowa. Photo by Charles R. Keyes. Courtesy of the State Historical Society of Iowa, Iowa City.

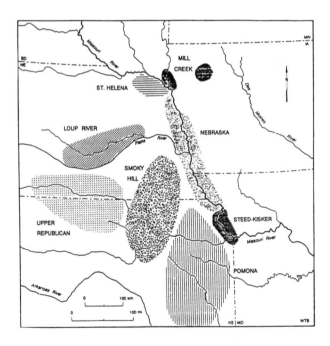

**9.2.** Distribution of regional phases of the Central Plains tradition. From Billeck 1993.

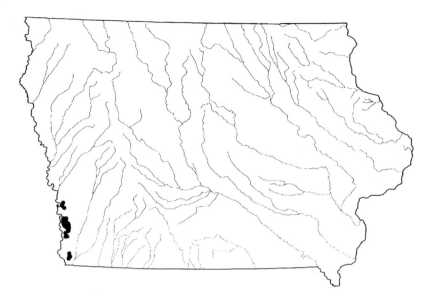

**9.3.** Recorded Nebraska phase sites in Iowa. Data compiled from site records. Office of the State Archaeologist, University of Iowa. Courtesy of Timothy S. Weitzel and Stephen C. Lensink.

Glenwood locality, and many others have been destroyed. Almost all sites occur within 4 km of the Missouri River valley. Sites exist along ridges and bluffs, on sideslopes and footslopes, and along the terraces of the Missouri River and its small tributaries, particularly the Keg and Pony Creek drainages (Billeck 1993:8) (fig. 9.4). In some areas, sites are probably underrepresented due to geomorphological processes. Those occurring in low-lying settings may be buried by alluvial and colluvial sediments (Billeck 1993:128). Although a few sites extend north into Pottawattamie and Harrison counties and south into Fremont County, by far the highest density is in western Mills County.

The concentration of Nebraska phase sites in Mills County is not just a reflection of the visibility of sites there or the more intense investigation of the area. The Glenwood locality in Mills County appears to have been intentionally chosen by Nebraska phase people (Billeck

1993:16). The scattered pattern of Glenwood sites along the bluffs and ridges may reflect a pioneer situation associated with the settlement of a relatively unoccupied area (Anderson and Zimmerman 1976; Zimmerman 1977a, 1977b). Although some remnant Late Woodland groups may have been present, Nebraska phase homesteaders probably were attracted to the region because of the presence of abundant stone, timber, and arable land. The strategic position of the sites immediately adjacent to the mouth of the Platte, one of the gateways to the Plains, must also be considered as a factor attracting settlement (Hedden 1997).

A relatively dispersed settlement pattern of unfortified farmsteads also implies that Glenwood people coexisted peacefully with one another and with adjacent groups. Resources, including nearby cropland, must have been sufficiently well distributed to prevent intergroup hostilities. The wide spacing of lodges across the

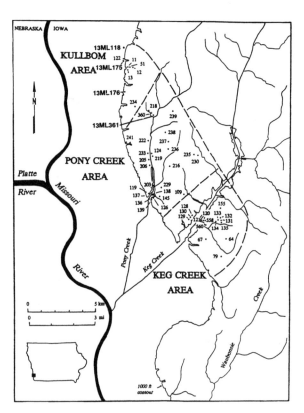

**9.4.** Location of Nebraska phase sites in the Glenwood locality in Iowa. From Billeck 1993.

landscape probably helped reduce competition for arable land and wild food resources.

While archaeologists can surmise some of the reasons why Nebraska phase people were attracted to the locality, others can only be imagined. If the region was selected for aesthetic, spiritual, or historic reasons, we probably will never know what these were. The oral histories of many historic American Indian groups describe particular events—dissension between families, fights over the division of game, personal wrongs committed between individuals, or natural disasters—that led their ancestors to seek out new territories. Unfortunately, the archaeological record rarely provides clues to such events.

At the time of initial settlement, Mills County would have been a mosaic environment of tall-grass prairie and open woodlands with a heavily dissected terrain of loess bluffs, small streams, and the Missouri River trench (Green et al. 1993). Site selection was doubtlessly affected by the availability of important resources, including access to fertile lowlands crucial to swidden farming, a readily available supply of water, and wood for fuel and house construction (Anderson and Zimmerman 1976; Tiffany and Abbott 1982). The bluffs themselves probably comprised one of the more heavily timbered areas along the river (Hotopp 1982). Excavations of house timbers and the identification of the wood used by Nebraska phase people indicate a deliberate selection of hardwoods for building material, especially elm (Billeck 1993; Hotopp 1978a). The position of many houses may have been chosen to take advantage of this favored resource. In addition, the region was plentifully supplied with easily obtainable Pennsylvanian- and Permian-age cherts. Certain Pennsylvanian-age cherts, generically referred to as Nehawka flint, have been recognized as the preferred material for chipped stone tools at Nebraska phase sites (Blakeslee and Caldwell 1979:34). The availability of lithic raw material was a magnet for early settlement by Central Plains peoples, whose technology was based primarily on stone resources (Ludwickson and Bozell 1993:146).

### Settlement Size and Duration

Unlike the small, compact settlements characteristic of Mill Creek communities, most Glenwood sites consist of dispersed, isolated farmsteads or small hamlets of lodges, and none appear to have been fortified. Burial patterns are virtually unknown. Although mounds are recorded in the vicinity of Nebraska phase sites, those whose affiliation is known are Woodland (Orr 1942; Proudfit 1881). The Kullbom site (13ML10), situated in a small valley that opens onto the Missouri River floodplain (Anderson 1961:54), represents the largest Nebraska phase cluster reported in Iowa. As many as 15 lodges, spaced 60 to 100 m apart, may once have existed at this location. While it is

**Plate 1.** Aerial photograph of the rectangular fortifications surrounding the Mill Creek Wittrock site, O'Brien County. Photo archives, Office of the State Archaeologist, University of Iowa.

**Plate 2.** Ridged agricultural fields (center) at the
Litka site, O'Brien County. Courtesy of Mary Helgevold.
Photo archives, Office of the State Archaeologist, University
of Iowa.

**Plate 3.** Excavation layout at the Sid's site, Keokuk County. Courtesy of David W. Benn. From Benn 1984a.

**Plate 4.** Water flotation at the multicomponent Frerichs site (13DK12), near Lake Okoboji, Dickinson County. Photo archives, Office of the State Archaeologist, University of Iowa.

**Plate 5.** Middle Woodland effigy pipe from Toolesboro Mounds, Louisa County, believed to be made of Elkhorn Creek pipestone from Illinois. Item in the Putnam Museum of History and Natural Science, Davenport, Iowa. Photo archives, Office of the State Archaeologist, University of Iowa.

**Plate 6.** Copper artifacts from Iowa sites. The rattail point (center) and spud (left) are from Allamakee County. On display, Iowa Hall, University of Iowa. Photo archives, Office of the State Archaeologist, University of Iowa.

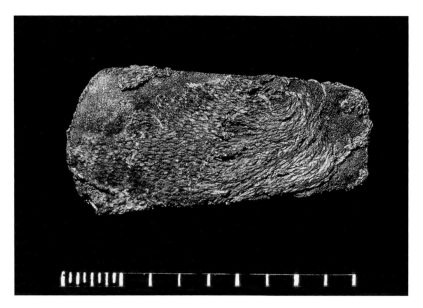

**Plate 7.** Copper ax with woven wrapping from a Hopewell mound at Toolesboro Mounds, Louisa County. Item in the Putnam Museum of History and Natural Science, Davenport, Iowa. Photo archives, Office of the State Archaeologist, University of Iowa.

**Plate 8.** Hopewell zoned vessel from the Cook Farm Mounds, Scott County. Item in the Putnam Museum of History and Natural Science, Davenport, Iowa. Photo archives, Office of the State Archaeologist, University of Iowa.

**Plate 9.** Middle Woodland Fish Farm Mounds State
Preserve, Allamakee County, a 300 ha preserve with
about 30 extant mounds. Photo by Jean Cutler Prior.
From *Iowa Geology* 1993.

Plate 10. Lane Farm Cord Impressed vessel from a Delaware County site (13DW43) mixes rocker stamping on the body with twisted cord or fabric impressions on the rim. Photo archives, Office of the State Archaeologist, University of Iowa.

Plate 11. "Downtown" Cahokia ca. A.D. 1100. From a painting by Lloyd K. Townsend. Courtesy of the Cahokia Mounds State Historic Site.

**Plate 12.** Shell gorget from the surface of Hadfields Cave, Jones County. On display, Iowa Hall, University of Iowa. Photo archives, Office of the State Archaeologist, University of Iowa.

**Plate 13.** Bird's-eye view of a Great Oasis community in northwest Iowa. On display, Iowa Hall, University of Iowa. Photo archives, Office of the State Archaeologist, University of Iowa.

**Plate 14.** The Amana fish weir or trap on the Iowa
River in Iowa County, a probable protohistoric or
early historic site. Earlier prehistoric peoples may also
have constructed such devices. Photo archives, Office of
the State Archaeologist, University of Iowa.

**Plate 15.** Bone and shell artifacts from Mill Creek sites in Plymouth County. Upper row: a marine whelk shell and carved bone amulet or possibly a bow guard from the Broken Kettle site; lower item from the Kimball site may represent a fish lure made of clamshell. On display, Iowa Hall, University of Iowa. Photo archives, Office of the State Archaeologist, University of Iowa.

**Plate 16.** Effigy pot representing a bird from the Broken Kettle site, Plymouth County. On display, Iowa Hall, University of Iowa. Photo archives, Office of the State Archaeologist, University of Iowa.

**Plate 17.** Post pattern and location of cache pits on the floor of an excavated Nebraska phase earthlodge in the Glenwood locality. Photo archives, Office of the State Archaeologist, University of Iowa.

**Plate 18.** Clamshell fish effigy from the Nebraska phase site 13ML176, Mills County, possibly used as a lure. Photo archives, Office of the State Archaeologist, University of Iowa.

**Plate 19.** Catlinite tablet with incised designs depicting a bison from the Blood Run National Historic Landmark, Lyon County. On display, Iowa Hall, University of Iowa. Photo archives, Office of the State Archaeologist, University of Iowa.

**Plate 20.** Iron trade axes and iron knife from protohistoric sites possibly associated with the Ioway. On display, Iowa Hall, University of Iowa. Photo archives, Office of the State Archaeologist, University of Iowa.

possible that this site was a village, it may also be that sites like Kullbom and other larger clusters such as those at the mouth of Pony Creek (Perry 1990a, 1998) grew by accretion, with kin-based groups reoccupying favorite locations (Anderson and Zimmerman 1976:152). Community clusters may have shifted to homesteads through time (Perry 1998).

Establishing the contemporaneity of lodges is difficult. Radiocarbon dating, with an error factor of usually more than 25 years, is too coarse-grained to determine whether houses that were abandoned after 10 to 15 years were contemporary with one another. During their residency of the Glenwood locality, the Nebraska phase population is believed to have occupied as many as 500 to 1,000 lodges (Billeck 1993:11). If the area was inhabited for 150 to 250 years, as suggested from radiocarbon evidence, the total population can be estimated by considering the possible duration and contemporaneity of lodges and the number of individuals living within them (Billeck 1993).

The life span of historic Plains Indian earthlodges was affected both by the quality of their construction and the wood used in the heavy support posts. The wood found in Glenwood lodges was primarily oak, walnut, or elm, species that were at least as hard or harder than the cottonwood used by historic earthlodge builders such as the Hidatsa, whose lodges were reported to have lasted a maximum of 12 years (Wilson 1978a). If a more conservative figure of 10 years is used to calculate the life span of the Glenwood lodges, then a simple mathematical formula whose variables include the life span per lodge (10 years), total occupation span of the locality (150 to 250 years), and minimum lodge density (500) can be used to estimate the number of lodges occupied at any one time and the population density. Either scenario supports data from Nebraska phase sites in other localities that suggest a relatively low population density of perhaps 200–500 people in a region that was occupied for about two centuries.

Population Estimate for the Nebraska Phase in the Glenwood Locality

500 lodges x 10 years = 5,000 ÷ 150 = 33 lodges or

500 lodges x 10 years = 5,000 ÷ 250 = 20 lodges

11 persons per lodge x 33 lodges = 363 people

11 persons per lodge x 20 lodges = 220 people or

15 persons per lodge x 33 lodges = 495 people

15 persons per lodge x 20 lodges = 300 people

### This Old House

Unlike the long, rectangular Mill Creek earthlodges, the typical house built by Glenwood people was usually large but had a square shape with rounded corners and an extended entryway whose orientation may have been determined by the landscape. Lodges placed on dissected bluff locations were constructed with the rear wall oriented parallel to the slope of the hill and the entryway exiting from the downslope wall. In less-confining environmental settings, the house orientation could be determined by factors other than concerns for drainage or the effort required to dig the house pit (Hotopp 1978a:162–163). Most entryways appear to face southeast or southwest, presumably to avoid prevailing winds and to take advantage of the sun.

Lodges were constructed within a semisubterranean pit up to 1 m in depth, and walls consisted of closely spaced timber posts. Vertical timbers positioned between the central fire pit and each corner supported the roof. Four central posts or occasionally four pairs of two or three posts were typical (fig. 9.5). Houses with sets of posts may represent larger structures or those designed to support a heavier roof covering. Overlapping or multiple posts may also reflect the replacement or repair of older posts (Blakeslee and Caldwell 1979:39). Charred timbers found at some sites indicate that hardwoods were preferred in construction, although other woods such as green ash, willow, plum, red cedar, and cottonwood were sometimes used. The floor area of a Nebraska phase lodge as calculated from 48 excavated houses ranged from 17 to 242 m$^2$ (Blakeslee and Caldwell 1979:36). Floors were flat to slightly dish-shaped and in eastern Nebraska occasionally were prepared with a clay lining (Blakeslee and Caldwell 1979:45).

The architectural features of the Glenwood lodge have encouraged archaeologists to consider the nature of the techniques and materials used in construction, as well as the builders' stylistic preferences. The excavation of the house pit and postholes, for instance, required certain digging implements, possibly bison scapula hoes, frontal bone scoops, or ulna picks, all of which are found in Central Plains tradition sites. Floor plans with posts of relatively uniform size and spacing suggest the use of a standard unit of measurement, perhaps the length of the human arm or pace. The location of the lodge corners may have been determined as it was among the Omaha, who measured the distance to the lodge walls from the central fireplace using a rawhide rope attached to a stick (Fletcher and LaFlesche 1972:97).

Judging from historic accounts of Plains earthlodge builders such as the Hidatsa, Arikara, and Pawnee, timbers would have been felled by burning and cutting and left to cure for a lengthy period of time before construction began. Once posts were set, construction of the wattle, daub, and sod walls began. Analysis of the impressions in daub and occasionally of charred organic remains indicates the kind of materials (bark, grass, reeds, thatch) that Nebraska phase people used to build up the walls. The roof pattern may have been conical, flat, or in some cases gabled. The position of central support posts and their distance to walls provide clues to the kind of roof possible. Too great a distance would not provide the necessary support for a long span of rafters. The builders would have had to consider the pitch of the roof, the weight of the rafters, the earthen cover, occasional snow, and possibly

**9.5.** Excavated house from a Nebraska phase site. Single post molds delineate a square-shaped house with rounded corners and extended entryway. Four central support posts surround a firepit with cache pits dotting the house floor. Photo archives, Office of the State Archaeologist, University of Iowa.

human weight (Hotopp 1978a:101). Among historic Plains earthlodge dwellers, the roof provided a convenient place for lounging and socializing, particularly by the men (fig. 9.6).

## A Day in the Life

In some instances Nebraska phase houses burned while they were still occupied. Destruction of a house by fire is evidenced archaeologically by the presence of layers of charcoal, burned timbers, and large amounts of fired daub. Though obviously unfortunate for their former inhabitants, this situation preserves something akin to "a day in the life" of a Glenwood household, a single instant captured in time. Unlike houses whose residents have moved on, those abandoned quickly because of fire contain objects left in place at the time of the disaster. By counting the number of once-whole pots, now crushed by burning and falling house timbers, the archaeologist can estimate the actual number of vessels being used by the household. The position of specific types of tool kits—the flintknapper's, the potter's, the cook's—can indicate the location of activity areas in various parts of the house. Storage pits open at the time of the fire can be distinguished by burned zones at the top or by a fire-reddened upper wall. Those whose contents were sealed or were already abandoned and closed will not show signs of burning. The contents of in-use pits may suggest the season of year the house fire occurred. A large number of abandoned and closed pits implies that the house was occupied for a relatively long time. These pieces of information, taken together, can help in calculating the size of the social group living in the lodge, as well as individual residents' skills and responsibilities.

In some Glenwood houses, a wide earthen bench was built around the central living area, possibly serving as a raised bed. Specific areas were probably allocated to certain family members. Larger structures may have been extended or multifamily dwellings. At some sites there are differences in the construction style,

**9.6.** Archaeologists believe that some Nebraska phase peoples occupied earthlodge structures not unlike later Pawnee peoples. Illustration by Mary M. Slattery.

internal features, and distribution of artifacts from one side of a house to another (Ludwickson and Bozell 1993). These differences suggest that different families may have built and occupied separate portions of the lodge. Smaller structures known at some Nebraska phase sites possibly served particular functions, such as confinement huts for women during menstruation and field houses set up to maintain and oversee gardens.

## Communities and Neighborhoods

The Nebraska phase sites in Iowa have more radiocarbon dates than almost any other group on the Plains (Billeck 1993:175). These dates indicate that the southern part of the locality was occupied by around A.D. 1150. Settlement then expanded northward, ending by A.D. 1300. No later prehistoric cultures are documented in the area, although the latest Glenwood sites show contact with Oneota communities. Some archaeologists maintain that the distinctive nature of the Iowa sites warrants their assignment to a separate phase within the Central Plains tradition (Ludwickson and Bozell 1993:153).

Research conducted in the 1960s assigned all the Glenwood sites to one of three geographic areas (see fig. 9.4). From south to north, these are the Keg Creek, Pony Creek, and Kullbom areas. Sites in the Keg Creek area occupy the southern part of the Glenwood locality along the lower drainage of Keg Creek. They all have a high percentage of ceramics with collared rims. Pony Creek sites, in the center of the locality, have intermediate percentages of collared jars. The Kullbom area is west of Pony Creek along the bluff line of the Missouri River. Sites here have ceramics with a low incidence of collared jars and a high percentage of shell tempering (Billeck 1993). Glenwood sites in general have a higher percentage of collared jars and decorated pottery than Nebraska phase sites elsewhere (Ludwickson and Bozell 1993:144).

Numerous studies over the years have attempted to develop a local sequence for the Nebraska phase sites in the Glenwood locality (Anderson 1961; Billeck 1993; Brown 1966; Hotopp 1978a, 1978b; Zimmerman 1971b, 1977a). The first of these studies correlated radiocarbon dates and ceramic seriation to suggest that sites in the three regions represented temporally sequential phases, with Keg Creek the earliest, followed by Pony Creek, and ending with the Kullbom phase (Anderson 1961). Although this scheme was challenged (Brown 1967a), further study of both ceramics and projectile point assemblages and abundant radiocarbon dates reinforce this tripartite division. This work postulates the existence of three partially coeval subphases that likely represent two or three kin-based communities moving throughout the locality over time (Anderson 1961; Anderson and Zimmerman 1976; Billeck 1993; Zimmerman 1977a).

Sites included in the early subphase (A.D. 1150–1200) occur in the Keg Creek area and near the mouth of Pony Creek. Stirling phase Mississippian influences, possibly derived indirectly through the Steed-Kisker sites in northwestern Missouri, sites in western Illinois, or Mill Creek communities, probably date to the early subphase (Billeck 1993:274). Nebraska phase people may have been living in both the Keg Creek and Pony Creek areas throughout the early and middle subphases (A.D. 1200–1250). Occupation of the Kullbom area and several sites in the Pony Creek and Keg Creek areas was primarily confined to the late subphase (A.D. 1250–1300) (Billeck 1993:182; Morrow 1995b). By this time, evidence for Oneota contact is present, and interaction with Mill Creek was apparently over.

## A Varied Diet

Although the subsistence economy of Glenwood people is not as well known as their settlement pattern, preliminary study suggests distinct differences from that of contemporary Mill Creek groups. Missing from Glenwood is evidence for intensive use of bison and certain other prairie resources. Bison were only a minor element in the diet of Glenwood people, who utilized a more diverse array of smaller mammals, birds, and aquatic fauna, as well as both domestic and wild plants. The evidence to date indicates use of a variety of microenvironments, including woodlands, backwater sloughs, small streams, and the Missouri River itself (Green ed. 1990a:42). This more generalized subsistence base is consistent with what is known for Central Plains sites elsewhere (Roper 1995).

Three recently excavated sites have contributed details about the Glenwood subsistence economy: the Wall Ridge site (13ML176) on a loess bluff overlooking the Missouri River (Croft and Semken 1994; Green ed. 1990a), the Millipede site (13ML361) in the Pony Creek drainage (Billeck 1992c), and 13ML175 on an alluvial/colluvial fan at the base of the Missouri River bluffs in the Kullbom area (Morrow 1995b). These sites reveal a subsistence pattern more similar to that of earlier Great Oasis and contemporary Mississippian peoples to the east and south (Green ed. 1990a:42). In addition to deer, elk, and bison, over 25 species of fish and 27 species of birds were found at Wall Ridge (Green ed. 1990a; Theler 1990b). Fish, particularly bullheads, some probably seined or trapped, represent the most abundant fauna present. Bone fishhooks and small fish-shaped objects cut from shell, possibly lures, suggest hook-and-line fishing as well (see plate 18). The Missouri River system proved an abundant source for freshwater clams used as food and as raw materials for tools (Green ed. 1990a; Hirst 1995).

Nebraska phase people were farmers. The location of sites near easily tillable land and the charred remains of both corn cobs and kernels found in Glenwood cache pits have long demonstrated that horticulture was an important part of the economy. Water flotation and paleobotanical analysis has confirmed the diversified nature of the subsistence economy. Cultigens include maize, squash, the common bean, sunflower, yellow gourd, and tobacco. In addition, goosefoot, marshelder, and little barley were possible domesticates. Cultivated little barley was the most abundant seed type found at Wall Ridge and represents the first reported archaeological occurrence on the Central or Eastern Plains (Green ed. 1990a). Barnyard grass and knotweed also may have been cultivated. Wild plants such as amaranth, wild rye, panic grass, purslane, cordgrass, elderberry, and bulrush were used. At Millipede, a mass of porcupine grass awns twisted in a ropelike arrangement suggests the preparation of brushes.

Stone axes or celts and scapula hoes, implements associated with the clearance and preparation of fields, are common artifacts at Nebraska phase sites. Some archaeologists propose that the prevalence of ground stone axes indicates the practice of swidden farming (Blakeslee 1987). Aboriginally, swidden farmers first cleared their fields of brush and timber by girdling trees with stone axes and then burning off the remaining vegetation. The resulting ash was tilled into the soil to increase nutrients. Prepared fields could be planted for several seasons until the soil was exhausted, at which time new fields were established.

Glenwood farmers may have used wooden digging sticks; the bone tip of such an object was reported from 13ML175 (fig. 9.7). Bison or elk scapula hoes found at Nebraska phase sites are different from those produced by Mill Creek people. The placement of the notch on the lower lateral edge of the element reveals that hafting occurred farther down the blade than on similar implements from northwest Iowa (fig. 9.8).

Nebraska phase hoes also tend to have worn notches on the edge of the glenoid cavity, another feature produced by hafting. Corn shellers made of freshwater mussels represent another type of tool associated with horticulture (Gradwohl 1982; Hirst 1995).

## Connections

Farming was evidently just one part of a seasonal subsistence round for Glenwood people that may also have involved long-distance hunts. The infrequent occurrence of bison remains and the fact that they represent processed items such as

A

**9.7.** Bone item, possibly a digging stick tip, from 13ML175 shown in three views with a cross section. Illustration by Toby Morrow. From Morrow 1995b.

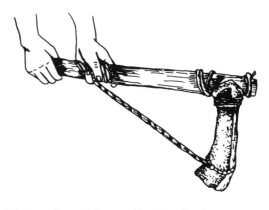

**9.8.** Type of scapula hoe used by Nebraska phase peoples. Illustration by Mary M. Slattery. From L. Alex 1980.

scapula tools, which could have been transported back to the village in finished form, may imply that hunts were conducted at some distance from the settlement or that Glenwood people traded for such items with groups to the west or north. Studies from sites like 13ML118 and 13ML175 also indicate that the chipped stone tool industry reflects more of a western orientation. Chert procurement ranged from the Missouri River bluffs on the Iowa side to the lower Platte River in eastern Nebraska, pointing out the possibility of regular contact with Nebraska phase people to the west. Flint Hills chert from the territory of the Smoky Hill phase hints at more distant western contacts (Morrow 1995b).

Unnotched projectile points from the Glenwood locality are larger and have more blunted tips and more massive flake scars than notched varieties, suggesting they were unfinished and in the early stages of manufacture or possibly had functions other than as projectiles. This is not the case for the Mill Creek or Oneota unnotched points, both of which appear to be completed items (Billeck 1993:186). Notched projectile points from Glenwood sites are triangular in shape, often with multiple side and basal notches (fig. 9.9). While this form resembles the Cahokia point, it is likely just part of a broader trend in weapon manufacture throughout the Midwest during this period (Billeck 1993).

While interaction with western communities seems well documented at Glenwood sites, contact with eastern societies, particularly Mississippian communities such as Cahokia, are less apparent and were probably more indirect. Archaeologists think that Mississippian items or influences reaching southwest Iowa were first filtered through Mill Creek communities or sites of the Steed-Kisker phase in Missouri. Such items and influences include red-slipped ceramics, effigy handles on pottery (fig. 9.10), seed jars, water bottles, low everted rim vessels, discoidals, ear spools, notched projectile points, and Southern Cult symbols (Billeck 1993:212–213).

Ceramics are the feature that most distinguishes Nebraska phase sites from other Central Plains groups. While some researchers have called for a reworking of the ceramic classification, four ware groupings and their component types are still used in southwest Iowa. These include direct jars with simple, straight rims (McVey ware); collared jars (Beckman ware), a distinctive Central Plains tradition form; collared S-shaped rim jars (Swoboda ware); and bowls and seed jars (Debilka ware) (fig. 9.11).

As the Glenwood ceramics have become better known, several temporal trends have been noted.

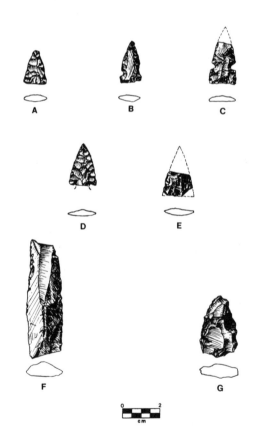

**9.9.** Chipped stone artifacts from 13ML175, Mills County: (A) Madison point; (B–C) side-notched Cahokia points; (D) side-notched point; (E) Madison point; (F) retouched blade; (G) biface. Illustrations by Toby Morrow. From Morrow 1995b.

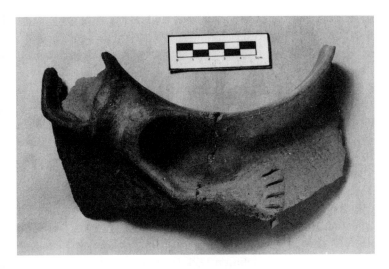

**9.10.** Effigy-handled pot from a Nebraska phase site, 13ML237, Mills County. On display, Iowa Hall, University of Iowa. Photo archives, Office of the State Archaeologist, University of Iowa.

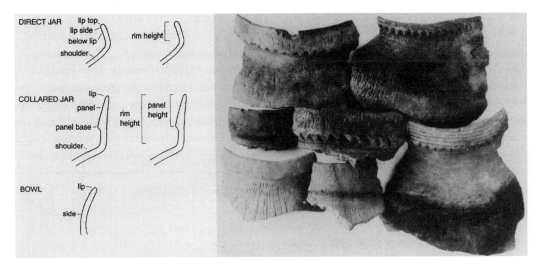

**9.11.** Rim profiles characteristic of Nebraska phase pottery (left) and Nebraska phase rim sherds from Mills County (right). Drawing from Billeck 1993; photo by Charles R. Keyes. Courtesy of the State Historical Society of Iowa, Iowa City.

In the early subphase sites, ceramic influences and possibly ceramic imports from Mill Creek and Steed-Kisker sites are present. Contact with Mississippian sites likewise seems confined to the early and middle subphase sites. Early sites have more bowls, the rare use of sand tempering, low rim height on direct jars, few decorated direct jars, and incised or diagonally cordmarked decoration on collared rims with a usually plain panel base. Late subphase sites show a greater incidence of higher rims on direct jars, a high frequency of decoration on the rim and lip, fewer bowls, more sand tempering, collared jars with notched panel bases, and Oneota influences, particularly Oneota designs (Billeck 1993).

### Exodus from Iowa

There seems little question that at the end of their Iowa residency in the thirteenth century, Nebraska phase people were interacting with intrusive Oneota groups. Items of Oneota origin occur at late subphase sites (Billeck 1993:275), and Nebraska phase pottery is purported to be in some Oneota components (Henning 1961: 15–16). By this time, there is no indication that Mill Creek was part of this network. Some archaeologists believe that the location of Nebraska phase settlements allowed them to interrupt Mill Creek trading connections. As a result, items suggestive of "friendly" interaction with Mill Creek, such as pottery, drop out of later Glenwood assemblages. According to this view, northerly late Nebraska phase sites were strategically positioned to interdict exports, chiefly bison products, slated for export from Mill Creek communities to sites like Cahokia. Warfare between Mill Creek and Nebraska phase peoples, who were possibly allied with Oneota communities, could account for the ultimate disappearance of both cultures from Iowa (Ludwickson and Bozell 1993:148). However, open hostility between Nebraska phase and Mill Creek communities has not been confirmed archaeologically. The desire for bison products and Plains lithic resources, including catlinite, reflected in

later Oneota sites could explain why Oneota people were attracted to territories and perhaps trading arteries formerly controlled by earlier Glenwood and Mill Creek communities. The fortifications found at many Mill Creek sites may reflect a perceived threat from Oneota groups as Oneota people began to extend their range into northwest Iowa. Whether Glenwood communities felt threatened by outsiders is unknown. No Glenwood sites are fortified, but all appear to have been abandoned after A.D. 1300.

Most archaeologists believe that Nebraska phase people moved westward and northward. In addition, despite some alternative hypotheses (Johnson 1991; Ludwickson and Bozell 1993; Steinacher et al. 1991), most researchers suggest that there is direct continuity between the Central Plains tradition and the later Coalescent tradition centered north of the Nebraska–South Dakota border. Initial Coalescent peoples invaded the territory of the Middle Missouri tradition in South Dakota during the thirteenth and fourteenth centuries A.D., sometimes with violent results (see Appendix 9.3). Protohistoric Coalescent sites are identified as the ancestral settlements of northern Caddoan-speaking Wichita, Arikara, and Pawnee peoples who were encountered by Spanish and French explorers in Kansas, Nebraska, and the Dakotas. Today, human remains and funerary items from Central Plains tradition sites are being repatriated to these tribes (Billeck 1996).

### APPENDIX 9.1.
### Central Plains Tradition

The Central Plains tradition, like the contemporary Middle Missouri tradition farther north, marks for the first time the establishment of a settled farming way of life in a broad region stretching from northwestern Missouri to the base of the Rocky Mountains and from the Kansas River to southern South Dakota. All of the members of the Central Plains tradition represent societies of semisedentary hunter-gatherers and horticulturists who shared similar artifact assemblages, settlement patterns, and house plans. Although specific geographic variations have been noted, common features shared by members of the tradition include the presence of corn and bean horticulture; housing comprised of semisubterranean, square to rectangular earth-covered lodges; globular ceramic vessels with simple (direct) and collared rims; and specific stone tools including side-notched and multiple-notched arrowpoints, alternatively beveled knives, and elongated end scrapers (Morrow 1995b:7).

In addition to the Nebraska phase, the Central Plains tradition includes the Upper Republican phase of north-central Kansas and south-central Nebraska and the Smoky Hill phase of northeastern Kansas and southeastern Nebraska. These three phases are believed to have begun earlier than the later members of the tradition, the St. Helena and Itskari (Loup River) phases of northeastern and north-central Nebraska, respectively. Related phases are the Pomona of eastern Kansas, the Solomon River of north-central Kansas (Blakeslee 1994), and Steed-Kisker, located along the Missouri River between Kansas City and St. Joseph, Missouri (Billeck 1993). The Steed-Kisker phase represents a mixture of Central Plains tradition traits and those related to contemporary Mississippian populations residing in the Cahokia area (Morrow 1995b:7). Early dates at Glenwood sites suggest the emergence of the tradition on the eastern edge of the Central Plains (Roper 1995:214).

## APPENDIX 9.2.
### Paul Rowe and Avocational Archaeology

Avocational archaeologists have played a major role in the understanding of Iowa's archaeological past. In Mills County Paul Rowe (1894–1968), was an active local archaeological researcher and careful record keeper. He and his colleagues investigated hundreds of archaeological sites throughout the county through surface collections and occasional excavation. He made notes about his finds, mapped the location of all Mills County sites of which he was aware, maintained regular correspondence with professional archaeologists, and was a founding member of the Iowa Archeological Society and the Society for American Archaeology. His work demonstrated the close relationship between sites of the Glenwood culture and other Nebraska phase sites of the Central Plains tradition (Green et al. 1992:1–4).

## APPENDIX 9.3.
### The Crow Creek Disaster and the Intrusion of Central Plains People into the Dakotas

The late thirteenth and fourteenth centuries on the northern Plains in many ways appear to have been a time of turmoil. Sites along the Missouri River in South Dakota were frequently fortified, and some show signs of destruction and death. Lodges were burned, people were killed, and some settlements were never reoccupied. It is at this time that there is a conjunction of sound evidence—archaeological, biological, and linguistic—for the intrusion of peoples from the Central Plains into the territory of the Middle Missouri tradition. This invasion was evidently met with considerable resistance by resident peoples. Early sites that reflect a Central Plains heritage retain many Central Plains tradition characteristics that were apparently modified as a result of contact with resident Middle Missouri tradition societies. These sites are classified into what is called the Initial variant of the Coalescent tradition. A cluster of such sites occurs between Chamberlain and Pierre, South Dakota, in the big bend of the Missouri River. One site that demonstrates the scale of confrontation among prehistoric groups at this time is the Crow Creek site just north of Chamberlain on the east bank of the Missouri River.

The Crow Creek site contains two components, an earlier Initial Middle Missouri village and a later Initial Coalescent village of the early fourteenth century. The numerous earthlodges that composed this second settlement were protected by a defensive system consisting of an interior ditch and wooden palisade with a number of bastions or loops on the palisade and ditch. These bastions are believed to have permitted the site defenders to fire arrows down their wall line at hostile intruders. A second defensive system, including a ditch some 38 m long, was under construction. The new wooden palisade had not yet been set when the village was attacked and overrun. Lodges were burned, and at least 500 residents were killed.

More than 90 percent of the dead uncovered at the Crow Creek site were scalped, and most were mutilated in other ways. Hands, feet, and tongues were cut off, and young and old were bludgeoned and shot with arrows. A relatively normal population ratio of males to females and young to old, as discerned from the skeletal remains, suggests that it was indeed the villagers who had lost in this violent incident. Had the attackers been vanquished, the remains should have reflected a high preponderance of adult males.

Sometime after the attack, people returned and placed the dead at the bottom of one end of the fortification ditch and covered the bodies with red ochre and a thin layer of clay from the Missouri River bottom. Whether the attack against this Central Plains population was instigated by resident Middle Missouri tradition peoples or another Coalescent community is unknown. While perhaps the most dramatic incident, Crow Creek is just one example of violence documented on the Plains during this period (Zimmerman et al. 1981; Zimmerman and Bradley 1993).

# 10   Late Prehistoric Oneota

Archaeologists purposely give arbitrary names to archaeological cultures to avoid names implying specific ethnic or linguistic associations. The names are often taken from geographical features, like Woodland or Mississippi, or from place names, like Blue Earth or Blue Island. Oneota, for instance, is the name of the geological formation, Oneota dolomite, that outcrops prominently along the Upper Iowa River within the home area of the Orr phase of Oneota culture in Allamakee County, Iowa. Charles R. Keyes applied the name Oneota to the archaeological culture which we now know as the Orr phase, which he believed was that of prehistoric Siouan speakers such as the Iowa. It is thus ironic that Oneota turns out to have been named for an Indian tribe after all, unintentionally I am sure.

Oneota is a name that came to the public attention in 1844 and 1845 when Henry R. Schoolcraft used it in the title for a work he called "Oneota, or Characteristics of the Red Race of America," and the name is of Indian origin. But what Indians? The Oneida, Schoolcraft tells us, [are] a tribe of the Iroquois Confederacy. Oneota is Schoolcraft's spelling of a word in the Oneida language that refers to a certain large boulder of "granite" (actually syenite) that figured in Oneida traditional history. The Oneida were the People of the Stone. This stone now stands in the Forest Hill Cemetery in Utica, New York. Oneota is just another spelling of Oneida, but the Oneida did not have an Oneota archaeological culture.
—Hall 1995:19

**ONE OF** the more contentious issues in midwestern archaeology centers around the last prehistoric tradition to leave its mark on Iowa, the Oneota. The very fact that Oneota sites are widely distributed over a 10-state area from Indiana to South Dakota and from southern Canada to Missouri and span half a millennium makes it unlikely that these are the remains of a single culture. And, although some Oneota sites bring us to the threshold of written history when we can begin to identify the archaeological remains of known peoples, such identifications are often more difficult to determine than we might imagine.

Archaeologists agree that Oneota sites are post-Woodland, that they are found all across the Prairie Peninsula, and that minimally they can be recognized by their shell-tempered, globular-shaped pottery (Henning 1970b; Tiffany 1979b) (fig. 10.1). It has been suggested that the requirement for strong, thermally efficient ceramic containers for simmering seed foods and extracting tallow from bones influenced many Eastern Woodland cultures to shift to shell-tempered pottery (Benn 1989b:254; Braun 1983; Bronitsky and Hammer 1986; Brown 1982; Steponaitis 1980). It is thought that most late Oneota sites represent the protohistoric locations of Siouan speakers (Griffin 1937; Keyes 1927b, 1951; Mott 1938), particularly the Chiwere-Winnebago whose descendants were the Ioway, Oto, Missouria, and Winnebago (including the Ho-Chunk of Wisconsin and Winnebago of Nebraska). It is also likely that some Dhegihan Sioux, such as the Kansa, Omaha-Ponca, and Dakota, and possibly Algonquian speakers, such as the Miami (Emerson and Brown 1992), left material remains archaeologists would identify as Oneota (see chapter 11) (Gibbon 1972, 1995; Hall 1993; Henning 1993; Tiffany 1998). Archaeologists have a harder time agreeing where Oneota people came from, how local sequences of Oneota sites might be related through time, whether individual sites are the remains of entire tribes or smaller social groups, and which specific historic groups Oneota represents (Appendix 10.1).

**10.1.** Oneota pottery. Photo by Charles R. Keyes. Courtesy of the State Historical Society of Iowa, Iowa City.

## Oneota in the Midwest

The term "Oneota" derives from an article written by Ellison Orr (Orr 1914) in which he describes ceramics found along the Oneota River, later renamed the Upper Iowa (Henning 1970b:3). Charles R. Keyes subsequently applied the name to archaeological materials from this area (Fishel 1995b; Henning 1970b; Keyes 1927b, 1951). Most of the more than 100 Oneota sites recorded in Iowa are concentrated in four primary regions: the Upper Iowa River area in the northeast, the central Des Moines valley, the Iowa Great Lakes region and the upper reaches of the Big and Little Sioux rivers in the northwest, and the uplands and floodplain of the Mississippi and the mouths of its tributary streams in the southeast (fig. 10.2). Elsewhere in Iowa, there are only sporadic instances of Oneota materials reported and no major sites (McKusick 1973).

Oneota sites occur on or near ecotones, where floodplain forest, upland forest, and prairie meet, suggesting the positioning of settlements to take advantage of a wide range of resources

(Tiffany 1979b:91). The subsistence of Oneota people generally shows a mixed economy based on large and small game hunting, wild plant harvesting, and wetland exploitation of marsh and water species, along with intensive horticulture of maize, beans, and squash.

As more is known about Oneota across its 1,600 km distribution and throughout its 500-year existence, however, differences in local subsistence practices can be demonstrated, as well as shifts in the overall economy through time. Some sites, for instance, reflect a greater or lesser emphasis on forest or prairie species. Wild rice and fish were staples at some Minnesota and Wisconsin locations. Bison were more important to groups situated closer to grasslands and may have increased in importance with the spread of the prairie eastward during certain climatic episodes. Corn was intensively grown by most if not all Oneota peoples, while cultivation of native American seed crops such as chenopodium evidently was abandoned by some communities (Tolmie 1992). Early Oneota people may have practiced floodplain gardening, relocating fields as soil fertility declined; later groups expanded their agricultural pursuits with ridged field systems in upland settings (Gallagher et al. 1985; Gallagher and Sasso 1987). The demands of the fur trade in the protohistoric period created new economic patterns, with animals such as bison and beaver taking on added significance as a source of hides.

Although Oneota sites have been dated as early as the late eleventh century A.D. in Wisconsin, Iowa sites consistently range between A.D. 1250 and 1700 (Boszhardt et al. 1995; Tiffany 1998). The latest Iowa sites almost certainly represent settlements of the protohistoric and early historic Ioway and probably the Missouria, Oto, Winnebago, Omaha, and Ponca. Hotly debated is the ultimate origin of the tradition. Some midwestern prehistorians view Oneota as a migration of people and a transplantation of Middle Mississippian culture from the Cahokia area followed by readjustment to new environmental settings. Others propose an in situ development in the upper Mississippi valley from Late Woodland cultures who had adopted corn agriculture within a mobile hunting and gathering pattern suited to the upper Mississippi valley and who were strongly affected by Middle Mississippian influences (Stoltman 1986c:32).

Since Oneota begins earlier in states such as Wisconsin (Overstreet 1995) and as there are as yet no sites in Iowa that confirm a Late Woodland to Oneota transition, sites here have shed little light on the origin of the tradition. Cordmarked, shell-tempered ceramics found at sites in southeastern Iowa that seem to blend Late Woodland and Oneota traits could relate to this transition, although at present the oldest sites apparently occur in the central Des Moines valley (Finn et al. 1986; Perry 1987; Tiffany 1979b, 1997b, 1998). It seems likely that resident Late Woodland people in Iowa were either absorbed

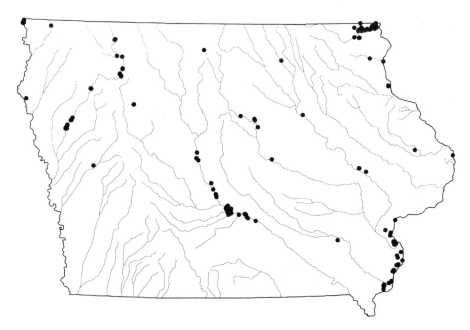

**10.2.** Recorded Oneota sites in Iowa. Data compiled from site records, Office of the State Archaeologist, University of Iowa. Courtesy of Timothy S. Weitzel and Stephen C. Lensink.

by intrusive Oneota people or adopted Oneota characteristics, essentially becoming "Oneota" themselves.

The relationship between Oneota and other late prehistoric cultures such as Glenwood and Mill Creek has already been discussed. Whether or not these groups directly interacted, it is certain that eventually Oneota expanded across the entire state, ranging westward into the Dakotas and Nebraska. Northwestern Iowa Oneota sites show utilization of lithic resources procured directly or indirectly from Plains sources (Fishel 1995b).

Oneota sites in Iowa have been grouped into seven phases. The Orr phase, named by Keyes in honor of Ellison Orr, originally included Oneota sites with Allamakee Trailed pottery found over a broad area of the Upper Midwest (fig. 10.3). The term "Orr phase" is now considered most appropriate when applied to the late Oneota sites of the Upper Iowa River valley in the northeastern part of the state (Betts 1996; Tiffany 1988, 1998). These sites are likely the settlements of the Ioway and possibly related peoples such as the Oto (Mott 1938; M. Wedel 1959). Sites of the Correctionville (Harvey 1979; Henning 1970b), Moingona (Benn 1991; DeVore 1990a, 1990b; Gradwohl 1967; Moffat et al. 1990; Osborn 1982), and Burlington phases (Tiffany 1979b) are the earliest known locations of Oneota people in the northwest, central, and southeastern parts of Iowa, respectively. Two additional phases, the Kelley phase and the Bailey Farm phase, include later prehistoric Oneota sites in southeast Iowa (Tiffany 1979b). The Okoboji phase has recently been proposed to include the protohistoric sites of the Iowa Great Lakes region—Harriman or Burr Oak (13CY1), Milford (13DK1), and Gillett Grove (13CY2) (Henning 1996c)—believed by most to represent Ioway and Oto occupations established around the turn of the seventeenth century. The historic Blood Run site (13LO2) near the mouth of the Big Sioux was likely occupied by several tribal groups, particularly the Dhegihan-Siouan-

speaking Omaha and Ponca, but with ceramic evidence suggesting a probable Ioway presence there as well (fig. 10.4).   .

Some archaeologists maintain that within local areas sequential Oneota sites that share similar materials reflect an ethnic or group continuity (Boszhardt 1994; Hall 1962; Harvey 1979; Henning 1970b; Wedel 1963). For instance, researchers in southwestern Wisconsin have outlined a succession of Oneota sites that extends from around A.D. 1300 to just before the time of European contact (Boszhardt 1994). This sequence is believed to reflect three centuries of occupation by a related group of people who ultimately became the Ioway. Such a model has also been outlined for Oneota remains in Iowa but has yet to be confirmed (Harvey 1979; Henning 1995).

As archaeologists have discovered (Henning 1995:67–68), Oneota sites are frequently complex, implying occupation or reoccupation for decades, sometimes by more than one tribe and sometimes by smaller segments of a tribe. Historically, Chiwere and Dhegiha-Siouan speakers were quite mobile, often traveling long distances. A sequence of local sites therefore may not represent continuous occupation by a group in an area. Historic settlements also were occupied by small segments of a tribe—bands, moieties, or even clans, or occasionally by combinations of these groups—who came together periodically and then disbanded. Some Siouan societies were grouped into Earth and Sky peoples (Tiffany 1997b:231). If most prehistoric Oneota sites represent ancestral Siouan groups such as these, we might expect similar patterns in the past. Thus the importance of kin-based groups like the clan or moiety in producing a site would also have to be assumed, and the possibility of coresidence by multiple ethnic groups might also have to be considered. Unfortunately, it is not easy to tease these subtle aspects of prehistoric social organization from the archaeological record.

We cannot even assume that the tribal groups named historically had the same ethnic identity

**10.3.** Allamakee Trailed vessels from the O'Regan site, Allamakee County. Photo archives, Office of the State Archaeologist, University of Iowa. From Wedel 1959.

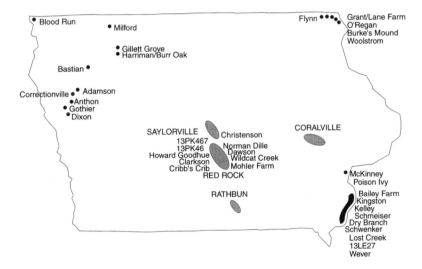

**10.4.** Oneota sites mentioned in the text. Map by Diana Brayton.

throughout long periods of prehistoric time (Gibbon 1995). The people first known to us as the Ioway in the seventeenth century may only have come to recognize themselves by that identity in the fairly recent past. We cannot be sure that the people who produced 400-year-old Oneota sites had that same identity. Perhaps they were the Ioway or Oto, perhaps not.

## The Oneota Pattern

There are broad similarities in sites of the Oneota tradition across the Prairie Peninsula. Sites share large, globular, shell-tempered vessels with constricted openings and opposing pairs of loop or strap handles (fig. 10.5). Decoration occurs on the lip, rim, shoulder, and handles. Shoulder

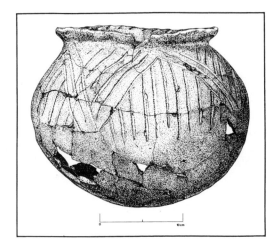

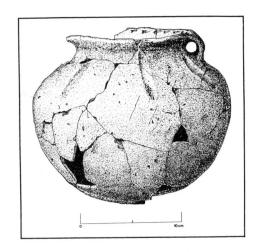

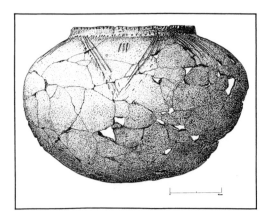

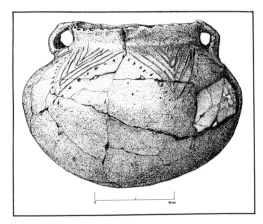

**10.5.** Pairs of opposing handles on reconstructed ceramic vessels from the Dixon site, Woodbury County. Illustrations by David M. Crawford. From Fishel 1995b.

decoration generally includes combinations of trailed lines, rectilinear motifs such as chevrons or triangles, and punctate fringing or filler. Some vessels, referred to as "pumpkin pots," have vertical, broad trailed lines extending from the shoulder down the body, as if in imitation of large squashes or pumpkins (fig. 10.6). Rims are frequently finished off with finger or tool indentations. The broad strap and narrower loop handles are attached to the rim at the lip or midway down the rim. Handles sometimes have horizontal notches or vertical grooves. Differences in ceramic attributes—rim height, the kind and attachment point of handles, and particularly variation in shoulder and lip decoration—are ways that archaeologists differentiate Oneota components from different time periods and locations. Indeed, archaeologists describe Oneota as a "ceramic culture."

The characterization of the Oneota way of life as a reasonably flexible one that successfully integrated hunting, fishing, collecting seasonally available resources, and farming also seems an accurate depiction (Wood 1995:78). Unlike

Middle Mississippian people to the south who could count on abundant resources available year-round in the alluvial bottomlands of the American Bottom, access to the upper Mississippi valley floodplain was constrained by annual flooding. As a result, Oneota people developed a mobile pattern of shifting cultivation in upland settings and seasonal exploitation of a variety of wild resources (Stoltman 1986c:32). This economy is reflected in the presence of many small, triangular, unnotched projectile points; snub-nosed end scrapers (fig. 10.7); scapula hoes; and a diversified faunal and floral record, almost always found in the context of abundant and often very large storage pits. Oneota sites are typically characterized by the presence of tens to thousands of such pits.

Beyond this there are only a few additional features that could, if removed from context, be suspected as being of Oneota origin. These would include catlinite pipes and tablets, often inscribed with superimposed anthropomorphic animal or mythical figures that resemble bird

men, bison, and serpents or symbols such as sunbursts, weeping eyes, and arrows (Bray 1963) (see plate 19). Such symbols are part of a larger group common throughout the eastern and midwestern United States referred to as the Southeastern Ceremonial Complex (Howard 1953, 1968; Waring and Holder 1945) and are believed to have originated within the Mississippian tradition. Interpreting the meaning of some of these symbols as suggested in recorded Siouan myths is one of the more fascinating aspects of Oneota studies (Benn 1989b).

These similarities have resulted in a certain pan-Oneota characterization of the late prehistoric in the Midwest. The lifeways of Oneota people were similar to one another and were evidently well suited to the environment of the Prairie Peninsula. There is also a definite redundancy in the material remains produced over a broad territory. Lithics and bone tools are broadly similar, and the ceramics suggest that decorative styles were shared between groups over a long period of time, their popularity shift-

**10.6.** Broad trailing on the shoulder of this Oneota vessel suggests a resemblance to a squash or pumpkin. Photo archives, Office of the State Archaeologist, University of Iowa.

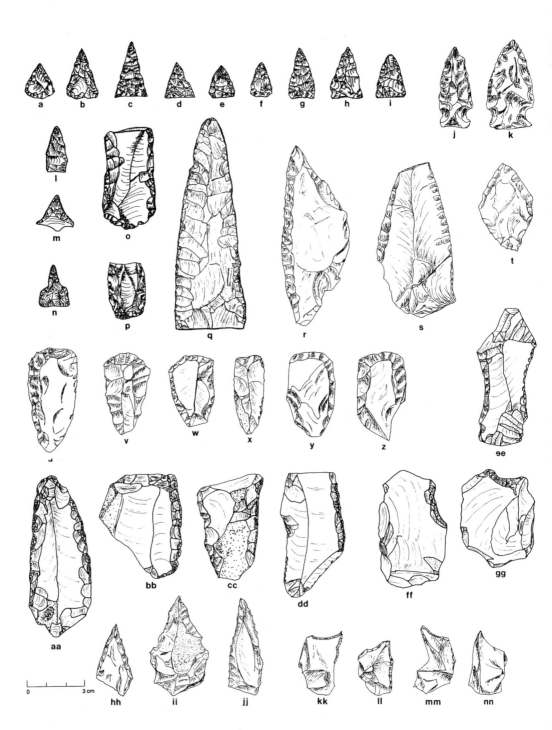

**10.7.** A lithic assemblage from the Moingona phase Cribb's Crib site in Washington County illustrates triangular projectile points (a–j) and scrapers (u–z, aa–dd) typical of many Oneota sites. From De Vore 1990a.

ing in concert over broad areas (Tiffany 1979b: 91, 100) (see Appendix 10.1).

The archaeological record can be deceiving, however. Perhaps it is a case of not recognizing "the trees for the forest." Doubtlessly, numerous individual societies with specific histories and many distinctive customs participated in the Oneota way of life. Different pottery styles may reflect these distinctions, or they may not. If Oneota is composed of numerous ethnic groups who shared similar pottery decoration across broad areas, these groups were also trading and mingling with one another as part of broad networks of exchange and communication. After years of such interaction, the pottery might appear very much the same (Fishel 1995b:48). A similar situation characterizes the Late Woodland. As local areas are becoming better known, archaeologists are attempting to understand the reasons for the apparent similarities in Oneota culture, as well as defining and explaining local differences. It remains to be seen whether the archaeological record is detailed enough and the archaeologist clever enough to perceive and interpret these details.

When the four main regions of Oneota settlement in Iowa are investigated more closely, the differences between Oneota materials become more apparent (Fishel 1995b:81). In each of these regions, archaeologists have begun to define local sequences and to link regions based on shared characteristics. Ultimately these local sequences may serve as the basis for understanding the development of Oneota in Iowa and its relationship to the tradition elsewhere in the Midwest.

## Southeast Iowa Oneota

Oneota sites in southeast Iowa are found throughout a 70 km extent of the Mississippi alluvial plain from just north of Fort Madison to just south of Muscatine in Lee, Des Moines, Louisa, and Muscatine counties (Tiffany 1979b). This area encompasses the lower portion of all major Mississippi River tributaries in southern Iowa, including the Iowa, Cedar, Skunk, and Des Moines rivers. More than 25 sites occur in both bluff and floodplain settings that would have positioned Oneota communities within reach of a wide range of resources and in some cases at strategic locations marking the confluence of inland waterways with the Mississippi River (Tiffany 1982c, 1997b). Oneota sites in both settings are woodland and riverine oriented and may be paired, suggesting the possibility of seasonal occupation between the two (Alex 1978; Tiffany 1982c:10, 1998:4). Briefly inhabited encampments or special purpose extractive sites, such as those recorded in the central Des Moines valley, are unknown in southeast Iowa.

Sites range in size from less than 1 to more than 20 ha in extent and include both diffuse settlements and compact villages (Alex 1971; Hollinger 1996; Tiffany 1979b:90–91). Some appear to have been occupied or successively reoccupied over long periods of time, and none are known to have been fortified (Henning 1995:72; Tiffany 1979b:91). Repeated testing and remote sensing at the McKinney site (13LA1) have not confirmed the presence of the enclosure first described in 1841 (Newhall 1841).

Early period sites like 13LE110 on the Wever terrace, Schmeiser (13DM101), Lost Creek (13LE8), and Kingston (13DM3) consistently date to the beginning of the fourteenth century (Joseph A. Tiffany, personal communication, 1998). Nineteen of 20 dates from 13LE110 alone center closely on A.D. 1300 (Henning 1995:68). Although some of these sites have also produced Woodland pottery, indicating the possibility of a local transition from Late Woodland to Oneota (Finn et al. 1986), the consensus of opinion supports the idea of a migration of Oneota people into the area. Radiocarbon dates indicate that the Moingona phase sites of central Iowa immediately precede those in the southeast. Ceramic similarities between the two areas might also imply some form of antecedent-descendant relationship.

The latest known Oneota occupations in southeast Iowa include more recent components at the Kelley (13DM140), Bailey Farm (13DM2), and McKinney sites. Since Euroamerican trade items evidently had not yet reached these locations, it seems prudent to assume that these sites were abandoned just prior to historic contact (Henning 1995).

While numerous post molds and lumps of daub with grass or twig impressions occur at some locations (Straffin 1971b), the southeast Iowa sites have not revealed house patterns. Elsewhere throughout the Midwest, ovoid wigwams, large longhouses, wall-trench structures, and even square earthlodges have been reported at Oneota sites (Bluhm and Liss 1961; Gibbon 1972; Hall 1962; Hill and Wedel 1936; Hollinger 1993, 1995; McKusick 1971b, 1973; Overstreet 1977; Tiffany 1979b). Changes seen in the size and plans of Oneota houses over time may be a

clue to changes in social organization (Hollinger 1993) (Appendix 10.2).

Storage pits are by far the most commonly encountered feature at southeast Oneota sites, and both bowl-shaped and bell-shaped forms occur (Henning 1995; Straffin 1971b) (fig. 10.8). At some sites these appear in huge numbers, with more than 1,600 at 13LE110 alone (Henning 1995). Pits that once served for storage were usually emptied and abandoned or filled with trash and garbage; when excavated, the pits yield large amounts of discarded bone, pottery, and lithics. At some sites, including McKinney and 13LE110 and 13LE327 on the Wever terrace, numerous burials existed within the village area or were concentrated in nearby cemeteries. Oneota burials investigated in southeast Iowa confirm the practice of inhumation in long oval pits or abandoned storage pits.

Oneota pottery found in early period sites

**10.8.** Overlapping storage/trash pits at the McKinney site, Louisa County. Large numbers of storage pits characterize most Oneota sites. Photo archives, Office of the State Archaeologist, University of Iowa.

such as Schmeiser (the type site for the Burlington phase), Schwenker (13DM82), Dry Branch (13DM80), and Kingston share tool-impressed lips or lip interiors, plain rims, and loop handles that frequently have horizontal notched or step-like decoration. Shoulder designs consist of medium-wide trailed lines forming chevrons, which are outlined by punctates and separated by vertical fields of parallel-trailed lines—the so-called nested chevron design. A circle and dot motif is also present on some vessel shoulders (Tiffany 1979b, 1997b) (fig. 10.9). Other ceramics from these sites include cordmarked and shell-tempered pottery and red-slipped rim and body sherds presumably from high-neck water bottles.

### Kingston

The Kingston site occupies 2 ha of a Mississippi River blufftop overlooking a short lateral valley bordered by steep, wooded ravines. The broad floodplain below was once marshy and poorly drained, and in the late nineteenth century boats were able to float almost to the base of the bluff (Straffin 1971b). A 35 m² area of the site excavated in 1968 revealed shallow cultural deposits. Most features had been destroyed by plowing, and existing ones consisted of refuse-filled storage pits and concentrations of burned earth. A small midden was encountered partly overlapping the northernmost mounds of the Malchow Group. Faunal remains reflect a floodplain and forest orientation.

Pottery from Kingston compares favorably with that found at the Schmeiser site, a floodplain settlement further south. Three radiocarbon dates obtained from Kingston places the occupation in the early fourteenth century (Joseph A. Tiffany, personal communication, 1998). The Kingston and Schmeiser sites have been classified within the Burlington phase of the Kingston locality, provisionally dated to the 1300s and thought to represent the early period of Oneota occupation in southeast Iowa. Burlington phase Oneota pottery is similar to that found in the Moingona, Correctionville, and Blue Earth

phases. The Wever site, placed within the Lost Creek locality north of Fort Madison (Tiffany 1997b) and also dated to the early 1300s, has pottery with similar lip and rim decoration but higher percentages of strap handles (Henning 1995). Shoulder decoration has not been reported in detail. Two other ceramic attributes—smoothed-over-cordmarking and the use of grog temper—may represent a regional characteristic of southeast Iowa Oneota sites in general (Henning 1995).

Components believed to be intermediate in age occur at the Kelley site in the Kingston locality, dated to the early 1400s. The Kelley pottery collection, which largely derives from a salvage excavation conducted in the fall of 1972 (Straffin 1972a; Tiffany 1997b), has more strap than loop handles frequently decorated with parallel, vertical lines. Rims tend to be curved, flaring, and shorter than those at Schmeiser and Kingston. Rim decoration consists of deep tool and finger impressions on the lip. Combinations of parallel vertical and diagonal to horizontal broad trailed bands, as well as alternating, oblique parallel lines that form triangles and other combinations, are common as shoulder decoration (Tiffany 1997b). Similar shoulder design elements occur at the Bastian site (13CK28) on the Little Sioux River (Henning 1970b; Tiffany 1979c), at Grant Village (13AM201) (McKusick 1973), and at the Lane Enclosure site (13AM200) in northeast Iowa (Tiffany 1979b). Sites of this intermediate period are believed to date to A.D. 1400–1500 (Tiffany 1997b:20).

Kelley and possibly Kingston have been proposed as exchange centers between Wisconsin Oneota and late Middle Mississippian groups (Henning 1995). These sites are strategically located for trade and have produced a small amount of nonlocal pottery and exotic items. With the decline of Mississippian centers in the fourteenth century, a number of Oneota sites possibly assumed an important role in the exchange system of the Midwest (Gibbon 1995). The high percentage of scrapers in some settle-

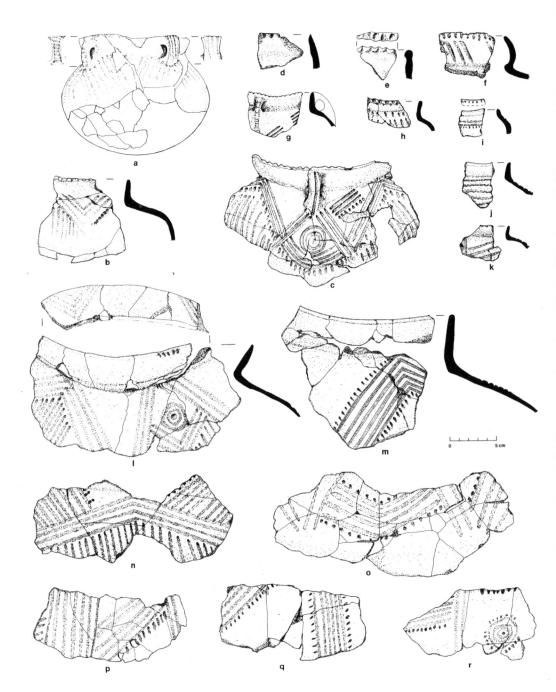

**10.9.** Oneota ceramics from the Cribb's Crib site in Washington County illustrate common motifs, including the nested chevron (m, n, o) and circle and dot (c, l, r). From De Vore 1990a.

ments points to hidework, probably of bison, as an important trade commodity. Later in time, Oneota people seem to have monopolized access to and trade in catlinite from the southwestern Minnesota quarries.

### McKinney

Ceramic cross-dating, radiocarbon evidence, and lithic items such as catlinite pipes and a hematite plaque decorated with a "thunderbird" (fig. 10.10) suggest a late Oneota occupation at the McKinney site in Louisa County. Ceramics include those with shoulder designs of punctate-filled triangles and "pumpkin pots." Similar ceramics occur in sites of the Bailey Farm phase in the Kingston locality and at Orr phase sites in northeastern Iowa. While the "pumpkin pot" vessel is generally considered to be a post–A.D. 1400 phenomenon, it also occurs in low percentages at components of earlier phases, such as Correctionville, Grant, Wever, and Kelley (Tiffany 1997b).

The McKinney site occupies an upland divide between the Iowa and Mississippi valleys (Tiffany 1988). It is an extensive site covering 20–24 ha of plowed farmland adjacent to the "principal group" of mounds at Toolesboro (Alex and Green 1995). Recorded as early as 1841 (Newhall 1841), it was first believed to be associated with an octagonal earthwork or enclosure described as 1 to 2 m in height with a rock foundation (*Annals of Iowa* 1957:488–489). Historic records indicate that plowing had largely removed signs of this feature by the time the Davenport Academy of Natural Sciences first conducted investigations of the area in 1875, although reportedly it remained visible under favorable conditions a century later (Henning 1970b:149).

Some archaeologists believe that this enclosure and a similar one associated with the Lane Enclosure in northeast Iowa are Middle Woodland in age (M. Wedel 1959; Tiffany 1988). If so, the McKinney earthwork is more appropriately viewed as a feature associated with the adjacent Toolesboro Mound Group and in this regard

would be similar to several Middle Woodland structures in the central Illinois valley and in Ohio (Alex and Green 1995). Aerial photographs reveal the possibility of a subsurface feature that may be a remnant of the McKinney enclosure (William Green, personal communication, 1997). Future excavation may clarify its age and cultural affiliation.

In addition to unrecorded collecting and looting during the twentieth century, weekend excavations were undertaken at the McKinney site by John H. Bailey, director of the Putnam Museum and the Quad Cities Archaeological Society in 1946 and 1947. Since then a number of archaeological and remote-sensing investigations have been conducted (Hollinger 1996; Slattery 1979; Slattery et al. 1975; Tiffany 1988).

Numerous overlapping subsurface storage pits, human burials, and occasional post molds can be attributed to the Oneota occupation at McKinney. The possibility that burials occurred within house structures—as documented at Oneota sites in the La Crosse, Wisconsin, area—has also been proposed (Hollinger 1996). Both woodland and riverine resources were exploited. In addition to corn and beans, inhabitants cultivated native crops of little barley and knotweed (Hollinger 1996). Earlier Oneota residents of the Wever terrace grew corn, beans, little barley, and marshelder. Squash and bottle gourd have also been identified at the Kelley site (R. Eric Hollinger, personal communication, 1997).

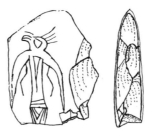

**10.10.** Hawk or thunderbird motif drawn on hematite from the McKinney site, Louisa County. Courtesy of R. Eric Hollinger.

While Oneota people were doubtlessly hunting bison, it is not known if large long-distance hunts were taking place at this time. Bison remains from southeast Iowa Oneota sites, though present, are scarce. Artifacts made of bison bone may have been brought in along with jerked meat and hides, possibly through trade (Henning 1995; Hollinger and Falk 1996). It is also possible that if long-distance hunts were taking place, much of the bone would have been left close to the kill and processing areas and returned to the village only in the form of bone tools (Sasso 1993).

Euroamerican items, including rolled copper or brass tubular beads and blue glass beads originally reported in collections from McKinney, suggest possible occupation by protohistoric Ioway (Henning 1970b:149; Mott 1938:255). It was once thought that McKinney and the nearby Oneota Poison Ivy site (13LA84) on the Iowa River floodplain might represent the twin villages of the Peoria first visited by Marquette and Joliet in their sojourn down the Mississippi in 1673 (Alex 1978). This scenario, however, now seems unlikely. While additional examples of rolled copper have been found in excavation, they are considered to be native-made artifacts, and other items suggestive of Euroamerican trade are absent. Thus the occupation at McKinney, while apparently late, appears to predate contact, perhaps ending in the late sixteenth to the early seventeenth centuries (R. Eric Hollinger, personal communication, 1998). The possibility of an earlier component in undisturbed portions of the site also has been proposed (Tiffany 1988). Archaeologists believe that the recently discovered Illiniwek Village State Historic site at the mouth of the Des Moines River in northeastern Missouri is a better candidate for Marquette and Joliet's landfall stop (see chapter 11).

## Central Iowa Oneota

The Moingona phase of the central Des Moines valley derives its name from the designation of the Des Moines River on eighteenth-century maps. Most of the sites in Warren, Polk, and Marion counties included in the Moingona phase were recorded and investigated in connection with the construction and filling of Lake Red Rock and Saylorville Lake (Benn and Rogers 1985; Gradwohl 1967, 1974:96). The Moingona phase was originally defined on the basis of village sites recorded south of the confluence of the Des Moines and Raccoon rivers, but additional research has demonstrated the existence of other site types as well as the presence of sites upriver in the vicinity of Saylorville Lake (Benn 1991; Benn and Rogers 1985; Perry 1992b). Geomorphic studies now suggest that additional Oneota components once situated on lower, more recent Holocene terraces may be buried under alluvium or have been eroded and destroyed by the meandering of the Des Moines River (Benn 1991; Benn and Bettis 1981).

Moingona phase sites are the earliest in Iowa. Calibrated radiocarbon dates place them in the latter half of the thirteenth century A.D. More than 25 sites occur in ecologically diverse settings, which include prairie-forest margins on the uplands and marshy abandoned channels dissecting the bottomland (Perry 1992b:7). The landscape position of sites and recovered subsistence data indicate a shifting settlement pattern with intermittent occupation of semipermanent villages followed by seasonal relocation to smaller communities and special purpose or extractive camps (De Vore 1990b:20; Roper 1986:323–328). A number of sites, including Christenson (13PK407) and Wildcat Creek (13MA209), provide evidence for periodic reoccupation (Benn 1991; Moffat et al. 1990).

Moingona phase sites include both large and small residential settlements, ranging from .5 to 12 ha, that occupied high, prairie-covered terraces in the upper Red Rock valley or uplands overlooking the main valley farther downstream (Gradwohl 1974; Perry 1992b). None of these sites appear to have been fortified. Extensive excavation has been conducted at Clarkson (13WA2) (Osborn 1982), Cribb's Crib

(13WA105) (De Vore 1990a), Mohler Farm (13MA30), Howard Goodhue (13PK1) (Gradwohl 1974), and Wildcat Creek (Moffat and Koldehoff 1990).

Additional site types in other settings discovered by more recent CRM research suggest that Moingona phase people were utilizing a broad territory extending over 150 km (Benn and Rogers 1985). These sites include seasonal encampments such as Christenson, located on an intermediate terrace at Saylorville Lake and associated with fall to winter hunting (Benn 1984b); Norman Dille (13MA208) and Dawson (13MA207), small floodplain settlements at Red Rock whose residents engaged in fishing and horticulture (Moffat and Koldehoff 1990); and 13PK46, also at Red Rock, a seasonally occupied village exhibiting a range of subsistence and processing activities (Perry 1992b). In addition, briefly occupied special purpose or extractive camps like 13PK467 exist (Perry 1992a, 1992b; Roper 1986).

Excavation and testing of over a third of the Moingona phase sites demonstrate the abundance of basinal, cylindrical, and bell-shaped storage pits, some lined with grass or matting as evidenced by thin layers of carbonized material at their base (Gradwohl 1974; Moffat and Koldehoff 1990; Osborn 1982). Similar features are reported from Oneota sites elsewhere, including McKinney, Kelley, and the Lane Enclosure in northeast Iowa. At Cribb's Crib and Wildcat Creek, large groups of storage pits were concentrated in particular areas and were not associated with known structures. A similar situation may have existed at 13LE110 in southeast Iowa. The presence of pits away from known structures may indicate that communal foodstuffs and other storables were hidden in particular areas of a settlement, perhaps for security reasons, when the residents abandoned the village.

Both house structures and household areas have been delineated at Oneota sites in the Red Rock and Saylorville areas. At Wildcat Creek, two house types were defined on the basis of five

large, shallow, basin-shaped depressions. One type was a large, rectangular structure with a row of large interior posts down the centerline and several interior fire pits. Similar houses, believed to have been dome-shaped and possibly covered with bark or mats, were reported at the Oneota Anker and Oak Forest sites in northern Illinois (Bluhm and Liss 1961; Moffat and Koldehoff 1990:106). The second house type at Wildcat Creek was thought to be wigwamlike and similar to oval-shaped structures from Oneota sites in Wisconsin, such as the Pipe site (Overstreet 1981a). At Wildcat Creek, small post molds were found surrounding the edge of the basinal depression (Moffat and Koldehoff 1990:106).

Oneota people at the Christenson site may have been living in light, bark- or reed-covered lodges similar to those of the nineteenth-century Ioway (Benn 1991:25). Although no post molds were found, three distinct areas of artifact clustering associated with hearths suggest the possible locations of such lodges (fig. 10.11). Household areas were also defined at Cribb's Crib based on similar concentrations of features and artifacts (De Vore 1990a). The occurrence of daub with what appears to be pole and fiber impressions from a number of Moingona phase sites provides additional evidence for the building materials used by central Iowa Oneota people. Other features identified at Moingona phase sites include hearths and earth ovens (Moffat and Koldehoff 1990). A sweat lodge, defined by the presence of a circular arrangement of burned rock and charcoal flecks, was reported at the Mohler Farm site (Gradwohl 1974:95).

Like Oneota sites elsewhere, Moingona phase burials occasionally occur in pits within the settlement area. At the Howard Goodhue site, the presence of a burial enclosure or charnel house was suggested by a curved arrangement of post holes surrounding the remains of 16 individuals lying in an extended fashion (Gradwohl 1974: 96). A child sprawled face down in a storage pit at the Clarkson site provides evidence of possible violence (Osborn 1982), as does an individual

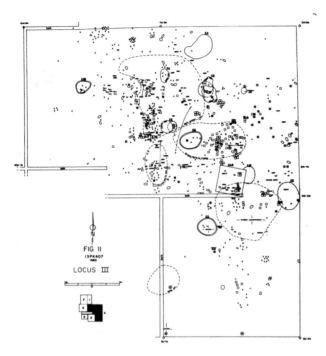

**10.11.** Concentrations of features and cultural materials at the Christenson site in Polk County may be the remains of houses. From Benn 1991.

from the Dawson site whose skull displayed possible scalp marks (McCorvie 1990:414). The presence of fortified sites and the frequent occurrence of human skeletal remains exhibiting signs of trauma mark the late prehistoric as a time when violence and warfare touched the lives of many midwestern societies.

Faunal and floral analyses have shown that a wide range of resources representing all available biotic communities in the central Des Moines valley were exploited by Oneota groups. Hunting centered on large ungulates, particularly white-tailed deer and to a lesser extent on bison and elk. Bison remains found in Moingona phase sites appear to be curated items, such as scapula hoes, suggesting acquisition elsewhere, possibly through trade. Numerous smaller mammals, fish, and freshwater mussels served as both food and sources of material culture (De Vore 1990b: 20). Moingona phase people, like Oneota groups

elsewhere, were adept farmers who positioned themselves to take advantage of arable soils and produced quantities of storable surpluses, particularly corn. At least two indigenous starchy grains, chenopodium and little barley, and two domesticated oily seeds, sunflower and marsh-elder, were grown in the central Des Moines valley, along with cucurbits, an eastern eight-row variety of maize, tobacco, and beans (Parker 1990). The abundant remains of hawthorns, grapes, wild cherries, and especially plums have led some to believe that these items were being processed, dried, and stored and that a form of aboriginal arboriculture may have been practiced (Parker 1990:367).

Ceramics from Moingona phase sites seem most similar to those of the Burlington phase in southeastern Iowa. In addition to the typical vessel form, bowls, water bottles, and miniature pots are known. Hematite inclusions in the paste are reported at a number of sites, although hematite may be a natural ingredient of certain local clays (De Vore 1990a). Some grit-tempered pottery occurs, and cordmarked shell-tempered vessels are reported at most sites, perhaps another link with the Burlington phase sites.

Rims at Moingona phase sites are straight and either upright or slightly everted (Osborn 1982:88). Both strap and loop handles attached at the lip are characteristic, most of the former decorated with broad trailed, vertical lines. Loop handles are usually plain but occasionally exhibit horizontal notches or grooves as found at Schmeiser and Kingston. Handles are attached both by riveting and molding. Vessels with plain lips are more common than at other Oneota phase sites in Iowa (De Vore 1990a:422). Interior tool-impressed lips occur frequently, as at both Burlington and Correctionville phase sites. Exterior tool impressions are reported at three Moingona phase sites, while finger punctations are known only from Cribb's Crib. Interior trailed rim design is found in about the same frequency as at sites of the Correctionville phase and commonly takes the form of chevrons. Shoulder decoration is dominated by nested chevrons outlined by sets of vertical or oblique trailed lines, often fringed or bordered by punctates. Crosses, concentric circles, and circles with crosses often occur within open design spaces (Osborn 1982:87). The use of punctates as a space filler is rare to nonexistent. Of 45 ceramic design components reported from five excavated Moingona phase sites in the Red Rock area, 7 were present at all five sites and are believed to be common at the majority of sites (Moffat et al. 1990:427) (fig. 10.12).

Moingona phase chipped and ground stone artifacts are similar to those of early phase Oneota sites in Iowa. They reveal that stone tool makers had access to local high-grade sedimentary and metamorphic rock but rarely good-quality cherts (Moffat et al. 1990). A preference for Burlington and Croton cherts from southeast Iowa required nonlocal contacts. Croton cherts were available in the Skunk River drainage about 40 km to the east and north, while sources of Burlington chert were found at a distance of 100 to 140 km downstream (Moffat et al. 1990:190).

Close social or political ties with Burlington phase groups could account for the high percentage of Burlington and Croton cherts in the central Des Moines valley (Moffat and Koldehoff 1990:440). The divide between the Des Moines and Skunk river valleys that served as a connection between Fort Madison and Fort Des Moines in historic times may have linked the southeast Iowa Oneota sites to those in the central Des Moines valley and to sites at the mouths of the Chariton and Grand rivers in Missouri. An isolated Oneota site at the bend of the Des Moines River near Keosauqua might represent a way station along this trail (Collins 1997:13, 14). Other nonlocal materials at Moingona phase sites include small amounts of copper and galena. Catlinite is not reported.

## Northwest Iowa Oneota

More than 22 Oneota sites have been recorded in nine counties in northwest Iowa, most found within the Little Sioux River valley, with a couple outliers on the Big Sioux and the Missouri (Fishel 1995b:83). Oneota sites in the Northwest Iowa Plains region—an area of dry, upland, tall-grass prairie, with timber restricted to stands and groves along major streams, rivers, and lakes (Harvey 1979:14)—consist of prehistoric and protohistoric villages and burials, including those in mounds. House types, such as at Dixon (13WD8), include rectangular structures of single post construction. The remains of hunting or processing sites or smaller special purpose camps are unknown in northwest Iowa. Prehistorically, bison would have been an abundant fauna, and archaeological investigation underscores the importance of this species to northwest Iowa Oneota people (Gibbon 1972).

Through time, site distribution appears to shift from lower terrace locations to the uplands (Harvey 1979). A similar trend is seen at Oneota

**10.12.** Shoulder design elements on Moingona phase pottery. Elements 1, 1A, 1E, 2, 3, 4D, and 5A are the most common motifs at the majority of Moingona phase sites. From De Vore 1990a.

sites in western Wisconsin (Sasso 1993). Archaeologists at one time believed that this settlement pattern reflected a decrease in farming or possibly the need for defense (Harvey 1979). The former now seems unlikely because paleobotanical research confirms the importance of corn farming to northwest Iowa Oneota people. Although later settlements seem to occur at greater distances from bottomland gardens, it may be that some Oneota farmers practiced a form of ridged field gardening on the uplands. A similar pattern has been documented at Oneota sites in Wisconsin (Gallagher and Sasso 1987; Gallagher

et al. 1985). By having a two-field system, Oneota people may have reduced the risks of an unsuccessful harvest by relying on floodplain crops during dry years and on upland gardens during wet ones when lower-lying fields were flooded (Withrow et al. 1991).

In general, the Oneota presence in northwest Iowa, though well established, remains poorly known. Controlled and limited excavations have been undertaken at only a few sites, including Dixon, Milford, Gillett Grove, and Blood Run. Unfortunately, most of these sites are also well known to local and regional collectors who for more than a century have removed hundreds of artifacts.

Prehistoric components are reported at Anthon (13WD10), Dixon, Gothier (13WD3), Correctionville (13WD6), Adamson (13WD7), Bastian, Harriman, and Postlewait (13PM11). The earliest of these, such as Dixon, date to the mid-fourteenth century and may be the product of Oneota populations moving out of the Blue Earth River valley of south-central Minnesota. Blue Earth sites like Vosberg and Humphrey Village in Faribault County, Minnesota, have produced materials, especially Correctionville pottery, similar to the early northwest Iowa sites (Gibbon 1983; Fishel 1995b). Correctionville pottery is also reported at the Leary site in Nebraska and at the Utz site in Missouri (Henning 1970b).

## A Local Sequence?

It is possible that Dixon, Gothier, Correctionville, and Bastian represent a sequential occupation of the Little Sioux valley through time and a movement of people from the floodplain to the uplands (Fishel 1995b:84). Although the assemblages from these sites have yet to be compared carefully, differences do exist. For example, ceramic decoration appears to decrease over time, while the occurrence of catlinite increases. Dixon residents relied on Plains lithic resources not yet documented at the other sites (Fishel 1995b; Fishel ed. 1999).

Although there are no radiocarbon dates from Gothier, both Correctionville and Bastian apparently date to the early sixteenth century (Fishel 1995:83–84; Joseph A. Tiffany, personal communication, 1998). These dates, plus ceramic similarities (Henning 1970b; Tiffany 1979c), may imply the presence of a single population migrating northward up the Little Sioux valley over time and switching from terrace locations at Dixon, Gothier, and Correctionville to the uplands at Bastian. A fifteenth-century date for Gothier would lend credence to such a scenario. Alternatively, it is possible that the contemporaneity implied by the dates from Correctionville

and Bastian are the result of a splitting of the Oneota into two contemporary villages during the 1500s (Fishel 1995b:84).

The suggested ceramic affiliation between the prehistoric northwest Iowa sites and the Minnesota Blue Earth sites led to the classification of sites from both areas into a so-called Correctionville–Blue Earth phase (Fishel 1995b; Gibbon 1983; Harvey 1979; Henning 1961, 1970b; M. Wedel 1959; Wilford 1945, 1955). In considering the 200 km distance between these two areas, slightly varying radiocarbon dates, and other ceramic differences, the idea of a single phase covering both areas seems highly unlikely. It is now proposed that the earlier northwest Iowa sites, particularly Dixon, Gothier, Correctionville, and Bastian, be placed in a Correctionville phase separate from the Blue Earth phase of Minnesota (Fishel 1995b).

Fishel (1995b) has compared the Dixon ceramic assemblage to ceramics from sites in central and southeast Iowa and Minnesota. The Dixon ceramic assemblage is similar to those from Moingona phase sites in the Des Moines valley and Burlington phase sites in southeast Iowa, which is to be expected since Dixon represents an early component. Dates suggest the presence of Oneota people in all three regions by the 1300s. The similarity between Dixon and Blue Earth phase materials may indicate a migration of Oneota peoples from Minnesota to northwest Iowa during the late A.D. 1200s (Fishel 1995b:90). Burlington phase sites could represent the movement of Moingona phase peoples into southeast Iowa (Henning 1995:73).

Protohistoric or early historic sites in northwest Iowa include Milford, Gillett Grove, Harriman, and Blood Run. All occur in the northern portion of the Little Sioux and Big Sioux valleys, and Gillett Grove may date as early as the late sixteenth century (Doershuk 1997; Shott and Doershuk 1996). Recently an Okoboji phase has been proposed to include these sites (Henning 1996c). European trade goods from Okoboji phase sites include glass beads, Jesuit finger rings, iron points, copper or brass wire coils, brass tinklers, and cones (Shott and Doershuk 1996; Tiffany and Anderson 1993). French Jesuit missionaries used finger rings, usually made of brass (fig. 10.13), as incentives to convert Native Americans. Later, the rings appear to have become trade items. Because the designs on these rings changed over time, particular styles can help pin down the age of occupation at a site (Cleland 1972).

Euroamerican accounts and tribal oral histories suggest that some of these sites were probably the settlements of the Ioway and Oto. These people were drawn westward by abundant bison herds and the opportunity to acquire furs for trade to Europeans. They may also have fled the effects of pandemic disease and the intrusion of new, mostly Algonquian-speaking peoples into their former territories (Henning 1996c). In addition, sites like Blood Run, and possibly earlier ones, might document the presence of other groups in the region, such as the Omaha.

### Blood Run

Blood Run—part of a 385 ha National Historic Landmark—is a complex of large and small components at the junction of Blood Run Creek and the Big Sioux River in Lyon County, Iowa, and

**10.13.** Jesuit finger ring from the Oneota Milford site, Dickinson County. On display, Iowa Hall, University of Iowa. Photo archives, Office of the State Archaeologist, University of Iowa.

Lincoln County, South Dakota. The site includes 276 mounds, stone circles, pitted boulders, and possibly a serpent effigy (Henning 1993; Henning and Long 1991; Schermer 1987:2–3). It is likely that a conglomerate of tribes occupied this location at the turn of the seventeenth century, perhaps the dominant groups being the Omaha and Ponca.

Much of the pottery from Blood Run is Oneota. The principal ware is a small jar with opposing handles, which is tempered with shell, grog, limestone, sand, or grit. One ceramic type is similar to the Allamakee Trailed type diagnostic of the Orr phase and suggests the presence of the Ioway and Oto at the site. Omaha oral tradition also describes encounters with the Arikara at Blood Run (Fletcher and La Flesche 1972:14), and ceramics typical of Arikara sites farther west occur (Henning 1993:259). The region fell within the territory of the Dakota at this time, and their presence might also be suspected.

European trade items at Blood Run—glass beads, kettles, kettle fragments, brass rolled tubular beads, brass tinklers, bracelets, finger rings, earrings, and iron knives—frequently accompany burials in the mounds.

In addition, items of chipped and ground stone, including catlinite pipes and plaques, have been found (Henning 1993:259). The abundance of catlinite artifacts, the proximity of the Blood Run site to the Minnesota quarries, and evidence of multiethnic occupation indicate that this site was a redistribution point for catlinite and other trade items to groups throughout the Midwest at this time.

While house patterns at Blood Run are unknown, small-scale investigations in 1985 uncovered more than 200 pit features. Fill from these pits was subjected to fine screening and flotation, producing one of the most detailed paleobotanical studies of an Oneota site in Iowa. The identified plant remains reflect exploitation of wetland, lowland, and upland wild resources, as well as the cultivation of corn and beans. This study concluded that native cultigens such as marshelder, goosefoot, and amaranth were no longer part of the gardens and that their wild counterparts were being utilized instead (Green et al. 1993).

## Northwest Iowa Trends

Several temporal trends in both site occupation and content have been noted in the northwest Iowa Oneota sequence. Earlier prehistoric sites are situated on lower terraces or the floodplain near the river or on old channels (Henning 1970b:153). Later sites are found on higher terraces or hilltops above the river. The incidence of bison remains appears to increase over time. While lithic assemblages are similar in many ways, side-notched projectile points occur more commonly at earlier sites and at sites such as Blood Run, where more Plains-oriented groups may have been present. Although limited lithic identification has been conducted, earlier sites have a higher incidence of lithic resources from central and eastern Kansas and Nebraska, including Smokey Hill, Flint Hills Green, and Florence B and D cherts. This may reflect Iowa residents traveling west for communal bison hunts or trade with western Oneota groups such as those of the White Rock phase of Kansas (Fishel 1995b; Logan 1994, 1995, 1996). More than one researcher has proposed that bison remains were procured at some distance from village sites (Fishel 1995b; Harvey 1979). The presence of Burlington chert and other eastern Iowa lithics suggests contact in that direction as well. Catlinite occurs at the early sites, although its incidence decidedly increases through time, and certain items, particularly disc pipes, are typically late.

Ceramics from northwest Iowa also exhibit some apparent trends. Strap handles predominate and at all prehistoric sites are attached to the vessel lip rather than below it. Loop handles are recorded in earlier sites. Ceramics from earlier sites in general have thinner vessel lips and lower rim heights, narrower trailed lines, and shoulder decoration of parallel trailed lines in-cluding chevrons, sometimes found in combination with punctate fringing. At the Dixon site, a few sherds with wide vertical finger trailing suggestive of the "pumpkin pots" and one sherd having what appears to be a punctate-filled zone were discovered (Fishel 1995b:50–51). Both traits characterize later Oneota pottery. Grit-tempered pottery occurs as a minor form at prehistoric sites.

The apparent co-occurrence of Chiwere- and Dhegiha-Siouan-speaking peoples at the protohistoric and early historic sites, particularly Blood Run, links Oneota materials to both of these ethnic traditions. This multiethnic affiliation for Oneota is also evidenced at the Utz village, a historic Missouria site in central Missouri (Bray 1991), and at the Fanning and King Hill sites (Henning 1970b; Raish 1979; W. Wedel 1959), late-seventeenth-century Kansa occupations in northeast Kansas and Missouri.

It is unknown if Oneota peoples occupied northwest Iowa continuously from the fourteenth century to protohistoric times. The Iowa Great Lakes locations such as Gillett Grove, Milford, and Harriman have been proposed as intrusive settlements of the Ioway and Oto following their withdrawal from their Upper Iowa locations in the late seventeenth century. Historic references and oral tradition suggest that the Ioway actually joined the Oto, who had already occupied the northwest Iowa region by this time (Mott 1938; Wedel 1976). Whether an earlier presence by either or both groups is represented in the sequence of prehistoric sites in the Big and Little Sioux valleys remains to be demonstrated. Charles R. Keyes (1951) thought that Oneota sites in northwest, central, and southeast Iowa might represent the remains of the Oto, while the later Orr phase sites of northeast Iowa seemed most securely tied to the Ioway. This remains an interesting, although untested, hypothesis, and recent study suggests a much more complicated picture than Keyes might even have imagined.

## Northeast Iowa Oneota

Oneota in northeast Iowa is best known from a group of tightly clustered protohistoric or early historic sites, mostly cemeteries, extending along the Upper Iowa River and secluded inland tributaries such as Bear Creek in Allamakee and Winneshiek counties and along Riceford Creek and the Root River in Houston County, Minnesota. Sites such as O'Regan (13AM21), Flynn (13AM43), Malone (13AM60), Woolstrom (13AM61), and Lane Enclosure in Iowa and Farley Village, Hogback, and Wilsey in Minnesota (Sasso 1993:342) contain glass beads, iron knives, brass ornaments, and other historic trade goods in association with items of native manufacture, particularly Allamakee Trailed pottery (see fig. 10.3). Allamakee Trailed vessels have fine lip-top notching and shoulder designs that include wide, vertical trailing or punctates filling rectilinear motifs. Wide strap handles fastened below the lip predominate. "Pumpkin pots" are common.

### The Orr Phase

Oneota sites in northeast Iowa belong to the Orr phase. Since the French first encountered Ioway peoples in this area in the 1670s and 1680s and since later Ioway recognized it as their homeland, Orr phase sites have been identified as the probable villages of the Ioway and related groups (Griffin 1937; Mott 1938; M. Wedel 1959).

The native-made artifacts found at Orr phase sites, including Allamakee Trailed pottery, resemble materials from the latest Oneota sites across the Mississippi River in the La Crosse, Wisconsin, area. At the latter sites, archaeologists have demonstrated three centuries of continuous Oneota occupation that seems to have ended just prior to historic contact (Boszhardt 1994, 1997b). None of the La Crosse area sites contain European trade items, and their absence suggests that people had abandoned southwestern Wisconsin and migrated westward to the Upper Iowa and Root rivers before European goods were

reaching them (Withrow et al. 1991) (see chapter 11).

With the exception of the Lane Enclosure, virtually all of the Orr phase Oneota sites investigated in northeast Iowa represent cemeteries of individual graves or intrusive burials in Woodland mounds, and none have been investigated recently. Sites such as Flynn, Burke's Mound (13AM67), Malone, and Woolstrom occur on Pleistocene terraces along the Upper Iowa River and in the narrower valleys of Bear and Riceford creeks, small tributaries of the Root River farther inland. Secluded locations indicate consideration of defense (Withrow et al. 1991). The presence of burials adjacent to habitation areas, as is characteristic of Oneota sites elsewhere, implies that Oneota people had little aversion to the proximity of the dead (Foster 1996). The analysis of Orr phase sites in Wisconsin suggests the presence of other ceramic types in addition to Allamakee Trailed (Betts 1996). Sites in northeast Iowa are greatly in need of a reanalysis in light of more recent findings elsewhere.

### The Lane Enclosure

The Lane Enclosure is the only Orr phase residential site excavated in northeast Iowa, although others are known. It was one of the first archaeological sites in the state to attract attention and was opened by Colonel P. W. Norris in 1882, who referred to it as the "pottery circle." Norris was conducting archaeological field surveys under the supervision of Cyrus Thomas and the Smithsonian Institution's Bureau of Ethnology. The site is composed of a circular to slightly polygonal earthwork described in 1894 as "4 feet in height with an interior ditch 1–3 feet in depth and 8–10 feet wide with an entrance on the south" (Thomas 1894 quoted in M. Wedel 1959). Excavations conducted by Norris and in the 1930s by Ellison Orr found no trace of a palisade associated with the ditch and earthwork but uncovered numerous refuse-filled storage pits dug into the earthwork, the ditch, and an adjacent borrow area. Oneota material also overlay the earthwork and was deposited within the ditch. Excavations in the 1960s revealed the existence of a palisade and identified an earlier prehistoric component (McKusick 1973) (fig. 6.37).

Earthworks occur at the Oneota Lane Enclosure and McKinney sites, but these sites are also associated with earlier Woodland components. At the Lane Enclosure, in fact, Oneota pits and debris were found dug into and covering the associated earthwork, suggesting the possibility that it belonged to an earlier component.

Subsistence data from the Lane Enclosure indicates year-round occupation. The economic pattern, similar to that seen in the La Crosse area, involved large game hunting (particularly deer and elk), floodplain foraging of wetland resources, and agriculture. Bison are represented only by scapulae. The occupation at the Lane Enclosure may represent a time when the hide and fur trade with Europeans had just begun. When first contacted, the wealth of the Ioway in bison hides and catlinite was of particular interest to the French (see chapter 11).

The question of an older prehistoric Oneota presence along the Upper Iowa has recently drawn renewed interest. Decades ago, the Grant Village on the Hartley Terrace produced evidence of longhouse structures where Oneota people may have lived in the thirteenth or fourteenth century (Boszhardt et al. 1995:213; McKusick 1971b, 1973) (fig. 10.14). Excavations suggested the presence of a compact settlement of .5 ha with houses constructed of poles and possibly covered by mats or bark. Residents were utilizing woodland and floodplain resources (Semken cited in McKusick 1973). The original interpretation of the site as a summer occupation (McKusick 1973:66–67) has since been challenged (Hollinger 1995). Although the large dimensions of the houses at the Grant Village site might have resulted from their reconstruction and reoccupation over time, large longhouses have been documented at Oneota sites elsewhere, such as the Tremaine site near La Crosse (Stevenson and Boszhardt 1993) (Appendix 10.2).

Certain ceramic attributes on Oneota pottery from the La Crosse area are temporally sensitive (Boszhardt 1989; Stevenson and Boszhardt 1993). Ceramics from the Grant Village site have shoulder designs of primarily narrow to medium trailed oblique lines and nested chevrons, lip-top finger or tool impressions, and some interior vertical and oblique tool marks. Wide strap handles attached at the lip and rims ranging from less than 30 to 50 mm in height predominate (McKusick 1973). These attributes suggest that the Grant Village pottery has elements similar to ceramics of the transitional early to late Pammel Creek phase of the Wisconsin sequence. Other northeast Iowa sites, including O'Regan, exhibit similarities to earlier Brice Prairie and Pammel Creek phase sites of southwest Wisconsin dating between the fourteenth and sixteenth centuries (Betts 1996).

The presence of prehistoric Oneota occupations along both the Upper Iowa and Root river localities is a crucial issue with regard to the possible long-term residence of Chiwere-Winnebago Siouan peoples. It seems reasonable that if the La Crosse area was inhabited for 300 years, Oneota people (i.e., prehistoric Ioway/Oto/Winnebago) might also have utilized the area just a few kilometers west across the Mississippi.

## Warhawks and Warriors

Although archaeologists do not believe that Oneota society was as nucleated or as hierarchical as that proposed for Mississippian chiefdoms, communities were probably larger than previously and the job of managing them may have fallen to important clan leaders. Among historic midwestern tribes, such leaders were often organized into councils composed of separate but complementary war and civil "chiefs." The authority of such individuals was supernaturally sanctioned and manifest in ceremonial clan bundles containing a variety of symbolic items and amulets, including the skins, feathers, beaks, claws, and talons of birds and mammals; human scalps; metal objects; stones; and small bags containing sweet

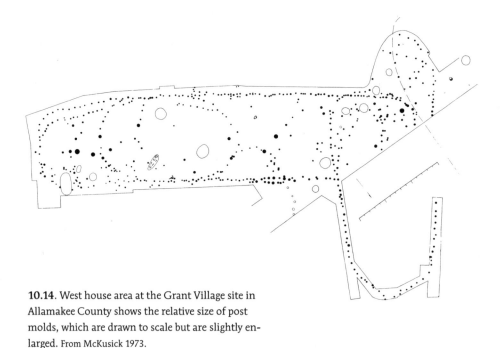

**10.14**. West house area at the Grant Village site in Allamakee County shows the relative size of post molds, which are drawn to scale but are slightly enlarged. From McKusick 1973.

grass, tobacco, and other important medicine. These bundles were passed down through particular clans, establishing a kind of spiritual contract between the supernatural and the people who held them (Foster 1994). Among the Ioway and Siouan peoples generally, each clan had one or more men who were keepers of the clan's war bundles and were in charge of military operations.

Some archaeologists believe that the symbolic authority of similar Oneota leaders is reflected in the iconography of the bird-men, hawk, or thunderbird motifs prominent on ceramics, tablets, and rock art and later expressed in the mythology of Chiwere-Siouan and related peoples. The nested chevron designs fringed with punctates on early Oneota ceramics and the punctate fillers characteristic of later sites are thought to be stylized renditions of the wings and spotted breasts of these hawk or falcon figures (Benn 1989b). In some cases, depictions of what seem to be half bird–half men are shown (see figs. 10.9 and 10.10). These motifs may derive from Mississip-

pian symbolism and relate to values placed on aggression and warfare, as was the case among later American Indian societies throughout the Midwest (Benn 1989b:252; Brown 1976). According to Paul Radin, "The skycreature-warrior theme was the dominant expression in the social and ritual structure of historic tribes. For instance among the Winnebago, the paired Thunderbird and Warrior clans in the Upper moiety controlled the major political functions of the village" (Radin 1923:439 quoted in Benn 1989b:252). The hawk-warrior seems to have been a pan-Oneota symbol and possibly the insignia of the clan leaders who inherited social advantages through descent and achieved positions of leadership through exploits in war and hunting (Benn 1989b:252).

Another interpretation of Oneota pottery decoration is that the motifs and designs symbolize the tripartite subdivision of the ancient "worlds" of Siouan and other native peoples. As such they would be allegorical symbols of shared lifeways, a statement that "we are a people." Among the

Ioway, the Above, or Sky, and the Below, or Sea, sandwich the earth, an island resting on the back of a great turtle placed there by a muskrat. "In the center was the invisible kettle-hole, the navel of the World, the axis mundi" (Foster 1996:1). In this interpretation, the bird or hawk motifs symbolize the sky or upper world, while the "pumpkin pots" serve as metaphors for the earth. Other symbols such as snakes or zigzag lines reflect the water. The circle and dot motif or the diamond within a diamond might then represent the "axis mundi," or center (Foster 1996). Chiwere-Winnebago-Siouan peoples generally thought of themselves as earth or sky people, and the moiety divisions of their society may reflect such groupings.

## Whither Oneota?

Any discourse on Oneota invariably brings to light more questions than answers. This is certainly true in Iowa. If Oneota sites first occur in the central Des Moines valley, for instance, where did their residents come from, and why were the sites abandoned by the protohistoric period? If Oneota people are immigrants, what happened to earlier Woodland communities? Are the Oneota responsible for the disappearance of Mill Creek peoples in Iowa? Could Mill Creek or even Glenwood peoples have become Oneota? Does Oneota represent the expansion of Siouan-speaking peoples throughout the Midwest? If so, what were their ties to the Mississippian world? How does archaeological evidence correlate with the oral traditions of Chiwere-Siouan speakers like the Ioway and Oto or Dhegiha-Siouan speakers like the Omaha, and with early French accounts?

"History," as one individual has said, "like archaeology, has its layers obscured by the passage of time" (Cramer 1998:36). Although the study of the Oneota tradition brings us to the very threshold of history, when we can add written descriptions and oral traditions to our arsenal of investigative methods, we still find the path obscured by the complexity of a record that has many layers.

## APPENDIX 10.1.
### Horizons

Researchers have utilized the concept of the horizon in organizing Oneota sites throughout the Midwest (Hall 1962; Overstreet 1978, 1995; Wedel 1963). Although found throughout a broad geographical territory, sites grouped within the same horizon are believed to share similar materials of a relatively specialized nature. As originally defined, the intended meaning of "horizon" was as a content and spatial unit (Willey and Phillips 1958). Archaeologists working on Oneota have increasingly assigned temporal parameters to horizons, creating what have effectively become sequential periods defined by a trait list of shared characteristics. The horizons as currently defined follow.

Emergent (A.D. ?–1000): represented by sites in eastern Wisconsin undergoing a transition to Oneota. Ceramics are distinguished by their lack of shoulder decoration and few handles. No known Iowa sites currently fit this description.

Developmental (A.D. 1000–1350): represented by fairly large settlements located on major waterways and seemingly occupied for long periods of time. Maize farming becomes more important than in the earlier periods, and beans are added to the list of cultivated plants grown by Oneota people. Pottery traits include the use of loop handles, some riveted, attached at the lip; tool-impressed lip interiors; punctate borders; and curvilinear designs. The Correctionville, Moingona, and Burlington phase sites all have been suggested as Developmental manifestations in Iowa.

Classic (A.D. 1350–1650): the period of widest Oneota distribution, largest populations concentrated in specific regions, more intensive cultivation, and wide exchange of materials such as catlinite, copper, bison scapulae, marine shell, and pottery. Early ceramic characteristics include punctate border zones, which are later replaced by punctate-filled zones. Large strap handles are common in eastern Wisconsin, while both loop and strap handles attached at the lip mark La Crosse, Wisconsin, area pottery. End scrapers outnumber triangular points, and scapula hoes are common. Use of copper and catlinite increases after 1500. The Wever and Dixon sites have been assigned to this horizon.

Historic (post–A.D. 1650): the period after contact with Euroamericans as noted by the presence of European trade items and the replacement of native technologies, effects of depopulation, and new economic pursuits related to fur/hide trade. Iowa sites that fit into this horizon include those with Allamakee Trailed pottery; and Orr phase sites in the northeast; and northwest Iowa locations including Blood Run, Gillette Grove, Harriman, and Milford, now part of the Okoboji phase.

## APPENDIX 10.2.
### Residence Patterns

Based on cross-cultural studies, anthropologists have proposed that in societies in which the newly married couple takes up residence with the wife's family (matrilocal residence) where related women are accustomed to living near or with one another, larger households and house sizes result. From these findings it has been predicted that societies with houses having a mean floor area between 79.2 and 270.8 m$^2$ could be inferred to have had matrilocal rules of residence. Archaeological evidence indicates that the size and floor plan of Oneota houses changed with time, at least in some locations. It is thought that these changes reflect shifts in social structure, specifically postmarital residence patterns. Smaller floor plans at early sites were replaced by houses with very large floor plans during the centuries just prior to European contact. This is believed to reflect a shift from a patrilocal to a matrilocal form of social organization (Hollinger 1995).

# 11   Protohistoric and Early Historic Sites Archaeology

We have seen this year at the home of the puants 7 or 8 families from a nation neutral between our Indians and the nadoessi who are at war. They are called aiaoua or mascouteins nadoessi. Their village which is 200 leagues from here toward the west is very large but poor, since their greatest wealth is in buffalo hides and red stone calumet pipes.

> —Father Louis Andre's account of the first known encounter between the Ioway and Europeans, 1676, quoted in Wedel 1986:15

THE STATE of Iowa and each state bordering it bear a name reflecting a rich Native American heritage, yet few midwesterners are aware of the details. The best-known native people living in Iowa today are the Meskwaki (Fox). While the Meskwaki are the only Native American people who maintain an independent settlement in Iowa, they were not the only historic native residents, nor were they the earliest. As many as 18 different groups may have resided in Iowa during the historic period. They include the Ioway, Oto, Winnebago, Omaha, Ottawa, Huron, Miami, Kitchigami, Mascouten, Chippewa, Sauk, Meskwaki, Potawatomi, Pawnee, Santee, Yankton, Moingwena, and Peoria. A comprehensive history of the state's indigenous peoples has yet to be written. This chapter presents the archaeological background of a few of the people encountered in Iowa at the time of historic contact.

The historic period in North America begins with the first written accounts by Europeans. However, historic documentation of the American continent was a time-transgressive phenomenon, as explorers and traders moved inland from the coasts. In many areas of the Midwest, including Iowa, the historic period did not begin until the French arrived in the mid to late seventeenth century. Throughout the eighteenth and nineteenth centuries, the Spanish, British, and Euroamericans had interests in and affected events in the area that would become the state of Iowa in 1846. The period of time when European trade goods and influences were reaching Iowa sites but prior to actual face-to-face contact between the French and native peoples is referred to as the protohistoric period.

The archaeological remains of all historic peoples who once occupied Iowa will never be identified. Their presence was often too fleeting to have left much of a trace. The acquisition of European technology also meant the abandonment of native-made artifacts that might help to identify particular groups. The archaeological sites left by others have long disappeared. To date fewer than 100 historic American Indian sites have been recorded. Linking historic groups to their prehistoric ancestors is especially difficult, as discussed in the previous chapter. The prehistoric remains of particular groups are not necessarily found in the area where those people first encountered Europeans, where they live today, or even in the area described in their own oral histories (Hall 1995:25).

A more fundamental problem is that the name or label assigned to historic American Indian groups by Europeans may have very little reality or temporal depth. While the allegiance of many Europeans was to a sociopolitical structure such as a nation or state, this was not the case for native peoples. Historical sources are full of references to groups of people Europeans identified as "tribes." In many instances this identification had little reality for the native people. Often more important was the clan, the moiety, or the band. The name the French assigned to the Meskwaki, for instance, was *Renard* (Fox), possibly because they first met a portion of the Fox clan. Social organization among many midwestern groups seems to have been quite fluid, and even a tribal affiliation was sometimes temporary and situational. Closely related groups intermarried, and the common practice of adopting captives or war prisoners helped integrate American Indian communities. The disruption created by the European invasion also quickly altered the makeup of native society. In some cases decentralization of political systems occurred as formerly well-organized tribes broke down into smaller segments.

In addition, although the European ethos was closely tied to a country or government, this was not true for most native peoples. While the individual surely knew the essence of what it meant to be Ioway, Meskwaki, or Winnebago, it was not easy to convey this to the priest, the trapper, the trader, or, later, the anthropologist. And when the archaeologist looks into the dark well of prehistoric time, it is even more difficult to identify a people from the bits and pieces of their material record.

Late protohistoric and early historic sites associated with the Ioway and related peoples are the best documented in the state and will be the focus of this chapter. Since the Meskwaki figure importantly in the later history of Iowa, archaeological evidence pertaining to their arrival and occupation also will be discussed. A concluding section takes a brief look at historic Euroamerican sites.

## Contact

Long before most resident American Indian groups ever came face-to-face with a European, the effects of European contact had already radiated like a series of shock waves across the continent (fig. 11.1). Within a few years the native situation was drastically altered as a result of depopulation from introduced disease, destruction and dislocation of settlements, massive migration, breakdown of social and political life, formation of new economic patterns, and the adoption of European technology. Even some of the so-called tribes described by the newcomers had only recently coalesced, the by-products of depopulation and new economic and political partnerships. For instance, nineteenth-century accounts of the Meskwaki, who first arrived in Iowa in the 1730s, are of a culture already greatly altered by decades of resettlement, confrontation, and economic and social changes. Their survival and eventual reoccupation of parts of the state under terms of their own making is one of the more successful stories in the generally dismal history of American Indian and Euroamerican relations.

The earliest protohistoric sites in Iowa probably date to the first decades of the 1600s and typ-

**11.1.** Oglala Sioux American-Horse's Winter Count 1780–1781 (left) illustrates the effect of a smallpox epidemic among the Dakota. Swan's Minneconjou Dakota Winter Count (right) depicts a measles epidemic among the Dakota in 1818–1819. From Mallery 1893.

ically contain artifacts of native manufacture alongside a few European trade items such as copper or brass tinklers, brass rings, glass beads, and iron knives acquired through American Indian intermediaries (see plate 20). As European kettles, metal cutting tools, weapons, and jewelry became more easily obtained and more desirable, pottery vessels, stone knives, arrows, and bone, quill, and shell ornaments were replaced by their brass, iron, and glass counterparts.

Sites in some parts of the country give witness to the effects of contagious diseases brought from western Europe and passed in a down-the-line fashion to American Indian peoples who had no natural resistance (Green 1993b). Post-contact population losses in the Americas may have been as high as 85 to 90 percent (Denevan 1992; Dobyns 1983; Driver 1964; Ramenofsky 1987; Stoffle et al. 1995), although such estimates have been challenged (Green 1993b; Henige 1986; Milner 1980; Ramenofsky 1990). While direct evidence for European-introduced disease in protohistoric Iowa is unknown, the scarcity of protohistoric sites in Illinois may reflect population losses there dating to the seventeeth and possibly even the sixteenth centuries (Emerson and Brown 1992). In addition, the pictographic calendars drawn by Plains peoples, known as winter counts, depict devastating epidemics of measles and smallpox as early as the late seventeenth century (Sundstrom 1997).

The early descriptions and maps made by Europeans add to our knowledge of native peoples, but these sources must be evaluated very carefully. Such accounts are partisan chronicles, limited in scope, selective in terms of what was recorded, and not always reliable. Often they were produced by individuals who had ulterior motives. Early French interests, for instance, were primarily economic, involving the desire to establish the fur trade. The French also promoted a course of religious conversion among the native groups they encountered. For this reason, the population figures reported for some native communities were inflated in order to demonstrate

to the church the number of souls that had been "saved." Because of the involvement of American Indian trappers and brokers in acquiring furs, both the French and the English, and later Euroamericans, played native groups against one another to suit mercantile interests and later military and territorial ones. Thus an unfavorable description of one people could serve as propaganda to justify their displacement at the hands of another with whom the Euroamericans were allied.

## Ethnohistory

The earliest historic documents and most of those that succeeded them for the next century are incomplete, often distorted records of native peoples facing unfamiliar and frequently dire circumstances. As a result, we cannot rely on written records alone to link the prehistoric period to the historic in Iowa. A combination of history, archaeology, linguistics, native oral history, and ethnohistory is required. Ethnohistory requires the critical examination of early documents with an eye to discovering information they might contain regarding native peoples. Both historians and ethnohistorians utilize government and church records, merchants' inventories and ledgers, and maps, letters, diaries, and journals of explorers and settlers. Although not intended as anthropological accounts, these sources can tell us much about the lives and cultures of native peoples at the time of contact. When combined with archaeological research and native oral and pictographic histories, such documents provide a more complete picture than would any one of these sources on their own.

## The Beaver Wars

Almost all of the American Indian groups known to have occupied Iowa in the historic period were speakers of languages that belong either to the Siouan or Algonquian language families, and almost all of these tribes at one time appear to have lived in territories to the east (fig. 11.2). During the early seventeenth century, the

Huron, an Iroquoian-speaking tribe of southern Ontario, were the major supplier of furs in trade with the French. At that time they acted as brokers between the tribes in the Great Lakes region who had access to the rich fur-bearing territories of southern Canada, Minnesota, and Wisconsin and the Europeans who were just beginning their stronghold in New France. During the middle of the century, eastern tribes, particularly the Five Nations of the Iroquois, began a concerted destruction of the Huron in an effort to gain access to the fur-bearing resources of the northwest and thus satisfy their desire for European trade goods (Hunt 1940; Mason 1986). This internecine warfare created a disruptive effect throughout the entire Great Lakes region and the Ohio valley, as wave after wave of Huron and neighboring peoples fled their former territories and came pouring through the Upper Peninsula seeking asylum along the shores of Lake Superior and Lake Michigan. Eventually the Iroquois would raid as far west as the Illinois valley, and some Huron and Ottawa briefly took refuge in Iowa. Resident groups in the western Great Lakes region, including the Dakota and possibly Cheyenne, were pushed or fled to more distant locations, including areas west of the Mississippi River.

In the wake of these disruptions, French contact and influence spread into interior portions of the continent, and trade was established with groups who formerly had been involved only secondhand. Realignment of many western Great Lakes peoples occurred as they scrambled to adjust to the newcomers and to put themselves in favorable positions to trade with the Europeans. It is at this time and as a result of these events that the names of Siouan- and Algonquian-speaking peoples first appear in the documents of French traders, explorers, and missionaries. Among these groups are the Ioway, Winnebago, Oto, Dakota, Meskwaki, Sauk, Menominee, Miami, Peoria, Moingwena, and Mascouten.

## The Ioway

The people the Meskwaki would displace in Iowa were Chiwere-Siouan speakers who called themselves Páxoche, though they were known by the Dakota Sioux as the ayúxba or Aiaouia—the Ioway. They are a group whose residency in the state stretches well into the prehistoric period. According to some Ioway, they have always lived here. Today many Ioway live on reservations on the Kansas-Nebraska border and in Oklahoma. At one time, however, they dominated the land between the two rivers, the *Nyitanga* (Mississippi) and *Nyishuje* (Missouri) (Foster 1996:1). Their story in Iowa allows us to bridge from prehistory to history at the time of contact.

When Europeans first reached the New World, there were over 400 distinct Native American languages belonging to a number of families. Siouan is one of these families. The Ioway are classified by linguists as Chiwere-Siouan speakers, most closely related to the Oto, Missouria, and Winnebago, with whom they share similarities of culture and traditional histories and whose languages are mutually intelligible. The Chiwere and Winnebago languages are considered a subgroup within the Mississippi Valley Branch of Siouan languages (Voegelin and Voegelin 1977). Another subgroup, the Dakota (the "Sioux" proper), includes the Eastern or Santee (the Dakota speakers), Middle or Yankton and Yanktonai (the Nakota speakers), and Western or Teton (the Lakota speakers) (see fig. 11.2).

Traditionally, the Ioway referred to the Winnebago as their "fathers" and to the Oto as their "brothers." Linguistic, archaeological, and physical anthropological evidence combine to suggest that the Ioway, Winnebago, and Oto became separate around 500 to 700 years ago, about the time of the Oneota dispersal in Iowa. The Dhegiha-Siouan languages—Quapaw, Osage, Kansa, and Omaha-Ponca—are another subgroup of the Mississippi Valley Branch. The Chiwere-Winnebago Siouan speakers may have

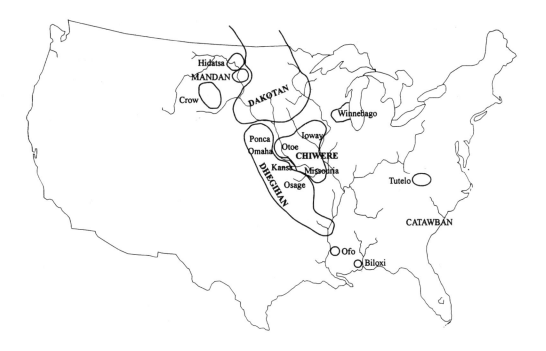

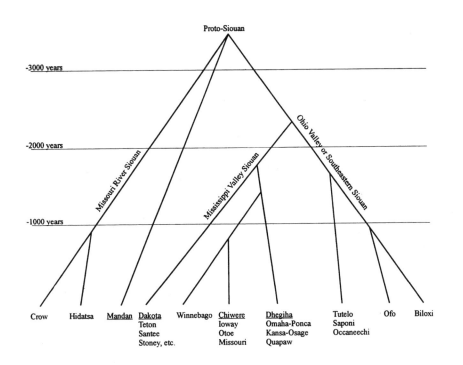

**11.2.** Top: Language groups classified within the Siouan language family. Bottom: Suggested time of split for Siouan languages. From Rankin 1997.

separated from Dhegiha-Siouan speakers around 1200 to 1500 years ago (Rankin 1997).

Although its origin is not without question, the name the Ioway called themselves, Páxoche, is traditionally believed to translate as "dusty/ashy/gray noses" or possibly "dusty/ashy/gray heads." This meaning is an integral part of a traditional Ioway migration story that recounts the time when the Ioway and related groups were camped on a sandbar by a great river, possibly the Mississippi. The blowing sand, a sudden dust devil, or possibly the ash from wayward campfires landed on their heads, inspiring their relatives to label them Páxoche (Blaine 1979; Wedel 1978).

The Ioway trace their roots to a place called Moka-Shutze (Mashuje), the Red Earth, possibly a reference to a spot along the Lake Michigan shore in Wisconsin (Skinner 1925) or to a mythical homeland shared with the Winnebago north of Lake Superior (Hall 1993:65). While there are traces of archaeological remains in eastern Wisconsin that could verify their Lake Michigan origin, more than 100 Oneota sites along terraces of the Mississippi valley near La Crosse, Wisconsin, suggest that between the fourteenth and seventeenth centuries Chiwere-Siouan speakers were residing there (Withrow et al. 1991). Late prehistoric Oneota sites of the Wisconsin Valley View phase occur on tributary streams away from the main river channel, possibly as a means of protection. Around A.D. 1600–1650 these settlements apparently were abandoned in favor of the Root River and Upper Iowa drainages to the west, territories that may already have been familiar to Oneota people (Betts 1996; Sasso 1993:340–342) (see figs. 10.4 and 11.3).

According to their own tradition, each of the seven original Ioway clans was founded by four animal brothers who became human beings (Skinner 1926). Four and seven are important numbers to Siouan-speaking peoples. The Ioway recognize seven cardinal directions: the Above, the Below, the East, the South, the West, the

North, and the Center (Foster 1996:1). By historic times each clan was patrilineal (members traced descent through the male line) and exogamous (members sought marriage partners outside their own clan). The Bear and the Buffalo clans were considered the most important, and paramount chiefs were chosen from these clans. Other clans included the Wolf, Pigeon, Elk, Thunder, Eagle, Red Earth, Snake, Beaver, and Owl (Skinner 1926). Each clan was divided into subclans who claimed descent from one of the four founding ancestors.

The first known written reference to people believed to be the Ioway occurs in an account by Nicholas Perrot, a French trader who around 1656 learned, probably from Ottawa and Huron informants, of a river that flowed from the west into the Mississippi and of a local people living near it. That river is believed to be the Upper Iowa. The French probably did not meet the Ioway until 1676, when the Jesuit Father Louis Andre encountered them trading at a Winnebago village south of Green Bay, Wisconsin. He described them as poor, their greatest wealth being in bison hides and calumet pipes. The description is a good example of a European's perspective and bias regarding the state of their "wealth."

### Prehistory to History

Ethnohistoric study, primarily of seventeenth- and eighteenth-century French accounts and maps, has produced a framework for understanding the location and movement of the Ioway and related peoples at the time of contact (Wedel 1976). Archaeological investigation of suspected Ioway sites and scrutiny of surviving oral tradition help round out this picture.

No one has contributed more to the ethnohistoric understanding of the Ioway than the late Mildred Mott Wedel (1912–1995) (Gradwohl 1997) (fig. 11.4). An Iowa native, Wedel spent much of her professional career examining early documents and proposing ways to tie history to prehistory in Iowa (Gradwohl 1997). She en-

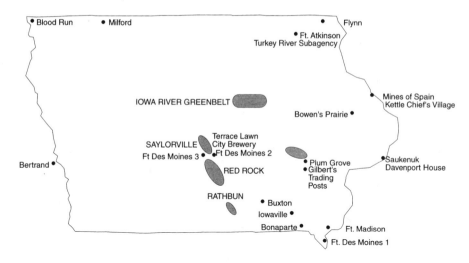

**11.3.** Historic sites mentioned in the text. Map by Diana Brayton.

couraged archaeologists to utilize the Direct Historical Approach (Strong 1935; Wedel 1938b), finding the historic sites of known peoples and linking them with earlier sites having similar remains (Wedel 1976). In this way, the location of historic groups might be retraced into more remote periods of prehistory.

At the time they emerge from the mists of prehistory in the mid to late seventeenth century, the Ioway seem to have shifted west, abandoning Wisconsin and concentrating their settlement on the Upper Iowa–Root River region of northeast Iowa and southeast Minnesota probably at Orr phase Oneota sites (see chapter 10). From their Upper Iowa villages, the Ioway apparently ventured west to hunt in the lake country of southern Minnesota and north-central Iowa. Sharing the western part of this region were the Oto, and possibly at times the Winnebago. This position seems for the most part to have given the three related groups neutral status between Algonquian speakers such as the Kickapoo, Mascouten, Potawatomi, Sauk, and Meskwaki to the east and the Dakota Sioux to the north. The similarity in the material culture of the Ioway, Oto, and Winnebago makes it virtually impossible to distinguish their individual sites.

**11.4.** Mildred Mott Wedel (1912–1995) on right wearing large hat. Keyes Collection. Courtesy of the State Historical Society of Iowa, Iowa City.

Oral tradition as well as numerous seven-teenth-century French documents and later references establish the presence of the Ioway in the Upper Iowa region at the time of first contact. These include a map presented by the Ioway chief Notchininga, or No-Heart (No Heart of Fear), to a council in Washington, D.C., in 1837 in support of the Ioway's claim to the territory of Iowa (Green 1995c, 1998; Warhus 1997) (fig. 11.5). The Ioway themselves, in fact, refer to their ancestral villages and burial sites in northeast Iowa in a petition submitted to President Andrew Jackson and the Congress in 1836. In it they state:

> No Indians of any other Tribe dare build his fire or make a moccasin track between the Mo. and Mississippi Rivers from the mouth of Missouri as high north as the head branch of the Calumet, upper Ioway, and Desmoines Rivers, without first having obtained the consent of the Ioway Nation of Indians. In fact this Country was all of theirs, and has been for hundreds of years. And this fact is susceptible of the clearest proof, even at this late date. Search at the mouth of the Upper Ioway River, (which has been the name of their Nation time out of mind) there see their dirt lodges, or Houses, the Mounds and remains of which are all plain to be seen, even at this day, and even more, the Country which they have just claim to, is spotted in various places with their ancient Towns and Villages, the existence of which no Nation can deny. (Blaine 1979:164)

It is likely that the trader Michel Accault first visited the Ioway at their villages on the Upper Iowa between 1677 and 1680. He was interested in procuring bison hides, a role for which the Ioway were well suited, having established hunting territories in the prairie area at the headwaters of the Upper Iowa and Cedar rivers and on the lower course of the Minnesota to the north. The Little Ice Age, beginning around 500 years ago, is believed to have brought episodes of cooler and moister conditions to the Midwest (Laird, Fritz, Grimm, and Mueller 1996; Wendland 1978: 281). While the effect of climatic change on the

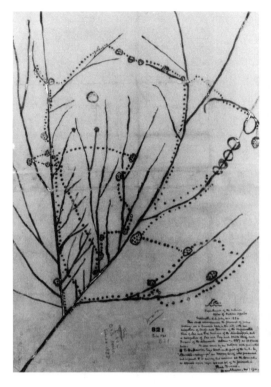

**11.5.** Map presented by Ioway delegation to U.S. Indian Commissioner, October 1837. Record Group 75, National Archives and Records Administration. Washington, D.C.

economy of native groups at this time is not well known, corn growing may have declined in some areas while bison hunting increased. Many groups, including the Ioway, seem to have shifted their territories and their economies to take advantage of the herds. In this way they were in a sense predisposed to the fur trade with the French.

According to Accault (Wedel 1986), in the early 1670s the Kickapoo and Miami had gained refuge for a number of years in the region of the Ioway and Oto after fleeing from the Illinois, who had already received firearms. It is believed that the Illinois, a loose alliance of central Algonquian-speaking groups, were acting as brokers in the trade with Europeans. Thus they were able to acquire certain items firsthand and, in turn, control the dissemination of these items to secondary tribes.

### Settlements across Iowa

Although the position of the "Páxoche" is noted for the first time on maps by Father Jacques Marquette and cartographer Louis Joliet after their voyage down the Mississippi in 1673, it does not appear that the Ioway met the famous priest and explorer at this time (Donnelly 1968; Hamilton 1970; Thwaites 1900; Weld 1903). Marquette and Joliet apparently learned of the Ioway while visiting the Peoria, one of the Illinois. The location of the encounter between the two Frenchmen and the Peoria is believed to have been at the mouth of the Des Moines River in northeastern Missouri. Archaeologists have confirmed the presence of early historic trade materials together with native-made shell-tempered Danner series pottery at the Illiniwek Village State Historic site. The historic items include copper and brass beads, tinklers, wire coils, and points; glass beads; iron blades, awls, and axes; gun parts; and a silver Jesuit finger ring of a type predating A.D. 1700 (Ehrhardt and Conrad 1994; Grantham 1993; Grantham et al. 1995). The Danner phase represents the archaeological remains of protohistoric and early historic Illinois groups, including the Peoria. When visited in 1673, the Peoria were reported to have had guns and other trade goods. The Illiniwek site provides confirmation of this. It apparently was a community consisting of large longhouses arranged in a regular fashion. This settlement pattern is consistent with other known sites, such as the Peoria village on the Illinois River described by the French in the 1680s (Deliette 1934).

The location of Marquette and Joliet's landfall visit at the mouth of the Des Moines is not without its contenders (Weld 1903). In 1973 the three hundredth anniversary of their voyage and encounter with the Peoria was reenacted and commemorated at Toolesboro, Iowa, at the mouth of the Iowa River. Oneota sites in the region, including McKinney and Poison Ivy, had been proposed

as the possible archaeological locations of the Algonquian villages they visited (Alex 1978). This hypothesis now seems untenable.

In 1685 the Ioway performed a colorful weeping ceremony to honor Nicholas Perrot when he and his party visited their village, possibly near the Zumbro River in southeastern Minnesota (Appendix 11.1). This marked the Ioway's initiation into the beaver trade with the French and put a premium on the lake country at the headwaters of the Cedar, Blue Earth, and Des Moines rivers, a favorable habitat for the animal. As a result, the Ioway traveled westward to hunt (Anderson 1973a, 1973b; Wedel 1986:42).

By the late 1600s the Ioway appear to have abandoned their villages on the Upper Iowa and relocated to northwestern Iowa and southwestern Minnesota. The direct involvement of upper Mississippi River tribes in the beaver trade with the French gave them immediate access to European trade goods. It also created a realignment of relationships with surrounding native groups. Algonquian-speaking peoples such as the Mascouten particularly resented being bypassed by the French and feared that the Siouan groups would obtain firearms. Hostilities ensued, Ioway villages were attacked, and by the late 1680s their residents fled westward to be near allies such as the Oto and Omaha, probably along the Little Sioux and Missouri rivers. This meant they were now infringing on the territory of the Dakota Sioux, with whom they had enjoyed generally amicable relations. Increasingly throughout the eighteenth century, the Dakota ranged into the region of the upper Des Moines and Cedar rivers. A Dakota village below the mouth of the Upper Iowa was later recorded on William Clark's map of 1810 (Mott 1938:280).

From the 1690s to the 1820s, descriptions and maps from French, English, Spanish, and American sources document the presence of the Ioway at various locations across the state, as does later archaeological evidence. French maps made during this time refer to Ioway locations that probably included temporary seasonal settlements and semisedentary villages. There is the possibility that the locations of only segments of the tribe (clans or moieties) are being referenced. It is not known if more than one major village was occupied at a time, although perhaps two contemporaneous or seasonal ones existed (Wedel 1976). While the Ioway apparently settled on or near the Missouri until the 1760s, they are known to have hunted throughout the territory that would later become the state of Iowa.

In the late 1680s the Ioway established a settlement on the Little Sioux River near Spirit Lake. By the early decades of the eighteenth century they lived at the mouth of the Big Sioux River, probably with other groups including the Omaha and Oto. In 1701–1702, at the invitation of the French, they resided for a brief period near Fort l'Huillier (Fort Vert) at the confluence of the Blue Earth and Minnesota rivers in southern Minnesota. They had been invited there by the trader and explorer Pierre-Charles Le Sueur, who hoped to obtain food supplies and labor to exploit suspected metal deposits. After this, they may have returned for a time to the Spirit Lake region and then established a succession of villages on the Little Sioux or in the Missouri–Big Sioux–Vermillion river region, before moving, probably in the 1740s, to the Missouri River near the Platte (Wedel 1988). During this time they also hunted farther south along the Little Sioux and Des Moines rivers (Harvey 1979; Wedel 1978).

Oneota sites in northwestern Iowa, including Gillett Grove, Milford, and Blood Run, and several in southeastern South Dakota (Alex 1994) are just a few of the potential archaeological manifestations of these early historic locations. Since the Oto are known to have occupied contiguous or nearby settlements (Mott 1938:258), any consideration of these sites as Ioway locations has to include the possibility that they could also represent the Oto. In the case of Blood Run and the South Dakota locations, Omaha-Ponca and Arikara affiliations are certainly a possibility as well. Since some of these sites, such as Milford, contain evidence suggestive of prehistoric Oneota occupations, they may represent spots occupied by Chiwere-Siouan speakers when they traveled inland to hunt earlier in their history (Tiffany 1997a).

A settlement in southwestern Iowa on the Missouri River near the mouth of the Platte and just south of Council Bluffs may represent one of the Ioway locations after 1740. The village was first recorded in a memoir by M. Louis Antoine Bougainville in 1757 and possibly noted later as an abandoned site by Lewis and Clark in 1804 and Henry Brackenridge in 1811. Unfortunately, archaeological evidence for the site seems to have been destroyed (Wedel 1988). This position would have placed the Ioway within striking distance of the hunting territory of the Caddoan-speaking Pawnee, who probably lived along the Platte (Wedel 1938b:279–289; Wedel 1981:10).

*Lifeways*

Archaeological evidence suggests that the lifeways and culture of the Ioway during the first century of European contact was largely a continuation of that inferred from prehistoric Oneota sites. The traditional culture of the Ioway seems to have retained elements of their historical association with the Great Lakes and Central Algonquian groups, as well as their growing contacts with the Plains and its peoples during historic times. Economically, the Ioway maintained a dual dependence on the hunt and the garden. This is reflected in the occupation of two kinds of settlements: relatively permanent year-round villages situated on river terraces or uplands where summer gardens could be established and where a riverine and floodplain foraging pattern could be employed; and the shifting campsites of nomadic bison hunters. There are tantalizing hints from early documentary sources that two permanent villages may have been maintained at one time. These might reflect division of the tribe into two major segments (moieties), each composed of several clans. Mildred Wedel (1986:50) estimated a population of perhaps 1,000 for the

Ioway around the beginning of the eighteenth century.

The permanent villages may have been composed of traditional elliptical or rectangular pole houses covered with layers of bark and mats, sized to accommodate nuclear or extended families (fig. 11.6). A larger, longer ceremonial house and smaller sweat lodges and menstrual huts would likely have been built elsewhere throughout the community. Inside the houses, benches or platform beds, fireplaces, hanging storage baskets, bark and hide containers, and underground storage pits for garden produce and perhaps valuables might be found. Shell-tempered pottery, bone and shell ornaments, and the whole complement of bone and stone tools handed down from Oneota traditions would gradually have been replaced with iron kettles; glass beads; brass, copper, and silver jewelry; and iron cutting tools acquired through trade. Drying racks, roasting pits, and additional storage pits would have made up some of the outside features. During the winter, when people were not away on the hunt, more sheltered settlement locations on the lower creek or river terraces or bottoms may have been favored.

If Ioway ancestors had practiced mound burial earlier in prehistory, this custom was apparently all but abandoned by the contact period. The remains of numerous individual interments occur in cemeteries situated near the permanent villages, such as the Flynn cemetery in Allamakee County (Bray 1961). Grave offerings include items thought to have use in the afterlife, as well as less utilitarian objects with symbolic and ceremonial importance. On the occasion of a burial, the family may have sponsored a give-away of personal items, a custom still important at such times. Scaffold burial also may have been practiced. The division of the historic Ioway into the sky and earth moieties prescribed separate burial customs for the member clans of each group, scaffolding for the former and interment for the latter (Benn 1989b; Skinner 1926).

Food crops grown by the Ioway at contact included maize, beans, squashes/pumpkins, and

**11.6.** An Ioway house. Courtesy of the National Anthropological Archives, Smithsonian Institution, Washington, D.C.

tobacco. In their calendar year April is called the cultivating moon (Skinner 1926) (Appendix 11.2). Traditionally, women prepared the fields and planted, tended, and harvested the crops, although only the men grew tobacco and sacred corn. Gardens were located on the lower terraces near rivers and creeks. A form of slash and burn field clearance was practiced. The Ioway at one time possibly prepared ridged fields as did the Winnebago. A characteristic complex of horticultural indicators—bison and elk scapula hoes, clamshell scrapers, storage pits, and charred seeds of domesticated plants—have been recovered from the protohistoric Upper Iowa River sites and those in northwest Iowa. Seed remains from these sites also attest to the use of wild forms of plants, including lambs' quarters, sunflowers, and various nuts, roots, and berries.

During the fall and winter and again in the summer the Ioway left their permanent villages to hunt. Such hunts sometimes involved an entire village and lasted two to three months. By the contact period if not earlier, the Ioway had probably adopted a form of the Plains bison skin tent while on the move. Although distant bison hunting was a feature of the Ioway past and continued even after their confinement to reservation life, its economic importance was heightened after trade was established with the French. Beaver, on the other hand, while possibly a dietary delicacy in early times, appears to have been of relatively short-lived importance to the Ioway economy and entirely associated with the fur trade of the late seventeenth century. By the mid-1700s acquisition of firearms and the horse significantly enhanced both the mobility and the hunting skills of the Ioway.

In the latter half of the 1700s the Ioway were once again drawn east to trade and into the often competing interests and hostilities of the Spanish, British, and Americans. By the middle of the century they conducted seasonal hunting excursions south and west into Missouri, north to southern Minnesota, and west across the Missouri River (Ingalls 1991a:11–12). For a time in

the 1760s they occupied two settlements in Illinois: the "Lower Ioway" village opposite the mouth of the Des Moines River and the "Upper Ioway" village south of the confluence of the Iowa and Mississippi rivers.

The presence of the Ioway on the Des Moines River is well documented in historic records from the beginning of the 1770s into the 1820s. Archaeological evidence at a sprawling site in the Des Moines River valley in northwest Van Buren County, later the location of the town of Iowaville (13VB124), may be one manifestation of this occupation. Although the site has never been excavated, large surface collections include historic trade beads, glass, pottery, iron tools, pipestone, European gunflints, and gun parts (Gourley 1990; Ingalls 1991a; Straffin 1972b; Till 1976). Oral tradition strongly associates the site with an Ioway occupation in the latter half of the eighteenth century. Surface collections match the historic description of goods the Ioway received from both the French and the British during this time. Typical French items include Jesuit finger rings (see chapter 10), hawk bells, metal tinklers, faience pottery cut into gorgets, liquor bottles, gun flints, and gun parts. British trade goods, such as gun spalls, gun flints, and gun parts, dominate later (Ingalls 1991a). The Ioway appear to have had a stronghold on Euroamerican trade in this portion of the Mississippi River until they were attacked, probably by the Sauk, and defeated at the Iowaville location in the early 1820s (Cole 1938; Fulton 1882; Houck 1909; Pickard 1893). After this time, the site was utilized by the Sauk (Gourley 1990:140).

During the first decades of the 1800s the Ioway were increasingly pushed about and forced to relocate as the result of strengthening American interests and settlement following the Louisiana Purchase in 1803. By this time, too, the Sauk and Meskwaki had arrived and were situating themselves in a more favorable position to trade and to press their own claims to territory in Iowa. The Ioway population also was reduced by epidemic disease, especially smallpox (Blaine

1979:81). Throughout this period, the Ioway territory included much of the state beyond the Iowa River watershed to the Des Moines, extending to the Spirit Lake locality, down the Little Sioux to the Missouri, and from there to the Grand and Gasconade rivers in Missouri. The early 1800s saw apparently simultaneous occupation of several villages on the Mississippi, Grand, Iowa, and Des Moines rivers. The War of 1812 contributed to polarization among the Ioway, some of whom supported the Americans, others the British (Foster 1996:3–4).

The peripheries of Ioway territory were claimed by, contested by, or shared with the Oto, Missouria, Kansa, Osage, Sauk, Meskwaki, Omaha, and Yankton Dakota (Blaine 1979:82). During these times hostilities ensued between the Ioway and many of these groups. The Sauk, Black Hawk among them, reportedly led the devastating attack against the Ioway around 1821 at Iowaville (Fulton 1882). For short periods the Ioway visited or lived with allies such as the Kickapoo in Illinois and the Winnebago in southern Wisconsin.

### Final Years in Iowa

By the 1820s the fate of the Ioway was charted by forces over which they had little control and by legislation they often little understood. This was literally the case when United States government agents failed to provide interpreters at treaty sessions. In a series of land cessions between 1824 and 1838, the Ioway relinquished territory east of the Missouri River and began life at the Great Nemaha River reservation in northeastern Kansas and southeastern Nebraska (Anderson 1973a, 1973b). The Ioway made an eloquent final appeal to the United States Indian Commissioner at a council convened in Washington, D.C., in 1837, opposing the claims of the Sauk and Meskwaki to cede and receive compensation for lands to which the Ioway laid ancient claim (Green 1995c; Tinnian 1998). Two individuals—Notchininga, or No Heart (fig.11.7), and Moving Rain (also Walking Rain)—presented the Ioway

case and as evidence displayed a large map drawn in heavy black charcoal illustrating the territory occupied by the Ioway for a period of nearly 200 years (Green 1995c; Lewis 1987). Their efforts in Washington brought them little gain, and in an 1838 treaty they ceded all their lands between the Missouri and Mississippi rivers.

At the Great Nemaha River reservation they were joined by some Sauk and, for a brief period, Winnebago. Occasionally, small groups of Ioway returned to Iowa for short stays. Two hundred briefly joined the Potawatomi, for instance, during their forced move from Lake Michigan to the Council Bluffs area between 1837 and 1847. The presence of the Potawatomi in Iowa is noted in a number of county histories (e.g., Hartman 1915). At least six widely scattered clusters of Potawatomi villages may have been established in southwestern Iowa throughout this period (Clifton 1977:320). One Potawatomi cemetery in

**11.7.** Notchininga, or No-Heart (1797–1862), in a portrait painted by Charles Bird King in Washington, D.C., 1837. Courtesy of the National Anthropological Archives, Smithsonian Institution, Washington, D.C.

Waubonsie State Park, named after a Potawatomi leader, was destroyed in 1930 (Billeck and Green 1994).

Between 1841 and 1845 a group of 14 Ioway made a momentous tour of Great Britain, Ireland, and France, accompanied by, among others, the painter George Catlin. The descriptions by one of their party, Wash-ka-mon-ya, provides interesting commentary on a Native American's impressions of European life and the social conditions he observed there (Blaine 1979; Catlin 1844; Stevenson 1993).

In the latter half of the nineteenth century a portion of the Ioway tribe moved to Indian Territory in present-day Oklahoma. This land was originally set aside for the relocation of Indian tribes forcibly removed from their territories to the east. Protesting allotment and the encroaching white settlement of their northern reservation and urged by other tribal groups in Indian Territory to join them, a group of Ioway were given reservation land adjacent to the Sauk and Meskwaki in 1883. After the Dawes Act of 1887, the Ioway at both the northern and southern locations were forced onto private allotments, and residual reservation properties were opened to white settlement. In the twentieth century the Ioway received additional compensation for their concessions of the previous century (Blaine 1979:319). Today, Ioway people live on the northern and southern reservations in Oklahoma, Kansas, and Nebraska, as well as in many other parts of the United States.

## Meskwaki

About the time the Ioway are first mentioned historically, the French Jesuit Father Claude Allouez encountered a trading party of Meskwaki along the southern shores of Lake Superior, probably in 1666 or 1667 (Edmunds and Peyser 1993:8; Thwaites 1896–1901). The Meskwaki are closely related linguistically and culturally to two other Central Algonquian peoples, the Sauk and Kickapoo. The Mascouten also spoke a similar dialect. French sources frequently refer to the Meskwaki by their Chippewa name, Outagami, translated as "people of the opposite shore." Early on, however, the French called them *Renard* (Fox), possibly because they first encountered members of the Fox clan. The four largest and possibly oldest Meskwaki clans are named Bear, Fox, Thunder, and Wolf. Traditionally the paramount chiefs were selected from the first three, war chiefs coming from the Fox clan and village or peace chiefs usually from the Bear clan. The Thunder clan also could supply village and war chiefs, but these chiefs usually played a secondary role in leadership positions (Blair 1911; Edmunds and Peyser 1993; Gearing 1970; Hagan 1958).

According to their oral history, the Meskwaki originated on the east coast of North America. The tribe was created by Wisaka, the Elder Brother, who remade the earth after it was destroyed by the manitous (spirit beings). Wisaka created all living things, including people. The name Meskwaki means Red Earth or Red Earth People, since according to the origin story Wisaka created the first humans with red earth or clay. After he created people and taught them the proper way to live, Wisaka left by the sea (Buffalo 1993a:11).

At the beginning of the contact period, the Meskwaki and other tribes in the western Great Lakes region may have been moving into territories depleted of earlier populations. Archaeologists have noted a paucity of sites in some areas just prior to direct European contact (Emerson and Brown 1992). Epidemic disease introduced with the arrival of Europeans on the southern and eastern coasts of North America may have spread rapidly from one native group to another along extensive midwestern trade networks (Green 1993b).

The Meskwaki are referred to by the Huron name Schenchiohrononon in documents the Hurons gave to the Jesuit priests after 1640 (Thwaites 1896–1901). Their first known contact with the French was recorded in 1656 by Father Gabriel Druillettes. At that time they may have had a total population of around 12,000 (Kay 1984:272). Researchers suggest that the Meskwaki, like other central Algonquians such as the Sauk, Kickapoo, Mascouten, and Potawatomi, retreated westward during the middle decades of the seventeenth century in the face of incursions by the Huron and other tribes fleeing the Iroquois. However, some evidence indicates that the Meskwaki may have migrated earlier (Edmunds and Peyser 1993:9).

After encountering the French on the south shore of Lake Superior at Chequamegon Bay in the 1660s, the Meskwaki were drawn to eastern Wisconsin, where they ranged over an area from the Wolf River south to northern Illinois and from Lake Michigan to the Mississippi (Bauxar 1978). By the late 1670s they were established on the Fox River, an area they occupied over the next half century despite periodic dislocations due to intertribal hostilities and their continual altercations with the French. According to their traditional history, the Ioway occasionally granted them sanctuary in Iowa.

### Attempted Genocide

In a series of wars between 1712 and 1738, the French, assisted by allied tribes, attempted to exterminate the Meskwaki and almost succeeded (Edmunds and Peyser 1993). The Meskwaki, whose early experiences had left them mistrustful of the French, disrupted French trading ventures with the Dakota and maintained hostilities with French-allied tribes such as the Chippewa, traditional enemies who were forced into Meskwaki territory in Wisconsin (Edmunds and Peyser 1993; Kay 1984). The French enlisted the help of tribes such as the Illinois and Miami, who were suffering from Meskwaki encroachment into their own lands, and negotiated positions of neutrality with groups such as the Ioway to prevent their allying with the Meskwaki.

In 1716, while occupying a stockaded settlement on the south shore of Big Lake Butte des Morts near the headwaters of the Fox River in central Wisconsin, the Meskwaki were set upon by 800 well-armed French soldiers from Fort Michilimackinac and their allied tribes. After three days and nights of siege, a cease-fire was negotiated (Mason 1986). The archaeological setting for this drama is the Bell site near Oshkosh. Here archaeologists excavated a time capsule of aboriginal life of the early eighteenth century. A Meskwaki community living within a fortified village of wall trench structures still produced traditional ceramics and stone tools at a time when they had already adopted numerous European items. Archaeologists have documented features of traditional culture, including evidence for bear ceremonialism and dog sacrifice at the site (Behm 1991; Blake and Cutler 1963; Wittry 1963).

In 1730, while attempting to seek refuge with the Iroquois farther east, the main body of Meskwaki suffered a resounding defeat at the hands of the French and allied tribes in northeastern Illinois. Some archaeologists believe that the Arrowsmith site in Mclean County, Illinois, provides archaeological confirmation of this incident (Stelle 1992). The Meskwaki lost close to 1,000 men, women, and children as they attempted to slip away through a storm following a 23-day seige and were set upon by the French and allied native groups (Stelle 1992; Temple 1966:91). Afterward, the French and their allies, who now included the Iroquois, pursued the survivors.

The Meskwaki and the Sauk, who proved steadfast allies throughout this period, eventually fled across the Mississippi into Iowa. They established fortified villages on the Wapsipinicon River in 1734. Pursued by the French who threatened to destroy both nations and permit the allied Christian-Iroquois and Huron groups to "eat them up," they met again the following year on the Des Moines, possibly near present-day Camp Dodge (Edmunds and Peyser 1993; Mott 1938:274). Entrenched in a large, fortified encampment on an island in the river, the Meskwaki and Sauk were able to stave off the French and their allies and force them to retreat. In 1737 the French government, having failed in its attempt at genocide, ended the wars by granting both the Meskwaki and Sauk a general pardon (Callender 1978:644).

### Residence in Iowa

Throughout the middle decades of the 1700s the Meskwaki and Sauk roamed over a broad territory, frequently relocating their villages. Both tribes increasingly occupied an area along the Mississippi River in northern Illinois and adjacent Iowa. This location placed them in a favorable position to hunt into Ioway lands, to take advantage of the lead mines at Dubuque, to trade with the British and dissuade other tribes like the Dakota from doing so, and to continue to conduct raids against the Illinois. By the late 1700s the Sauk had established the village of Saukenuk at the confluence of the Rock and the Mississippi rivers. Saukenuk was described in early accounts by Zebulon Pike in 1805 and John Hays in 1812 (Bluhm 1962; Hedman 1993; McKusick and Slack 1962). It remained an important settlement until the Black Hawk War of 1832, although the tribe also occupied other locations. Excavations at Crawford Farm, believed to be the site of Saukenuk, uncovered the remains of house structures; trash, storage, and fire pits; and two burial areas. Materials within the pits included trade silver, glass beads, metal utensils, gun parts, and liquor bottles. Lead spew, shot, and shot molds confirmed the involvement of the residents in lead mining and in the production of ammunition either for trade or for their own use (Hedman 1993:537).

One of the difficulties in identifying the archaeological sites of the Meskwaki and other specific groups in the historic period is the lack of diagnostic artifacts, especially pottery, whose individual styles often are correlated with particular ethnic groups. Once European-made kettles, ceramics, iron knives, and jewelry replaced their indigenous counterparts, the archaeological remains of native peoples are less distinct. Historical archaeologists, trained in both archival research and the analysis of time-diagnostic artifacts, can help. The manufacture of items such as glass trade beads or imported ceramics usually occurred within known time intervals. The discovery of these artifacts can help to establish the time of occupation of a site and, in conjunction with written and oral sources, suggest the cultural identity of its inhabitants. Gun flints, for instance, were imported by both the French and British from different sources in Europe (Hirst 1991). Their presence at a Native American site can indicate with whom the occupants were trading and help pinpoint the likely period of interaction.

In the late eighteenth century the Meskwaki established villages on the Iowa side of the Mississippi, while returning on occasion to Wisconsin well into the 1800s. Over the next half century they and the Sauk increasingly pressed their claims to territory in Iowa. Settlements are reported at various locations throughout the eastern and southern portions of the state, including areas along most of the Mississippi River tributaries. The Meskwaki occupied villages from the Turkey River and the Mines of Spain (Dubuque) southward to Davenport across from the mouth of the Rock River. In 1805 Zebulon Pike reported three Meskwaki villages: the first on the western bank of the Mississippi north of the Rock River rapids; the second near the lead mines at Dubuque; and the third on the right bank of the Turkey River not far from its confluence with the Mississippi. Morrell Marston in 1820 listed small villages at the first two locations as well as near the mouth of the Wapsipinicon (Mott 1938). In addition to a main village at Saukenuk, Sauk communities were found from the Rock River to the mouth of the Des Moines. Both tribes also ranged south and west into Missouri. Based on the age of the associated artifacts and the records of Sauk occupation of the area at that time, an early-nineteenth-century burial site excavated in Lee County was probably that of a Sauk woman (Fisher and McKusick 1980).

### Mines of Spain

The Meskwaki presence in the Dubuque area was tied to their role in the mining, smelting, and trade in lead beginning in the late 1700s. The lead industry was second in economic importance only to the fur trade in the upper Mississippi valley. Other tribes such as the Ioway and later the Winnebago were involved in these activities between 1780 and 1840. Native peoples had known of this resource for centuries. Archaic peoples traded crystals and nodules of galena, the mineral from which lead in this area is derived, to as far away as Louisiana (Walthall 1981). Prehistorically, galena was worked into small artifacts such as plummets and beads and was often ground to form a paint or sprinkled as a powder.

The French were the first Europeans to become aware of the ore deposits in the tri-state area of Iowa, Wisconsin, and Illinois. By the middle of the seventeenth century the French were mining and smelting lead for their personal use and for trade with Native Americans and others. This further encouraged native mining and smelting, and lead from Native American mines was being traded as early as 1688 (Abbott 1988:2). When the French ceded the western portion of the upper Mississippi to the Spanish in 1762, large-scale enterprises began. Julien Dubuque was granted mining rights from the Meskwaki in 1788 (Blaine 1979:109; Walthall 1981:18). Dubuque received confirmation of his grant from the Spanish governor in 1796 and called his 14 by 33 km purchase the Mines of Spain (Walthall 1981:19). By the time of his death in 1810, Dubuque had amassed a sizable fortune from his commercial ventures in the upper Mississippi valley.

Numerous archaeological investigations in the Mines of Spain Historic District have confirmed the Meskwaki presence in the Dubuque area (Abbott 1982b, 1983, 1988; DeVore et al. 1991; Finney 1992b; McKusick comp. 1968; Mehrer 1990; Schermer 1988; Schermer and Kurtz 1986). Prior to Dubuque's land grant, the Meskwaki apparently lived near the mouth of Catfish Creek in order to guard the mines. Dubuque situated his operations near their village, a settlement known as Kettle Chief's village. According to those who visited Kettle Chief's village prior to its abandonment in 1830, as many as 70 buildings existed, including lodges and a council house (Finney 1992b:14). Archaeological investigations at the Herod site (13DB62) at the mouth of Catfish Creek apparently uncovered part of Kettle Chief's village. Additional archaeological sites in the Dubuque area include mines, smelters, forges, and blacksmith operations associated with the lead industry, as well as farmsteads and other features linked to the Euroamerican occupation (Finney 1992b).

### Fort Madison

Although the Meskwaki and the Sauk were closely associated after the mid-1700s and beginning in 1804 were treated by the federal government as one tribe, the two had separate leaders who in councils acted as representatives of independent tribes (Buffalo 1993a:11). In an 1804 treaty with the United States government, a small number of Sauk ceded territory east of the Mississippi, creating resentment and dissension between the two tribes. As the United States prepared for war with Britain and possibly some pro-British Sauk and Meskwaki, the American government sought greater control over the two tribes. As a result, land for a trading post and nearby fort a short distance above the confluence of the Des Moines and the Mississippi rivers was purchased from the Sauk and Meskwaki. In 1809 construction was completed on Fort Bellevue, soon renamed Fort Madison. It was the first United States army outpost in the upper Mississippi valley and became the focal point for a flourishing trade with the Native Americans. Tons of lead and thousands of bales of furs were exchanged for huge quantities of guns, blankets, dry goods, kettles, traps, and other manufactured goods (Jackson 1966:46; McKusick 1980:78).

Archaeological investigation at the site of Fort Madison (13LE10) was undertaken in 1965 prior to the installation of an underground water tank in the parking lot of the Sheaffer Pen company (fig. 11.8). The remnants of the old fort were believed to lie beneath this property. Excavation uncovered the remains of blockhouses, the stockade, enlisted men's barracks, and officers' quarters. These discoveries added new information to what was known about the fort from the historical records. Basement storage rooms not indicated on nineteenth-century plans of the structure were found, and the presence of a "rotated" type of blockhouse was confirmed. Numerous artifacts helped to distinguish between the location of the enlisted men's barracks and the officers' quarters. These artifacts show that both enlisted men and officers used china and silver utensils and smoked clay pipes (Jackson 1966; McKusick 1980; McKusick and Archie 1966; Williams 1980a). Later excavations at the site established that the cellar beneath the

officers' quarters had been enlarged some 20 years following the fort's abandonment and was part of the Madison House hotel (Hansman 1987).

Fort Madison was part of the American system of military garrisons and trading posts, or "factories," on the western frontier. They were established after the Louisiana Purchase in 1803 to create stability, reduce the influence of British traders, and promote the economic dependency of native peoples. By extending credit to American Indians, debts might be repaid by cession of their lands. Once such cessions were under way and native groups were relocated, military garrisons sometimes functioned to prevent further incursions by American settlers. This was a relatively short-lived protection of Indian interests, however. The voracious appetite for land among Americans soon forced cession of most American Indian property west of the Mississippi (Blaine 1979:103; Kurtz 1986).

When the War of 1812 began, Native Americans proved divided in their loyalties. The British

**11.8.** Blockhouse 3 foundation excavated at Fort Madison. Photo archives, Office of the State Archaeologist, University of Iowa. From McKusick 1980.

promised the Sauk they could retain their Iowa and Illinois lands if England won the war. Many American Indians who favored the Americans were induced to settle for a time on the Missouri River to lessen their chances of joining the British. Others, mostly Sauk, the so-called British Band, remained loyal to England and continued hostilities against American interests even after a treaty was signed between the Sauk and the United States in 1816. During this period Fort Madison was repeatedly attacked and in 1813 was finally abandoned and burned by its fleeing regiment in order to render it useless to the British.

### Black Hawk's War

Throughout the first three decades of the nineteenth century the Sauk and Meskwaki were parties, either singly or together, to six different treaties with the American government (Gourley 1990:24). Black Hawk, a celebrated warrior and leader of the Sauk who helped rout the Americans from Fort Madison, maintained British sympathies (Black Hawk 1932). He attempted to resist the growing American incursion and tried to reoccupy former Sauk land in Illinois. Other Sauk, under the growing leadership of Keokuk, and most of the Meskwaki, remained neutral. This resistance culminated in the so-called Black Hawk War of 1832. In this dismal episode, the 65-year-old Sauk leader and several hundred of his followers attempted to reoccupy their old territory and if necessary make a stand against the Americans. Abandoned by promises of support from allies and realizing that they were outnumbered by federal troops and the Illinois militia, including a young Abraham Lincoln, the band tried repeatedly and unsuccessfully to surrender. After a four-month pursuit by several thousand soldiers and American Indian mercenaries, mostly Dakota, the increasingly ragged and starving group was finally defeated at Bad Axe Creek in southwestern Wisconsin. Many of the group, including women and children, were gunned down as they attempted to cross the Mississippi. After Black Hawk was defeated, the govern-

ment appointed Keokuk as "head chief" of the so-called Sauk and Meskwaki Nation. Both tribes were forced to relinquish about 2.5 million ha of land along the eastern border of Iowa—known as the Black Hawk Purchase—and to move to small reserves in Iowa (fig. 11.9). Because Keokuk and the Meskwaki had not participated in the Black Hawk War, some of the Sauk and Meskwaki were awarded a small, 100 km² territory within the Black Hawk Purchase along the lower reaches of the Iowa River. Within this area, called the Keokuk Reserve, were the villages of Keokuk and most of the Meskwaki, including Wapello and Poweshiek (Green 1983). The so-called Half Breed tract, reserved by treaty in 1824, was an area of land in Lee County near the mouth of the Des Moines River set aside for the offspring of Sauk-Meskwaki and Euroamericans (Gourley 1990:118).

The first Fort Des Moines, established on the Des Moines River 19 km upstream from its confluence with the Mississippi, was built in 1834 within the Half Breed tract. Archaeological testing of the presumed fort area in 1966 failed to locate any structures (McKusick 1975b). Greater success resulted from archival and archaeological investigation of Fort Des Moines 2. The post was established at the confluence of the Raccoon and Des Moines rivers following an 1842 treaty that provided the Meskwaki a temporary stay in Iowa. After 1845 they were to be removed south of the Missouri River. Archival evidence predicted the location of structures such as the officers' quarters and dragoon barracks, and archaeological investigation generally confirmed these features. A hearth from one of the officers' quarters produced coins, buttons, clay pipe fragments, bottle and window glass, and ceramics. Evidence of earlier prehistoric and later historic components was also found (Gourley 1990; Henning et al. 1982).

From the time of the Black Hawk Purchase until relocation outside of Iowa after 1845, the Meskwaki and Sauk shifted their locations as they ceded more land. From the Mississippi and

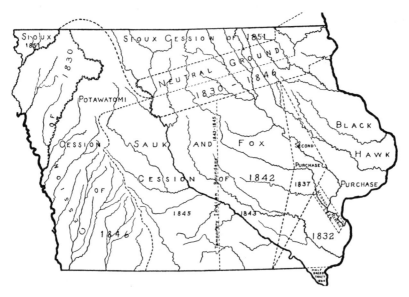

**11.9.** Historic American Indian land cessions in Iowa. From Auman 1957.

lower Iowa, Cedar, Skunk, and Des Moines rivers, individual bands of the two tribes moved upriver in a northwesterly direction to new settlements. Twenty-five Meskwaki or Sauk villages are documented for this period, and the positions of 14 of these have been determined (Gourley 1990). All of the known villages are located at the edge of broad prairie flanking a major stream (Gourley 1990). Like the Ioway, the Meskwaki traditionally followed a seasonal cycle of spring planting, a mid-summer hunt, a late summer harvest, and dispersal into small groups for the winter. All of the documented settlements are considered to be spring-summer horticultural villages. These locations remained fairly stable, with the same groups returning annually. The transitory hunting camps or winter quarters are more difficult to locate and identify, although accounts by early settlers, such as Aristarchus Cone's description of a "Sue" attack on a Meskwaki winter camp in Muscatine County, may help (Gourley 1990; Throne 1951:64).

### Final Years in Iowa

Throughout the historic period, the Meskwaki, perhaps even more than the Ioway, seem to have fissioned into small, highly mobile bands or kinship groups headed by individual leaders. This may well have been prompted by the fur trade itself (Herold et al. 1990:99). In most cases, historical documentation furnishes specific information about the later settlements, their leaders, and when the villages were established and abandoned. The everyday life within the village is not usually discussed, however, and for earlier locations the written records are virtually silent. Fortunately, both oral history and archaeology can help. Villages of three Meskwaki leaders—Poweshiek, Wacoshashe, and Totokonock—occupied between 1832 and 1838 are documented along the Iowa River south and west of Iowa City (Gourley 1990; Peterson 1997). One of Poweshiek's villages was estimated to have had a population of 1,700 to 2,000 and may have had a fortification to protect against the Dakota (Fugle

1954:4). The approximate location of this village is known and could contain archaeological materials. Wacoshashe's 1830s' village probably has been destroyed by a gravel quarry (Peterson 1996a). Limited investigations of some Meskwaki and Sauk settlements thought to date between 1843 and 1845 also have been undertaken (Perry 1990b). These sites include Wishecomaque's village and cemetery (Sauk) and Pasheshemoni's village and possible burial area (Meskwaki), all on the Des Moines River in Polk County.

In 1835 Keokuk's band reportedly established itself on the left bank of the Des Moines River in northwestern Van Buren County on property later sold for the town of Iowaville, itself abandoned around 1870. An archaeological site covering 2 to 3 ha exists at this location. Although the site has not been excavated, it occupies a landscape setting typical of known villages and has produced historic artifacts that are time diagnostic of the period (Straffin 1972b; Till and Nansel 1981b). It seems likely that this is the spot where the Ioway were defeated in 1821.

In 1836 and 1842 the Meskwaki and Sauk were forced to relinquish all territory in Iowa and were assigned to reservations, first in Kansas and later in Oklahoma. At the 1837 council with the commissioner of Indian Affairs in Washington, the Ioway contested the right of the Meskwaki and Sauk to cede territories they considered their own. Refuting this was Keokuk, whose argument is hauntingly similar to the declarations of nineteenth-century Euroamerican settlers. "This country I have gained by fighting. Therefore, I claim it. Our people once inhabited the country about the Great Lakes. We were driven off. You don't hear me claiming the country I was driven off. This is my country. I have fought for it" (Keokuk quoted in Blaine 1979: 169).

Although the Meskwaki were officially removed to reservations outside Iowa after 1845, some never left, and others returned (Green 1976, 1983). In 1856 the Iowa state legislature authorized the Meskwaki to purchase land in the state. One year later tribal leaders, including descendants of Poweshiek's group, bought land along the Iowa River and created the Meskwaki Settlement near Tama. Some of the Potawatomi soon followed, settling near Marshalltown (Clifton 1977:349). Although the Bureau of Indian Affairs refused to recognize the Meskwaki as a separate tribe, it did acknowledge that they were a distinct band, the "Sacs and Foxes of Iowa." Today the Meskwaki Settlement consists of over 1300 ha.

## Lifeways

The traditional Meskwaki lifeways combined hunting, gathering, and horticulture. The arrival of Europeans also put a premium on trapping and trade in hides and lead. Bear and deer were preferred game, but elk and bison were also hunted. Prior to their settlement in Iowa, the Meskwaki left their villages in Wisconsin during the summer to travel to Iowa on hunting expeditions for bison. After acquiring increasing numbers of horses late in the eighteenth century, they hunted westward to the Missouri River, trading with the Oto and Omaha (Edmunds and Peyser 1993:203). Gardens producing corn, squash, pumpkin, beans, and melons were situated along the river bottoms. A wide variety of wild plants supplemented the diet, including wild potatoes, ground nuts, hickory nuts, walnuts, hazelnuts, and fruit such as plums, grapes, raspberries, and strawberries. Like many northern tribes, the Meskwaki made maple sugar in the spring, but unlike some others, wild rice was never a staple (Jones 1939; Smith 1928).

The Meskwaki summer village was characterized by the use of rectangular pole houses covered with elm bark. Large enough to accommodate extended families, these structures had platforms or benches covered with rush mats along each side and interior storage pits for dried crops. After the harvest, village members disbanded into smaller groups to occupy the winter hunting grounds where round bark- or reed-covered houses were constructed (fig. 11.10).

The last summer village in Iowa was occupied between 1857 and 1902 and consisted of about 75 houses. It was burned by the federal government following a smallpox epidemic. Winter camps were still in use until after World War II, and the round winter house has become part of the modern Pow-Wow (Buffalo 1993b:11).

The often fierce Meskwaki resistance to Euroamerican encroachment apparently insured the survival of much of their traditional culture. This is particularly true in the areas of religion, ceremony, and language. One example is the Green Corn dance, an activity traditionally associated with the corn harvest in August or September, which today takes the form of the annual Pow-Wow (Buffalo 1993a:12) (Appendix 11.3). The ability of the Meskwaki to be somewhat selective in the assimilation of Euroamerican customs also has enhanced their adaptation and survival as a tribe.

### Yankton-Santee

In 1825 the Neutral Line was drawn from the mouth of the Upper Iowa River to the Big Sioux River in the western part of the state as a buffer between the Meskwaki and Sauk and their traditional enemies, the Santee and Yankton (see fig. 11.9). Both the Yankton and Santee had occasionally occupied parts of central and northwestern Iowa during the historic period. The Yankton are reported to have used the area of western Iowa more intensively and over a greater length of time than did any of the Dakota subtribes (Henning 1983:4.87). Field notes of the Lewis and Clark expedition for 1804 describe the Yankton as inhabiting the James, Des Moines, and "Sioux" rivers (Howard 1972:287). They also ranged into the southeastern part of the state, where they caused considerable anguish for the Ioway, Sauk, and Meskwaki. The 1837 account by Aristarchus Cone describes just one of many violent encounters (Throne 1951:64). Back-and-forth raiding between the Santee and Yankton and the Potawatomi also occurred during the latter's tenure in the state (Clifton 1977:327).

Although the Yankton and Santee had ceded their lands in Iowa by mid century, the Santee ultimately would write one of the final chapters of American Indian resistance in Iowa with the raids of the Dakota leader Inkpaduta and the incidents surrounding the Spirit Lake Massacre and the capture of Abbie Gardner and others in 1857.

### Winnebago

A 32-km-wide strip on either side of the Neutral Line was established in 1830 as a Neutral Ground where neither Sauk, Meskwaki, nor Dakota were allowed unless permitted by treaty or other negotiations. In treaties signed in 1832 and 1837, the Winnebago, banished from their Wisconsin territories, were given a 64 km stretch in the easternmost portion of this region and in 1842 were forced to move there. Fort Atkinson was built in 1840 to contain the tribe within the Neutral Ground and to prevent unhappy members from returning home. The fort also functioned to prevent illegal entry of white traders, smugglers, and squatters (Merry and Green 1989:2). The Turkey River Subagency was established at the same time, the second of two Winnebago subagencies in Iowa. Many Winnebago settlements existed within a 40 km area of the subagency, where supplies and annuity payments were doled out and facilities such as a school, mill, and model farm were located.

Fort Atkinson has been the scene of extensive archaeological investigations (McKusick 1976; Merry 1988; Reque 1944; Stanley 1992) and reconstruction. Documentary evidence and field studies have indicated the potential for research at the two Winnebago subagencies, trading posts, encampments, habitations, and cemeteries (Merry and Green 1989; Peterson 1995a, 1996b; Rogers 1993a; Stanley 1995; Williams 1980b) (fig. 11.11). Excavations at the Turkey River Subagency discovered two building foundations, including what was probably the school. Many of the 19,000 artifacts found were believed to be pieces of writing slate (Peterson 1996b).

**11.10.** A Meskwaki winter dwelling. Courtesy of the
State Historical Society of Iowa, Iowa City.

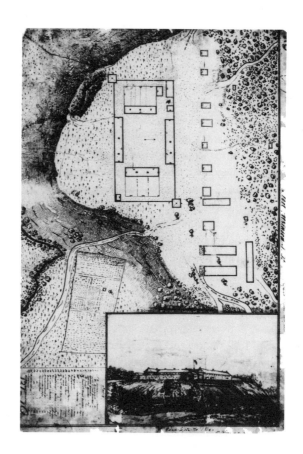

**11.11.** Fort Atkinson, Iowa Territory, drawn
September 1842 by Lt. Reynolds. National Archives,
Washington, D.C. From Merry and Green 1989.

Future excavation at the Winnebago villages may determine more about the living conditions of these people during their stay in Iowa. In 1848 most of the Winnebago were removed to a reservation at Fort Snelling, Minnesota, although small parties occasionally reoccupied northeast Iowa for almost a century (Carman 1988). Modern descendants of the Winnebago are the Ho-Chunk of Wisconsin and the Winnebago of Nebraska.

## Euroamerican and African American Sites Archaeology

Illegal Euroamerican squatters crossed the Mississippi to claim land prior to 1832. It was not until the Black Hawk Purchase, however, that the pioneer settlement of Iowa Territory was officially permitted and a land rush began. By 1851 all American Indian lands in Iowa had been ceded to the federal government, and the GLO surveys quickly parceled this property for sale.

Dozens of archaeological sites in eastern Iowa illustrate the early historic period succession from trading and military posts and squatters camps to homesteads and the first town sites with associated industries such as ceramic and brick works; grain, lumber, and fabric mills; and rock and mineral quarries (Rogers and Gradwohl 1995; Stanley 1992, 1995; Swisher 1940, 1961; Tandarich 1977). Across the state, archaeological investigations of Euroamerican domestic sites (Charlton et al. 1988; Donham 1985; Finney 1992b; Henning 1988; Higginbottom and Bakken 1990; McKay 1979, 1988; Peterson 1995b; Richner 1997; Rogers 1994b; Snow 1996) and commercial sites (Abbott 1988; Ballard 1984; Finney and Snow 1991; Merry 1989; Rogers and Page 1997; Rogers 1996) have contributed significantly to our knowledge of the territorial period and early statehood, the ethnicity of towns and farmsteads (De Vore 1993, 1994a, 1994b; Gradwohl and Osborn 1984; Reynolds 1970; Rogers 1990, 1996), and the location of military and transportation facilities (McKusick 1975b, 1975c, 1975d, 1976, 1980; McKusick and Archie

1966; Merry and Green 1989; Peterson 1996b; Rogers 1991, 1993b, 1994a; Snow 1993, 1996; Stanley 1995; Tuftee 1993). Even sites in urban areas occasionally come to light as the result of testing prior to new construction, surprising modern residents with details of life in earlier neighborhoods often unrecorded in conventional accounts (Rogers 1996). In many cases archaeological and archival research permits a close look into specific events and the lives of individual families and well-known communities, something the study of more remote periods of prehistory rarely permits. The following examples provide a small sampling of the Euroamerican and African American site investigations in Iowa.

### Gilbert's Trading Post

In 1836 the first of three trading posts was established south of present-day Iowa City at the edge of the Keokuk Reserve. This was an American Fur Company post under John Gilbert. Settlements of perhaps 2,000 Meskwaki led by Poweshiek and Wacoshashe, who in 1836 had been moved to the Keokuk Reserve, were located nearby. In 1839 Johnson County was opened to Euroamerican settlement, and the Meskwaki moved their villages up the Iowa River to the vicinity of Marengo.

Archaeological reconnaissance along the Iowa River south of Iowa City in 1995–1996 and documentary evidence, including American Fur Company records in St. Louis, helped to establish the location of Gilbert's first post at the confluence of Snyder Creek and the Iowa River (Iowa *Archeological Society Newsletter* 1996). Three other fur-trade-era sites were also recorded. Testing uncovered thousands of small artifacts and several borrow pits dug as sources of clay chinking used in building the trading house. Trade items found in the excavations and noted on the American Fur Company inventories included hand-wrought nails, gun parts, clay pipe fragments, gun flints, glass, and beads. Portions of a mouth organ or jaw harp and a strike-a-light were two of the more unusual items found. The faunal remains and the food commodities listed on the inventories suggest that by the 1830s the Meskwaki were dependent on traders, not only for manufactured goods like cloth, guns, and jewelry, but also for food supplies and items such as buffalo robes (Peterson 1997). These materials were transported up the Mississippi by steamboat, then transferred to rafts for shipment directly to the posts. Credit extended to native peoples for purchased items was often deducted from the annuities they received and, if these failed to cover their debts, by land cessions. The information from Gilbert's Trading Post and nearby fur-trade-era sites provides new insights into pioneer life and the relationship between traders and American Indians.

*Bowen's Prairie*

Bowen's Prairie, located between the north and south forks of the Maquoketa River in Jones County, has been proposed as a historic archaeological district. Reconnaissance survey and excavations were conducted in the project area, and a number of sites were determined eligible for the National Register of Historic Places (Snow 1996). Test excavations were conducted at the first cheese factory in Jones County, at the town site of Bowen's Prairie itself, at one of two post office locales in the district, and at the Moses Collins farmstead (13JN196) settled between ca. 1834 and ca. 1839, the earliest Euroamerican occupation in the region.

GLO records indicate that Moses Collins established his homestead prior to the arrival of the government surveyors. The remnants of a small, semicircular brick structure uncovered on the property were interpreted as evidence of the small cabin that served as an informal tavern and trading post run by Collins just after the land was opened to Euroamerican settlement following the Black Hawk War. The cabin was situated on the old Military Road, which followed an earlier wagon trail. Two additional trails crossed the Military Road in the same vicinity, so the tavern would have been in a favorable position to serve as a meeting place. Associated artifacts included imported English ceramics, bottles, pipe fragments, beads, gun parts, ammunition, and shot (Snow 1996:126–127).

A later structure, interpreted as a house, was composed of soft mud bricks probably made nearby and had a limestone foundation. The homemade nature of the bricks suggests that the house was built prior to the 1860s, when a professional brickmaker is known to have moved into Monticello Township, and most likely before 1851, when Moses Collins sold the house lot.

Redware and whiteware dominate the ceramic assemblage from the house site. Other artifacts included glass bottles of various sorts, window glass, cutlery, lamp chimneys, buttons, glass beads, buckles, a hat pin, brass and iron rivets, writing slates, kaolin pipe fragments, children's toys, and sewing items such as a brass thimble and a brass hook and eye. Pieces of flintlock rifles, lead shot, mini balls, and cartridges are consistent with the mid-nineteenth-century occupation of the site. A small amount of animal bone, shell, and egg shell fragments attest to the inhabitants' diet.

The excavation of the Collins homesite provides a good example of the kind of historic settlement archaeology that is possible in Iowa. While historic records may indicate the name of early families who settled in an area, learning about the nature of their everyday life, their standard of living, and interactions with the outside world is often greatly aided by archaeological clues.

*Bonaparte Pottery Works*

The Bonaparte Pottery site in Van Buren County exemplifies nineteenth-century commercialism in Iowa. The enterprise operated between 1866 and 1895, producing utilitarian ceramics, construction and paving bricks, drainage and sewer tiles, well tubing, and chimney stacks (Rogers and Gradwohl 1995). Architectural and archaeological investigation of the site following the 1993 flood uncovered numerous intact features, including the foundation of the factory building, and a large quantity of artifacts, especially the stoneware produced on site. While archival information provided a general history of the operation and its commerce, archaeological investigation produced new insights. Detailed study of the stoneware, for instance, showed the influence of individual potters on ceramic styles and the shift from hand-thrown to mold-made vessels (Rogers et al. 1995).

### Plum Grove

Plum Grove (13JH311) was the home of Robert Lucas, first governor of the Iowa Territory, 1838–1841. Located in Iowa City, it is another historic site that has been the scene of numerous archaeological investigations. Lucas built the house in 1844 from local quarry stone and brick made in Iowa City. He lived in the house with his wife, Friendly, and four children until his death in 1853. Archaeological investigation, historic documents, and oral histories tell of changes in the property over the 150 years of its history and provide a well-rounded view of life in a fairly comfortable nineteenth-century Iowa residence on the frontier of urban expansion (Charlton et al. 1988) (fig. 11.12). Excavations at Terrace Hill (13PK53), the governor's property in Des Moines; the Mackey, Miles, and Hayhurst houses at the Herbert Hoover National Historic site in West Branch; and the Colonel Davenport House on Rock Island Arsenal are good examples of historical archaeology at sites whose residents were well known (Henning 1988; McKay 1979, 1988; Richner 1997; Sudderth 1992).

### Mormon Hand Cart Trail and Settlements

In February 1846 members of the Church of Jesus Christ of Latter-day Saints, or Mormons, left Nauvoo, Illinois, and began their 2,000-km trek across the Midwest to Utah. Their route across southern Iowa is now part of a National Historic Trail. Several semipermanent settlements, including Mt. Pisgah and Garden Grove, were founded along the way to serve as resting places and to provide supplies and shelter for Mormon

11.12. A cistern excavated in the center of a barn at Plum Grove, Johnson County, was probably used by the nineteenth-century residents to collect rainwater from the roof for livestock. From Charlton et al. 1988.

pioneers who followed over the next six years (De Vore 1994a, 1994b). Historical descriptions, including the journals and diaries of settlers, and archaeological evidence bear witness to the substantial efforts that went into these settlements and to the hardships faced by their residents (De Vore 1993, 1994a, 1994b). Thousands of hectares of land were cleared and planted, and numerous log cabins, mills, communal meeting houses, and other structures were built. Hundreds reportedly died and were buried in community cemeteries and along the trail.

Ten years later, seven additional companies comprising about 2,000 new converts temporarily settled near Coralville in Johnson County, having traveled across the eastern United States by train (Loren Horton, personal communication 1999; Perry 1991b:8; Tandarich 1976). Lacking wagons and oxen necessary to supply the whole party, the Mormon leadership proposed that the journey be completed on foot using wooden handcarts to carry personal possessions and household items (Iowa Writers Program 1941:43). These handcarts were supposedly built by Iowa City carpenters and blacksmiths from materials supplied by the Mormon church (Hixon 1975).

In 1991 the location of an unmarked cemetery (13JH593) along a lower course of a tributary of Clear Creek was reported to archaeologists conducting CRM investigation in preparation for a bridge replacement on Interstate 80. The cemetery was believed to represent the burial of a small number of Mormon emigrants; however, test excavation could not confirm this (Perry 1991b). The paucity of finds at this site underscores the extremely ephemeral nature of the handcart venture. Considering that these travelers were carting meager possessions and stopping for brief periods, their nearly invisible record in Johnson County is not difficult to understand.

### City Brewery, Des Moines

The year 1884 saw the closing of the City Brewery in Des Moines, one of numerous commercial and residential buildings on the city's crowded west side. Built as a modest two-story brick structure by two German immigrants, Joseph and George Hierb, in the early 1850s and later expanded, it served as a local tavern for neighbors and workers until its demise. By 1894 all but two of the brewery's buildings had been demolished and covered with fill, victims of the state's prohibition legislation (Rogers and Page 1997). More than 100 years later, the Des Moines Metropolitan Transit Authority's plan to construct a new downtown transportation facility resulted in salvage of archaeological and historic data about the brewery and the west side neighborhood of which it was a part. Particularly interesting was the information about consumer behavior, subsistence, ethnic affiliation, and health and sanitation recovered from privies and refuse deposits. For instance, while beer mugs and shot glasses were prevalent in the early deposits, the occurrence of liquor bottles later is believed to reflect changing drinking habits and the easing of prohibition laws that promoted increased consumption of hard liquor (Rogers 1996; Rogers and Page 1997).

### Buxton

Buxton in Monroe County was a planned, predominantly African American coal-mining community established in 1900 by the Consolidation Coal Company, a subsidiary of the Chicago and North Western Railroad. It lasted until the 1920s, when the coal company changed its base of operations and the residents were forced to move. The townsite was abandoned and within a short period was reclaimed as farmland (Gradwohl and Osborn 1984). In 1980 an interdisciplinary study of Buxton included oral history, photographic study, and archaeological investigations. Researchers learned about commercial, social, and ethnic aspects of the community not known from the documentary data alone. The locations of a prominent hotel, the home of the mine superintendent, and the town cemetery, all missing on contemporary plat maps, were discovered. Historical accounts and archaeological remains together illustrated the local, national, and international commercial networks in which Buxton residents participated. They also confirmed that not all employees "owed their souls" to the Monroe Mercantile Company store (Gradwohl and Osborn 1984:166). Items purchased from other businesses or through mail order included china and glassware, alcoholic patent medicines, and revolvers. Perhaps the most important aspect of the Buxton investigation is that it represents one of the few archaeological studies of an African American community outside the South or the urban centers on the East Coast. Oral testimony from surviving Buxton residents and their descendants, combined with archaeology and historic accounts, verified a relatively high standard of life for the citizens of this unusual community.

### Steamboat Bertrand

Finally, mention must be made of what many would probably consider the least likely kind of archaeological site associated with a landlocked state such as Iowa—a shipwreck. The importance of steamboating is well known to most Iowans. River transport was a primary means of travel and commerce throughout the Midwest until the first railroads reached west to the Mississippi in 1855. The fortunes of many communities and individuals along the Mississippi were intricately tied to the steamboats, keelboats, and rafts whose cargoes supplied both the necessities and luxuries of life (Bowers et al. 1990:6). As many as 74 steamboat wrecks are believed to lie buried in the silt of the Mississippi and Missouri rivers and their navigable tributaries in Iowa (Bowers et al. 1990:16). Excavation of the steamboat *Bertrand* in 1968 and 1969 near DeSoto Landing on the Nebraska side of the Missouri River north of Omaha has demonstrated the rich potential of

this class of remains (Petsche 1974) (fig. 11.13). The *Bertrand,* bound with abundant stores for the Montana gold fields, struck a timber snag in 1865 and sank in shallow water. Although salvage operations commenced immediately, the brief diversion of the salvage crew to an upstream wreck left enough time for the notorious currents of the Missouri River to bury the boat in silt for almost 100 years. The recovery and conservation of intact foodstuffs, tools, mining equipment, and household goods at a state-of-the-art center in the DeSoto Bend National Wildlife Refuge in Harrison County, Iowa, preserve a virtual time capsule of the everyday necessities the *Betrand* carried to the mining frontier more than a century ago.

**11.13.** Excavating the steamboat *Bertrand.* Much of the cargo had already been removed when this photo was taken. Courtesy of the Nebraska State Historical Society. From Bowers et al. 1990.

## APPENDIX 11.1.

### Weeping Ceremony of the Ioway in Welcoming Nicholas Perrot to Their Village

The interview with these newcomers was held in so peculiar a manner that it furnished cause for laughter. They approached the Frenchman [Perrot], weeping hot tears, which they let fall into their hands along with saliva, and with other filth which issued from their noses, with which they rubbed their heads, faces, and garments of the French; all these caresses made their stomachs revolt. On the part of those savages there were only shouts and yells, which were quieted by giving them some knives and awls. At last, after having made a great commotion, in order to make themselves understood—which they could not do, not having any interpreter—they went back [to their people]. Four others of their men came, at the end of a few days, of whom there was one who spoke Islinois [sic]; this man said that their village was nine leages [sic] distant, on the bank of the river, and the French went there to find them. At their arrival, the women fled; some gained the hills, and others rushed into the woods which extended along the river, weeping, and raising their hands towards the sun. Twenty prominent men presented the calumet to Perrot, and carried him upon a buffalo-skin into the cabin of the chief, who walked at the head of this procession. When they had taken their places on the mat, this chief began to weep over Perrot's head, bathing it with his tears, and with moisture that dripped from his mouth and his nose; and those who carried the guest did the same to him. These tears ended, the calumet was again presented to him; and the chief caused a great earthen pot, which was filled with tongues of buffaloes, to be placed over the fire. These were taken out as soon as they began to boil, and were cut into small pieces, of which the chief took one and placed it in his guest's mouth; Perrot tried to take one for himself, but the chief refused until he had given it to him, for it is their custom to place the morsels in the guest's mouth when he is a captain, until the third time, before they offer the dish. He could not forbear spitting out this morsel, which was still all bloody (those same tongues were cooked that night in an iron pot); immediately some men, in great surprise, took their calumet, and perfumed them with tobacco-smoke. Never in the world were seen greater weepers than those peoples; their approach is accompanied with tears, and their adieu is the same. (quoted from the writings of Nicholas Perrot by Baqueville de La Potherie in Blair 1911:1:368–369)

## APPENDIX 11.2.

### The Ioway Months of the Year

January: Bear Jumping Moon
February: Big Bear Jumping Moon
March: Frog Moon
April: Cultivating Moon
May: Nothing to do Moon
June: Little Flowers Moon
July: Big Flowers Moon
August: Buffalo Rutting Moon
September: Frost in Animal Beds Moon
October: Elk Whistling Moon
November: Deer Rutting Moon
December: Raccoon Rutting Moon
(Skinner 1926:294–295)

## APPENDIX 11.3.

### Meskwaki Pow-Wow

The annual Meskwakis Pow-Wow originated from the traditional religious and social beliefs of the Meskwakis tribe. Today it is not so much a religious event but more of a social gathering. The modern Meskwakis Pow-Pow is derived from the Green Corn Dance, "Field Days," and other social events of the tribe in its early years. The "Green Corn Dance" was an annual event that took place during the harvesting of crops. This generally happened in August or occasionally in September if the corn crop matured late. During this event, some of the fresh crop was cooked for the feasting and the rest would be boiled and dried. The dried corn would then be placed in sacks and buried in deep pits located in the summer houses. The dancing and feasting that accompanied the harvest would last two to three weeks, and now and then would be interrupted with horse racing, gambling, and ball playing ("no-rules", "Lacross" etc.). After all harvesting, dancing and feasting was completed, the families would go their separate ways and return to their winter hunting grounds.

In the winter of 1901–1902, a smallpox epidemic swept through the village resulting in the deaths of many people. The following spring the Federal government burned the last village the Meskwakis would ever have. After that, the tribe no longer lived close together in their summer homes (wickiups) or planted in a community garden, but lived in small scattered housing built by the Federal government. They planted and harvested separately on their own. This new living situation eliminated the need for a common harvest. However, the tribe fixed in their cultural ways, still craved for a social gathering. A location was established near the old village site and an event that took the place of the Green Corn Dance was still established. The "Field Days" as it came to be known lasted about a week with dancing, games and horse racing. It was a general social gathering without the harvest.

The Field Days were held from 1902 to 1912 and during those years more and more tourists and visitors were in attendance. With some organization and planning, the Field Days had the possibility of becoming a major commercial enterprise. In 1912, the Chief appointed 15 men to plan for 1913. The men appointed decided to change the name from Field Days to "Pow-Wow." The first pow-wow was held at the same location. Five wickiups were arranged in a circle to enclose a dance area and dancers performed the Meskwakis Bean, Buffalo Head, Snake, Swan, and Shawnee dances, along with general war dances. The War dance is the most colorful and up-tempo event to view.

Today the Meskwakis pow-wow is the only one of its kind in Iowa. It is held annually on the only Indian Settlement in the Hawkeye state. During the four-day affair, the gathering of the tribes celebrate the end of summer in numerous ways, playing cards, softball games, and performing in full regalia the dances that have been handed down for generations. The Meskwakis pow-wow is a time of reaffirmation and hope, a time of worship and kinship—and, it is above all, a time of friendship and making of new acquaintances. (Buffalo, 1993a:12)

# 12 Stewardship: The Eleventh Hour

The mounds are rapidly being destroyed and thousands of valuable relics exhumed and carried to the eastern States and foreign countries every year, and soon these remains of the work of a laborious race will have forever vanished from sight, and almost from memory, save what knowledge of them may be stored up in the collections made by those who have appreciated the importance of the work before it is too late. —Pratt 1885:217

**ARCHAEOLOGY** has come a long way since the days when the moundbuilder problem was the focus of antiquarian concern. Iowa's prehistoric and historic outline has been established, the environments and lifeways of its earlier residents are better known, and each new site promises information to help in the reconstruction of the past. Nevertheless, our increasing knowledge has, in some cases, barely kept pace with the destruction of sites.

Throughout the twentieth century urban expansion, natural resources development, and agriculture have resulted in a loss of Iowa's prehistoric and historic heritage. Modern buildings and highways are often constructed in locations that were equally attractive to earlier peoples, resulting in the disruption of areas having a high site density. Farming has had a bittersweet effect on archaeological remains. The plow has exposed evidence of sites that might not have been discovered. Thanks to many farmers the importance of these remains is recognized and brought to the archaeologist's attention. At the same time, the context of artifacts has been disturbed, and some sites, particularly mounds, have been obliterated by plowing.

Sites are also lost to age-old forces of destruction. Erosion from wind and water takes its toll on archaeological remains. The Poison Ivy site,

an Oneota component in Louisa County, was washed away by the Iowa River before it was ever well studied. The flood of 1993 damaged many sites, and salvage excavations at well-known locations such as Phipps and Helen Smith were undertaken in the hopes of retrieving information exposed as the result of high water levels and erosion (Billeck 1995; Fishel 1995a). Damming of rivers—with the raising and lowering of water levels to decrease flood potential and improve irrigation—continues to accelerate natural stream erosion.

The looting of sites also persists, despite greater public awareness and stronger protective legislation. A market for artifacts creates the impetus for some of this "pothunting." No matter how innocent their motives, people who purchase artifacts for private collections unwillingly contribute to the wanton destruction of archaeological sites. Just about everyone interested in archaeology appreciates the beauty and originality of prehistoric and historic artifacts. However, these remains are valuable in the scientific sense only because, when found in context, they extend our knowledge of human history back thousands of years before written records and document the rich cultural heritage of native peoples. Everyone should be given the opportunity to learn about this history and heritage.

In Iowa we are fortunate in having a public that, in general, is sensitive to its prehistoric and historic past. Many sites have been recognized and saved because of the efforts of people who are interested in Iowa's cultural resources and understand their worth. Numerous public and private historic and conservation organizations—including the State Historical Society, the Office of the State Archaeologist, the Iowa State Preserves Board, county and municipal historical commissions, and especially the Iowa Archeological Society—have been exemplary in this regard. The Iowa State Preserves system is one of only a few in the country that include cultural resources along with natural resources in their preservation efforts. The Iowa Archeological Society has played an integral part in educating the public for almost half a century (fig. 12.1; Appendix 12.1).

Only by becoming aware of our cultural heritage and educating others can we hope to insure its continued protection. Archaeological sites on state and federal properties can be protected through stronger legislation. If we are familiar with sites on private land before they are threatened, we can draw attention to them and perhaps persuade their owners to protect them or permit their study. Private companies in Iowa have sometimes supported archaeological investigation of threatened sites on their property although not required to do so by law (Snow 1994), and archaeologists rarely encounter opposition to their research on privately owned land.

By informing others of the nature and importance of cultural remains, by sharing our interests and concerns, and by periodically checking on the status of known sites in an area, we can help to remove archaeological sites from the endangered species list. Federal agencies like the Corps of Engineers and the U.S. Forest Service have sponsored archaeological site-stewardship programs. Local, state, and private organizations could do the same. Surely if individuals and organizations are willing to lend time and assistance in "adopting" Iowa's highways, they might be willing to become sponsors and stewards of Iowa sites, the archaeological highways to the past.

**12.1.** Members of the Iowa Archeological Society working at the Mill Creek Lange site in O'Brien County. Photo by Stephen C. Lensink.

## APPENDIX 12.1.
### Avocational Opportunities

The Iowa Archeological Society offers the best opportunities for people to become involved in local archaeology. The Society is an organization of professional and avocational archaeologists interested in learning about and protecting Iowa's prehistoric past. Its quarterly newsletter describes recent discoveries throughout the state, reviews relevant books, and announces archaeological events. An annual journal contains more extensive articles on various aspects of Iowa archaeology. The Society usually conducts two annual meetings where avocational and professional archaeologists gather to share information, display their finds, and discuss Iowa's archaeological past. Since 1974 the Society has sponsored a number of field school opportunities (Tiffany 1974) and beginning in 1976 offered a certification program in survey, excavation, and lab methods. Individual chapters also sponsor local meetings and field opportunities.

In addition to cosponsoring the certification program and field schools, the Office of the State Archaeologist has its own program in public education, offering a series of educational pamphlets on Iowa prehistory, a number of films and filmstrips on various aspects of prehistory and history, and numerous publications. A Web site (http://www.uiowa.edu/~osa/) provides additional information and has links to other informative sites. Information on all of these resources is available by contacting the Office of the State Archaeologist, University of Iowa, 700 Clinton Street Building, Iowa City, Iowa 52242.

Field opportunities in other states and abroad are published annually in the periodical *Archaeological Fieldwork Opportunities Bulletin* offered through the Archaeological Institute of America, Order Department, Kendall-Hunt Publishing, 4050 Westmark Dr., Dubuque, IA 52002. A nationwide program, "Passport in Time," developed by the U.S. Forest Service, offers public participation in archaeological and historic preservation projects throughout the country. Information is available from Passports in Time Clearinghouse, P.O. Box 31315 Tucson AZ 85751-1315.

# Glossary

activity area   a concentration of archaeological materials (artifacts/features/ecofacts) whose context and association suggest the former location of a particular activity at an archaeological site

allotment   a parcel of land

artifacts   portable objects humanly made or used

assemblage   all of the various classes of artifacts found together at one site

atlatl   a Nahuatl (central Mexican) word for spear-thrower

attribute   the smallest distinguishing feature of an artifact

auger   a coring device used to sample subsurface deposits

bands   small (20–25), egalitarian societies related through kinship with social differentiation based on age and gender alone

base camp   home base or campsite from which groups set out to hunt and collect food and other resources and then return

Beringia   wide land mass joining northwestern North America to northeastern Siberia; created as a result of lowered sea levels during glacial episodes

biface or bifacial artifact   a stone worked or flaked on two sides

bipolar core reduction   a method of detaching flakes from a stone core by resting the core on an anvil and striking perpendicular to the core. The core is then reversed against the anvil and the process repeated, producing diametrically opposed striking platforms on the core. The resulting bipolar flakes have characteristic platforms and bulbs of percussion on one end, leaving the other end with typical shattered or severed attributes.

calibration   the process of converting radiocarbon dates to calendar dates

ceramics   pottery artifacts

chert   a hard, dense, cryptocrystalline rock of sedimentary origin

chiefdom   a society in which corporate groups such as clans become ranked and one or more may assume positions of dominance or leadership for the acquisition, control, and redistribution of goods and services within the society as a whole.

chipped stone artifacts   stone tools fashioned by percussion and pressure flaking techniques

component   a single episode of use or occupation at a site

**coprolites**   ancient feces

**cord-impressed**   cord impressions visible as the result of pressing a piece of cord or fabric into the vessel surface as a decorative and/or manufacturing technique

**cord-marking or cord-roughening**   cord impressions visible as linear marks on the vessel surface as a result of working the vessel walls with a cord-wrapped paddle.

**cross-dating**   dating sites relative to one another based on the similar artifacts they contain

**Cultural Resource Management (CRM)**   contract archaeology resulting from compliance with local, state, and federal legislation

**culture history**   the sequence of cultural events characteristic of an area; roughly equivalent to the historian's time line of historic events

**culture process**   the mechanisms and processes by which human societies change

**daub**   clay or mud usually tempered with grass or other plant materials that was used as plastering and waterproofing material over a wall composed of small, interlaced timbers called wattle.  Frequently daub survives in an archaeological site because it has burned and becomes baked.  This often occurs if the house caught fire during the time it was occupied or burned after it was abandoned

**Dawes Act or General Allotment Act (1887)**   intended to assign to individual Native Americans allotments of land varying from 40 to 160 acres plus agricultural equipment and seed. Most of the remaining reservation land was to be sold off to Euroamericans, with the proceeds going to the tribe. From the time the Dawes Act was passed until the Indian Reorganization Act in 1934, American Indians lost 60 percent of their lands

**debitage**   stone flakes bearing no signs of further use or modification; sometimes called waste flakes.

**dendrochronology**   tree-ring dating

**direct historical approach**   a method of working back from the historic into the prehistoric period by identifying the archaeological sites of known peoples and using the diagnostic features to propose the ethnic identity of older ancestral sites

**direct percussion flaking**   directly hitting or striking flakes from a core or another flake with an implement such as a hammerstone or antler billet or by knocking the core or flake against a stationary anvil

**ecofacts**   archaeological evidence—seeds, pollen, mollusks, bone, shell, chemical changes in the soil—relevant to dietary, environmental, and climatic reconstruction

**ethnographic analogy**   utilizing descriptions of the lifeways of people in the recent past as a guide to infer the function and meaning of archaeological remains

**Euroamericans**   human inhabitants of North America of European descent

**fauna**   animals

**features**   nonportable cultural remains found at a site, such as burials, hearths, storage pits, and post molds

**fire-cracked rock**   lithic material (including chert, limestone, granite, and hematite) that shows discoloration or breakage, indicating it has been fractured by heat.  Fire-cracked rock often occurs in huge quantities at some sites, suggesting cooking and roasting processes such as stone boiling and pit roasting. Close examination of fire-cracked rock often reveals that discarded ground stone tools were recycled as a source for heating and cooking

**flake**   a smaller piece or chip struck from a stone core or another flake

**flint**   generally equivalent to chert

**flora**   plants

**flute** long, thin channel flake

**fusilinid** fossiliferous; refers to poorly known cherts from Pennsylvanian-age deposits in southwestern Iowa

**geomorphology** the study of landforms

**ground stone artifacts** stone artifacts produced by pecking, grinding, and polishing

**hammerstone** a stone used to strike flakes from a core or other flake

**heat treating** the application of heat to certain types of stone to increase their knapability; heat treating often creates a change in the color and patina of the rock

**historical archaeology** the archaeology of periods for which there are also written records

**Holocene (Recent) epoch** post-Pleistocene; the interglacial of the past 10,000 years

**horizon** broadly shared styles or similarities in culture content

**Hypsithermal** period of Holocene warming when climatic conditions throughout the Midwest were warmer and drier than present

**Ice Age** typically refers to the Pleistocene epoch

**indirect percussion** detaching a flake from a core or another flake by hitting an intermediary object such as an antler, bone, stone, or piece of wood held between the core and the striking implement

**in situ** in place, undisturbed

**isotope** one of two or more forms of an atomic element that share the same atomic number but vary in atomic mass due to the number of neutrons (i.e., $^{13}C$ and $^{14}C$)

**lanceolate** leaf-shaped

**lithics** stone artifacts

**malacology** the study of mollusks or snails

**mano** hand-held grinding stone used to crush and grind materials on a metate

**megafauna** big game or big animals

**metate** stationary rock against which materials are ground

**midden** accumulation of garbage or trash

**multicomponent** more than one period of use or occupation at a site

**Native American Graves Protection and Repatriation Act (NAGPRA)** federal law passed in 1990 requiring federal agencies and most museums in the United States to inventory Native American human remains, burial artifacts, sacred objects, and objects formerly owned communally by tribes and make them available (repatriate) to those tribes who can demonstrate a clear affiliation

**Native Americans** American Indian and Inuit (Eskimo) peoples; also referred to in Canada as First Nations

**occupation** a single episode of site use

**ossuary** a grave site containing multiple burials rather than inhumations in single graves

**paleobotany/archaeobotany** the study of ancient plant remains

**paleosol** ancient soil

**palynology** the study of pollen

**paste** the material from which ceramics are made; includes the plastic clay and the aplastic inclusions or temper

**period** an increment of time

**phase**   a group of contemporary components within a locality that share a similarity of content and are assumed to be related in some way

**Pleistocene**   the most recent Ice Age, a geologic epoch spanning the period between 1,700,000 and 10,000 years ago

**pothunting**   looting archaeological sites

**potsherds**   pieces of pottery

**preform**   a flake roughly worked into shape, marking the beginning stage in the manufacture of a biface

**prehistory**   before written history

**pressure flaking**   detaching a smaller flake from another stone by applying pressure along the flake edge or to the surface with an implement of stone, antler, or bone

**proton magnetometer or gradiometer**   remote sensing device used to detect subsurface deposits (typically features such as hearths and pits) by measuring the difference in magnetism in buried remains

**provenience**   the context of archaeological remains, including their location and relationship to others

**Quaternary**   the geological time period containing the Pleistocene and Holocene epochs

**RCYBP**   Radiocarbon years before present, conventionally set at A.D. 1950, when radiocarbon dating became a common archaeological tool; RCYBP and B.P. are often used interchangeably to indicate a date in years before present which has not been calibrated

**rockshelter**   rock overhang or cave utilized by humans

**site**   any location exhibiting evidence of past human use or habitation

**stratigraphy**   the study of the superimposed natural or cultural layers at a site

**survey**   the deliberate search for archaeological remains

**temper**   inclusions (sand, stone, shell) added to clay to counteract breakage as the result of expansion and contraction during drying and firing

**tradition**   long-term trajectories of similar culture content

**transformational processes**   the natural and human impacts to an archaeological site from the time of occupation

**uniface or unifacial artifact**   a stone worked or flaked on one side only

**wattle**   see daub

**Wisconsin**   the fourth stage of the Pleistocene epoch in North America; it is followed by the early Holocene epoch

# Bibliography

Abbott, Larry R.
1980   Upland Soil Development in Iowa. Paper presented at the 92nd session of the Iowa Academy of Science, Indianola. Copy on file, Office of the State Archaeologist, University of Iowa, Iowa City.

1982a   Environmental Setting. In *A Preliminary Report on the Arthur Site, East Okoboji Lake, Iowa,* edited by Joseph A. Tiffany, pp. 7–14. Research Papers Vol. 7, No. 1. Office of the State Archaeologist, University of Iowa, Iowa City.

1982b   *An Archaeological Assessment of the Mines of Spain Area, Dubuque County, Iowa.* Contract Completion Report 195. Office of the State Archaeologist, University of Iowa, Iowa City.

1983   *The Cultural Resources of the Mines of Spain Area, Dubuque County, Iowa.* Contract Completion Report 206. Office of the State Archaeologist, University of Iowa, Iowa City.

1988   Frontier Lead Mining in the Upper Mississippi Valley. *Journal of the Iowa Archeological Society* 35:1–15.

Abbott, Larry R., and Shirley J. Schermer
1983   *The Pooler Site (13WB215).* Research Papers Vol. 8, No. 3. Office of the State Archaeologist, University of Iowa, Iowa City.

Abbott, Larry R., and Joseph A. Tiffany
1986   Archaeological Context and Upland Soil Development: The Midwest U.S.A. Example. Ms. on file, Office of the State Archaeologist, University of Iowa, Iowa City.

Adair, James
1775   *History of the American Indians.* E. and C. Dilly, London.

Agogino, George A., and W. D. Frankforter
1960   A Paleo-Indian Bison-Kill in Northwest Iowa. *American Antiquity* 25:414–415.

Ahern, Lawrence D.
1938   *Down One Hundred Years.* Wallace-Homestead, Des Moines, Iowa.

Ahler, Stanley A.
1995   Survey of Area B/F Preceramic Archaeology. In *Archaeology of the Medicine Crow Site Complex (39BF2), Buffalo County, South Dakota,* edited by Stanley A. Ahler and Dennis L. Toom, pp. 177–187. Report of Investigations 51. Illinois State Museum, Springfield.

Alex, Lynn M.
1973   *An Analysis of Fish Utilization at Four Initial Middle Missouri Sites.* Unpublished Master's thesis, Department of Anthropology, University of Wisconsin–Madison.

1976   1976 I.A.S. Field School. Iowa Archeological Society *Newsletter* 82:3–10.

1978   The Poison Ivy Site: A New Oneota Site in Southeastern Iowa. *Journal of the Iowa Archeological Society* 25:78–91.

1980   *Exploring Iowa's Past: A Guide to Prehistoric Archaeology.* University of Iowa Press, Iowa City.

1993   Sources for *Busycon* Specimens Found in Initial Middle Missouri Sites in South Dakota. Paper presented at the 51st Annual Plains Anthropological Conference, Saskatoon, Saskatchewan. Copy on file, Office of the State Archaeologist, University of Iowa, Iowa City.

1994   Oneota and the Olivet Phase, South Dakota. *Newsletter of the South Dakota Archaeological Society* 24(1):1–4.

1996   Hot Pits and Hot Rocks: An Introduction.

Paper presented at the 54th Annual Plains Anthropological Conference, Iowa City. Copy on file, Office of the State Archaeologist, University of Iowa, Iowa City.

Alex, Lynn M., Mark Anderson, and Shirley Schermer
1998    A Stratigraphic Profile of Public Archaeology in Iowa. Paper presented at the 63rd Annual Meeting of the Society for American Archaeology, Seattle.

Alex, Lynn M., and William Green
1995    *Toolesboro Mounds National Historic Landmark Archaeological Analysis and Report.* Research Papers Vol. 20, No. 4. Office of the State Archaeologist, University of Iowa, Iowa City.

Alex, Lynn M., and Joseph A. Tiffany
1996    Southeast Iowa Woodland and Oneota Sites Tour. In *Field Trip Guide: Southeast Iowa Woodland and Oneota Sites,* pp. 1–14. 54th Annual Plains Anthropological Conference, Iowa City. Copy on file, Office of the State Archaeologist, University of Iowa, Iowa City.

Alex, Robert A.
1968    *The Rock Run Shelter: A Stratified Woodland Site in East-Central Iowa.* Unpublished Master's thesis, Department of Anthropology, University of Iowa, Iowa City.

1970    An Interpretation of Havana and Spring Hollow Incised Pottery in Eastern Iowa. Ms. on file, Office of the State Archaeologist, University of Iowa, Iowa City.

1971    Upper and Plains Mississippian. Ms. on file, Office of the State Archaeologist, University of Iowa, Iowa City.

1973    Architectural Features of Houses at the Mitchell Site (39DV2), Eastern South Dakota. *Plains Anthropologist* 18:149–159.

1976    Problem Oriented Contract Archaeology and Some Thoughts on the Prehistory of Eastern Iowa. *The Keystone: Newsletter of the Charles R. Keyes Chapter of the Iowa Archeological Society* 1:5–10.

1980    Contents of a Soil Sample from the Great Oasis Site at Oakwood Lakes State Park. *Newsletter of the South Dakota Archaeological Society* 10(1):1–3.

1981a    *The Village Cultures of the Lower James Valley, South Dakota.* Unpublished Ph.D. dissertation, Department of Anthropology, University of Wisconsin–Madison.

1981b    Village Sites off the Missouri River. In *The Future of South Dakota's Past,* edited by Larry J. Zimmerman and Lucille C. Stewart, pp. 39–45. Special Publication of the South Dakota Archaeological Society No. 2. University of South Dakota Archaeology Laboratory, Vermillion.

Anderson, Adrian D.
1954    Stone Artifacts from the Glenwood Area: A Report on Dig 7, a House-Site. *Journal of the Iowa Archeological Society* 4(2):2–16.

1957    Report on Turin Skeleton No. 3. Iowa Archeological Society *Newsletter* 19:4–5.

1958    Suggested Manner of Mound Construction. Iowa Archaeological Society *Newsletter* 28:7.

1961    The Glenwood Sequence: A Local Sequence for a Series of Archeological Manifestations in Mills County. *Journal of the Iowa Archeological Society* 10(3):1–101.

1971a    Review of Iowa River Valley Archaeology. In *Prehistoric Investigations,* edited by Marshall B. McKusick, pp. 1–23. Report 3. Office of the State Archaeologist, University of Iowa, Iowa City.

1971b    The Late Woodland Walters Site. In *Prehistoric Investigations,* edited by Marshall B. McKusick, pp. 24–52. Report 3. Office of the State Archaeologist, University of Iowa, Iowa City.

1973    Phase III Highway Salvage Archaeology: 1966–1969. In *Archaeological Explorations along Iowa Highways,* by Marshall B. McKusick, James Boylan, and John Hotopp, pp. 21–26. Submitted to the Iowa Department of Transportation, Ames. Copy on file, Office of the State Archaeologist, University of Iowa, Iowa City.

Anderson, Adrian, and Barbara Anderson
1960    Pottery Types of the Glenwood Focus. *Journal of the Iowa Archeological Society* 9(4):12–39.

Anderson, Adrian D., and Joseph A. Tiffany
1972    Rummells-Maske: A Clovis Find-Spot in Iowa. *Plains Anthropologist* 17:55–59.

Anderson, Adrian D., and Larry J. Zimmerman
1976    Settlement-Subsistence Variability in the Glenwood Locality, Southwestern Iowa. *Plains Anthropologist* 21:141–154.

Anderson, David G.

1990 The Paleoindian Colonization of Eastern North America: A View from the Southeastern United States. In *Early Paleoindian Economies of Eastern North America,* edited by Kenneth Tankersley and B. L. Isaac, pp. 163–216. Research in Economic Anthropology Supplement 5. JAI, Greenwich, Connecticut.

Anderson, Duane C.

1969 Mill Creek Culture: A Review. *Plains Anthropologist* 14:137–143.

1970 The Catlinite Amulet Site (13CK64). *Northwest Chapter of the Iowa Archeological Society Newsletter* 18 (2):3–12.

1973a Ioway Ethnohistory: A Review Pt. 1. *Annals of Iowa* 41:1228–1241.

1973b Iowa Ethnohistory: A Review Pt. 2. *Annals of Iowa* 42:41–59.

1974 Message from the President. Iowa Archaeological Society *Newsletter* 72:1.

1975a The Development of Archaeology in Iowa: An Overview. *Proceedings of the Iowa Academy of Science* 82:71–86.

1975b The Manufacture of Long Nosed God Masks and Other Items from Marine Shell. Iowa Archeological Society *Newsletter* 77:9–10.

1975c A Long-Nosed God Mask from Northwest Iowa. *American Antiquity* 40:326–329.

1975d *Western Iowa Prehistory.* Iowa State University Press, Ames.

1976 *A Dugout Canoe from Montgomery County, Iowa.* Research Papers Vol. 1, No. 4. Office of the State Archaeologist, University of Iowa, Iowa City.

1977 *The Crim Site (13ET403).* Research Papers Vol. 2, No. 9. Office of the State Archaeologist, University of Iowa, Iowa City.

1980 Stone Tool Assemblages from the Cherokee Site. In *The Cherokee Excavations: Holocene Ecology and Human Adaptations in Northwestern Iowa,* edited by Duane C. Anderson and Holmes A. Semken, Jr., pp. 197–238. Academic Press, New York.

1981a *Mill Creek Ceramics: The Complex from the Brewster Site.* Report 14. Office of the State Archaeologist, University of Iowa, Iowa City.

1981b *Eastern Iowa Prehistory.* Iowa State University Press, Ames.

1985a *Excavations at the Wittrock Site (13OB4): A Compilation of Information Pertaining to Projects Conducted in 1959 and 1965.* Research Papers Vol. 10, No. 1. Office of the State Archaeologist, University of Iowa, Iowa City.

1985b Models of Mill Creek Midden Formation: Implications for Future Research. *Proceedings of the Iowa Academy of Science* 92:53–57.

1985c Mesquakie Chief Poweshiek's Feathered Cape. *Plains Anthropologist* 30:161–164.

1986 The Wittrock Excavations: Implications for the Study of Culture Process within the Initial Variant of the Middle Missouri Tradition. *North American Archaeologist* 7:215–241.

1987a The Keystone Site (13JK23): A Multicomponent Rockshelter in Jackson County, Iowa. *Journal of the Iowa Archaeological Society* 34:1–6.

1987b Toward a Processual Understanding of the Initial Variant of the Middle Missouri Tradition: The Case of the Mill Creek Culture of Iowa. *American Antiquity* 52:522–537.

1994 *Stone, Glass, and Metal Artifacts from the Milford Site (13DK1): An Early 18th Century Oneota Occupation in Northwest Iowa.* Research Papers Vol. 19, No. 5. Office of the State Archaeologist, University of Iowa, Iowa City.

Anderson, Duane C. (editor)

1969 Unusual Items Found during Salvage Operations at the Williams Site (13PM50). *Northwest Chapter of the Iowa Archeological Society Newsletter* 19(6):12–13.

1973 A New Archaic Site. *Northwest Chapter of the Iowa Archeological Society Newsletter* 21(1):2.

Anderson, Duane C., and David A. Baerreis

1973 The Rock Creek Ossuary, Iowa (13PM65). *Proceedings of the Iowa Academy of Science* 80:185–191.

Anderson, Duane C., Michael Finnegan, John Hotopp, and Alton K. Fisher

1977 *Archaeology and Indian Religion: Precedents and Data from an Archaic Cemetery in Western Iowa.* Research Papers Vol. 2, No. 3. Office of the State Archaeologist, University of Iowa, Iowa City.

1978 The Lewis Central School Site (13PW5): A Resolution of Ideological Conflicts at an Archaic Ossuary in Western Iowa. *Plains Anthropologist* 23:183–219.

Anderson, Duane C., and Holmes A. Semken, Jr. (editors)

1980   *The Cherokee Excavations: Holocene Ecology and Human Adaptations in Northwestern Iowa.* Academic Press, New York.

Anderson, Duane C., and Richard Shutler, Jr.

1974   Summary and Conclusions. The Cherokee Sewer Site (13CK405): A Preliminary Report of a Stratified Paleo-Indian/Archaic Site in Northwestern Iowa. *Journal of the Iowa Archeological Society* 21:155–172.

1978   The Cherokee Sewer Site (13CK405): A Summary and Assessment. In *Bison Procurement and Utilization: A Symposium,* edited by Leslie B. Davis and Michael Wilson, pp. 132–139. Memoir 14. *Plains Anthropologist,* Lincoln, Nebraska.

Anderson, Duane C., Richard Shutler, Jr., and Wayne M. Wendland

1980   The Cherokee Sewer Site and the Cultures of the Atlantic Climatic Episode. In *The Cherokee Excavations: Holocene Ecology and Human Adaptations in Northwestern Iowa,* edited by Duane C. Anderson and Holmes A. Semken, Jr., pp. 257–274. Academic Press, New York.

Anderson, Duane C., and Michael Spriestersbach

1982   The Stone Tool Assemblage. In *A Preliminary Report on the Arthur Site, East Okoboji Lake,* edited by Joseph A. Tiffany, pp. 86–118. Research Papers Vol. 7, No. 1. Office of the State Archaeologist, University of Iowa, Iowa City.

Anderson, Duane C., and Joseph A. Tiffany

1987   A Caddoan Trade Vessel from Northwestern Iowa. *Plains Anthropologist* 32:93–96.

Anderson, Duane C., Joseph A. Tiffany, Michael Fokken, and Patricia M. Williams

1979   The Siouxland Sand and Gravel Site (13WD402): New Data and the Application of Iowa's New State Law Protecting Ancient Cemeteries. *Journal of the Iowa Archeological Society* 26:119–145.

Anderson, Duane C., Joseph A. Tiffany, and Fred W. Nelson

1986   Recent Research on Obsidian from Iowa Archaeological Sites. *American Antiquity* 51:837–852.

Anderson, Duane C., Joseph A. Tiffany, and James M. Zalesky

1981   A Preliminary Report on the M.A.D. Sites (13CF101 and 13CF102), Crawford County, Iowa. In *Archaeology of the M.A.D. Sites at Denison, Iowa,* by David W. Benn, pp. V-1–V-62. Division of Historic Preservation, Iowa State Historical Department, Iowa City. Copy on file, Office of the State Archaeologist, University of Iowa, Iowa City.

Anderson, Duane C., and Patricia M. Williams

1974   Western Iowa Proboscidians. *Proceedings of the Iowa Academy of Science* 81:185–191.

Anderson, Mark L.

1995   *Archaeological Excavations at the Cowan Site: A Phase II Investigation of 13WD88, Primary Roads Project NHS-75-1(54)-19-97 a.k.a. 91-97060-1, Woodbury County, Iowa.* Project Completion Report Vol. 18, No. 10. Office of the State Archaeologist, University of Iowa, Iowa City.

1996a   Great Oasis: Who, What, Where, When, and Why? Paper presented at the 54th Annual Plains Anthropological Conference, Iowa City. Copy on file, Office of the State Archaeologist, University of Iowa, Iowa City.

1996b   Where Are the Great Oasis Sites in Iowa? . . . A View from the Cowan Site. Paper presented at the 54th Annual Plains Anthropological Conference, Iowa City. Copy on file, Office of the State Archaeologist, University of Iowa, Iowa City.

1998   Application of Computer Scanned and Manipulated Aerial Photographic Images during Archaeological Survey: Investigating Mounds in Northeast Iowa. Paper presented at the 63rd Annual Meeting of the Society for American Archaeology, Seattle. Copy on file, Office of the State Archaeologist, University of Iowa, Iowa City.

Anderson, Wayne I.

1983   *Geology of Iowa: Over Two Billion Years of Change.* Iowa State University Press, Ames.

Anfinson, Scott F.

1979   Great Oasis Phase. In *A Handbook of Minnesota Prehistoric Ceramics,* compiled and edited by Scott F. Anfinson, pp. 87–94. Occasional

Publications in Minnesota Anthropology 5. Minnesota Archaeological Society, St. Paul.

1982 The Prehistoric Archaeology of the Prairie Lakes Region: A Summary from a Minnesota Perspective. *Journal of the North Dakota Archaeological Association* 1:65–90.

1997 *Southwestern Minnesota Archaeology: 12,000 Years in the Prairie Lake Region.* Minnesota Prehistoric Archaeological Series No. 14. Minnesota Historical Society, St. Paul.

Anfinson, Scott F. (compiler and editor)

1979 *A Handbook of Minnesota Prehistoric Ceramics.* Occasional Publications in Minnesota Anthropology 5. Minnesota Historical Society, St. Paul.

*Annals of Iowa*

1957 The Ebenezer Alden Jr. Letters from Iowa Territory. *Annals of Iowa* 33:472–509.

Artz, Joe A.

1991 *Prehistory, History, and Geomorphology of the Mississippi River Valley in the Montrose Bottoms, A Phase I Archaeological Survey of Primary Roads Project F-61-1(55)--20-56 a.k.a. PIN 79-56040-U.S. 61, Lee County, Iowa.* Project Completion Report Vol. 14, No. 9. Office of the State Archaeologist, University of Iowa, Iowa City.

1993a *Phase II Investigations at 13MR267, Marshall County, Iowa.* Project Completion Report Vol. 16, No. 8. Office of the State Archaeologist, University of Iowa, Iowa City.

1993b The Preservation of Cultural Stratigraphy in Loess-Mantled Terrains of Iowa. *Journal of the Iowa Archeological Society* 40:50–65.

1993c *Phase II Archaeological Investigations at 13RN59: A Late Archaic Campsite in Ringgold County, Iowa, Primary Roads Project STP-2-4(28)--2C-80 a.k.a. PIN 85-80020-2, Ringgold County, Iowa.* Project Completion Report Vol. 16, No. 53. Office of the State Archaeologist, University of Iowa, Iowa City.

1995 *Archaeology of the Eisele's Hill Locality: Phase II Test Excavations at Six Sites in Muscatine County, Iowa.* Project Completion Report Vol. 18, No. 30. Office of the State Archaeologist, University of Iowa, Iowa City.

1996 The Geoarchaeology of Southeast Iowa: Scale and Process in an Evolving Landscape. In *Field Trip Guide: Southeast Iowa Geoarchaeology,* pp. 1–27. 54th Annual Plains Anthropological Conference, Iowa City. Copy on file, Office of the State Archaeologist, University of Iowa, Iowa City.

Arzigian, Constance M.

1987 The Emergence of Horticultural Economies in Southwestern Wisconsin. In *Emergent Horticultural Economies of the Eastern Woodlands,* edited by William F. Keegan, pp. 217–242. Occasional Paper No. 7. Center for Archaeological Investigations, Southern Illinois University, Carbondale.

Arzigian, Constance M., Robert F. Boszhardt, Holly P. Halverson, and James L. Theler

1994 The Gundersen Site: An Oneota Village and Cemetery in La Crosse, Wisconsin. *Journal of the Iowa Archeological Society* 41:3–75.

Asch, David L.

1992 Prehistoric Agriculture in Iowa. In *Crops of Ancient Iowa: Native Plant Use and Farming Systems,* by David L. Asch and William Green, pp. 9–108. Office of the State Archaeologist, University of Iowa. Submitted to the Leopold Center for Sustainable Agriculture, Iowa State University, Ames. Copy on file, Office of the State Archaeologist, University of Iowa, Iowa City.

1996 Archaeobotanical Analysis. In *Excavations at the Maxwell Site (13DA264): A Great Oasis Settlement in Central Iowa,* by John F. Doershuk and Fred A. Finney, pp. 29–37. Contract Completion Report 445. Office of the State Archaeologist, University of Iowa, Iowa City.

Asch, David L., and Nancy B. Asch

1985 Prehistoric Plant Cultivation in West-Central Illinois. In *Prehistoric Food Production in North America,* edited by Richard I. Ford, pp. 149–203. Anthropological Papers 75. Museum of Anthropology, University of Michigan, Ann Arbor.

Asch, David L., and Nancy Asch Sidell

1992 Archaeobotany. In *Early Woodland Occupations at the Ambrose Flick Site in the Sny Bottom of West-Central Illinois,* edited by C. Russell Stafford, pp. 177–293. Research Series 10. Center for American Archeology, Kampsville Archeological Center, Kampsville, Illinois.

Asch, David L., Kenneth B. Farnsworth, and Nancy B. Asch

1979    Woodland Subsistence and Settlement in West Central Illinois. In *Hopewell Archaeology: The Chillicothe Conference,* edited by David S. Brose and N'omi Greber, pp. 80–85. Kent State University Press, Kent, Ohio.

Asch, David L., and William Green

1992    *Crops of Ancient Iowa: Native Plant Use and Farming Systems.* Office of the State Archaeologist, University of Iowa. Submitted to the Leopold Center for Sustainable Agriculture, Iowa State University, Ames. Copy on file, Office of the State Archaeologist, University of Iowa, Iowa City.

Ashworth, Michael J., and Marshall McKusick

1964    *Archeological Resources of Saylorville Reservoir Drainage, Iowa.* Office of the State Archaeologist, University of Iowa. Submitted to the National Park Service. Copy on file, Office of the State Archaeologist, University of Iowa, Iowa City.

Association of Iowa Archaeologists

1993    Guidelines for Geomorphological Investigations in Support of Archaeological Investigations in Iowa. *Journal of the Iowa Archeological Society* 40:1–19.

Atkinson, R. J. C.

1953    *Field Archaeology.* Methuen, London.

Auman, F. A.

1957    Dispossession of the Tribe. *Palimpsest* 38: 33–96.

Baerreis, David A.

1953    Blackhawk Village Site (DA5) Dane County, Wisconsin. *Journal of the Iowa Archeological Society* 2(4):5–20.

1968    Artifact Descriptions: Bone, Stone and Shell. In Climatic Change and the Mill Creek Culture of Iowa, Part 1, edited by Dale R. Henning, pp. 107–191. *Journal of the Iowa Archeological Society* 15.

Baerreis, David A., and Robert A. Alex

1974    An Interpretation of Midden Formation: The Mill Creek Example. In *Aspects of Upper Great Lakes Anthropology: Papers in Honor of Lloyd A. Wilford,* edited by Elden Johnson, pp. 143–148. Minnesota Prehistoric Archaeology Series 11. Minnesota Historical Society, St. Paul.

Baerreis, David A., and Reid A. Bryson

1965    Climatic Episodes and the Dating of the Mississippian Cultures. *Wisconsin Archeologist* 46:203–220.

Baerreis, David A., Margie L. Staab, Robert A. Alex, Donna H. Scott, Lynn M. Betzler, Andrew Fortier, John E. Dallman, Raymond Treat, John Kelly, Larry A. Conrad, Ericka Thrash, and Edward Lugenbeal

1970    Environmental Archaeology in Western Iowa. *Northwest Chapter of the Iowa Archeological Society Newsletter* 18(5):3–15.

Bailey, Anthony W.

1977    *A Report on the Bennett-Roth Site, 11-HE-62: A Surface-Collected Site in Henderson County, Illinois.* Unpublished Master's thesis, Department of Anthropology, Northern Illinois University, DeKalb.

Baker, Richard G., E. Arthur Bettis III, and Diana G. Horton

1993    Late Wisconsinan–Early Holocene Riparian Paleoenvironment in Southeastern Iowa. *Geological Society of America Bulletin* 105: 206– 212.

Baker, Richard G., E. Arthur Bettis III, R. Sanders Rhodes, and George R. Hallberg

1986    Wisconsinan Ice-Marginal Biotic Environments in Iowa. Paper presented at the Ninth Biennial Meeting of the American Quaternary Association, Urbana, Illinois. Copy on file, Office of the State Archaeologist, University of Iowa, Iowa City.

Baker, Richard G., E. Arthur Bettis III, D. P. Schwert, Diana G. Horton, Craig A. Chumbley, L. A. Gonzalez, and M. K. Reagan

1996    Holocene Paleoenvironments of Northeast Iowa. *Ecological Monographs* 66:203–224.

Baker, Richard G., Craig A. Chumbley, Patricia M. Witinok, and Hyung K. Kim

1990    Holocene Vegetational Changes in Eastern Iowa. *Journal of the Iowa Academy of Science* 97:167–177.

Baker, Richard G., Louis J. Maher, Craig A. Chumbley, and Kent L. Van Zant

1992    Patterns of Holocene Environmental Change in the Midwestern United States. *Quaternary Research* 37:379–389.

Baker, Richard G., D. P. Schwert, E. Arthur Bettis III, and Craig A. Chumbley
1993　Impact of Euro-American Settlement on a Riparian Landscape in Northeast Iowa, Midwestern USA: An Integrated Approach Based on Historical Evidence, Floodplain Sediments, Fossil Pollen, Plant Macrofossils, and Insects. *The Holocene* 34:314–323.

Baker, Richard G., and Kent L. Van Zant
1980　Holocene Vegetational Reconstruction in Northwestern Iowa. In *The Cherokee Excavations: Holocene Ecology and Human Adaptations in Northwestern Iowa,* edited by Duane C. Anderson and Holmes A. Semken, Jr., pp. 123–138. Academic Press, New York.

Baker, Richard G., Kent L. Van Zant, and James J. Dulian
1980　Three Late Glacial Pollen and Plant Macrofossil Assemblages from Iowa. *Palynology* 4:197–203.

Baker, Richard G., and Mary K. Whelan
1992　Eastern Iowa Paleoenvironments and Cultural Change: Introduction and Paleoecological Background. Paper presented at the 57th Annual Meeting of the Society for American Archaeology, Pittsburgh. Copy on file, Office of the State Archaeologist, University of Iowa, Iowa City.

Ballard, David N., Jr.
1984　Nineteenth-Century Mills and Milling Industries in Story County, Iowa. *Journal of the Iowa Archeological Society* 31:137–190.

Balme, J., and W. Beck (editors)
1994　*Women in Archaeology.* Department of Prehistory, Research School of Pacific Studies, Australian National University, Canberra.

Banks, Roger
1965　Excavations at the Beals Site (13CK62). *Northwest Chapter of the Iowa Archeological Society Newsletter* 14(5):4–7.
1967　Museum Notes. Description of the Bolte Catlinite Tablet from the Blood Run Site, 13LO2. *Northwest Chapter of the Iowa Archeological Society Newsletter* 15(2):5–7.
1969　Resistivity Surveying Attempt at 13PM25. *Northwest Chapter of the Iowa Archeological Society Newsletter* 17(4):2–8.

Banks, Roger, and David Lilly
1965　A Preliminary Description of a Mill Creek Cemetery Near the Broken Kettle Midden Mound. *Northwest Chapter of the Iowa Archeological Society Newsletter* 13(1):2–11.
1968　Early Investigations of the Broken Kettle Mound (13PM1). *Northwest Chapter of the Iowa Archeological Society Newsletter* 16(5):3–5.

Bardwell, Jennifer
1981　*The Paleoecological and Social Significance of the Zooarchaeological Remains from the Central Plains Tradition Earthlodges of the Glenwood Locality, Mills County, Iowa.* Unpublished Master's thesis, Social Studies, University of Iowa, Iowa City.

Barnhardt, Michael L., David C. Dycus, Edward B. Jelks, Frederick W. Lange, Floyd R. Mansberger, Joseph S. Phillippe, and Frederick S. Thomas
1983　Preliminary Cultural Resources Survey and Geomorphological Assessment of Selected Areas in Navigation Pool 16, Mississippi River. *Wisconsin Archeologist* 64:9–110.

Barrett, Stephen A.
1933　Ancient Aztalan. *Bulletin of the Public Museum of the City of Milwaukee* Vol. 13.

Baugh, Timothy G.
1991　*The Avoca Site (14JN332): Excavation of a Grasshopper Fall Phase Structure, Jackson County, Kansas.* Contract Archeology Publication No. 8. Kansas State Historical Society, Topeka.

Bauxar, J. Joseph
1978　History of the Illinois Area. In *Northeast,* edited by Bruce G. Trigger, pp. 594–601. Handbook of North American Indians, Vol. 15, W. C. Sturtevant, general editor. Smithsonian Institution, Washington, D.C.

Beals, Joe
1965a　Simonsen Site Revisited. *Northwest Chapter of the Iowa Archeological Society Newsletter* 13(5):3–5.
1965b　Another Pipestone Plaque. *Northwest Chapter of the Iowa Archeological Society Newsletter* 13(4):6.

Beaubien, Paul L.
1952　Preliminary Notes on an Archaeological Pro-

ject in Northeastern Iowa. *Journal of the Iowa Archeological Society* 1(3):3–5.

1953    Cultural Variation within Two Woodland Mound Groups of Northeastern Iowa. *American Antiquity* 19:56–66.

Behm, Jeffery A.

1991    Recent Excavations at the Bell Site (47-WN-9), Winnebago County, Wisconsin. Ms. on file, Office of the State Archaeologist, University of Iowa, Iowa City.

Behrman, Sara (compiler)

1983    *Selected Sources on the Mesquakie Indians.* Research Papers Vol. 8, No. 1. Office of the State Archaeologist, University of Iowa, Iowa City.

Beissel, D., K. L. Brown, M. E. Brown, and K. Zimmerman

1984    *Cultural Resources Investigations of the Upper Minnesota River (639) Project, Deuel and Grant Counties, South Dakota, and Lac Qui Parle and Yellow Medicine Counties, Minnesota.* University of South Dakota Archaeology Laboratory. Submitted to the U.S. Army Corps of Engineers, St. Paul District. Copy on file, University of South Dakota Archaeology Laboratory, Vermillion.

Bell, Robert E.

1958    *Guide to the Identification of Certain American Indian Projectile Points.* Oklahoma Anthropological Society, Special Bulletin 1.

1960    *Guide to the Identification of Certain American Indian Projectile Points.* Oklahoma Anthropological Society, Special Bulletin 2.

Benchley, Elizabeth D., Michael L. Gregg, and Mark J. Dudzik

1977    *Recent Investigations at Albany Mounds Whiteside County, Illinois.* Illinois Archaeological Survey Circular No. 2. Illinois State Museum, Springfield.

Benchley, Elizabeth D., Harold Hassen, and William Billeck

1979    *Final Report of Archaeological Investigations at the Sloan Site (11-Mc-86) FAS Project 1210, Mercer County, Illinois.* Report of Investigations No. 36. Archaeological Research Laboratory, University of Wisconsin–Milwaukee. Copy on file, Office of the State Archaeologist, University of Iowa, Iowa City.

Benchley, Elizabeth D., Blane Nansel, Clark A. Dobbs, Susan M. Thurston Myster, and Barbara H. O'Connell

1997    *Archeology and Bioarcheology of the Northern Woodlands.* Arkansas Archeological Survey Research Series No. 52. Arkansas Archeological Survey, Fayetteville.

Benn, David W.

1976    *The Woodland Cultures of Northeast Iowa (A.D. 300–800): A Perspective from Hadfields Cave Site.* Unpublished Ph.D. dissertation, Department of Anthropology, University of Wisconsin–Madison.

1978    The Woodland Ceramic Sequence in the Culture History of Northeastern Iowa. *Midcontinental Journal of Archaeology* 3:215–283.

1979    Some Trends and Traditions in Woodland Cultures of the Quad-State Region in the Upper Mississippi River Basin. *Wisconsin Archeologist* 60:47–82.

1980    *Hadfields Cave: A Perspective on Late Woodland Culture in Northeastern Iowa.* Report 13. Office of the State Archaeologist, University of Iowa, Iowa City.

1981    *Archaeology of the M.A.D. Sites at Denison, Iowa.* Division of Historic Preservation, Iowa State Historical Department, Iowa City. Copy on file, Office of the State Archaeologist, University of Iowa, Iowa City.

1982a   The Ceramic Assemblage. In *A Preliminary Report on the Arthur Site, East Okoboji Lake, Iowa,* edited by Joseph A. Tiffany, pp. 38–86. Research Papers Vol. 7, No. 1. Office of the State Archaeologist, University of Iowa, Iowa City.

1982b   Arthur Site Ceramics in Regional Perspective. In *A Preliminary Report on the Arthur Site, East Okoboji Lake, Iowa,* edited by Joseph A. Tiffany, pp. 161–188. Research Papers Vol. 7, No. 1. Office of the State Archaeologist, University of Iowa, Iowa City.

1983a   Diffusion and Acculturation in Woodland Cultures on the Western Prairie Peninsula. In *Prairie Archaeology: Papers in Honor of David A. Baerreis,* edited by Guy E. Gibbon, pp. 75–85. Publications in Anthropology No. 3. University of Minnesota, Minneapolis.

1983b   *Evaluation of Archaeological Resources for Pro-*

posed Construction and Improvements in Pleasant Creek Reservoir, Linn County, Iowa: 1983. Report CAR-595. Center for Archaeological Research, Southwest Missouri State University, Springfield. Copy on file, Office of the State Archaeologist, University of Iowa, Iowa City.

1984a Archaeological Salvage Excavations at Sid's Site (13KK16): A Woodland Campsite in Keokuk County, Iowa: 1983. Report CAR-574. Center for Archaeological Research, Southwest Missouri State University, Springfield. Copy on file, Office of the State Archaeologist, University of Iowa, Iowa City.

1984b Excavations at the Christenson Oneota Site 13PK407, Central Des Moines Valley, Iowa. Report CAR-592. Center for Archaeological Research, Southwest Missouri State University, Springfield. Copy on file, Office of the State Archaeologist, University of Iowa, Iowa City.

1985 Interpretive Overview of Cultural Resources in Saylorville Lake, Iowa. Report CAR-627 (II). Center for Archaeological Research, Southwest Missouri State University, Springfield. Copy on file, Office of the State Archaeologist, University of Iowa, Iowa City.

1986 The Western Iowa Rivers Basin: An Archaeological Overview. Report CAR-677. Center for Archaeological Research, Southwest Missouri State University, Springfield. Iowa River Basin Report Series Vol. 3. Office of Historic Preservation, Des Moines. Copy on file, Office of the State Archaeologist, University of Iowa, Iowa City.

1987 Archaeology in the Mississippi River Floodplain at Sand Run Slough, Iowa. Report CAR-690. Center for Archaeological Research, Southwest Missouri State University, Springfield. Copy on file, Office of the State Archaeologist, University of Iowa, Iowa City.

1989a Another View of the Hanging Valley Site (13HR28). Plains Anthropologist 34:179–181.

1989b Hawks, Serpents, and Bird-Men: Emergence of the Oneota Mode of Production. Plains Anthropologist 34:233–260.

1990 Depositional Stratigraphy, Site Context, and Prehistoric Cultural Overview. In Holocene Alluvial Stratigraphy and Selected Aspects of the Quaternary History of Western Iowa, by E. Arthur Bettis III, pp. 75–86. Midwest Friends of the Pleistocene 37th Field Conference. Iowa Quaternary Studies Group Contribution 36. University of Iowa, Iowa City.

1991 The Christenson Oneota Site, 13PK407. Journal of the Iowa Archeological Society 38:16–55.

1992 Archaeological Overview of the Upper Mississippi River Valley, Rock Island District. In Late Wisconsinan and Holocene Alluvial Stratigraphy, Paleoecology, and Archaeological Geology of East-Central Iowa, by E. Arthur Bettis III, Richard G. Baker, William Green, Mary K. Whelan, and David W. Benn, pp. 63–82. Guidebook Series 12. Iowa Quaternary Studies Group Contribution 51. Iowa Department of Natural Resources. Copy on file, Office of the State Archaeologist, University of Iowa, Iowa City.

1993 Review of Phase 3 Investigations at 13LC17: A Randolph Phase Winter Camp in the White Breast Creek Valley, Lucas County, Iowa by Donna C. Roper. Journal of the Iowa Archeological Society 40:95–96.

1995 Woodland People and the Roots of Oneota. In Oneota Archaeology Past, Present, and Future, edited by William Green, pp. 91–139. Report 20. Office of the State Archaeologist, University of Iowa, Iowa City.

1996 Trajectories of Ceramic Change across Iowa. Paper presented at the 61st Annual Meeting of the Society of American Archaeology, New Orleans. Copy on file, Office of the State Archaeologist, University of Iowa, Iowa City.

1997 Where Are Late Archaic and Early Woodland Sites Buried in Iowa? Paper presented at the 55th Annual Plains Anthropological Conference, Boulder, Colorado. Copy on file, Office of the State Archaeologist, University of Iowa, Iowa City.

Benn, David W. (editor)

1976 Pleasant Creek II: A Preliminary Report of Site Salvage in 1975. In Cultural Resource Surveys 1976-1979, edited by David W. Benn, pp. 1–17. Luther College Archaeological Research Laboratory, Decorah, Iowa. Copy on file, Office of the State Archaeologist, University of Iowa, Iowa City.

1981a   *Archaeological Investigations at the Rainbow Site, Plymouth County, Iowa.* Luther College Archaeological Research Center, Decorah, Iowa. Copy on file, Office of the State Archaeologist, University of Iowa, Iowa City.

1981b   The Rainbow Site, Stratigraphy and Features. In *Archaeological Investigations at the Rainbow Site, Plymouth County, Iowa,* edited by David W. Benn, pp. 75–153. Luther College Archaeological Research Center, Decorah, Iowa. Copy on file, Office of the State Archaeologist, University of Iowa, Iowa City.

1981c   Paleobotany. In *Archaeological Investigations at the Rainbow Site, Plymouth County, Iowa,* edited by David W. Benn, pp. 315–328. Luther College Archaeological Research Center, Decorah, Iowa. Copy on file, Office of the State Archaeologist, University of Iowa, Iowa City.

1987   *Big Sioux River Archaeological and Historic Resources Survey, Lyon County, Iowa: Volume 1.* Report CAR-705. Center for Archaeological Research, Southwest Missouri State University, Springfield. Copy on file, Office of the State Archaeologist, University of Iowa, Iowa City.

1990   *Woodland Cultures on the Western Prairies: The Rainbow Site Investigations.* Report 18. Office of the State Archaeologist, University of Iowa, Iowa City.

Benn, David W., Jeffrey D. Anderson, and E. Arthur Bettis III

1994   *Archeological and Geomorphological Surveys in Pools 21–22, Upper Mississippi River.* Bear Creek Archeology No. 238, Cresco, Iowa. Submitted to the U.S. Army Corps of Engineers, Rock Island District. Copy on file, Office of the State Archaeologist, University of Iowa, Iowa City.

Benn, David W., and E. Arthur Bettis III

1979   *Archaeological Investigations and Culture-Historical Interpretations in the Volga Lake Project, Fayette County, Iowa.* Luther College Archaeological Research Center, Decorah, Iowa. Copy on file, Office of the State Archaeologist, University of Iowa, Iowa City.

1981   *Archaeological and Geomorphological Survey of the Downstream Corridor, Saylorville Lake, Iowa.* Luther College Archaeological Research Center, Decorah, Iowa. Submitted to the U.S. Army Corps of Engineers District, Rock Island District. Copy on file, Office of the State Archaeologist, University of Iowa, Iowa City.

Benn, David W., E. Arthur Bettis III, and R. Clark Mallam

1978   *Archeological Investigations at the Keller Mounds (13AM69) and Related Manifestations: Insights into Woodland Indian Mythology.* Research Papers Vol. 3, No. 3. Office of the State Archaeologist, University of Iowa, Iowa City.

1993   Cultural Transformations in the Keller and Bluff Top Mounds. In *Prehistory and Human Ecology of the Western Prairies and Northern Plains: Papers in Honor of Robert A. Alex (1941–1988),* edited by Joseph A. Tiffany, pp. 53–73. Memoir 27. *Plains Anthropologist,* Lincoln, Nebraska.

Benn, David W., E. Arthur Bettis III, and R. C. Vogel

1988   *Archaeology and Geomorphology in Pools 17–18, Upper Mississippi River.* Report CAR-714. Center for Archaeological Research, Southwest Missouri State University, Springfield, and Geological Survey Bureau, Iowa Department of Natural Resources, Iowa City. Submitted to the U.S. Army Corps of Engineers, Rock Island District. Copy on file, Office of the State Archaeologist, University of Iowa, Iowa City.

Benn, David W., and Martha H. Bowers

1994   *Phase I Cultural Resource Study of U.S. Highway 34 Improvements Des Moines to Burlington Corridor, Wapello, Jefferson, and Henry Counties, Iowa.* DE-163-2 (12)--2A-51. Cultural Resource Group, Louis Berger and Associates, East Orange, New Jersey. Submitted to the Office of Project Planning, Iowa Department of Transportation, Ames. Copy on file, Office of the State Archaeologist, University of Iowa, Iowa City.

Benn, David W., and William Green

1997   Late Woodland Cultures West of the Mississippi Valley in Iowa. Paper presented at the Urbana Late Woodland Conference, University of Illinois, Champaign-Urbana. Copy on file, Office of the State Archaeologist, University of Iowa, Iowa City.

Benn, David W., and David M. Hovde

1981 *Intensive Survey of Archaeological Site 13AN52 Rathbun Lake, Iowa.* Luther College Archaeological Research Center, Decorah, Iowa. Copy on file, Office of the State Archaeologist, University of Iowa, Iowa City.

Benn, David W., and Derrick J. Marcucci

1981 *A Survey of Selected Rock Shelter Archaeological Sites in Eastern Iowa.* Division of Historic Preservation, State Historical Society of Iowa, Iowa City. Copy on file, Office of the State Archaeologist, University of Iowa, Iowa City.

Benn, David W., and Leah D. Rogers

1985 *Interpretive Overview of Cultural Resources in Saylorville Lake, Iowa.* 2 vols. Report CAR-627. Center for Archaeological Research, Southwest Missouri State University, Springfield. Submitted to the U.S. Army Corps of Engineers, Rock Island District. Copy on file, Office of the State Archaeologist, University of Iowa, Iowa City.

Benn, David W., Shirley J. Schermer, and Jonathan Sellars

1992 *Excavations of Human Remains from the Sand Run West Site (13LA38) Louisa County, Iowa.* Bear Creek Archeology, No. 150, Decorah, Iowa. Submitted to the U.S. Army Corps of Engineers, Rock Island District. Copy on file, Office of the State Archaeologist, University of Iowa, Iowa City.

Benn, David W., and Dean M. Thompson

1977 The Young Site, Linn County, Iowa, and Comments on Woodland Ceramics. *Journal of the Iowa Archeological Society* 24:1–61.

Bentancourt, Phil P.

1965 A Description of Certain Engraved Artifacts from the Utz Oneota Site. *Plains Anthropologist* 10:256–270.

Berres, Thomas, Kenneth Farnsworth, and Randall Hughes

1993 Northern Illinois Pipestone and Hopewellian Exchange Systems. Paper presented at the 58th Annual Meeting of the Society for American Archaeology, St. Louis. Copy on file, Office of the State Archaeologist, University of Iowa, Iowa City.

Bettis, E. Arthur, III

1979 Holocene Alluvial Fill Sequences and Their Bearing on the Location and Preservation of Prehistoric Cultural Resources in Smoky Hollow Subwater Shed, Woodbury County, Iowa. Paper presented at the 37th Annual Plains Conference, Kansas City, Missouri. Copy on file, Office of the State Archaeologist, University of Iowa, Iowa City.

1981 Geology of the MAD Sites. In *Archaeology of the M.A.D. Sites at Denison, Iowa,* by David W. Benn, pp. IIA-1–IIA-121. Division of Historic Preservation, Iowa State Historical Department, Iowa City. Copy on file, Office of the State Archaeologist, University of Iowa, Iowa City.

1988 Quaternary History, Stratigraphy, Geomorphology, and Pedology. In *Archaeology and Geomorphology in Pools 17-18, Upper Mississippi River,* by David W. Benn, E. Arthur Bettis III, and R. C. Vogel, pp. 18–91. Report CAR-714. Center for Archaeological Research, Southwest Missouri State University, Springfield, and Geological Survey Bureau, Iowa Department of Natural Resources, Iowa City. Submitted to the U.S. Army Corps of Engineers, Rock Island District. Copy on file, Office of the State Archaeologist, University of Iowa, Iowa City.

1990 *Holocene Alluvial Stratigraphy and Selected Aspects of the Quaternary History of Western Iowa.* Midwest Friends of the Pleistocene 37th Field Conference. Iowa Quaternary Studies Group Contribution 36. Copy on file, Office of the State Archaeologist, University of Iowa, Iowa City.

Bettis, E. Arthur, III, Richard G. Baker, William Green, Mary K. Whelan, and David W. Benn

1992 *Late Wisconsinan and Holocene Alluvial Stratigraphy, Paleoecology, and Archaeological Geology of East-Central Iowa.* Guidebook Series 12. Iowa Quaternary Studies Group Contribution 51. Iowa Department of Natural Resources. Copy on file, Office of the State Archaeologist, University of Iowa, Iowa City.

Bettis, E. Arthur, III, and David W. Benn

1984 An Archaeological and Geomorphological Survey in the Central Des Moines River Valley, Iowa. *Plains Anthropologist* 29:211–227.

1988 Landscapes and Man in Pools 17–18 Upper

Mississippi River. *Illinois Archaeological Survey Newsletter* 3(2):3–9.

1989    Geologic Context of Paleoindian and Archaic Occupations in a Portion of the Mississippi Valley, Iowa and Illinois. *Current Research in the Pleistocene* 6:85–86.

Bettis, E. Arthur, III, and Edwin R. Hajic

1995    Landscape Development and the Location of Evidence of Archaic Cultures in the Upper Midwest. In *Archaeological Geology of the Archaic Period in North America,* edited by E. Arthur Bettis III, pp. 87–113. Special Paper 297. Geological Society of America, Boulder, Colorado.

Bettis, E. Arthur, III, and Bernard E. Hoyer

1986    *Late Wisconsinan and Holocene Landscape Evolution and Alluvial Stratigraphy in the Saylorville Lake Area, Central Des Moines River Valley, Iowa.* Open-File Report 86-1. Geological Survey Bureau, Iowa Department of Natural Resources, Iowa City. Copy on file, Office of the State Archaeologist, University of Iowa, Iowa City.

Bettis, E. Arthur, III, and J. P. Littke

1987    *Holocene Alluvial Stratigraphy and Landscape Development in Soap Creek Watershed, Appanoose, Davis, Monroe, and Wapello Counties.* Open-File Report 87-2. Geological Survey Bureau, Iowa Department of Natural Resources, Iowa City. Copy on file, Office of the State Archaeologist, University of Iowa, Iowa City.

Bettis, E. Arthur, III, Deborah J. Quade, and Timothy J. Kemmis

1996    *Hogs, Bogs, and Logs: Quaternary Deposits and Environmental Geology of the Des Moines Lobe.* Geological Survey Bureau Guidebook Series 18. Geological Survey Bureau, Iowa Department of Natural Resources, Iowa City. Copy on file, Office of the State Archaeologist, University of Iowa, Iowa City.

1982    *Interrelations of Cultural and Fluvial Deposits in Northwest Iowa.* Guidebook for the Spring 1982 Meeting of the Association of Iowa Archaeologists. Copy on file, Office of the State Archaeologist, University of Iowa, Iowa City.

Betts, Colin

1996    Reexamining the Orr Phase. Paper presented at the 54th Annual Plains Anthropological Conference, Iowa City.

Billeck, William T.

1985    Archaeological Investigations at the Smith Site: A Multi-component Early to Late Woodland Habitation in Southeast Iowa. Paper presented at the 43rd Annual Plains Anthropological Conference, Iowa City. Copy on file, Office of the State Archaeologist, University of Iowa, Iowa City.

1986a   Investigations at 13WS122—The Davis Creek Site, Lithics. In *Archaeological Investigations along the F-518 Corridor,* edited by Stephen C. Lensink, pp. 177–197. Iowa Quaternary Studies Contribution 9. Copy on file, Office of the State Archaeologist, University of Iowa, Iowa City.

1986b   Investigations at 13WS126—The Prymek Site, Lithics. In *Archaeological Investigations along the F-518 Corridor,* edited by Stephen C. Lensink, pp. 115–142. Iowa Quaternary Studies Contribution 9. Office of the State Archaeologist, University of Iowa, Iowa City.

1986c   Excavations at the Smith Site (13LA2), Louisa County, Iowa: 1955 and 1985. Paper presented at the 36th Annual Meeting of the Iowa Archeological Society, Iowa City. Copy on file, Office of the State Archaeologist, University of Iowa, Iowa City.

1986d   Garden Beds in Black Hawk County. Iowa Archeological Society *Newsletter* 36(4):5–6.

1987    Functional Variation at Two Short-Term, Multicomponent Sites in Black Hawk County, Iowa. *Journal of the Iowa Archeological Society* 34:7–22.

1991    Triangular Projectile Point Stages of Manufacture at the Late Woodland Sweeting Site, 13WS61 Washington County, Iowa. *Journal of the Iowa Archeological Society* 38:11–15.

1992a   Personal communication. In A Checklist of Plains Ceramic Types and Wares, assembled by William B. Butler and J. J. Hoffman. *South Dakota Archaeology* 16:61.

1992b   Archaeological Survey of Paul Rowe Sites in Mills County, Iowa. *Journal of the Iowa Archeological Society* 39:66–90.

1992c   Excavations at the Millipede Site: A Nebraska

Phase Earthlodge in Mills County, Iowa. Iowa Archeological Society *Newsletter* 42(1):1–2.

1993   *Time and Space in the Glenwood Locality: The Nebraska Phase in Western Iowa.* Unpublished Ph.D. dissertation, Department of Anthropology, University of Missouri–Columbia.

1994   Corner-Tang Artifacts in the Paul Rowe Collection. *Journal of the Iowa Archeological Society* 41:140–144.

1995   *Excavations at the Helen Smith Site (13LA71): Early and Late Woodland in Southeast Iowa.* Contract Completion Report 446. Office of the State Archaeologist, University of Iowa, Iowa City.

1996   The Pawnee Repatriation Case, an Example of Repatriation at the National Museum of Natural History. Paper presented at the 54th Annual Plains Anthropological Conference, Iowa City.

Billeck, William T., and William Green

1994   *Archaeological Investigations in Waubonsie State Park, Fremont County, Iowa.* Research Papers Vol. 19, No. 3. Office of the State Archaeologist, University of Iowa, Iowa City.

Billeck, William T., and Paul R. Rowe

1992   Excavation Reports by Paul Rowe: 13ML272, 13ML297, 13ML299, and 13ML396. *Journal of the Iowa Archeological Society* 39:91–98.

Binford, Lewis R.

1978   Dimensional Analysis of Behavior and Site Structure: Learning from an Eskimo Hunting Stand. *American Antiquity* 43:330–361.

1980   Willow Smoke and Dogs' Tails: Hunter-Gatherer Settlement Systems and Archaeological Site Formation. *American Antiquity* 45:4–20.

Black Hawk

1932   *Life of Ma-Ka-Tai-Me-She-Kia-Kiak, or Black Hawk.* Reprinted. State Historical Society of Iowa, Iowa City. Originally published 1834, Boston.

Blaine, Martha R.

1979   *The Ioway Indians.* University of Oklahoma Press, Norman.

Blair, Emma H. (editor)

1911   *The Indian Tribes of the Upper Mississippi Valley and Region of the Great Lakes.* 2 vols. Arthur H. Clark, Cleveland.

Blake, Leonard W., and Hugh C. Cutler

1963   Plant Materials from the Bell Site, Wn9, Wisconsin. *Wisconsin Archeologist* 44:70–71.

Blakeslee, Donald J.

1975   *The Plains Interband Trade System: An Ethnohistoric and Archaeological Investigation.* Unpublished Ph.D. dissertation. Department of Anthropology, University of Wisconsin–Milwaukee.

1987   Swidden Horticulture on the Great Plains: Explaining Plains Village Settlement Patterns. Paper presented at the 45th Annual Plains Conference, Columbia, Missouri.

1988   *St. Helena Archaeology: New Data, Fresh Interpretations.* Reprints in Anthroplogy Vol. 39, J. & L. Reprint, Lincoln, Nebraska.

1990   A Model for the Nebraska Phase. *Central Plains Archaeology* 2:29–56.

1994   The Archaeological Context of Human Skeletons in the Northern and Central Plains. In *Skeletal Biology in the Great Plains: Migration, Warfare, Health, and Subsistence,* edited by Douglas W. Owsley and Richard L. Jantz, pp. 9–32. Smithsonian Institution, Washington D.C.

Blakeslee, Donald J., and Warren W. Caldwell

1979   *The Nebraska Phase: An Appraisal.* Reprints in Anthropology Vol. 18. J. & L. Reprint, Lincoln, Nebraska.

Blitz, John H.

1988   Adoption of the Bow in Prehistoric North America. *North American Archaeology* 9:123–145.

Bluhm, Elaine A.

1962   An Indian Site near Rock Island, Illinois: An Example of Historic Archaeology. Paper presented at the 27th Annual Meeting of the Society for American Archaeology, Tucson, Arizona. Copy on file, Office of the State Archaeologist, University of Iowa, Iowa City.

Bluhm, Elaine A., and A. Liss

1961   The Anker Site. In *Chicago Area Archaeology*, ed. by Elaine A. Bluhm, 89–138. *Illinois Archaeological Survey Bulletin* 3.

Boszhardt, Robert F.

1989   Ceramic Analysis and Site Chronology of the Pammel Creek Site. *Wisconsin Archeologist* 70:41–94.

1994    Oneota Group Continuity at La Crosse: The Brice Prairie, Pammel Creek, and Valley View Phases. *Wisconsin Archeologist* 75:173–236.

1995    Additional Western Lithic Sources for Hopewell Bifaces in the Upper Mississippi River Valley. Paper presented at the 53rd Annual Plains Anthropological Conference, Laramie, Wyoming.

1997a   The Re-Discovery of Pipestone Quarries in the Baraboo Hills. *Archaeology News* 17(1):1. Mississippi Valley Archaeology Center and the La Crosse Area Archaeological Society, La Crosse, Wisconsin.

1997b   Ceramics from the Sand Lake Archaeological District, Wisconsin. *Journal of the Iowa Archeological Society* 44:139–159.

Boszhardt, Robert F., Wendy Holtz, and Jeremy Nienow

1995    A Compilation of Oneota Radiocarbon Dates as of 1995. In *Oneota Archaeology: Past, Present, and Future,* edited by William Green, pp. 203–227. Report 20. Office of the State Archaeologist, University of Iowa, Iowa City.

Boszhardt, Robert F., James L. Theler, and Thomas F. Kehoe

1986    The Early Woodland Stage. In *Introduction to Wisconsin Archaeology,* edited by William Green, James B. Stoltman, and Alice B. Kehoe, pp. 243–262. *Wisconsin Archeologist* 67: 163–395.

Bower, John, and E. Arthur Bettis III

1991    Chronology of the Archaic Period in Central Iowa. Ms. on file, Office of the State Archaeologist, University of Iowa, Iowa City.

Bowers, Alfred W.

1950    *Mandan Social and Ceremonial Organization.* University of Chicago Press, Chicago.

Bowers, Martha H., Hans Muessig, and Lowell J. Soike

1990    Historic Shipwrecks of Iowa. *Journal of the Iowa Archeological Society* 37:4–39.

Bowles, John B.

1975    *Distribution and Biogeography of Mammals of Iowa.* Special Publications No. 9. Museum, Texas Tech University, Lubbock.

Bozell, John R., and John Ludwickson

1994    *Nebraska Phase Archeology in the South Bend Locality.* Highway Archeology Program, Nebraska State Historical Society. Submitted to the Nebraska Department of Roads and the Federal Highway Administration. Copy on file, Office of the State Archaeologist, University of Iowa, Iowa City.

Bradley, Bruce A.

1993    Paleoindian Flaked Stone Technology in the North American High Plains. In *From Clovis to Kostienki: Upper Paleolithic–Paleo-Indian Adaptations,* edited by Olga Soffer and N. D. Praslov, pp. 251–262. Plenum Press, New York.

Bradley, Lawrence E.

1988    *Subsistence and Settlement at Rathbun Reservoir Area in South Central Iowa.* University of South Dakota Archaeology Laboratory, Vermillion.

Braun, David P.

1983    Pots as Tools. In *Hammer Theory of Archaeological Research,* edited by James A. Moore and Arthur S. Keene, pp. 107–134. Academic Press, New York.

Braun, David P., James B. Griffin, and Paul F. Titterington

1982    *The Snyders Mounds and Five Other Mound Groups in Calhoun County, Illinois.* Technical Reports No. 13. Research Reports in Archaeology Contribution 8. Museum of Anthropology, University of Michigan, Ann Arbor.

Bray, Robert T.

1961    The Flynn Cemetery: An Orr Focus Oneota Burial Site in Allamakee County. *Journal of the Iowa Archeological Society* 10(4):15–25.

1963    Southern Cult Motifs from the Utz Oneota Site, Saline County, Missouri. *Missouri Archaeologist* 25:1–40.

1991    The Utz Site: An Oneota Village in Central Missouri. *Missouri Archaeologist* 52:1–146.

Broihahn, John H.

1997    The Blosser (13BN125) and Old Moser (13BN130) Sites. *Journal of the Iowa Archeological Society* 44:7–83.

Broihahn, John H., and David M. Gradwohl

1997    A Grass Rope Ware Vessel and Associated Artifacts from the Central Des Moines River Valley, Iowa. *Plains Anthropologist* 42:375–380.

Bronitsky, Gordon, and Robert Hammer
1986    Experiments in Ceramic Technology: The Effects of Various Tempering Materials on Impact and Thermal Shock Resistance. *American Antiquity* 51:89–101.

Brose, Davis S., and N'omi Greber (editors)
1979    *Hopewell Archaeology: The Chillicothe Conference.* Kent State University Press, Kent, Ohio.

Brown, James A.
1976    The Southern Cult Reconsidered. *Midcontinental Journal of Archaeology* 1:115–135.
1982    What Kind of Economy Did the Oneota Have? In *Oneota Studies,* edited by Guy E. Gibbon, pp. 107–112. Publications in Anthropology No. 1. University of Minnesota, Minneapolis.

Brown, James A., Richard A. Kerber, and Howard D. Winters
1990    Trade and the Evolution of Exchange Relations at the Beginning of the Mississippian Period. In *The Mississippian Emergence,* edited by Bruce D. Smith, pp. 251–280. Smithsonian Institution Press, Washington, D.C.

Brown, James A., and Robert K. Vierra
1983    What Happened in the Middle Archaic? Introduction to an Ecological Approach to Koster Site Archaeology. In *Archaic Hunters and Gatherers in the American Midwest,* edited by James L. Phillips and James A. Brown, pp. 165–195. Academic Press, New York.

Brown, James A., Roger W. Willis, Mary A. Barth, and George K. Neuman
1967    *The Gentleman Farm Site, LaSalle County, Illinois.* Reports of Investigations 12. Illinois State Museum, Springfield.

Brown, Lionel A.
1966    Temporal and Spatial Order in the Central Plains. *Plains Anthropologist* 11:294–301.
1967a   *Pony Creek Archaeology.* River Basin Surveys. Publications in Salvage Archaeology No. 5. Office of Anthropology, Smithsonian Institution, Lincoln, Nebraska.
1967b   Archaeology of the Rathbun Reservoir, Iowa. *Journal of the Iowa Archeological Society* 14:1–36.

Broyles, Betty J.
1971    *Second Preliminary Report: The St. Albans Site, Kanahwa County, West Virginia.* Report of Archaeological Investigations 3. West Virginia Geological and Economic Survey, Morgantown.

Bryson, Reid A., and David A. Baerreis
1968    Introduction and Project Summary. In Climatic Change and the Mill Creek Culture of Iowa, Part 1, edited by Dale R. Henning, pp. 1–34. *Journal of the Iowa Archeological Society* 15.

Bryson, Reid A., David A. Baerreis, and Wayne M. Wendland
1970    The Character of Late-Glacial and Post-Glacial Climatic Changes. In *Pleistocene and Recent Environments of the Central Great Plains,* edited by Wakefield Dort, Jr., and J. Knox Jones, Jr., pp. 53–74. Special Publication 3. Department of Geology, University Press of Kansas, Lawrence.

Bryson, Reid A., and Wayne M. Wendland
1967    Tentative Climatic Patterns for Some Late-Glacial and Post-Glacial Episodes in Central North America. In *Life, Land and Water,* edited by William J. Mayer-Oakes, pp. 271–298. Occasional Papers No. 1. Department of Anthropology, University of Manitoba, Winnipeg.

Buechler, Jeffrey
1982    Test Excavations at the Volunteer Site (39BK8). *South Dakota Archaeology* 6:1–31.

Buffalo, Johnathan
1993a   A Brief History of the Mesquaki Pow-Wow. *The Legend* (October 1993) 12.
1993b   Introduction to Mesquaki History. *The Legend* (October 1993) 11.
1993c   Part II—Introduction to Mesquaki History. *The Legend* (December 1993) 4.
1994    Part III—Introduction to Mesquaki History. *The Legend* (April 1994) 6–7.

Buikstra, Jane E.
1979    Contributions of Physical Anthropologists to the Concept of Hopewell: A Historical Perspective. In *Hopewell Archaeology: The Chillicothe Conference,* edited by David J. Brose and N'omi Greber, pp. 220–233. Kent State University Press, Kent, Ohio.

Buikstra, Jane E., Jill Bullington, Douglas K. Charles, Della C. Cook, Susan R. Frankenberg, Lyle W. Konigsberg, Joseph B. Lambert, and Liang Xui

1987    Diet, Demography and the Development of Horticulture. In *Emergent Horticultural Economies of the Eastern Woodlands,* edited by William F. Keegan, pp. 67–86. Occasional Paper No. 7. Center for Archaeological Investigations, Southern Illinois University, Carbondale.

Buikstra, Jane E., Jerome Rose, and George Milner
1989    Maize Consumption in the Prehistoric Mississippi Valley: ∂ 13C Values and Diet. Paper presented at the 54th Annual Meeting of the Society for American Archeology, Atlanta. Copy on file, Office of the State Archaeologist, University of Iowa, Iowa City.

Butler, William B., and J. J. Hoffman (editors)
1992    A Checklist of Plains Ceramic Types and Wares. *South Dakota Archaeology* 16:1–105.

Caldwell, James R.
1958    *Trend and Tradition in the Prehistory of the Eastern United States.* Memoir 88. American Anthropological Association, Washington, D.C.

Caldwell, Warren W.
1961    *Archaeological Investigations at the Coralville Reservoir, Iowa. River Basin Surveys Papers* No. 22. Bulletin 179, pp. 79–148. Bureau of American Ethnology, Smithsonian Institution, Washington, D.C.

Callender, Charles
1978    Fox. In *Northeast,* edited by Bruce G. Trigger, pp. 636–647. Handbook of North American Indians, Vol. 15, Smithsonian Institution, Washington, D.C.

Cantwell, Anne-Marie
1987    Havana Tradition Patterns of Chert Procurement: Economic and Political Implications for the Central Illinois Valley and Beyond. *Wisconsin Archeologist* 68:22–43.

Carman, Mary R.
1988    The Last Winnebago in Northeast Iowa. *Journal of the Iowa Archeological Society* 35:72–76.

Catlin, George
1844    *Unparalleled Exhibition: The Fourteen Ioway Indians and Their Interpreter, Just Arrived from the Upper Missouri, near the Rocky Mountains.* W. S. Johnson, London.

Chapman, Carl H.
1975    *The Archaeology of Missouri, I.* University of Missouri Press, Columbia.

1980    *The Archaeology of Missouri, II.* University of Missouri Press, Columbia.

Charles, Douglas K., and Jane E. Buikstra
1983    Archaic Mortuary Sites in the Central Mississippi Drainage: Distribution, Structure, and Behavioral Implications. In *Archaic Hunters and Gatherers in the American Midwest,* edited by James L. Phillips and James A. Brown, pp. 117–145. Academic Press, New York.

Charlton, Thomas H., Cynthia Otis Charlton, Stephen C. Lensink, and James A. Sartain
1988    Historical Archaeology at Plum Grove. *Journal of the Iowa Archeological Society* 35:40–69.

Childe, V. Gordon
1951    *Man Makes Himself.* New American Library, New York.

Chumbley, Craig A., Richard G. Baker, and E. Arthur Bettis III
1990    Midwestern Holocene Paleoenvironments Revealed by Floodplain Deposits in Northeastern Iowa. *Science* 249:272–274.

Clark, Frances
1984    Knife River Flint and Interregional Exchange. *Midcontinental Journal of Archaeology* 9:173–198.

Clark, J. S.
1990    Fire and Climate Change during the Last 150 · Years in Northwestern Minnesota. *Ecological Monographs* 60:135–159.

Clark, Jerry
1971    Malone Terrace Oneota Site. In *Prehistoric Investigations,* edited by Marshall B. McKusick, pp. 80–85. Report 3. Office of the State Archaeologist, University of Iowa, Iowa City.

Clayton, Lee, W. B. Bickey Jr., and W. J. Stone
1970    Knife River Flint. *Plains Anthropologist* 15:282–290.

Cleland, Charles E.
1972    From Sacred to Profane: Style Drift in the Decoration of Jesuit Finger Rings. *American Antiquity* 37:202–210.

Clifton, James A.
1977    *The Prairie People: Continuity and Change in Potawatomie Indian Culture, 1665-1965.* Regents Press of Kansas, Lawrence.

Cole, Cyrenus
1938    *I Am a Man: The Indian Black Hawk.* State Historical Society of Iowa, Iowa City.

Cole, Fay-Cooper, and Thorne Deuel
1937    *Rediscovering Illinois.* University of Chicago Press, Chicago.

Collins, James M.
1985    Prehistoric Investigations at the Marriott Site, Van Buren County, Iowa. Luther College Archaeological Research Center, Decorah, Iowa. Ms. on file, Office of the State Archaeologist, University of Iowa, Iowa City.

1989    The Des Moines Rapids and Western Oneota Socio-Political Patterns. *Journal of the Steward Anthropological Society* 18:165–186.

1990    *Human Adaptations to Holocene Landscapes in the Iowa River Greenbelt.* Contract Completion Report 290. Office of the State Archaeologist, University of Iowa, Iowa City.

1991    *The Iowa River Greenbelt: An Archaeological Landscape.* Special Publication. Office of the State Archaeologist, University of Iowa, Iowa City.

1995    Lithic Technology and Temporal Variation at a Chert Workshop in Central Iowa. *Journal of the Iowa Archeological Society* 42:8–20.

1996a   *The Archaeology of the Dolomite Ridge Site. Archaeological Data Recovery at 13DB428, Primary Roads Projects TPN-52-2(17)--2J-31, Dubuque County, Iowa.* Project Completion Report Vol. 19, No. 10. Office of the State Archaeologist, University of Iowa, Iowa City.

1996b   *A Phase I Archaeological Evaluation of the Carroll Rock Shelter (13DB486), Primary Roads Project STP-52-2(17)-2J--31 a.k.a. PIN 71-31060-1, Dubuque County, Iowa.* Project Completion Report Vol. 19, No. 28. Office of the State Archaeologist, University of Iowa, Iowa City.

1997    *Prehistoric Archaeology of the Marriott Site: Archaeological Data Recovery at 13VB455 Van Buren County, Iowa.* Research Papers Vol. 22, No. 2. Office of the State Archaeologist, University of Iowa, Iowa City.

Collins, James M., E. Arthur Bettis III, and Timothy J. Kemmis
1991    *Archaeological and Geomorphological Investigations at the Bash Site.* Project Completion Report Vol. 14, No. 85. Office of the State Archaeologist, University of Iowa, Iowa City.

Collins, James M., and Linda Forman
1995    *Phase II Archaeological Salvage of the Buck Creek Mounds (13CT34 and 13CT36), Local Systems Project GRS-1792(2), Clayton County, Iowa.* Project Completion Report Vol. 18, No. 14. Office of the State Archaeologist, University of Iowa, Iowa City.

Collins, James M., and William Green
1988    Archaeological Survey in the Turkey River Valley. In *Archaeological and Paleoenvironmental Studies in the Turkey River Valley, Northeastern Iowa,* edited by William Green, pp. 110–130. Research Papers Vol. 13, No. 1. Office of the State Archaeologist, University of Iowa, Iowa City.

Collins, James M., Richard W. Slaughter, David L. Asch, K. Kris Hirst, and John L. Cordell
1997    A Brief Evaluation of the Carroll Rock Shelter, Dubuque County, Iowa. *Journal of the Iowa Archeological Society* 44:84–101.

Conard, Henry S.
1952    *The Vegetation of Iowa: An Approach toward a Phystosociologic Account.* Studies in Natural History Vol. 19, No. 4. State University of Iowa, Iowa City.

Conard, Nicholas, David L. Asch, Nancy B. Asch, David Elmore, Harry Gove, Meyer Rubin, James A. Brown, Michael D. Wiant, Kenneth B. Farnsworth, and Thomas G. Cook
1984    Accelerator Radiocarbon Dating Evidence for Prehistoric Horticulture in Illinois. *Nature* 308:443–446.

Conrad, Lawrence A.
1981    *An Introduction to the Archaeology of Upland West Central Illinois: Preliminary Archaeological Survey of the Canton to Quincy Corridor for the Proposed FAP-407 Highway Project.* Report of Investigations 2. Archaeological Research Laboratory, Western Illinois University, Macomb.

1986    The Late Archaic/Early Woodland Transition in the Interior of West-Central Illinois. In *Early Woodland Archeology,* edited by Kenneth B. Farnsworth and Thomas E. Emerson, pp. 301–325. Kampsville Seminars in Archeology 2. Center for American Archeology Press, Kampsville, Illinois.

1991    The Middle Mississippian Cultures of the

Central Illinois Valley. In *Cahokia and the Hinterlands,* edited by Thomas E. Emerson and R. Barry Lewis, pp. 119–156. University of Illinois Press, Urbana and Chicago.

Cook, D. C., and Jane E. Buikstra
1979    Health and Differential Survival in Prehistoric Populations: Prenatal Dental Defects. *American Journal of Physical Anthropology* 51:649–664.

Cook, David
1975a   *Archaeological Resources Management Plan: Known Archaeological Resources of the Chariton River Basin.* Division of Historic Preservation, Iowa State Historical Department, Iowa City.
1975b   *Archaeological Management Plan: Known Archaeological Resources of the Iowa-Cedar Rivers Basin.* Division of Historic Preservation, Iowa State Historical Department, Iowa City.

Cook, Thomas G.
1976    *Koster: An Artifact Analysis of Two Archaic Phases in West-Central Illinois.* Prehistoric Records No. 1. Northwestern Archeological Program, Northwestern University, Evanston, Illinois.

Cooper, Paul L.
1949    Recent Investigations in Fort Randall and Oahe Reservoirs, South Dakota. *American Antiquity* 14:300–310.

Cooper, Tom C. (editor)
1982    *Iowa's Natural Heritage.* Iowa Natural Heritage Foundation and the Iowa Academy of Sciences, Des Moines.

Cordell, John, William Green, and Derrick Marcucci
1991    The Paul Sagers Archaeological Collection. *Journal of the Iowa Archeological Society* 38:5–10.

Cowan, C. Wesley
1997    Evolutionary Changes Associated with the Domestication of *Cucurbita pepo:* Evidence from Eastern Kentucky. In *People, Plants, and Landscapes: Studies in Paleoethnobotany,* edited by K. Gremillion, pp. 63–85. University of Alabama Press, Tuscaloosa.

Crabtree, Don
1972    *An Introduction to Flintworking.* Occasional Papers of the Idaho State University Museum, Pocatello, Idaho, 28.

Cramer, Ann
1998    Pioneer Legacy. In *Federal Archeology Program: Secretary of Interior's Report to Congress 1994–1995,* by Daniel Haas, pp. 36–37. U.S. Department of the Interior, National Park Service, Washington, D.C.

Crichton, Michael
1990    *Jurassic Park.* Knopf, New York.

Crismon, Sandra, and William Green
1992    Rediscovering Glenwood Earthlodges: The McDowell "Digs," 1938–47. *Journal of the Iowa Archeological Society* 39:15–65.

Crites, Gary D.
1991    Investigations into Early Plant Domesticates and Food Production in Middle Tennessee: A Status Report. *Tennessee Anthropologist* 16:69–87.

Croft, Darin A., and Holmes Semken, Jr.
1994    Distribution of Mammalian Osteological Elements Recovered from Waterscreened Features, House Fill, and Overburden of the Wall Ridge Earthlodge (13ML176), Mills County, Iowa. *Current Research in the Pleistocene* 11:65–67.

Dallman, John E.
1983    *A Choice of Diet: Response to Climatic Change.* Report 16. Office of the State Archaeologist, University of Iowa, Iowa City.

Damon, P. E., C. W. Ferguson, A. Long, and E. I. Wallick
1974    Dendrochronologic Calibration of the Radiocarbon Time Scale. *American Antiquity* 39:350–366.

Daniels, Raymond B., and Robert H. Jordan
1966    *Physiographic History and the Soils, Entrenched Stream Systems, and Gullies, Harrison County, Iowa.* Technical Bulletin 1348. U.S. Department of Agriculture, Washington, D.C.

Davis, Donald D., and Paul R. Rowe
1960    Further Notes on the Glenwood Culture: The Stille Site. *Journal of the Iowa Archeological Society* 9(3):13–17.

Dean, S.
1881    *Antiquities of Mills County, Iowa.* Annual Report of the Smithsonian Institution for 1879, pp. 528–532. Smithsonian Institution, Washington, D.C.

Deetz, James
1965 *The Dynamics of Stylistic Change in Arikara Ce-
    ramics*. Illinois Studies in Anthropology No. 4.
    University of Illinois Press, Urbana.
1967 *Invitation to Archaeology*. Natural History
    Press, Garden City, New Jersey.

Deliette, Pierre
1934 Memoir of DeGannes Concerning the Illinois
    Country [1721]. In *The French Foundations*,
    compiled by Theodore C. Pease and Raymond
    C. Werner, pp. 302–395. Collections of the Il-
    linois State Historical Library 23. Illinois State
    Historical Library, Springfield.

Deller, D. B., and C. J. Ellis
1988 Early Paleo-Indian Complexes in Southwest-
    ern Ontario. In *The Late Pleistocene and Early
    Holocene Paleoecology and Archaeology of the
    Eastern Great Lakes Region*, edited by R. S.
    Laub, N. G. Miller, and D. W. Steadman, pp.
    251–263. Bulletin of the Buffalo Society of
    Natural Sciences Vol. 33. Buffalo, New York.

DeMott, Rodney C., Derrick J. Marcucci, and Joyce A.
    Williams
1992 Chippea Lithic Materials. In *The Archaeology
    of the Cahokia Mounds ICT-III: Testing and
    Lithics*. Illinois Cultural Resources Study 9.
    Illinois Historic Preservation Agency, Spring-
    field.

Denevan, W. M.
1992 The Pristine Myth: The Landscape of the
    Americas in 1492. In The Americas before and
    after 1492: Current Geographical Research,
    edited by Karl W. Butzer, pp. 369–385. *Annals
    of the Association of American Geographers* 82.

Deuel, Thorne
1958 *American Indian Ways of Life: An Interpretation
    of the Archaeology of Illinois and Adjoining
    Areas*. Story of Illinois Series No. 9. Illinois
    State Museum, Springfield.

Deuel, Thorne (editor)
1952 *Hopewellian Communities in Illinois*. Scientific
    Papers Vol. 5. Illinois State Museum, Spring-
    field.

De Vore, Steven L.
1984 *The Cribb's Crib Site (13WA105): The Archae-
    ology and Ecology of an Oneota Village in the
    Central Des Moines Valley*. Unpublished

Master's thesis, Department of Anthropology,
    Iowa State University, Ames.
1990a The Cribb's Crib Site (13WA105): The Ar-
    chaeology and Ecology of an Oneota Village
    in the Central Des Moines Valley. *Journal of
    the Iowa Archeological Society* 37:46–87.
1990b *Moingona Phase Oneota Subsistence Strategies:
    Examples from the Central Des Moines River
    Valley*. Research Papers Vol. 15, No. 3. Office
    of the State Archaeologist, University of Iowa,
    Iowa City.
1993 *The Quest for the Latter-Day Saints at Garden
    Grove: Archeological Reconnaissance at
    13DT110*. National Park Service, Denver.
    Copy on file, Office of the State Archaeologist,
    University of Iowa, Iowa City.
1994a *Archeological Assessment of a Mormon Trail
    Crossing (13CA32), Cass County, Iowa*. Na-
    tional Park Service, Denver. Copy on file, Of-
    fice of the State Archaeologist, University of
    Iowa, Iowa City.
1994b *Archeological Assessment of the Mt. Pisgah Set-
    tlement, Union County, Iowa*. National Park
    Service, Denver. Copy on file, Office of the
    State Archaeologist, University of Iowa, Iowa
    City.

De Vore, Steven L., Kay Simpson, Joyce McKay, Shirley
    J. Schermer, and Larry R. Abbott
1991 The Dubuque Lead Mining District: The Ar-
    chaeological Investigations and Management
    Concerns for the Frontier Lead Mining Indus-
    try, 1788–1865. Paper presented at the 1991
    Annual Meeting of the Society for Historical
    Archaeology, Richmond, Virginia. Copy on
    file, Office of the State Archaeologist, Univer-
    sity of Iowa, Iowa City.

DeWys-VanHecke, Amy J.
1990 Pine Creek Masters Project. Department of
    Anthropology, University of Iowa. Ms. on file,
    Office of the State Archaeologist, University of
    Iowa, Iowa City.

Dillehay, Thomas (editor)
1997 *Monte Verde: A Late Pleistocene Settlement in
    Chile*, Vol. 2, *The Archaeological Context*.
    Smithsonian Institution, Washington, D.C.

Dinsmore, James J.
1994 *A Country So Full of Game: The Story of Wildlife
    in Iowa*. University of Iowa Press, Iowa City.

Dobyns, Henry

1983   *Their Number Became Thinned.* University of Tennessee Press, Knoxville.

Doershuk, John F.

1996   Excavations at the Maxwell Site (13DA264): A Great Oasis Structure in Dallas County, Iowa. Paper presented at the 54th Annual Plains Anthropological Conference, Iowa City. Copy on file, Office of the State Archaeologist, University of Iowa, Iowa City.

1997   Recent Excavations at the Gillett Grove Site, Clay County, Iowa. Iowa Archeological Society *Newsletter* 47(3):1–3.

Doershuk, John F., and Fred A. Finney

1996   *Excavations at the Maxwell Site (13DA264): A Great Oasis Settlement in Central Iowa.* Contract Completion Report 445. Office of the State Archaeologist, University of Iowa, Iowa City.

Donham, Theresa K.

1982   Chronology of the Ceramic Period. In *The Cannon Reservoir Human Ecology Project,* edited by Michael J. O'Brien, Robert E. Warren, and Dennis E. Lewarch, pp. 117–130. Academic Press, New York.

1985   *The Seth Richards and James Marriott House Sites: Historic Context and Material Culture.* Luther College Archaeological Research Center, Decorah, Iowa. Copy on file, Office of the State Archaeologist, University of Iowa, Iowa City.

Donnelly, J. P.

1968   *Jacques Marquette, S.J. 1637–1675.* Loyola University Press, Chicago.

Dorale, Jeffrey A., Luis A. Gonzalez, Mark K. Reagan, David A. Pickett, Michael T. Murrell, and Richard G. Baker

1992   A High-Resolution Record of Holocene Climate Change in Speleotherm Calcite from Cold Water Cave, Northeast Iowa. *Science* 258:1628–1630.

Doudy, Willis, and Sandra Burke

1995   *Population (1850–1990) and Population Estimates (1990) for Incorporated Places in Iowa.* Census Services, Iowa State University, Ames.

Driver, Harold E. (editor)

1964   *The Americas on the Eve of Discovery.* Prentice-Hall, Englewood Cliffs, New Jersey.

Drucker, Philip

1965   *Cultures of the North Pacific Coast.* Chandler Publishing, San Francisco.

Dunne, Michael

1997   *Paleoethnobotany at the Gast Spring Site (13LA152).* Unpublished Master's paper, Department of Anthropology, University of Iowa, Iowa City.

Edmonds, R. David, and Joseph L. Peyser

1993   *The Fox Wars: The Mesquakie Challenge to New France.* University of Oklahoma Press, Norman.

Edwards, William C.

1983   *A Macro- and Micro-Technological Analysis of Four Great Oasis Ceramic Assemblages.* Unpublished Master's thesis, Department of Anthropology, University of Iowa, Iowa City.

1993   Great Oasis Ceramics: Communication by Design. *Journal of the Iowa Archeological Society* 40:20–49.

Ehrhardt, Kathleen, and Lawrence A. Conrad

1994   Recent Investigations at Illiniwek Village State Historic Site, Clark County, Missouri. Paper presented at the 51st Southeastern Archaeological Conference and the 39th Midwest Archaeological Conference, Lexington, Kentucky.

Ekland-Olson, Carolyn Lee

1981   *Holly Fine Engraved: Some New Light on an Old Type.* Unpublished Master's thesis, Department of Anthropology, University of Texas, Austin.

Emerson, Patricia M., and Harlan R. Finney

1984   *Archaeological and Geomorphological Data Recovery at Saylorville Lake, Polk County, Iowa,* Vols. 1–3. Impact Services, Mankato, Minnesota. Copy on file, Office of the State Archaeologist, University of Iowa, Iowa City.

Emerson, Patricia M., Harlan R. Finney, Frederick W. Lange, and David S. Radford

1984   *The Cultural Resources and Geomorphology of Coralville Lake, Johnson County, Iowa.* Impact Services, Mankato, Minnesota. Submitted to the U.S. Army Corps of Engineers, Rock Island District. Copy on file, Office of the State Archaeologist, University of Iowa, Iowa City.

Emerson, Thomas E.

1991   The Apple River Mississippian Culture of Northwestern Illinois. In *Cahokia and the Hin-*

*terlands: Middle Mississippian Cultures of the Midwest,* edited by Thomas E. Emerson and R. Barry Lewis, pp. 164–182. University of Illinois Press, Urbana and Chicago.

Emerson, Thomas E., and James A. Brown
1992 The Late Prehistory and Protohistory of Illinois. In *Calumet and Fleur-De-Lys,* edited by John A. Walthall and Thomas E. Emerson, pp. 77–128. Smithsonian Institution Press, Washington, D.C.

Emerson, Thomas E., and Andrew C. Fortier
1986 Early Woodland Cultural Variation, Subsistence, and Settlement in the American Bottom. In *Early Woodland Archeology,* edited by Kenneth B. Farnsworth and Thomas E. Emerson, pp. 475–522. Kampsville Seminars in Archeology Vol. 2. Center for American Archeology Press, Kampsville, Illinois.

Emerson, Thomas E., and Dale L. McElrath
1983 A Settlement-Subsistence Model of the Terminal Late Archaic Adaptation in the American Bottom. In *Archaic Hunters and Gatherers in the American Midwest,* edited by James L. Phillips and James A. Brown, pp. 219–242. Academic Press, New York.

Ennis, J. Harold
1951 Charles Reuben Keyes (Obituary). *Journal of the Iowa Archeological Society* 1(1):14–16.

Esarey, Duane
1986a Red Ocher Mound Building and Marion Phase Associations: A Fulton County, Illinois, Perspective. In *Early Woodland Archeology,* edited by Kenneth B. Farnsworth and Thomas E. Emerson, pp. 231–243. Kampsville Seminars in Archeology Vol. 2. Center for American Archeology Press, Kampsville, Illinois.
1986b Protohistoric Oneota Material from the Clear Lake Site, Illinois. *Journal of the Iowa Archeological Society* 33:75–82.

Faegri, Knut, and John Iversen
1964 *Textbook of Pollen Analysis.* Hafner, New York.

Farnsworth, Kenneth B.
1986 Black Sand Culture Origins and Distribution. In *Early Woodland Archeology,* edited by Kenneth B. Farnsworth and Thomas E. Emerson, pp. 634–651. Kampsville Seminars in Archeology Vol. 2. Center for American Archeology Press, Kampsville, Illinois.

Farnsworth, Kenneth B., and David L. Asch
1986 Early Woodland Chronology, Artifact Styles, and Settlement Distribution in the Lower Illinois Valley Region. In *Early Woodland Archeology,* edited by Kenneth B. Farnsworth and Thomas E. Emerson, pp. 326–457. Kampsville Seminars in Archeology Vol. 2. Center for American Archeology Press, Kampsville, Illinois.

Farnsworth, Kenneth B., and Thomas E. Emerson (editors)
1986 *Early Woodland Archeology.* Kampsville Seminars in Archeology Vol. 2. Center for American Archeology Press, Kampsville, Illinois.

Farnsworth, Kenneth B., and Ann L. Koski
1985 *Massey and Archie: A Study of Two Hopewellian Homesteads in the Western Illinois Uplands.* Research Series 3. Center for American Archeology, Kampsville Archeological Center, Kampsville, Illinois.

Farquharson, R. J.
1876 Recent Archaeological Discoveries at Davenport Iowa, of Copper Axes, Cloth, etc., Supposed to Have Come Down to Us from a Pre-Historic People, Called the Mound-Builders. *Proceedings of the Davenport Academy of Natural Sciences* 1:117–142.

Fawcett, William B., Jr.
1988 Changing Prehistoric Settlement along the Missouri River: Timber Depletion and the Historic Context. *Plains Anthropologist* 33:67–94.

Feder, Kenneth L.
1996 *The Past in Perspective.* Mayfield, Mountain View, California.

Finn, Michael R.
1982 *The Merrimac Mills Site (13JF92): A Study of Site Positioning and Mobile Strategy of an Upland Archaic Site in Southeast Iowa.* Unpublished Master's thesis, Department of Anthropology, University of Iowa, Iowa City.

Finn, Michael R., Michael J. Fokken, and John Hotopp
1986 *Phase I and II Cultural Resource Investigations of the U.S. 61 Corridor (Wever Bypass), Lee County, Iowa, F-61-4(24)--20-56.* Cultural Resource Group, Louis Berger and Associates, East Orange, New Jersey. Copy on file, Office

of the State Archaeologist, University of Iowa, Iowa City.

Finney, Fred A.

1992a  Hartley Fort Revisited: Late Woodland, Mill Creek, and Middle Mississippian Culture Contact in Northeast Iowa. Paper presented at the 37th Midwest Archaeological Conference, Grand Rapids, Michigan. Copy on file, Office of the State Archaeologist, University of Iowa, Iowa City.

1992b  *Mid to Late-Nineteenth-Century Rural Households in the Upper Mississippi Valley Lead District: Phase III Excavations at the Mouth of Catfish Creek in the Mines of Spain Recreation Area, Dubuque County, Iowa.* Contract Completion Report 350. Office of the State Archaeologist, University of Iowa, Iowa City.

1993  *Cahokia's Northern Hinterland as Viewed from the Fred Edwards Site in Southwest Wisconsin: Intrasite and Regional Evidence for Production, Consumption, and Exchange.* Unpublished Ph.D. dissertation, Department of Anthropology, University of Wisconsin–Madison.

1994  Hartley Terrace Archaeology. In *Archaeological Resources of Allamakee County, Iowa: A Guidebook for the Association of Iowa Archaeologists Annual Field Trip June 4, 1994,* compiled and edited by Lori A. Stanley, pp. 29–37. Luther College, Decorah, Iowa. Copy on file, Office of the State Archaeologist, University of Iowa, Iowa City.

1995  Lithic Analysis. In *Excavations at the Phipps Site (13CK21): New Perspectives on Mill Creek Culture,* by Richard L. Fishel, pp. 51–68. Contract Completion Report 443. Office of the State Archaeologist, University of Iowa, Iowa City.

Finney, Fred A., Russell P. Baldner, and E. Arthur Bettis III

1993  The 1993 Field Season at the Hartley Fort in Northeast Iowa. Paper presented at the 38th Midwest Archaeological Conference, Milwaukee.

Finney, Fred A., and R. Eric Hollinger

1994  A New Look at Some Old Sites on the Hartley Terrace in Northeast Iowa. Paper presented at the 51st Southeastern Archaeological Conference and the 39th Midwest Archaeological Conference, Lexington, Kentucky. Copy on file, Office of the State Archaeologist, University of Iowa, Iowa City.

Finney, Fred A., and Matthew S. Logan

1993  Palisades-Dows State Preserve. In *Archaeological Inventory Survey and Potential of Selected Iowa State Preserves,* by Fred A. Finney, pp. 14–22. Research Papers Vol. 18, No. 3. Office of the State Archaeologist, University of Iowa, Iowa City.

Finney, Fred A., and Susan R. Snow

1991  Small-Scale, Soft-Mud Brickmaking Facilities in the Mid-Nineteenth Century: An Archaeological Example from Iowa. *Journal of the Iowa Archeological Society* 38:66–72.

Finney, Fred A., and James B. Stoltman

1991  The Fred Edwards Site: A Case of Stirling Phase Culture Contact in Southwestern Wisconsin. In *New Perspectives on Cahokia: Views from the Periphery,* edited by James B. Stoltman, pp. 229–252. Monographs in World Archaeology No. 2. Prehistory Press, Madison, Wisconsin.

Fishel, Richard L.

1995a  *Excavations at the Phipps Site (13CK21): New Perspectives on Mill Creek Culture.* Contract Completion Report 443. Office of the State Archaeologist, University of Iowa, Iowa City.

1995b  *Excavations at the Dixon Site (13WD8): Correctionville Phase Oneota in Northwest Iowa.* Contract Completion Report 442. Office of the State Archaeologist, University of Iowa, Iowa City.

1996  A Reanalysis of Mill Creek Midden Formation. *Journal of the Iowa Archeological Society* 43:119–127.

1997  Medicine Birds and Mill Creek–Middle Mississippian Interaction: The Contents of Feature 8 at the Phipps Site (13CK21). *American Antiquity* 62:538–553.

Fishel, Richard L., ed.

1999  *Bison Hunters of the Western Prairies: Excavations at the Dixon Site (13WD8): Woodbury County, Iowa.* Report 21. Office of the State Archaeologist, University of Iowa, Iowa City.

Fisher, Alton K.

1984  Human Skeleton Found on Banks of Nodaway River in Page County, Iowa, at Site

13PA39. In *Miscellaneous Reports on Iowa Archaeology*, pp. 74–80. Research Papers Vol. 9, No. 2. Office of the State Archaeologist, University of Iowa, Iowa City.

1986 Human Skeletal Material from the Boone Mound (13BN29). In *Miscellaneous Reports on Iowa Archaeology*, pp. 40–47. Research Papers Vol. 11, No. 1. Office of the State Archaeologist, University of Iowa, Iowa City.

Fisher, Alton K., W. D. Frankforter, Joseph A. Tiffany, Shirley J. Schermer, and Duane C. Anderson

1985 Turin: A Middle Archaic Burial in Western Iowa. *Plains Anthropologist* 30:195–218.

Fisher, Alton K., and Marshall McKusick

1980 A Historic Period Aboriginal Burial from Lee County, Iowa (13LE136). In *Miscellaneous Reports on Iowa Archaeology*, pp. 65–71. Research Papers Vol. 5, No. 1. Office of the State Archaeologist, University of Iowa, Iowa City.

Flanders, Richard E.

1960 A Reexamination of Mill Creek Ceramics: The Robinson Technique. *Journal of the Iowa Archeological Society* 10(2):iv–34.

1977 The Soldow Site, 13HB1: An Archaic Component from North Central Iowa. *Journal of the Iowa Archeological Society* 24:125–147.

Flanders, Richard E., and Rex Hansman

1961 A Woodland Mound Complex in Webster County, Iowa. *Journal of the Iowa Archeological Society* 11(1):1–12.

Fletcher, Alice C., and Francis La Flesche

1972 *The Omaha Tribe.* 2 vols. Reprinted. University of Nebraska Press, Lincoln. Originally published 1911, 27th Annual Report, Bureau of American Ethnology, Smithsonian Institution, Washington, D.C.

Fokken, Michael J., and Michael R. Finn

1984 *Iowa's Great River Road, Louisa County, Phase III Archaeological Mitigation at the Michael's Creek Segment of County Road X61, GRS-8028(2).* Cultural Resource Group, Louis Berger and Associates, East Orange, New Jersey. Copy on file, Office of the State Archaeologist, University of Iowa, Iowa City.

Ford, Richard I.

1977 Evolutionary Ecology and the Evolution of Human Ecosystems: A Case Study from the Midwestern U.S.A. In *Explanation of Prehistoric Change,* edited by James N. Hill, pp. 153–184. University of New Mexico Press, Albuquerque.

Foster, Lance M.

1994 *Sacred Bundles of the Ioway Indians.* Unpublished Master's thesis, Department of Anthropology, Iowa State University, Ames.

1996 The Ioway and the Landscape of Southeast Iowa. *Journal of the Iowa Archeological Society* 43:1–5.

Fowler, Melvin L.

1955 Ware Groupings and Decorations on Woodland Ceramics in Illinois. *American Antiquity* 20:213–225.

1973 Midwestern Prehistory, Cognitive Dissonance and Conspicuous Assumptions: An Essay. In Archaeology in the '70s—Mitigating the Impact. *Missouri Archaeologist* 35(1–2):45–54.

1989 *The Cahokia Atlas: A Historical Atlas of Cahokia Archaeology.* Studies in Illinois Archaeology No. 6. Illinois Historic Preservation Agency, Springfield.

Fowler, Melvin L., and Robert L. Hall

1975 Archaeological Phases at Cahokia. In *Perspectives in Cahokia Archaeology,* edited by James A. Brown, pp. 1–14. Illinois Archaeological Survey Bulletin 10. Urbana, Illinois.

Frankforter, W. D.

1953 Trinomial Site Numbering System. *Journal of the Iowa Archeological Society* 3(1):3–7.

1959 A Pre-Ceramic Site in Western Iowa. *Northwest Chapter of the Iowa Archaeological Society Newsletter* 7(2):1–13.

1961 Meaning of the "Archaic" and Possible Relationships. *Journal of the Iowa Archeological Society* 10(4):26–31.

Frankforter, W. D. (editor)

1955 Early Indian Skeletons at Turin, Iowa. *Northwest Chapter of the Iowa Archaeological Society Newsletter* 3(5):4–6.

1959a Excavation at the Simonsen Site. *Northwest Chapter of the Iowa Archeological Society Newsletter* 7(4):2–3.

1959b Geologic Field Trip in Northeastern Nebraska. *Northwest Chapter of the Iowa Archeological Society Newsletter* 7(4):3–4.

1961 News and Notes from the Museum. *North-*

*west Chapter of the Iowa Archeological Society Newsletter* 9(3):4–5.

Frankforter, W. D., and George A. Agogino

1959a   Recent Pre-Ceramic Archeological Developments in Western Iowa. *Journal of the Iowa Archaeological Society* 9(1):13–19.

1959b   Archaic and Paleo-Indian Archaeological Discoveries in Western Iowa. *Texas Journal of Science* 11:482–491.

1960   The Simonsen Site: Report for the Summer of 1959. *Plains Anthropologist* 5:65–70.

Frantz, W.

1958a   The Wissler Site, 25CD12, Cedar County, Nebraska. Ms. on file, Nebraska State Historical Society, Lincoln.

1958b   The Burney Site, 25CD21, Cedar County, Nebraska. Ms. on file, Nebraska State Historical Society, Lincoln.

Frese, Millie

1993   Maria Pearson (Running Moccasins). *Goldfinch* 15(2):21–23.

Frison, George C.

1978   *Prehistoric Hunters of the High Plains.* Academic Press, New York.

1989   Experimental Use of Clovis Weaponry and Tools on African Elephants. *American Antiquity* 54:766–784.

1991   *Prehistoric Hunters of the High Plains.* 2nd ed. Academic Press, New York.

Frison, George C., Michael Wilson, and Diane J. Wilson

1976   Fossil Bison and Artifacts from an Early Altithermal Period Arroyo Trap in Wyoming. *American Antiquity* 41:28–57.

Fritz, Gayle J.

1990   Multiple Pathways to Farming in Precontact Eastern North America. *Journal of World Prehistory* 4:387–435.

Fugle, Eugene

1954   A Fox Village Site. *Journal of the Iowa Archeological Society* 4(1):4–15.

1957   *Introduction to the Artifact Assemblages of the Big Sioux and Little Sioux Foci.* Unpublished Master's thesis, Department of Sociology and Anthropology, State University of Iowa, Iowa City.

1962   Mill Creek Culture and Technology. *Journal of the Iowa Archeological Society* 11(4):3–126.

Fulmer, Darrell, John Hotopp, and Alton K. Fisher

1977   *The Lambert Site 13VB82.* Contract Completion Report 71. Office of the State Archaeologist, University of Iowa, Iowa City.

Fulton, Alexander R.

1882   *The Red Men of Iowa.* Mills, Des Moines.

Gallagher, James P., Robert F. Boszhardt, Robert F. Sasso, and Katherine Stevenson

1985   Oneota Ridged Field Agriculture in Southwestern Wisconsin. *American Antiquity* 50:605–612.

Gallagher, James P., and Robert F. Sasso

1987   Investigations into Oneota Ridged Field Agriculture on the Northern Margin of the Prairie Peninsula. *Plains Anthropologist* 32:141–151.

Gass, Jacob

1877a   A Connected Account of the Explorations of Mound No. 3, Cook's Farm Group. *Proceedings of the Davenport Academy of Natural Sciences* 2:92–97.

1877b   Report of Exploration of Mound No. 10, Cook's Farm Group. *Proceedings of the Davenport Academy of Natural Sciences* 2:141–142.

1883a   Exploration of Mounds in Louisa County, Iowa. *Proceedings of the Davenport Academy of Natural Sciences* 3:140–146.

1883b   Mounds near Muscatine. *Proceedings of the Davenport Academy of Natural Sciences* 3:191.

Gearing, Frederick O.

1970   *The Face of the Fox.* Aldine, Chicago.

Gero, Joan M., and Margaret W. Conkey (editors)

1991   *Engendering Archaeology: Women and Prehistory.* Blackwell Press, Oxford.

Gibbon, Guy E.

1972   Cultural Dynamics and the Development of the Oneota Life-way in Wisconsin. *American Antiquity* 37:166–185.

1982   Oneota Origins Revisited. In *Oneota Studies,* edited by Guy E. Gibbon, pp. 85–89. Publications in Anthropology No. 1. University of Minnesota, Minneapolis.

1983   The Blue Earth Phase of Southern Minnesota. *Journal of the Iowa Archeological Society* 30:1–84.

1986   Does Minnesota Have an Early Woodland? In *Early Woodland Archeology,* edited by Kenneth B. Farnsworth and Thomas E. Emerson, pp. 84–91. Kampsville Seminars in Archeology

Vol. 2. Center for American Archeology Press, Kampsville, Illinois.

1991 The Middle Mississippian Presence in Minnesota. In *Cahokia and the Hinterlands: Middle Mississippian Cultures of the Midwest,* edited by Thomas E. Emerson and R. Barry Lewis, pp. 207–220. University of Illinois Press, Urbana and Chicago.

1993 The Middle Missouri Tradition in Minnesota: A Review. In *Prehistory and Human Ecology of the Western Prairies and Northern Plains: Papers in Honor of Robert A. Alex (1941–1988),* edited by Joseph A. Tiffany, pp. 169–187. Memoir 27. *Plains Anthropologist,* Lincoln, Nebraska.

1995 Oneota at the Periphery: Trade, Political Power, and Ethnicity in Northern Minnesota and on the Northeastern Plains in the Late Prehistoric Period. In *Oneota Archaeology: Past, Present, and Future,* edited by William Green, pp. 175–199. Report 20. Office of the State Archaeologist, University of Iowa, Iowa City.

1998 Old Copper in Minnesota: A Review. *Plains Anthropologist* 43:27–50.

Gibbon, Guy E. (editor)

1982 *Oneota Studies.* Publications in Anthropology No. 1. University of Minnesota, Minneapolis.

Gillen, Timothy V.

1993 Possible Great Oasis and Initial Middle Missouri Relationships at Split Rock Creek, Minnehaha County, South Dakota. *Newsletter of the South Dakota Archaeological Society* 23(1):1–3.

Gilmore, Melvin R.

1977 *Uses of Plants by the Indians of the Missouri River Region.* University of Nebraska Press, Lincoln.

Glenn, Elizabeth J.

1974 *Physical Affiliations of the Oneota Peoples.* Report 7. Office of the State Archaeologist, University of Iowa, Iowa City.

Goldman-Finn, Nurit, William Green, and E. Arthur Bettis III

1991 The Archaic-Woodland Transition in the Upper Mississippi Valley. Paper presented at the 36th Annual Midwest Archaeological Conference, La Crosse, Wisconsin. Copy on

file, Office of the State Archaeologist, University of Iowa.

Gourley, Kathryn E.

1983 *The Southern Iowa Rivers Basin: An Archaeological Overview.* Iowa River Basins Report Series Vol. 1. Office of Historic Preservation, Iowa State Historical Department, Des Moines.

1984 *The Skunk River Basin, an Archaeological Overview.* Iowa River Basins Report Series Vol. 2. Office of Historic Preservation, Iowa State Historical Department, Des Moines.

1990 *Locations of Sauk, Meskwakie and Associated Euro-American Sites 1832 to 1845: An Ethnohistoric Approach.* Unpublished Master's thesis, Department of Anthropology, Iowa State University, Ames.

Gradwohl, David M.

1965 Salvage Archaeology at 13PK33, the Charles D. Johnson Mound, in Polk County, Iowa. Paper presented at the 23rd Annual Plains Anthropological Conference, Topeka, Kansas.

1967 A Preliminary Précis of the Moingona Phase, an Oneota Manifestation in Central Iowa. Paper presented at the 24th Annual Plains Anthropological Conference, Lincoln, Nebraska.

1969 *Prehistoric Villages in Eastern Nebraska.* Publication No. 4. Nebraska State Historical Society, Lincoln.

1973 *Final Report on Investigation of Archaeological Sites in Red Rock Reservoir, Iowa, as Covered in Contracts 14-10-0232-820 and 14-10-0232-1164 between the National Park Service and Iowa State University.* Research Report. Iowa State University Archaeological Laboratory, Ames. Copy on file, Office of the State Archaeologist, University of Iowa, Iowa City.

1974 Archaeology of the Central Des Moines River Valley: A Preliminary Survey. In *Aspects of Great Lakes Anthropology: Papers in Honor of Lloyd Wilford,* edited by Elden Johnson, pp. 90–102. Minnesota Prehistoric Archaeology Series 11. Minnesota Historical Society, St. Paul.

1975 *Final Report on the Investigation of Archaeological Sites in Saylorville Reservoir, Iowa, as Covered in Four Contracts between the National*

*Park Service and Iowa State University.* Research Report. Iowa State University Archaeological Laboratory, Ames.

1978    The Native American Experience in Iowa: An Archaeological Perspective. In *The Worlds between Two Rivers: Perspectives on American Indians in Iowa,* edited by Gretchen M. Bataille, David M. Gradwohl, and C. L. P. Silet, pp. 26–53. Iowa State University Press, Ames.

1982    Shelling Corn in the Prairie-Plains: Archaeological Evidence and Ethnographic Parallels beyond the Pun. In *Plains Indian Studies: A Collection of Essays in Honor of John C. Ewers and Waldo R. Wedel,* edited by D. H. Ubelaker and H. J. Viola, pp. 135–156. Smithsonian Contribution to Anthropology 30. Smithsonian Institution, Washington, D.C.

1996    Great Oasis Manifestations in the Central Des Moines River Valley. Paper presented at the 54th Annual Plains Anthropological Conference, Iowa City.

1997    Pioneer Woman in Iowa Archaeology and Prairie-Plains Ethnohistory: Mildred Mott Wedel. *Journal of the Iowa Archeological Society* 44:1–6.

Gradwohl, David M., and Nancy M. Osborn
1972    *Stalking the Skunk: A Preliminary Survey and Appraisal of Archaeological Resources in the Ames Reservoir, Iowa.* Papers in Anthropology No. 1. Iowa State University, Ames.

1973    *Site Seeking in Saylorville.* Research Report. Iowa State University Archaeology Laboratory, Ames. Copy on file, Office of the State Archaeologist, University of Iowa, Iowa City.

1974    *More Site Seeking in Saylorville.* Research Report. Iowa State University Archaeology Laboratory, Ames. Copy on file, Office of the State Archaeologist, University of Iowa, Iowa City.

1975    *Still More Site Seeking in Saylorville.* Research Report. Iowa State University Archaeology Laboratory, Ames. Copy on file, Office of the State Archaeologist, University of Iowa, Iowa City.

1976    *Continued Site Seeking in Saylorville.* Research Report. Iowa State University Archaeology Laboratory, Ames. Copy on file, Office of the

State Archaeologist, University of Iowa, Iowa City.

1984    *Exploring Buried Buxton: Archaeology of an Abandoned Iowa Coal Mining Town with a Large Black Population.* Iowa State University Press, Ames.

Graham, R. W., C. Vance Haynes, D. L. Johnson, and Marvin Kay
1981    Kimmswick: A Clovis-Mastodon Association in Eastern Missouri. *Science* 213:1115–1117.

Graham, R. W., and Marvin Kay
1988    Taphonomic Comparisons of Cultural and Noncultural Faunal Deposits at the Kimmswick and Barnhart Sites, Jefferson County, Missouri. In *Late Pleistocene and Early Holocene Paleoecology and Archaeology of the Eastern Great Lakes Region,* edited by R. S. Laub, N. G. Miller, and D. W. Steadman, pp. 227–240. Bulletin of the Buffalo Society of Natural Sciences Vol. 33. Buffalo, New York.

Grantham, Larry
1993    The Illini Village of the Marquette and Jolliet Voyage of 1673. *Missouri Archaeologist* 54:1–20.

Grantham, Larry D., William B. Butler, Steven L. De Vore, and James W. Walker
1995    Geophysical Investigations at Illiniwek Village State Historic Site: A 17th Century Illini Village in Northeast Missouri. Paper presented at the 53rd Annual Plains Anthropological Conference, Laramie, Wyoming.

Gray, Jean (editor)
1995    The Proof Is in the Pipestone. *Nature of Illinois* 3(1):4–5. Nature of Illinois Foundation, Chicago.

Green, Michael
1976    *A Chronicle of the Meskwakis in Iowa, 1845–1856.* Report to the U.S. Bureau of Indian Affairs. Copy on file, Office of the State Archaeologist, University of Iowa, Iowa City.

1983    "We Dance in Opposite Directions": Meskwakis (Fox) Separatism from the Sac and Fox Tribe. *Ethnohistory* 30:129–140.

Green, William
1984    Protohistoric Depopulation in the Upper Midwest. Paper presented at the 28th Midwest Archaeological Conference, Evanston,

Illinois. Copy on file, Office of the State Archaeologist, University of Iowa, Iowa City.

1986    Prehistoric Woodland Peoples in the Upper Mississippi Valley. In *Prehistoric Mound Builders of the Mississippi Valley*, edited by James B. Stoltman, pp. 17–25. Putnam Museum of History and Natural Sciences, Davenport, Iowa.

1987    *Between Hopewell and Mississippian: Late Woodland in the Prairie Peninsula as Viewed from the Western Illinois Uplands.* Unpublished Ph.D. dissertation, Department of Anthropology, University of Wisconsin–Madison.

1990    Durst Style Artifacts Dated to about 600–800 B.C. Iowa Archeological Society *Newsletter* 40(4):4.

1991    New Data on Glenwood Life. Iowa Archeological Society *Newsletter* 41(3):1–2.

1992    Charles Reuben Keyes and the History of Iowa Archaeology. *Journal of the Iowa Academy of Sciences* 99:80–85.

1993a   A Prehistoric Frontier in the Prairie-Peninsula: Late Woodland Upland Settlement and Subsistence Patterns. *Illinois Archaeology* 5:201–214.

1993b   Examining Protohistoric Depopulation in the Upper Midwest. *Wisconsin Archeologist* 74:290–323.

1993c   *Mapping of the Toolesboro Mounds Historic Site (13LA29), Louisa County, Iowa.* Contract Completion Report 378. Office of the State Archaeologist, University of Iowa, Iowa City.

1994    Ioway Cartography, History, and Archaeology. Iowa Archeological Society *Newsletter* 44(2):7.

1995a   Botanical Analysis at the Cowan Site. In *Archaeological Excavations at the Cowan Site,* by Mark L. Anderson pp. 32–38. Project Completion Report Vol. 18, No. 10. Office of the State Archaeologist, University of Iowa, Iowa City.

1995b   Floral Remains. In *Test Excavations at the Kuehn Site (13DA110): The Great Oasis Component,* by Stephen C. Lensink and Fred A. Finney, p. 16. Contract Completion Report 440. Office of the State Archaeologist, University of Iowa, Iowa City.

1995c   The 1837 Ioway Map: Ethnohistory, Geography, and Archaeology. Paper presented at the Annual Meeting of the American Society for Ethnohistory, Kalamazoo, Michigan.

1995a   The Middle-Late Woodland Transition in the Prairie Peninsula. Paper presented at the 61st Annual Meeting of the Society of American Archaeology, New Orleans. Copy on file, Office of the State Archaeologist, University of Iowa, Iowa City.

1998    Ioway Cartography, Ethnohistory, and Archaeology. Paper presented at the 56th Annual Plains Anthropological Conference, Bismarck, North Dakota. Copy on file, Office of the State Archaeologist, University of Iowa, Iowa City.

Green, William (editor)

1988    *Archaeological and Paleoenvironmental Studies in the Turkey River Valley, Northeastern Iowa.* Research Papers Vol. 13, No. 1. Office of the State Archaeologist, University of Iowa, Iowa City.

1990a   *Glenwood Culture Paleoenvironment and Diet: Analysis of Plant and Animal Remains from the Wall Ridge Earthlodge (13ML176), Mills County, Iowa.* Research Papers Vol. 15, No. 6. Office of the State Archaeologist, University of Iowa, Iowa City.

1990b   Finds of the Year. Iowa Archaeological Society *Newsletter* 40(2):4.

1992    *Mills County Archaeology: The Paul Rowe Collection and Southwestern Iowa Prehistory.* Research Papers Vol. 17, No. 5. Office of the State Archaeologist, University of Iowa, Iowa City.

1994    *Agricultural Origins and Development in the Midcontinent.* Report 19. Office of the State Archaeologist, University of Iowa, Iowa City.

Green, William, and David L. Asch

1996    Great Oasis Agriculture: New Archaeobotanical Data from Central and Northwestern Iowa. Paper presented at the 54th Annual Plains Anthropological Conference, Iowa City. Copy on file, Office of the State Archaeologist, University of Iowa, Iowa City.

Green, William, and John F. Doershuk

1996    Summary and Site Significance. In *Excavations at the Maxwell Site (13DA264): A Great Oasis Settlement in Central Iowa,* by John F. Doershuk and Fred A. Finney, pp. 38–39. Contract Completion Report 445. Office of the State Archaeologist, University of Iowa, Iowa City.

1998 Cultural Resource Management and American Archaeology. *Journal of Archaeological Research* 6(2):121–167.

Green, William, Chérie E. Haury, and John L. Cordell

1992 Documenting Southwestern Iowa Prehistory through the Paul Rowe Collection. *Journal of the Iowa Archeological Society* 39:1–14.

Green, William, Doug W. Jones, and Claire Tolmie

1993 Late Prehistoric and Protohistoric Plant Use on the Eastern Plains: New Evidence from Western Iowa. Paper presented at the 58th Annual Meeting of the Society of American Archaeology, St. Louis. Copy on file, Office of the State Archaeologist, University of Iowa, Iowa City.

Green, William, and Leah D. Rogers

1995 *Wickiup Hills Natural Area Archaeological Survey.* Research Papers Vol. 20, No. 1. Office of the State Archaeologist, University of Iowa, Iowa City.

Green, William, and Shirley J. Schermer

1988 The Turkey River Mound Group (13CT1). In *Archaeological and Paleoenvironmental Studies in the Turkey River Valley, Northeastern Iowa,* edited by William Green, pp. 131–198. Research Papers Vol. 13, No. 1. Office of the State Archaeologist, University of Iowa, Iowa City.

Green, William, and Rebecca Wallace

1991 Woodland Community Definition at the Gast Farm Site (13LA12), Louisa County, Iowa. Paper presented at the 36th Midwest Archaeological Conference, La Crosse, Wisconsin. Copy on file, Office of the State Archaeologist, University of Iowa, Iowa City.

Green, William, Mary K. Whelan, E. Arthur Bettis III, and Richard G. Baker

1994 Archaeological and Paleoenvironmental Investigations at the Gast Spring Alluvial Fan (13LA152), Southeastern Iowa. Paper presented at the 51st Southeastern Archaeological Conference and the 39th Midwest Archaeological Conference, Lexington, Kentucky.

Copy on file, Office of the State Archaeologist, University of Iowa, Iowa City.

Gregg, Michael L.

1974 Three Middle Woodland Sites from Henderson County, Illinois: An Apparent Congruity with Middle Woodland Subsistence-Settlement Systems in the Lower Illinois Valley. *Wisconsin Archeologist* 55:231–245.

Griffin, James B.

1937 The Archaeological Remains of the Chiwere Sioux. *American Antiquity* 2:180–181.

1946 Cultural Change and Continuity in Eastern United States Archaeology. In *Man in Northeastern North America,* edited by Frederick Johnson, pp. 37–95. Papers of the Robert S. Peabody Foundation for Archeology Vol. 3. Andover, Maryland.

1948 Letter dated April 2, 1948, to Charles R. Keyes. On file, Keyes Collection, State Historical Society of Iowa, Iowa City.

1952a Culture Periods in Eastern United States Archaeology. In *Archeology of Eastern United States,* edited by James B. Griffin, pp. 352–364. University of Chicago Press, Chicago.

1952b Some Early and Middle Woodland Pottery Types in Illinois. In *Hopewellian Communities in Illinois,* edited by Thorne Deuel, pp. 93–129. Scientific Papers 5. Illinois State Museum, Springfield.

Griffin, James B. (editor)

1952 *Archeology of Eastern United States.* University of Chicago Press, Chicago.

Grinnell, George B.

1892 *Blackfoot Lodge Tales.* Scribner, New York.

Grissell, Lois A.

1946 *An Analysis of a Prehistoric Indian Village Site Near Cedar Rapids, Iowa.* Unpublished Master's thesis, Department of History, University of Iowa, Iowa City.

Guldner, Ludwig F.

1960 *Vascular Plants of Scott and Muscatine Counties.* Botanical Publication No. 1. Davenport Public Museum, Davenport, Iowa.

Gunnerson, James H.

1952 Some Nebraska Culture Pottery Types. *Plains Archaeological Conference Newsletter* 5(3):39–49.

Haas, Daniel R.

1983 *Walker-Gilmore: A Stratified Woodland Period Occupation in Eastern Nebraska.* Laboratory Notebook No. 6. Division of Archeological Research, University of Nebraska, Lincoln.

Haberman, Thomas W.

1993a The Randall Phase Component at the Dirt Lodge Village Site, Spink County, South Dakota: Late Woodland/Early Plains Village Transitions on the Northeastern Plains. In *Prehistory and Human Ecology of the Western Prairies and Northern Plains: Papers in Honor of Robert A. Alex (1941-1988),* edited by Joseph A. Tiffany, pp. 75-116. Memoir 27. *Plains Anthropologist,* Lincoln, Nebraska.

1993b The Bonander Site, 39MH012: A Great Oasis Occupation in Southeast South Dakota. *South Dakota Archaeology* 17:1-34.

Hagan, William T.

1958 *The Sac and Fox Indians.* University of Oklahoma Press, Norman.

Hainlin, Sheila W.

1992 *Analysis of the Archaic Lithic Artifacts from the Buchanan Site, 13SR153, Ames, Iowa.* Unpublished Master's thesis, Department of Anthropology, Iowa State University, Ames.

Hajic, Edwin R.

1990 *Koster Site Archeology I: Stratigraphy and Landscape Evolution.* Research Series Vol. 8. Center for American Archeology, Kampsville, Illinois.

1989 *Late Pleistocene and Holocene Landscape Evolution, Depositional Subsystems and Stratigraphy in the Lower Illinois River Valley and Adjacent Central Mississippi River Valley.* Unpublished Ph.D. dissertation, Department of Geology, University of Illinois, Urbana.

Hall, Robert L.

1961 An Archaeological Investigation in the Gavin's Point Area, Yankton County, South Dakota. *Museum News 22(7).* W. H. Over Museum, State University of South Dakota, Vermillion.

1962 *The Archaeology of Carcajou Point.* 2 vols. University of Wisconsin Press, Madison.

1967 The Mississippian Heartland and Its Plains Relationship. *Plains Anthropologist* 12:175-183.

1979 In Search of the Ideology of the Adena-Hopewell Climax. In *Hopewell Archaeology: The Chillicothe Conference,* edited by David S. Brose and N'omi Gerber, pp. 258-265. Kent State University Press, Kent, Ohio.

1983 Who's Sioux in Eastern Wisconsin? Paper presented at the 28th Midwest Archaeological Conference, Iowa City.

1991 Cahokia Identity and Interaction Models of Cahokia Mississippian. In *Cahokia and the Hinterlands: Middle Mississippian Cultures of the Midwest,* edited by Thomas E. Emerson and R. Barry Lewis, pp. 3-34. University of Illinois Press, Urbana and Chicago.

1993 Red Banks, Oneota, and the Winnebago: Views from a Distant Rock. *Wisconsin Archeologist* 74:10-79.

1995 Relating the Big Fish and the Big Stone: Reconsidering the Archaeological Identity and Habitat of the Winnebago in 1634. In *Oneota Archaeology Past, Present, and Future,* edited by William Green, pp. 19-30. Report 20. Office of the State Archaeologist, University of Iowa, Iowa City.

Hallberg, George R., E. Arthur Bettis III, and Jean C. Prior

1984 Geologic Overview of the Paleozoic Plateau Region of Northeastern Iowa. *Proceedings of the Iowa Academy of Science* 91:3-11.

Hallberg, George R., Bernard E. Hoyer, and Gerald A. Miller

1974 The Geology and Paleopedology of the Cherokee Sewer Site. The Cherokee Sewer Site (13CK405): A Preliminary Report of a Stratified Paleo-Indian/Archaic Site in Northwestern Iowa. *Journal of the Iowa Archeological Society* 21:17-49.

Hamilton, R. N.

1970 *Marquette's Exploration: The Narrative Reexamined.* University of Wisconsin Press, Madison.

Hamon, J. Hill

1961 Bird Remains from a Sioux Indian Midden. *Plains Anthropologist* 6:208-212.

Hannus, L. Adrien

1974 The Heath Site, 13ML15. *Newsletter of the South Dakota Archaeological Society* 5(1):6-19.

1990 Mammoth Hunting in the New World. In *Hunters of the Recent Past,* edited by L. B. Davis and Borian O. K. Reeves, pp. 47–67. Unwin-Hyman, London.

Hannus, L. Adrien, R. Peter Winham, and Edward J. Lueck

1986   *Cultural Resource Reconnaissance Survey of Portions of Moody, Lincoln and Union Counties, South Dakota.* Archeological Contract Series 26. Archeology Laboratory of the Center for Western Studies, Augustana College, Sioux Falls, South Dakota.

Hansman, John

1987   An Archaeological Problem at Old Fort Madison. *Plains Anthropologist* 32:217–231.

Hare, Timothy

1992   Blade Core Technology at the Gast Farm Site (13LA12): The Acquisition and Processing of Warsaw Tabular Chert during the Middle Woodland Period. Paper presented at the 57th Annual Meeting of the Society for American Archaeology, Pittsburgh.

Harlan, Edgar R.

1908   Boone Mound Exploration. *Annals of Iowa* 3rd series 8:467–469.

Harn, Alan D.

1971   *The Prehistory of Dickson Mounds: A Preliminary Report.* Dickson Mounds Museum Anthropological Studies No. 1. Illinois State Museum, Springfield.

1991   The Eveland Site: Inroad to Spoon River Mississippian Society. In *New Perspectives on Cahokia: Views from the Periphery,* edited by James B. Stoltman, pp. 129–153. Monographs in World Archaeology No. 2. Prehistory Press, Madison, Wisconsin.

Harrison, Charles E.

1880   Exploration of Mound No. 11 Cook's Farm Group, and Discovery of an Inscribed Tablet of Limestone. *Proceedings of the Davenport Academy of Natural Sciences* 2:221–224.

1885   Report of Mound Exploration near Pine Creek, Muscatine County, Iowa. *Proceedings of the Davenport Academy of Natural Sciences* 4:197–198.

Harrison, Charles E., and William H. Pratt

1893   Additional Explorations at Toolesboro. *Proceedings of the Davenport Academy of Natural Sciences* 5:43–44.

Hartman, John C. (editor)

1915   *History of Black Hawk County, Iowa, and Its People.* 2 vols. S. J. Clarke, Chicago.

Harvey, Amy E.

1971   *Challenge and Response, Environment and Northwest Iowa Oneota.* Unpublished Ph.D. dissertation, Department of Anthropology, University of Wisconsin–Madison.

1979   *Oneota Culture in Northwestern Iowa.* Report 12. Office of the State Archaeologist, University of Iowa, Iowa City.

Haug, James K.

1977   Great Oasis Site in Marshall County. *Newsletter of the South Dakota Archaeological Society* 7(2):5.

1981a  *Excavations at the Winter Site and at Hartford Beach Village, 1980–1981.* South Dakota Archaeological Research Center, Rapid City.

1981b  Preliminary Report on the 1980–81 Excavations at the Winter Site (39DE5) and the Hartford Beach Village (39RO5). *Newsletter of the South Dakota Archaeological Society* 11(4):1–7.

1983   Winter and Hartford Beach Site Carbon Dates Received. *Newsletter of the South Dakota Archaeological Society* 13(1):4.

Haury, Chérie E.

1993   Profiles in Iowa Archeology: Theodore Hayes Lewis: The Northwestern Archaeological Survey in Iowa. *Journal of the Iowa Archeological Society* 40:82–87.

Headley, Robert K., Jr.

1971   *The Origin and Distribution of the Siouan-Speaking Tribes.* Unpublished Ph.D. dissertation, Department of Anthropology, Catholic University of America, Washington, D.C.

Hedden, John G.

1996   Two Recently Identified Late Archaic Sites in Western Iowa. *Journal of the Iowa Archeological Society* 43:139–144.

1997   The Glenwood GIS Project: A New Tool for Studying the Central Plains Tradition in Western Iowa. Paper presented at the 55th Annual Plains Anthropological Conference, Boulder, Colorado. Copy on file, Office of the State Archaeologist, University of Iowa, Iowa City.

Hedman, Kristin

1993   Skeletal Remains from a Historic Sauk Village

(11RI81), Rock Island County, Illinois. *Illinois Archaeology* 5(1–2):537–548.

Heizer, Robert F., and John A. Graham

1967 *A Guide to Field Methods in Archaeology.* National Press, Palo Alto, California.

Henige, David

1986 Primary Source by Primary Source? On the Role of Epidemics in New World Depopulation. *Ethnohistory* 33:293–312.

Henning, Amy E.

1966 The Beals Site: Great Oasis and Woodland Components. Paper presented at the 24th Annual Plains Anthropological Conference, Lincoln, Nebraska.

Henning, Dale R.

1961 Oneota Ceramics in Iowa. *Journal of the Iowa Archeological Society* 11(2):1–64.

1967 Mississippian Influences on the Eastern Plains Border: An Evaluation. *Plains Anthropologist* 12:184–194.

1969a University of Nebraska Archaeological Research in Northwest Iowa. *Northwest Chapter of the Iowa Archeological Society Newsletter* 17(5):3–5.

1969b Ceramics from the Mill Creek Sites. In Climatic Change and the Mill Creek Culture of Iowa, Part 2, edited by Dale R. Henning, pp. 192–280. *Journal of the Iowa Archeological Society* 15.

1970a University of Nebraska Excavations in Northwest Iowa. Iowa Archeological Society *Newsletter* 57:3–5.

1970b Development and Interrelationships of Oneota Culture in the Lower Missouri River Valley. *Missouri Archaeologist* 32:1–180.

1971a Great Oasis Culture Distributions. In *Prehistoric Investigations*, edited by Marshall B. McKusick, pp. 125–133. Report 3. Office of the State Archaeologist, University of Iowa, Iowa City.

1971b Origins of Mill Creek. *Journal of the Iowa Archeological Society* 18:6–13.

1982 *Evaluative Investigations of Three Landmark Sites in Northwest Iowa.* Luther College Archaeological Research Center, Decorah, Iowa. Submitted to the Division of Historic Preservation, State Historical Society of Iowa.

1983a Attenuated Mississippian Sites near "Down-town" Cahokia. Paper presented at the 48th Annual Meeting of the Society for American Archaeology, Pittsburgh.

1983b The Initial Variant of the Middle Missouri Tradition. In *Archaeology of the Northern Border Pipeline: Minnesota I,* edited by G. J. Hudak, pp. 4.42–4.65. Archaeological Field Services, Stillwater, Minnesota.

1988 Excavations of the South Lawn Area, Terrace Hill. *Journal of the Iowa Archeological Society* 35:31–39.

1990 Appendix G: Landowner Collections. In *Phase I Cultural Resource Investigation of the Burlington to Des Moines Highway Corridor: Section II, Iowa Counties: Mahaska, Wapello, Monroe, and Jefferson, DE-163-2(11)--2A-62,* edited by Craig M. Hudak, pp. G1–G34. BRW, Minneapolis. Submitted to the Iowa Department of Transportation.

1991 Great Oasis and Emergent Mississippian: The Question of Trade. *Journal of the Iowa Archeological Society* 38:1–4.

1992a *A Study of Pottery from the Blood Run Site (13LO2), 1985 Excavations.* Luther College Archaeological Research Center, Decorah, Iowa.

1992b Cultural Adaptations to the Prairie Environment: The Ioway Example. *Proceedings of the Twelfth North American Prairie Conference 1990,* edited by Daryl D. Smith and Carol A. Jacobs, pp. 193–194. University of Northern Iowa, Cedar Falls.

1993 The Adaptive Patterning of the Dhegiha Sioux. *Plains Anthropologist* 38:253–264.

1995 Oneota Evolution and Interactions: A View from the Wever Terrace, Southeast Iowa. In *Oneota Archaeology: Past, Present, and Future,* edited by William Green, pp. 65–88. Report 20. Office of the State Archaeologist, University of Iowa, Iowa City.

1996a The Archeology of Two Great Oasis Sites in the Perry Creek Valley, Northwest Iowa. *Journal of the Iowa Archeological Society* 43:7–118.

1996b The Perry Creek Phase: Terminal Great Oasis? Paper presented at the 54th Annual Plains Anthropological Conference, Iowa City.

1996c Oneota, the Western Manifestations. Paper

presented at the 54th Annual Plains Anthropological Conference, Iowa City.

1998   Response to "Comments." *Journal of the Iowa
Archeological Society* 45:101–107.

Henning, Dale (compiler)

1980   *A Prehistoric Cultural Resources Survey in the
Proposed Perry Creek Reservoir*. Technical Report No. 80-10. Division of Archaeological
Research, Department of Anthropology, University of Nebraska, Lincoln.

1982   *Subsurface Testing Program: Proposed Perry
Creek Dam and Reservoir Area, Plymouth
County, Iowa*. Technical Report No. 82-05.
Division of Archaeological Research, Depart-
ment of Anthropology, University of Ne-
braska, Lincoln.

Henning, Dale R. (editor)

1968   Climatic Change and the Mill Creek Culture
of Iowa, Part 1. *Journal of the Iowa Archeological Society* 15.

1969   Climatic Change and the Mill Creek Culture
of Iowa, Part 2. *Journal of the Iowa Archeological Society* 16.

Henning, Dale R., and Duane C. Anderson

1985   *The Blood Run Archeological Site: A Landmark
in Plains-Midwestern Prehistory*. Luther College Archaeological Research Center, Decorah, Iowa, and Office of the State Archaeologist, University of Iowa, Iowa City.

Henning, Dale R., and Elizabeth R. P. Henning

1978   Great Oasis Ceramics. In *Some Studies of Minnesota Prehistoric Ceramics: Papers Presented at
the First Council for Minnesota Archeology Symposium, 1976*, edited by Alan R. Woolworth
and Mark A. Hall, pp. 12–26. Occasional
Publications in Minnesota Anthropology No.
2. Minnesota Historical Society, St. Paul.

Henning, Dale R., and Barbara Beving Long

1991   *Annotated Bibliography for Blood Run Research*.
Four Mile Research Company, Cresco, Iowa.
Copy on file, Office of the State Archaeolo-
gist, University of Iowa, Iowa City.

Henning, Dale R., and Martin Q. Peterson

1965   Re-Articulated Burials from the Upper Iowa
River Valley. *Journal of the Iowa Archeological
Society* 13:1–16.

Henning, Dale R., Jacqueline E. Saunders, Theresa K.
Donham, and Rolfe Mandel

1982   *Cultural Resources of the CBD Loop Arterial
Project Area: Phase I Investigation*. Brice,
Petrides, Waterloo, Iowa. Submitted to the
City of Des Moines, Iowa.

Henning, Dale R., and Shirley J. Schermer

1985   Blood Run Excavations—1985. Iowa Archeological Society *Newsletter* 35(3):1–2.

Henning, Elizabeth R. P.

1981   Great Oasis and the Middle Missouri Tradition. In *The Future of South Dakota's Past*,
edited by Larry J. Zimmerman and Lucille
Stewart, pp. 33–38. Special Publication of the
South Dakota Archaeological Society No. 2.
University of South Dakota Archaeology Laboratory, Vermillion.

1983   Protohistoric and Historic Indian Occupation. In *An Archaeological Reconnaissance of the
Northern Border Pipeline for the Northern
Plains Natural Gas Company—Iowa Segment*,
1:4.82–4.102. Archaeological Field Services,
G. Joseph Hudak, principal investigator. Copy
on file, Office of the State Archaeologist, University of Iowa, Iowa City.

1985   Initiating the Resource Protection Planning
Process in Iowa. Office of Historic Preserva-
tion, Iowa State Historical Department, Iowa
City.

Herold, Elaine Bluhm

1970   Hopewell Burial Mound Builders. *Palimpsest*
51:497–528.

Herold, Elaine Bluhm (editor)

1971   *The Indian Mounds at Albany, Illinois*. Davenport Museum Anthropological Papers No. 1.
Davenport, Iowa.

Herold, Elaine Bluhm, Patricia J. O'Brien, and David
J. Wenner Jr.

1990   Part I: Hoxie Farm and Huber: Two Upper
Mississippian Archaeological Sites in Cook
County, Illinois. In *At the Edge of Prehistory:
Huber Phase Archaeology in the Chicago Area*,
edited by James A. Brown and Patricia J.
O'Brien, pp. 1–119. Center for American Ar-
cheology, Kampsville, Illinois. Submitted to
the Illinois Department of Transportation.

Higginbottom, Dan, and Kent Bakken

1990   An Examination of the Material Culture from

Two Turn-of-the-Century Midwestern Farmsteads. Ms. on file, Office of the State Archaeologist, University of Iowa, Iowa City.

Hill, A. T., and Marvin Kivett

1941   Woodlandlike Manifestations in Nebraska.
*Nebraska History Magazine* 21(3):146–243.

Hill, A. T., and Waldo R. Wedel

1936   Excavations at the Leary Indian Village and
Burial Site, Richardson County, Nebraska.
*Nebraska History Magazine* 17(1):2–73.

Hill, Mark, and Stephen C. Lensink

1986   Investigations at 13W561, The Sweeting site,
7.2. Excavation Methodology and Results. In
*Archaeological Investigations along the F-518
Corridor,* edited by Stephen C. Lensink, pp.
63–73. Iowa Quaternary Studies Contribution 9. University of Iowa, Iowa City.

Hirst, K. Kris

1991   The Great Gunflint Debate. *Journal of the
Iowa Archeological Society* 38:62–65.

1993   *Archaeological Investigations on Elk Creek.
Phase II Investigations at 13DT07 Primary
Roads Project STP-2-5(18)--20-27 a.k.a. PIN
85-27010-2, Decatur County, Iowa.* Project
Completion Report Vol. 16, No. 47. Office of
the State Archaeologist, University of Iowa,
Iowa City.

1995   Analysis of Shell Artifacts at the Phipps Site.
In *Excavations at the Phipps Site (13CK21):
New Perspectives on Mill Creek Culture,* by
Richard L. Fishel, pp. 98–102. Contract Com-
pletion Report 443. Office of the State Ar-
chaeologist, University of Iowa, Iowa City.

1997   A Buried Archaic Groundstone Axe Workshop
in Crawford County Found by Avocational Archaeologist Delmar Rath. Iowa Archeological
Society *Newsletter* 47(2):2–3.

Hirst, K. Kris, and Joseph A. Artz

1993   *Archaeological and Geomorphological Investiga-
tions at the Diagonal Dune Site, Phase II Inves-
tigations at 13RN54 Primary Roads Project
FN-66-1(9)-21–80 a.k.a. PIN 90-8004-1
Ringgold County, Iowa.* Project Completion
Report Vol.16, No. 29. Office of the State
Archaeologist, University of Iowa, Iowa City.

*History of Johnson County Iowa.*

1883   *History of Johnson County Iowa.* Iowa City.

Hixon, Charlene

1975   The Handcart Expeditions of 1856 in Johnson
County, Iowa. Ms on file, State Historical Society of Iowa, Iowa City.

Hobson, Matt

1983   Allamakee Petroglyphs. Iowa Archeological
Society *Newsletter* 105:6–7.

Hodges, Denise C.

1989   *Pine Creek Mounds.* Miscellaneous Reports on
Iowa Archaeology. Office of the State Archaeologist, University of Iowa, Iowa City.

Hodgson, Nancy J.

1992   *Ancient Agriculture in Iowa: Paleoethnobotany
of the Weaver Occupation at Gast Farm
(13LA12), Louisa County, Iowa.* Unpublished
Master's thesis, Department of Anthropology,
University of Iowa, Iowa City.

Hoeffecker, John F., W. Roger Powers, and Ted Goebel

1993   The Colonization of Beringia and the Peopling
of the New World. *Science* 259:46–53.

Hoffman, J. J.

1965   *An Appraisal of the Archeological Resources of the
Rathbun Reservoir, Iowa.* River Basin Surveys.
Smithsonian Institution, Lincoln, Nebraska.

Hoffman, J. J.

1972   *The History of Decatur County, Iowa.* Decatur
County Historical Society, Leon, Iowa.

Hole, Frank, and Robert F. Heizer

1965   *An Introduction to Prehistoric Archaeology.*
Holt, Rinehart, and Winston, New York.

Holland, Thomas Dean

1983   Osteological Analysis of the Boone Mound
Assemblage. Prepared for the Division of Historic Preservation. Iowa State Historical Department, Iowa City. Copy on file, Office of
the State Archaeologist, University of Iowa,
Iowa City.

Holley, George R.

1989   *The Archaeology of the Cahokia Mounds ICT-II:
Ceramics.* Illinois Cultural Resources Study
No. 11. Illinois Historic Preservation Agency,
Springfield.

Hollinger, R. Eric

1993   *Investigating Oneota Residence through Domes-
tic Architecture.* Unpublished Master's thesis,
Department of Anthropology, University of
Missouri–Columbia.

1995   Residence Patterns and Oneota Cultural Dynamics. In *Oneota Archaeology: Past, Present,*

*and Future,* edited by William Green, pp. 141–174. Report 20. Office of the State Archaeologist, University of Iowa, Iowa City.

1996    Recent Investigations at the McKinney Oneota Village in Southeastern Iowa. Paper presented at the 41st Midwest Archaeological Conference, Beloit, Wisconsin.

Hollinger, R. Eric, and Carl Falk

1996    Reassessing Late Prehistoric Patterns of Bison Exploitation in the Midwest. Paper presented at the 54th Annual Plains Anthropological Conference, Iowa City.

Holman, Margaret B.

1984    The Identification of Late Woodland Maple Sugaring Sites in the Upper Great Lakes. *Midcontinental Journal of Archaeology* 9:63–89.

1986    Historic Documents and Prehistoric Sugaring: A Matter of Cultural Context. *Midcontinental Journal of Archaeology* 11:125–131.

Holman, Margaret B., and Kathryn Egan

1985    Processing Maple Sap with Prehistoric Techniques. *Journal of Ethnobiology* 5:61–75.

Horan, J. D.

1972    *The McKenney-Hall Portrait Gallery of American Indians.* Crown, New York.

Hotopp, John A.

1977    *Archaeological Explorations along Iowa Highways.* Submitted to the Iowa Department of Transportation. Copy on file, Office of the State Archaeologist, University of Iowa, Iowa City.

1978a   *A Reconsideration of Settlement Patterns, Structures, and Temporal Placement of the Central Plains Tradition in Iowa.* Unpublished Ph.D. dissertation, College of Education, University of Iowa.

1978b   Glenwood: A Contemporary View. In *The Central Plains Tradition: Internal Developments and External Relationships,* edited by Donald J. Blakeslee, pp. 109–133. Report 11. Office of the State Archaeologist, University of Iowa, Iowa City.

1982    Some Observations on the Central Plains Tradition in Iowa. In *Plains Indian Studies: A Collection of Essays in Honor of John C. Ewers and Waldo R. Wedel,* edited by D. H. Ubelaker and H. J. Viola, pp. 173–192. Smithsonian Contribution to Anthropology 30. Smithsonian Institution, Washington, D.C.

Hotopp, John, David Cook, and Anton Till

1979    *Iowa Highway Archaeology Annual Report 1978-1979.* Contract Completion Report 173. Office of the State Archaeologist, University of Iowa, Iowa City.

Houck, Louis (editor)

1909    *The Spanish Regime in Missouri.* R. R. Donnelley, Chicago.

Howard, Calvin D.

1990    The Clovis Point: Characteristics and Type Description. *Plains Anthropologist* 35:255–262.

Howard, James H.

1953    The Southern Cult in the Northern Plains. *American Antiquity* 19:130–138.

1968    *The Southern Ceremonial Complex and Its Interpretation.* Memoir No. 6. Missouri Archaeological Society, Columbia.

1972    Notes on the Ethnogeography of the Yankton Dakota. *Plains Anthropologist* 17:281–307.

Howard, W. E.

1949    A Means to Distinguish Skulls of Coyotes and Domestic Dogs. *Journal of Mammalogy* 30:169–171.

Howe, Samuel S. (editor)

1882    Indian Mounds. *Annals of Iowa* n.s. 1:33–38.

Hoyer, Bernard E.

1980    The Geology of the Cherokee Sewer Site. In *The Cherokee Excavations: Holocene Ecology and Human Adaptations in Northwestern Iowa,* edited by Duane C. Anderson and Holmes A. Semken, Jr., pp. 21–66. Academic Press, New York.

Hudak, G. Joseph

1976    *Woodland Ceramics from the Pedersen Site.* Scientific Publications of the Science Museum of Minnesota, n.s., Vol. 3, No. 2. Science Museum of Minnesota, St. Paul.

Hudak, G. Joseph, and Elden Johnson

1975    *An Early Woodland Pottery Vessel from Minnesota.* Scientific Publications of the Science Museum of Minnesota, n.s., Vol. 2, No. 4. Science Museum of Minnesota, St. Paul.

Hunt, George T.

1940    *The Wars of the Iroquois: A Study in Intertribal*

*Trade Relations.* University of Wisconsin Press, Madison.

Hurley, William M.

1986 The Late Woodland Stage: Effigy Mound Culture. In *Introduction to Wisconsin Archaeology,* edited by William Green, James B. Stoltman and Alice B. Kehoe, pp. 283–301. *Wisconsin Archeologist* 67:163–395.

Hurt, Wesley R., Jr.

1951 *Report of the Investigation of the Swanson Site, 39BR16, Brule County, South Dakota.* Archaeological Studies Circular No. 3. South Dakota Archaeological Commission, Pierre.

1952 *Report on the Investigations of the Scalp Creek Site, 39GRI, and the Ellis Creek Site, 39GR2, Gregory County, South Dakota.* Archaeological Studies Circular No. 4. South Dakota Archaeological Commission, Pierre.

1954 Pottery Types of the Over Focus, South Dakota. In *Prehistoric Pottery of the Eastern United States,* edited by James B. Griffin. Museum of Anthropology, University of Michigan, Ann Arbor.

Ingalls, Marlin

1991a Proto-Historic and Historic Indians of Eastern Iowa and Their Artifacts in the Collections of the Office of the State Archaeologist. Ms. on file, Office of the State Archaeologist, University of Iowa, Iowa City.

1991b Excavation at Davenport House Site. Iowa Archeological Society *Newsletter* 41(1):4.

Iowa Archeological Society *Newsletter*

1958 A Further Report on the SUI Summer Dig. Iowa Archeological Society *Newsletter* 27:1–3.

1996 Find of the Year: John Gilbert's First Trading Post. Iowa Archeological Society *Newsletter* 46(4):7.

Iowa Writers Program

1941 *Johnson County History.* Iowa Writers Project of the WPA, Des Moines.

Ives, John C.

1955a Turin Man. Iowa Archeological Society *Newsletter* 16:3–5.

1955b Glenwood Ceramics. *Journal of the Iowa Archeological Society* 4(3–4):2–32.

1962 Mill Creek Pottery. *Journal of the Iowa Archeological Society* 11(3):3–59.

Jackson, C. V., and M. A. McConaughy

1983 Rench Site Structural Evidence and Associated Ceramic Remains. Paper presented at the 48th Annual Meeting of the Society for American Archaeology, Pittsburgh.

Jackson, Donald

1966 Old Fort Madison—1803–1813. *Palimpsest* 47:1–62.

Jaehnig, Manfred E. W.

1975 *The Prehistoric Cultural Ecology of Eastern Iowa as Seen from Two Woodland Rock Shelters.* Unpublished Ph.D. dissertation, Department of Anthropology, University of Wisconsin–Madison.

Jans-Langel, Carmen, and Richard L. Fishel

1995 Faunal Analysis. In *Excavations at the Phipps Site (13CK21): New Perspectives on Mill Creek Culture,* by Richard L. Fishel, pp. 38–50. Contract Completion Report 443. Office of the State Archaeologist, University of Iowa, Iowa City.

Johnson, Alfred E.

1976 A Model of the Kansas City Hopewell Subsistence-Settlement System. In *Hopewellian Archaeology in the Lower Missouri Valley,* edited by Alfred E. Johnson, pp. 7–15. Publications in Anthropology 8. University of Kansas, Lawrence.

1979 Kansas City Hopewell. In *Hopewell Archaeology: The Chillicothe Conference,* edited by David S. Brose and N'omi Greber, pp. 86–93. Kent State University Press, Kent, Ohio.

1981 The Kansas City Hopewell Subsistence and Settlement System. *Missouri Archaeologist* 42:69–79.

1991 Kansa Origins: An Alternative. *Plains Anthropologist* 36:57–65.

Johnson, Craig M.

1974 House Number Four at the Broken Kettle West Site (13PM25). Ms. on file, Department of Anthropology, University of Nebraska, Lincoln.

1996 *A Chronology of Middle Missouri Plains Village Sites.* Submitted to the Department of Anthropology, National Museum of Natural History, Smithsonian Institution. Copy on file, Office of the State Archaeologist, University of Iowa, Iowa City.

Johnson, Elden
1969   Decorative Motifs on Great Oasis Pottery. *Plains Anthropologist* 14:272–276.
Johnson, Paul C.
1972   *Mammalian Remains Associated with Nebraska Phase Earth Lodges in Mills County, Iowa.* Unpublished Master's thesis, Department of Geology, University of Iowa, Iowa City.
Johnson, Roger, and Terry Birk
1983   *A Phase II Intensive Archaeological Survey of Site 13LE143, Lee County, Iowa.* Contract Completion Report 208. Office of the State Archaeologist, University of Iowa, Iowa City.
Johnston, Richard B.
1967   *The Hitchell Site.* River Basin Surveys Publications in Salvage Archaeology No. 3. Office of Anthropology, Smithsonian Institution, Lincoln, Nebraska.
Jones, Douglas W.
1993   *Finding a Niche for Lamb's Quarters in Mill Creek Subsistence Patterns: The Role of Chenopodium Utilization in Mill Creek Agricultural Systems.* Unpublished Master's thesis, Department of Anthropology, University of Iowa, Iowa City.
Jones, William
1939   *Ethnography of the Fox Indians.* Bureau of American Ethnology Bulletin 125. Smithsonian Institution, Washington, D.C.
Justice, Noel D.
1987   *Stone Age Spear and Arrow Points of the Midcontinental and Eastern United States.* Indiana University Press, Bloomington.
Kant, Joanita
1979   Salvage Excavations at the Hofer Mound (39HT2). *South Dakota Archaeology* 3:91–113.
Kay, Jeanne
1984   The Fur Trade and Native American Population Growth. *Ethnohistory* 31:265–287.
Kehoe, Thomas F.
1966   The Small, Side-notched Point System of the Northern Plains. *American Antiquity* 31:827–841.
1973   *The Gull Lake Site: A Prehistoric Bison Drive Site in Southwestern Saskatchewan.* Milwaukee Museum Publications in Anthropology and History No. 1.

Kemmis, Timothy J.
1991   *Glacial Landforms, Sedimentology, and Depositional Environments of the Des Moines Lobe, Northern Iowa.* Unpublished Ph.D. dissertation, Department of Geology, University of Iowa, Iowa City.
Kemmis, Timothy J., George R. Hallberg, and A. J. Lutenegger
1981   Depositional Environments of Glacial Sediments and Landforms on the Des Moines Lobe, Iowa. Iowa Geological Survey Guidebook No. 6. Copy on file, Office of the State Archaeologist, University of Iowa, Iowa City.
Keslin, Richard O.
1958   A Preliminary Report on the Hahn (Dg 1 and Dg 2) and Horicon (Dg 5) Sites, Dodge County, Wisconsin. *Wisconsin Archeologist* 39:191–273.
Key, Patrick J.
1994   Relationships of the Woodland Period on the Northern and Central Plains: The Craniometric Evidence. In *Skeletal Biology in the Great Plains: Migration, Warfare, Health, and Subsistence,* edited by Douglas W. Owsley and Richard L. Jantz, pp. 179–188. Smithsonian Institution Press, Washington, D.C.
Keyes, Charles R.
1920   Some Materials for the Study of Iowa Archeology. *Iowa Journal of History and Politics* 18:357–370.
1925   Progress of the Archaeological Survey of Iowa. *Iowa Journal of History and Politics* 23:339–352.
1927a  Field Notes of July 1, 1927. On file, Keyes Collection, State Historical Society of Iowa, Iowa City.
1927b  Prehistoric Man in Iowa. *Palimpsest* 8:185–229.
1928a  The Hill-Lewis Archeological Survey. *Minnesota History* 9:96–108.
1928b  Prehistoric Red Men. *Palimpsest* 9:33–37.
1929   Some Methods and Results of the Iowa Archeological Survey. *Wisconsin Archeologist* 8:135–143.
1930   A Unique Survey. *Palimpsest* 11:214–226.
1933   Shall Iowa Have National Monuments? *Iowa Journal of History and Politics* 31:31–46.

1934　Antiquities of the Upper Iowa. *Palimpsest* 15:321–354.

1941a　Letter of January 25, 1941, to Mrs. John C. Hartman. On file, Keyes Collection, State Historical Society of Iowa, Iowa City.

1941b　An Outline of Iowa Archaeology. *Proceedings of the Iowa Academy of Science* 48:91–98.

1943　James Sherman Minott. *Palimpsest* 24:1–40.

1949　Four Iowa Archaeologies with Plains Affiliations. *Proceedings of the 5th Plains Conference for Archeology,* pp. 96–97. Notebook No. 1. Laboratory of Anthropology, University of Nebraska, Lincoln.

1951　Prehistoric Indians in Iowa. *Palimpsest* 32:281–344.

Kim, Hyung K.

1986　*Late-Glacial and Holocene Environment in Central Iowa: A Comparative Study of Pollen Data from Four Sites.* Unpublished Ph.D. dissertation, Department of Geology, University of Iowa, Iowa City.

King, Maureen L., and Sergei B. Slobodin

1996　A Fluted Point from the Uptar Site, Northeastern Siberia. *Science* 273:634–636.

Kivett, Marvin F.

1952　*Woodland Sites in Nebraska.* Publications in Anthropology No. 1. Nebraska State Historical Society, Lincoln.

1962　Logan Creek Complex. Paper presented at the 20th Annual Plains Anthropological Conference, Lincoln, Nebraska.

Knauth, Otto

1963　The Mystery of the Crosses. *Annals of Iowa* 37:81–91.

Krantz, Grover S.

1959　Distinctions between the Skulls of Coyotes and Dogs. *Kroeber Anthropological Society Papers* 21:40–42.

Krause, Richard

1969　Correlation of Phases in Central Plains Prehistory. In *Two House Sites in the Central Plains: An Experiment in Archaeology,* edited by W. Raymond Wood, pp. 82–96. Memoir 6. *Plains Anthropologist,* Lincoln, Nebraska.

Kurtz, Royce D.

1986　*Economic and Political History of the Sauk and Mesquakie: 1780's–1845.* Unpublished Ph.D.

dissertation, Department of Anthropology, University of Iowa, Iowa City.

Laird, Kathleen R., Sherilyn C. Fritz, Eric C. Grimm, and Pietra G. Mueller

1996　Century-Scale Paleoclimatic Reconstruction from Moon Lake, a Closed-Basin Lake in the Northern Great Plains. *Limnology and Oceanography* 41:890–902.

Laird, Kathleen, Sherilyn C. Fritz, Kirk A. Maasch, and Brian F. Cummings

1996　Greater Drought Intensity and Frequency before AD 1200 in the Northern Great Plains, USA. *Nature* 384:552–554.

Lehmer, Donald J.

1951　Pottery Types from the Dodd Site, Oahe Reservoir, South Dakota. *Plains Archaeological Conference Newsletter* 4(2):13–25.

1954　*Archaeological Investigations in the Oahe Dam Area, South Dakota, 1950–1951.* River Basin Survey Papers No. 7. Bureau of American Ethnology Bulletin 158. Smithsonian Institution, Washington, D.C.

1971　*Introduction to Middle Missouri Archeology.* Anthropological Papers 1. National Park Service, U.S. Department of the Interior, Washington, D.C.

Lehmer, Donald J., and Warren W. Caldwell

1966　Horizon and Tradition in the Northern Plains. *American Antiquity* 31:511–516.

Leigh, Steven R.

1988　Comparative Analysis of the Elizabeth Middle Woodland Artifact Assemblage. In *The Archaic and Woodland Cemeteries at the Elizabeth Site in the Lower Illinois Valley,* edited by Douglas K. Charles, Steven R. Leigh, and Jane E. Buikstra, pp. 191–217. Research Series 7. Center for American Archeology, Kampsville Archeological Center, Kampsville, Illinois.

Lensink, Stephen C.

1968　*An Analysis of Ceramic Material from the Boone Mound (13BN30) and an Associated Woodland Village (13BN29) in Central Iowa.* Unpublished Honor's thesis, Department of Sociology and Anthropology, Iowa State University, Ames.

1984　*A Quantitative Model of Central-Place Foraging among Prehistoric Hunter-Gatherers.* Unpub-

lished Ph.D. dissertation, Department of Anthropology, University of Iowa, Iowa City.

1991  Possible Ridged Fields at Two Sites of the Initial Middle Missouri Tradition in Northwestern Iowa. Paper presented at the 49th Annual
Plains Anthropological Conference, Lawrence, Kansas.

1992  Rethinking Mill Creek Radiocarbon Chronol-
ogy. Paper presented at the 50th Annual
Plains Anthropological Conference, Lincoln,
Nebraska.

1993a  Episodic Climatic Events and Mill Creek Culture Change: An Alternative Explanation. In
*Prehistory and Human Ecology of the Western
Prairies and Northern Plains: Papers in Honor
of Robert A. Alex (1941–1988)*, edited by Joseph A. Tiffany, pp. 189–197. Memoir 27.
*Plains Anthropologist*, Lincoln, Nebraska.

1993b  A Reanalysis of Eastern Initial Middle Missouri Radiocarbon Dates and the Implications
for the Timing of Long-distance Trade with
Middle Mississippian Centers. Paper presented at the 38th Midwest Archaeological
Conference, Milwaukee.

1994  The Role of Fortification in the Eastern Initial
Variant of the Middle Missouri Tradition.
Paper presented at the 52nd Annual Plains
Anthropological Conference, Lubbock, Texas.
Copy on file, Office of the State Archaeolo-
gist, University of Iowa, Iowa City.

1996  The Temporal Relationship of Great Oasis and
the Initial Variant of the Middle Missouri Tradition. Paper presented at the 54th Annual
Plains Anthropological Conference, Iowa
City. Copy on file, Office of the State Archaeologist, University of Iowa, Iowa City.

1997  Beginnings of the Middle Missouri Tradition:
New Data on Climate and Chronology. Paper
presented at the 55th Annual Plains Anthropological Conference, Boulder, Colorado.

1998a  A New Chronology for the Initial Variant of
the Middle Missouri Tradition. *Plains Anthropologist*, in press.

1998b  The Transition to Nucleated Village Life on
the Eastern Edge of the Great Plains. Paper
presented at the 63rd Annual Meeting of the
Society for American Archaeology, Seattle.

Lensink, Stephen C. (editor)

1986  *Archaeological Investigations along the F-518
Corridor*. Iowa Quaternary Studies Contribution 9. University of Iowa, Iowa City.

Lensink, Stephen C., and Fred A. Finney

1994  Dealing with Risk in the Initial Middle Missouri Variant: Local Subsistence Systems and
Regional Interaction Networks. Paper presented at the 59th Annual Meeting of the Society for American Archaeology, Anaheim,
California.

1995  *Test Excavations at the Kuehn Site (13DA110):
The Great Oasis Component*. Contract Completion Report 440. Office of the State Archaeologist, University of Iowa, Iowa City.

Lensink, Stephen C., Fred A. Finney, and Richard I.
Fishel

1995  Rethinking Mill Creek Settlement and Agricultural Systems: New Data from the Phipps,
Double Ditch and Litka Sites. Paper presented
at the 60th Annual Meeting of the Society for
American Archaeology, Minneapolis.

Lensink, Stephen C., and William Gartner

1994  Early Agricultural Field Systems from the
Upper Midwest and Eastern Plains. Paper presented at the 51st Southeastern Archaeological Conference and the 39th Midwest Archaeological Conference, Lexington, Kentucky.

Lepper, Bradley T.

1996  The Newark Earthworks and the Geometric
Enclosures of the Scioto Valley: Connections
and Conjectures. In *A View from the Core: A
Synthesis of Ohio Hopewell Archaeology*, edited
by Paul J. Pacheco, pp. 225–240. Ohio Archaeological Council, Columbus.

Lewis, G. Malcolm

1987  Indian Maps: Their Place in the History of
Plains Cartography. In *Mapping the North
American Plains: Essays in the History of Car-
tography*, edited by Frederick C. Luebke, Fran-
cis W. Kaye, and Gary E. Mouton, pp. 63–80.
University of Oklahoma Press, Norman.

Lewis, Theodore H.

1890  Effigy Mounds in the Valley of the Big Sioux
River, Iowa. *Science* 15:275.

*Life*

1955  A Fifteen Year Mystery Gets 9,000 Years

Older. *Life Magazine* 39(September 19): 59–60.

Lillie, Robin

1990a  Analysis of Human Skeletal Remains from Broken Kettle West Site, 13PM25, Plymouth County, Iowa. In *Reports on Iowa Burial Sites: Archaeology and Osteology,* edited by Mary C. Allen, pp. 37–39. Research Papers Vol. 15, No. 5. Office of the State Archaeologist, University of Iowa, Iowa City.

1990b  Analysis of Human Skeletal Remains from 13WD55, Woodbury County, Iowa. In *Reports on Iowa Burial Sites: Archaeology and Osteology,* edited by Mary C. Allen, pp. 106–107. Research Papers Vol. 15, No. 5. Office of the State Archaeologist, University of Iowa, Iowa City.

Lillie, Robin M., and Shirley J. Schermer

1990  Analysis of Human Skeletal Remains from 13WD402, Siouxland Sand and Gravel Site, Woodbury County, Iowa. In *Reports on Iowa Burial Sites: Archaeology and Osteology,* edited by Mary C. Allen, pp. 112–125. Research Papers Vol. 15, No. 5. Office of the State Archaeologist, University of Iowa, Iowa City.

Lindley, Clarence

1876  Mound Explorations in 1875. *Proceedings of the Davenport Academy of Natural Sciences* 1:111–113.

Little, Elizabeth A.

1987  Inland Waterways in the Northeast. *Midcontinental Journal of Archaeology* 12:55–76.

Little, James A.

1890  *From Kirtland to Salt Lake City.* James A. Little, Salt Lake City.

Logan, Brad

1994  The White Rock Phase and Late Prehistoric Dynamics of the Central Plains. Paper presented at the 52nd Annual Plains Anthropological Conference, Lubbock, Texas.

1995  Late Prehistoric Oneota Migration to the Central Plains. Paper presented at the 60th Annual Meeting of the Society for American Archaeology, Minneapolis.

1996  Oneota Far West: The White Rock Phase. Paper presented at the 54th Annual Plains Anthropological Conference, Iowa City.

Logan, Wilfred D.

1952/  Archeological Investigation of Spike Hollow
1953   Rock Shelter, Allamakee County, Iowa. *Journal of the Iowa Archeological Society* 2(2–3):4–30.

1959  *Analysis of Woodland Complexes in Northeastern Iowa.* Unpublished Ph.D. dissertation, Department of Anthropology, University of Michigan, Ann Arbor.

1971  Final Investigation of Mound 33, Effigy Mounds National Monument. *Journal of the Iowa Archeological Society* 18:29–45.

1976  *Woodland Complexes in Northeastern Iowa.* Publications in Archaeology 15. National Park Service, U.S. Department of the Interior, Washington, D.C.

Lopinot, Neal H.

1987  Archaeobotany. In *Archaeology in the Mississippi River Floodplain at Sand Run Slough, Iowa,* by David W. Benn, pp. 195–221. Report CAR-690. Center for Archaeological Research, Southwest Missouri State University, Springfield.

Lothson, Gordon A.

1976  *The Jeffers Petroglyphs Sites.* Minnesota Prehistoric Archaeology Series 12. Minnesota Historical Society, St. Paul.

Loy, T. H.

1983  Prehistoric Blood Residues: Detection on Tool Surfaces and Identification of Species of Origin. *Science* 220:1269–1271.

Luchterhand, Kubet

1970  *Early Archaic Projectile Points and Hunting Patterns in the Lower Illinois Valley.* Illinois Archaeological Survey Monograph No. 2. Reports of Investigations. Illinois State Museum, Springfield.

Luckenbach, Al, Ellen Dugan, Richard Levy, David Pollack, and Charles Niquette

1988  *Archaeological Investigations at Rathbun Lake, Iowa.* Environmental Consultants, Dallas, Texas.

Ludvigson, Greg A., E. Arthur Bettis III, and Bernard E. Hoyer

1994  Mapping for the Next Century. *Iowa Geology 1994,* No. 19:22–27. Geological Survey Bureau, Iowa Department of Natural Resources, Iowa City.

Ludwickson, John, Donald Blakeslee, and John
  O'Shea
1981    *Missouri National Recreational River: Native
        American Cultural Resources.* Nebraska State
        Historical Society. Submitted to the Heritage
        Conservation and Recreation Service, Inter-
        agency Archaeological Services, Denver. U.S.
        Army Corps of Engineers, Omaha District.
Ludwickson, John, and John R. Bozell
1993    Perspectives on the Late Prehistory of the
        South Bend Locality. In *Nebraska Phase Arche-
        ology in the South Bend Locality,* by John R. Bo-
        zell and John Ludwickson, pp. 109-133. Ne-
        braska State Historical Society, Lincoln.
Lueck, Edward J., R. Peter Winham, L. Adrien Hannus, and Lynette Rossum
1995    The Map, of the Map, of the Map, of the Map:
        Tracking the Blood Run Archaeological Site.
        *Journal of the Iowa Archaeological Society*
        42:21–43.
Lynch, E. P., H. C. Fulton, Charles E. Harrison, and
  Charles H. Preston
1893    Mound Explorations at Toolesboro, Louisa
        County, Iowa. *Proceedings of the Davenport
        Academy of Natural Sciences* 5:37–42.
Mallam, R. Clark
1971    Fluted Projectile Points from Allamakee and
        Winneshiek Counties. Iowa Archeological
        Society *Newsletter* 61:4–7.
1976a   The Mound-Builders: An American Myth.
        *Journal of the Iowa Archeological Society*
        23:145–175.
1976b   *The Iowa Effigy Mound Manifestation: An Inter-
        pretive Model.* Report 9. Office of the State
        Archaeologist, University of Iowa, Iowa City.
1978    An Old Copper Complex Artifact from Win-
        neshiek County. Iowa Archeological Society
        *Newsletter* 90:2–5.
1979    A Cut and Perforated Mandible from the
        Quandahl Rockshelter, Winneshiek County,
        Iowa. *Journal of the Iowa Archeological Society*
        26:29–36.
Mallam, R. Clark, and E. Arthur Bettis III
1979    *Mound Investigations in Garnavillo Township,
        Clayton County, Iowa.* Research Papers Vol. 4,
        No. 2. Office of the State Archaeologist, Uni-
        versity of Iowa, Iowa City.
1980    *The Iowa Northern Archaeological Project.*

Luther College Archaeological Research
  Center, Decorah, Iowa.
Mallery, Garrick
1893    Picture-Writing of the American Indians. In
        *Tenth Annual Report of the Bureau of Ethnology
        to the Secretary of the Smithsonian Institution
        1888-1889,* by John W. Powell, pp. 25–822.
        Smithsonian Institution, Washington, D.C.
Marcucci, Derrick J.
1977    Poison Ivy Obsidian. *The Keystone: Newsletter
        of the Charles R. Keyes Chapter of the Iowa
        Archeological Society* 2:4–6.
1993    Mississippian-style Artifacts from Eastern
        Iowa. Iowa Archeological Society *Newsletter*
        43(2):2.
1997    *An Inventory and Assessment of Selected Prehis-
        toric Mound Sites in Jackson County, Iowa.* Pre-
        pared for the Jackson County Historic Preser-
        vation Commission. Copy on file, Office of
        the State Archaeologist, University of Iowa,
        Iowa City.
1998    The Jackson County Indian Mound Survey.
        Iowa Archeological Society *Newsletter*
        48(1):1–3.
Marcucci, Derrick J., David W. Benn, and Toby
  Morrow
1994    *Archaeological Investigations to Determine Na-
        tional Register of Historic Places Eligibility of
        Rockshelters 13JH188, 13JK189, and 13JK98,
        Jackson County, Iowa.* Submitted to the Ma-
        quoketa Historic Preservation Commission,
        Maquoketa, Iowa.
Marcucci, Derrick J., Susan L. Gade, Julie T. Morrow,
  and Toby T. Morrow (editors and compilers)
1993    *An Introduction to the Prehistory and History of
        Maquoketa, Jackson County, Iowa.* Association
        of Iowa Archaeologists 1993 Field Trip Guide.
        Maquoketa, Iowa.
Marcucci, Derrick J., Fred W. Nelson, and Raymond
  V. Sidrys
1978    Poison Ivy Obsidian Source Identification.
        *Journal of the Iowa Archeological Society*
        25:92–99.
Markman, Charles W.
1986    Above the American Bottom: The Late Wood-
        land–Mississippian Transition in Northeast-
        ern Illinois. Paper presented at the 51st An-

nual Meeting of the Society for American Archaeology, New Orleans.

Markman, Charles W. (editor)

1988   *Putney Landing: Archaeological Investigations at a Havana-Hopewell Settlement on the Mississippi River, West-Central Illinois.* Report of Investigations No. 15. Department of Anthropology, Northern Illinois University, DeKalb.

Marquardt, William H.

1996   Unearthing Support for Archaeology. *Chronicle of Higher Education,* June 7, 1996. http://chronicle.com.

Marquardt, William H., and Patty Jo Watson

1983   The Shell Mound Archaic of Western Kentucky. In *Archaic Hunters and Gatherers in the American Midwest,* edited by James L. Phillips and James A. Brown, pp. 323–329. Academic Press, New York.

Martin, Paul S.

1973   The Discovery of America. *Science* 179:969–974.

Martin, Paul S., and Richard G. Klein (editors)

1984   *Quaternary Extinctions: A Prehistoric Revolution.* University of Arizona Press, Tucson.

Mason, Carol I.

1986   The Historic Period in Wisconsin Archaeology. *Wisconsin Archeologist* 67:370–392.

1987   Maple Sugaring Again; or the Dog That Did Nothing in the Night. *Canadian Journal of Archaeology* 11:99–107.

1990   Indians, Maple Sugaring and the Spread of Market Economies. In *The Woodland Tradition in the Western Great Lakes: Papers Presented to Elden Johnson,* edited by Guy E. Gibbon, pp. 37–43. Publications in Anthropology No. 4. University of Minnesota, Minneapolis.

Mason, Otis T.

1891   Aboriginal Skin Dressing: A Study Based on Material in the U.S. National Museum. *Report of the U.S. National Museum for 1889,* Section 3:553–589. Washington, D.C.

McAllister, Patricia A.

1972   The Larson Site (13PM61): Great Oasis or Mill Creek—or Both? *Northwest Chapter of the Iowa Archeological Society Newsletter* 20(5):3–8.

McCorvie, Mary R.

1990   Analysis of Human Skeletal Material. In *Archaeological Data Recovery at Five Prehistoric Sites, Lake Red Rock, Marion County, Iowa,* by Charles R. Moffat, Brad Koldehoff, Kathryn E. Parker, Lucretia S. Kelly, Mary R. McCorvie, and Joseph Craig. Cultural Resources Management Report No. 133. American Resources Group, Carbondale, Illinois.

McElrath, Dale L., Thomas E. Emerson, Andrew C. Fortier, and J. L. Phillips

1984   Late Archaic Period. In *American Bottom Archaeology: A Summary of the FAI-270 Project Contribution to the Culture History of the Mississippi River Valley,* edited by Charles J. Bareis and James W. Porter, pp. 34–58. University of Illinois Press, Urbana.

1993   Mule Road: A Newly Defined Late Archaic Phase in the American Bottom. In Highways to the Past: Essays on Illinois Archaeology in Honor of Charles J. Bareis, edited by Thomas E. Emerson, Andrew C. Fortier, and Dale L. McElrath, pp. 148–157. *Illinois Archaeology* 5.

McGregor, John C.

1947   Museum Exhibits of Illinois Hopewellian Artifacts. *Journal of the Illinois State Archaeological Society* (old series) 4(4):8.

1952   The Havana Site. In *Hopewellian Communities in Illinois,* edited by Thorne Deuel, pp. 43–92. Scientific Papers Vol. 5. Illinois State Museum, Springfield.

McKay, Joyce

1979   *Historical Archaeology at Terrace Hill.* Division of Historic Preservation, Iowa State Historical Department, Iowa City.

1988   The Investigation of the Landscaping at Terrace Hill through Historical Archaeology. *Journal of the Iowa Archeological Society* 35:16–30.

McKenney, Thomas L., and James Hall

1933/  *The Indian Tribes of North America.* 3 vols. J. 1934   Grant, Edinburgh.

McKern, William C.

1939   The Midwestern Taxonomic Method as an Aid to Archaeological Culture Study. *American Antiquity* 4:301–313.

McKusick, Marshall B.

1963   Ancient Iowa Lives On in Indian Rock Drawings. *Iowan* 11(40):40–44.

1964a   Exploring Turkey River Mounds. *Palimpsest* 45:473–485.

1964b   *Men of Ancient Iowa*. Iowa State University Press, Ames.

1964c   Prehistoric Man in Northeastern Iowa. *Palimpsest* 45:465–496.

1964d   Discovering the Hartley Fort. *Palimpsest* 45:487–494.

1965   Discovering an Ancient Indian Fort. *Iowa Conservationist* 24(1):6–7.

1968   Manuscript and field notes for site 13DB17. Ms. on file, Office of the State Archaeologist, University of Iowa, Iowa City.

1969   The Late Woodland Hartley Fort. Ms. on file, Office of the State Archaeologist, University of Iowa, Iowa City.

1970   *The Davenport Conspiracy*. Report 1. Office of the State Archaeologist, University of Iowa, Iowa City.

1971a   Art that Pre-Dates Columbus. *Iowan* 19(4): 8–13, 52.

1971b   Oneota Longhouses. In *Prehistoric Investigations*, edited by Marshall B. McKusick, pp. 86–94. Report 3. Office of the State Archaeologist, University of Iowa, Iowa City.

1973   *The Grant Oneota Village*. Report 4. Office of the State Archaeologist, University of Iowa, Iowa City.

1975a   A Perspective of Iowa Prehistory 1841–1928. *The Wisconsin Archeologist* 56:16–54.

1975b   Ft. Des Moines (1834–37): An Archaeological Test. *Annals of Iowa* 42(7):513–522.

1975c   Fort Atkinson Artifacts. *Palimpsest* 56:15–21.

1975d   *The Iowa Northern Border Brigade*. Report 8. Office of the State Archaeologist, University of Iowa, Iowa City.

1976   Fort Atkinson, Iowa: Archaeological Dimensions of an Historic Site. Ms. on file, Office of the State Archaeologist, University of Iowa, Iowa City.

1979   Documenting Iowa Prehistory: 1928–1964. *Wisconsin Archeologist* 60:3–25.

1980   *Fort Madison, Iowa: 1808–1813*. Research Papers Vol. 5, No. 2. Office of the State Archaeologist, University of Iowa, Iowa City.

1991   *The Davenport Conspiracy Revisited*. Iowa State University Press, Ames.

McKusick, Marshall B. (compiler)

1968   Dubuque Mines of Spain. Published sources. Ms. on file, Office of the State Archaeologist, University of Iowa, Iowa City.

McKusick, Marshall B., and Adrian D. Anderson

1966   Jollyville Hill Field Notes (13LE12). Ms. on file, Office of the State Archaeologist, University of Iowa, Iowa City.

McKusick, Marshall B., and David Archie

1966   Tale of Two Forts: Exploring Old Fort Madison and Old Fort Atkinson. *Iowan* 15(1):10–13, 50–51.

McKusick, Marshall B., James Boylan, and John A. Hotopp

1973   *Archaeological Explorations along Iowa Highways*. Submitted to the Iowa Department of Transportation. Copy on file, Office of the State Archaeologist, University of Iowa, Iowa City.

McKusick, Marshall B., and Joe Ries

1964   *Archaeological Resources of the Rathbun Reservoir Drainage, Iowa*. State University of Iowa, Iowa City.

McKusick, Marshall B., and Charles Slack

1962   Historic Sauk Indian Art and Technology. *Journal of the Iowa Archeological Society* 12(1):1–22.

McNerney, Michael J.

1987   The Effigy Complex of the Nebraska Phase and the Problem of Nebraska Phase–Mississippian Relationships. *Journal of the Iowa Archeological Society* 34:23–50.

McNerney, Michael J., David G. Stanley, Jeffrey D. Anderson, and Leah D. Rogers

1988   *Archaeological Site Testing, Lake Red Rock, Iowa: Pool Raise Project, 1987 Season*, vols. 1–5. Cultural Resources Management Report No. 127. American Resources Group, Carbondale, Illinois.

McNett, Charles W. (editor)

1985   *Shawnee Minisink Site: A Stratified Paleoindian-Archaic Site in the Upper Delaware Valley of Pennsylvania*. Academic Press, Orlando, Florida.

Mead, Barbara

1981   Seed Analysis of the Meehan-Schell Site (13BN110), a Great Oasis Site in Central

Iowa. *Journal of the Iowa Archeological Society* 28:15–90.

Mehrer, Mark W.

1989 *Site Protection Project at 13PA38, the McCall Site, Primary Roads Project Fn-71-1(15) --21-73 a.k.a. PIN 88-73020-1, Page County, Iowa.* Project Completion Report Vol. 12, No. 41. Office of the State Archaeologist, University of Iowa, Iowa City.

1990 *Archaeological Survey of the Julien Dubuque Monument Area, Mines of Spain, Dubuque County, Iowa.* Contract Completion Report 286. Office of the State Archaeologist, University of Iowa, Iowa City.

Meltzer, David J.

1989 Why Don't We Know When the First People Came to North America? *American Antiquity* 54:471–490.

1997 Monte Verde and the Pleistocene Peopling of the Americas. *Science* 276:754–755.

Meltzer, David J., and Jim I. Mead

1984 North American Late Quaternary Extinctions and the Radiocarbon Record. In *Quaternary Extinctions: A Prehistoric Revolution,* edited by Paul S. Martin and R. G. Klein, pp. 440–450. University of Arizona Press, Tucson.

Meltzer, David J., and Bruce D. Smith

1986 Paleoindian and Early Archaic Subsistence Strategies in Eastern North America. In *Foraging, Collecting and Harvesting: Archaic Period Subsistence and Settlement in the Eastern Woodlands,* edited by Sarah W. Neusius, pp. 3–31. Occasional Paper No. 6. Center for Archaeological Investigations, Southern Illinois University, Carbondale.

Merry, Carl A.

1988 The Archaeology of Fort Atkinson (13WH57): A Guide to Sources. In *Archaeological and Paleoenvironmental Studies in the Turkey River Valley, Northeastern Iowa,* edited by William Green, pp. 200–216. Research Papers Vol. 13, No. 1. Office of the State Archaeologist, University of Iowa, Iowa City.

1989 Historical Archaeology at the Kendallville Flouring Mill. *Journal of the Iowa Archaeological Society* 36:66–81.

Merry, Carl A., and William Green

1989 Sources for Winnebago History in Northeast-ern Iowa, 1837–1848. *Journal of the Iowa Archeological Society* 36:1–8.

Miller, Dennis R.

1977 Another Dugout Canoe from the Nishnabotna River. Iowa Archeological Society *Newsletter* 86:5.

Miller, Jim

1998 Teaching Archaeology in the 21st Century. Summary report to National Association of State Archaeologists. Society for American Archaeology Workshop, Wakulla Springs, Florida.

Miller, Terry

1986 SEM Analysis. In *Archaeological Investigations along the F-518 Corridor,* edited by Stephen C. Lensink, pp. 98–104. Iowa Quaternary Studies Contribution 9. University of Iowa, Iowa City.

Milner, George R.

1980 Epidemic Disease in the Postcontact Southeast: A Reappraisal. *Midcontinental Journal of Archaeology* 5:39–56.

Moffat, Charles R., and Brad Koldehoff

1989 The Moingona Phase Reconsidered: Recent Research at Oneota Sites in the Des Moines River Valley, Iowa. Paper presented at the 34th Midwest Archaeological Conference, Iowa City.

1990 Overview of Oneota Studies at Lake Red Rock. In *Archaeological Data Recovery at Five Prehistoric Sites, Lake Red Rock, Marion County, Iowa,* by Charles R. Moffat, Brad Koldehoff, Kathryn E. Parker, Lucretia S. Kelly, Mary R. McCorvie, and Joseph Craig. Cultural Resources Management Report No. 133 pp. 417–465. American Resources Group, Carbondale, Illinois.

Moffat, Charles R., Brad Koldehoff, and Mary R. McCorvie

1988 *Archaeological Data Recovery at the Cormorant Site (13MA387): A Multicomponent Woodland and Oneota Site at Lake Red Rock.* Cultural Resources Management Report No. 128. American Resources Group, Carbondale, Illinois.

Moffat, Charles R., Brad Koldehoff, Kathryn E. Parker, Lucretia S. Kelly, Mary R. McCorvie, and Joseph Craig

1990 *Archaeological Data Recovery at Five Prehistoric*

*Sites, Lake Red Rock, Marion County, Iowa.* 2 vols. Cultural Resources Management Report No. 133. American Resources Group, Carbondale, Illinois.

Montet-White, Anta

1968   *The Lithic Industries of the Illinois Valley in the Early and Middle Woodland Period.* Anthropological Papers No. 35. Museum of Anthropology, University of Michigan, Ann Arbor.

Moore, J. A.

1983   The Trouble with Know-It-Alls: Information as a Social and Ecological Resource. In *Archaeological Hammers and Theories,* edited by J. A. Moore and Arthur S. Keene, pp. 173–191. Academic Press, New York.

Morgan, David T., David L. Asch, and C. Russell Stafford

1986   Marion and Black Sand Occupations in the Sny Bottom of the Mississippi Valley. In *Early Woodland Archeology,* edited by Kenneth B. Farnsworth and Thomas E. Emerson, pp. 207–230. Kampsville Seminars in Archeology Vol. 2. Center for American Archeology Press, Kampsville, Illinois.

Morrow, Juliet E.

1994   Preliminary Survey of Iowa Fluted Points. Paper presented at the 52nd Annual Plains Anthropological Conference, Lubbock, Texas.

1996   *The Organization of Early Paleoindian Lithic Technology in the Confluence Region of the Mississippi, Illinois, and Missouri Rivers.* Unpublished Ph.D. dissertation, Department of Anthropology, Washington University, St. Louis.

Morrow, Juliet E., and Toby A. Morrow

1994   Preliminary Fluted Point Survey in Iowa. *Current Research in the Pleistocene* 11:47–48.

1996   Fluted Point Complexes in the Midwest: A Technological and Morphological Review. Paper presented at the 41st Midwest Archaeological Conference, Beloit, Wisconsin.

Morrow, Toby A.

1981   Making Ground Stone Axes. Iowa Archeological Society *Newsletter* 99:4–6.

1984   *Iowa Projectile Points.* Special Publication. Office of the State Archaeologist, University of Iowa, Iowa City.

1994   A Key to the Identification of Chipped-Stone Raw Materials Found on Archaeological Sites in Iowa. *Journal of the Iowa Archeological Society* 41:108–129.

1995a  *Phase I Archaeological Survey of Avenue of the Saints between Mount Pleasant and the Missouri Line, Lee and Henry Counties, Iowa.* Contract Completion Report 430. Office of the State Archaeologist, University of Iowa, Iowa City.

1995b  *Phase III Excavations at 13ML118 and 13ML175, Mills County, Iowa.* Contract Completion Report 469. Office of the State Archaeologist, University of Iowa, Iowa City.

1996a  Clovis Blade Tool Found in Lee County. Iowa Archeological Society *Newsletter* 46(4):1–2.

1996b  Folsom Points and Preforms in Iowa. Paper presented at the 54th Annual Plains Anthropological Conference, Iowa City. Copy on file, Office of the State Archaeologist, University of Iowa, Iowa City.

1996c  *Phase III Excavations at the Ed's Meadow Site (13DM712), Local Systems Project P-64, a.k.a. FHWA 143160, Des Moines County, Iowa.* Contract Completion Report 480. Office of the State Archaeologist, University of Iowa, Iowa City.

1996d  Lithic Analysis. In *Excavations at the Maxwell Site (13DA264): A Great Oasis Settlement in Central Iowa,* by John F. Doershuk and Fred A. Finney, pp. 17–27. Contract Completion Report 445. Office of the State Archaeologist, University of Iowa, Iowa City.

1996e  Lithic Refitting and Archaeological Site Formation Processes: A Case Study from the Twin Ditch Site, Green County, Illinois. In *Stone Tools: Theoretical Insights into Human Prehistory,* edited by George H. Odell, pp. 345–373. Plenum Press, New York.

1997a  Prehistoric Context of Southeast Iowa. In *Sand Road Heritage Corridor, Johnson County, Iowa: Archaeology and History of Indian and Pioneer Settlement,* by Cynthia L. Peterson, pp. 4–18. Contract Completion Report 492. Office of the State Archaeologist, University of Iowa, Iowa City.

1997b  *Archaeological Monitoring of Step Reconstruction at Horse Thief Cave (13JN8), Wapsipinicon State Park, Jones County, Iowa.* Contract

Completion Report 565. Office of the State Archaeologist, University of Iowa, Iowa City.

Morse, Dan F., and Albert C. Goodyear III
1973 The Significance of the Dalton Adz in Northeast Arkansas. *Plains Anthropologist* 18:316–322.

Mott, Mildred
1938 The Relation of Historic Indian Tribes to Archaeological Manifestations in Iowa. *Iowa Journal of History and Politics* 36:227–314.

Munson, Patrick J.
1982 Marion, Black Sand, Morton, and Havana Relationship: An Illinois Valley Perspective. *Wisconsin Archeologist* 63:1–17.
1986a Black Sand and Havana Tradition Ceramic Assemblages and Culture History in the Central Illinois River Valley. In *Early Woodland Archeology,* edited by Kenneth B. Farnsworth and Thomas E. Emerson, pp. 280–300. Kampsville Seminars in Archeology 2. Center for American Archeology Press, Kampsville, Illinois.
1986b Marion, Black Sand, Morton, and Havana Relationship: An Illinois Valley Perspective. In *Early Woodland Archeology,* edited by Kenneth B. Farnsworth and Thomas E. Emerson, pp. 642–651. Kampsville Seminars in Archeology 2. Center for American Archeology Press, Kampsville, Illinois.

Musil, R. R.
1988 Functional Efficiency and Technological Change: A Hafting Tradition Model for Prehistoric North America. In *Early Human Occupation in Far Western North America: The Clovis-Archaic Interface,* edited by Judith A. Willig, C. Melvin Aikers, and John L. Fagan, pp. 373–387. Anthropological Papers No. 21. Nevada State Museum, Carson City.

Mutel, Cornelia F.
1989 *Fragile Giants: A Natural History of the Loess Hills.* University of Iowa Press, Iowa City.

Mutel, Cornelia F., and Mary Swander (editors)
1994 *Land of the Fragile Giants.* University of Iowa Press, Iowa City.

Myer, W. E.
1922 Field Work in South Dakota and Missouri. *Smithsonian Miscellaneous Collections* 72(15):118–122.

Nansel, Blane
1992 Hopewellian Interaction in the Central and Upper Mississippi River Valley: A View from Gast Farm. Paper presented at the 57th Annual Meeting of the Society for American Archaeology, Pittsburgh. Copy on file, Office of the State Archaeologist, University of Iowa, Iowa City.
1996 How Green Were Their Valleys: Examining the Havana Tradition through Frontiers and Boundaries Research. Paper presented at the 61st Annual Meeting of the Society for American Archaeology, New Orleans. Copy on file, Office of the State Archaeologist, University of Iowa, Iowa City.

Nations, Brenda K., Richard G. Baker, and E. Arthur Bettis III
1989 A Holocene Pollen and Plant Macrofossil Record from the Upper Mississippi Valley. *Current Research in the Pleistocene* 6:58–60.

Neuman, Robert W.
1960 Truman Mound Site, Big Bend Reservoir Area, South Dakota. *American Antiquity* 26:78–92.
1964 *The Good Soldier Site (39LM238), Big Bend Reservoir, Lyman County, South Dakota.* River Basin Survey Papers No. 37. Bureau of American Ethnology Bulletin 189. Smithsonian Institution, Washington, D.C.
1975 *The Sonota Complex and Associated Sites on the Northern Great Plains.* Publications in Anthropology No. 6. Nebraska State Historical Society, Lincoln.

Neverett, Margot S.
1995 Faunal Remains. In *Excavations at the Helen Smith Site (13LA71) Louisa County, Iowa: Early and Late Woodland in Southeast Iowa,* by William Billeck, pp. 10.1–10.28. Contract Completion Report 446. Office of the State Archaeologist, University of Iowa, Iowa City.
1996 Social and Economic Aspects of Subsistence: Exploring the Middle to Late Woodland Transition through Zooarchaeological Analysis. Paper presented at the 61st Annual Meeting of the Society for American Archaeology, New Orleans.

Neverett, Margot S., William Green, Rebecca L. Wallace, and Mary K. Whelan
1993 Further Investigations of the Weaver Occupa-

tion at the Gast Farm Site (13LA12), South-eastern Iowa. Paper presented at the 38th Midwest Archaeological Conference, Milwau-kee. Copy on file, Office of the State Archae-ologist, University of Iowa, Iowa City.

Newell, H. Perry, and Alex D. Krieger
1949   *The George C. Davis Site, Cherokee County, Texas.* Memoirs of the Society for American Archaeology No. 5.

Newhall, John B.
1841   *Sketches of Iowa, or, the Emmigrants Guide.* J. H. Colton, New York.

Nicholson, Beverly A.
1989   Modeling a Horticultural Complex in South-Central Manitoba during the Late Prehistoric Period—The Pelican Lake Focus. Paper pre-sented at the 47th Annual Plains Conference, Sioux Falls, South Dakota.

Nickerson, William B.
1908   Exploration of a Part of the Albany, Illinois Group of Burial Mounds. Unpublished field report on file, Putnam Museum of History and Natural Science, Davenport, Iowa.
1912   Explorations in the Albany Mound Group. Ms. on file, Putnam Museum of History and Natural Science, Davenport, Iowa.

O'Brien, Michael J., Robert E. Warren, and Dennis E. Lewarch (editors)
1982   *The Cannon Reservoir Human Ecology Project: An Archaeological Study of Cultural Adaptations in the Southern Prairie Peninsula.* Academic Press, New York.

O'Brien, Michael J., and W. Raymond Wood
1998   *The Prehistory of Missouri.* University of Mis-souri Press, Columbia.

O'Brien, Patricia A.
1971   Valley Focus Mortuary Practices. *Plains Anthropologist* 16:165–182.

Odell, George H.
1994   The Role of Stone Bladelets in Middle Wood-land Society. *American Antiquity* 59:102–120.

Olsen, Stanley J.
1960   *Post-Cranial Skeletal Characters of Bison and Bos.* Papers of the Peabody Museum of Archaeology and Ethnology Vol. 35, No. 4. Harvard University, Cambridge.
1964   *Mammal Remains from Archaeological Sites: Part 1: Southeastern and Southwestern United States.* Papers of the Peabody Museum of Ar-chaeology and Ethnology Vol. 56, No. 1. Har-vard University, Cambridge.
1968   *Fish, Amphibian and Reptile Remains from Archaeological Sites, Part 1: Southeastern and Southwestern United States.* Papers of the Pea-body Museum of Archaeology and Ethnology Vol. 56, No. 2. Harvard University, Cam-bridge.

O'Neal, Charles F.
1958   *The Ethnohistory of the Ioway.* Unpublished Master's thesis, Department of Sociology and Anthropology, University of Iowa, Iowa City.

Orr, Ellison
1913   Mounds and Mound Explorations in North-eastern Iowa. *Proceedings of the Iowa Academy of Science* 20:257–260.
1914   Indian Pottery of the Oneota or Upper Iowa River Valley in Northeastern Iowa. *Proceedings of the Iowa Academy of Science* 21:231–239.
1917a   Notable Mound Groups in and Near the Pro-posed Government Park at McGregor, Iowa. *Proceedings of the Iowa Academy of Science* 24:43–46.
1917b   Preserving the Indian Mounds along the Mis-sissippi River. *Iowa Conservation* 1(3):44–46.
1940   Sundry Archaeological Papers and Mem-oranda Vol. 12. Ms. on file, Office of the State Archaeologist, University of Iowa, Iowa City.
1942   Report of an Archaeological Survey of Mills County, Iowa. Submitted to the State Histori-cal Society of Iowa. Copy on file, Office of the State Archaeologist, University of Iowa, Iowa City.
1949   The Enlarged Crevices of Northeastern Iowa. *Minnesota Archaeologist* 15(1):7–23.
1963   Iowa Archeological Reports 1934–1939. Ar-chives of Archaeology Microcard Series No. 20. Society for American Archaeology, Univer-sity of Wisconsin Press, Madison.

Osborn, Nancy M.
1976   *The Clarkson Site (13WA2): An Oneota Man-ifestation in the Central Des Moines River Val-ley.* Unpublished Master's thesis, Department of Sociology and Anthropology, Iowa State University, Ames.
1982   The Clarkson Site (13WA2): An Oneota Man-ifestation in the Central Des Moines River.

*Journal of the Iowa Archeological Society*
29:1–108.

Osborn, Nancy M., and David M. Gradwohl

1980 Emergency Archaeological Investigations at
13PK154 (The DeArmond/Barrier Dam Site),
Saylorville Reservoir, Iowa. *Journal of the Iowa
Archeological Society* 27:61–96.

1981 *Saylorville Stage 2 Contract Completion Report:
Archaeological Excavations in the Saylorville
Lake Project, Iowa.* Iowa State University
Archaeological Laboratory, Ames.

1982 *Saylorville Stage 3 Contract Completion Report:
Testing of Priority 1 Archaeological Sites
1980-1981.* Iowa State University Archaeological Laboratory, Ames.

Osborn, Nancy M., David M. Gradwohl, and Randall
M. Thies

1978 *Emergency Archaeological Investigations at the
Saylorvillage Site (13PK165), a Late Woodland
Manifestation within the Saylorville Reservoir,
Iowa.* Iowa State University Archaeological
Laboratory, Ames. Submitted to the U.S. Her-
itage Conservation and Recreation Service,
Interagency Archeological Services, Denver.

1989 The Archaeology of the Saylorvillage Site
(13PK65): A Late Woodland Manifestation
on the Des Moines River. *Journal of the Iowa
Archeological Society* 36:9–38.

Oschwald, W. R., F. F. Reicken, R. I. Dideriksen, W. H.
Scholtes, and F. W. Schaller

1965 *Principal Soils of Iowa.* Special Report No. 42.
Cooperative Extension Service, Iowa State
University, Ames.

Overstreet, David F.

1977 Wisconsin Binomial Pottery Types and
Oneota Prehistory. *Wisconsin Archeologist*
58:144–164.

1978 Oneota Settlement Patterns in Eastern Wisconsin: Some Considerations in Time and
Space. In *Mississippian Settlement Patterns,*
edited by Bruce D. Smith, pp. 21–52. Academic Press, New York.

1981a Investigations at the Pipe Site (47-Fd-10) and
Some Perspectives on Eastern Wisconsin
Oneota Prehistory. *Wisconsin Archeologist*
62:365–525.

1981b Review of *Oneota Culture in Northwestern
Iowa. Plains Anthropologist* 26:87–89.

1984 *Archaeological Reconnaissance Survey of Pool
10, Upper Mississippi River, Grant and Crawford Counties, Wisconsin, and Allamakee and
Clayton Counties, Iowa.* Reports of Investigations No. 139. Great Lakes Archaeological Research Center, Wauwatosa, Wisconsin.

1985 *Archaeological Investigations at Coralville Lake,
Iowa.* Reports of Investigations No. 156. Great
Lakes Archaeological Research Center, Wau-
watosa, Wisconsin.

1995 The Eastern Wisconsin Oneota Regional Continuity. In *Oneota Archaeology: Past, Present,
and Future,* edited by William Green, pp.
33–64. Report 20. Office of the State Archaeologist, University of Iowa, Iowa City.

Overstreet, David F., Larry Doebert, Gary W. Henschel, Phil Sander, and David Wasion

1996 Two Red Ocher Mortuary Contexts from
Southeastern Wisconsin—The Henschel Site
(47 Sb 29), Sheboygan County and the Barnes
Creek Site (47 Kn 41), Kenosha County. *Wisconsin Archeologist* 77:36–62.

Owsley, Douglas W., Darcy F. Morey, and William B.
Turner

1981 Inferring History from Crania: Biological Distance Comparisons of Mill Creek and Early
Middle Missouri Tradition Crania with Mandan and Arikara Population Samples. *Plains
Anthropologist* 26:301–310.

Paarmann, J. Herman

1914 Explorations in the Albany Mound Group.
Ms. on file, Putnam Museum of History and
Natural Science, Davenport, Iowa.

Pacheco, Paul J. (editor)

1996 *A View from the Core: A Synthesis of Ohio Hopewell Archaeology.* Ohio Archaeological Council, Columbus.

Palmer, Harris A., and James B. Stoltman

1976 The Boaz Mastodon: A Possible Association of
Man and Mastodon in Wisconsin. *Midcontinental Journal of Archaeology* 1:163–177.

Parker, Kathryn E.

1990 Oneota Botanical Remains. In *Archaeological
Data Recovery at Five Prehistoric Sites, Lake Red
Rock, Marion County, Iowa,* by Charles R.
Moffat, Brad Koldehoff, Kathryn E. Parker,
Lucretia S. Kelly, Mary R. McCorvie, and Jo-
seph Craig. Cultural Resources Management

Report No. 133, pp. 347–368. American Resources Group, Carbondale, Illinois.

Pauketat, Timothy, and Thomas E. Emerson (editors)

1997    *Cahokia: Domination and Ideology in the Mississippian World.* University of Nebraska Press, Lincoln.

Pauketat, Timothy R., and Neal H. Lopinot

1997    Cahokian Population Dynamics. In *Cahokia: Domination and Ideology in the Mississippian World,* edited by Timothy R. Pauketat and Thomas E. Emerson, pp. 103–123. University of Nebraska Press, Lincoln.

Peck, J. L. E., O. H. Montzheimer, and William J. Miller

1914    *Past and Present of O'Brien and Osceola Counties, Iowa.* B. F. Bowen, Indianapolis, Indiana.

Perino, Gregory

1966    Three Late Woodland Projectile Point Types from Illinois. Paper presented at the 24th Annual Plains Anthropological Conference, Lincoln, Nebraska.

1968    *Guide to the Identification of Certain American Indian Projectile Points.* Special Bulletin of the Oklahoma Anthropological Society No. 3.

1971    *Guide to the Identification of Certain American Indian Projectile Points.* Special Bulletin of the Oklahoma Anthropological Society No. 4.

Perkins, D. A. W.

1897    *History of O'Brien County, Iowa.* Brown and Saenger, Sioux Falls, South Dakota.

Perkins, Edward S.

1991    Diameter Estimated from Potsherd Rims. Iowa Archeological Society *Newsletter* 41(4):4–5.

Perry, Michael J.

1982    *Phase II Investigation GRS-8028(2) Louisa County, Local Roads.* Project Completion Report Vol. 5, No. 41. Office of the State Archaeologist, University of Iowa, Iowa City.

1984    *Test Excavations at Sites 13MC23, 13MC32, 13MC33, and 13MC88.* Project Completion Report Vol. 7, No. 363. Office of the State Archaeologist, University of Iowa, Iowa City.

1985    *Phase II Excavations at Sites 13LN226 and 13LN236, RS-4834(5), Linn County, Local Roads.* Project Completion Report Vol. 8, No. 228. Office of the State Archaeologist, University of Iowa, Iowa City.

1987    Late Woodland Ceramics in Southeastern Iowa: A Perspective from the Lower Skunk Valley. *Journal of the Iowa Archeological Society* 34:57–62.

1990a   *A Phase I Archaeological Survey of Local Systems Project LC-9091-4 and LC9293-3, Mills County, Iowa.* Project Completion Report Vol. 13, No. 113. Office of the State Archaeologist, University of Iowa, Iowa City.

1990b   *A Supplemental Phase I Archaeological Survey of Primary Roads Project F-500-1(2) and (5)-20-77 a.k.a. PIN 77-77190-1, 2, 3, Polk County, Iowa.* Project Completion Report Vol. 13, No. 34. Office of the State Archaeologist, University of Iowa, Iowa City.

1991a   Middle Woodland Field Camps in the Cedar Valley. *Journal of the Iowa Academy of Science* 98:109–117.

1991b   *A Phase I Archaeological Survey of Primary Roads Project IR-8--6(138)241--12-52 a.k.a. PIN 89-52110-1, Johnson County, Iowa.* Project Completion Report Vol. 14, No. 45. Office of the State Archaeologist, University of Iowa, Iowa City.

1992a   *Phase II Test Excavations in the Central Des Moines Valley, Primary Roads Project F-500-1 (5 and 20)--20-77 a.k.a. PIN 77-77190-1 and 3, Polk County, Iowa.* Project Completion Report Vol. 15, No. 25. Office of the State Archaeologist, University of Iowa, Iowa City.

1992b   Recent Investigations of Moingona Phase Oneota Components in the Upper Red Rock Region, Central Des Moines River Valley, Iowa. Paper presented at the 50th Annual Plains Anthropological Conference, Lincoln, Nebraska.

1993    13IW216: An Apparent Keyes Phase Component in the Amana Locality, Eastern Iowa. Paper presented at the 38th Midwest Archaeological Conference, Milwaukee.

1996    The Woodland Period. A Brief Culture History of Iowa. www.uiowa.edu/~osa/cultural/wood.htm.

1998    An Archaeological Survey of the Lower Pony Creek Valley: Implications for Glenwood Locality Settlement Pattern. *Central Plains Archaeology* 6(1):35–36.

Petersen, William J.
1951   Charles Reuben Keyes. *Palimpsest* 32:281–284.

Petersen, William J. (editor)
1957   Indians of Iowa. *Palimpsest* 38:33–96.

Peterson, Cynthia L.
1995a  *The Turkey River Winnebago Subagency (13WH111), 1840–1848: An Archaeological Investigation of Locus A and Surrounding Subagency-Era Sites.* Contract Completion Report 441. Office of the State Archaeologist, University of Iowa, Iowa City.
1995b  *The Smith and Owens Homestead, 1848–1851: An Archaeological Investigation of Site 13DA232, Dallas County, Iowa.* Contract Completion Report 439. Office of the State Archaeologist, University of Iowa, Iowa City.
1996a  Summer Discoveries: John Gilbert's Trading Post, 1836–1837 and the Turkey River Winnebago Subagency, 1840–1848. Lecture presented at the Iowa Society of the Archaeological Institute of America, University of Iowa, Iowa City.
1996b  *The Turkey River Winnebago Subagency, 1840–1848: An Archaeological Investigation of Locus A and Surrounding Subagency-Era Sites.* Unpublished Master's thesis, Department of Anthropology, University of Nevada, Reno.
1997   *Sand Road Heritage Corridor, Johnson County, Iowa: Archaeology and History of Indian and Pioneer Settlement.* Contract Completion Report 492. Office of the State Archaeologist, University of Iowa, Iowa City.

Peterson, Drexel A., Jr.
1967a  A First Report on the Excavation of a Great Oasis Site, 13PM25. *Newsletter of the Northwest Chapter of the Iowa Archeological Society* 15(4):3–8.
1967b  *A Ceramic Sequence for Northwest Iowa.* Unpublished Senior Honors Thesis, Department of Anthropology, Harvard University, Cambridge.
1968a  Mississippian Influences in the Plains. Ms. on file, Office of the State Archaeologist, University of Iowa, Iowa City.
1968b  Floor Plan for House 1, Broken Kettle West Site (13PM25). Map on file, Office of the State Archaeologist, University of Iowa, Iowa City.

Petsche, Jerome E.
1974   *The Steamboat* Bertrand: *History, Excavation, and Architecture.* Publications in Archaeology 11. National Park Service, U.S. Department of the Interior, Washington, D.C.

Phillips, James L., and James A. Brown (editors)
1983   *Archaic Hunters and Gatherers in the American Midwest.* Academic Press, New York.

Pickard, J. L.
1893   The Iowa Indians. *Annals of Iowa,* 3rd series 1:14.

Plank, Pryor
1908   The Iowa, Sac, and Fox Indian Mission and Its Missionaries, Rev. Samuel M. Irvin and Wife. *Kansas State Historical Society Transactions* 10:312–325.

Porter, James
1969   The Mitchell Site and Late Prehistoric Exchange Systems at Cahokia: A.D. 1000 ± 300. In *Explorations into Cahokia Archaeology,* edited by Melvin L. Fowler, pp. 137–164. Bulletin No. 7. Illinois Archaeological Survey, University of Illinois, Champaign-Urbana.

Powers, H. C.
1910   Opening of an Indian Mound near Sioux City. *Records of the Past* 9:309–311.

Pratt, William H.
1876a  Report of Explorations of the Ancient Mounds of Albany, Whiteside County, Illinois. *Proceedings of the Davenport Academy of Natural Sciences* 1:99–104.
1876b  Report of Explorations of the Ancient Mounds at Toolesboro, Louisa County, Iowa. *Proceedings of the Davenport Academy of Natural Sciences* 1:106–111.
1885   Report of the Curator. *Proceedings of the Davenport Academy of Natural Sciences* 4:216–217.

Price, T. Douglas, and James A. Brown
1985   Aspects of Hunter-Gatherer Complexity. In *Prehistoric Hunters-Gatherers,* edited by T. Douglas Price and James A. Brown, pp. 3–20. Academic Press, New York.

Price, T. Douglas, and Gary M. Feinman
1993   *Images of the Past.* Mayfield Publishing, Mountain View, California.

Prior, Jean C.
1991   *Landforms of Iowa.* University of Iowa Press, Iowa City.

Prior, Jean C. (editor)
1994   *Iowa Geology 1994.* Geological Survey Bureau, Iowa Department of Natural Resources, Iowa City.

Proudfit, S. V.
1881   Antiquities of the Missouri Bluffs. *American Antiquarian* 3:271–280.

Pyle, Katherine B.
1980   The Cherokee Large Mammal Fauna. In *The Cherokee Excavations: Holocene Ecology and Human Adaptations in Northwestern Iowa,* edited by Duane C. Anderson and Holmes A. Semken, Jr., pp. 171–196. Academic Press, New York.

Radin, Paul
1920   *The Autobiography of a Winnebago Indian.* University of California Press, Berkeley.
1923   *The Winnebago Tribe.* Annual Report of the Bureau of American Ethnology 37. Smithsonian Institution, Washington, D.C.

Raish, Carol B.
1979   *King Hill (23BN1), Fanning (14DP1) and Leary (25RH1): A Study of Oneota Ceramic Variability.* Unpublished Master's thesis, Department of Anthropology, University of Nebraska, Lincoln.

Ramenofsky, Ann F.
1987   *Vectors of Death: The Archaeology of European Contact.* University of New Mexico Press, Albuquerque.
1990   Loss of Innocence: Explanations of Differential Persistence in the Sixteenth Century Southeast. In *Columbian Consequences,* vol. 2, edited by D. H. Thomas, pp. 31–48. Smithsonian Institution Press, Washington, D.C.

Rankin, Robert L.
1997   Oneota and Historical Linguistics. Paper presented at the 1997 Oneota Conference, Iowa City. Copy on file, Office of the State Archaeologist, University of Iowa, Iowa City.

Reeves, Brian O. K.
1973a  The Nature and Age of the Contact between the Laurentide and Cordilleran Ice Sheets in the Western Interior of North America. *Arctic and Alpine Research* 5(1):1–16.

1973b  The Concept of the Altithermal Cultural Hiatus in Northern Plains Prehistory. *American Anthropologist* 75:1221–1253.
1983   Bergs, Barriers, and Beringia: Reflections on the Peopling of the New World. In *Quaternary Coastlines and Marine Archaeology,* edited by P. M. Masters and N. C. Fleming, pp. 389–411. Academic Press, New York.

Reid, Kenneth C.
1980   *A Reconnaissance Survey of Prehistoric Cultural Resources in the Nodaway River Basin, Southwestern Iowa.* Archaeology Laboratory, Department of Social Behavior, University of South Dakota, Vermillion. Copy on file, Office of the State Archaeologist, University of Iowa, Iowa City.
1983   The Nebo Hill Phase: Late Archaic Prehistory in the Lower Missouri Valley. In *Archaic Hunters and Gatherers in the American Midwest,* edited by James L. Phillips and James A. Brown, pp. 11–40. Academic Press, New York.
1990   Simmering Down: A Second Look at Ralph Linton's "North American Cooking Pots." In *Hunter-Gatherer Pottery from the Far West,* edited by Joanne M. Mack, pp. 7–18. Anthropological Papers No. 23. Nevada State Museum, Carson City.

Reque, Sigurd
1944   History of Old Fort Atkinson. Fort Atkinson Research File, Ms. 173. Ms. on file, State Historical Society of Iowa, Iowa City.

Reynolds, John D.
1966   Historic Archaeology in the Red Rock Reservoir, Iowa, 1966. Paper presented at the 24th Annual Plains Anthropological Conference, Lincoln, Nebraska.
1970   *Coalport and Its Relationship to the Early Historic Pottery Industry in the Des Moines River Valley.* Unpublished Master's thesis, Department of Anthropology, Iowa State University, Ames.
1979   *The Grasshopper Falls Phase of the Plains Woodland.* Anthropological Series No. 7. Kansas State Historical Society, Topeka.
1981   The Grasshopper Falls Phase: A Newly Defined Plains Woodland Cultural Historical Integration Phase in the Central Plains. *Missouri Archaeologist* 42:85–96.

Rhodes, R. Sanders, II, and Holmes A. Semken, Jr.

1986 Quaternary Biostratigraphy and Paleoecology of Fossil Mammals from the Loess Hills Region of Western Iowa. *Proceedings of the Iowa Academy of Science* 93:94–130.

Richner, Jeffrey J.

1997 *Archeology in Herbert Hoover's Neighborhood: 1989 Excavations at the L. Miles and E. S. Hayhurst Houses, West Branch, Iowa.* Midwest Archeological Center Technical Report No. 51. National Park Service, Lincoln, Nebraska.

Riegger, Hal

1972 *Primitive Pottery.* Van Nostrand Reinhold, New York.

Riggle, Stan

1981 The Late Woodland Transition in the Central Mississippi Valley: A.D. 700–1100. *South Dakota Archaeology* 5:5–18.

Riley, Thomas J., Charles Moffat, and Glen Freimuth

1981 Prehistoric Raised Fields in the Upper Midwestern United States: An Innovation in Response to Marginal Growing Conditions. *North American Archaeologist* 2(2):101–116.

Ritzenthaler, Robert E.

1946 The Osceola Site, an "Old Copper" Site near Potosi, Wisconsin. *Wisconsin Archeologist* 27:53–70.

1967 *A Guide to Wisconsin Indian Projectile Point Types.* Milwaukee Public Museum Popular Science Series 11.

Ritzenthaler, Robert T. (editor)

1957 The Old Copper Culture of Wisconsin. *Wisconsin Archeologist* 38:185–329.

Ritzenthaler, Robert, and George J. Quimby

1962 *The Red Ochre Culture of the Upper Great Lakes and Adjacent Areas.* Fieldiana: Anthropology, Vol. 36, No. 11. Field Museum of Natural History, Chicago.

Rodell, Roland L.

1991 The Diamond Bluff Site Complex and Cahokia Influence in the Red Wing Locality. *In New Perspectives on Cahokia: Views from the Periphery,* edited by James B. Stoltman, pp. 253–280. Monographs in World Archaeology No. 2. Prehistory Press, Madison, Wisconsin.

1997 *The Diamond Bluff Site Complex: Time and Tradition in the Northern Mississippi Valley.* Unpublished Ph.D. dissertation, Department of Anthropology, University of Wisconsin–Milwaukee.

Roetzel, Kathleen A., Richard A. Strachan, Robert Douglas, Michael Eigen, and Patricia Emerson

1980 *An Archaeological and Architectural Historical Survey of Maquoketa Caves State Park, Jackson County, Iowa.* Impact Services, Mankato, Minnesota.

Rogers, Leah D.

1990 *Preservation Partnerships Phase II: Monona and Woodbury Counties, Iowa.* Submitted to the Bureau of Historic Preservation, State Historical Society of Iowa, Des Moines, and Monona/Woodbury Preservation Partnership Commission.

1991 *Archival and Archaeological Investigation of the Fountainbleau Townsite, Harrison County, Iowa.* Submitted to the Harrison County Historic Preservation Commission and the Bureau of Historic Preservation, State Historical Society of Iowa, Des Moines. Copy on file, Office of the State Archaeologist, University of Iowa, Iowa City.

1993a *Archaeological and Historical Survey of the Turkey River Subagency Site (13WH111) and Vicinity, Winneshiek County.* Contract Completion Report 379. Office of the State Archaeologist, University of Iowa, Iowa City.

1993b *Early Transportation Development in Harrison County, Iowa: Archaeological and Architectural Survey.* Submitted to the Harrison County Historic Preservation Commission and the Historic Preservation Bureau, State Historical Society of Iowa, Des Moines. Copy on file, Office of the State Archaeologist, University of Iowa, Iowa City.

1994a *Early Transportation Development in Monona County, Iowa: Archaeological and Architectural Survey.* Submitted to the Harrison and Monona County Historic Preservation Commissions and the Historic Preservation Bureau, State Historical Society of Iowa, Des Moines. Copy on file, Office of the State Archaeologist, University of Iowa, Iowa City.

1994b *Archaeological Monitoring of the Mansion Foundation Restoration Project, Brucemore Historic Site, Cedar Rapids, Iowa.* Copy on file, Office of the State Archaeologist, University of Iowa, Iowa City.

1996   *"It Was Some Brewery." Data Recovery of the City Brewery Site, 13PK661, Des Moines,* Iowa. Submitted to the Des Moines Metropolita Transit Authority, Des Moines, Iowa.

Rogers, Leah D., and Brad Koldehoff

1987   *Archaeological Site Testing, Lake Red Rock, Iowa: Pool Raise Project, 1986 Season.* Cultural Resources Management Report No. 125. American Resources Group, Carbondale, Illinois.

Rogers, Leah D., and David M. Gradwohl

1995   Pottery Industry in Iowa. In *The Bonaparte Pottery Site (13VB200): a.k.a. the Parker-Hanback-Wilson Pottery: Archaeological and Historical Investigations,* by Leah D. Rogers, Cynthia L. Peterson, Maria F. Schroeder, and Fred A. Finney, pp. 12–16. Contract Completion Report 444. Office of the State Archaeologist, University of Iowa, Iowa City.

Rogers, Leah D., and William Green

1995   *Wickiup Hill Natural Area Archaeological Survey.* Research Papers Vol. 20, No. 3. Office of the State Archaeologist, University of Iowa, Iowa City.

Rogers, Leah D., and William C. Page

1997   *Walking to Work: Victorian Life in Des Moines.* Submitted to the Federal Transit Administration and Des Moines Metropolitan Transit Authority, Des Moines, Iowa.

Rogers, Leah D., Cynthia L. Peterson, Maria F. Schroeder, and Fred A. Finney

1995   *The Bonaparte Pottery Site (13VB200): a.k.a. the Parker-Hanback-Wilson Pottery: Archaeological and Historical Investigations.* Contract Completion Report 444. Office of the State Archaeologist, University of Iowa, Iowa City.

Roggman, Arnold D.

1974   Aulwes Site. Iowa Archeological Society *Newsletter* 73:3–8.

1990   Aulwes Field Site Clayton County, Iowa, Lower Buck Creek Bench. Iowa Archeological Society *Newsletter* 40(4):2–3.

Roosa, W. B.

1965   Some Great Lakes Fluted Point Types. *Michigan Archaeologist* 11(3–4):89–102.

Roper, Donna C.

1984   *A Cultural Resources Reconnaissance at Lake Red Rock, Iowa.* Report R-2596. Gilbert/Commonwealth, Jackson, Michigan. Submitted to the U.S. Army Corps of Engineers, Rock Island District.

1986   *Archaeological Survey and Testing at Lake Red Rock, Iowa: The 1984 and 1985 Seasons.* Report R-2821. Gilbert/Commonwealth, Jackson, Michigan. Submitted to the U.S. Army Corps of Engineers, Rock Island District.

1992   *Phase 3 Investigations at 13LC17: A Randolph Phase Winter Camp in the White Breast Creek Valley, Lucas County, Iowa.* Submitted to the Iowa Department of Transportation. IDOT Project Reference BRF-65-2(3)--20-59.

1994   A Randolph Phase Winter Camp in the White Breast Creek Valley. *Journal of the Iowa Archeological Society* 41:76–107.

1995   Spatial Dynamics and Historical Process in the Central Plains Tradition. *Plains Anthropologist* 40:203–221.

Roper, Donna C., and Beverly E. Bastian

1986   *A Cultural Resources Management Plan for Lake Red Rock, Iowa.* Report R-2715. Gilbert/Commonwealth, Jackson, Michigan. Submitted to the U.S. Army Corps of Engineers, Rock Island District.

Rowe, John H.

1958   Archaeology as a Career. *Journal of the Iowa Archeological Society* 7:17–33.

1961   Stratigraphy and Seriation. *American Antiquity* 26:324–330.

Rowe, Paul

1952a  Early Horizons of Mills County, Iowa. Part I, Evidences of Early Man. *Journal of the Iowa Archeological Society* 1(3):6–13.

1952b  Early Horizons of Mills County, Iowa. Part II, Prepottery Sites. *Journal of the Iowa Archeological Society* 2(1):3–10.

Ruhe, Robert V.

1969   *Quaternary Landscapes in Iowa.* Iowa State University Press, Ames.

Ruppé, Reynold J.

1954   An Archaic Site at Olin, Iowa. *Journal of the Iowa Archeological Society* 3(4):12–15.

1955a  Archaeology Students Excavate Prehistoric Indian Village near Cherokee, Iowa. *On Iowa* 30(6):4–5.

1955b  Cherokee and Turin, Iowa: Archaeological Ex-

cavations Reveal More Knowledge about Prehistoric Man. *State University of Iowa Staff
Magazine* 6(2):6–20, 30–31.

1955/ Iowa Archaeology: I. The Earliest Indians of
1956    Iowa. *Journal of the Iowa Archeological Society*
        5:2–10.

1956    Archaeological Investigations of the Mill
        Creek Culture of Northwestern Iowa. *Year-
        book of the American Philosophical Society*
        1955:335–339.

1960    The Westwood Site: A Middle Woodland Bur-
        ial Mound. *Journal of the Iowa Archeological
        Society* 9(3):20–23.

Ruth, Amy

1993    Protecting Indian Burial Sites. *Goldfinch*
        15(2):23.

Salzer, Robert J.

1986    The Middle Woodland Stage. In Introduction
        to Wisconsin Archaeology, edited by William
        Green, James B. Stoltman, and Alice B. Kehoe,
        pp. 263–282. *Wisconsin Archeologist* 67: 163–
        395.

1990    Red Horn and the Williams-Goggin Hypothe-
        sis. Paper presented at the 35th Midwest Ar-
        chaeological Conference, Evanston, Illinois.

Sasso, Robert F.

1993    La Crosse Region Oneota Adaptations:
        Changing Late Prehistoric Subsistence and
        Settlement Patterns in the Upper Mississippi
        Valley. *Wisconsin Archeologist* 74:324–369.

Schermer, Shirley J.

1983    *Coralville Reservoir Shoreline Survey.* Research
        Papers Vol. 8, No. 2. Office of the State Ar-
        chaeologist, University of Iowa, Iowa City.

1987    *Preliminary Report on the 1986 Limited Survey
        at the Blood Run National Historic Landmark
        Site Lyon County, Iowa.* Contract Completion
        Report 248. Office of the State Archaeologist,
        University of Iowa, Iowa City.

1988    *Mines of Spain 1987 Archaeological Field School.*
        Research Papers Vol. 13, No. 2. Office of the
        State Archaeologist, University of Iowa, Iowa
        City.

1992    *Discovering Archaeology: An Activity Guide for
        Educators.* Special Publication. Office of the
        State Archaeologist, University of Iowa, Iowa
        City.

1996    Iowa Rockshelters Tour. In *Field Trip Guide:*

        *Iowa Rockshelters,* pp. 1–14. 54th Annual
        Plains Anthropological Conference, Iowa
        City. Copy on file, Office of the State Archae-
        ologist, University of Iowa, Iowa City.

Schermer, Shirley J., and Royce Kurtz

1986    *Archaeological and Historical Studies, Mines of
        Spain, Dubuque, Iowa.* Contract Completion
        Report 242. Office of the State Archaeologist,
        University of Iowa, Iowa City.

Schermer, Shirley J., and Douglas W. Owsley

1987    Analysis of Human Skeletal Material from the
        Hanging Valley Site (13HR28). In *Miscella-
        neous Reports on Iowa Archaeology,* pp. 13–53.
        Research Papers Vol. 12, No. 1. Office of the
        State Archaeologist, University of Iowa, Iowa
        City.

Schermer, Shirley J., and Joseph A. Tiffany

1985    Environmental Variables as Factors in Site Lo-
        cation: An Example from the Upper Midwest.
        *Midcontinental Journal of Archaeology*
        10:215–240.

Scholtz, James A.

1958    Description of Pottery Vessels Recovered from
        Burial Chamber of a Middle Woodland Burial
        Mound. Iowa Archeological Society *Newsletter*
        28:7–13.

Scott, Donna H.

1979    Analysis of the Avifauna from Five Sites in
        Northwestern Iowa. *Journal of the Iowa Arche-
        ological Society* 26:43–79.

Seeman, Mark F.

1979    *The Hopewell Interaction Sphere: The Evidence
        for Interregional Trade and Structural Complex-
        ity.* Prehistory Research Series Vol. 5, No. 2.
        Indiana Historical Society, Indianapolis.

Semenov, S. A.

1964    *Prehistoric Technology.* Translated by M. W.
        Thompson. Cory, Adams, and MacKay,
        London.

Semken, Holmes, Jr.

1980    Holocene Climatic Reconstructions Derived
        from Three Micromammal Bearing Cultural
        Horizons of the Cherokee Sewer Site, North-
        western Iowa. In *The Cherokee Excavations: Ho-
        locene Ecology and Human Adaptations in
        Northwestern Iowa,* edited by Duane C. An-
        derson and Holmes A. Semken, Jr., pp. 67–99.
        Academic Press, New York.

Shane, Orin
1991    *Final Report to the Minnesota Historical Society
        for Contract 90-C2443: Radiocarbon Assays of
        Bone from the Browns Valley Skeleton.* Science
        Museum of Minnesota, St. Paul.

Shay, C. Thomas
1978    Late Prehistoric Bison and Deer Use in the
        Eastern Prairie-Forest Border. In *Bison Pro-
        curement and Utilization: A Symposium*, edited
        by Leslie B. Davis and Michael Wilson, pp.
        194–212. Memoir 14. Plains Anthropologist,
        Lincoln, Nebraska.

Shepard, Anna O.
1956    *Ceramics for the Archaeologist.* Publication
        609. Carnegie Institute of Washington,
        Washington, D.C.

Shippee, J. M.
1948    Nebo Hill, a Lithic Complex in Western Mis-
        souri. *American Antiquity* 14:29–32.
1967    *Archaeological Remains in the Area of Kansas
        City: The Woodland Period, Early, Middle, Late.*
        Research Series No. 5. Missouri Archaeologi-
        cal Society, Columbia.

Shott, Michael J.
1993    Spears, Darts, and Arrows: Late Woodland
        Hunting Techniques in the Upper Ohio Valley.
        *American Antiquity* 58:425–443.

Shott, Michael J., and John F. Doershuk
1996    Recent Investigations at the Gillett Grove
        (13CY2) Oneota Site, Clay County, Iowa.
        Paper presented at the 41st Midwest Archae-
        ological Conference, Beloit, Wisconsin. Copy
        on file, Office of the State Archaeologist, Uni-
        versity of Iowa, Iowa City.

Shutler, Richard, Jr.
1974    Bone Artifacts. The Cherokee Sewer Site
        (13CK405): A Preliminary Report of a Strati-
        fied Paleo-Indian/Archaic Site in Northwest-
        ern Iowa. *Journal of the Iowa Archeological So-
        ciety* 21:93–96.

Shutler, Richard, Jr., and Duane C. Anderson
1974    Introduction. The Cherokee Sewer Site
        (13CK405): A Preliminary Report of a Strati-
        fied Paleo-Indian/Archaic Site in Northwest-
        ern Iowa. *Journal of the Iowa Archeological So-
        ciety* 21:1–15.

Shutler, Richard, Jr., Duane C. Anderson, George A.
        Hallberg, Bernard E. Hoyer, Gerald A. Miller,
        Katherine E. Butler, Holmes A. Semken Jr.,
        David A. Baerreis, Robert C. Koeppen,
        Lawrence A. Conrad, and Joseph A. Tiffany
1974    The Cherokee Sewer Site (13CK405): A
        Preliminary Report of a Stratified Paleo-
        Indian/Archaic Site in Northwestern Iowa.
        *Journal of the Iowa Archeological Society*
        21:1–175.

Shutler, Richard, Jr., Duane C. Anderson, Lise S.
        Tatum, and Holmes A. Semken Jr.
1980    Excavation Techniques and Synopsis of Re-
        sults Derived from the Cherokee Project. In
        *The Cherokee Excavations: Holocene Ecology and
        Human Adaptations in Northwestern Iowa*,
        edited by Duane C. Anderson and Holmes A.
        Semken, Jr., pp. 1–20. Academic Press, New
        York.

Shutler, Richard Jr., and Thomas H. Charlton
        (editors)
1980    *Southeast Iowa Lake Calvin Area Paleo-Indian
        Survey*, Department of Anthropology, Univer-
        sity of Iowa, Iowa City. Submitted to the Divi-
        sion of Historic Preservation, Iowa State His-
        torical Department, Iowa City.

Shwartz, Marion
1997    *A History of Dogs in the Early Americas.* Yale
        University Press, New Haven.

Silverberg, Robert
1968    *Moundbuilders of Ancient America: The Archae-
        ology of a Myth.* New York Graphic Society,
        Greenwich, Connecticut.

Simons, D. B., Michael J. Shott, and H. T. Wright
1984    The Gainey Site: Variability in a Great Lakes
        Paleo-Indian Assemblage. *Archaeology of East-
        ern North America* 12:266–279.

Skinner, Alanson
1915    *Societies of the Iowa, Kansa and Ponca Indians.*
        Anthropological Papers of the American Mu-
        seum of Natural History Vol. 11, No. 9.
1925    Traditions of the Iowa Indians. *Journal of
        American Folklore* 38:425–506.
1926    Ethnology of the Iowa Indians. *Bulletin of the
        Public Museum of the City of Milwaukee*
        5(4):181–354.

Slattery, Richard G.
1979    Further Testing at the McKinney Oneota Vil-

lage Site (13LA1). *Journal of the Iowa Archeological Society* 26:81–94.

Slattery, Richard G., George A. Horton, and Michael
E. Ruppert

1975    The McKinney Village Site: An Oneota Site in
Southeastern Iowa. *Journal of the Iowa Archeological Society* 22:35–61.

Smith, Bruce D.

1987    *Rivers of Change: Essays on Early Agriculture in
Eastern North America.* Smithsonian Institution Press, Washington, D.C.

Smith, Huron H.

1928    Ethnobotany of the Mesquakie Indians. *Bulletin of the Public Museum of the City of Milwaukee* 4:175–326.

1933    Ethnobotany of the Forest Potawatomi Indians. *Bulletin of the Public Museum of the City of
Milwaukee* 7:1–230.

Snortland, J. Signe

1994    Northern Plains Woodland Mortuary Practices. In *Skeletal Biology in the Great Plains,*
edited by Douglas W. Owsley and Richard L.
Jantz, pp. 51–70. Smithsonian Institution
Press, Washington, D.C.

Snow, Susan R.

1993    *Phase II Investigations at the Cromwell Train
Depot (13UN149), Union County, Iowa.* Con-
tract Completion Report 366. Office of the
State Archaeologist, University of Iowa, Iowa
City.

1994    *Archaeological Investigations at the Thompson-
Ballard Site (13SR166): An Archaic Base Camp
in Story County, Iowa.* Contract Completion
Report 395. Office of the State Archaeologist,
University of Iowa, Iowa City.

1996    *Phase I and Phase II Investigations of Seven Sites
within the Proposed Historic District of Bowen's
Prairie, U.S. 151 (NHS-151-3[84]--19-57),
Segment 4, Jones County, Iowa Volume I: Text.*
Contract Completion Report 477. Office of
the State Archaeologist, University of Iowa,
Iowa City.

Springer, James W., and Stanley R. Witkowski

1982    Siouan Historical Linguistics and Oneota Archaeology. In *Oneota Studies,* edited by Guy E.
Gibbon, pp. 69–83. Publications in Anthropology No. 1. University of Minnesota, Minneapolis.

Stafford, C. Russell

1992a   Radiocarbon Dates and Chronology. In *Early
Woodland Occupations at the Ambrose Flick Site
in the Sny Bottom of West-Central Illinois,*
edited by C. Russell Stafford, pp. 95–104. Research Series 10. Center for American Archeology, Kampsville Archeological Center,
Kampsville, Illinois.

1992b   Ambrose Flick and Marion Settlement and
Subsistence. In *Early Woodland Occupations at
the Ambrose Flick Site in the Sny Bottom of
West-Central Illinois,* edited by C. Russell Stafford, pp. 294–307. Research Series 10. Center
for American Archeology, Kampsville Archeological Center, Kampsville, Illinois.

Stafford, C. Russell (editor)

1985    *The Campbell Hollow Archaic Occupations: A
Study of Intrasite Spatial Structure in the Lower
Illinois Valley.* Research Series 4. Center for
American Archaeology, Kampsville Archeo-
logical Center, Kampsville, Illinois.

1992    *Early Woodland Occupations at the Ambrose
Flick Site in the Sny Bottom of West-Central Illi-
nois.* Research Series 10. Center for American
Archeology, Kampsville Archeological Center,
Kampsville, Illinois.

Stanley, David G.

1987    Lithic Analysis. In *Archaeology in the Mississippi River Floodplain at Sand Run Slough, Iowa,*
by David W. Benn, pp. 98–179. Report CAR-
690. Center for Archaeological Research,
Southwest Missouri State University, Springfield.

1992    *Archeological Investigation of the Fort Atkinson
Locality Associated with a Proposed Wastewater
Treatment Facility, City of Fort Atkinson, Win-
neshiek County, Iowa.* BCA Report 85. Bear
Creek Archeology, Decorah, Iowa.

1995    *Phase I Archeological Reconnaissance Survey of
the Yellow River Mission Property, Yellow River
State Forest, Allamakee County, Iowa.* BCA Report 359. Bear Creek Archeology, Cresco,
Iowa.

Stanley, David G., J. D. Anderson, and Leah D. Rogers

1988    *Archaeological Site Testing, Lake Red Rock, Iowa:
Pool Raise Project, 1987 Season.* 5 vols. Cultural Resources Management Report No. 127.

American Resources Group, Carbondale, Illinois.

Starr, Frederick

1887a   Mounds and Lodge Circles in Iowa. *American Antiquarian* 9(6):361–363.

1887b   Shell Heap at Cedar Rapids, Iowa. *American Antiquarian* 9(5):303.

1897a   Bibliography of Iowa Antiquities. *Proceedings of the Davenport Academy of Natural Sciences* 6:1–124.

1897b   Summary of the Archaeology of Iowa. *Proceedings of the Davenport Academy of Natural Sciences* 6:53–124.

1897c   Circular of Suggestions Regarding Work in Archaeology. *Proceedings of the Davenport Academy of Natural Sciences* 6:340–343.

Steinacher, Terry L., John Ludwickson, Gayle F. Carlson, and Rob Bozell

1991   An Evaluation of Central Plains Tradition–Pawnee Ancestry. Paper presented at the 49th Annual Plains Anthropological Conference, Lawrence, Kansas.

Stelle, Lenville J.

1992   History and Archaeology: The 1730 Meskwakis Fort. In *Calumet and Fleur-De-Lys,* edited by John A. Walthall and Thomas E. Emerson, pp. 265–307. Smithsonian Institution Press, Washington, D.C.

Steponaitis, Vincas P.

1980   *Ceramics, Chronology, and Community Patterns at Moundville, a Late Prehistoric Site in Alabama.* Unpublished Ph.D. dissertation, Department of Anthropology, University of Michigan, Ann Arbor.

Stevens, J. Sanderson

1980   Survey Results. In *Southeast Iowa Lake Calvin Area Paleo-Indian Survey,* edited by Richard Shutler Jr. and Thomas H. Charlton, pp. 55–63. Department of Anthropology, University of Iowa, Iowa City. Submitted to the Division of Historic Preservation, Iowa State Historical Department, Iowa City.

Stevens, J. Sanderson, and Joseph A. Tiffany

1977   *The Williams Site (13HN10): A Multicomponent Village in Southeast Iowa.* Research Papers Vol. 2, No. 7. Office of the State Archaeologist, University of Iowa, Iowa City.

Stevenson, J. E.

1879   The Mound Builders. *American Antiquarian* 2:89–104.

Stevenson, Katherine, and Robert F. Boszhardt

1993   *The Current Status of Oneota Sites and Research in Western Wisconsin.* The Oneota Study Unit in Region 6, 1993 Update. Reports of Investigations 163. Mississippi Valley Archaeology Center, University of Wisconsin–La Crosse.

Stevenson, Winona

1993   Beggars, Chickabobbooags, and Prisons: Páxoche (Ioway) Views of English Society, 1844–45. *American Indian Culture and Research Journal* 17(4):1–23.

Steventon, Raymond L., and John E. Kutzbach

1990   University of Wisconsin Radiocarbon Dates XXVI. *Radiocarbon* 32:209–228.

Stoffle, Richard W., Kristine L. Jones, and Henry F. Dobyns

1995   Direct European Immigrant Transmission of Old World Pathogens to Numic Indians during the Nineteenth Century. *American Indian Quarterly* 19:181–203.

Stoltman, James B.

1973   The Overhead Site (47LC 20), an Orr Phase Site near La Crosse, Wisconsin. *Wisconsin Archeologist* 54:2–35.

1979   Middle Woodland Stage Communities of Southwestern Wisconsin. In *Hopewell Archaeology: The Chillicothe Conference,* edited by David S. Brose and N'omi Greber, pp. 122–139. Kent State University Press, Kent, Ohio.

1980   Review of *Koster, an Artifact Analysis of Two Archaic Phases in Westcentral Illinois,* by Thomas Glen Cook. *Journal of the Iowa Archeological Society* 27:135–139.

1986a   The Archaic Tradition. In Introduction to Wisconsin Archaeology, edited by William Green, James B. Stoltman, and Alice B. Kehoe, pp. 207–238. *Wisconsin Archeologist* 67:163–395.

1986b   The Prairie Phase: An Early Woodland Manifestation in the Upper Mississippi Valley. In *Early Woodland Archeology,* edited by Kenneth B. Farnsworth and Thomas E. Emerson, pp. 121–136. Kampsville Seminars in Archeology Vol. 2. Center for American Archeology Press, Kampsville, Illinois.

1986c The Appearance of the Mississippian Cultural Tradition in the Upper Mississippi Valley. In *Prehistoric Mound Builders of the Mississippi Valley,* edited by James Stoltman, pp. 26–34. Putnam Museum of History and Natural Science, Davenport, Iowa.

1986d Introduction. In *Prehistoric Mound Builders of the Mississippi Valley,* edited by James B. Stoltman, pp. 1–3. Putnam Museum of History and Natural Science, Davenport, Iowa.

1989 A Quantitative Approach to the Petrographic Analysis of Ceramic Thin Sections. *American Antiquity* 54:147–160.

1990 The Woodland Tradition in the Prairie du Chien Locality. In *The Woodland Tradition in the Western Great Lakes: Papers Presented to Elden Johnson,* edited by Guy E. Gibbon, pp. 239–259. Publications in Anthropology No. 4. University of Minnesota, Minneapolis.

1991 Ceramic Petrography as a Technique for Documenting Cultural Interaction: An Example from the Upper Mississippi Valley. *American Antiquity* 56:103–120.

1993 A Petrographic Perspective on Ceramic Production and Exchange during the Period A.D. 1000–1200 in the American Bottom and Its Northern Hinterlands. Paper presented at the 58th Annual Meeting of the Society for American Archaeology, St. Louis. Copy on file, Office of the State Archaeologist, University of Iowa, Iowa City.

Stoltman, James B., and George W. Christiansen

1997 The Late Woodland Stage in the Driftless Area of the Upper Mississippi Valley. Paper presented at the Urbana Late Woodland Conference, University of Illinois, Champaign-Urbana. Copy on file, Office of the State Archaeologist, University of Iowa, Iowa City.

Stoltman, James B., and Fred A. Finney

1991 Cahokia and Its Northern Hinterlands: The Migration Hypothesis Reconsidered. Paper presented at the 56th Annual Meeting of the Society for American Archaeology, New Orleans.

Storey, Glen R.

1997 The Population of Ancient Rome. *Antiquity* 71:966–978.

Straffin, Dean F.

1971a Wolfe Havana Hopewell Site. In *Prehistoric Investigations,* edited by Marshall B. McKusick, pp. 53–65. Report 3. Office of the State Archaeologist, University of Iowa, Iowa City.

1971b *The Kingston Oneota Site.* Report 2. Office of the State Archaeologist, University of Iowa, Iowa City.

1972a Kelley Site Field Notes. Manuscript on file, Office of the State Archaeologist, University of Iowa, Iowa City.

1972b Iowaville: A Possible Historic Ioway Site on the Lower Des Moines. *Proceedings of the Iowa Academy of Science* 79:44–46.

Strong, William D.

1935 *An Introduction to Nebraska Archaeology.* Smithsonian Miscellaneous Collections Vol. 93, No. 10. Smithsonian Institution, Washington, D.C.

Struever, Stuart

1964 The Hopewell Interaction Sphere in Riverine–Western Great Lakes Culture History. In *Hopewellian Studies,* edited by Joseph R. Caldwell and Robert J. Hall, pp. 85–106. Scientific Papers Vol. 12. Illinois State Museum, Springfield.

1968 Woodland Subsistence-Settlement Systems in the Lower Illinois Valley. In *New Perspectives in Archeology,* edited by Sally R. Binford and Lewis R. Binford, pp. 285–312. Aldine, Chicago.

Stuart, George E., and Francis P. McManamon

1996 *Archaeology and You.* Society for American Archaeology, Washington, D.C.

Stuiver, M., and P. J. Reimer

1986 A Computer Program for Radiocarbon Age Calibration. *Radiocarbon* 28:1022–1030.

1993 Extended $^{14}$C Database and Revised CALIB Radiocarbon Calibration Program. *Radiocarbon* 35:215–230.

Styles, Bonnie, Steven R. Ahler, and Melvin L. Fowler

1983 Modoc Rock Shelter Revisited. In *Archaic Hunters and Gatherers in the American Midwest,* edited by James L. Phillips and James A. Brown, pp. 261–297. Academic Press, New York.

Sudderth, W. E.

1992 *Salvage Archeology at the Herbert Hoover National Historic Site: The Mackey House.* Technical Report 12. Midwest Archeological Center, Lincoln, Nebraska.

Sundstrom, Linea
1997   Smallpox Used Them Up. *Ethnohistory* 44:303–343.

Swenson, Fern
1987   Prehistoric Ceramics from the Naze Site. In *Archaeological Excavation at the Naze Site (32SN246)*, edited by Michael L. Gregg, pp. 123–183. University of North Dakota, Grand Forks. Submitted to the USDI Bureau of Reclamation.

Swisher, Jacob
1940   *Iowa, Land of Many Mills*. State Historical Society of Iowa, Iowa City.
1961   Iowa, Land of Many Mills. *Palimpsest* 42:1–32.

Syms, E. Leigh
1977   *Cultural and Ecological Dynamics of the Ceramic Period in Southwestern Manitoba*. Memoir 12. *Plains Anthropologist*, Lincoln, Nebraska.

Tabeau, Pierre Antoine
1939   *Tabeau's Narrative of Loisel's Expedition to the Upper Missouri*, edited by Annie Heloise Abel. University of Oklahoma Press, Norman.

Tainter, Joseph A.
1983   Woodland Social Change in the Central Midwest: A Review and Evaluation of Interpretive Trends. *North American Archaeologist* 4:141–161.

Tandarich, John P.
1976   *An Archaeological Survey of the Mormon Handcart Camp and Cemetery*. Contract Completion Report 3. Office of the State Archaeologist, University of Iowa, Iowa City.
1977   *Final Report of Archaeological Investigations at the Site of the Ottumwa Generating Station, Chillicothe, Iowa*. Contract Completion Report 73. Office of the State Archaeologist, University of Iowa, Iowa City.

Tandarich, John P., and Loren Horton
1976   A Memorial Bibliography of Charles R. Keyes and Ellison J. Orr. *Journal of the Iowa Archeological Society* 23:45–143.

Tankersley, Kenneth B.
1989   A Close Look at the Big Picture: Early Paleoindian Lithic Resource Procurement in the Mid-western United States. In *Eastern Paleoindian Lithic Resource Use*, edited by C. J. Ellis and J. C. Lothrop, pp. 259–292. Westview, Boulder, Colorado.

Tankersley, Kenneth B., and B. L. Isaac (editors)
1990   *Early Paleoindian Economies of Eastern North America*. Research in Economic Anthropology Supplement 5. JAI, Greenwich, Connecticut.

Tatum, Lise S.
1980   A Seasonal Subsistence Model for Holocene Bison Hunters on the Eastern Plains of North America. In *The Cherokee Excavations: Holocene Ecology and Human Adaptations in Northwestern Iowa*, edited by Duane C. Anderson and Holmes A. Semken, Jr., pp. 149–169. Academic Press, New York.

Tatum, Lise S., and Richard Shutler, Jr.
1980   Bone Tool Technology and Subsistence Activity at the Cherokee Sewer Site. In *The Cherokee Excavations: Holocene Ecology and Human Adaptations in Northwestern Iowa*, edited by Duane C. Anderson and Holmes A. Semken, Jr., pp. 239–255. Academic Press, New York.

Taylor, R. E., C. Vance Haynes Jr., and Minze Stuiver
1996   Clovis and Folsom Age Estimates: Stratigraphic Context and Radiocarbon Calibration. *Antiquity* 70:515–525.

Temple, Wayne C.
1977   *Indian Villages of the Illinois Country*. Scientific Papers Vol. 2, Part 2. Illinois State Museum, Springfield.

Theler, James L.
1983   *Woodland Tradition Economic Strategies: Animal Resource Utilization in Southwestern Wisconsin and Northeastern Iowa*. Unpublished Ph.D. dissertation, Department of Anthropology, University of Wisconsin–Madison.
1987   *Woodland Tradition Economic Strategies: Animal Resource Utilization in Southwestern Wisconsin and Northeastern Iowa*. Report 17. Office of the State Archaeologist, University of Iowa, Iowa City.
1990a  A Possible Oneota Freshwater Mussel Cache Intended for Ceramic Tempering Material. *Journal of the Iowa Archeological Society* 37:1–3.
1990b  Progress Report on the Analysis of Fish and Gastropod Remains from the Wall Ridge Site

(13ML176). In *Glenwood Culture Paleoenvironment and Diet: Analysis of Plant and Animal Remains from the Wall Ridge Earthlodge (13ML176), Mills County, Iowa,* edited by William Green, pp. 21–28. Research Papers Vol. 15, No. 6. Office of the State Archaeologist, University of Iowa, Iowa City.

Thomas, Cyrus
1885    Ancient Works in Iowa. *American Antiquarian* 7(4):212–214.

1887a    *Ancient Mound in Johnson County (Iowa).* Annual Report of the Smithsonian Institution for 1887. Smithsonian Institution, Washington, D.C.

1887b    *Burial Mounds of the Northern Sections of the United States.* Fifth Annual Report of the Bureau of American Ethnology, 1881–1884, pp. 2–45. Smithsonian Institution, Washington, D.C.

1894    *Report on Mound Explorations of the Bureau of Ethnology.* Twelfth Annual Report of the Bureau of American Ethnology, 1890–1891, pp. 1–730. Smithsonian Institution, Washington, D.C.

Thomas, Terry
1992    Luck of the Irish. *Central States Archaeological Journal* 39:166–167.

Thompson, Dean M., and David W. Benn
1983    *An Archaeological Survey of the Benson Valley (13WD50) in Woodbury County, Iowa.* Division of Historic Preservation, State Historical Society of Iowa, Des Moines. Copy on file, Office of the State Archaeologist, University of Iowa, Iowa City.

Thompson, Dean M., and Alton K. Fisher
1977    *The Hickenbottom Site (13JF52): Salvage Excavation of a Boone Focus Burial from Jefferson County, Southeastern Iowa.* Research Papers Vol. 2, No. 5. Office of the State Archaeologist, University of Iowa, Iowa City.

Thompson, Theron
1879    *Mounds in Muscatine County, Iowa, and Rock Island County, Illinois.* Annual Report of the Smithsonian Institution for 1879, pp. 359–363. Smithsonian Institution, Washington, D.C.

Throne, Mildred (editor)
1951    The Memories of Aristarchus Cone. *Iowa Journal of History* 49(1):51–72.

Thwaites, Reuben G. (editor)
1896/    *The Jesuit Relations and Allied Documents,* 73
1901    vols. Burrow Brothers, Cleveland.

1969    *Original Journals of the Lewis and Clark Expedition, 1804–1806.* Arno Press, New York.

Tiffany, A. S.
1876a    Report on the Results of an Excursion to Albany, Illinois, Nov. 7th and 8th, 1873. *Proceedings of the Davenport Academy of Natural Sciences* 1:104–106.

1876b    Mound Explorations in 1875. *Proceedings of the Davenport Academy of Natural Sciences* 1:113–114.

Tiffany, Joseph A.
1975    University of Wisconsin–Madison Archaeological Research at the Chan-ya-ta Mill Creek Site, Buena Vista County, Iowa. Iowa Archeological Society *Newsletter* 76:3–11.

1977    Artifacts from the Sharp's Site: A Sterns Creek Component in Southwestern Iowa. *Journal of the Iowa Archeological Society* 24:84–124.

1978a    Middle Woodland Pottery Typology from Southwest Iowa. *Plains Anthropologist* 23:169–182.

1978b    Discoidals from Mill Creek Sites. Iowa Archeological Society *Newsletter* 87:6–12.

1978c    *A Model of Changing Settlement Patterns for the Mill Creek Culture of Northwest Iowa: An Analysis from the Chan-ya-ta Site (13BV1), Buena Vista County, Iowa.* Unpublished Ph.D. dissertation, Department of Anthropology, University of Wisconsin–Madison.

1979a    The Logo of the Office of the State Archaeologist. Iowa Archeological Society *Newsletter* 94:7–11.

1979b    An Overview of Oneota Sites in Southeastern Iowa: A Perspective from the Ceramic Analysis of the Schmeiser Site, 13DM101, Des Moines County, Iowa. *Proceedings of the Iowa Academy of Science* 86:89–101.

1979c    *An Archaeological Survey of the Bastian Oneota Site (13CK28), Cherokee County, Iowa.* Research Papers Vol. 4, No. 1. Office of the State Archaeologist, University of Iowa, Iowa City.

1980    Late Woodland Pottery in Northeastern Iowa

as Seen from the Hartley Fort. Paper presented at the 38th Annual Plains Anthropological Conference, Iowa City.

1981a   A Compendium of Radiocarbon Dates for Iowa Archaeological Sites. *Plains Anthropologist* 26:55–73, 172.

1981b   The Williams Site (13HN10) Ceramics. *South Dakota Archaeology* 5:85–95.

1982a   Hartley Fort Ceramics. *Proceedings of the Iowa Academy of Science* 89:133–150.

1982b   *Chan-ya-ta: A Mill Creek Village*. Report 15. Office of the State Archaeologist, University of Iowa, Iowa City.

1982c   Site Catchment Analysis of Southeast Iowa Oneota Sites. In *Oneota Studies*, edited by Guy Gibbon, pp. 1–13. Publications in Anthropology No. 1, University of Minnesota, Minneapolis.

1983   An Overview of the Middle Missouri Tradition. In *Prairie Archaeology: Papers in Honor of David A. Baerreis*, edited by Guy E. Gibbon, pp. 87–108. Publications in Anthropology No. 3. University of Minnesota, Minneapolis.

1986a   The Early Woodland Period in Iowa. In *Early Woodland Archeology*, edited by Kenneth B. Farnsworth and Thomas E. Emerson, pp. 159–170. Kampsville Seminars in Archeology Vol. 2. Center for American Archeology Press, Kampsville, Illinois.

1986b   Ceramics from the F-518 Project. In *Archaeological Investigations along the F-518 Corridor*, edited by Stephen C. Lensink, pp. 227–245. Iowa Quaternary Studies Contribution 9. University of Iowa, Iowa City.

1986c   The Mississippian Tradition and Iowa's Prehistoric Peoples. In *Prehistoric Mound Builders of the Mississippi Valley*, edited by James B. Stoltman, pp. 35–39. Putnam Museum of History and Natural Science, Davenport, Iowa.

1987   *Modeling Mill Creek-Mississippian Interaction*. Iowa Quaternary Studies Contribution 12. University of Iowa, Iowa City.

1988   Preliminary Report on Excavations at the McKinney Oneota Village Site (13LA1) Louisa County, Iowa. *Wisconsin Archeologist* 69:227–312.

1991a   Modeling Mill Creek–Mississippian Interaction. In *New Perspectives on Cahokia: Views from the Periphery*, edited by James B. Stoltman, pp. 319–347. Monographs in World Archaeology No. 2. Prehistory Press, Madison, Wisconsin.

1991b   Models of Mississippian Culture History in the Western Prairie Peninsula: A Perspective from Iowa. In *Cahokia and the Hinterlands: Middle Mississippian Cultures of the Midwest*, edited by Thomas E. Emerson and R. Barry Lewis, pp. 183–192. University of Illinois Press, Urbana.

1997a   Ceramics from the Milford Site (13DK1): A Post-Contact Oneota Village in Northwest Iowa. *South Dakota Archaeology* 19–20:49–86.

1997b   Ceramics from the Kelley Site: Perspectives on the Oneota Tradition in Southeast Iowa. *Plains Anthropologist* 42:205–236.

1998   Southeast Iowa Oneota: A Review. *The Wisconsin Archeologist* 79:147–164.

Tiffany, Joseph A. (editor)

1982   *A Preliminary Report on the Arthur Site, East Okoboji Lake, Iowa*. Research Papers Vol. 7, No. 1. Office of the State Archaeologist, University of Iowa, Iowa City.

Tiffany, Joseph A., and Larry R. Abbott

1982   Site-Catchment Analysis: Applications to Iowa Archaeology. *Journal of Field Archaeology* 9(3):313–322.

Tiffany, Joseph A., Larry R. Abbott, and Duane C. Anderson

1977   *Archaeological Investigations at the Proposed Site of the Sutton Coal Mine, Monroe, Iowa*. Research Papers Vol. 2, No. 15. Office of the State Archaeologist, University of Iowa, Iowa City.

Tiffany, Joseph A., and Kimberly J. Adams

1998   Ceramics from the Phipps (13CK21): A Mill Creek Culture Site in Northwest Iowa. *Journal of the Iowa Archeological Society* 45:19–47.

Tiffany, Joseph A., and Lynn M. Alex

1999   Symbolism and Ritual in the Emerging Plains Village Pattern: The West Des Moines and Paardekooper Great Oasis Sites. Paper presented at the 64th Annual Meeting of the Society for American Archaeology, Chicago.

Tiffany, Joseph A., Lynn M. Alex, and Mark L. Anderson

1998 Comments on "The Archaeology of Two Great Oasis Sites in the Perry Creek Valley, Northwest Iowa." *Journal of the Iowa Archeological Society* 45:95–99.

Tiffany, Joseph A., and Duane C. Anderson

1993 The Milford Site (13DK1): A Postcontact Oneota Village in Northwest Iowa. In *Prehistory and Human Ecology of the Western Prairies and Northern Plains: Papers in Honor of Robert A. Alex (1941–1988)*, edited by Joseph A. Tiffany, pp. 283–306. Memoir 27. *Plains Anthropologist*, Lincoln, Nebraska.

Tiffany, Joseph A., Shirley J. Schermer, James L. Theler, Douglas W. Owsley, Duane C. Anderson, E. Arthur Bettis III, and Dean M. Thompson

1988 The Hanging Valley Site (13HR28): A Stratified Woodland Burial Locale in Western Iowa. *Plains Anthropologist* 33:219–259.

1989 Reply to Benn's Comments on the Hanging Valley Site (13HR28). *Plains Anthropologist* 34:271–272.

Till, Anton

1976 Archaeological Investigations of the Black Hawk Historic-Archaeological District: Davis, Van Buren, and Wapello Counties. Ms. on file, Office of the State Archaeologist, University of Iowa, Iowa City.

1977 Louisa County Archaeology. In *Iowa's Great River Road Cultural and Natural Resources, Vol. II: Archaeology, Geology, and Natural Areas*, by John Hotopp, pp. 187–276. Contract Completion Report 108. Office of the State Archaeologist, University of Iowa, Iowa City.

Till, Anton, David Cook, and John A. Hotopp

1979 *The Landis Site (13DA12): A Great Oasis Component in the Raccoon River Valley, Dallas County, Iowa*. Project Completion Report Vol. 2, No. 76. Office of the State Archaeologist, University of Iowa, Iowa City.

Till, Anton, and Blane H. Nansel

1981a Area XV Cultural Resources Surveys: Jefferson County Archaeology. Submitted to the Division of Historic Preservation, Iowa State Historical Department, Iowa City. Copy on file,

Office of the State Archaeologist, University of Iowa, Iowa City.

1981b Area XV Cultural Resources Survey, Van Buren County Archaeology, Vol. 1. Submitted to the Division of Historic Preservation, Iowa State Historical Department, Iowa City, Iowa.

Timberlake, Robert

1981 *Darr-es-Shalom: The Culture History and Ecology of a Stratified Archaic through Woodland Archaeological Site, Polk County, Iowa*. Unpublished Master's thesis, Department of Sociology and Anthropology, Iowa State University, Ames.

Tinnian, Raymond

1998 Iowa Indians Visit Washington, D.C. Unpublished manuscript in possession of author.

Titus, S., J. K. Johnson, C. R. McGimsey, and J. D. Anderson

1991 *Phase II Archaeological Investigations within the Northern Border Pipeline Expansion/Extension Project Corridor Harper, Iowa to the Mississippi River*. Cultural Resources Management Report No. 168. American Resources Group, Carbondale, Illinois.

Tolmie, Clare

1992 *Archaeobotany and Paleoethnobotany of Blood Run (13LO2), Lyon County, Iowa*. Unpublished Master's thesis, Department of Anthropology, University of Iowa, Iowa City.

Toole, William L.

1868 Sketches and Incidents Relating to the Settlement of Louisa County. *Annals of Iowa* 6:45–54.

Transeau, Edgar N.

1935 The Prairie Peninsula. *Ecology* 16:423–437.

Treat, Raymond, John Kelly, and Larry A. Conrad

1970 Seeds. In Environmental Archaeology in Western Iowa, by David A. Baerreis, Margie L. Staab, Robert A. Alex, Donna Scott, Lynn M. Betzler, Andrew Fortier, John E. Dallman, Raymond Treat, John Kelly, Larry Conrad, Ericka Thrash, and Edward Lugenbeal, pp. 10–12. *Northwest Chapter of the Iowa Archeological Society Newsletter* 18(5).

Tuftee, Matthew

1993 A New Perspective on Fort Des Moines: A Site Report. Ms. on file, Office of the State Archaeologist, University of Iowa, Iowa City.

Van Hyning, Thompson

1910a  The Boone Mound. *Records of the Past* 9:157–162.

1910b  The Boone Mound. *Archaeological Bulletin* 1(4):92–94.

Van Nest, Julieann

1987  *Holocene Stratigraphy and Geomorphic History of the Buchanan Drainage, a Small Tributary to the South Skunk River near Ames, Story County, Iowa.* Unpublished Master's thesis, Department of Geology, University of Iowa, Iowa City.

1995  Geological Investigations. In *Excavations at the Helen Smith Site (13LA71): Early and Late Woodland in Southeast Iowa,* by William T. Billeck, pp. 5.1–5.13. Contract Completion Report 446. Office of the State Archaeologist, University of Iowa, Iowa City.

1995  Geomorphological Analysis. In *Excavations at the Phipps Site (13CK21): New Perspectives on Mill Creek Culture,* by Richard I. Fishel, pp. 16–24. Contract Completion Report 443. Office of the State Archaeologist, University of Iowa, Iowa City.

Van Nest, Julieann and Gregory A. Vogel

1999  Geoarchaeological Record of Holocene Mississippi River Floods in the Sny Bottom of Western Illinois. Paper presented at the 64th Annual Meeting of the Society for American Archaeology, Chicago.

Van Zant, Kent L.

1979  Late Glacial and Postglacial Pollen and Plant Macrofossils from Lake West Okoboji, Northwestern Iowa. *Quaternary Research* 12:358–380.

Van Zant, Kent L., and George R. Hallberg

1979  *A Late Glacial Pollen Sequence from Northeastern Iowa: Sumner Bog Revisited.* Iowa Geological Survey Technical Information Series 3.

Vawser, Anne M. Wolley, and Holley E. Hampton

1997  Relocating Features at the Blood Run/Rock Island National Historic Landmark: An Oneota Site. Paper presented at the 55th Annual Plains Anthropological Conference, Denver.

Vehik, Susan C.

1983  Middle Woodland Mortuary Practices along the Northeastern Periphery of the Great Plains: A Consideration of Hopewellian Inter-

actions. *Midcontinental Journal of Archaeology* 8:211–255.

Vis, Robert B., and Dale R. Henning

1969  A Local Sequence for Mill Creek Sites in the Little Sioux River Valley. *Plains Anthropologist* 14:253–271.

Voegelin, C. F., and F. M. Voegelin

1977  *Classification and Index of the World's Languages.* Elsevier, New York.

Vogel, Virgil J.

1983  *Iowa Place Names of Indian Origin.* University of Iowa Press, Iowa City.

Walker, Danny N., and George C. Frison

1982  Studies of Amerindian Dogs, 3: Prehistoric Wolf/Dog Hybrids from the Northwestern Plains. *Journal of Archaeological Science* 9:125–172.

Walthall, John A.

1981  *Galena and Aboriginal Trade in Eastern North America.* Scientific Papers Vol. 17. Illinois State Museum, Springfield.

Walthall, John A., and Thomas E. Emerson (editors)

1992  *Calumet and Fleur-De-Lys.* Smithsonian Institution Press, Washington, D.C.

Wandsnider, LuAnn

1997  The Roasted and the Boiled: Food Composition and Heat Treatment with Special Emphasis on Pit-Hearth Cooking. *Journal of Anthropological Archaeology* 16:1–48.

Ward, Duren

1903a  Historico-Anthropological Possibilities in Iowa. *Iowa Journal of History and Politics* 1:47–76.

1903b  Anthropological Instruction in Iowa. *Iowa Journal of History and Politics* 1:312–328.

1904  Some Iowa Mounds, an Anthropological Survey. *Iowa Journal of History and Politics* 2:34–68.

1905a  The Investigations of the Okoboji Mounds and Their Finds. *Iowa Journal of History and Politics* 3:427–435.

1905b  Second Yearly Meeting of the Iowa Anthropological Association. *Iowa Journal of History and Politics* 3:442–458.

Warhus, Mark

1997  *Another America: Native American Maps and the History of Our Land.* St. Martin's Press, New York.

Waring, A. J., Jr., and Preston Holder
1945  A Prehistoric Ceremonial Complex in the Southeastern United States. *American Anthropologist* 47:1–34.

Watson, Patty Jo
1989  Early Plant Cultivation in the Eastern Woodlands of North America. In *Foraging and Farming: The Evolution of Plant Exploitation,* edited by D. Harris and G. Hillman, pp. 555–571. Unwin Hyman, London.

1991  Origins of Food Production in Western Asia and Eastern North America: A Consideration of Interdisciplinary Research in Anthropology and Archaeology. In *Quaternary Landscapes,* edited by L. Shane and E. Cushing, pp. 1–37. University of Minnesota Press, Minneapolis.

Weaver, J. E.
1960  Floodplain Vegetation of the Central Missouri Valley and Contacts of Woodland with Prairie. *Ecology Monograph* 30:37–64.

Weaver, J. E., and T. J. Fitzpatrick
1934  The Prairie. *Ecology Monograph* 4:111–295.

Webster, Clement L.
1889  *Ancient Mounds in Johnson County, Iowa.* Annual Report of the Smithsonian Institution for 1887. Smithsonian Institution, Washington, D.C.

Wedel, Mildred M.
1959  Oneota Sites on the Upper Iowa River. *Missouri Archaeologist* 21(2–4):1–181.

1963  Note on Oneota Classification. *Wisconsin Archeologist* 44:118–122.

1974  LeSueur and the Dakota Sioux. In *Aspects of Upper Great Lakes Anthropology: Papers in Honor of Lloyd A. Wilford,* edited by Elden Johnson, pp. 151–171. Minnesota Historical Society, St. Paul.

1976  Ethnohistory: Its Payoffs and Pitfalls for Iowa Archeologists. *Journal of the Iowa Archeological Society* 23:1–44.

1978  A Synonymy of Names for the Ioway Indians. *Journal of the Iowa Archeological Society* 25:49–77.

1981  The Ioway, Oto, and Omaha Indians in 1700. *Journal of the Iowa Archeological Society* 28:1–13.

1986  Peering at the Ioway Indians through the Mist of Time: 1650–circa 1700. *Journal of the Iowa Archeological Society* 33:1–74.

1988  The 1804 "Old Ioway Village" of Lewis and Clark. *Journal of the Iowa Archeological Society* 35:70–71.

Wedel, Waldo R.
1938a  Hopewellian Remains near Kansas City, Missouri. *Proceedings of the U.S. National Museum* 86:99–106.

1938b  *The Direct-Historical Approach in Pawnee Archaeology,* Smithsonian Miscellaneous Collections Vol. 97, No. 7. Smithsonian Institution, Washington, D.C.

1940  Culture Sequence in the Central Great Plains. In *Essays in Historical Anthropology of North America,* pp. 291–352. Smithsonian Miscellaneous Collections 100. Smithsonian Institution, Washington, D.C.

1943  *Archaeological Investigations in Platte and Clay Counties, Missouri.* U.S. National Museum Bulletin 183.

1959  *An Introduction to Kansas Archaeology.* Bureau of American Ethnology Bulletin 174. Smithsonian Institution, Washington, D.C.

1961  *Prehistoric Man on the Great Plains.* University of Oklahoma Press, Norman.

Wegner, Steven A.
1979  Analysis of Seed Remains from the Chan-ya-ta Site (13BV1), a Mill Creek Village in Northwestern Iowa. *South Dakota Archaeology* 3:1–80.

Weichman, Michael S.
1975  *The Johnson County-Coralville Reservoir Road Improvement Project.* Research Report 20. Environmental Research Center, Iowa City.

1976a  *A Preliminary Archaeological, Architectural, and Historical Reconnaissance within the Upper Chariton River Valley: Appanoose County, Iowa, and Putnam County, Missouri.* Research Report 24. Environmental Research Center, Iowa City.

1976b  *An Intensive Survey of the Archaeological, Architectural, and Historical Resources within the Proposed Lodge Complex Project, Lake Rathbun, Iowa.* Research Report 25. Environmental Research Center, Iowa City.

Weichman, Michael S., and John Tandarich
1974  *An Overview of Known Archaeological Resources*

within the Iowa River Valley: Coralville Reservoir to the Cedar River. Research Report 10.
Environmental Research Center, Iowa City.

Weitzel, Timothy S.
1992   *A Ceramic Analysis of the Weaver Community
at Gast Farm (13LA12), Southeastern Iowa.*
Unpublished Master's thesis, Department of
Anthropology, University of Iowa, Iowa City.

Weitzel, Timothy S., and William Green
1994   Weaver Ceramics from the Gast Farm Site
(13LA12), Southeastern Iowa. *Journal of the
Iowa Archeological Society* 41:130–139.

Weld, L. G.
1903   Joliet and Marquette in Iowa. *Iowa Journal of
History and Politics* 1:3–16.

Weltfish, Gene
1965   *The Lost Universe: Pawnee Life and Culture.*
University of Nebraska Press, Lincoln.

Wendland, Wayne M.
1978   Holocene Man in North America: The
Ecological Setting and Climatic Background.
*Plains Anthropologist* 23:273–287.
1980   Holocene Climatic Reconstructions on the
Prairie Peninsula. In *The Cherokee Excavations:
Holocene Ecology and Human Adaptations in
Northwestern Iowa,* edited by Duane C.
Anderson and Holmes A. Semken, Jr., pp.
139–148. Academic Press, New York.

Wheeler, Richard
1949   *Appraisal of the Archaeological Resources of the
Coralville Reservoir, Iowa River, Iowa.* River Basin Surveys, Smithsonian Institution, Lincoln, Nebraska.
1952   Plains Ceramic Analysis: A Checklist of Features and Descriptive Terms. *Plains Archaeological Conference Newsletter* 5(2):29–36.

Whelan, Mary K., and William Green
1991   Archaeological Fieldwork and Analysis. In
*Upper Mississippi River Prehistory and Paleo-
environmental Project: Final Report,* by Mary K.
Whelan, Richard Baker, E. Arthur Bettis III,
and William Green, pp. 2–12. Iowa Science
Foundation Grant No. ISF-90-24. Copy on
file, Office of the State Archaeologist, University of Iowa, Iowa City.

Whelan, Mary K., Margot Neverett, and Kristin D.
Sobolik
1992   The Gast Farm Site (13LA12) Faunal Re-

mains: Early-Late Woodland Subsistence Patterns in Southeastern Iowa. Paper presented
at the 57th Annual Meeting of the Society for
American Archaeology, Pittsburgh. Copy on
file, Office of the State Archaeologist, University of Iowa, Iowa City.

White, Charles A.
1868   Indian Mounds. *Annals of Iowa* 6:19–22.

Whiteford, Andrew H.
1970   *North American Indian Arts.* Golden Press,
New York.

Whittaker, William E.
1997   *The Cherokee Site Revisited: Prehistoric Adaptation and Change in the Eastern Great Plains.*
Unpublished Master's thesis, Department of
Anthropology, University of Iowa, Iowa City.
1998   The Cherokee Excavations Revisited: Bison
Hunting on the Eastern Plains. *North American Archaeologist* 19:293–316.

Wilford, Lloyd A.
1945   Three Villages of the Mississippian Pattern in
Minnesota. *American Antiquity* 11:32–40.
1950a  The Great Oasis Village Site. Copy on file, Office of the State Archaeologist, University of
Iowa, Iowa City.
1950b  The Low Village Site. Copy on file, Office of
the State Archaeologist, University of Iowa,
Iowa City.
1955   A Revised Classification of the Prehistoric
Cultures of Minnesota. *American Antiquity*
21:130–142.
1960   A Sickle from the Great Oasis Site in Minnesota. *Plains Anthropologist* 5:28–29.

Willey, Gordon R.
1956   *Prehistoric Settlement Patterns in the New
World.* Viking Fund Publications in Anthropology 23. Greenwood Press, Westport,
Connecticut.

Willey, Gordon R., and Philip Phillips
1958   *Method and Theory in American Archaeology.*
University of Chicago Press, Chicago.

Willey, Gordon, and Jeremy A. Sabloff
1974   *A History of American Archaeology.* W. H. Free-
man, San Francisco.

Willey, P., and Thomas E. Emerson
1992   The Osteology and Archaeology of the Crow
Creek Massacre. In *Prehistory and Human
Ecology of the Western Prairies and Northern*

*Plains: Papers in Honor of Robert A. Alex (1941-1988),* edited by Joseph A. Tiffany, pp. 227-270. Memoir 27. *Plains Anthropologist,* Lincoln, Nebraska.

Williams, Bradley B.

1980a *Fort Madison.* Educational Series. Office of the State Archaeologist, University of Iowa, Iowa City.

1980b *Fort Atkinson Historic Preserve: Technical Report: Historical Analysis and Planning Recommendations.* Prepared for Iowa State Preserves Advisory Board, Des Moines, Iowa Conservation Commission.

Williams, Patricia M.

1975 The Williams Site (13PM50): A Great Oasis Component in Northwest Iowa. *Journal of the Iowa Archeological Society* 22:1-33.

Wilson, Gilbert L.

1977 *Agriculture of the Hidatsa Indians: An Indian Interpretation.* Studies in the Social Sciences No. 9, 1917. University of Minnesota, Minneapolis. Reprints in Anthropology Vol. 5, J.& L. Reprints, Lincoln, Nebraska.

1978a *The Hidatsa EarthLodge.* Anthropological Papers of the American Museum of Natural History 33, Pt. V, 1934. Reprints in Anthropology Vol. 11, J. & L. Reprints, Lincoln, Nebraska.

1978b *The Horse and Dog in Hidatsa Culture.* Anthropological Papers of the American Museum of Natural History 15, Pt. II, 1924. Reprints in Anthropology Vol. 10, J. & L. Reprints, Lincoln, Nebraska.

Winkler, M. G., A. M. Swain, and J. E. Kutzbach

1986 Middle Holocene Dry Period in the Northern Midwestern United States: Lake Levels and Pollen Stratigraphy. *Quaternary Research* 25:235-250.

Wissler, Clark

1910 *Material Culture of the Blackfoot Indians.* Anthropological Papers of the American Museum of Natural History 5. Trustees, New York.

Withrow, Randall M.

1983 *An Analysis of Lithic Resource Selection and Processing at the Valley View Site (47LC34).* Unpublished Master's thesis, Department of Anthropology, University of Minnesota, Minneapolis.

Withrow, Randall M., James P. Gallagher, and Roland Rodell

1991 Oneota Orr Phase and the Seventeenth Century Ioway. Paper presented at the 56th Annual Meeting of the Society for American Archaeology, New Orleans.

Wittry, Warren L.

1959a Archeological Studies of Four Wisconsin Rock Shelters. *Wisconsin Archeologist* 40:137-267.

1959b The Raddatz Rockshelter, Sk5, Wisconsin. *Wisconsin Archeologist* 40:33-69.

1963 The Bell Site, Wn9, an Early Historic Fox Village. *Wisconsin Archeologist* 44:1-57.

Witzke, Brian J., Robert M. McKay, Bill J. Bunker, and Frederick J. Woodson

1990 *Stratigraphy and Paleoenvironments of Mississippian Strata in Keokuk and Washington Counties, Southeast Iowa.* Geological Survey Bureau Guidebook Series 10. Prepared for the 54th Tri-State Geological Field Conference, Geological Survey Bureau, Iowa Department of Natural Resources, Iowa City.

Wolforth, Thomas

1995 An Analysis of the Distribution of Steuben Punctated Ceramics. *Wisconsin Archeologist* 76: 27-47.

Wood, W. Raymond

1995 Historic Indians. In *Holocene Human Adaptations in the Missouri Prairie-Timberlands,* edited by W. Raymond Wood, Michael J. O'Brien, Katherine A. Murray, and Jerome C. Rose, pp. 78-87. Research Series No. 54. Arkansas Archeological Survey, Fayetteville.

Woods, William (editor)

1992 *Late Prehistoric Agriculture: Observations from the Midwest.* Studies in Illinois Archaeology No. 8. Illinois Historic Preservation Agency, Springfield.

Wormington, H. Marie

1957 *Ancient Man in North America.* Popular Series No. 4. Denver Museum of Natural History, Denver.

Wray, Donald E., and Richard S. MacNeish

1961 *The Hopewellian and Weaver Occupations of the Weaver Site, Fulton County, Illinois.* Scientific

Papers Vol. 7, No. 2. Illinois State Museum, Springfield.

Yarnell, Richard A.

1989 A Survey of Prehistoric Crop Plants in Eastern North America. In New World Paleoethnobotany: Collected Papers in Honor of Leonard W. Blake, edited by E. Voigt and D. Pearsall, pp. 47–59. *Missouri Archaeologist.*

1993 The Importance of Native Crops during the Late Archaic and Woodland Periods. In *Foraging and Farming in the Eastern Woodlands,* edited by C. M. Scarry, pp. 13–26. University of Florida Press, Gainesville.

Zalesky, James

1977 A Collection of Surface Finds from East-Central Iowa. Ms. on file, Office of the State Archaeologist, University of Iowa, Iowa City.

Zalucha, L. Anthony

1982 *Methodology in Paleoethnobotany: A Study in Vegetational Reconstruction Dealing with the Mill Creek Culture of Northwestern Iowa.* Unpublished Ph.D. dissertation, Department of Anthropology, University of Wisconsin–Madison.

Zieglowsky, Debby, and James Zalesky

1981 The Coralville Reservoir: A Status Report. In Miscellaneous Reports on Iowa Archaeology, pp. 229–246. Research Papers Vol. 6, No. 4. Office of the State Archaeologist, University of Iowa, Iowa City.

Zimmerman, Larry J.

1971a Skadeland Mill Creek Culture Site. In *Prehistoric Investigations,* edited by Marshall B.

McKusick, pp. 114–124. Report 3. Office of the State Archaeologist, University of Iowa, Iowa City.

1971b *The Glenwood Taxonomic Problem.* Unpublished Master's thesis, Department of Anthropology, University of Iowa, Iowa City.

1977a The Glenwood Local Sequence: A Re-examination. *Journal of the Iowa Archeological Society* 24:62–83.

1977b *Prehistoric Locational Behavior: A Computer Simulation.* Report 10. Office of the State Archaeologist, University of Iowa, Iowa City.

1985 *Peoples of Prehistoric South Dakota.* University of Nebraska Press, Lincoln.

Zimmerman, Larry J., and Lawrence E. Bradley

1993 The Crow Creek Massacre: Initial Coalescent Warfare and Speculations about the Genesis of Extended Coalescent. In *Prehistory and Human Ecology of the Western Prairies and Northern Plains: Papers in Honor of Robert A. Alex (1941–1988),* edited by Joseph A. Tiffany, pp. 215–226. Memoir 27. *Plains Anthropologist,* Lincoln, Nebraska.

Zimmerman, Larry J., Lawrence E. Bradley, Richard A. Fox, Jr., and Brian L. Molyneaux

1994 Response to the Geomorphological Guidelines. *Journal of the Iowa Archeological Society* 41:1–2.

Zimmerman, Larry J., John B. Gregg, and Pauline S. Gregg

1981 Para-mortem Osteopathology in the Crow Creek Massacre Victims. *South Dakota Journal of Medicine* 34(2):7–12.

# Index